Brief Contents

Unit 1 Reading to Write 1

1. Understanding the Active Reading Process 3
2. Building Vocabulary for Reading and Writing 33
3. Understanding the Writing Process 58
4. Understanding Introductions, Body Paragraphs, and Conclusions 106
5. Thinking, Reading, and Writing Critically 132
6. Reading and Writing about Different Kinds of Texts 165

Unit 2 Reading and Writing Essays 197

7. Reading and Writing Exemplification Essays 199
8. Reading and Writing Narrative Essays 214
9. Reading and Writing Cause-and-Effect Essays 230
10. Reading and Writing Comparison-and-Contrast Essays 246
11. Reading and Writing Argument Essays 263
12. Additional Options for Organizing Essays 284

Unit 3 Research 339

13. Finding and Evaluating Sources 341
14. Documenting Sources in MLA or APA Style 358

Unit 4 Basic Grammar Guide 381

15. Understanding Verbs 383
16. Understanding Nouns and Pronouns 398
17. Understanding Adjectives and Adverbs 421
18. Writing Simple, Compound, and Complex Sentences 430
19. Writing Varied Sentences 453
20. Using Parallelism 467
21. Using Words Effectively 474
22. Run-Ons 491
23. Fragments 504
24. Subject-Verb Agreement 521
25. Illogical Shifts 534
26. Misplaced and Dangling Modifiers 542
27. Using Commas 549
28. Using Apostrophes 564
29. Understanding Mechanics 571

Unit 5 Reading Essays 587

30. Readings for Writers 588

FOCUS
on READING and WRITING
ESSAYS

Second Edition

Laurie G. Kirszner
University of the Sciences, Emeritus

Stephen R. Mandell
Drexel University

in collaboration with reading specialists

Dr. Lana Myers
Lone Star College

Dr. Michelle Francis
West Valley College

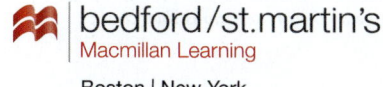

Boston | New York

For Bedford/St. Martin's
Vice President, Editorial, Macmillan Learning Humanities: Edwin Hill
Executive Program Director, English: Leasa Burton
Senior Program Manager, Developmental English: Karita France dos Santos
Marketing Manager: Azelie Fortier
Director of Content Development, Humanities: Jane Knetzger
Senior Development Editor: Gillian Cook
Senior Content Project Manager: Edward Dionne
Senior Workflow Project Manager: Jennifer Wetzel
Production Supervisor: Brianna Lester
Senior Media Project Manager: Rand Thomas
Media Editor: Angela Beckett
Manager of Publishing Services: Andrea Cava
Project Management: Lumina Datamatics, Inc.
Composition: Lumina Datamatics, Inc.
Text Permissions Editor: Kalina Ingham
Photo Permissions Editor: Angela Boehler
Permissions Associate: Allison Ziebka
Photo Researcher: Brittani Morgan, Lumina Datamatics, Inc.
Director of Design, Content Management: Diana Blume
Text Design: Claire Seng-Niemoeller
Cover Design: William Boardman
Cover Image: Juan Carlos Vindas/Getty Images
Printing and Binding: LSC Communications

Copyright © 2019, 2015 by Bedford/St. Martin's

All rights reserved. No part of this book may be reproduced, stored in a retrieval system, or transmitted in any form or by any means, electronic, mechanical, photocopying, recording, or otherwise, except as may be expressly permitted by the applicable copyright statutes or in writing by the Publisher.

Manufactured in the United States of America.

1 2 3 4 5 6   23 22 21 20 19 18

For information, write: Bedford/St. Martin's, 75 Arlington Street, Boston, MA 02116

ISBN   978-1-319-05500-4   (Student Edition)
ISBN   978-1-319-13219-4   (Loose-Leaf Edition)

Acknowledgments
Text acknowledgments and copyrights appear at the back of the book on pages 643–644, which constitutes an extension of the copyright page. Art acknowledgments and copyrights appear on the same page as the art selections they cover.

Preface

Our goal in this new edition of *Focus on Reading and Writing: Essays* was to create an engaging, integrated text that motivates students to improve their reading and writing skills and that gives them the tools to do so. **TEST**, our unique assessment tool, is designed specifically for this purpose. The letters **TEST** stand for **T**hesis, **E**vidence, **S**ummary, and **T**ransitions, the key elements of effective essays. Thus, **TEST** helps students to keep in mind the four key elements to look for as they **read** and enables them to make sure all these elements are also present in the essays they **write**.

In addition to this important student-tested assessment tool, *Focus on Reading and Writing* reflects our core pedagogical belief—that students learn best by practicing a new skill or concept in the context of their own work. Accordingly, throughout Units 1 and 2, chapters begin by prompting students to consider their prior knowledge of a subject; then, they are encouraged to expand their knowledge of this subject as they learn and practice active reading strategies; finally, they are asked to apply these new skills in their own writing.

With a complete grammar guide and twenty-three professional reading selections, this comprehensive text gets students reading, writing, and thinking critically in preparation for academic, career, and life success. Arresting images and a contemporary design appeal to today's ever-more-visual learners, as do the graphic organizers we have included as chapter review exercises in Unit 1 and as exercises for understanding essay organization in Unit 2.

With the help of two reading specialists, we have built a book with a truly integrated approach to reading and writing instruction. We are confident in the book's pedagogy, flexibility, and accessibility; it is our hope that this second edition of *Focus on Reading and Writing* will motivate and empower students to become critical readers and confident writers.

Organization

Focus on Reading and Writing has a flexible organization that permits instructors to teach various topics in the order that works best for them and for their students. The book is divided into three sections, which are color-coded to help students and instructors more easily navigate the book:

- **Units 1–3,** Chapters 1–14, offer a comprehensive discussion of the reading and writing processes. Included in these units are eleven full-length professional essays, several excerpts from professional writing, and numerous student writing examples as well as detailed information on working with and documenting sources.

- **Unit 4,** Chapters 15–29, is a thorough yet accessible review of sentence skills, grammar, punctuation, and mechanics with ample practice activities.
- **Unit 5,** Chapter 30, offers a thematically organized selection of twelve additional professional essays. Each essay is preceded by a brief headnote and a "Before you read" prompt and is followed by critical reading, thinking, and discussion questions as well as by two writing prompts.

Features

TEST — A unique tool that inspires student confidence and independence: This simple and unique assessment tool helps students to remember the key elements to look for as they read professional and other college-level texts and as they revise their own writing. Thus TEST prepares them to work independently to analyze their reading and empowers them to revise their own writing with confidence.

Focus on Reading and Writing prompts: These prompts introduce a connected strand of activities, a hallmark of the Kirszner/Mandell approach, that prompts students to activate their prior knowledge on the topic of a chapter's central reading, sends them back to the reading as they practice active reading strategies, and prompts them to apply the new skills they are learning in their own writing.

Reading Tips: Featured in the grammar chapters, these marginal tips appear next to connected discourse practice exercises and essay-length editing exercises, encouraging students to practice active and critical reading skills as they master important writing skills.

Graphic organizers: Used as chapter review exercises in Unit 1 and as exercises for understanding essay organization in Unit 2, these graphic organizers visually aid students in understanding the reading and writing processes.

FYI boxes: Throughout the book, these boxes highlight useful information and explain difficult concepts.

Word Power boxes: Marginal Word Power boxes help students build their vocabulary by defining unfamiliar words that appear in the text's explanations and reading selections.

New to This Edition

- **Improved TEST tool:** The TEST tool has been streamlined to make it more effective for analyzing readings and writing essays. Chapter 1 explains in depth how to apply TEST to identify key elements in professional essays and other college-level texts, and Chapter 3 describes how students can use TEST to evaluate their own written work.
- **Enhanced Chapter 1:** A new section focuses on how to use TEST to identify stated and implied main ideas, supporting evidence, summary statements, and transitions in college texts. A new reading by Colin Powell, "What Makes American Citizenship Possible," illustrates the elements of TEST, helping students to identify them, and is also the source of examples used to demonstrate other reading strategies discussed in the chapter. In addition, new content has been added on paraphrasing, summary coverage has been expanded, mark-up and annotation strategies have been clarified, and a new box, "Preparing to Read" has been added.
- **Enhanced Chapter 3:** A new section demonstrates how students can use TEST to evaluate their essays for an effective thesis, sufficient and appropriate evidence, a strong conclusion, and transitions to ensure coherence. A new box, "Additional Strategies," provides useful tips for finding and generating ideas.
- **New coverage of implied main idea:** Chapter 5 now includes a section on identifying implied ideas and provides guidelines on how to recognize them, plus a practice exercise.
- **Reconfigured patterns chapters (7–12) now provide enhanced reading coverage:** The TEST tool has been more deeply embedded into these chapters, and reading and writing strategies are now more seamlessly integrated. Students use the TEST tool (modified for the specific pattern) first to read and analyze a professional reading and then to analyze a student essay. Next, they follow a student writer as he or she writes an essay and TESTs it, and finally they write and evaluate their own essays.
- **New themes and readings in Unit 5: Reading Essays:** Chapter 30 has been significantly revised and now contains twelve readings, nine of which are new to this edition. Selections are organized into four thematic groups, three of which are also new: Technology and Science, Working and Learning, and Identity and Self-Image.
- **Separate research and documentation chapters:** Chapter 13: Working with Sources from the first edition of *Focus on Reading and Writing* has been broken into two shorter, more accessible, chapters: Chapter 13: Finding and Evaluating Sources and Chapter 14: Documenting Sources in MLA and APA Style. MLA examples have been updated throughout both to reflect the changes outlined in the *MLA Handbook Eighth Edition*.

- **New Grammar Exercises:** A number of practices in the grammar chapters (15–29) have been replaced or updated to provide current and engaging exercise options.

We're all in. As always.

Bedford/St. Martin's is as passionately committed to the discipline of English as ever, working hard to provide support and services that make it easier for you to teach your course your way.

Find **community support** at the Bedford/St. Martin's English Community (community.macmillan.com), where you can follow our *Bits* blog for new teaching ideas, download titles from our professional resource series, and review projects in the pipeline.

Choose **curriculum solutions** that offer flexible custom options, combining our carefully developed print and digital resources, acclaimed works from Macmillan's trade imprints, and your own course or program materials to provide the exact resources your students need. Our approach to customization makes it possible to create a project uniquely suited for your students, and based on your enrollment size, return money to your department.

Rely on **outstanding service** from your Bedford/St. Martin's sales representative and editorial team. Contact us or visit macmillanlearning.com to learn more about any of the options below.

Choose from Alternative Formats of *Focus on Reading and Writing*

Bedford/St. Martin's offers a range of formats. Choose what works best for you and your students:

- *Paperback.* To order the second edition, use ISBN 978-1-319-05500-4.
- *Loose-leaf edition.* The loose-leaf edition does not have a traditional binding; its pages are loose and hole punched to provide flexibility and a low price to students. To order the second edition, use ISBN 978-1-319-13219-4.
- *Popular e-book formats.* For details of our e-book partners, visit **macmillanlearning.com/ebooks**.

Select Value Packages

Add value to your text by packaging the following Bedford/St. Martin's resource with *Focus on Reading and Writing* at a significant discount. Contact your sales representative for more information.

LaunchPad Solo for Readers and Writers allows students to work on what they need help with the most. At home or in class, students learn at their own pace, with instruction tailored to each student's unique needs. *LaunchPad Solo for Readers and Writers* features:

- **Pre-built units that support a learning arc.** Easy-to-assign units include a pre-test, multimedia instruction, and a post-test that assesses what students have learned about a particular topic such as critical reading, the writing process, research and using sources, grammar, style, mechanics, and help for multilingual writers. Many units also include brief, accessible videos that illustrate the concepts at hand.
- **Diagnostics that help establish a baseline for instruction.** Eight diagnostics are available to identify areas of strength and areas for improvement on topics related to grammar and reading. The diagnostics offer visual reports that show performance by topic, class, and student as well as comparison reports that track improvement over time.
- **LearningCurve adaptive quizzing.** The pre-built units include LearningCurve, game-like online quizzing that adapts to what students already know and helps them focus on what they need to learn. LearningCurve links to supplemental study pages to support students as they work through topics.
- **Twenty-five reading selections with comprehension quizzes.** Assign a range of classic and contemporary readings directly from LaunchPad Solo for Readers and Writers. Each reading includes a Lexile® measure to help instructors connect students with the right level of challenge.
- **Access to Exercise Central.** Exercise Central is a growing bank of grammar, punctuation, style, writing, and research exercises, ready-made for instructors to add to any unit.
- **The ability to monitor student progress.** Use the gradebook to see which students are on track and which need additional help with specific topics.

Order ISBN 978-1-319-23234-4 to package *LaunchPad Solo for Readers and Writers* with the *Focus on Reading and Writing* text at a significant discount. Order ISBN 978-1-319-23231-3 to package *LaunchPad Solo for Readers and Writers* with the looseleaf version of *Focus on Reading and Writing*, also at a significant discount. Students who rent or buy a used book can purchase access and instructors may request free access at **macmillanlearning.com/readwrite**.

Instructor Resources

You have a lot to do in your course. We want to make it easy for you to find the support you need—and to get it quickly.

- **The Instructor's Edition of** *Focus on Reading and Writing* contains answers to all grammar practice exercises as well as many of the exercises throughout the reading and writing instructional material, in addition to teaching ideas, reminders, and cross-references. ISBN: 978-1-319-13375-7
- **The** *Classroom Resources and Instructor's Guide: Focus on Reading and Writing*, 2e is available as a PDF that can be downloaded from macmillanlearning.com. Visit the instructor resources tab for *Focus on Reading and Writing*. In addition to chapter overviews and teaching tips, the instructor's manual includes an overview of integrated reading and writing courses, tips for teaching reading and for teaching writing, sample syllabi, a chapter-by-chapter guide to teaching using the text, and answers to exercises and activities. ISBN: 978-1-319-24074-5

Acknowledgments

In our work on *Focus on Reading and Writing*, we have benefited from the help of a great many people.

We are grateful to our reading consultants, Michelle Francis of West Valley College and Lana Myers of Lone Star College, for their expert advice and guidance. Additionally, we thank Randee Falk, who made important contributions to the research chapter, and Jessica Carroll, who made valuable contributions to exercises and writing activities.

Instructors throughout the country have contributed suggestions and encouragement at various stages of the book's development. For their collegial support, we thank Amy Petersen Ambrosious, *Alvin Community College*; Joe Antinarella, *Tidewater Community College*; Elizabeth Baldridge, *Illinois Central College*; Pamela Bilton Beard, *Houston Community College, Southwest*; Andrea Berta, *University of Texas at El Paso*; Donna Beverly, *Montgomery Community College*; Marilyn Black, *Middlesex Community College*; Reed Breneman, *Wake Technical Community College*; Robyn Browder, *Tidewater Community College*; Marta Brown, *Community College of Denver*; Elizabeth Buchanan, *Porterville College*; Susan Buchler, *Montgomery Community College*; Gricelle Cano, *Houston Community College*; Patti Casey, *Tyler Junior College*; Annette Cole, *Tarrant County College*; Cathy Colton, *College of Lake County*; Lori Conrad, *University of Arkansas*; Michael Cox, *Mitchell Community College*; Linda Crawford, *McLennan Community College*; Patricia Davis, *Houston Community College, Southwest*; Syble S. Davis, *Houston Community College-Central*; Cynthia DeLauder, *Spokane Falls Community College*; Lynn Dornink, *Northeastern University*; Mary Dubbé, *Thomas Nelson Community College*; Dr. Joy Eichner-Lynch, *Contra Costa College*; Maryann Errico, *Georgia Perimeter College*; Richard Farias, *Alamo Colleges*,

San Antonio; Jennifer Ferguson, *Cazenovia College*; Judith Gallagher, *Tarrant County College*; Kris Giere, *Ivy Tech Community College of Indiana*; Virginia Gleason, *Tarrant County College*; Angie Gordon, *Trinity Valley Community College*; Priscilla Hall, *Wytheville Community College*; Beth Hashemzadeh, *Bluefield State College*; Sharon Hayes, *Community College of Baltimore*; Thomasa Henry, *Tarrant County College*; Dr. Patricia Hill-Miller, *Central Piedmost Community College*; Ferdinand Hunter, *Gateway Community College*; Janis Innis, *Houston Community College*; Kimberley Koledoye, *Houston Community College*; Tamara Kuzmenkov, *Tacoma Community College*; Mimi Leonard, *Wytheville Community College*; Desmond Lewis, *Houston Community College*; Jennifer Martin, *Salem Community College*; Beverly Mason, *Paul D. Camp Community College*; Margaret McClain, *Arkansas State University*; Precious Mckenzie, *Rocky Mountain College*; Georgene Bess Montgomery, *Clark Atlanta College*; Robbi Muckenfuss, *Durham Technical Community College*; Alexis Nelson, *Spokane Falls Community College*; Nicole Oechslin, *Piedmont Virginia Community College*; Sandra Padilla, *El Paso Community College*; Catherine Parra, *Northern Virginia Community College*; Elaine Pascale, *Suffolk University*; Pam Price, *Greenville Technical College*; Rhonda Pruitt, *John Tyler Community College*; Paula Rash, *Caldwell Community College and Technical Institute*; Mary Reed, *Lord Fairfax Community College*; Mancy M. Risch, *Caldwell Community College and Technical Institute*; Jennifer Riske, *Northeast Lakeview College*; Linda Robinett, *Oklahoma City Community College*; David Roloff, *University of Wisconsin–Stevens Point*; Becky Rudd, *Citrus College*; Stacey Said, *Northern Virginia Community College*; Charis Sawyer, *Johnson County Community College*; Pattie See, *University of Wisconsin–Eau Claire*; Vanessa Sekinger, *Germanna Community College*; Gail Shearer, *Madison Area Technical College*; Kitty Spires, *Midlands Technical College*; Catherine Swift, *University of Central Arkansas*; Lawrence L. Szigeti, *John Abbott College*; Kerry Thomas, *Rufus King International School*; Jason Todd, *Xavier University of Louisiana*; Annie Tsui, *Houston Community College-Central*; Patricia Tymon, *Virginia Highlands Community College*; Beverly Van Citters, *Citrus College*; Nancy Warren, *Paul D. Camp Community College*; Jeanine Williams, *Community College of Baltimore;* Lisa Wilmot, *Tacoma Community College*; Kenneth Wilson, *Cuyahoga Community College*; and Dr. Gaye Winter, *Mississippi Gulf Coast Community College-Perkinston Campus.*

At Bedford/St. Martin's, we thank Jessica Gould and Edward Dionne for guiding the book ably through production, and Claire Seng-Niemoeller for overseeing the book's design. Many thanks also go to Lauren Arrant, marketing manager, and Azelie Fortier, market development manager. We would also like to thank Karita France dos Santos, Program Manager for Developmental English, for her help and encouragement. We especially want to thank Paola Garcia-Muniz and Suzy Chouljian, our editorial assistants, who did the almost impossible job of manuscript preparation. And finally, we thank our editor, Gillian

Cook. The deep knowledge and extensive experience she applied to this project made it a better book, and we are grateful to her for all her hard work.

It almost goes without saying that *Focus on Reading and Writing* could not exist without our students, whose work inspired the sample sentences, paragraphs, and essays in this book. We thank all of them, past and present, who allowed us to use their work.

We are grateful in addition for the continued support of our families. Finally, we are grateful for the survival and growth of the writing partnership we entered into when we were graduate students. We had no idea then of the wonderful places our collaborative efforts would take us. Now, we know.

Laurie G. Kirszner

Stephen R. Mandell

Contents

Preface v

unit 1 Reading to Write 1

1 Understanding the Active Reading Process 3

  1a Before You Read 4
    Creating a Reading Schedule 4
    Assessing Prior Knowledge 6
    Understanding Your Purpose 7
    Previewing 7
      Skimming 7 ▪ *Scanning* 8

  1b As You Read 10
    TESTing a Text 11
    Colin Powell, *What American Citizenship Makes Possible* 12
    Marking Up a Text 15
    Annotating a Text 18

  1c After You Read 21
    Outlining 21
    Summarizing and Paraphrasing 23
      Summarizing 23 ▪ *Paraphrasing* 24
    Reviewing and Self-Quizzing 25

  1d Writing a Response Paragraph 26

  Chapter Review 28

Science Source

2 Building Vocabulary for Reading and Writing 33

  2a Understanding Your Vocabularies 34

2b **"Knowing" Words** 35
Activating Your Schemata 35
Amy Tan, *Excerpt from "Mother Tongue"* 36
Understanding Denotations, Connotations, Synonyms, and Antonyms 37
   Denotations 37 ■ *Connotations* 38 ■ *Synonyms and Antonyms* 39

2c **Acquiring New Words** 40
Learning from Reference Tools 41
   Using a Dictionary 41 ■ *Using a Thesaurus* 42 ■
   Using the Internet 42
Learning from Context Clues 42
   Definition/Synonym Clues 43 ■ *Example Clues* 43 ■
   General Information Clues 43 ■ *Contrast Clues* 44
Learning from Your Coursework 45
   Using Concept Cards 45 ■ *Using Mnemonics* 46 ■
   Using Visual Cues 47
Learning from Roots, Prefixes, and Suffixes 47
   Using Roots 48 ■ *Using Prefixes* 49 ■ *Using Suffixes* 50
Learning from Your Reading 51

2d **Using New Words in Your Writing** 52
Chapter Review 55

3 Understanding the Writing Process 58

3a Understanding Essay Structure 59

Aimee Groth, *Why Working at Starbucks for Three Weeks Was the Toughest Job I've Ever Had* 62

Richard Levine/Alamy Stock Photo

3b Moving from Assignment to Topic 64

3c Finding Ideas to Write about 66
Freewriting 66
Brainstorming 67
Keeping a Journal 69
Clustering 70

3d Stating Your Thesis 72

3e Choosing Supporting Points 78

3f Making an Outline 80

3g Drafting Your Essay 82

3h TESTing Your Essay 85
  TESTing for a Thesis 85
  TESTing for Evidence 85
  TESTing for a Summary 87
  TESTing for Transitions 87

3i Revising Your Essay 89

3j Editing Your Essay 95

3k Proofreading Your Essay 96

Chapter Review 101

4 Understanding Introductions, Body Paragraphs, and Conclusions 106

4a Reading Paragraphs 107

4b Writing Introductions 109
  Beginning with a Narrative 110
  Beginning with a Question (or a Series of Questions) 110
  Beginning with a Definition 111
  Beginning with a Quotation 111
  Beginning with a Surprising Statement or Statistic 111

4c Body Paragraphs 114
  Body Paragraphs Should Be Unified 117
  Body Paragraphs Should Be Coherent 119
  Body Paragraphs Should Be Well Developed 122

4d Conclusions 124
  Concluding with a Narrative 125
  Concluding with a Recommendation 125
  Concluding with a Quotation 126
  Concluding with a Prediction 126

Chapter Review 128

mavo/Shutterstock.com

5 Thinking, Reading, and Writing Critically 132

5a Identifying Audience, Purpose, and Tone 133
  The Writer's Audience 133
  The Writer's Purpose 134
  The Writer's Tone 136

Michael Ventura/Alamy Stock Photo

5b Identifying Connotations and Figurative Language   139
  Connotations   139
  Figurative Language   140

5c Identifying the Main Idea   141
  Identifying Implied Main Ideas   142

5d Identifying Major and Minor Supporting Points   143

5e Evaluating the Writer's Ideas   145
  Distinguishing between Fact and Opinion   145
  Making Inferences   148
  Identifying Bias   152

5f Reading and Writing Critically   153
  Summarizing   154
  Analyzing   155
  Synthesizing   157
  Evaluating   159
  Jamie Lincoln Kitman, *Google Wants Driverless Cars, but Do We?*   159

Chapter Review   163

6 Reading and Writing about Different Kinds of Texts   165

Ivonne Wierink/Shutterstock;
sbarabu/Shutterstock;
Lauren Burke/Getty Images;
Photodisc/Getty Images

6a Reading Written Texts   166
  Textbooks   166
  News Articles   168
  Business Documents   171
  Web Pages   172
  Blogs   174

6b Reading Visual Texts   177
  Previewing a Visual   177
  Marking Up and Annotating a Visual   182

6c Types of Visuals   183
  Charts, Graphs, and Tables   183
  Maps   185
  Diagrams   186
  Photographs   188
  Editorial Cartoons   189
  Advertisements   191

Chapter Review   193

Contents xvii

Unit 2 Reading and Writing Essays 197

7 Reading and Writing Exemplification Essays 199

7a Read an Exemplification Essay 200

Keshia Mcclantoc, *In Defense of the Small-Town Library* 202

travelib/Alamy Stock Photo

7b Analyzing a Student Essay: Exemplification 205

7c Writing an Exemplification Essay 208

Following a Student Writer 210

Chapter Review 213

8 Reading and Writing Narrative Essays 214

8a Reading a Narrative Essay 215

Lynda Barry, *The Sanctuary of School* 217

© Lynda Barry. Used with permission by Drawn & Quarterly

8b Analyzing a Student Essay: Narration 221

8c Writing a Narrative Essay 224

Following a Student Writer 225

Chapter Review 229

9 Reading and Writing Cause-and-Effect Essays 230

9a Reading a Cause-and-Effect Essay 232

John Edgar Wideman, *The Seat Not Taken* 233

NICHOLAS KAMM/Getty Images

9b Analyzing a Student Essay: Cause and Effect 237

9c Writing a Cause-and-Effect Essay 240

Following a Student Writer 241

Chapter Review 245

10 Reading and Writing Comparison-and-Contrast Essays 246

- **10a** Reading a Comparison-and-Contrast Essay 247
  - **Steven Conn,** *The Twin Revolutions of Lincoln and Darwin* 249
- **10b** Analyzing a Student Essay: Comparison and Contrast 252
- **10c** Writing a Comparison-and-Contrast Essay 256
  - Following a Student Writer 257
- **Chapter Review** 262

North Wind Picture Archives/Alamy Stock Photo; PRISMA ARCHIVO/Alamy Stock Photo

11 Reading and Writing Argument Essays 263

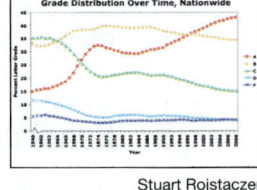

- **11a** Reading an Argument Essay 264
  - Inductive and Deductive Argument 266
  - **Mary Sherry,** *In Praise of the F Word* 269
- **11b** Analyzing a Student Essay: Argument 272
- **11c** Writing an Argument Essay 276
  - Following a Student Writer 277
- **Chapter Review** 283

Stuart Rojstaczer

12 Additional Options for Organizing Essays 284

- **12a** Description 284
  - Reading a Descriptive Essay 285
  - **Rachel Carson,** *A Fable for Tomorrow* 287
  - Analyzing a Student Essay: Description 290
  - Writing a Descriptive Essay 292
- **12b** Process 297
  - Reading a Process Essay 297
  - **Amy Ma,** *My Grandmother's Dumpling* 299
  - Analyzing a Student Essay: Process 306
  - Writing a Process Essay 308
- **12c** Classification 313
  - Reading a Classification Essay 313
  - **Scott Russell Sanders,** *The Men We Carry in Our Minds* 315

Analyzing a Student Essay: Classification   319
Writing a Classification Essay   322

12d Definition   325

Reading a Definition Essay   326

Julia Alvarez, *What Is a* Quinceañera?   328

Analyzing a Student Essay: Definition   331
Writing a Definition Essay   334

unit 3 Research   339

13 Finding and Evaluating Sources   341

13a Finding Information   341

Finding Information in the Library   342
Evaluating Library Sources   343
   Questions to Ask When Evaluating Library Sources   343
Finding Information on the Internet   344
Evaluating Internet Sources   344

13b Using Sources in Your Writing   347

Paraphrasing   347
Summarizing   348
Quoting   348
Working Sources into Your Writing   349
Synthesizing   350

13c Using Sources Ethically   350

Guideline 1: Document Ideas from Your Sources   352   ■   *Guideline 2: Place Borrowed Words in Quotation Marks*   352   ■   *Guideline 3: Use Your Own Phrasing*   352   ■   *Guideline 4: Distinguish Your Ideas from the Source's Ideas*   353

Chapter Review   354

14 Documenting Sources in MLA or APA Style   358

14a MLA Documentation Style   358

MLA In-Text Citation   358
   Sample In-Text Citations   359
The Works-Cited List   360
   Sample Works-Cited Entries   360
Sample MLA-Style Paper   363

14b APA Documentation Style 368
    APA In-Text Citation   368
        Sample In-Text Citations   368
    The Reference List   370
        Sample Reference List Entries   370
    Sample APA-Style Paper   373
Chapter Review   377

unit 4 Basic Grammar Guide   381

15 Understanding Verbs   383

15a Regular Verbs   383

15b Irregular Verbs   384

15c Problem Verbs: *Be*   386

15d Problem Verbs: *Can/Could* and *Will/Would*   387
    Can/Could   387
    Will/Would   387

15e Regular Past Participles   389

15f Irregular Past Participles   390

15g The Present Perfect Tense   393

15h The Past Perfect Tense   395

Chapter Review   396

16 Understanding Nouns and Pronouns   398

16a Identifying Nouns   398

16b Forming Plural Nouns   398

16c Identifying Pronouns   400

16d Pronoun-Antecedent Agreement   402

16e Identifying Problem Areas with Agreement   403
    Compound Antecedents   404
    Indefinite Pronoun Antecedents   405
    Collective Noun Antecedents   407

16f   Vague and Unnecessary Pronouns   408
   Vague Pronouns   408
   Unnecessary Pronouns   409

16g   Understanding Pronoun Case   410
   Subjective Case   410
   Objective Case   410
   Possessive Case   411

16h   Identifying Problem Areas with Pronoun Case   412
   Pronouns in Compounds   412
   Pronouns in Comparisons   413
   Who and *Whom*, *Whoever* and *Whomever*   415

16i   Reflexive and Intensive Pronouns   416
   Reflexive Pronouns   417
   Intensive Pronouns   417

Chapter Review   419

17 Understanding Adjectives and Adverbs   421

17a   Identifying Adjectives and Adverbs   421

17b   Comparatives and Superlatives   424
   Forming Comparitives and Superlatives   424
      Adjectives   424   ■   *Adverbs*   425
   Solving Special Problems with Comparitives and Superlatives   425

Chapter Review   428

18 Writing Simple, Compound, and Complex Sentences   430

Simple Sentences   430

18a   Identifying Subjects in Simple Sentences   430

18b   Identifying Prepositional Phrases in Simple Sentences   431

18c   Identifying Verbs in Simple Sentences   433
   Action Verbs   433
   Linking Verbs   434
   Helping Verbs   435

Compound Sentences   437

18d   Forming Compound Sentences with Coordinating Conjunctions   437

18e   Forming Compound Sentences with Semicolons   440

18f Forming Compound Sentences with Transitional Words and Phrases 442

Complex Sentences 445

18g Forming Complex Sentences with Subordinating Conjunctions 445

18h Forming Complex Sentences with Relative Pronouns 448

Chapter Review 450

19 Writing Varied Sentences 453

19a Varying Sentence Types 453

19b Varying Sentence Openings 454
Beginning with Adverbs 454
Beginning with Prepositional Phrases 456

19c Combining Sentences 457
Using *-ing* Modifiers 457
Using *-ed* Modifiers 458
Using a Series of Words 460
Using Appositives 462

19d Mixing Long and Short Sentences 463

Chapter Review 465

20 Using Parallelism 467

20a Recognizing Parallel Structure 467

20b Using Parallel Structure 468
Paired Items 468
Items in a Series 469
Items in a List or in an Outline 469

Chapter Review 471

21 Using Words Effectively 474

21a Using Specific Words 474

21b Using Concise Language 476

21c Using Similes and Metaphors 478

21d Avoiding Slang 479

21e Avoiding Clichés 480

21f   Avoiding Sexist Language   481
21g   Identifying Commonly Confused Words   483
Chapter Review   489

22 Run-Ons   491

22a   Recognizing Run-Ons   491

22b   Correcting Run-Ons   492
Use a Period to Create Two Separate Sentences   493
Use a Coordinating Conjunction to Connect Ideas   494
Use a Semicolon to Connect Ideas   495
Use a Semicolon and a Transitional Word or Phrase to Connect Ideas   496
Use a Dependent Word to Connect Ideas   498

Chapter Review   501

23 Fragments   504

23a   Recognizing Fragments   504

23b   Missing-Subject Fragments   506

23c   Phrase Fragments   508
Appositive Fragments   508
Prepositional Phrase Fragments   509
Infinitive Fragments   509

23d   *-ing* Fragments   511

23e   Dependent-Clause Fragments   513

Chapter Review   518

24 Subject-Verb Agreement   521

24a   Understanding Subject-Verb Agreement   521

24b   Compound Subjects   522

24c   *Be*, *Have*, and *Do*   523

24d   Words between Subject and Verb   525

24e   Collective Noun Subjects   526

24f   Indefinite Pronoun Subjects   527

24g   Verbs before Subjects   529

Chapter Review   531

25 Illogical Shifts 534
- **25a** Shifts in Tense 534
- **25b** Shifts in Person 535
- **25c** Shifts in Voice 537

Chapter Review 540

26 Misplaced and Dangling Modifiers 542
- **26a** Correcting Misplaced Modifiers 542
- **26b** Correcting Dangling Modifiers 544

Chapter Review 547

27 Using Commas 549
- **27a** Commas in a Series 549
- **27b** Commas with Introductory Phrases and Transitional Words and Phrases 550
  - Introductory Phrases 551
  - Transitional Words and Phrases 551
- **27c** Commas with Appositives 553
- **27d** Commas with Nonrestrictive Clauses 554
- **27e** Commas in Dates and Addresses 556
  - Dates 557
  - Addresses 557
- **27f** Unnecessary Commas 558

Chapter Review 561

28 Using Apostrophes 564
- **28a** Apostrophes in Contractions 564
- **28b** Apostrophes in Possessives 565
  - Singular Nouns and Indefinite Pronouns 565
  - Plural Nouns 566
- **28c** Incorrect Use of Apostrophes 567

Chapter Review 569

29 Understanding Mechanics 571

- **29a** Capitalizing Proper Nouns 571
- **29b** Punctuating Direct Quotations 574
    - Identifying Tag at the Beginning 575
    - Identifying Tag at the End 575
    - Identifying Tag in the Middle 575
    - Identifying Tag between Two Sentences 576
- **29c** Setting Off Titles 577
- **29d** Using Hyphens 579
- **29e** Using Abbreviations 580
- **29f** Using Numbers 581
- **29g** Using Semicolons, Colons, Dashes, and Parentheses 582
    - Semicolons 582
    - Colons 582
    - Dashes 582
    - Parentheses 582

Chapter Review 584

unit 5 Reading Essays 587

30 Readings for Writers 588

Reading and Writing 590

- **Amy Tan,** *Mother Tongue* 590
- **Richard Lederer,** *The Case for Short Words* 596
- **Noah Lewis,** *For Trans People Like Me, Pronouns Are about More Than Grammatical Correctness* 600

Technology and Science 604

- **Sherry Turkle,** *The Flight from Conversation* 604
- **Alex Hern,** *Don't Know the Difference between Emoji and Emoticons? Let Me Explain* 610
- **Michael Pollan,** *Why 'Natural' Doesn't Mean Anything Anymore* 613

Working and Learning 618

    Toni Morrison, *The Work You Do, the Person You Are* 618

    Jennine Capó Crucet, *Taking My Parents to College* 622

    Naomi Rosenberg, *How to Tell a Mother Her Child Is Dead* 626

Identity and Self-Image 629

    Nikita, *Growing Up a Desi Girl: What It Means to Be between Two Worlds* 629

    Jacqueline Woodson, *When a Southern Town Broke a Heart* 633

    Umapagan Ampikaipakan, *That Oxymoron, the Asian Comic Superhero* 637

Acknowledgements 643
Index 645
Revision Symbols 662

unit 1
Reading to Write

1. **Understanding the Active Reading Process** 3
2. **Building Vocabulary for Reading and Writing** 33
3. **Understanding the Writing Process** 58
4. **Understanding Introductions, Body Paragraphs, and Conclusions** 106
5. **Thinking, Reading, and Writing Critically** 132
6. **Reading and Writing about Different Kinds of Texts** 165

1 Understanding the Active Reading Process

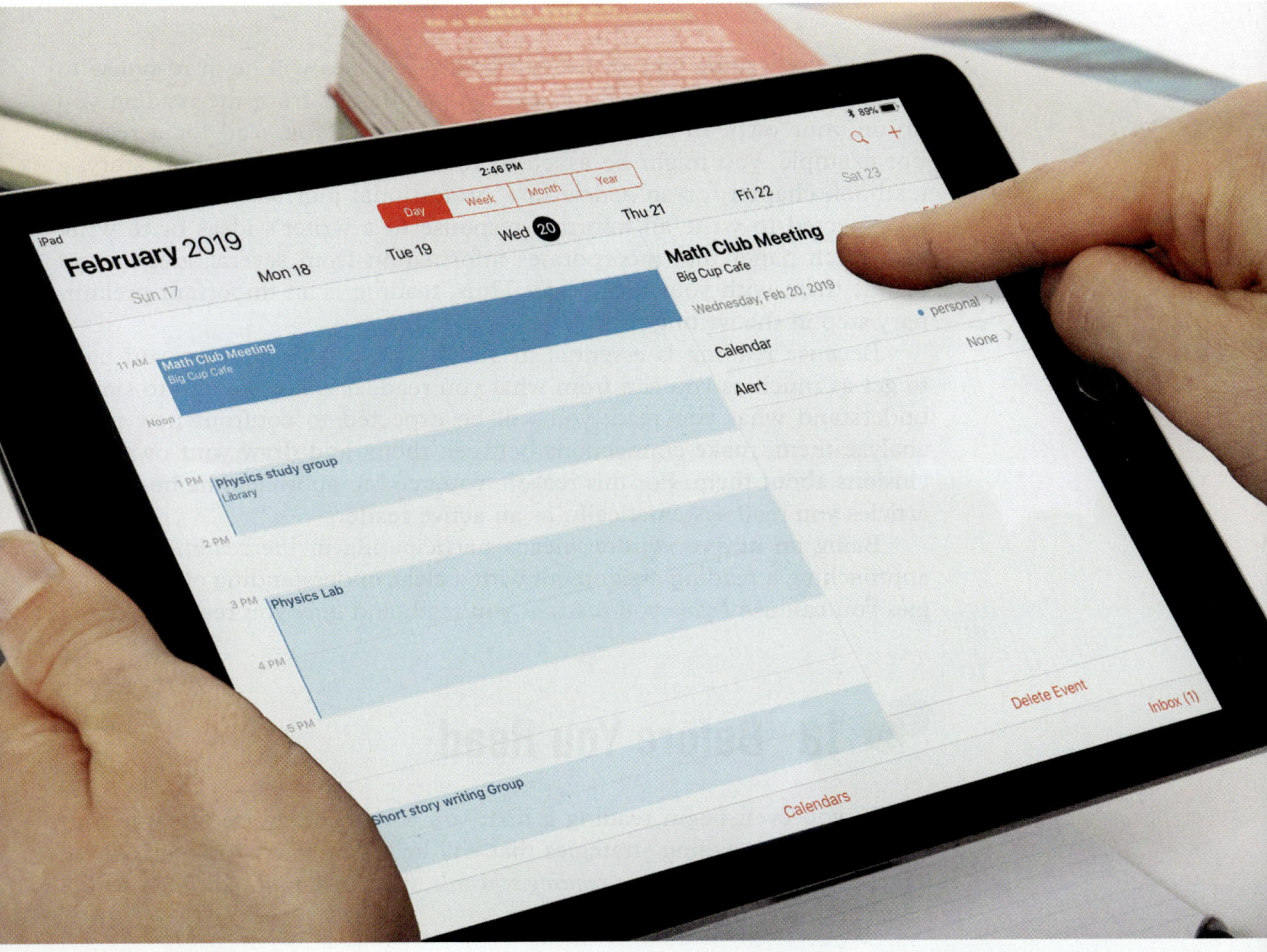

Science Source

FOCUS on reading and writing
Think about what you already know about how to manage your time. Later in this chapter, you will read and write about a passage on this topic.

> **PREVIEW**
>
> In this chapter, you will learn to
> - use active reading strategies before you read (1a).
> - use active reading strategies as you read (1b).
> - use active reading strategies after you read (1c).
> - write a response paragraph (1d).

Most of the writing you do in your college courses will be in response to reading. The reading you do in college is different from the reading you do on your own. In college, you read a lot, and you read for a reason. For example, you might be asked to read a news article, a short story, a textbook chapter, or an article in a professional journal. You might then be expected to write an informal response to a writer's ideas or to write a research paper that incorporates information from several sources and blends them with your own ideas. Thus, reading is an important preliminary step in the writing process.

Because reading is essential in all of your college courses, you need to get as much as you can from what you read. It is not enough to simply understand what you read; you will be expected to confront new ideas, analyze them, make connections between them, and draw your own conclusions about them. For this reason, you need to approach the books and articles you read systematically, as an active reader.

Being an **active reader** means participating in the reading process: approaching a reading assignment with a clear understanding of the strategies you can use *before* you read, *as* you read, and *after* you read.

1a Before You Read

Before you even begin reading a text, you should be aware of some preliminary active reading strategies that will help you when you read. These strategies include *creating a reading schedule, assessing prior knowledge, understanding your purpose,* and *previewing.*

Creating a Reading Schedule

As a college student, you have a lot to do, so planning your reading and study time is very important. One useful time-management strategy is creating a **reading schedule** that maps out how many pages you will read and when you will read them.

For example, if you are assigned to read thirty-six pages in your biology textbook, and the time you have available is between 3 p.m. Monday and 11 a.m. Wednesday, you could map out a reading schedule like the following one.

36 pages/3 days = 12 pages per day
Monday: Read pages 1–12 (7:30–8:45 p.m.)
Tuesday: Read pages 13–24 (3:15–4:30 p.m.)
Wednesday: Read pages 25–36 (7:30–8:45 a.m.)
TOTAL PAGES = 36

When creating your reading schedule, be sure to specify exact times for your reading. If you have blocked out specific times, you will be less likely to procrastinate. Also, be realistic about the number of pages you will read each time, and give yourself more time than you think you will need.

PRACTICE

For practice, create a reading schedule like the one illustrated above for an assignment in one of your classes.

FYI

Preparing to Read

Active reading requires your full attention. Following these guidelines will help you focus as you read:

- **Find a quiet place to study.** If you will be constantly interrupted in your home or dorm room, find an alternative spot, such as the college library, your local library, a coffee shop, or a bookstore.
- **Read in the same place and at the same time each day.** Block out regular times for reading, and then list your assignments for each week. Once you develop a routine of reading in the same place and at the same time, you'll find it easier to focus, and concentrated reading will become a useful habit.
- **Read when you are alert.** Choose a time of day when you're not hungry or tired.

(Continued)

- **Avoid distractions.** Turn off the television. Silence your cell phone; ignore texts; and resist visiting Facebook, YouTube, Snapchat, Instagram, or Twitter. Every time you look at your TV or cell phone, you'll lose your concentration.
- **Break readings into manageable chunks.** Don't try to finish a long reading in one sitting. Instead, try breaking a chapter into sections and stopping at the end of each section to make sure you have understood what you have just read. You might also write a brief summary or use a graphic organizer to help you make sense of the new information. Be sure to reread any passages you find confusing.
- **Build in breaks.** Stop at the end of a chapter, a long section, or an article to stretch your legs, get coffee, or take a short walk.
- **Build in rewards for completing assignments.** Once you've completed your reading for the day, reward yourself. For example, text with a friend or order pizza.

Assessing Prior Knowledge

> **WORD POWER**
>
> **assessing** measuring; determining the value, extent, or significance
>
> **prior** preceding in time or order

Another strategy that you can engage in before reading is to **assess your prior knowledge**—that is, ask yourself what you already know about a subject and what you still need (or want) to know about it. Assessing your prior knowledge will help you to decide how much time you will need to read and which specific reading strategies to use. For example, if you already know a good deal about animal and plant cells, reading a chapter about them may not be very difficult for you. However, if you have no idea how animal and plant cells are different, you will probably have to spend more time reading the chapter in your biology textbook.

To assess your prior knowledge, start by asking the following questions.

> **QUESTIONS FOR ASSESSING PRIOR KNOWLEDGE**
> - Can you predict what the reading material will be about?
> - What do you already know about the subject?
> - How is the text similar to (or different from) other texts you have read?
> - Is there anything in your background that helps you relate to or understand the material?
> - How interested are you in this subject?
> - What do you hope to learn from your reading?

Understanding Your Purpose

Before you begin to read, you should make sure you have a clear understanding of your **purpose** for reading. For example, are you reading to study for a test or quiz? For a research project? To locate information? To complete an assignment? Understanding your purpose, like assessing your prior knowledge, can help you to decide how much time you will need and what reading strategies you will use. For example, if you are reading to prepare for an informal discussion with your study group, you will not need to read as carefully as you might if you were studying for an exam.

> **QUESTIONS FOR UNDERSTANDING YOUR PURPOSE**
> - Why are you reading?
> - Will you be expected to discuss what you are reading? If so, will you discuss it in class? In a conference with your instructor?
> - Will you have to write about what you are reading? If so, will you be expected to write an informal response (for example, a journal entry) or a more formal one (for example, an essay)?
> - Will you be tested on the material?

FYI

Deciding on a Reading Strategy

You will need to adjust your reading strategy based on your purpose or on the type of text you are reading. For example, if you are reading an essay about something you have little or no knowledge about, and you will be tested on it, you will likely use more than one active reading strategy; if you will be discussing a reading in class, you may want to construct an outline of the important points. As you practice reading actively, you will begin to know which strategies are best for which purposes.

Previewing

Once you have set up a reading schedule, assessed your prior knowledge, and established your purpose for reading, you are ready to **preview**, focusing on *skimming* and *scanning* the text.

Skimming

When you **skim** a text, you read it quickly, to get a sense of the writer's main idea and key supporting points. This strategy is particularly useful when you need to read many pages in a short amount of time. (Skimming can also help you determine if a text will be useful to you.)

As you skim, you look at the text's **visual signals**: the title, the author's name, the first paragraph (which often contains a thesis statement or overview), and the last paragraph (which often contains a summary of the writer's points). You might also look at each paragraph's first sentence, which is often the topic sentence. As you skim, you should also look at other visual signals for clues to content and emphasis—for example, headings, boxed text, and images. (Later on, as you read, you will look at **verbal signals**—the words and phrases the writer uses to indicate which points are emphasized and how ideas are arranged.)

> **GUIDELINES FOR SKIMMING**
>
> When skimming a text, look for these visual signals:
>
> - The title
> - The author's name
> - The opening paragraph, searching for the sentence that best expresses the main idea
> - The closing paragraph, searching for a summary of the writer's ideas
> - Each paragraph's first sentence
> - Headings and subheadings
> - *Italicized* and **boldfaced** words
> - Numbered lists
> - Bulleted lists (like this one)
> - Graphs, charts, tables, diagrams, photographs, and other visuals
> - Any information that is in color

Scanning

Scanning is a purposeful, focused look at a text to locate specific information—often to enable you to answer specific questions about the material. For example, if you need to prepare for a quiz or answer questions on a worksheet, you would scan the text, looking only for specific words and phrases that will give you the information you need.

> **GUIDELINES FOR SCANNING**
>
> When scanning a text, look for the following elements:
>
> - Bulleted or numbered lists that might enumerate the writer's key points
> - **Bold faced** or *italicized* words

WORD POWER

enumerate to name one by one

- Organizational words such as *first*, *second*, *third*, *next*, and *finally*
- Proper nouns (capitalized)
- Numbers
- Words set in quotation marks
- Specific words or ideas related to information you are looking for

When you have finished previewing, you should have a general sense of what the writer wants to communicate.

FOCUS on reading and writing

Below is a discussion of time management from a first-year college textbook. In preparation for class discussion and other activities that will be assigned throughout this chapter, **skim** the textbook passage. As you skim, try to identify the writer's main idea and key supporting points and perhaps jot them down for future reference.

TIME-MANAGEMENT STRATEGIES

Learning to manage your time is very important for success in college. Here are some strategies you can adopt to make this task easier:

1. ***Use an organizer.*** New electronic tools are constantly being developed to help you stay organized. For example, Schoolbinder, a free online organizer, can help you manage your time and create a study schedule. If you have trouble blocking out distractions when you are studying, a site like StudyRails can be helpful. For a small monthly fee, this site will help you plan a study schedule and alert you to when it's time to focus on schoolwork. It can also be programmed to block your go-to recreational sites during hours when you should be studying.

    You can use the calendar function on your smartphone or tablet to keep track of deadlines and appointments (see the example on page 3). At the beginning of the semester, enter key pieces of information from each course syllabus—for example, the date of every quiz and exam and the due date of every paper. (Set the alert function of your calendar two or three days in advance so you have enough time to prepare.)

    As the semester progresses, continue to add assignments and deadlines. In addition, enter information such as days when a class will be canceled or will meet in the computer lab or in the library, reminders to bring a particular book or piece of equipment to class, and appointments with instructors or other college personnel. (If you'd like, you can also note reminders and schedule appointments that are not related to school — for example, changes in your work hours, a dental appointment, or lunch with a friend.) Some students also like to keep a separate month-by-month "to do" list. Deleting completed items can give you a feeling of accomplishment — and make the road ahead look shorter.

2. *Use a calendar.* Buy a large wall calendar, and post it where you will see it every morning — on your desk, on the refrigerator, or wherever you keep your phone, your keys, and your ID. At the beginning of the semester, fill in important dates such as school holidays, work commitments, exam dates, and due dates for papers and projects. When you return from classes each day, update the calendar with any new information you have entered into your organizer.

3. *Plan ahead.* If you think you will need help from a writing center tutor to revise a paper that is due in two weeks, don't wait until day thirteen to make an appointment; all the tutoring slots may be filled by then. To be safe, make an appointment about a week in advance.

4. *Learn to enjoy downtime.* When you have a free minute, take time for yourself — and don't feel guilty about it.

FOCUS on reading and writing

Look once again at "Time-Management Strategies." This time, **scan** the passage to look for the following details, noting where you found each piece of information:

- Examples of electronic tools that can help you stay organized
- Suggestions for the best places to put a calendar
- How far in advance you should make an appointment with a writing center tutor

 ## 1b As You Read

Once you have finished previewing a text, it is time to begin reading. Two active reading strategies — *marking* up a text and *annotating* a text — can aid your comprehension as you read. In addition, at some point in this stage of the reading process, you will find it helpful to **TEST** the text you are reading.

TESTing a Text

The letters that spell **TEST** form an acronym for the four basic elements of an essay: **t**hesis (main idea), **e**vidence, **s**ummary, and **t**ransitions. **TEST** is a reading strategy that you can use to help you identify these elements in the professional essays and other texts you will encounter in your college courses. As you will discover in Chapter 3, **TEST** is also a writing strategy that you can use to help you take inventory of the elements in the essays you compose (see p. 85). Using **TEST** to survey a text will help you to get a general idea of what you are reading; it can also help you to see the logic of the writer's discussion and the relationship between the key ideas and the evidence that supports them.

> **WORD POWER**
> **acronym** a word formed from the first letters of a series of words

T **Thesis**—Look for the thesis or **main idea**, which is sometimes stated directly, often (but not always) in the opening paragraphs and often, but not always, in a single sentence. Try to decide why the writer placed the main idea where it is. If the main idea is **implied** (suggested), try to decide why it is not explicitly stated. Try to write a sentence that states the main idea in your own words.

E **Evidence**—Look for the evidence that supports the writer's main idea. This evidence can be in the form of facts, examples, statistics, anecdotes based on the writer's observations or experiences, or the opinions of experts. Think about why the writer chose these types of evidence rather than others. Consider whether different evidence or additional support is needed and whether any evidence is irrelevant or unnecessary. Also, ask yourself what information the writer might have omitted, and why. Finally, think about what you can **infer** from the evidence presented (see 5e Evaluating the Writer's Ideas).

S **Summary**—Look for a statement that lists or summarizes the writer's key points or the essay's main idea. (Often, this summary appears in the closing paragraphs.) If no summary is included, write a sentence that could serve as a summary statement.

T **Transitions**—Look for transitional words and expressions that connect ideas within and between paragraphs. How do these transitions help you to understand the writer's ideas and follow his or her train of thought? Look for **transitional paragraphs**, paragraphs whose purpose is not to supply evidence but rather to move readers from one section of the essay to the next.

When you read essays by professional writers, you should always look for the four **TEST** elements. In some cases, however, you may not be able to easily identify these elements. This is because professional writers may prefer to experiment with them. For example, they may imply a thesis instead of stating it directly or suggest, rather than explicitly summarizing, their main points. In a long or complex professional essay, particularly one whose main idea is controversial, the main idea may appear at the end instead of near the beginning. In addition, the conclusion may not include a summary statement; it may simply suggest the main idea and not summarize it at all.

Despite these variations, looking for the four **TEST** elements as you read is important because it will help you to identify the main idea and the evidence that supports it. This in turn will aid your comprehension and enable you to respond in writing to the writer's ideas.

In the following essay, "What American Citizenship Makes Possible," by Colin Powell, the **TEST** elements have been identified for you.

What American Citizenship Makes Possible
Colin Powell

Taking the Oath of Allegiance to the U.S., June 20, in Washington, DC

1   Many years ago, after I had become a four-star general and then chairman of the Joint Chiefs of Staff, *The Times* of London wrote an article observing that if my parents had sailed to England rather than New York, "the most they could have dreamed of for their son in the military was to become a sergeant in one of the lesser British regiments."

2   Only in America could the son of two poor Jamaican immigrants become the first African-American, the youngest person and the first

ROTC graduate from a public university to hold those positions, among many other firsts. My parents arrived—one at the Port of Philadelphia, the other at Ellis Island—in search of economic opportunity, but their goal was to become American citizens, because they knew what that made possible.

3   Immigration is a vital part of our national being because people come here not only to build a better life for themselves and their children, but to become Americans. With access to education and a clear path to citizenship, they routinely become some of the best, most-patriotic Americans you'll ever know. That's why I am a strong supporter of immigration-law reform: America stands to benefit from it as much as, if not more than, the immigrants themselves.

4   Contrary to some common misconceptions, neighborhoods with greater concentrations of immigrants have lower rates of crime and violence than comparable nonimmigrant neighborhoods, according to a 2015 report from the National Academies of Sciences, Engineering, and Medicine. Foreign-born men age 18–39 are jailed at one-quarter the rate of native-born American men of the same age.

5   Today's immigrants are learning English at the same rate or faster than earlier waves of newcomers, and first-generation arrivals are less likely to die from cardiovascular disease or cancer than native-born people. They experience fewer chronic health conditions, have lower infant-mortality and obesity rates, and have a longer life expectancy.

6   My parents met and married here and worked in the garment industry, bringing home $50 to $60 a week. They had two children: my sister Marilyn, who became a teacher, and me. I didn't do as well as the family hoped; I caused a bit of a crisis when I decided to stay in the Army. "Couldn't he get a job? Why is he still in the Army?"

7   We were a tightknit family with cousins and aunts and uncles all over the place. But that family network didn't guarantee success. What did? The New York City public education system.

8   I'm a public-education kid, from kindergarten through to Morris High School in the South Bronx and, finally, City College of New York. New York University made me an offer, but tuition there was $750 a year. Such a huge sum in 1954! I would never impose that on my parents, so it was CCNY, where back then tuition was free. I got a B.S. in geology and a commission as an Army second lieutenant, and that was that. And it all cost my parents nothing. Zero.

9   After CCNY, I was lucky to be among the first group of officers commissioned just after the Army was desegregated. I competed against West Pointers, against grads from Harvard and VMI and the Citadel and other top schools. And to my surprise, I discovered I had gotten a pretty good education in the New York City public schools. Not only in geology and the military, but also in wider culture. I had learned a little about music, about Chaucer's *Canterbury Tales* and theater and things like that. I got a complete education, all through public schools, and it shapes me to this day.

[T] Transitions

10   This amazing gift goes back to 1847 when the Free Academy of the City of New York was created with a simple mandate: "Give every child the opportunity for an education." And who would pay for it? The citizens and taxpayers of New York City and State. They did it and kept at it when the Academy became CCNY in 1866, because they knew that poor immigrants were their children. They were the future.

11   They still are. Today some 41 million immigrants and 37.1 million U.S.-born children of immigrants live in the U.S. Taken together, the first and second generations are one-quarter of the population. While some countries, like Japan and Russia, worry that population decline threatens their economies, America's economic future vibrates with promise from immigrants' energy, creativity, and ambition.

[E] Evidence

12   Every one of these people deserves the same educational opportunities I had. It wasn't, and isn't, charity to immigrants or to the poor. Those early New Yorkers were investing in their own future by making education and citizenship accessible to "every child." They knew it—and what a future it became!

13   We still have that model. But today too many politicians seem to think that shortchanging education will somehow help society. It does not. It hurts society. We need people who know that government has no more important function than securing the terrain, which means opening the pathways to the future for everyone, educating them to be consumers, workers, leaders, and citizens.

[S] Summary

14   We are all immigrants, wave after wave over several hundred years. And every wave makes us richer: in cultures, in language and food, in music and dance, and in intellectual capacity. We should treasure this immigrant tradition, and we should reform our laws to guarantee it.

15   In this political season, let us remember the most important task of our government: making Americans. Immigrants—future Americans—make America better every single day.

★ ★ ★

In this essay, retired General and former Secretary of State Colin Powell presents a powerful argument about the value of immigrants. Noting that he himself is the son of immigrants, he uses narration, exemplification, and other patterns of development to convince readers that his position is valid.

Instead of stating his thesis explicitly in a single sentence at the end of the first paragraph, a technique that serves beginning writers well, he presents his main idea in paragraph 3, after first introducing himself and establishing his status as a son of immigrants. Paragraph 3 then explains his main idea: that immigrants "become American" and thus become patriotic citizens—and that this in turn benefits the nation.

Powell's essay includes helpful transitions between paragraphs, such as "They were the future. They still are" (paras. 10–11), as well as a transitional paragraph (para. 7). He also includes a summary (para. 14) that stresses the importance of immigrants, and he closes with a strong appeal to his audience (para. 15).

Marking Up a Text

When you **mark up** a text, you use underlining and symbols to identify key ideas. This active reading strategy will help you to understand the writer's ideas and make connections among them when you reread. Be selective as you proceed. You will eventually be rereading every underlined word, phrase, and sentence—so set off only the most important information.

> **MARKING UP A TEXT**
> - Underline key ideas—for example, topic sentences.
> - Box or circle words or phrases you want to remember.
> - Place a check mark (✓) or star (★) next to an important idea.
> - Place double check marks (✓✓) or double stars (★★) next to an especially significant idea.
> - Draw lines or arrows to connect related ideas. ⟶
> - Put a question mark (?) beside a word or idea that you need to look up.
> - [Bracket] text you want to set off.
> - Number the writer's key supporting points or examples.

FYI

Knowing What to Mark Up

You want to identify what is important—but how do you *know* what is important?

- *Look for visual signals.* As a general rule, you should look for the same **visual signals** you looked for when you did your previewing. Many of the ideas you will need to set off will probably be found in material that is visually set off from the rest of the text—opening and closing paragraphs, lists, and so on.
- *Look for verbal signals.* At this stage, you should also look for **verbal signals**—words and phrases that often introduce key points. (These are listed in the box on page 16.)

Together, these visual and verbal signals will give you clues to the writer's meaning and emphasis.

> **VERBAL SIGNALS**
> - Repeated words and phrases
> - Phrases that signal emphasis ("The *primary* reason"; "The *most important* idea")
> - Words that signal addition (*also, in addition, furthermore*)
> - Words that signal time sequence (*first, after, then, next, finally*)
> - Words that identify causes and effects (*because, as a result, for this reason*)
> - Words that introduce examples (*for example, for instance*)
> - Words that signal comparison (*likewise, similarly*)
> - Words that signal contrast (*unlike, although, in contrast*)
> - Words that signal contradiction (*however, on the contrary*)
> - Words that signal a narrowing of the writer's focus (*in fact, specifically, in other words*)
> - Words that signal summaries or conclusions (*to sum up, in conclusion*)

Here is how one student used underlining and symbols to mark up an excerpt from the newspaper article "What American Citizenship Makes Possible," by Colin Powell.

Model Marked-Up Text

We were a tightknit family with cousins and aunts and uncles all over the place. But that family network didn't guarantee success. What did? The New York City public education system.

I'm a public-education kid, from kindergarten through to Morris High School in the South Bronx and, finally, City College of New York. New York University made me an offer, but tuition there was $750 a year. Such a huge sum in 1954! I would never impose that on my parents, so it was CCNY, where back then tuition was free. I got a B.S. in geology and a commission as an Army second lieutenant, and that was that. And it all cost my parents nothing. Zero.

After CCNY, I was lucky to be among the first group of officers commissioned just after the Army was desegregated. I competed against West Pointers, against grads from Harvard and VMI and the Citadel and other top schools. And to my surprise, I discovered I had gotten a pretty good education in the New York City public schools. Not only in geology and the military, but also in wider culture. I had learned a little about music, about Chaucer's "Canterbury Tales" and theater and things like that. I got a complete education, all through public schools, and it shapes me to this day.

This amazing gift goes back to 1847 when the Free Academy of the City of New York was created with a simple mandate: "Give every child the opportunity for an education." And who would pay for it? The citizens and taxpayers of New York City and State. They did it and kept at it when the Academy became CCNY in 1866, because they knew that poor immigrants * were their children. They were the future.

The student who marked up the passage above was preparing to write an essay about whether public colleges should be free. Because the passage included no visual signals apart from the paragraph divisions, she looked carefully for verbal signals.

The student began by underlining the writer's main idea in the passage's first paragraph: that New York City public schools made him a success. She then circled the key terms *success, lucky, amazing gift,* and *opportunity,* which she thought conveyed a sense of the writer's impression of his public school education, and she drew lines to connect these related terms.

The student underlined sentences that supported the main idea, drawing an arrow to connect two related points ("I'm a public-education kid" and "I got a complete education, all through public schools, and it shapes me to this day.") She also bracketed an unfamiliar reference to desegregating the army and put a question mark beside it to remind herself to look it up.

Finally, she underlined and starred some of the passage's closing lines, which she thought summarized the main idea: that poor immigrants, like Powell himself, have benefited from their free education and owe their success to the New York City schools.

PRACTICE

1-2 Review the marked-up passage on pages 16 and 17. How would your own underlining and symbols on this passage be similar to or different from the sample student's? How does the purpose for your reading affect what you might set off?

FOCUS on reading and writing

Reread "Time-Management Strategies" (p. 10). As you reread, underline and star the main idea, box and circle key words, checkmark important points, draw lines and arrows to connect related ideas, and so on. Be sure to circle each unfamiliar word and put a question mark above it so that you will remember to look it up later on.

FYI

Using Context Clues

Before you turn to a dictionary to determine the meaning of an unfamiliar word, see if you can figure out the meaning from context clues in the text. (See 2c Acquiring New Words (p. 40) for information on how to use context clues to expand your vocabulary.)

Annotating a Text

Once you have marked up a passage, your next step is to *annotate* it. **Annotating** a passage means reading critically and making notes—of questions, reactions, reminders, and ideas for writing or discussion—in the margins or between the lines. (If you run out of room on the page, you can use sticky notes.) Keeping an informal record of ideas as they occur to you will prepare you for class discussion and for writing. This is the first step in engaging with the text on a deeper level, one in which you analyze and evaluate it.

As you read, keeping the following questions in mind will help you make useful annotations.

> **QUESTIONS FOR ANNOTATING**
> - What is the writer saying? What do you think the writer is suggesting or implying? What makes you think so?
> - What is the writer's purpose (his or her reason for writing)?
> - What kind of audience is the writer addressing?
> - Is the writer responding to another writer's ideas?
> - What is the writer's main idea? Is it stated or implied? Can you restate the main idea in your own words?

- How does the writer support his or her points? Does the writer use facts? Expert opinion? Personal experiences or observations?
- Does the writer include enough supporting details and examples?
- How does the writer signal a shift from one point to the next?
- Does the writer summarize the main idea or key points? If so, where?
- What is the writer's main idea?
- What pattern of development does the writer use to arrange his or her ideas? Is this pattern the best choice?
- Does the writer seem well informed? Reasonable? Fair?
- Do you understand the writer's vocabulary?
- Do you understand the writer's ideas?
- Do you agree with the points the writer is making?
- How are the ideas presented in this reading selection like (or unlike) those presented in other selections you have read?

FYI

Making Useful Annotations

As you annotate, remember that you should not write too much or too little; good annotations fit in the margins or on a small sticky note. You should *not* write your annotations on a separate sheet of paper. If you do, you will be tempted to write too much, and you can easily lose track of where a particular note belongs or what point it comments on. (Moreover, if you lose the sheet of paper, you will also lose all your notes and thoughts.)

Think of annotations as a study aid that you can consult when you return to the text a few days later. Brief, useful annotations will help you follow the writer's ideas and remember what is most important in the text.

The following passage, which reproduces the student's marking from pages 16–17, also includes her annotations.

Model Annotating

We were a tightknit family with cousins and aunts and uncles all over the place. But that family network didn't guarantee success. What did? The New York City public education system.

I'm a public-education kid, from kindergarten through to Morris High School in the South Bronx and, finally, City College of New York. New York University made me an offer, but tuition there was $750 a year. Such a huge sum in 1954! I would never impose that on my parents, so it was CCNY, where back then tuition was free. I got a B.S. in geology and a commission as an Army second lieutenant, and that was that. And it all cost my parents nothing. Zero.

After CCNY, I was lucky to be among the first group of officers commissioned just after the Army was desegregated. I competed against West Pointers, against grads from Harvard and VMI and the Citadel and other top schools. And to my surprise, I discovered I had gotten a pretty good education in the New York City public schools. Not only in geology and the military, but also in wider culture. I had learned a little about music, about Chaucer's "Canterbury Tales" and theater and things like that. I got a complete education, all through public schools, and it shapes me to this day.

This amazing gift goes back to 1847 when the Free Academy of the City of New York was created with a simple mandate: "Give every child the opportunity for an education." And who would pay for it? The citizens and taxpayers of New York City and State. They did it and kept at it when the Academy became CCNY in 1866, because they knew that poor immigrants * were their children. They were the future.

Margin annotations:
- Is CCNY still free?
- Why is he surprised to find his education was good?
- U.S. Army segregated until 1948 (through WWII)

In her marginal annotations, the student wrote a brief explanation of the reference to army segregation and asked two questions. She thought that answers to these questions would give her information that would help her develop ideas for her paper on whether public colleges should be free.

FOCUS on reading and writing

Reread "Time-Management Strategies" (p. 9). This time, refer to the Questions for Annotating (p. 18), and use them to guide you as you write down your own thoughts and questions in the margins of the passage. Note where you agree or disagree with the writer, and briefly explain why. Briefly summarize any points you think are particularly important. Take time to look up any unfamiliar words you have circled and to write brief definitions. Think of these annotations as your preparation for discussing the passage in class—and, eventually, for writing about it.

FOCUS on reading and writing

Exchange books with another student, and read his or her highlighting and annotations on "Time-Management Strategies." How are your written responses similar to the other student's? How are they different? Do your classmate's responses help you to see anything new about the passage? Looking again at your own annotations, consider how you might use them to write a response to the suggestions in "Time-Management Strategies."

1c After You Read

After you finish reading, some additional active reading strategies—*outlining*, *summarizing* and *paraphrasing*, *reviewing*, and *self-quizzing*—will enable you to better retain and use the information you have acquired. Once you have a command of the material, you will be prepared to express your reactions by writing a *response paragraph*.

Outlining

Outlining a text is an active reading strategy that you can use to help you understand it. Unlike a **formal outline**, which follows strict conventions, an **informal outline** is just a list of a passage's key ideas and supporting points in the order in which they are presented. After you have made an informal outline of a passage, you should be able to see which ideas are more important than others, as well as how the ideas are related.

FYI

Constructing an Informal Outline

To construct an informal outline, follow these guidelines:

1. Write or type the passage's main idea at the top of a sheet of paper. (This will remind you of the writer's focus and help keep your outline on track.)
2. At the left margin, record the most important idea of the first body paragraph or first part of the passage.
3. Indent the next line a few spaces, and list the examples or details that support this idea.
4. As ideas become more specific, indent further. (Ideas that have the same degree of importance are indented the same distance from the left margin.)

Repeat the process with each body paragraph or part of the passage.

The student who marked up and annotated the excerpt from Colin Powell's "What American Citizenship Makes Possible" (p. 12) made the following informal outline to help her understand the writer's ideas.

Model Outline

<u>Main idea</u>: According to Colin Powell, he — like many other children from poor immigrant families — owes his success to the free public education he received.

    New York City public school experience
        Attended free public elementary and high school
        Attended CCNY
            Free tuition
            B.S. degree
            Army commission
    Army experience
        Became officer
        Realized his education had been good
            Geology and military
            "Wider culture"

FOCUS on reading and writing

Make an informal outline of "Time-Management Strategies" (p. 9). Refer to your underlining, symbols, and annotations as you construct your outline. When you have finished, check to make certain your outline accurately represents the writer's emphasis and the relationships among his or her ideas.

Summarizing and Paraphrasing

Once you have **TEST**ed, marked up, annotated, and outlined a passage, you may want to *summarize* or *paraphrase* it to help you understand it better.

Summarizing

A **summary** is a brief restatement, *in your own words*, of a passage's main idea. A summary does not include supporting examples and details, and it does not include your own ideas or opinions. For this reason, a summary is always much shorter than the original passage—usually no longer than a few sentences.

> **GUIDELINES FOR WRITING A SUMMARY**
>
> 1. Reread your source, and review your outline.
> 2. Consulting your outline, restate the passage's main idea *in your own words*, using synonyms wherever possible and using your own syntax. If you decide to use a distinctive word or phrase from the original passage, put it in quotation marks.
> 3. To avoid accidentally using the exact same language as the original, do not look at the passage when you are writing your summary.
> 4. Be sure to identify the author and title of the source.
> 5. Reread the original passage once again to make sure you have accurately summarized the main idea and key supporting details and that you have not included any unrelated or unnecessary material. Also, check to make sure you have not accidentally used the source's exact wording or sentence structure. (If you have, you will have committed **plagiarism**. See 13c Using Sources Ethically (p. 350).)

The student who marked up, annotated, and outlined the excerpt from "What American Citizenship Makes Possible" (p. 16 Model Marked-Up Text; p. 20 Model Annotating; p. 22 Model Outline) wrote the following summary. Note that her summary includes the author's name and the title of the source.

In "What American Citizenship Makes Possible," Colin Powell attributes his success in life to the free public education he received from kindergarten through college and stresses the value of free college education, particularly for children of immigrants (like himself).

FOCUS on reading and writing

Write a summary of "Time-Management Strategies" (p. 9). Use your informal outline to guide you, and keep your summary brief—no more than two or three sentences long.

Paraphrasing

When you **paraphrase**, you put a writer's words into your own, substituting different vocabulary and sentence structure for the writer's. The act of paraphrasing helps you to understand a text better because it requires you to think about exactly what the writer means to say and how he or she says it.

As is the case with summaries, paraphrases do not include your own ideas or your opinions of the writer's statements. Unlike a summary, however, a paraphrase can be the same length as (or longer than) the original.

> ### GUIDELINES FOR WRITING A PARAPHRASE
> 1. Read the passage carefully.
> 2. Draft your paraphrase, following the order and emphasis of the original. Be sure to include the passage's main idea as well as the key supporting examples and details. Use your own syntax, use synonyms wherever possible, and put any distinctive words you borrow in quotation marks.
> 3. Reread your paraphrase, comparing it to the original source to make sure it reflects its meaning and emphasis, and does not include any of the source's distinctive wording or sentence structure.
> 4. Be sure to include an in-text citation that references your Works Cited List.

The student who summarized the Colin Powell passage above paraphrased a few sentences to help her understand his ideas.

ORIGINAL EXCERPT

> I discovered I had gotten a pretty good education in the New York City public schools. Not only in geology and the military, but also in wider culture. I had learned a little about music, about Chaucer's *Canterbury Tales* and theater and things like that. I got a complete education, all through public schools, and it shapes me to this day.

PARAPHRASE

> Powell learned that his New York City public school education was better than he had thought, giving him a foundation in "wider culture" as well as in subjects such as geology and in military topics. He discovered he had also learned something about subjects such as music, literature, and theater. The public school education he received "shapes [him] to this day" (p. 13).

The student writer knew that she had to avoid using the original excerpt's distinctive words or sentence constructions. When she came across distinctive phrases that were hard to put into different words, she kept the original words but put them in quotation marks to indicate that they were used in her source. (When she had to change the source's *me* to *him* to make it fit into her sentence, she set *him* in brackets to indicate her change.) She was also careful to retain the order and emphasis of Powell's ideas. (For more information on writing summaries and paraphrases, see 13b Using Sources in Your Writing.

Reviewing and Self-Quizzing

In order to remember the information you have read, you should review it carefully and quiz yourself after you read.

When you **review**, you repeat information so that you can remember and use it. Typically, this review strategy works best when you have only five to seven items (or concepts) to remember. For example, if you need to remember the sequence of key U.S. immigration laws, the relative distance of planets from the sun, or the muscles in the shoulder, you can just list these items and study them until you have memorized them. This strategy will help to prepare you for class discussion or for writing an exam answer. (You can also use **mnemonic** devices to help you remember items. See p. 46 Using Mnemonics.)

Self-quizzing helps you make connections to the information so you can truly learn it. If you want to remember information for a long time—and understand it—you will find this strategy helpful. Self-quizzing not only helps you identify important information, but it also helps you apply information to a specific situation—for example, on an exam.

Self-quizzing involves creating thoughtful questions from the information in a text. You can create three kinds of questions:

1. **Literal questions** test your comprehension of factual material. If you scan the text, you will find the answers to these questions. For example, to answer the question, "When did the Free Academy of the City University of New York become City College?," you can point to the answer—"1866"—in the third paragraph of the passage from the Colin Powell essay.

2. **Inferential questions** are those that go beyond facts; they ask you to look at the ideas in the text and **infer** (figure out) what the writer means. For example, if you asked, "Does the writer believe that all public colleges should be free?," you would have to review your highlighting to see what the text suggests about Powell's personal opinion.

3. **Evaluative questions** force you to go beyond the literal meaning of the text and make a judgment or generate an opinion about the material. For example, if you asked, "Do I believe that Powell's success is really largely due to his access to a free college education? What in my experience has led me to believe that my answer is correct?," you would have to think about your own experiences and observations in light of what you have read.

Once you create your questions, you can use them as you study and interact with the text. Keep in mind that different kinds of questions serve different purposes. For example, if you were taking a multiple-choice quiz, you might want to focus on creating literal study questions, but if you were preparing for class discussion or taking an essay exam, it might be helpful to practice answering inferential and evaluative questions.

PRACTICE 1-3

To practice self-quizzing, work with another student to create one literal question, one inferential question, and one evaluative question for one of the model student essays in Unit 2 of this book. Write your questions without the answers on a sheet of paper. Then, trade questions with another group, and answer their questions while they answer yours.

1d Writing a Response Paragraph

After you have marked up and annotated a reading selection, you are ready to write about it—perhaps in a **response paragraph**, in which you record your reactions to the writer's ideas.

Because a response paragraph is informal, no special guidelines or rules govern its format or structure. As in any paragraph, however, you should include a topic sentence, support the topic sentence with specific evidence (examples and details), use complete sentences, and link sentences with appropriate transitions. In a response paragraph, informal style and personal opinions are acceptable.

The student who marked up, annotated, outlined, summarized, and paraphrased material from "What American Citizenship Makes Possible," wrote the following response paragraph.

Model Response

In "What American Citizenship Makes Possible," General Colin Powell, former U.S. Secretary of State, discusses the ways in which immigrants enrich the United States. Summarizing his own experience as the son of poor Jamaican immigrants, Powell stresses the value of the free public education he received not just in elementary and high school but also through college, and he identifies this education as the key factor that led to his professional success. This seems like an exaggeration. He probably had many other important personal experiences and professional interactions that could have led to his success. Besides, a private college—even one he had to borrow money to attend—might have provided an even better education. By stressing how fortunate he was, and how greatly he benefited, Powell seems to suggest that the "amazing gift" he received from New York City should be widely available today to students like him. If it were, he believes, it would provide a valuable opportunity for immigrants who cannot afford private college tuition. However, immigrant children could fund their education at private colleges with the help of loans, work-study, and tuition scholarships. Thus, Powell's point—that the children of poor immigrants should have access to free public college education—is questionable. These children may be "the future" of our country, as he says, but that does not mean that their college education should be subsidized.

The process of writing this paragraph was very helpful to the student. The questions she asked suggested some interesting ideas that she could explore in class discussion or in a more fully developed piece of writing.

FOCUS on reading and writing

Now that you have practiced the complete active reading process with the textbook excerpt on page 9, "Time-Management Strategies," write a response paragraph that explains your thoughts about the time-management strategies presented in the excerpt. In your paragraph, you can discuss why these strategies would (or would not) be useful to you, or you can write about strategies you already use to manage your time. When you have finished, **TEST** what you have written.

Science Source

CHAPTER REVIEW

REVIEW ACTIVITY

Graphic Organizer: *Active Reading Strategies*

Drawing on the information you learned in Chapter 1, use the graphic organizer that follows on page 29 to map the various strategies that can be applied before, during, and after reading. Also include a brief explanation of how you plan to use each reading strategy this semester.

Chapter Review

Before Reading Strategies

Strategy 1: _Creating a reading schedule_

I will apply strategy 1 by _Reading at least 15 pages of each textbook on Mon. – Thurs. between 7:00–9:00 p.m._

Strategy 2: _____

I will apply strategy 2 by _____

Strategy 3: _____

I will apply strategy 3 by _____

Strategy 4: _____

I will apply strategy 4 by _____

During Reading Strategies

Strategy 1: _____

I will apply strategy 1 by _____

Strategy 2: _____

I will apply strategy 2 by _____

After Reading Strategies

Strategy 1: _____

I will apply strategy 1 by _____

Strategy 2: _____

I will apply strategy 2 by _____

Strategy 3: _____

I will apply strategy 3 by _____

Strategy 4: _____

I will apply strategy 4 by _____

Chapter Review

COLLABORATIVE ACTIVITY

Fill in the crossword puzzle on page 31 with the help of the clues listed below. Answers to clues that fall under the heading "Across" will appear only in the boxes ordered from left to right in the puzzle. Answers to clues that fall under the heading "Down" will appear only in boxes ordered from top to bottom in the puzzle. The answers are drawn from the key terms in Chapter 1 (which are set in boldface), and page numbers are provided to guide you back to the proper place in the chapter.

Hint: Five of the answers consist of two-word terms.

Example (1 Across):

The words and phrases the writer uses to indicate which points are emphasized and how ideas are arranged: VERBAL SIGNALS

ACROSS

2. The words and phrases the writer uses to indicate which points are emphasized and how ideas are arranged (see p. 16)
8. A plan that maps out how many pages you will read and when you will read them (two words) (see p. 4)
9. A reading strategy that helps you identify an essay's four key elements (see p. 11)
10. Clues to content and emphasis, such as headings, boxed text, and images (see p. 8)
13. Taking a purposeful, focused look at a text to locate specific information (see p. 8)
14. Tools to help you manage your time (see p. 9)
16. Putting a passage into your own words (see p. 24)

DOWN

1. Using underlining and symbols to identify key ideas (see p. 15)
3. A process involving strategies that include creating a reading schedule, assessing prior knowledge, understanding your purpose, and previewing (two words) (see p. 4)
4. A technique to help you understand the structure of a reading assignment as well as the ideas it communicates (see p. 21)
5. What you already know about a subject and what you still need (or want) to know about it (two words) (see p. 6)
6. Your reason for reading, such as for pleasure, for information, or to complete an assignment (see p. 7)
7. Writing a brief restatement, in your own words, of a passage's main idea (see p. 23)
11. Reading critically and making notes—of questions, reactions, reminders, and ideas for writing or discussion—in the margins or between the lines (see p. 18)
12. Reading a text quickly and trying to get a sense of the writer's main idea and key supporting points (see p. 7)
15. Repeating information so that you can remember and use it (see p. 25)

Chapter Review

Review checklist

✔ Being an active reader involves using strategies before, during, and after you read to help you retain and use the information in the text.

✔ Before you read, you should assess your prior knowledge, set a purpose for your reading, and preview the text. (See 1a.)

✔ As you read, **TEST** the text to help you identify its key elements. Also, mark up and annotate the text to help you identify the writer's key ideas. (See 1b.)

✔ After you read, outlining, summarizing, paraphrasing, reviewing, and self-quizzing can help you remember what you have read. (See 1c.)

✔ Once you have marked up and annotated a text, you can write a response paragraph to record your reactions to the writer's ideas. (See 1d.)

2 Building Vocabulary for Reading and Writing

FOCUS on reading and writing
List some things that you already know about taking standardized tests. Later in this chapter, you will read and write about a passage on this topic.

PREVIEW

In this chapter, you will learn to
- understand your vocabularies (2a).
- "know" words (2b).
- acquire new words (2c).
- use new words in your writing (2d).

Words are everywhere. Between the time you entered kindergarten and the time you entered the college classroom, you learned thousands of words. However, there are still many words left to learn. Learning these new words—and using those that you already know correctly and effectively—are important keys to becoming a better reader and writer.

In addition, recent studies have found a definite link between a person's vocabulary and success. This should come as no surprise because your ability to express yourself depends on your command of the language. It makes sense that the more words you understand and can use the easier it will be to present your ideas clearly and convincingly. In other words, a larger vocabulary increases your options in life and has a powerful effect on how well you will do both in school and on the job.

In order to build a stronger vocabulary, you need to be aware of the different vocabularies you use, understand what it means to "know" a word, learn how to acquire new words, and practice using new words in your writing.

2a Understanding Your Vocabularies

When people refer to "vocabulary," they are actually talking about four separate vocabularies: a *listening vocabulary*, a *reading vocabulary*, a *speaking vocabulary*, and a *writing vocabulary*. If you want to be a better reader, writer, learner, and speaker, you need to work on improving all four of these vocabularies.

1. Your **listening vocabulary** consists of the words you hear daily—in conversation, on television, or in song lyrics. This is the first vocabulary that you develop as a child. Your listening vocabulary is part of your **receptive vocabulary**—the words you generally understand, but may not know well enough to use.

2. Your **reading vocabulary**, which is also part of your receptive vocabulary, consists of the words you recognize when you read. It develops as you begin to learn to read, usually early in elementary school.

This vocabulary is generally your largest; many words in your reading vocabulary are not part of your speaking or writing vocabularies. This is especially true of discipline-specific words, such as *jurisprudence*, *tort*, *acidification*, *arbitrage*, *antigen*, *meniscus*, *conditioning*, *titration*, and *algorithm*.

3. Your **speaking vocabulary** consists of the words you use in conversation. It comes from interacting with people around you as you communicate orally. Your speaking vocabulary is part of your **expressive vocabulary**—the words that you know well enough to use when you speak and write. (Your expressive vocabulary is generally smaller than your receptive vocabulary.)

4. Your **writing vocabulary** is also a part of your expressive vocabulary. It consists of the words you use when you write, and it is the last vocabulary to develop. For most people, it is their most limited vocabulary because it is much more difficult to use a word effectively in writing than it is to recognize it when listening or reading. Many words in your speaking vocabulary are part of your writing vocabulary, but academic words—such as *simile*, *deduce*, *empirical*, *logarithm*, and *paradigm*—are much more common in your writing vocabulary.

2b "Knowing" Words

When you learn a new word, your ultimate goal is to be able to use it in all four of your vocabularies. In other words, you want to achieve **full knowledge** of the word—to recognize it in conversation, use it correctly when you speak, understand its meaning when you come across the word in your reading, and use it accurately in your writing.

Activating Your Schemata

People come to college with different degrees of knowledge. According to one theory, the knowledge you have is organized into individual units, each of which is called a **schema**. These **schemata** (plural of schema), or units of existing knowledge, help you understand new material, and they expand as you acquire this new information. In other words, as you read, you gain information from the text as well as from what you already know about the subject of the text. As you read further, the information that you have just acquired helps you understand and interpret new information. When you gain new knowledge, you create new schemata or expand (or revise) existing ones.

This concept holds true when you learn new words. When you first encounter a word, you create a schema for that word and expand it as you learn more about the word. Every time you encounter this word, you access the schema associated with it. As you see the word in different contexts, you add to your knowledge about how the word is used.

For example, when you look at the title of the following passage by Amy Tan, you might have some idea what the writer means by the words *mother tongue*. If so, you have automatically activated your prior knowledge—or schema—for that phrase as soon as you read it.

FOCUS on reading and writing

The passage that follows is excerpted from "Mother Tongue," an essay by Amy Tan. ("Mother Tongue" is included in Chapter 30, p. 590.) In preparation for class discussion and writing that will be assigned later in this chapter, read the passage. Then, choose one of the following terms from the essay—a term that you already know—to use in Practice 2-1.

Terms: *sociologists, immigrant families, IQ tests, SAT, math*

Excerpt from "Mother Tongue"

Amy Tan

1   I think my mother's English almost had an effect on limiting my possibilities in life as well. Sociologists and linguists probably will tell you that a person's developing language skills are more influenced by peers. But I do think that the language spoken in the family, especially in immigrant families which are more insular, plays a large role in shaping the language of the child. And I believe that it affected my results on achievement tests, I.Q. tests, and the SAT. While my English skills were never judged as poor, compared to math, English could not be considered my strong suit. In grade school I did moderately well, getting perhaps B's, sometimes B-pluses, in English and scoring perhaps in the sixtieth or seventieth percentile on achievement tests. But those scores were not good enough to override the opinion that my true abilities lay in math and science, because in those areas I achieved A's and scored in the ninetieth percentile or higher.

2   This was understandable. Math is precise; there is only one correct answer. Whereas, for me at least, the answers on English tests were always a judgment call, a matter of opinion and personal experience. Those tests were constructed around items like fill-in-the-blank sentence completion, such as, "Even though Tom was _____, Mary thought he was _____." And the correct answer always seemed to be the most bland combinations of thoughts, for example, "Even though Tom was shy, Mary thought he was charming," with the grammatical structure "even though" limiting the correct answer to some sort of semantic opposites, so you wouldn't get answers

like, "Even though Tom was foolish, Mary thought he was ridiculous." Well, according to my mother, there were very few limitations as to what Tom could have been and what Mary might have thought of him. So I never did well on tests like that.

3   The same was true with word analogies, pairs of words in which you were supposed to find some sort of logical, semantic relationship—for example, "*Sunset* is to *nightfall* as _____ is to _____." And here you would be presented with a list of four possible pairs, one of which showed the same kind of relationship: *red* is to *stoplight*, *bus* is to *arrival*, *chill* is to *fever*, *yawn* is to *boring*: Well, I could never think that way. I knew what the tests were asking, but I could not block out of my mind the images already created by the first pair, "*sunset* is to *nightfall*"—and I would see a burst of colors against a darkening sky, the moon rising, the lowering of a curtain of stars. And all the other pairs of words—red, bus, stoplight, boring—just threw up a mass of confusing images, making it impossible for me to sort out something as logical as saying: "A sunset precedes nightfall" is the same as "a chill precedes a fever." The only way I would have gotten that answer right would have been to imagine an associative situation, for example, my being disobedient and staying out past sunset, catching a chill at night, which turns into feverish pneumonia as punishment, which indeed did happen to me.

PRACTICE 2-1   Activate your schemata for the term you chose from the Tan passage. Then list five pieces of information you already know about this term.

PRACTICE 2-2   Working with another student, read each other's lists, and add information you know about both terms. Together, you will be building your schemata by adding to each other's knowledge of the word.

Understanding Denotations, Connotations, Synonyms, and Antonyms

To achieve full knowledge of a word—that is, to learn what a word means and how to use it—you need to understand the word's *denotations*, *connotations*, *synonyms*, and *antonyms*.

Denotations

The **denotation** of a word is its literal meaning—the definition of the word that you find in a dictionary. This **formal definition** has a three-part structure:

1. The word being defined
2. The general class to which the word belongs
3. The qualities or characteristics that distinguish the word from the other words in the class

TERM	CLASS	DIFFERENTIATION
A graphic novel	is a work of fiction	that tells its story through a series of pictures.
Democracy	is a form of government	in which supreme power rests with the people.
Geology	is a science	that deals with the study of the earth.

PRACTICE 2-3 Create your own formal definitions by filling in the following templates.

A disaster movie is _____ that _____
_____.

Happiness is _____ that _____
_____.

A tablet is _____ that _____
_____.

Connotations

The **connotations** of a word are its shared emotional associations or underlying meanings. For example, *angry* has the same denotation as *furious* and *livid*, but the words have different connotations, depending on who is speaking and why. Would you be angry, furious, or livid if someone wrecked your car? (It might depend on how old your car was.) Connotations can be positive or negative (*sunshine*, *peace*, and *rainbow* have positive connotations for most people), more or less forceful (*furious* is more forceful than *angry*), and sometimes neutral, depending on context.

Whenever you are in doubt about the connotation of a word, look up the word's definition in a dictionary. (It never hurts to double-check your understanding of a word's precise meaning.) Sometimes a word's connotation is quite different from its denotation. For example, even though the words *aggressive* and *assertive* have the same general denotations, their connotations are quite different: *aggressive* suggests that a person is pushy or hostile while *assertive* implies confidence and assurance.

PRACTICE 2-4

Look up each of the following word pairs in a dictionary. Then, working in small groups, consider how their connotations differ:

demonstration / riot

handicap / disability

illegal alien / undocumented worker

smile / smirk

thrifty / frugal

Synonyms and Antonyms

Another important aspect of learning words is becoming familiar with their synonyms and antonyms. **Synonyms** are words that have the same or similar meanings (for example, *happy* and *euphoric*). **Antonyms** are words that have opposite meanings (for example, *happy* and *distraught*).

Even though two words are synonyms, they may not have the same connotations. You may be *happy*, but not necessarily *euphoric*.

PRACTICE 2-5

Look at the following list of words and think of as many synonyms and antonyms as you can for each word. Next, working in pairs, decide if each synonym and antonym has generally positive or negative connotations. The first item has been filled in for you.

1. **Smart**

    a. Synonyms: *clever; intelligent*

    Connotations: *positive*

    b. Antonyms: *stupid; uninformed*

    Connotations: *negative*

2. **Slim**

    a. Synonyms: _____

    Connotations: _____

    b. Antonyms: _____

    Connotations: _____

3. **Enthusiastic**

   a. Synonyms: _____

   Connotations: _____

   b. Antonyms: _____

   Connotations: _____

4. **Fake**

   a. Synonyms: _____

   Connotations: _____

   b. Antonyms: _____

   Connotations: _____

5. **Young**

   a. Synonyms: _____

   Connotations: _____

   b. Antonyms: _____

   Connotations: _____

FOCUS on reading and writing

What words in the Amy Tan passage on page 36, "Mother Tongue" are not familiar to you? List those words, look them up, and supply some synonyms and antonyms for each. Do the synonyms have the same connotations as the original words? If not, how are they different?

 ## 2c Acquiring New Words

> **WORD POWER**
>
> **acquire** to gain or obtain for oneself

Now that you understand what it means to "know" a word, you will want to learn how to achieve full knowledge of the words you come across in your college classes and textbooks. We acquire new vocabulary words from five sources: *reference tools*; *using context clues*; *coursework*; *using roots, prefixes, and suffixes*; and *reading*.

Learning from Reference Tools

Many people believe that looking up words in a dictionary is the easiest way to learn new words, but other reference tools—such as a thesaurus and the Internet—can also help you acquire new vocabulary words.

Using a Dictionary

A **dictionary** is often the first resource for defining new words. Many online dictionaries have a spell-check feature that enables you to find a word even if you don't know its exact spelling.

Although some dictionaries list the oldest definition first (often preceded by the word *archaic*), many list the most common usage first. Some dictionaries also tell you whether a word's usage is slang or formal. Be sure to read all the listed definitions so that you can identify the definition that best fits the **context**—the parts of a sentence before and after a word that provide clues to its meaning—in which you found the word.

The **boldfaced** words after the definition tell you the other parts of speech that can be formed from the word. These are useful because they show you how to change the word from a verb to a noun or from an adjective to an adverb. (The parts of speech are abbreviated: *v.* for verb, *n.* for noun, *adj.* for adjective, and *adv.* for adverb.)

Now, suppose you encountered the unfamiliar word *portage* in the following sentence.

> As they stood on the shore, they thought the *portage* looked daunting, but it had to be completed before the journey could continue.

The online version of *Merriam-Webster's Collegiate Dictionary*, at *merriam-webster.com*, lists the following definitions of *portage*.[1]

---

por-tage **noun** 1 : the labor of carrying or transporting

2 *archaic* : the cost of carrying : <u>porterage</u>

3 *a* : the carrying of boats or goods overland from one body of water to another or around an obstacle (as a rapids)
b : the route followed in making such a transfer

Which definition of *portage* best corresponds to how the word is used in the example sentence?

---

[1] By permission. From Merriam-Webster.com © 2018 by Merriam-Webster, Inc. https://www.merriam-webster.com/dictionary/portage.

Using a Thesaurus

A **thesaurus** lists words in groups of **synonyms** (words that have the same meanings) and sometimes also **antonyms** (words that have opposite meanings). By consulting a thesaurus, you can vary your vocabulary and make your writing more interesting. Remember that words that seem to mean the same thing will often have subtle differences in meanings, so you should not automatically assume you can substitute one word you find in a thesaurus for another.

For example, if you wanted to find a synonym for the word *daunting*, which appears in the example sentence on page 41, you could consult an online thesaurus, where you might find the following suggested synonyms.

Synonyms: intimidating, discouraging, disheartening, dismaying

Which of the synonyms for *daunting* do you think would work best in the sentence on page 41?

Using the Internet

Many websites and smartphone applications can help you learn new words. By downloading the following free apps, you can easily and painlessly expand your vocabulary:

- **Vocabulary.com** uses a game interface to make learning new words fun. It claims to be able to personalize questions for the user.
- **A Word A Day widget** shows you a new word every day. It includes the definition of the word as well as several examples of usage.
- **Freerice.com** quizzes you on the definitions of words. For each answer you get right, Free Rice donates ten grains of rice to the United Nations' World Food Programme.
- **Vocab Genius** uses flashcards geared to your level of competence. It claims to show cards in the precise pattern for maximum absorption.

Learning from Context Clues

You can often figure out the meaning of a word by looking at its **context**—the words around it. **Context clues** are hints in the text that can help you figure out the meaning of unfamiliar words that you encounter as you read. If you learn the different types of context clues, you will be able to determine the meanings of words without having to constantly stop to look them up. Learning to use context clues is especially important for reading textbooks, which contain many subject-specific words.

There are four types of context clues: *definition/synonym clues, example clues, general information clues*, and *contrast clues*.

Definition/Synonym Clues

Definition/synonym clues signal a definition of a word. These types of clues are common in nonfiction writing, such as textbooks or journal articles. Definition/synonym clues can often be identified by their use of certain words (*or*, *means*, *such as*) or by parentheses or pairs of commas or dashes.

> *Example*
>
> The Gates Foundation's *philanthropy*—charitable donations to numerous educational institutions and AIDS research—is impressive.

Based on this definition/synonym context clue, what do you think *philanthropy* means?

Example Clues

Example clues state the word or concept and then list examples of that word or concept. These clues can often be identified by their use of a colon or by their use of certain expressions (*including*, *such as*, *for example*).

> *Example*
>
> Many once-deadly *maladies*, such as polio, diphtheria, and tetanus, have been wiped out in the United States by vaccination programs.

Based on this example context clue, what do you think *maladies* means?

General Information Clues

General information clues provide readers with the ideas surrounding a specific word or concept; readers must piece the ideas together to determine the word or concept's definition. These are the hardest clues to use and understand. You will likely have to read some sentences that come before or after the word or concept in order to understand the definition.

> *Example*
>
> One of my coworkers is a *sycophant*. She constantly flatters our supervisor. When he looks tired, she tells him that he looks great. When she comes back from lunch, she brings him his favorite latte. Once, she even left work early to pick up office supplies for him. She thinks she's helping her career, but most of us think that our supervisor is simply taking advantage of her.

Based on these *general information* context clues, what do you think *sycophant* means?

Contrast Clues

Contrast clues help readers figure out the meaning of an unfamiliar word by using a word that has the opposite meaning. Contrast clues are sometimes called **antonym clues** because they are often the word's antonym. Words and phrases such as *however*, *in contrast*, *unlike*, and *but* can indicate that another word has the opposite meaning of the unknown word.

> *Example*
>
> For years, coaches praised his athletic skills, but more recently they have begun to *disparage* him.

Based on this *contrast* context clue, what do you think *disparage* means?

PRACTICE 2-6

Read the following excerpts from two professional essays, and use context clues to help you determine the definitions of the boldfaced words. Then, identify the type of context clues you used for each word.

1. It isn't every day that the definition of a common English word that is **ubiquitous** in common parlance is challenged in federal court, but that is precisely what has happened with the word "natural." During the past few years, some 200 class-action suits have been filed against food manufacturers, charging them with misuse of the adjective in marketing such edible **oxymorons** as "natural" Cheetos Puffs, "all-natural" Sun Chips, "all-natural" Naked Juice, "100 percent all-natural" Tyson chicken nuggets and so forth. The plaintiffs argue that many of these products contain ingredients—high-fructose corn syrup, artificial flavors and colorings, chemical preservatives and genetically modified organisms—that the typical consumer wouldn't think of as "natural."

   —From "Why 'Natural' Doesn't Mean Anything Anymore" by Michael Pollan (p. 613)

   Definition (ubiquitous): _____

   Context clue type: _____

   Definition (oxymoron): _____

Context clue type: _____

Context clue type: _____

2. I had made an error in naively assuming that **assimilating** wholeheartedly would make my life easier, but the truth is: whiteness didn't fit. And somehow, full on Indian-ness didn't either, given that I was (mostly) raised and schooled in America. I didn't feel as though I could relate to either fairly.
 —From "Growing Up a Desi Girl: What It Means to Be Between Two Worlds" by Nikita (p. 629)

Definition (assimilating): _____

_____

Context clue type: _____

Learning from Your Coursework

You spend a good deal of time in college listening to lectures and reading textbooks, so it makes sense that you learn new words from these hours of listening, reading, and taking notes. In order to learn about a given **discipline** or field of study, you must be able to understand **discipline-specific words**—the key words experts use in discussing the discipline.

For example, in a communications course, you will learn the term *rhetoric* and what that means in the context of persuasion. You might hear this word initially in a lecture, and then come across it in a chapter of the textbook. After these encounters with the word, you should realize that you need to learn its meaning in order to understand and write about the course's subject matter.

To learn the meaning of discipline-specific words, you can use three different strategies: *concept cards*, *mnemonics*, and *visual cues*.

Using Concept Cards

Concept cards can be 3- by 5-inch index cards or online flash cards that you create with a smartphone or tablet. On the front of each card, you write the word you want to learn, its part of speech, and its source (the sentence in which you found the word); on the back you record the definition, synonym, antonym, and an image to help you remember the definition of the word. Studying concept cards can help you master the words you want to know.

Concept cards are useful because they are portable. You can study them on a bus, in a doctor's office waiting room, or whenever you have a few spare moments.

Example

Front of card

	Part of Speech
WORD	
Source	

Back of card

Definition: (find this in the dictionary)

Synonyms: (find these in the thesaurus)

Antonyms: (you can often find these in a thesaurus or by using online search tools)

Image: (you can either draw this or find it on the Internet)

PRACTICE 2-7

Use the information you have learned in this section of the chapter to fill in the back of the concept card below for the word *eloquence*.

Front of card

noun
eloquence
"You don't have to be a great author, statesman, or philosopher to tap into the energy and eloquence of small words." (p. 596, from Richard Lederer, "The Case for Small Words")

Back of card

Definition:

Synonyms:

Antonyms:

Image:

Using Mnemonics

Mnemonics are strategies such as short rhymes, memorable phrases, or acronyms (new words created from the first letters of other words) that help you remember information. They do this by tying new information to images or concepts that you can easily remember. The acronym *FANBOYS*, for example, is a mnemonic designed to help you remember the coordinating conjunctions *for, and, nor, but, or, yet,* and *so*. Another mnemonic is the familiar rhyme, "*I* before *E* except after *C*." You can invent your own mnemonics to help you remember words. For example, to learn the word *ingot* (a block of metal), you could remember "*I got* a metal block."

PRACTICE 2-8

Working in pairs, try to create mnemonics to help you remember the meanings of two new words from this chapter.

Using Visual Clues

Visual clues are pictures or images that help you to remember a word's definition. By representing the word with a picture, you are more easily able to fix the word in your mind and remember it. For example, if you wanted to learn the meaning of the word *effervescent* ("the escape of gas from a liquid and the bubbling that results"), you could associate it with the picture of a cold-relief tablet dissolving in water.

You can draw a picture on the back of a 3- by 5-inch note card or cut-and-paste an image from a website to the back of an electronic flash card.

FYI

You can often find useful images by entering the word you want to remember in the Google search box and then clicking on the Images tab at the top of the search page.

PRACTICE 2-9

Look up the meaning of each word below in a dictionary, and then think of a visual clue that will help you remember it. Then, find or draw your own visual clue for each word. Finally, make a concept card for each word, including your visual clues.

pyrotechnics	vocational
ego	referendum
sequence	introspection

Learning from Roots, Prefixes, and Suffixes

English has taken many of its words from other languages, such as Latin and French. An important (and effective) strategy for learning new words is learning word parts: **roots**, **prefixes**, and **suffixes**. When you come across an unknown word, you can attempt to determine the meaning of the word by identifying its parts. By learning common roots, prefixes, and suffixes, you can often figure out the meanings of words simply by using these word-part clues.

Using Roots

Taking the basic part of a word—called a **root**—and adding prefixes and suffixes to it is the way many English words are formed. The chart below lists some of the most common roots, their meanings, and examples of words that include those roots.

COMMON ROOTS

ROOT	DEFINITION	EXAMPLE
aqua	water	aquarium
auto	self	automatic
bene	good	benefit
bio	life	biology
chrono	time	chronology
graph	writing	graphic
hydr	water	hydration
jud	judge	judicial
man	hand	manual
nym	name	antonym
pater	father	paternal
phon	sound	telephone
port	to carry	portable
psych	mind	psychology
spect	to look	inspect
struct	to build	construct
tele	far off	telescope
vac	empty	vacuum

Because the roots of English words come from many different languages, it is sometimes helpful when you encounter a new word to think of other words that have the same root that you already know the meaning of. For example, if you know that *vacuum* has the root *vac*, which means "empty," you can figure out that when you *vacate* an apartment, you leave it "empty of occupants."

PRACTICE
2-10 Using the list of Common Roots and their meanings, try to determine the meaning of each of the following words, and write that meaning on the lines. Finally, look up the words in a dictionary, and see how close you came to the actual definitions.

1. benevolent: _____

2. chronic: _____

3. evacuate: _____

4. export: _____

5. biography: _____

Using Prefixes

Prefixes are letters or groups of letters that have a specific meaning and are added before a root (as in *pre-*, which means "before") to change its meaning. For example, the prefix *contra-* means "against." If you see this prefix in front of the root *dict-*, which means "speak," then you can figure out the meaning of the word *contradict*: "to speak against, or in opposition to." By learning the meanings of some common prefixes, you can determine the meanings of many unfamiliar words. The chart below lists the most common prefixes, their meanings, and examples of words that include those prefixes.

COMMON PREFIXES

PREFIX	DEFINITION	EXAMPLE
anti-	against	antibiotic
bi-	two	bimonthly
con-	together	congregation
contra-	against	contradict
ex-	out	exhale
inter-	between	international
intra-	within	intramural
mal-	bad, wrong	malware
mini-	small	miniature
multi-	many	multiplex
non-	not	nonpartisan
pent-	five	pentagon
post-	after	postgame
pre-	before	prehistoric
semi-	half	semicircle
super-	above	superior
trans-	across	transmit
uni-	one	unity

PRACTICE 2-11 Choose five prefixes from the Common Prefixes list. Then, list as many words as you can that contain each of the prefixes. If you don't know the exact meaning of a word, look it up in a dictionary.

Using Suffixes

Suffixes are groups of letters that are added to the end of a word, often changing its part of speech. When the part of speech changes, the word's meaning changes as well. For example, *educate* is a verb meaning "to give moral or social instruction to." If you add the suffix *-tion* to the verb *educate*, it becomes the noun *education*, meaning "the process of giving or receiving instruction." (Like prefixes, suffixes cannot stand alone as words.) English has very few suffixes that form verbs and adverbs; a large number of suffixes, however, form nouns and adjectives. The chart below lists some common suffixes, their meanings, and examples of words that include those suffixes.

COMMON SUFFIXES

VERB SUFFIX	DEFINITION	EXAMPLE
-en	to cause or become	cheapen
-ate	cause to be	activate
-ify, -fy	to make or cause	magnify
-ize	to make, to give	memorize

ADVERB SUFFIX

The only regular adverb suffix is *–ly*, as in *quickly* or *wisely*.

ADJECTIVE SUFFIX	DEFINITION	EXAMPLE
-al	capable	comical
-ic	pertaining to	democratic
-ly	at specific intervals	hourly
-ous	full of	porous
-less	lack of	toothless
-ish	having the qualities of	ticklish

NOUN SUFFIX	DEFINITION	EXAMPLE
-ance, -ence	the quality of	competence
-arium	place for	aquarium
-ary	place for	dictionary
-ics	the science or art of	economics
-ism	quality or doctrine of	capitalism
-ology	the study of	biology

PRACTICE 2-12

Consult the Common Suffixes chart to help you determine what part of speech each suffix below creates. Then, think of an example (other than the ones listed in the chart) of a word that uses that suffix.

1. *-ism*

    Part of speech: _____ Example word: _____

2. *-ly*

    Part of speech: _____ Example word: _____

3. *-ish*

    Part of speech: _____ Example word: _____

4. *-ic*

    Part of speech: _____ Example word: _____

5. *-ize*

    Part of speech: _____ Example word: _____

Learning from Your Reading

All the strategies previously discussed are effective, but the single best way to improve your vocabulary is by reading as much as possible. Finding time to read for pleasure is difficult when you have large amounts of course work as well as other responsibilities. However, you can improve your vocabulary by setting realistic reading goals. Try reading one magazine article a day, subscribing to an online newspaper, or regularly reading a trustworthy blog.

Keep in mind that reading passively will not improve your vocabulary. You need to look up and study any new words you encounter—and ideally, use them in conversation and in writing. As you read, keep a list of the words you don't know. Create your own personal dictionary that lists each word, its definition, and the sentence in which the word appeared.

You can keep your personal dictionary in a computer file or in the front of your binder, and you can add to it each time you come across a word you do not know. Here is an example of an entry you might make in your dictionary.

Word	Sentence	Definition
malodorous	The early stages of the process can be a bit **malodorous**, so it's recommended that you follow the ancient custom of relocating to a well-ventilated tent.	foul smelling

FYI

Keep the following points in mind as you go about learning new words:

- It takes time to learn new words.
- In order to truly know a word, you have to be able to use it in your reading, writing, and speaking.
- It is all right to know only the most commonly used definition of a word; you don't have to know all of its meanings and usages.
- If you encounter an unfamiliar word while reading, you don't always have to stop and look it up; you can use the word's context to help you. However, if it is a word in a textbook for a class, you should be sure you know exactly what it means because it may be key to your understanding of the subject matter.

2d Using New Words in Your Writing

As you study new words and their meanings, try using some of these words in conversation or in writing. Remember, the ultimate goal of your vocabulary-building process is *full knowledge* of a word—not just the ability to understand a word when you hear it, use it correctly in conversation, and figure out its meaning when you read it, but also to use it correctly and with confidence in your writing.

Using New Words in Your Writing

Full Knowledge
"I can use this word in my speaking, reading, and writing vocabularies."

↑

Meaning Knowledge
"I understand the connotations, synonyms, and antonyms of this word."

↑

Denotation Knowledge
"I can tell someone else the definition of this word."

↑

Some Knowledge
"I have seen it or heard it, but I can't define it."

↑

No Knowledge
"I have never seen it or heard it."

PRACTICE

2-13 Below are six words you have read in this chapter's discussions of vocabulary building. Use the context in which each word appears to help you understand its meaning. Then, use each word in a new sentence:

standardized (p. 33)
ultimate (p. 35)
reference (p. 40)
context (p. 40)
discipline (p. 45)
mnemonic (p. 46)

FOCUS on reading and writing

Reread the list you made at the start of this chapter (about things you know about taking standardized tests) and also reread the passage from Amy Tan's essay "Mother Tongue" (p. 36). Then, **write** a response paragraph discussing your experiences with taking standardized tests. How are your experiences like and unlike Tan's? Did your family's language play a role in your performance on these tests? If so, how? Try to use two or three of the new words you have learned in this chapter in your paragraph. When you have finished, **TEST** what you have written.

CHAPTER REVIEW

REVIEW ACTIVITY

Graphic Organizer: *Building Vocabulary*

Chapter 2 identified the different types of vocabularies and explained how to build your vocabulary for reading and writing. Using the Graphic Organizer on page 56, fill in the main concepts presented in the chapter, and provide examples as required.

COLLABORATIVE ACTIVITY

Create (or find) a visual for each unfamiliar word you identified in the Focus on reading and writing box on page 40. (For example, for the word *percentile*, you might draw a percent sign.) Then, trade your pictures with another student, and have your classmate try to guess which words you are representing.

Chapter Review

Graphic Organizer

The four types of vocabularies:

1. Listening
2. _____
3. _____
4. _____

These vocabularies all influence my: _____

I can improve my vocabularies by: _____

Reference tools

An example of a reference tool is a:

dictionary or thesaurus.

A context clue is a: _____

My coursework this semester includes the following classes: _____

A root is: _____

Example of a root: _____

Vocabularies are expanded through these tools and methods.

I can get more vocabulary practice by reading more of these types of texts: _____

A prefix is: _____

Example of a word with a prefix: _____

A suffix is: _____

Example of a word with a suffix: _____

Review checklist

✔ You have listening, reading, speaking, and writing vocabularies, and you must work on each one if you want to improve your overall vocabulary. (See 2a.)

✔ "Knowing" a word means you are able to use that word in your listening, reading, speaking, and writing vocabularies. (See 2b.)

✔ You acquire new words through reference tools; context clues; coursework; roots, prefixes, and suffixes; and reading. (See 2c.)

✔ As you build your vocabulary, it is important for you to practice using new words correctly in your writing. (See 2d.)

3 Understanding the Writing Process

Richard Levine/Alamy Stock Photo

FOCUS on reading and writing

Think about the different jobs you've had and the challenges you faced. Then, list a few ideas about each job. Later in this chapter, you will read an essay about a challenging job and write an essay about the most difficult job you've ever had.

PREVIEW

In this chapter, you will learn to
- understand essay structure (3a).
- move from assignment to topic (3b).
- find ideas to write about (3c).
- state your thesis (3d).
- choose supporting points (3e).
- make an outline (3f).
- draft your essay (3g).
- TEST your essay (3h).
- revise your essay (3i).
- edit and proofread your essay (3j–3k).

Writing is not something that you do just in school; writing is a life skill. If you can write clearly, you can express your ideas convincingly to others—in school, on the job, and in your community.

- In college, you often write essays in response to reading—for example, in essays, on exams, or in research papers.
- At work, you might write a memo, a letter, a proposal, or a report.
- As a member of your community, you might write a letter or email to a government agency or to the editor of your local newspaper.
- In your personal life, you might respond to emails, post on social-networking sites and blogs, and text friends.

As you can see, writing is an important activity. If you can write, you can communicate; if you can communicate effectively, you have a good chance of succeeding in school and beyond.

When you write an essay, you begin by planning what you will write about and then move on to organizing your ideas, drafting, TESTing, revising, and editing and proofreading. In this chapter, you will learn strategies that you can use as you move through the writing process.

 ## 3a Understanding Essay Structure

In your college courses, you are frequently asked to write an **essay**—a group of paragraphs on a single subject.

- The essay's first paragraph—the **introduction**—begins with opening remarks that create interest and frequently ends with a **thesis statement** that presents the essay's main idea. (For more on introductions, see 4a (p. 107).)
- The **body** of the essay consists of several body paragraphs that support the thesis statement. Each **body paragraph** often begins with a **topic sentence** that states the main idea of the paragraph. The other sentences in the paragraph support the topic sentence with **evidence**—details and examples. (For more on body paragraphs, see 4b (p. 109).)
- **Transitional words and phrases** lead readers from sentence to sentence and from paragraph to paragraph. (For a list of transitions, see Frequently Used Transitional Words and Phrases (p. 120).)
- The last paragraph—the **conclusion**—ends the essay. The conclusion often includes a **summary statement** that reinforces the thesis. (For more on conclusions, see 4c (p. 114).)

FYI

The first letters of these four key elements—**T**hesis statement, **E**vidence, **S**ummary statement, and **T**ransitions—spell **TEST**. Before you begin the revision process, you can **TEST** your draft to see whether it includes all the elements of an effective essay.

Sample Essay

Introduction
: **Opening remarks** introduce the subject being discussed in the essay. The essay's main idea is presented in the **thesis statement**.

First body paragraph
: The **topic sentence** states the essay's first point.
Evidence supports the topic sentence.
Transitional words and phrases connect the examples and details and show how they are related.

Second body paragraph
: The **topic sentence** states the essay's second point.
Evidence supports the topic sentence.
Transitional words and phrases connect the examples and details and show how they are related.

> The **topic sentence** states the essay's third point.
> **Evidence** supports the topic sentence.
> **Transitional words and phrases** connect the examples and details and show how they are related.

— Third body paragraph

> The **summary statement** reinforces the thesis, summarizing the essay's main idea. **Concluding remarks** present the writer's final thoughts on the subject.

— Conclusion

The following essay by Jennifer Chu illustrates the structure of an essay. (Note that transitional words and phrases are underlined in blue.)

Becoming Chinese American

Although I was born in Hong Kong, I have spent most of my life in the United States. However, my parents have always made sure that I did not forget my roots. They always tell stories of what it was like to live in Hong Kong. To make sure my brothers and sisters and I know what is happening in China, my parents subscribe to Chinese-language television channels. When we were growing up, we would watch the celebration of the Chinese New Year, the news from Asia, and Chinese movies and music videos. <u>As a result</u>, even though I am an American, I value traditional Chinese culture.

Introduction

Thesis statement

The Chinese language is an important part of my life as a Chinese American. <u>Unlike</u> some of my Chinese friends, I do not think that the Chinese language is unimportant. <u>In fact</u>, I spend most Saturdays in a Chinese-heritage school learning Mandarin, a standard variety of spoken and written Chinese. I do this for a number of reasons. <u>First</u>, I feel that it is my duty as a Chinese American to learn Chinese so that I can pass it on to my children. <u>In addition</u>, knowing Chinese enables me to communicate with my relatives. Because my parents and grandparents do not speak English well, Chinese is our main form of communication. <u>Finally</u>, Chinese helps me identify with my culture. When I speak Chinese, I feel connected to a culture that is over five thousand years old. Without the Chinese language, I would not be who I am.

Topic sentence (states essay's first point)

First body paragraph

Evidence (supports topic sentence)

Chinese food is <u>another important part</u> of my life as a Chinese American. <u>One reason</u> for this is that everything we Chinese people eat has a history and a meaning. At a birthday meal, <u>for example</u>, we serve long noodles and buns in the shape of peaches. This is because we believe that long noodles represent long life and that peaches are served in heaven.

Topic sentence (states essay's second point)

Second body paragraph

Evidence (supports topic sentence)

Another reason is that to Chinese people, food is a way of reinforcing ties between family and friends. For instance, during a traditional Chinese wedding ceremony, the bride and the groom eat nine of everything. This is because the number nine stands for the Chinese words "together forever." By taking part in this ritual, the bride and groom start their marriage by making Chinese customs a part of their life together.

Topic sentence (states essay's third point)

Third body paragraph

Evidence (supports topic sentence)

Religion is the most important part of my life as a Chinese American. At various times during the year, Chinese religious festivals bring together the people I care about the most. During Chinese New Year, my whole family goes to the Buddhist temple, where we say prayers and welcome others with traditional New Year's greetings. After leaving the temple, we all go to Chinatown and eat dim sum until the lion dance starts. As the colorful lion dances its way down the street, people beat drums and throw firecrackers to drive off any evil spirits that may be around. Later that night, parents give children gifts of money in red envelopes that symbolize joy and happiness in the coming year.

Summary statement (reinforces essay's thesis)

Conclusion

My family has taught me how important it is to hold on to my Chinese culture. When I was six, my parents sent me to a Chinese-American grade school. My teachers thrilled me with stories of Fa Mulan, the Shang Dynasty, and the Moon God. I will never forget how happy I was when I realized how special it is to be Chinese. This is how I want my own children to feel. I want them to be proud of who they are and to pass their language, history, and culture on to the next generation.

PRACTICE
3-1

Following is an essay written by Aimee Groth for *Business Insider* about her experience working at Starbucks. Read the essay, and then answer the questions that follow it.

Why Working at Starbucks for Three Weeks Was the Toughest Job I've Ever Had

Aimee Groth

1   A few months ago, I had the opportunity to work for Starbucks as a barista. I had recently moved to New York City, and I was freelancing at the time. But I had to get a part-time job in order to pay next month's rent. So one afternoon, I printed off a stack of resumes, and hand-delivered them to nearly 30 Starbucks in Lower Manhattan and one in Brooklyn. Only one manager called me back: the one from Brooklyn, just a few blocks from

my apartment—and the last store I visited. She offered me the job at $10/hour; and if I worked part-time for three months, I'd be eligible for health insurance. I'd later find out that the store is located next to the busiest transit hub in Brooklyn, which makes it the busiest Starbucks outside of Manhattan. My initial idea of working a leisurely part-time job was completely false. This was going to be hard work—and a lot of it.

2   My first day was deceptively easy—watching videos of Starbucks CEO Howard Schultz on the store's laptop with my fellow three trainees, and taste-testing coffee and tea. We had some pamphlets that explained the drinks, and our task was to memorize all of them—including some several dozen variations of shots, sizes and flavors. We tried making a few of these with our trainers at the bar, but it wasn't easy. There was usually a steady stream of 20-some people waiting in line, and there simply wasn't the space or environment to train properly. It was always chaotic, with several people on the floor, calling orders, shifting from station to station, and asking you to get out of the way. Not to mention 10 customers waiting at the end of the bar for their drinks.

3   My first real 7:30 a.m. shift was jarring. The intensity of what goes on behind the counter is simply not visible from the customer's point of view. During the peak morning hours, we'd work through around 110 people every half hour with seven employees on the floor. Since there was no chance my new colleagues—or "partners," as Starbucks calls its employees—and I would ever memorize all the drinks, we handled everything else: brewing and changing coffees (staying on top of which ones are decaf, light and bold roasts, while rotating them via Starbucks' "coffee cadence" using 2-minute timers and grinding the beans, having them all prepared to brew—and never leaving one pot sitting longer than 30 minutes without dumping, since it's no longer "fresh"), marking drinks (there's a complicated shorthand that you've got to memorize, while translating what a customer is saying into "Starbucks speak" and calling it properly), rotating pastries, the food case, and tossing hot items into the oven—all while managing the register. Just as I was tempted to remind my coworkers that they were new once, too, I wanted to tell customers that I was way over-qualified for this job, and hoped they'd see me on the street in normal clothes, not in khakis, a black T-shirt, bright-green apron and baseball cap.

4   On my third day, my boss handed my fellow trainee—who would later disappear after a 10-minute break never to return—and me a mop and supplies to clean the bathroom, because the toilet was broken. It turned out not to be so horrible, but again, I quickly learned to swallow my pride.

5   We got two 10-minute breaks and one unpaid 30-minute break for every 8 hours on the floor. There we'd have to decide between running next door to use the restroom (because ours always had a line of customers in front of it), quickly eating a bag lunch (there was never time to stand in line and buy something from the store), or making a cell phone call. If you're lucky, you got to sit down on the one chair in the break room, or on the ladder, because there were never any open seats in the store.

6   Some of my coworkers were more demanding than others. Most were nice and welcoming. And there were office politics. On more than one occasion I walked into the break room to see someone crying, or talking about other coworkers. I mostly avoided this, until what would be my last week on the job. I told my boss that I got a new, full-time job, and could work until I started at *Business Insider*. But the next day my name disappeared from the schedule.

7   For many people, service industry jobs are not a supplementary income or short-term solution. And hats off to them—especially those who do it without even complaining.

1. Underline the essay's thesis statement.
2. Underline the topic sentence of each body paragraph.
3. What point does the first body paragraph make? What evidence supports this point?
4. What point does the second body paragraph make? What evidence supports this point?
5. What point does the third body paragraph make? What evidence supports this point?
6. What point does the fourth body paragraph make? What evidence supports this point?
7. What point does the fifth body paragraph make? What evidence supports this point?
8. What transitions does the essay include? How do they connect the essay's ideas?
9. Does this essay have a clear summary statement? If so, what is it? If not, write one on the lines below.

_____

_____

 ## 3b Moving from Assignment to Topic

Many essays you write in college begin as **assignments** given to you by your instructors. Before you focus on any assignment, however, you should take time to think about your **purpose** (what you want to accomplish by writing your essay) and your **audience** (the people who will read your essay). Once you have considered these issues, you are ready to move on to thinking about the specifics of your assignment.

The following assignments are typical of those you might be given in a composition class:

- Discuss some things you would change about your school.
- What can college students do to improve the environment?
- Discuss an important decision you made during the past few years.

Because these assignments are so general, you need to narrow them before you can start to write. What *specific* things would you change? *Exactly* what could you do to improve the environment? Answering these questions will help you narrow these assignments into **topics** that you can write about.

ASSIGNMENT	TOPIC
Discuss some things you would change about your school.	Three things I would change to improve the quality of life on campus
What can college students do to improve the environment?	The campus recycling project

Jared White, a student in a first-year composition course, was given the following assignment.

ASSIGNMENT

Discuss an important decision you made during the past few years.

Jared narrowed this assignment to the following topic.

TOPIC

Deciding to go back to school

Throughout the rest of this chapter, you will be following Jared's writing process.

PRACTICE

3-2 Decide whether the following topics are narrow enough for an essay of five or six paragraphs. If a topic is suitable, write *OK* next to it. If it is not, write a revised version of the same topic that is narrow enough for a brief essay.

Examples

Successful strategies for quitting smoking ___OK___

Horror movies ___1950s Japanese monster movies___

1. Instructional design models in elementary education _____
2. Dangers to the environment of Arctic oil drilling _____
3. The economic consequences of increasing the minimum wage _____
4. Online retail businesses _____
   _____
5. Marketing new smart-phone apps _____

DECIDE on a topic
Look back at the Focus on Reading and Writing prompt on page 58. To find a topic you can write about, you need to decide which job to focus on. Begin by reviewing your list of ideas about the different jobs you've had.

FYI
Visit the Study Guides and Strategies website (studygs.net/writing/prewriting.htm) to learn how to use one of the graphic organizers or to find other information about the writing process.

3c Finding Ideas to Write About

Before you start writing about a topic, you need to find out what you have to say about it. Sometimes ideas may come to you easily. More often, you will have to use specific strategies—such as *freewriting*, *brainstorming*, *keeping a journal*, or *clustering*—to help you come up with ideas.

Freewriting

When you **freewrite**, you write for a set period of time—perhaps five minutes—without stopping, and you keep freewriting even if what you are writing doesn't seem to have a point or a direction. Your goal is to relax and let ideas flow without worrying whether or not they are related—or even if they make sense. Sometimes you can freewrite without a topic in mind, but at other times, you can focus on a specific topic. This is called **focused freewriting**.

When you finish freewriting, read what you have written. Then, underline or highlight any ideas that you think you might be able to use. If you find an idea that you want to explore further, freewrite again, using that idea as a starting point.

Jared White wrote the following focused freewriting on the topic "deciding to go back to school."

> Deciding to go back to school. When I graduated high school, I swore I'd never go back to school. Hated it. Couldn't wait to get out. What was I thinking? How was I supposed to support myself? My dad's friend needed help. He taught me how to paint houses. I made good money, but it was boring. I couldn't picture myself doing it forever. Even though I knew I was going to have to go back to school, I kept putting off the decision. Maybe I was lazy. Maybe I was scared — probably both. I had this fear of being turned down. How could someone who had bad grades all through high school go to college? Also, I'd been out of school for six years. And even if I did get in (a miracle!), how would I pay for it? How would I live? Well, here I am — the first one in my family to go to college.

Jared's freewriting

PRACTICE 3-3

Reread Jared White's freewriting. If you were advising Jared, which ideas would you tell him to explore further? Why?

FREEWRITE

Choose two of the jobs you have been thinking about, and freewrite about each of them. Then, choose the job you think was the most challenging. Circle the ideas about this job that you would like to explore further in an essay.

Brainstorming

Unlike freewriting, **brainstorming** is sometimes written in the form of a list and sometimes scattered all over a page. You don't have to use complete sentences; single words or phrases are fine. After you have recorded as much information as you can, you can look over your brainstorming and decide which ideas are useful and which ones are not, underlining, starring, or boxing important ideas. You can also ask questions, draw arrows to connect important ideas, and even draw pictures or diagrams.

Usually you brainstorm on your own, but at times you may find it useful to do **collaborative brainstorming**, working with other students to find ideas. Sometimes your instructor may ask you and other students to brainstorm together. At times the class may even brainstorm as a group while your instructor writes down the ideas you think of. Whenever you brainstorm, however, your goal is the same: to come up with as much material about your topic as you can.

Here are Jared's brainstorming notes about his decision to go back to school.

Deciding to Go Back to School

Money a problem

Other students a lot younger

Paying tuition — how?

No one in family went to college

Friends not in college

Couldn't see myself in college

Considered going to trade school

Computer programmer?

Grades bad in high school

Time for me to grow up

Wondered if I would get in

Found out about community college

Admission requirements not bad

Afraid — too old, looking silly

Took time to get used to routine

Found other students like me

Liked studying

Jared's brainstorming

PRACTICE

3-4 Which ideas in Jared's brainstorming notes would you advise him to explore further? Why?

BRAINSTORM

Review your freewriting. Then, brainstorm about the job you plan to write about. What ideas about this job did you get from brainstorming that you did not get from freewriting?

Keeping a Journal

A **journal** is a computer file or notebook in which you keep an informal record of your personal insights, reactions, and ideas. In your journal, you can reflect, question, summarize, or even complain. Your journal is also a place where you record ideas about your assignments, note possible ideas to write about, and jot down interesting facts. Here you can try to resolve a problem, restart a stalled project, argue with yourself about your topic, or comment on a draft. You can also try out different versions of sentences; list details or examples; or keep a record of things you read, see, or hear.

Journal writing works best when you write regularly, preferably at the same time each day, so that it becomes a habit. Once you have started making regular entries in your journal, take the time every week or so to go back and read over what you have written. You may find ideas that you want to explore in further journal entries or to use in an essay.

Following is an entry in Jared's journal that he eventually used in his essay about returning to school.

> When I was working as a house painter, I had a conversation that helped convince me to go to college. One day, I started talking to the guy whose house I was painting. I told him that I was painting houses until I figured out what I was going to do with the rest of my life. He asked me if I had considered going to college. I told him that I hadn't done well in high school, so I didn't think college was for me. He told me that I could probably get into the local community college. That night I looked at the community college's website to see if going to college might be a good idea.

Jared's journal entry

WRITE journal entries

Write at least two journal entries for the topic you have been exploring for this chapter: the most difficult job you've ever had. Which of your entries do you want to explore further? What material could you use in your essay?

Clustering

Clustering, sometimes called *mapping*, is another strategy you can use to find ideas to write about. When you cluster, you begin by writing your topic in the center of a sheet of paper. Then, you branch out, writing relevant ideas on the page in groups, or clusters, around the topic. As you add new ideas, you circle them and draw lines to connect the ideas to one another and to the topic at the center. (These lines will look like a spider web or the spokes of a wheel.) As you move from the center out to the corners of the page, your ideas will be more and more specific.

Sometimes, one branch of your cluster diagram will give you all the material you need. At other times, you may decide to write about the ideas from several branches or to choose one or two ideas from each branch. If you find you need additional material after you finish your first cluster diagram, you can repeat the process on a new sheet of paper, this time beginning with a topic from one of the branches.

Jared's cluster diagram on the topic of deciding to go back to school appears below.

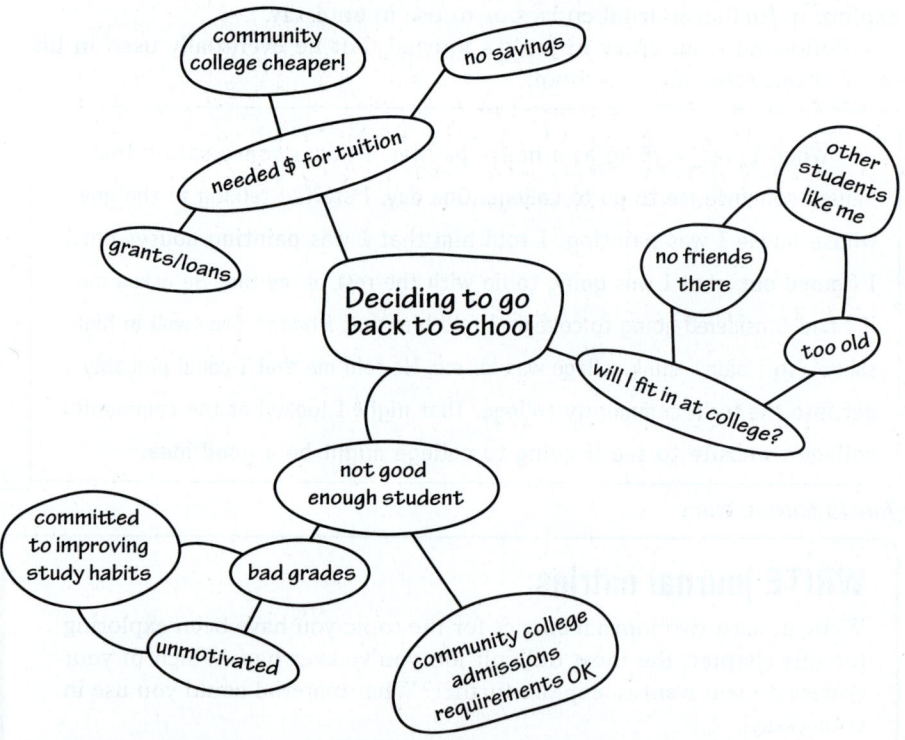

Jared's cluster diagram

Draw a cluster diagram

Draw a cluster diagram for your essay on your most difficult job. Was this method of finding ideas useful? Why or why not?

Additional Strategies

Here are some additional tips for finding ideas that you can use in your essays:

- *Get ideas from conversations.* Your family, your classmates, your coworkers, your friends, and your instructors can give you ideas for your essays. If you discuss your writing projects with others, they can suggest avenues for further exploration or provide you with facts and examples that you can use to support your points. Remember, however, to **document** the ideas or words of others that you use in your essays. (See Chapter 14 for information on documentation.)

- *Get ideas from the media.* Almost everything you see or read online — web pages, blog posts, podcasts, tweets, YouTube videos, television programs, and Facebook posts — can be a source of ideas. For this reason, you should record in your journal interesting facts and ideas that you get from these sources. Before you use this material, however, you should evaluate it to make sure that it is reliable. (See 13a for information on finding and evaluating sources.) In addition, be sure to record the bibliographic information you will need to document all your sources. (See Chapter 14 for information on documenting sources.)

- *Get ideas from research.* Sometimes the only way to get important information is to do research. This is especially true if you are writing about a topic with which you are unfamiliar. By consulting the books, magazine articles, and scholarly journals in your college library or online, you get necessary background information and explore new and interesting ideas. Research also enables you to gain insight into opposing points of view, develop your own ideas about your subject, and gather information to support your points. (See Chapter 13 for information about using sources.)

PRACTICE 3-5

Look at Jared's cluster diagram on deciding to go back to school. How is it similar to his brainstorming on the same subject (p. 68)? How is it different? If you were advising Jared, which branches of the cluster diagram would you suggest that he develop further? Why? Would you add any branches? What other sources of information could Jared have used? Be prepared to discuss your suggestions with the class or in a small group.

3d Stating Your Thesis

After you have gathered information about your topic, you need to decide on a thesis for your essay. You do this by reviewing the ideas from your brainstorming, freewriting, journal entries, or cluster diagrams and then asking, "What is the main point I want to make about my topic?" The answer to this question is the **thesis** of your essay. You express this point in a **thesis statement**: a single sentence that clearly expresses the main idea that you will discuss in the rest of your essay.

Keep in mind that each essay has just *one* thesis statement. The details and examples in the body of the essay all support (expand, discuss, or explain) this thesis statement.

TOPIC	THESIS STATEMENT
Three things I would change to improve the quality of life on campus	If I could change three things to improve life on campus, I would create a mentorship program for incoming students, increase student access to physical and mental health facilities, and provide students with information on student loans and money management.
The campus recycling project	Because attempts to recycle in the past have had limited results, our campus should develop a new program to reduce, reuse, and recycle waste.

Like a topic sentence in a paragraph, a thesis statement in an essay tells readers what to expect. An effective thesis statement has three important characteristics:

1. *An effective thesis statement makes a point about a topic, expressing the writer's opinion or unique view of the topic. For this reason, it must do more than state a fact or announce what you plan to write about.*

   A statement of fact is not an effective thesis statement because it gives you nothing to develop in your essay. After all, how much can you say about the *fact* that many older students are returning to school? Likewise, an announcement of what you plan to discuss gives readers no indication of the position you will take on your topic. Remember, an effective thesis statement makes a point.

STATEMENT OF FACT	Many older students are returning to school.
ANNOUNCEMENT	In this essay, I will discuss older students going back to school.

2. *An effective thesis statement is clearly worded and specific.*

   The vague thesis statement below gives readers no sense of the ideas the essay will discuss. It does not say, for example, *why* returning to school is difficult for older students. Remember, an effective thesis statement is specific.

VAGUE THESIS STATEMENT	Returning to school is difficult for older students.

3. *An effective thesis often indicates the purpose of your essay.*

   For example, if you are writing an *analytical essay,* an essay that breaks an idea into its parts, your thesis statement should suggest this purpose.

> An analysis of older students returning to school shows that most have three reasons for doing so: to advance their careers, to increase their potential earnings, and to set an example. (The essay that follows discusses the major reasons that older students have for returning to college.)

   If you are writing an essay that *explains* something, your thesis statement should make this purpose clear.

> The life of an older student attending college revolves around studying, working, and trying to find time for family and friends. (The essay that follows explains how returning students allocate their time.)

   Finally, if you are writing to *change people's views,* your thesis should indicate your intent.

> One of the easiest ways for older adults to return to school is to put their personal, professional, and prior academic experience to good use. (The essay that follows presents the evidence to convince readers that returning students should seek college credit for life experience.)

> **FYI**
>
> **Evaluating Your Thesis Statement**
>
> Once you have a thesis statement, you need to evaluate it to determine if it is effective. Asking the following questions will help you decide:
>
> - Is my thesis statement a complete sentence?
> - Does my thesis statement clearly express the main idea I will discuss in my essay?
> - Is my thesis statement specific and focused? Does it make a point that I can cover within my time and page limits?
> - Does my thesis statement make a point about my topic—not just state a fact or announce what I plan to write about?
> - Does my thesis statement avoid vague language?
> - Does my thesis statement avoid statements like "I think" or "In my opinion"?
> - Does my thesis statement suggest my essay's purpose?

After freewriting, brainstorming, and reviewing his journal entries and cluster diagram, Jared decided on a topic and wrote the following effective thesis statement for his essay.

> **EFFECTIVE THESIS STATEMENT** Although I realized it would be difficult in some ways, I decided that if I really wanted to attend college full-time, I could.

Jared knew that his thesis statement had to be a complete sentence that made a point about his topic and that it should be both clearly worded and specific. In addition, it should suggest his essay's purpose. When he reviewed his thesis statement, he felt sure that it satisfied these criteria and expressed an idea he could develop in his essay.

PRACTICE 3-6

Indicate whether each of the following items is a statement of fact (*F*), an announcement (*A*), a vague statement (*VS*), or an effective thesis (*ET*).

Examples

My drive to school takes more than an hour. ___F___

I hate my commute between home and school. ___VS___

1. Students who must commute a long distance to school are at a disadvantage compared to students who live close by. _____

2. In this paper, I will discuss cheating. _____

3. Schools should establish specific policies to discourage students from cheating. _____

4. Despite the efforts of the bottled water industry to suggest otherwise, plastic water bottles are causing a great deal of harm to the environment. _____

5. Television commercials are designed to sell products. _____

6. Effective television commercials use verbal and visual cues to create consumer interest in a product. _____

7. Children of teenage mothers face many challenges. _____

8. Young people are starting to abuse alcohol and drugs at earlier ages than in the past. _____

9. Opioid abuse is a major problem in our society. _____

10. Families can do several things to help children avoid alcohol and drugs. _____

PRACTICE 3-7

Label each of the following thesis statements *F* if it is a statement of fact, *A* if it is an announcement, *VS* if it is a vague statement, or *ET* if it is an effective thesis. Revise those that are not effective thesis statements.

Examples

The World Health Organization has warned that people can get sick from drinking unclean water. ___*F*___

Possible rewrite: The World Health Organization should make access to clean water its first priority in disease prevention.

A few simple changes could make the dining halls safer for students with food allergies. ___ET___

1. *Internet privacy* is the ability of people to control the storing, repurposing, displaying, and selling of personal information to third parties. _____

2. To compete with web-based businesses, brick-and-mortar businesses will have to take drastic action. _____

3. My essay will show that self-driving cars are better than human drivers. _____

4. Highway speed limits are ineffective. _____

5. Honor codes are the best way for universities to stop students from cheating. _____

6. Studying abroad enables college students to gain independence and self-confidence. _____

7. The National Weather Service predicts this will be an average year for hurricanes. _____

8. By teaching me critical problem-solving skills, the army prepared me well for a career in engineering. _____

9. Sugary soda is high in calories and low in nutritional value. _____

10. People have their own definitions of justice. _____

PRACTICE

3-8 Rewrite the following vague statements as effective thesis statements.

Example

Vaccinations are useful in preventing disease.

Possible rewrite: Although some parents refuse to have their children vaccinated, vaccinations are critical for the control and eradication of life-threatening diseases, such as polio, rubella, and mumps.

1. At times, Uber is a better option than a taxi.
2. Student loans should be forgiven.
3. Infomercials are sometimes misleading.
4. Cheerleading is a sport.
5. Online dating can be challenging.

PRACTICE 3-9 A list of broad topics for essays follows. Select five of these topics, narrow them, and generate a thesis statement for each.

1. Careers
2. Reality television
3. U.S. immigration policies
4. Music
5. Texting in class
6. Required courses
7. Computer games
8. Disciplining children
9. Street sense
10. The cost of tuition

PRACTICE 3-10 Read the following groups of statements. Then, write a thesis statement that could express the main point of each group.

1.
- *Gap year* is a term that refers to a year that students take off before they go to college.
- Many college students spend most of their time studying and socializing with their peers.
- Studies show that high school students who take a year off before they go to college get better grades.
- Many students take community-service jobs in order to broaden their interests and to increase their social awareness.

2.
- Some people post too much personal information on social-networking sites.
- Child predators frequently use social-networking sites to find their victims.
- Some experts believe that people can become addicted to social-networking sites.
- Employers have fired employees because of information they have seen on their employees' social-networking sites.

3.
- A student at Indiana University at Bloomington was able to create her own major in environmental ethics.
- Drexel University has begun recruiting students who would design their own majors.
- Some students get bored with traditional majors that force them to choose from a rigid list of courses.
- Many employers are impressed with students who design their own majors.

4.
- One way to pay for college is to get a job.
- The majority of students supplement their college tuition with loans or grants.
- According to the College Board, only 22 percent of all federal aid for college tuition goes to scholarships.
- Some students enlist in the armed forces and become eligible for tuition assistance programs.

5.
- You can save time in the kitchen by washing and putting away items as you cook.
- Keep your kitchen well stocked so that you will not have to run to the store to get an ingredient.
- Keep your countertops free of clutter so you don't have to put things away before you cook.
- Shred things like cheese in advance and store them in plastic bags.

Richard Levine/Alamy Stock Photo

STATE your thesis

Review your freewriting, brainstorming, journal entries, and cluster diagram. Then, write a thesis statement for your essay about the most difficult job you've ever had.

3e Choosing Supporting Points

Once you have decided on a thesis statement, it is time to look over your freewriting, brainstorming, journal entries, and cluster diagram again to identify the **evidence** (details and examples) that best supports your thesis.

The evidence you present should convince readers of the validity of your thesis. In order to so, your evidence must be both *sufficient* and *relevant*. The amount of evidence you need depends on your thesis. It makes sense that the more general or far-reaching your thesis, the more evidence you will need to support it. In addition, all of your evidence should clearly support the claim you are making. For example, if you are discussing math education in elementary school, you would not support it with information about math education in middle school.

> **QUESTIONS TO ASK ABOUT EVIDENCE**
> - Have I provided evidence to support each point I make?
> - Do I explain my evidence in enough detail?
> - Is all of my evidence relevant to the point it is supposed to support?

When Jared looked over the notes he had accumulated, he saw that his brainstorming had given him so much to work with that he didn't need to use the material he'd come up with through clustering and journal writing. At this point, he reviewed his brainstorming notes, crossing out several points that he thought would not support his thesis.

Deciding to Go Back to School: Pros and Cons

Money a problem
Other students a lot younger
Paying tuition — how?
No one in family went to college
Friends not in college
Couldn't see myself in college
~~Considered going to trade school~~
~~Computer programmer?~~
Grades bad in high school
Wondered if I would get in
Found out about community college
Admission requirements not bad
Afraid — too old, looking dumb
~~Took time to get used to routine~~
Found other students like me
Liked studying

Jared's list of supporting points

PRACTICE 3-11

Review Jared's list of supporting points above. Do you see any points he crossed out that you think he should have kept? Do you see any other points he should have crossed out?

3f Making an Outline

After you have selected the points you think will best support your thesis, you should make an **informal** (or **scratch**) **outline**. This informal outline enables you to organize your ideas and keeps you focused as you write. Begin your informal outline by writing down your main points. Then, under each main point, list the supporting points. Arrange them in the order in which you will discuss them (for example, from general to specific, or from least important to most important). (Keep in mind, that as you construct your outline, you will most likely think of additional ideas.)

When Jared looked over his list of supporting points, he saw that they fell into three groups of excuses for not going back to school: not being able to pay tuition, not being a good student in high school, and not being able to picture himself in college. He arranged his points under these three headings to create the following informal outline.

Excuse 1: Not being able to pay tuition

    Needed to work to live

    Didn't have much money saved

    Found out about community college (low tuition)

    Found out about grants, loans

Excuse 2: Not being a good student in high school

    Got bad grades in high school: wasn't motivated and didn't work

    Looked into admission requirements at community college — doable!

    Made a commitment to improve study habits

Excuse 3: Not being able to picture myself in college

    No college graduates in family

    Friends not in college

    Afraid of being too old, looking dumb

    Found other students like me

    Found out I liked studying

Jared's informal outline

PRACTICE 3-12

Look over Jared's informal outline. Do you think his arrangement is effective? Can you suggest any other ways he might have arranged his points?

> ## FYI
>
> ### Preparing a Formal Outline
>
> An informal outline like the one that Jared prepared is usually all you need to plan a short essay. However, some writers—especially when they are planning a longer, more detailed essay—prefer to use formal outlines.
>
> **Formal outlines** use a combination of numbered and lettered headings to show the exact order and the relative importance of the ideas you will discuss. For example, the most important (and most general) ideas are assigned a Roman numeral; the next most important ideas are assigned capital letters. Each level develops the idea above it, and each new level is indented.
>
> Here is a formal outline of the points that Jared planned to discuss in his essay:
>
> *Thesis statement:* Although I realized it would be difficult in some ways, I decided that if I really wanted to attend college full-time, I could.
>
> I. Difficulty: Money
>   A. Needed to work to live
>   B. Didn't have much money saved
>   C. Found out about community college (low tuition)
>   D. Found out about grants/loans
> II. Difficulty: Academic record
>   A. Got bad grades in high school
>   1. Didn't care
>   2. Didn't work
>   B. Found out about reasonable admission requirements at community college
>   C. Committed to improving study habits
> III. Difficulty: Imagining myself as a student
>   A. Had no college graduates in family
>   B. Had no friends who went to college
>   C. Felt anxious
>   1. Too old
>   2. Out of practice at school
>   D. Found other students like me
>   E. Discovered I like studying

MAKE an informal outline

Review your freewriting, brainstorming, journal entries, and cluster diagram. Then, list the points you plan to use to support your thesis statement. Cross out any points that do not support your thesis statement. Finally, group the remaining points into an informal outline that will guide you as you write.

 ## 3g Drafting Your Essay

After you have decided on a thesis for your essay and have arranged your supporting points in the order in which you will discuss them, you are ready to draft your essay.

FYI

Using Patterns of Essay Development

Writers have a variety of options for developing ideas in an essay. These options, which are discussed and illustrated in Unit 2 of this text, include *exemplification, narration, description, process, cause and effect, comparison and contrast, classification, definition,* and *argument*. Sometimes an essay combines several of these **patterns of development**; often, however, a single pattern dominates. Recognizing a pattern or patterns that emerge as you draft can help you arrange ideas in your essays.

    At this stage of the writing process, you should not worry about spelling or grammar or about composing a perfect introduction or conclusion. Your main goal is to get your ideas down so that you can react to them. Remember that the draft you are writing will be revised, so leave extra space between lines as you type. Follow your outline, but don't hesitate to depart from it if you think of new points.

    As you draft your essay, be sure that it has a **thesis-and-support** structure—that it states a thesis and supports it with evidence. Include a **working title**, a temporary title that you will revise later so that it accurately reflects the content of your completed essay. This working title will help you focus your ideas.

    Following is the first draft of Jared's essay.

Going Back to School

I was out of school for six years after I graduated from high school. The decision to return to school was one I had a lot of difficulty making. I had been around enough to know that without more education, I'd never get anywhere in life, but I always found reasons for not taking the plunge. However, after a lot of thinking, I realized that my reasons for not going to college were just excuses. Although I realized it would be difficult in some ways, I decided that if I really wanted to attend college full-time, I could.

My first excuse for not going to college was that I couldn't afford to go to school full-time. I had worked since I finished high school, but I hadn't put much money away. I kept wondering how I would pay for books and tuition. I needed to support myself and pay for rent, food, and car expenses. I was working as a house painter, and a house I was painting belonged to a college instructor. Painting wasn't hard work, but it was boring. I'd start in the morning and work without a break until lunch. We began talking. When I told him about my situation, he told me I should look at our local community college. He also told me about some loans and grants I'd probably be able to apply for. I went online and looked at the college's website. I found out that tuition was one hundred dollars a credit, less than I thought it would be. If I got just one of the grants he mentioned, I might be able to make it.

Now that I had taken care of my first excuse, I had to deal with my second — that I hadn't been a good student in high school. When I was a teenager, I didn't care much about school. School bored me to death. Probably as a result, I got bad grades. Now that I was considering going back to school, though, I wondered what price I would have to pay for my laziness and immaturity. The answer to this question was not as bad as I thought it would be. According to the community college's website, all I needed to be admitted was a high school diploma and county residence. I would have to take some placement tests, but I would be judged on my ability, not my high school grades. I knew I could do better if I made a real effort to study harder and smarter. The website was easy to navigate, and I had no problem finding information.

(continued)

(continued from previous page)

    I had a hard time picturing myself in college. No one in my family had ever gone to college. My friends were just like me; they all went to work right after high school. I had no role model or mentor who could give me advice. I thought I was just too old for college. After all, I was probably at least six years older than most of the students. How would I be able to keep up with the younger students in the class? I hadn't opened a textbook for years, and I'd never really learned how to study. Most of my fears disappeared during my first few weeks of classes. I saw a lot of students who were as old as I was, and some were even older. Studying didn't seem to be a problem, either. I actually enjoyed learning. History, which had put me to sleep in high school, suddenly became interesting. So did math and English. It soon became clear to me that I was going to like being in college.

    Going to college as a full-time student has changed my life, both personally and financially. I am no longer the same person I was in high school. I allowed laziness and insecurity to hold me back. Now, I have options that I didn't have before. When I graduate from community college, I plan to transfer to the state university and get a four-year degree.

Jared's first draft

PRACTICE 3-13 What changes would you suggest Jared make to his draft? What might he add? What might he delete? Which of his supporting details and examples do you find most effective? Why?

DRAFT your essay

Draft an essay about your most difficult job. When you finish your draft, give your essay a working title.

3h TESTing Your Essay

Before you begin revising, you should **TEST** your essay. **TEST**ing will tell you whether you essay includes the basic elements it needs to be effective.

T Thesis
E Evidence
S Summary
T Transitions

TESTing for a Thesis

The first thing you do when you **TEST** your essay is to make sure it has a clear thesis (**T**) that identifies the essay's main idea. By stating the main idea, your thesis helps to unify your essay. When Jared **TEST**ed the draft of his essay, he decided that his thesis statement clearly stated his main idea. (His marginal note appears below.)

Jared's Introduction

I was out of school for six years after I graduated from high school. The decision to return to school was one I had a lot of difficulty making. I had been around enough to know that without more education, I'd never get anywhere in life, but I always found reasons for not taking the plunge. However, after a lot of thinking, I realized that my reasons for not going to college were just excuses. <u>Although I realized it would be difficult in some ways, I decided that if I really wanted to attend college full-time, I could.</u>

Thesis clearly states what I want to say about going to college.

TESTing for Evidence

The next thing you do when you **TEST** your essay is to check your evidence (**E**) to make sure that the body of your essay includes enough examples and details to support your thesis. Remember that without evidence, your essay is simply a series of unsupported general statements. A well-developed essay includes enough evidence to explain, illustrate, and clarify the points you are making.

When Jared **TEST**ed his draft for evidence, he decided that he should add more examples and details in his body paragraphs and delete some irrelevant ones. (His marginal notes appear below.)

Jared's Body Paragraphs

Are details about painting necessary?

Add more about how I thought I could cover tuition.

Evidence [E]

My first excuse for not going to college was that I couldn't afford to go to school full-time. I had worked since I finished high school, but I hadn't put much money away. I kept wondering how I would pay for books and tuition. I needed to support myself and pay for rent, food, and car expenses. I was working as a house painter, and a house I was painting belonged to a college instructor. Painting wasn't hard work, but it was boring. I'd start in the morning and work without a break until lunch. We began talking. When I told him about my situation, he told me I should look at our local community college. He also told me about some loans and grants I'd probably be able to apply for. I went online and looked at the college's website. I found out that tuition was one hundred dollars a credit, less than I thought it would be. If I got just one of the grants he mentioned, I might be able to make it.

Give example of Boredom.

Evidence [E]

Are details about the website relevant?

Now that I had taken care of my first excuse, I had to deal with my second—that I hadn't been a good student in high school. When I was a teenager, I didn't care much about school. School bored me to death. Probably as a result, I got bad grades. Now that I was considering going back to school, though, I wondered what price I would have to pay for my laziness and immaturity. The answer to this question was not as bad as I thought it would be. According to the community college's website, all I needed to be admitted was a high school diploma and county residence. I would have to take some placement tests, but I would be judged on my ability, not my high school grades. I knew I could do better if I made a real effort to study harder and smarter. The website was easy to navigate, and I had no problem finding information.

Evidence [E]

Evidence seems OK here.

I had a hard time picturing myself in college. My friends were just like me; they all went to work right after high school. I had no role model or mentor who could give me advice. I thought I was just too old for college. After all, I was probably at least six years older than most of the students. How would I be able to keep up with the younger students in the class? I hadn't opened a textbook for years, and I'd never really learned how to study. Most of my fears disappeared during my first few weeks of classes. I saw a lot of students who were as old as I was, and some were even older. Studying didn't seem to be a problem, either. I actually enjoyed learning. History, which had put me to sleep in high school, suddenly became interesting. So did math and English. It soon became clear to me that I was going to like being in college.

TESTing for a Summary

The third thing you do when you **TEST** your essay is to look at your conclusion and make sure that it includes a **summary (S)** of your ideas. Most often, your conclusion will begin with a summary (or a summary statement), which reinforces your essay's thesis. By reinforcing your thesis, this summary helps to **unify** your essay.

When Jared **TEST**ed his draft, he saw that it included a summary statement that reinforced the main idea of his essay. (His marginal note appears below.)

Jared's Conclusion

<u>Going to college as a full-time student has changed my life, both personally and financially.</u> I am no longer the same person I was in high school. I allowed laziness and insecurity to hold me back. Now, I have options that I didn't have before. When I graduate from community college, I plan to transfer to the state university and get a four-year degree.

Conclusion is too short, but summary statement is OK.

TESTing for Transitions

The last thing you do when you **TEST** your essay is to make sure that it includes **transitions (T)**—words and phrases that connect your ideas. Make sure you have included all the transitions you need to tell readers how one sentence (or paragraph) is connected to another. Including transitions makes your essay **coherent**, with its sentences arranged in a clear, logical sequence that helps readers understand your ideas.

By linking sentences and paragraphs, transitions emphasize the relationship between ideas and help readers understand your essay's logic. By reminding readers of what has come before, transitions prepare readers for new information and help them understand how it fits into the discussion. In this sense, transitions are the glue that holds the ideas in your essay together.

Transitions are categorized according to their function. For example, they may indicate **time order** (*first, second, now, next, finally,* and so on), **spatial order** (*above, behind, near, next to, over,* and so on), or **logical order** (*also, although, therefore, in fact,* and so on). (For a full list of transitions, see 4c, p. 120.) When Jared **TEST**ed his draft for transitions, he realized that although he had included some transitional words and phrases, he needed to add more of them to connect his ideas. (His marginal notes appear on the following page.)

Jared's Thesis + Body Paragraphs

Although I realized it would be difficult in some ways, I decided that if I really wanted to attend college full-time, I could.

My first excuse for not going to college was that I couldn't afford to go to school full-time. I had worked since I finished high school, but I hadn't put much money away. I kept wondering how I would pay for books and tuition. I needed to support myself and pay for rent, food, and car expenses. I was working as a house painter, and a house I was painting belonged to a college instructor. Painting wasn't hard work, but it was boring. I'd start in the morning and work without a break until lunch. We began talking. When I told him about my situation, he told me I should look at our local community college. He also told me about some loans and grants I'd probably be able to apply for. I went online and looked at the college's website. I found out that tuition was one hundred dollars a credit, less than I thought it would be. If I got just one of the grants he mentioned, I might be able to make it.

Need to show relationship between ideas in these paragraphs.

 Transitions

Now that I had taken care of my first excuse, I had to deal with my second — that I hadn't been a good student in high school. When I was a teenager, I didn't care much about school. School bored me to death. Probably as a result, I got bad grades. Now that I was considering going back to school, though, I wondered what price I would have to pay for my laziness and immaturity. The answer to this question was not as bad as I thought it would be. According to the community college's website, all I needed to be admitted was a high school diploma and county residence. I would have to take some placement tests, but I would be judged on my ability, not my high school grades. I knew I could do better if I made a real effort to study harder and smarter. The website was easy to navigate, and I had no problem finding information.

Add better transition between these two paragraphs.

I had a hard time picturing myself in college. No one in my family had ever gone to college. My friends were just like me; they all went to work right after high school. I had no role model or mentor who could give me advice.

Add transition here.

I thought I was just too old for college. After all, I was probably at least six years older than most of the students. How would I be able to keep up with the younger students in the class? I hadn't opened a textbook in years, and I'd never really learned how to study. Most of my fears disappeared during my first few weeks of classes. I saw a lot of students who were as old as I was, and some were even older. Studying didn't seem to be a problem, either. I actually enjoyed learning. History, which had put me to sleep in high school, suddenly became interesting. So did math and English. It soon became clear to me that I was going to like being in college.

> **TEST your essay**
> **TEST** your draft to make sure it includes all the elements of an effective essay. If any elements are missing, add them now.

3i Revising Your Essay

Once you have **TEST**ed your essay, you can move on to revise it. When you revise, you resee, rethink, reevaluate, and rewrite your work. Some of the changes you make—such as adding, deleting, or rearranging sentences or even whole paragraphs—will be major. Others will be relatively small—for example, adding or deleting words or phrases.

> **FYI**
>
> Remember that revising is not the same as editing and proofreading. When you revise, you look at issues that affect the over-all organization and content of your essay. **Editing** and **proofreading** occur when you address smaller issues like grammar, word choice, spelling, typos, and punctuation. For this reason, you revise first, edit next, and proofread last.

Before you begin revising, put your essay aside for a while. This "cooling-off" period allows you to see your draft more objectively when you return to it. When you are ready to revise, keep in mind that the revision process is usually not a neat one. It is a good idea, therefore, to revise on hard copy and not on the computer screen. On hard copy, you are able to see a full page—or even two or three pages next to each other—as you revise. Revising on hard copy also gives you more options in terms of how you interact with your draft: You can draw arrows, underline, cross out, and write above lines and in the margins. When you have finished, you can type your changes into your document. Be careful, though, not to delete sentences or paragraphs until you are certain you do not need them. Instead, move unwanted material to the end of your draft—or save multiple dated drafts.

Revision can take many forms. You can receive feedback on your draft from other students, from your instructor, or from tutors in the writing center. In addition, you can use an outline to check your organization or a revision checklist to make sure you don't miss any important items. In the end, you have to determine what strategy (or combination of strategies) works best for you.

The following chart lists some commonly used revision strategies and explains the advantages of each:

STRATEGIES FOR REVISING	
STRATEGY	**ADVANTAGES**
FACE-TO-FACE CONFERENCE WITH INSTRUCTOR  Blend Images - Hill Street Studios/Getty Images	■ Provides one-to-one feedback that can't be obtained in the classroom ■ Builds a student-teacher relationship ■ Enables you to collaborate with your instructor ■ Allows you to ask questions that you might not ask in a classroom setting
WRITING CENTER 	■ Offers you a less formal, less stressful environment than an instructor conference ■ Enables you to get help from trained tutors (both students and professionals) ■ Provides a perspective other than the instructor's ■ Offers specialized help to students whose first language is not English
PEER REVIEW 	■ Enables students working on the same assignment to share insights with one another ■ Gives you the experience of writing for a real audience ■ Gives you several different readers' reactions to your work ■ Enables you to benefit from your classmates' ideas

STRATEGY	ADVANTAGES
ELECTRONIC COMMUNICATION WITH INSTRUCTOR 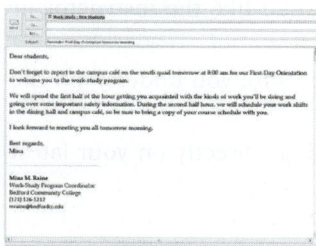	■ Enables you to submit email questions before a draft is due ■ Gives you quick answers to your questions ■ Enables instructors to give feedback by annotating drafts electronically ■ Enables you to react to your instructor's responses when you have time ■ Eliminates time spent traveling to instructor's office
REVISION CHECKLIST 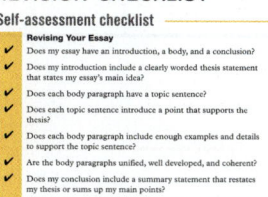	■ Gives you a tool that enables you to revise in an orderly way ■ Enables you to learn to revise independently ■ Enables you to focus on specific aspects of your writing
OUTLINE YOUR DRAFT 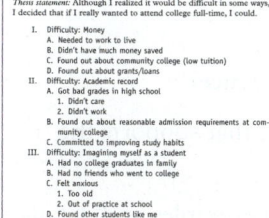	■ Enables you to see if you have left out important points ■ Enables you to see if your essay follows a particular pattern of development ■ Enables you to see the relationship between your thesis and your body paragraphs

FYI

Getting the Most Out of a Conference

If you need help at any point in the writing process, you can get it from your instructor or from a tutor in your school's writing center. Following the guidelines below will help you get the most out of your conferences:

- Make an appointment in advance, either by phone or by email.
- Arrive on time; instructors and tutors often schedule several appointments in a row, and if you are late, you may miss your appointment entirely.

(continued)

(continued from previous page)

- Bring a copy of your assignment.
- Bring all drafts and prewriting notes for the assignment you are working on.
- Bring a list of specific questions you would like the instructor or tutor to answer.
- Pay attention, ask your questions, and be sure you understand the answers.
- Write the instructor's or tutor's suggestions directly on your latest draft.
- Schedule a follow-up appointment if necessary.

Remember, your instructor or tutor will answer questions and make recommendations, but he or she will *not* revise or edit your work for you. That is your job.

Self-assessment checklist

Revising Your Essay

✔ Does my essay have an introduction, a body, and a conclusion?

✔ Does my introduction include a clearly worded thesis statement that states my essay's main idea?

✔ Does each body paragraph have a topic sentence?

✔ Does each topic sentence introduce a point that supports the thesis?

✔ Does each body paragraph include enough examples and details to support the topic sentence?

✔ Are the body paragraphs unified, well developed, and coherent?

✔ Does my conclusion include a summary statement that restates my thesis or sums up my main points?

When Jared finished **TEST**ing his essay, he decided to schedule a conference with his instructor to discuss how to revise and polish it. He made sure to follow the guidelines in the FYI box Getting the Most Out of a Conference on page 91. During the conference, Jared's instructor pointed out several places where she thought he should add more detail. For example, she thought his introduction started too abruptly and should be expanded. She also thought that Jared should give readers a sense of what he was like as a student in high school.

Jared's first draft, with his handwritten revisions—including those he made after he TESTed his draft—appears below. Notice that when Jared typed his draft, he left extra space so he could write more easily between the lines and in the margins.

Starting Over
~~Going Back to School~~

^I was out of school for six years after I graduated from high school. The decision to return to school was one I had a lot of difficulty making. I had been around enough to know that without more education, I'd never get anywhere in life, but I always found reasons for not taking the plunge. However, after a lot of thinking, I realized that my reasons for not going to college were just excuses. Although I realized it would be difficult in some ways, I decided that if I really wanted to attend college full-time, I could.

The other day, my sociology instructor mentioned that half the students enrolled in college programs across the country are twenty-five or older. His remark caught my attention because I am one of those students.

My first excuse for not going to college was that I couldn't afford to go to school full-time. I had worked since I finished high school, but I hadn't put much money away. I kept wondering how I would pay for books and tuition. I *also* needed to support myself and pay for rent, food, and car expenses. *The solution to my problem came unexpectedly.* I was working as a house painter, and a house I was painting belonged to a college instructor. ~~Painting wasn't hard work, but it was boring. I'd start in the morning and work without a break until lunch.~~ *During my lunch break, we* began talking. When I told him about my situation, he told me I should look at our local community college. He also told me about some loans and grants I'd probably be able to apply for. *Later,* I went online and looked at the college's website. I found out that tuition was one hundred dollars a credit, less than I thought it would be. If I got just one of the grants he mentioned, I might be able to make it.

The money I'd saved, along with what I could make painting houses on the weekends, could get me through.

Now that I had taken care of my first excuse, I had to deal with my second—that I hadn't been a good student in high school. When I was a teenager, I didn't care much about school. *In fact, school* ~~School~~ bored me ~~to death~~. Probably as a result, I got bad grades. Now that I was considering going

In class, I would stare out the window or watch the second hand on the clock move slowly around. I never bothered with homework. School just didn't interest me.

back to school, though, I wondered what price I would have to pay for my laziness and immaturity. The answer to this question was not as bad as I thought it would be. According to the community college's website, all I needed to be admitted was a high school diploma and county residence. I would have to take some placement tests, but I would be judged on my ability, not my high school grades. I knew I could do better if I made a real effort to study harder and smarter. ~~The website was easy to navigate, and I had no problem finding information.~~

My biggest problem still bothered me: I had a hard time picturing myself in college. No one in my family had ever gone to college. My friends were just like me; they all went to work right after high school. I had no role model or mentor who could give me advice. Besides, I thought I was just too old for college. After all, I was probably at least six years older than most of the students. How would I be able to keep up with the younger students in the class? I hadn't opened a textbook for years, and I'd never really learned how to study. However, most ~~Most~~ of my fears disappeared during my first few weeks of classes. I saw a lot of students who were as old as I was, and some were even older. Studying didn't seem to be a problem either. I actually enjoyed learning. History, which had put me to sleep in high school, suddenly became interesting. So did math and English. It soon became clear to me that I was going to like being in college.

Going to college as a full-time student has changed my life, both personally and financially. I am no longer the same person I was in high school. In the past, I allowed laziness and insecurity to hold me back. Now, I have options that I didn't have before. When I graduate from community college, I plan to transfer to the state university and get a four-year degree. *The other day, one of my instructors asked me if I had ever considered becoming a teacher. The truth is, I never had, but now I might. I'd like to be able to give kids like me the tough, realistic advice I wish someone had given me.*

(Add this new paragraph right before the conclusion.) The one question that still haunts me is why it took me six years to address my excuses and overcome my fears. The most obvious answer is that I was afraid, afraid of failure and afraid of looking stupid if I didn't succeed, but that was not the full answer. When I look back on my life, I realize that nothing in my environment steered me toward college. In fact, most of the people I knew actively discouraged me from trying to aim higher. In high school, my friends bragged about how many courses they had failed. If someone got a good grade, the others teased him. We got together almost every night and fooled around, so serious studying was out of the question. Many of my relatives were no better. In tenth grade, I told my father that I wanted to go to college. He looked at me for a second and said that if I went, I would probably change so much that I would not be part of the family. My mother was the only person who believed in me. She always told me I was smart and should aim higher. Even though I pretended not to listen to her, my mother's faith in me was one of the reasons I decided to return to school.

PRACTICE 3-14

Working in a group of three or four students, answer the following questions:

- What kind of material did Jared add to his draft?
- What did he delete?
- Why do you think he made these changes?
- Do you agree with the changes he made?

Be prepared to discuss your reactions to these changes with the class.

> ## REVISE your essay
> Choose one or two of the additional revision strategies from the Strategies for Revising chart on page 90, and continue revising your essay.

Richard Levine/Alamy Stock Photo

3j Editing Your Essay

Once you are finished revising, your next step is to edit your essay. When you **edit,** you check grammar and sentence structure. Then, you look at punctuation, mechanics, and spelling. As you edit, think carefully about the questions in the Self-assessment checklist below.

Self-assessment checklist

Editing Your Essay

EDITING FOR COMMON SENTENCE PROBLEMS

✔ Have I avoided run-ons? (See Chapter 22.)

✔ Have I avoided sentence fragments? (See Chapter 23.)

✔ Do my subjects and verbs agree? (See Chapter 24.)

✔ Have I avoided illogical shifts? (See Chapter 25.)

✔ Have I avoided dangling and misplaced modifiers? (See Chapter 26.)

EDITING FOR GRAMMAR

✔ Are my verb forms and verb tenses correct? (See Chapter 15.)

✔ Have I used nouns and pronouns correctly? (See Chapter 16.)

✔ Have I used adjectives and adverbs correctly? (See Chapter 17.)

EDITING FOR PUNCTUATION AND MECHANICS

✔ Have I used commas correctly? (See Chapter 27.)

✔ Have I used apostrophes correctly? (See Chapter 28.)

✔ Have I used capital letters where they are required? (See Chapter 29a.)

✔ Have I used quotation marks correctly where they are needed? (See Chapter 29b.)

3k Proofreading Your Essay

Your last step is to proofread. When you **proofread** your essay, you look for typos, check your formatting, and double-check for anything you might have missed while you were editing. Remember that Spell Check and Grammar Check tools are helpful starting points in the editing process, but they can also introduce errors, so as you proofread, check any words whose spelling you are not sure of. It is also a good idea to print your essay and proofread a hard copy because it is easy to miss typos and other small errors on a computer screen.

Now, look at your essay's format. The **format** of an essay is the way it looks on a page—for example, the size of the margins, the placement of page numbers, and the amount of space between lines. Most instructors expect you to follow a certain format when you type an essay. The model essay format illustration that follows is commonly used in composition classes. Before you hand in an essay, you should make sure that it follows this model (or the guidelines your instructor gives you).

Essay Format: *Sample First Page*

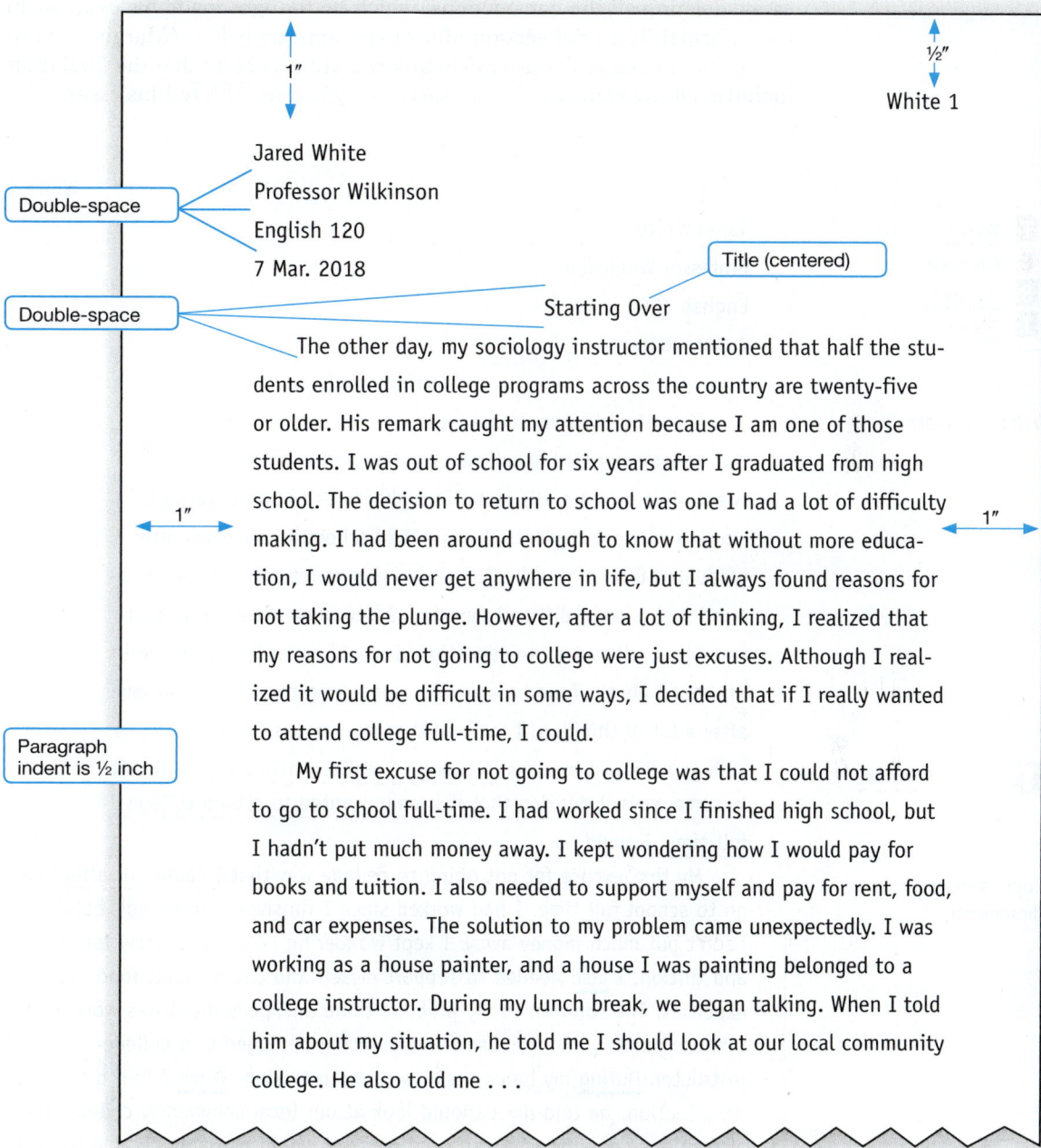

Jared White
Professor Wilkinson
English 120
7 Mar. 2018

Starting Over

    The other day, my sociology instructor mentioned that half the students enrolled in college programs across the country are twenty-five or older. His remark caught my attention because I am one of those students. I was out of school for six years after I graduated from high school. The decision to return to school was one I had a lot of difficulty making. I had been around enough to know that without more education, I would never get anywhere in life, but I always found reasons for not taking the plunge. However, after a lot of thinking, I realized that my reasons for not going to college were just excuses. Although I realized it would be difficult in some ways, I decided that if I really wanted to attend college full-time, I could.

    My first excuse for not going to college was that I could not afford to go to school full-time. I had worked since I finished high school, but I hadn't put much money away. I kept wondering how I would pay for books and tuition. I also needed to support myself and pay for rent, food, and car expenses. The solution to my problem came unexpectedly. I was working as a house painter, and a house I was painting belonged to a college instructor. During my lunch break, we began talking. When I told him about my situation, he told me I should look at our local community college. He also told me . . .

Note: The bottom margin of each page should be one inch.

When his revisions were complete, Jared edited and proofread his essay, deleting all the contractions, which he thought made his essay seem too informal. The final version of his essay appears below. (Marginal annotations have been added to highlight key features.) Note that the final draft includes all the elements Jared looked for when he **TEST**ed his essay.

White 1

Jared White
Professor Wilkinson
English 120
7 Mar. 2018

Starting Over

Introduction

The other day, my sociology instructor mentioned that half the students enrolled in college programs across the country are twenty-five or older. His remark caught my attention because I am one of those students. I was out of school for six years after I graduated from high school. The decision to return to school was one I had a lot of difficulty making. I had been around enough to know that without more education, I would never get anywhere in life, but I always found reasons for not taking the plunge. However, after a lot of thinking, I realized that my reasons for not going to college were just excuses. Although I realized it would be difficult in some ways, I decided that if I really wanted to attend college full-time, I could.

Thesis statement

Topic sentence (first point)

My first excuse for not going to college was that I could not afford to go to school full-time. I had worked since I finished high school, but I hadn't put much money away. I kept wondering how I would pay for books and tuition. I also needed to support myself and pay for rent, food, and car expenses. The solution to my problem came unexpectedly. I was working as a house painter, and a house I was painting belonged to a college instructor. During my lunch break, we began talking. When I told him about my situation, he told me I should look at our local community college. He also told me about some loans and grants I would probably be able to apply for. Later, I went online and looked at the college's website. I found out that tuition was one hundred dollars a credit, less than I thought it would be. If I got just one of the grants he mentioned, I might be able to make it. The money I had saved, along with what I could make painting houses on the weekends, could get me through.

Evidence

 **Transitions**

White 2

Now that I had taken care of my first excuse, I had to deal with my second—that I had not been a good student in high school. When I was a teenager, I didn't care much about school. In fact, school bored me. In class, I would stare out the window or watch the second hand on the clock move slowly around. I never bothered with homework. School just didn't interest me. Probably as a result, I got bad grades. Now that I was considering going back to school, though, I wondered what price I would have to pay for my laziness and immaturity. The answer to this question was not as bad as I thought it would be. According to the community college's website, all I needed to be admitted was a high school diploma and county residence. I would have to take some placement tests, but I would be judged on my ability, not my high school grades. I knew I could do better if I made a real effort to study harder and smarter.

My biggest problem still bothered me: I had a hard time picturing myself in college. No one in my family had ever gone to college. My friends were just like me; they all went to work right after high school. I had no role model or mentor who could give me advice. Besides, I thought I was just too old for college. After all, I was probably at least six years older than most of the students. How would I be able to keep up with the younger students in the class? I had not opened a textbook for years, and I had never really learned how to study. However, most of my fears disappeared during my first few weeks of classes. I saw a lot of students who were as old as I was, and some were even older. Studying didn't seem to be a problem, either. I actually enjoyed learning. For example, history, which had put me to sleep in high school, suddenly became interesting. So did math and English. It soon became clear to me that I was going to like being in college.

The one question that still haunts me is why it took me six years to address my excuses and overcome my fears. The most obvious answer is that I was afraid, afraid of failure and afraid of looking stupid if I didn't succeed, but that was not the full answer. When I look back on my life, I realize that nothing in my environment steered me toward college. In fact, most of the people I knew actively discouraged me from trying to aim higher. In high school, my friends bragged about how many courses they had failed. If someone got a good grade, the others teased him. We got together almost every night and fooled around, so serious studying was out of the question. Many of my relatives were no better. In tenth grade, I told my father that I wanted to go to college. He looked at me for a second and said that if I went, I would probably change so much that I would not be part of the

White 3

family. My mother was the only person who believed in me. She always told me I was smart and should aim higher. <u>Even though</u> I pretended not to listen to her, my mother's faith in me was one of the reasons I decided to return to school.

<u>Going to college as a full-time student has changed my life, both personally and financially.</u> I am no longer the same person I was in high school. In the past, I allowed laziness and insecurity to hold me back. Now, I have options that I didn't have before. When I graduate from community college, I plan to transfer to the state university and get a four-year degree. The other day, one of my instructors asked me if I had ever considered becoming a teacher. The truth is, I never had, but now I might. I would like to be able to give kids like me the tough, realistic advice I wish someone had given me.

S Summary

Conclusion

PRACTICE
3-15

Reread the final draft of Jared White's essay. Working in a group of three or four students, answer these questions:

- Do you think this draft is better than his first draft (shown on page 83)?
- What other changes could Jared have made?

Be prepared to discuss your group's answers with the class.

EDIT and proofread your essay

Edit your draft, using the Self-assessment checklist, "Editing Your Essay" on page 96 to guide you. Then, proofread your essay for typos and other errors. Finally, make sure that your essay's format follows your instructor's guidelines.

CHAPTER REVIEW

REVIEW ACTIVITY

1. The following student essay is missing its thesis statement and topic sentences and has no summary statement. First, write an appropriate thesis statement on the lines provided. (Make sure your thesis statement clearly communicates the essay's main idea.) Then, write the topic sentences for the second, third, and fourth paragraphs. Finally, add a summary statement in the conclusion.

   Preparing for a Job Interview

   A lot of books and many websites give advice on how to do well on a job interview. Some recommend practicing your handshake, and others suggest making eye contact. This advice is useful, but not many books tell how to get mentally prepared for an interview. [Thesis statement:] _____

   _____

   _____

   _____

   [Topic sentence for the second paragraph:] _____

   _____

   _____

   _____

   Feeling good about how you look is important, so you should probably wear a dress or skirt (or, for males, a jacket and tie) to an interview. Even if you will not be dressing this formally on the job, try to make a good first impression. For this reason, you should never come to an interview dressed in jeans or shorts. Still, you should be careful not to overdress. For example, wearing a suit or a dressy dress to an interview at a fast-food restaurant might make you feel good, but it could also make you look as if you do not really want to work there.

[Topic sentence for the third paragraph:] _____

_____

_____

Going on an interview is a little like getting ready to compete in a sporting event. You have to go in with the right attitude. If you think you are not going to be successful, chances are that you will not be. So, before you go on any interview, spend some time building your confidence. Tell yourself that you can do the job and that you will do well in the interview. By the time you get to the interview, you will have convinced yourself that you are the right person for the job.

[Topic sentence for the fourth paragraph:] _____

_____

_____

Many people go to an interview knowing little or nothing about the job. They expect the interviewer to tell them what they will have to do. Someone who has taken the time to do his or her homework, however, impresses most interviewers. For this reason, you should always do some research before you go on an interview — even for a part-time job. Most of the time, your research can be nothing more than looking at the company's website, but this kind of research really pays off. Being able to talk about the job can give you a real advantage over other candidates. Sometimes the interviewer will be so impressed that he or she will offer you a job on the spot.

[Summary statement:] _____

_____

_____

Of course, following these suggestions will not guarantee that you get a job. You still have to do well at the interview itself. Even so, getting mentally prepared for the interview will give you an advantage over people who do almost nothing before they walk in the door.

2. Now, using the topic sentence below, write another body paragraph that you could add to the essay above. (This new paragraph will go right before the essay's conclusion.)

Another way to prepare yourself mentally is to anticipate and answer some typical questions interviewers ask.

_____

_____

_____

_____

COLLABORATIVE ACTIVITY

Graphic Organizer: *Finding Ideas to Write About*

This chapter identified six strategies for finding ideas to write about. Fill in these six strategies in the graphic organizer on page 104, and then write a brief description of each strategy.

Chapter Review

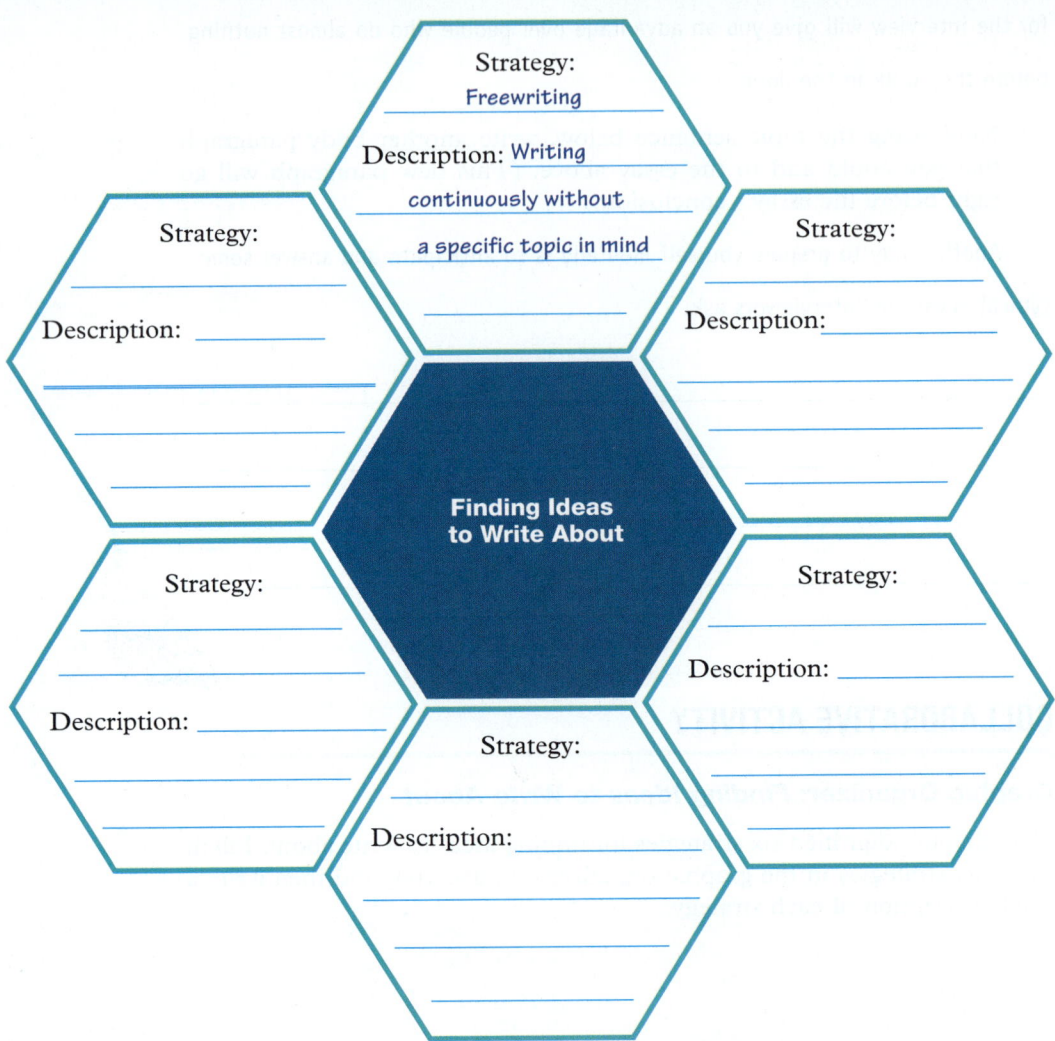

Strategy: Freewriting
Description: Writing continuously without a specific topic in mind

Review checklist

Writing an Essay

- ✔ Most essays have a thesis-and-support structure. The thesis statement presents the main idea, and the body paragraphs support the thesis. (See 3a.)

- ✔ Begin by focusing on your assignment, purpose, and audience to help you find a topic. (See 3b.)

- ✔ Find ideas to write about. (See 3c.)

- ✔ Identify your main idea, and develop an effective thesis statement. (See 3d.)

- ✔ List the points that best support your thesis (see 3e), and arrange them in the order in which you plan to discuss them, creating an informal outline of your essay. (See 3f.)

- ✔ Write your first draft, making sure your essay has a thesis-and-support structure. (See 3g.)

- ✔ **TEST** your essay. (See 3h.)

- ✔ Revise your essay. (See 3i.)

- ✔ Edit (see 3j) and proofread (see 3k) your essay.

4 Understanding Introductions, Body Paragraphs, and Conclusions

mavo/Shutterstock.com

FOCUS on reading and writing

Every job has different challenges: they can be fast-paced, physically demanding, dangerous, or even repetitive and boring. Now that you have identified the challenges in your job and completed the first draft of your essay, it is time to work on developing your introduction, body paragraphs, and conclusion.

> **PREVIEW**
>
> In this chapter, you will learn to
> - read an essay's paragraphs (4a).
> - write an introduction (4b).
> - write body paragraphs (4c).
> - write a conclusion (4d).

A well-constructed thesis-and-support essay is more than a collection of paragraphs. It begins with an **introduction** that includes a **thesis statement**—the sentence that states the main idea that the essay will develop. The next part of the essay—the **body**—includes several paragraphs that develop, support, or explain the essay's thesis. The essay's **conclusion** reinforces the thesis and ideally brings the essay to an effective and memorable close. As you read essays, you should evaluate these components carefully because they can help you understand the writers' ideas.

 ## 4a Reading Paragraphs

The **introduction** sets the tone for the essay. When you read an essay's introduction, ask the following questions:

- *How does the introduction prepare readers for the essay to follow?* What important information does the introduction provide? Does it give an overview of the essay? Does it provide necessary background information?

- *What strategy does the writer use?* Does the introduction tell readers why they should care about an issue? How does it make them want to read further? For example, does it relate an anecdote, present facts and examples, or define a key term? Is this strategy successful? What other strategy could the writer have used?

- *Does the introduction include a thesis statement?* Does the writer explicitly state the thesis? Is the wording clear? How could it be strengthened? Does the thesis help you to identify the writer's purpose? How? Is the thesis **implied**? (See 5c, Identifying Implied Main Ideas.) If so, why did the writer choose not to state it directly?

The **body paragraphs** develop the main idea of the essay. Each body paragraph discusses one key point backed up by evidence. When you read an essay's body paragraphs, ask the following questions:

- *Does each body paragraph have a **topic sentence**?* Is the topic sentence clearly worded? Is it concise? How could it be strengthened? Does the topic sentence identify the main point of the paragraph? Does it indicate how the body paragraph relates to the essay's thesis? Where is the topic sentence located? If it's not the first sentence of the paragraph, why not? If the paragraph does not have a topic sentence, why not? How do the topic sentences help guide readers through the essay?

- *Does each body paragraph have enough **evidence**?* Does the body paragraph include facts and examples that support the main idea? If more evidence is needed, where should it be added? Should the writer have used different kinds of evidence? If so, what kinds?

- *Does the body paragraph have a **summary**?* Does this summary restate the paragraph's main idea? How does the summary reinforce the paragraph's main idea? If the paragraph does not have a sentence that summarizes its content, does it need one?

- *Does each body paragraph include **transitional words and phrases**?* What transitions has the writer used? Has the writer used transitional paragraphs as well as transitional words and phrases? What relationship do the transitions signal? Do the transitions help readers follow the logic of the discussion? How? Has the writer used the right kind of transitions? Should the writer have used more transitions or different transitions?

The **conclusion** often stays with readers long after they have finished an essay. It is the writer's last chance to emphasize important points and to influence readers. When you read an essay's conclusion, ask the following questions:

- *What point (or points) does the writer emphasize in the conclusion?* Does the conclusion refer back to the thesis? Does the conclusion restate the essay's main points? Does it encourage readers to consider broader issues?

- *What strategy does the writer use?* What is the writer's concluding strategy? Does the writer propose a course of action or a solution to a problem? Would another concluding strategy have been more effective?

- *Does the writer end with a summary of the essay's main points?* If not, should it have? Does the conclusion reinforce the essay's thesis? How?

- *Is the conclusion effective?* Is the conclusion similar in tone to the rest of the essay? Does the conclusion give readers a sense of closure? If so, how? Is the conclusion memorable? Will it stick in readers' minds?

> You can use **TEST** as you read to help you understand the structure and content of an essay's body paragraphs.
>
> **T** ■ Topic Sentence
> **E** ■ Evidence
> **S** ■ Summary
> **T** ■ Transitions

As you read the essays in this book, you should evaluate their introductions, body paragraphs, and conclusions to see how different writers achieve their goals. This kind of focused reading can make you a stronger writer. The student and professional essays in Unit 2 and the readings in Chapter 30 can all serve as good models for your own writing. In addition, the specific guidelines for understanding introductions, body paragraphs, and conclusions discussed in this chapter can help you as you write and revise.

4b Writing Introductions

An **introduction** is the first thing people see when they read your essay. If your introduction is interesting, it will engage readers and make them want to read further. If it is not, readers may lose interest and stop reading.

Your introduction should be a full paragraph that moves from general to specific ideas. It should begin with some general **opening remarks** that will draw readers into your essay. The **thesis statement**, a specific sentence that presents the main idea of your essay, usually comes at the end of the introduction. (Later, when you are a more experienced writer, you can experiment with different placement options.) The following diagram illustrates the shape of an introduction.

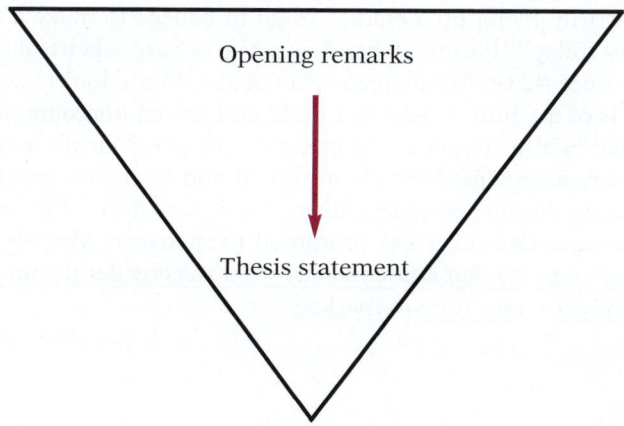

Here are some options you can experiment with when you write your introductions. (In each of the sample introductory paragraphs that follow, the thesis statement is underlined and labeled.)

Beginning with a Narrative

You can begin an essay with a narrative drawn from your own experience or from a current news event.

> On the first day my sister and I attended school in America, our parents walked us directly to the entrance of our new classroom. Even though she barely spoke any English, Mom tried earnestly to teach us how to ask for permission to use the bathroom: "Can I go to the bathroom?" Like parrots, she had us repeat this question over and over. At the time, neither of us realized that the proper way of asking for permission is "May I go to the bathroom?" This grammar slip did not matter, though, because we forgot the question as soon as our parents left. Reluctantly, we entered the classroom, more timid than two mice trying not to awaken a sleeping cat. <u>We didn't know yet that going to school where English was the only language spoken would prove to be very challenging.</u> [Thesis statement]
>
> —Hilda Alvarado (student)

Beginning with a Question (or a Series of Questions)

Asking one or more questions at the beginning of your essay is an effective strategy. Because readers expect you to answer the questions, they will want to read further.

> Is it worth giving up a chance to go to college to make a respectable salary today? "For me it was," says Mario Sarno, general manager of Arby's store #219. At nineteen years of age, Mario looks like a salesman. He is of medium height and build and has an outgoing personality that makes him stand out. As general manager, Mario's major tasks are to maintain the fast-food environment and to ensure that customers are happy. At the age of seventeen, Mario was noticed by an Arby's corporate supervisor and was promoted to manager. <u>Mario's positive experience suggests that students may want to consider the advantages of going directly into the job market.</u> [Thesis statement]
>
> —Lucus J. Anemone (student)

Beginning with a Definition

A definition at the beginning of your essay can give readers important information. As the following introduction shows, a definition can help explain a complicated idea or a confusing concept.

> Stereotypes are generalized beliefs about people based on their belonging to a specific group. Stereotypes can be relatively harmless, or they can be quite negative, as in the case of gender or racial stereotypes. Recent research has shown that stereotypes are difficult to change. This is because people tend to select information that confirms their preconceived ideas. Even though most adults claim that they do not have biases, most actually do. The result is that we unconsciously characterize people and act on these misguided beliefs. <u>By understanding the causes of stereotyping, we can take steps to move beyond these generalizations and judge individuals on their personal merits.</u> — Thesis statement
>
> Duc Le (student)

Beginning with a Quotation

An appropriate saying or some interesting dialogue can draw readers into your essay.

> According to the environmentalist Paul Watson, "We'll lose more species of plants and animals between 2000 and 2065 than we've lost in the last 65 million years." We humans are causing this problem by over-harvesting, degrading, and destroying habitats. Our activities also threaten entire ecosystems, as when clear-cutting forests or over-planting causes desertification or deforestation. In addition, toxic runoff from farm lands gets into streams and eventually flows into oceans, where it degrades and destroys marine ecosystems. As a result, biodiversity is declining, and a decrease in biodiversity can harm humans. <u>We can slow down and possibly stop this destruction if we act now to increase government support for actions that conserve our natural resources and protect our ecosystems.</u> — Thesis statement
>
> Veronica Platt (student)

Beginning with a Surprising Statement or Statistic

You can begin your essay with a surprising or unexpected statement. Because your statement takes readers by surprise, it catches their attention.

Thesis statement

> Some of the smartest people I know never went to college. In fact, some of them never finished high school. They still know how to save 20 percent on the price of a dinner, fix their own faucets when they leak, get discounted prescriptions, get free rides on a bus to Atlantic City, use public transportation to get anywhere in the city, and live on about twenty-two dollars a day. Some people would call them old and poor, but I would call them survivors who have learned to make it through life on nothing but a Social Security check. <u>These survivors are my grandparents' friends, and they have taught me many things I cannot learn in school.</u>
>
> —Sean Ragas (student)

FYI

What to Avoid in Introductions

When writing an introduction, avoid the following:

- Beginning your essay by announcing what you plan to write about.

  PHRASES TO AVOID

  This essay is about . . .
  In my essay, I will discuss . . .

- Apologizing for your ideas.

  PHRASES TO AVOID

  Although I don't know much about this subject . . .
  I might not be an expert, but . . .

FYI

Choosing a Title

Every essay should have a **title** that suggests the subject of the essay and makes people want to read it. Here are a few tips for properly formatting your title:

- Capitalize all words except for articles (*a, an, the*), prepositions (*at, to, of, around,* and so on), and coordinating conjunctions (*and, but,* and so on), unless they are the first or last word of the title.
- Do not bold, underline, or italicize your title or enclose it in quotation marks. Do not type your title in all capital letters.
- Center the title at the top of the first page. Double-space between the title and the first line of your essay.

As you consider a title for your paper, think about the following options:

- *A title can highlight a key word or term that appears in the essay.*
  Why "Natural" Doesn't Mean Anything Anymore
- *A title can be a straightforward announcement.*
  My First Police Stop
- *A title can express a point of view or state a position.*

  For Trans People Like Me, Pronouns Are About More Than Grammatical Correctness
- *A title can be a familiar saying or a quotation from the essay itself.*
  The Work You Do, The Person You Are

PRACTICE 4-1

Look through the student essays in Unit 2, and find one introduction you think is particularly effective. Be prepared to explain the strengths of the introduction you chose.

PRACTICE 4-2

Using the different options for creating titles discussed in the FYI box above, write two titles for each of the essays described below:

1. A student writes an essay about three people who disappeared mysteriously: Amelia Earhart, aviator; Ambrose Bierce, writer; and Jimmy Hoffa, union leader. In the body paragraphs, the student describes the circumstances surrounding their disappearances.

2. A student writes an essay arguing against doctors' letting people select the gender of their babies. In the body paragraphs, she presents reasons why she thinks it is unethical.

3. A student writes an essay explaining why America should elect a woman president. In the body paragraphs, he gives his reasons.

FOCUS on reading and writing

Reread the essay that you wrote in Chapter 3 about the most difficult job you've ever had. Evaluate your introduction. Then, choose one of the strategies discussed in 4b and write a new introduction. Which introduction—the old one or the new one—do you think is more effective? Why?

4c Body Paragraphs

The middle part of your essay is the **body**—the paragraphs that develop and support your thesis statement. Each body paragraph begins with a **topic sentence** that indicates the main idea the paragraph will discuss, and it goes on to support that idea with **evidence**—examples and details. **Transitional words and phrases** help readers follow the discussion. Often, the paragraph ends with a **summary** (or summary statement) that reinforces the main idea.

Body Paragraphs

> The **topic sentence** states the main idea of the paragraph.
> **Evidence** supports the main idea.
> **Transitional words and phrases** show the connections among ideas.
> A **summary** often ends the paragraph.

Every body paragraph should support your essay's thesis. If your thesis states that there are four reasons for high unemployment, then each of your body paragraphs should discuss one of these reasons. The topic sentence should identify the reason, and the rest of the paragraph should develop this point with examples and details.

Introduction

    ... Despite optimistic predictions to the contrary, unemployment will remain high for **four reasons**.

First body paragraph

    The **first reason** unemployment will remain high is . . .

Second body paragraph

    The **second reason** unemployment will remain high is . . .

Third body paragraph

    The **third reason** unemployment will remain high is . . .

Fourth body paragraph

    The **fourth reason** unemployment will remain high is . . .

Conclusion

    Even though some experts believe that the economy is improving, the truth is that unemployment will continue to be high. . . .

> ### Constructing Effective Topic Sentences
>
> The first step in writing effective body paragraphs is to construct effective topic sentences. As you draft your topic sentences, keep the following guidelines in mind:
>
> - **A topic sentence should be a complete sentence.** Like any sentence, a topic sentence should have a subject and a verb and express a complete thought.
> - **A topic sentence should make a point about the idea you plan to discuss.** For this reason, it should be more than just an announcement of what you plan to write about.
>
> | ANNOUNCEMENT | TOPIC SENTENCE |
> |---|---|
> | Now I am going to discuss another characteristic of a hero. | Another characteristic of heroes is that they take action instead of waiting for others to act. |
>
> - **A topic sentence should present an idea that you can discuss in a single paragraph.** If your topic sentence is too broad, you will not be able to develop it in a single paragraph. If it is too narrow, you will not be able to say much about it.
>
> **TOPIC SENTENCE TOO BROAD**
> Students with jobs have additional challenges.
>
> **TOPIC SENTENCE TOO NARROW**
> The tutoring center closes at 5 p.m.
>
> **EFFECTIVE TOPIC SENTENCE**
> The tutoring center's limited hours present another problem.

PRACTICE 4-3

The following paragraphs do not have topic sentences. Think of a topic sentence that expresses each paragraph's main idea, and write it on the lines above the paragraphs.

Example

Possible answer: Rock and roll originated in African American music but was reinterpreted by white performers.

Early 1950s African American musicians included performers such as Johnny Ace, Big Joe Turner, and Ruth Brown. Groups like the Drifters and the Clovers were also popular. By the mid-1950s, white performers such as Bill Haley and the Comets, Jerry Lee Lewis, and

Elvis Presley were imitating African American music. Their songs had a beat and lyrics that appealed to a white audience. Eventually, this combination of black and white musical styles became known as rock and roll.

1. _____

First, you have to find a suitable job to apply for. Once you decide to apply, you have to compose your résumé and cover letter to send them to the potential employer. Then, when you are invited in for an interview, you need to decide what you are going to wear and prepare a list of questions to ask your potential employer. Next, review your résumé, and practice answering questions that the interviewer might ask you. At the interview, speak slowly and clearly, make eye contact, and answer all questions directly and honestly. After the interview, send a note to the person who interviewed you, thanking him or her and reinforcing your interest in the job. Finally, if everything goes well, you will get an email or a phone call offering you the job.

2. _____

There are no written records left by the Native Americans themselves. Most of the early European settlers in North America were more interested in staying alive than in writing about the Native Americans. In addition, as the westward expansion took place, the Europeans encountered the Native Americans in stages, not all at once. Also, the Native Americans spoke at least fifty-eight different languages, which made it difficult for the Europeans to speak with them. Most important, by the time scholars decided to study Native American culture, many of the tribes no longer existed. Disease and war had wiped them out.

Because the body paragraphs of your essay carry the weight of the discussion, they are the most important (and longest) part of your essay. To be effective, each body paragraph should not only clearly support the essay's thesis but also be *unified*, *coherent*, and *well developed*.

Body Paragraphs Should Be Unified

A body paragraph is **unified** when all its sentences support the main idea stated in the **topic sentence**. Just as a thesis statement presents the essay's main idea, the topic sentence in a paragraph presents the paragraph's main idea. If the sentences in a body paragraph wander from the main idea stated in the topic sentence, the paragraph lacks unity.

The following paragraph is not unified because it contains sentences that do not support the paragraph's topic sentence. (These sentences have been crossed out.)

> The weak economy has led many people to move away from the rural Ohio community where I was raised. Over the years, farmland has become more and more expensive. Years ago, a family could buy each of its children twenty-five acres on which they could start farming. Today, the average farmer cannot make enough money to buy this amount of land, and those who choose not to farm have few alternatives. ~~After I graduate, I intend to return to my town and get a job there. Even though many factories have moved out of the area, I think I will be able to get a job. My uncle owns a hardware store, and he told me that after I graduate, he will teach me the business. I think I can contribute something to both the business and the community.~~ Young people just cannot get good jobs anymore. Factories have moved out of the area and taken with them the jobs that many young people used to get after high school. As a result, many eighteen-year-olds have no choice but to move away to find employment.

The following revised paragraph is unified. It discusses only the idea that is stated in the topic sentence.

> The weak economy has led many people to move away from the rural Ohio community where I was raised. Over the years, farmland has become more and more expensive. Years ago, a family could buy each of its children twenty-five acres on which they could start farming. Today, the average farmer cannot make enough money to buy this amount of land, and those who choose not to farm have few alternatives. Young people just cannot get good jobs anymore. Factories have moved out of the area and taken with them the jobs that many young people used to get after high school. As a result, many eighteen-year-olds have no choice but to move away to find employment.

PRACTICE 4-4

The following paragraph is not unified because some sentences do not support the topic sentence. First, underline the topic sentence. Then, cross out any sentences that do not support the topic sentence.

> Although many people still get down on one knee to propose, others have found more creative ways to pop the question. Using Jumbotrons, computer games, or even zero-gravity chambers, some people are making the moment truly memorable. Last year, one English graffiti artist asked his girlfriend to marry him by spray-painting his proposal on the side of a building. In 2011, a man used the Sunday crossword puzzle *in The Washington Post* to propose to his girlfriend. As she completed the puzzle, she saw that the answers to several of the clues spelled out her name and a question. Weddings are also becoming more unusual. Some couples are choosing to get married while skydiving or riding bicycles. One couple recently got married in a shark tank. Several brave people have also proposed on television. By buying ad space and recording a brief video clip, they appear on the screen during a favorite show. People are clearly using their imaginations to ask this age-old question in unexpected ways.

Body Paragraphs Should Be Coherent

A body paragraph is **coherent** if its sentences are arranged in a clear, logical order.

Transitional words and phrases create **coherence** by indicating how ideas are connected in a paragraph—for example, in *time order*, *spatial order*, or *logical order*. By signaling the order of ideas in a paragraph, these words and phrases make it easier for readers to follow your discussion:

- You use **time** signals to show readers the order in which events occurred.

    > In 1883, my great-grandfather came to this country from Russia.

- You use **spatial** signals to show readers how people, places, and things stand in relation to one another. For example, you can move from top to bottom, from near to far, from right to left, and so on.

    > Next to my bed is a bookcase that also serves as a room divider.

- You use **logical** signals to show readers how ideas are connected. For example, you can move from the least important idea to the most important idea or from the least familiar idea to the most familiar idea.

    > Certain strategies can help you do well in college. First, you should learn to manage your time effectively.

Because transitional words and phrases create coherence, a paragraph without them can be difficult to understand. You can avoid this problem by checking to make sure you have included all the words and phrases that you need to link the ideas in your paragraph.

The following body paragraph, from Amy Chua's *Battle Hymn of the Tiger Mother*, uses transitional words and phrases, repeated key words, and pronouns to create coherence. (Note that the transitions are shaded.)

> What Chinese parents understand is that nothing is fun until you're good at it. To get good at anything, you have to work, and children on their own never want to work, which is why it is crucial to override their preferences. This often requires fortitude on the part of their parents because the child will resist; things are always the hardest at the beginning, which is where Western parents tend to give up. But if done properly, the Chinese strategy produces a virtuous circle. Tenacious practice, practice, practice is crucial for excellence; rote repetition is underrated in America. Once a child starts to excel at something—whether it's math, piano, pitching, or ballet—he or she gets praise, admiration, and satisfaction. This builds confidence and makes the once not-so-fun activity fun. This in turn makes it easier for the parent to get the child to work even more.

> **WORD POWER**
> **fortitude** strength, determination
> **tenacious** determined or stubborn

Frequently Used Transitional Words and Phrases

Sequence or Addition

again	first, . . . second, . . . third	next
also	furthermore	one . . . another
and	in addition	still
besides	last	too
finally	moreover	

Time

afterward	finally	simultaneously
as soon as	immediately	since
at first	in the meantime	soon
at the same time	later	subsequently
before	meanwhile	then
earlier	next	until
eventually	now	

Comparison

also	likewise
in comparison	similarly
in the same way	

Body Paragraphs 4c

Contrast

although	in contrast	on the one hand . . .
but	instead	on the other hand . . .
conversely	nevertheless	still
despite	nonetheless	whereas
even though	on the contrary	yet
however		

Examples

for example	specifically
for instance	that is
in fact	thus
namely	

Conclusions or Summaries

as a result	in summary
in conclusion	therefore
in short	thus

Causes or Effects

as a result	so
because	then
consequently	therefore
since	

PRACTICE 4-5

Read the following paragraph carefully. Then, select transitional words and phrases from the accompanying aphabetized list, and write them in the appropriate blanks. When you have finished, reread your paragraph to make sure that it is coherent.

TRANSITIONS

after	by 1904
at first	for centuries
before	however
in fact	in 1897

The history of Jell-O is full of surprising setbacks. _____ Jell-O became "America's Most Famous Dessert," gelatin struggled for attention. _____, people experimented with the substance, but no one could make it appealing. By adding flavored syrup _____, Pearle B. Wait was the first to make gelatin taste good. Wait's wife, May, named the product Jell-O. _____, Wait could not market his new creation and ended up selling the company to Frank Woodward for $450 in 1899. _____, he had supposedly tried to sell the company for even less money. _____ failing to find buyers, Woodward started a major marketing campaign. He advertised in magazines and gave out free Jell-O cookbooks. _____, Jell-O was finally on its way to becoming the country's best-known dessert.

Body Paragraphs Should Be Well Developed

A body paragraph is **well developed** when it includes enough evidence. **Evidence** consists of the examples and details that support your statements. To make a convincing point, you need to support it with evidence. For example, it is one thing to say that gun violence has torn your neighborhood apart, but it is much more effective to follow this general statement with examples of specific incidents of gun violence in your community. The same is true when you describe something you have observed. You could, for example, say that a certain area of campus is peaceful. This statement means little to readers, however, unless you follow it with the details—the tall trees, the grass, the silence—that explain what you mean.

A paragraph is **well developed** when it includes enough evidence to explain and support its main idea. The following paragraph does not include enough evidence to support its main idea.

> Although pit bulls have a bad reputation, they actually make good pets. Part of their problem is that they can look frightening. Actually, though, pit bulls are no worse than other breeds of dogs. Even so, the bad publicity they get has given them a bad reputation. Pit bulls really do not deserve their bad reputation, though. Contrary to popular opinion, pit bulls can (and do) make friendly, affectionate, and loyal pets.

The following revised paragraph now includes enough evidence to support the main idea stated in the topic sentence.

> Although pit bulls have a bad reputation, they actually make good pets. Part of their problem is that they can look frightening. Their wide, powerful jaws, short muscular legs, and large teeth are ideally suited for fighting, and they were bred for this purpose. In addition, some pit bulls—especially males—can be very aggressive toward

both people and other dogs. Actually, though, pit bulls are no worse than other breeds of dogs. As several recent newspaper articles have pointed out, the number of reported bites by pit bulls is no greater than the number of bites by other breeds. In fact, some breeds, such as cocker spaniels, bite more frequently than pit bulls. Even so, the bad publicity they get has given them a bad reputation. The problem is that whenever a pit bull attacks someone, the incident is reported on the evening news. Contrary to popular opinion, pit bulls can (and do) make friendly, affectionate, and loyal pets.

Note: Length alone is no guarantee that a paragraph includes enough supporting evidence for your main idea. A long paragraph that consists of one generalization after another will still not include enough support for the topic sentence.

You should **TEST** every body paragraph after you finish drafting. **TEST**ing will tell you whether or not it includes all the elements of an effective paragraph.

Topic sentence

Evidence

Summary

Transitions

PRACTICE 4-6

Provide two or three specific pieces of evidence (examples or details) to support each of the following topic sentences.

1. When it comes to feeding a family, there are several cost-effective alternatives to fast food.

2. A romantic relationship with a coworker can create serious problems.

3. Choosing the right career is harder than I thought it would be.

PRACTICE 4-7

The paragraph that follows does not include enough supporting evidence. Suggest some examples and details that might help the writer develop the topic sentence more fully.

Young adults who move back in with their parents after college face many challenges. Feeling dependent on one's parents after living away from home can be frustrating. Living at home can restrict a person's freedom. Also, some parents can be overbearing and treat the young graduate as if he or she is a child. Of course, the success of the living situation depends on how well the college graduate and his or her parents communicate. Despite these drawbacks, living at home for a while after college can make sense.

PRACTICE 4-8

Choose two body paragraphs from one of the essays in Chapter 30, "Readings for Writers." Using the criteria discussed in 4c, decide whether the paragraphs are unified, coherent, and well developed. Be prepared to discuss your decisions with the class.

FOCUS on reading and writing

Reread the essay that you wrote in Chapter 3 about the most difficult job you've ever had. Check to make sure that all your body paragraphs support your essay's thesis. Then, evaluate your body paragraphs, and revise and edit them as necessary to make them unified, coherent, and well developed.

 ## 4d Conclusions

Because your conclusion is the last thing readers see, they often judge your entire essay by its effectiveness. For this reason, conclusions should be planned, drafted, and revised carefully.

Like an introduction, a **conclusion** should be a full paragraph. It should include a **summary** of the writer's key points or a summary statement that reinforces the essay's thesis. It should end with some general **concluding remarks**. The following diagram illustrates the shape of a conclusion.

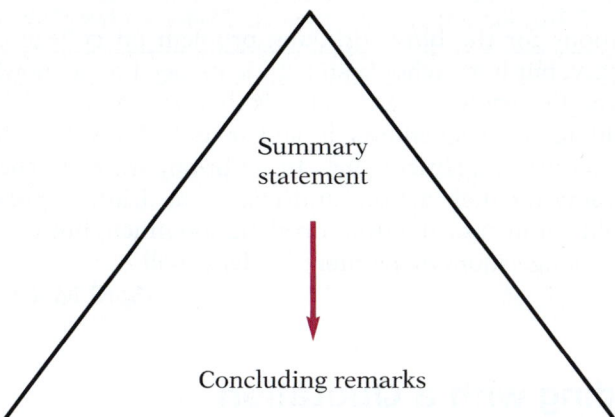

Here are some options you can experiment with when you write your conclusions. (In each of the sample concluding paragraphs that follow, the summary statement is underlined and labeled.)

Concluding with a Narrative

A narrative conclusion can bring an event discussed in the essay to a logical, satisfying close.

> <u>I went to Philadelphia with my boys to share the thing my father and I had shared—a love for history.</u> [Summary statement] Unfortunately, they were more interested in horse-and-buggy rides, overpriced knickknacks, the tall buildings, and parades. As we walked into Independence Hall, though, I noticed that the boys became quiet. They felt it. They felt the thick historical air around us. I watched them look around as the guide painted a vivid picture of the times and spoke of the marches down Broad Street and the clashing of ideas as our forefathers debated and even fought for freedom. I felt my husband behind me and took my eyes off of my boys to turn to the left; I could almost see my father. I almost whispered out loud to him, "We were here."
> —Shannon Lewis (student)

Concluding with a Recommendation

Once you think you have convinced readers that a problem exists, you can make recommendations in your conclusion about how the problem should be solved.

Summary statement

> Solutions for the binge-drinking problem on college campuses are not easy, but both schools and students need to acknowledge the problem and to try to solve it. Schools that have an alcohol-free policy should aggressively enforce it, and schools that do not have such a policy should implement one. In addition, students should take responsibility for their actions and resolve to drink responsibly. No one should get hurt or die from drinking too much, but if something does not change soon, many more students will.
>
> —April Moen (student)

Concluding with a Quotation

A well-chosen quotation—even a brief one—can be an effective concluding strategy. In the following paragraph, from a public health exam, the quotation reinforces the main idea of the essay.

Summary statement

> The Pure Food and Drug Act is the most important regulatory statute in the history of the United States. In his message to Congress, Theodore Roosevelt announced that the Pure Food and Drug Act would "secure the health and welfare of the consuming public." After weeks of debate the bill was passed on February 12, 1906. Nearly one hundred years after its passage, this act continues to protect the American public from mislabeled or misrepresented food and drug products. It makes sure that manufacturers list active ingredients and follow standards that are established by law. Since its enactment, millions of consumers have benefitted from improved food quality and the knowledge that products they bought were safe.
>
> Rose Erlich (student)

Concluding with a Prediction

This type of conclusion not only sums up the thesis but also looks to the future.

Summary statement

> Whether people like it or not, texting is not going to go away anytime soon. This generation and future generations are going to use "text speak" and become even more comfortable with communicating via text messages. Texting has already had a large impact on today's world. In fact, texting has helped put the written word back into our lives, making people more comfortable with the skill of writing, & it's a fast, EZ way 2 communic8.
>
> —Courtney Anttila (student)

FYI

What to Avoid in Conclusions

When writing a conclusion, avoid the following:

- Introducing new ideas. Your conclusion should sum up the ideas you discuss in your essay, not open up new lines of thought.
- Apologizing for your opinions, ideas, or conclusions. Apologies will undercut your readers' confidence in you.

    PHRASES TO AVOID

    At least that is my opinion . . .

    I could be wrong, but . . .

- Using unnecessary phrases to announce your essay is coming to a close.

    PHRASES TO AVOID

    In summary, . . .

    In conclusion, . . .

PRACTICE 4-9

Choose a conclusion from one of the essays in Chapter 30 that you think is particularly effective. Be prepared to explain the strengths of the conclusion you chose.

FOCUS on reading and writing

Reread the essay that you wrote in Chapter 3 about the most difficult job you've ever had. Evaluate your conclusion. Then, choose one of the strategies discussed in 4d, and write a new conclusion. Which conclusion—the old one or the new one—do you think is more effective? Why?

CHAPTER REVIEW

REVIEW ACTIVITY

The following student essay has an undeveloped introduction and conclusion. Decide what introductory and concluding strategies would be best for the essay. Then, rewrite both the introduction and the conclusion. Then, suggest an interesting title for the essay.

This essay is about three of the most dangerous jobs. They are piloting small planes, logging, and fishing.

Flying a small plane can be dangerous. For example, pilots who fly tiny planes that spray pesticides on farmers' fields do not have to comply with the safety rules for large airplanes. They also have to fly very low in order to spray the right fields. This leaves little room for error. Also, pilots of air-taxis and small commuter planes die in much greater numbers than airline pilots do. In some places, like parts of Alaska, there are long distances and few roads, so many small planes are needed. Their pilots are four times more likely to die than other pilots because of bad weather and poor visibility. In general, flying a small plane can be very risky.

Another dangerous job is logging. Loggers always are at risk of having parts of trees or heavy machinery fall on them. Tree trunks often have odd shapes, so they are hard to control while they are being transported. As a result, they often break loose from equipment that is supposed to move them. In addition, weather conditions, like snow or rain, can cause dangers. Icy or wet conditions increase the risk to loggers, who can fall from trees or slip when they are sawing a tree. Because loggers often work in remote places, it is very hard to get prompt medical aid. For this reason, a wound that could easily be treated in a hospital may be fatal to a logger.

Perhaps the most dangerous occupation is working in the fishing industry. Like loggers, professional fishermen work in unsafe conditions. They use heavy machinery to pull up nets and to move large amounts of fish. The combination of icy or slippery boat decks and large nets and cages makes the job unsafe. The weather is often very bad, so fishermen are at risk of falling overboard during a storm and drowning. In fact, drowning is the most common cause of death in this industry. Also, like logging, fishing is done far from medical help, so even minor injuries can be very serious.

In conclusion, piloting, logging, and fishing are three of the most dangerous occupations.

Now, evaluate the body paragraphs of the essay above. Choose one body paragraph, and strengthen it by adding some examples and details.

COLLABORATIVE ACTIVITY

Graphic Organizer: *Introductions, Body Paragraphs, and Conclusions*

The components of introductions, body paragraphs, and conclusions are presented in the graphic organizer on page 130. Work with another student to fill in the organizer with any information that is missing.

Chapter Review

Introduction

_____ begins the essay and presents the thesis statement.

A thesis statement is:
_____

Write a thesis statement for the following essay topic: "Rising college tuition and fees"
_____
_____

Write a thesis statement for the following essay topic: "Reducing childhood obesity"
_____
_____

Body Paragraphs

_____ should be unified, coherent, and well developed.

A body paragraph is unified when it includes
_____

A body paragraph is coherent when it includes
_____

A body paragraph is well developed when it includes
_____

Conclusion

_____ brings the essay to an effective close.

The conclusion should include
_____ and _____

Review checklist

✔ **Introductions and Conclusions**

✔ The essays you read have introductions, body paragraphs, and conclusions. You should evaluate these components carefully because they can help you understand the writers' ideas. (See 4a.)

✔ The introduction of your essay should include opening remarks and a thesis statement. (See 4b.) You can begin an essay with any of the following options.

A narrative	A quotation
A question	A surprising statement
A definition	

✔ Your title should suggest the subject of your essay and make people want to read further. (See 4b.)

✔ Your body paragraphs should be unified, coherent, and well developed. They should also clearly support the essay's thesis. (See 4c.)

✔ The conclusion of your essay should include a summary statement and some general concluding remarks. (See 4d.) You can conclude an essay with any of the following options.

A narrative	A quotation
A recommendation	A prediction

5 Thinking, Reading, and Writing Critically

Michael Ventura/Alamy Stock Photo

FOCUS on reading and writing

Brainstorm to discover what you already know about how the use of electronic devices affects the way we communicate with one another. Then, preview the essay "The Flight from Conversation," by Sherry Turkle (p. 604).

> **PREVIEW**
>
> In this chapter, you will learn to
> - identify audience, purpose, and tone (5a).
> - identify connotations and figurative language (5b).
> - identify the main idea (5c).
> - identify major and minor supporting points (5d).
> - evaluate the writer's ideas (5e).
> - read and write critically (5f).

In Chapter 1, you learned about the active reading process, a series of activities that enable you to identify key information and to determine the meaning of a text. In this chapter, we will take this process a step further and discuss some strategies that will help you to think critically about the texts you read—and eventually, to write about them. Keep in mind that thinking critically about a text does *not* mean challenging every idea you encounter. What **thinking critically** *does* mean is considering a writer's motives, weighing evidence, evaluating both the strengths and weaknesses of a text, keeping an open mind, and seeing connections between your own ideas and those in the text.

5a Identifying Audience, Purpose, and Tone

As you begin to think critically about a text, you should consider its intended *audience*, its *purpose*, and its *tone*.

The Writer's Audience

The writer's **intended audience** is the group of readers the writer wants to address. The publication in which a piece of writing appears can provide clues about its intended audience. For example, an article about childhood obesity in a popular magazine such as *Discover* or the digital edition of *Newsweek* is written for an intended audience that has only a general knowledge of the subject. However, an article in a scholarly journal, such as *Nature* or *The New England Journal of Medicine*, is aimed at an intended audience that knows a great deal about the subject—for example, researchers or medical doctors.

Identifying the intended audience of a piece of writing is helpful because it enables you to consider how the writer's view of the audience has determined the text's level and content. For example, has the writer included definitions of key terms and explanations of basic concepts, or are readers expected to know them?

> **Identifying the Writer's Intended Audience**
>
> To help identify the intended audience of a piece of writing, ask the following questions:
>
> - **Age** Does anything in the text—for example, slang or cultural references—indicate that it is aimed at a particular age group?
> - **Education level** How much education does the writer assume readers have? Does the text's vocabulary reveal the writer's assumptions?
> - **Biases** Does the writer expect readers to have preconceived ideas about the subject?
> - **Knowledge** Does the writer expect readers to know a lot (or a little) about the subject? How much space does the writer devote to defining terms, explaining concepts, and providing background information?

FOCUS on reading and writing

Now that you have previewed Sherry Turkle's essay about the differences between electronic and face-to-face communication, go back and read it, marking it up and annotating it. Who do you think is the intended audience for this essay? What led you to your conclusion?

The Writer's Purpose

In general, a writer has one of three **primary purposes**:

- To **inform** readers about something
- To **explain** something to readers
- To **persuade** readers to do something or to act in a certain way

In addition to this primary purpose, a writer often has one or more **secondary purposes**. For example, in a blog post, a writer's main purpose might be to inform readers about the dangers of performance-enhancing drugs. His secondary purpose might be to persuade readers not to take them.

Keep in mind that there is a difference between *informing*, *explaining*, and *persuading*. When writers **inform**, they present information and let readers draw their own conclusions. When writers **explain**, they interpret information, adding their own insights and judgments. When writers **persuade**, they try to change readers' minds—in other words, they try to convince readers that one side of an issue is preferable to another. Sometimes they even try to move readers to action.

Determining the Writer's Purpose

To determine the writer's purpose, consider the following:

- **Statements** Writers frequently make statements that reveal their primary purpose. For example, does a writer say that he or she wants to *inform* readers about the advantages of recycling or that he or she wants to *convince* them to recycle? (You can often discover a writer's purpose by looking at an essay's thesis statement.)

- **Knowledge about the writer** The more you know about a writer, the more accurately you can determine his or her purpose. For example, if you know that a writer is a scientist, you might assume that his or her purpose is to inform. If the writer is an environmental activist, however, you might assume that his or her purpose is to further that cause. Keep in mind, however, that you can't just assume that one writer is always out to inform and another is always out to persuade. You should base your conclusion about the writer's purpose on what he or she says, not on your preconceptions.

- **Knowledge about the publication** The type of publication in which an article appears can provide clues about a writer's purpose. For example, an article in *National Geographic* might present information about the damage caused by the *Exxon Valdez* oil spill in a straightforward way. An article in a publication sponsored by Exxon, however, might have a different purpose—for example, to publicize the company's support for its environmental efforts.

FOCUS on reading and writing

Referring to "The Flight from Conversation," by Sherry Turkle (p. 604), which you have now marked up and annotated, consider why Turkle wrote this essay. What did she hope to accomplish?

The Writer's Tone

The **tone** of a piece of writing indicates a writer's attitude toward readers or toward his or her subject. Just as people use various tones when speaking, written texts can also have different tones. Unlike speakers, who can create tone by changing their emphasis, timing, or volume, writers create tone largely through their choice of words.

A writer's purpose usually determines tone. For example, textbooks call for an *objective* tone, with an emphasis on facts and clear explanations and the use of relatively formal language. Creative literature and personal essays, however, often use a *subjective* tone, relying on informal language and words that communicate feelings and opinions. Other types of writing can convey different types of tone—for example, an email to a friend can be intimate, a letter to a customer can be polite, and an editorial in a newspaper can be critical.

Because a writer's tone can affect how you respond to a piece of writing, you should be aware of it when you read (as you should be aware of your own tone when you write). For example, an angry or sarcastic tone might indicate that a writer is biased; a conciliatory tone might suggest that a writer is fair and will consider opposing points of view.

> **Describing Tone**
>
> You can use any of the words below to describe a writer's tone. Keep in mind that this is just a sampling of the words that can be used to characterize tone.
>
> | | | |
> |---|---|---|
> | aloof | emotional | sad |
> | ambivalent | friendly | sarcastic |
> | angry | happy | sentimental |
> | apathetic | hostile | serious |
> | appreciative | insincere | sincere |
> | authoritative | ironic | subjective |
> | bitter | objective | sympathetic |
> | critical | playful | tender |
> | distant | respectful | |

Identifying Audience, Purpose, and Tone 5a 137

> **Determining a Writer's Tone**
>
> The following questions can help you identify a writer's tone:
> - How does the writer communicate his or her attitude to readers? Which word in the box on page 136 best describes this attitude?
> - How does the writer use adverbs and adjectives in descriptions (see 16a)?
> - What connotations do the writer's words have (see 2b and 5b)?

PRACTICE

Read the following short passages. Choose the word from the box on page 136 that best describes each writer's tone. Note which words helped you determine the tone of the passage.

1. My summer job at a fast-food restaurant was my all-time worst job because of the endless stream of rude customers, the many boring and repetitive tasks I had to perform, and my manager's insensitive treatment of employees.—Sarah Herman (student)

2. First, no government agency can accurately determine what is healthy for everyone. Different people have different health needs, different calorie requirements, and different abilities to tolerate certain foods. Therefore, any standard that the government adopts is bound to favor some people and penalize others. For example, low-income citizens are at a disadvantage because they cannot find or afford what the government has decided is "healthy." Jessica Mar (student)

3. When I think back on my childhood I remember the conversations around the dinner table, the family celebrations, the visits to my grandparents (both now dead), the evenings my friends and I played in the streets until dark, and the mystery that seemed to surrounded everything. Most of all, I see my mother, whose influence still guides me. Until the day she died, she never stopped believing in me—despite my many faults—and never stopped pushing me to greater heights. Everything I am today, I owe to her. Max Delgado (student)

FOCUS on reading and writing

Review "The Flight from Conversation," by Sherry Turkle (p. 604), as well as your underlining and symbols. How would you describe Turkle's tone in this essay? What words and phrases led you to your conclusion?

138   5a   Chapter 5   Thinking, Reading, and Writing Critically

PRACTICE 5-2   Graphic Organizer: *Audience, Purpose, and Tone*

In the following graphic organizer, fill in the details about audience, purpose, and tone. Be sure to provide examples where required.

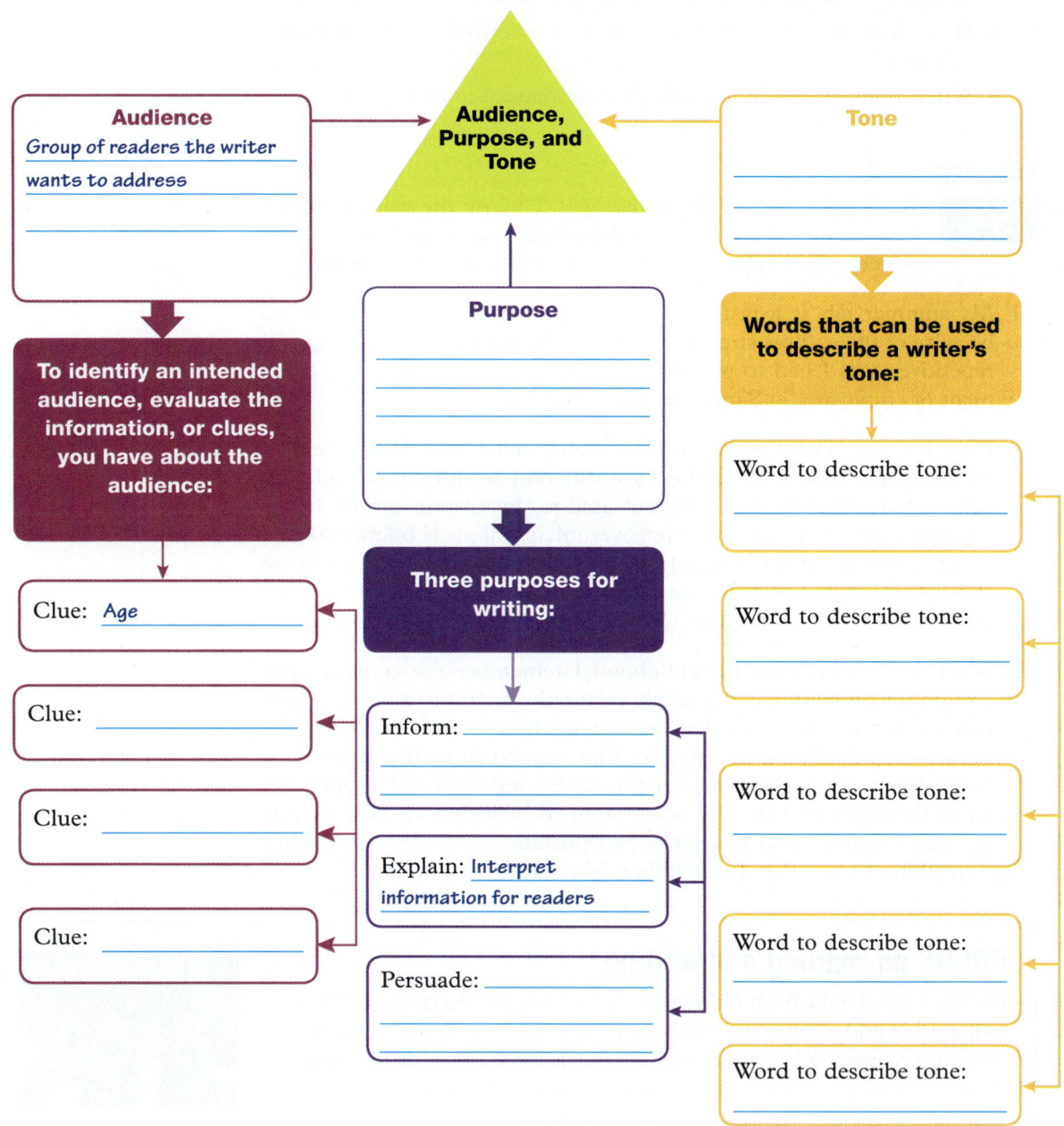

5b Identifying Connotations and Figurative Language

As you think critically about a text, your goal is to interpret what the writer is saying.

Connotations

Learning connotations of words can help you to accomplish this goal. A word's **connotations** are its emotional or cultural associations—apart from its literal (or **denotative**) meanings. (See 2b for more on connotations and denotations.)

Because no two words have exactly the same connotations, when you read and write, you should be sensitive to the different shades of meaning that various words have. Don't say *cheap* when you mean *inexpensive*, or *vagrant* when you mean *homeless person*. Although these words may have similar meanings, they have decidedly different connotations.

PRACTICE 5-3 Consider the different connotations of the three words in each group listed below. Which words have positive connotations? Which have negative connotations? Which are neutral? (Not every group includes all three categories.)

1. disabled / handicapped / differently abled
2. confident / proud / conceited
3. teacher / professor / instructor
4. invest / save / speculate
5. inquisitive / curious / nosy

> **FOCUS on reading and writing**
>
> Throughout "The Flight from *Conversation* (p. 604)," Turkle uses pairs of words to express the differences between electronic and face-to-face conversation. For example, she says that although we are constantly *connected* to one another, we do not actually have *conversations*. Find four or five of these word pairs in Turkle's essay, and be prepared to explain how the connotations of the two words in each pair differ.

Figurative Language

When you read a text, keep in mind that not everything a writer says should be taken literally. Sometimes writers use **figurative language**, describing something by comparing it to something else. For example, when a writer describes a neighborhood as a "food desert" or an athlete as moving "as fast as a cheetah on the Serengeti," he or she is using figurative language.

Figurative language allows writers to expand language beyond the literal meaning of words. It enables them to surprise readers with unexpected—and sometimes memorable—comparisons, suggesting that a neighborhood without stores can be like a desert and that an athlete can be as thrilling to watch as a cheetah running across a wide African plain. Remember, though, that figurative language only makes sense if you understand that the comparison the writer is making is not to be taken literally. (The neighborhood is not really a "desert," and the runner is not really "as fast as a cheetah.")

There are three basic types of figurative language—*simile*, *metaphor*, and *personification*:

- A **simile** uses the words *like* or *as* to compare two unlike things.

    > Her smile was like sunshine.

- A **metaphor** compares two unlike things without using the words *like* or *as*.

    > Her smile was a light that brightened the room.

- **Personification** suggests a comparison between a nonliving thing and a person by giving the nonliving thing human traits.

    > The sun smiled down on the crowd.

PRACTICE 5-4

Identify each of the following as a simile (*s*), a metaphor (*m*), or personification (*p*).

1. Life is a fashion show.
2. The sunlight seemed to dance across the water.
3. Her laugh hung in the air like a song.
4. Love is a battlefield.
5. Time stood still.
6. The DNA molecule is shaped like a twisted ladder.

7. "Life without love is like a tree without blossoms or fruit." (Kahlil Gibran)
8. The ocean sparkled like diamonds.
9. America is a melting pot.
10. "I wandered lonely as a cloud." (William Wordsworth)

> **FOCUS on reading and writing**
>
> Review "The Flight from Conversation," by Sherry Turkle (p. 604). Where in her essay does Turkle use figurative language? How does each use of figurative language help her make her point about how communication has changed?

 ## 5c Identifying the Main Idea

One of the first things you do when you think critically about a text is look for the writer's main idea—the key point the text is making. As you have already learned, writers frequently express this main idea in a **thesis statement** that often—but not always—appears in the introduction.

For example, in "The Case for Short Words" (p. 596), Richard Lederer expresses his main idea in a thesis statement at the end of his essay's introductory paragraph. This strategy enables him to communicate the main idea to readers before he goes on to support it with examples in the rest of his essay.

> When you speak and write, there is no law that says you have to use big words. Short words are as good as long ones, and short, old words—like *sun* and *grass* and *home*—are best of all. <u>A lot of small words, more than you might think, can meet your needs with a strength, grace, and charm that large words do not have.</u>

Sometimes, however, a writer may decide to state the main idea later in an essay. This is a good strategy when a writer is dealing with a controversial topic and wants to prepare readers for a main idea that may disturb or even shock them.

To locate a text's main idea, follow the active reading process outlined in Chapter 1, identifying verbal and visual signals that point to important information and marking the text as you read to highlight the writer's key points.

Identifying Implied Main Ideas

Many times, however, a writer will decide that presenting a main idea in a thesis statement does not suit his or her purpose. This is often the case for narrative or descriptive essays, in which a writer may want readers to come to understand the thesis as they read. Because the writer wants readers to see the main idea unfold gradually, he or she will imply the main idea rather than explicitly state it. Just because the main idea is implied, however, doesn't mean the essay has no focus; in fact, all the essay's paragraphs still have to work together to develop a single main idea.

If an essay you are reading has an **implied main idea**, identifying it can be a challenge, but doing so is an important part of the critical reading process. Even though there is no explicit thesis statement, you can identify the main idea by reviewing the details the writer chose to include and noting how these details are arranged.

> ### Guidelines for Identifying an Implied Main Idea
>
> - *Identify the essay's topic.* Summarize this topic in a word or two.
> - *Look at the essay's body paragraphs.* Consider what points each paragraph makes. If the body paragraphs have clear topic sentences, note what points these sentences make.
> - *Look at the essay's transitions.* Decide what ideas these transitions emphasize. Consider the logical organization they suggest.
> - *Decide how all the essay's elements are connected.* Consider what larger idea these elements suggest.
> - *Summarize this idea in a sentence.* Check to make sure that this sentence covers all the ideas in the essay. If it does, you have identified the essay's main idea.

FYI

Stating Your Main Idea

Although professional writers may not always include an explicitly stated main idea at the beginning of an essay or paragraph, it is a good idea for you to do so. This strategy will help keep you on track as you write and help readers follow your discussion as they read.

PRACTICE 5-5

Choose one professional essay from the readings in Unit 2 or Chapter 30, and answer these questions:

- If the main idea is explicitly stated, why did the writer choose to state it instead of implying it? Where is it stated? Why did the writer decide to locate this statement here instead of elsewhere in the essay?
- If the main idea is implied, why did the writer decide not to state the main idea directly?

FOCUS on reading and writing

Look again at the essay "The Flight from Conversation," by Sherry Turkle (p. 604). Summarize Turkle's main idea. Does she state this main idea directly, or does she imply it? Do you think this was the right choice?

Michael Ventura/Alamy Stock Photo

5d Identifying Major and Minor Supporting Points

In addition to identifying the main idea of a passage, you should also be able to identify its major and minor supporting points.

The **major supporting points** are the points that provide important information about the main idea. They relate directly to the main idea and establish the structure of the discussion. **Minor supporting points** provide additional information about the major supporting points. They supply the **evidence** (examples and details) that develops the major points and enables readers to understand exactly what a writer is saying. By evaluating the strength of a writer's major and minor supporting points, readers can determine how effectively they support the main idea.

The following diagram illustrates the relationship between the main idea and the major and minor supporting points:

Main Idea
Major Point
Major Point
Major Point
Minor Points
Minor Points
Minor Points

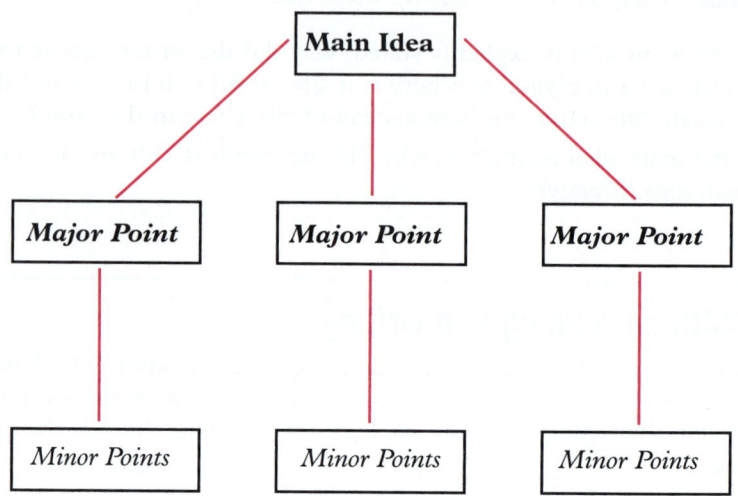

You can use this diagram to help you evaluate the essay "Starting Over" by Jared White on pages 98–99. The following diagram shows how the major and minor supporting points of Jared's essay support his essay's main idea:

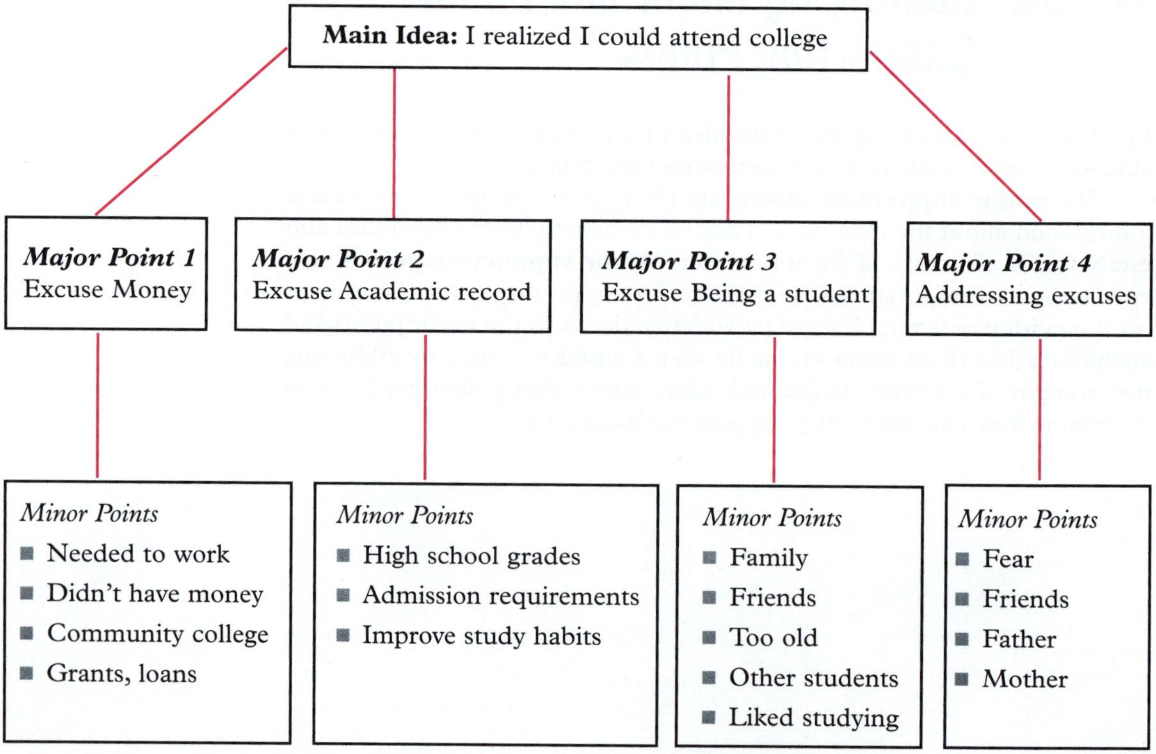

Main Idea: I realized I could attend college
Major Point 1
Excuse Money
Major Point 2
Excuse Academic record
Major Point 3
Excuse Being a student
Major Point 4
Addressing excuses
Minor Points
Needed to work
Didn't have money
Community college
Grants, loans
Minor Points
High school grades
Admission requirements
Improve study habits
Minor Points
Family
Friends
Too old
Other students
Liked studying
Minor Points
Fear
Friends
Father
Mother

You can also use this strategy to identify and evaluate the major and minor points in your own essays.

PRACTICE 5-6 Diagram an essay that you have written for this course (or for another course). Then, decide whether you included enough major supporting points as well as sufficient minor supporting points.

> ### FOCUS on reading and writing
> Reread "The Flight from Conversation," by Sherry Turkle (p. 604). Construct a diagram that shows the relationship between the essay's main idea and its major and minor supporting points.

5e Evaluating the Writer's Ideas

When you think critically about a text, you should not simply accept the writer's ideas. You should carefully evaluate these ideas as well as the **evidence** that the writer uses to support them. To do this, you need to understand the difference between fact and opinion, and you need to learn to make inferences from what you read as well as to identify bias in a text.

Distinguishing between Fact and Opinion

A **fact** is a statement that can be proven to be true. Facts are usually established through experience and observation. An **opinion** is a belief or an expression of values. It can never be fully established, and for that reason, is debatable. In other words, a fact is a statement that can be verified, but an opinion is a statement that can never be proven conclusively. Consider the following statements:

> **Fact:** Football is a game played by two teams with eleven players on each side and an oval ball.
>
> **Opinion:** Because football players have a high incidence of concussions, steps should be taken to make the game less dangerous.

> **WORD POWER**
> **substantiated** supported with proof or evidence

Because the first statement can be substantiated, it is a fact. The second statement, however, expresses a personal belief, and for this reason, is an opinion. No amount of evidence can demonstrate beyond a doubt that the second statement is true. The best you can do is to convince people that the position has merit and is therefore worth considering. As you read, be on the alert for words, such as *should* in the sentence above, that may introduce personal opinions, not facts.

Words That Indicate an Opinion

assume	right/wrong
believe	opinion
best/worst	ought
good/bad	seems
great	should

When you identify an opinion in your reading, you need to determine if it is *supported* or *unsupported*. An **unsupported** opinion is not backed up by facts, examples, or **expert opinion**—the testimony of someone with expertise in the particular subject under discussion. A **supported opinion** includes facts, examples, and expert opinion to back it up. Consider the following examples:

> **Unsupported Opinion:** It is important to save the wilderness from development.
>
> **Supported Opinion:** It is important to save the wilderness from development. According to the Wilderness Society website, only 110 million acres of true wilderness remain in the United States. Experts warn that oil and natural gas drilling and logging as well as commercial development are threatening this national legacy (Baden and Stroup). As environmentalist John Griffith points out, it is time to enact legislation that will protect the wilderness for future generations (37).

The unsupported opinion above is simply an expression of the writer's personal beliefs. The supported opinion, however, is backed up by material from the Wilderness Society website as well as from two environmental experts. For this reason, it is much more convincing than the unsupported opinion.

As you read, keep in mind that even if a writer supports an opinion, you still can question it or disagree with it. Support—even a great deal of support—does not turn an opinion into a fact, although it can make it more convincing.

Evaluating Support

As you read, evaluate how effectively the writer supports his or her opinions. The more convincing the support, the more willing you should be to consider (and possibly, to accept) the writer's ideas. To be effective, support should be *accurate, relevant, representative, sufficient,* and *reliable*:

- **Accurate** support is truthful.
- **Relevant** support applies directly to the issue being discussed.
- **Representative** support gives a balanced picture of the issue.
- **Sufficient** support contains enough evidence to back up the statement.
- **Reliable** support is drawn from trustworthy sources.

PRACTICE 5-7

Read the following statements and decide whether each is Fact (*F*); Unsupported Opinion (*UO*); or Supported Opinion (*SO*).

1. The Treaty of Versailles ended World War I on June 28, 1919. _____
2. The Treaty of Versailles, which ended World War I, was a misguided attempt to penalize Germany for the war. _____
3. According to the economist John Maynard Keynes, the Treaty of Versailles did almost nothing to stabilize Europe. _____
4. Rachel Carson's book *Silent Spring* was published in 1962. _____
5. Rachel Carson's book *Silent Spring* helped start the modern American environmental movement. _____
6. Salsa now outsells ketchup in the United States. _____
7. A recent study revealed that many people believe professional athletes are overpaid. _____
8. In 2017, LeBron James, basketball player for the Cleveland Cavaliers, earned $24 million in salary and $54 million in endorsements. _____
9. According to Mothers Against Drunk Driving (MADD), we must do more to eliminate drunk driving. _____
10. According to the Mothers Against Drunk Driving (MADD) website, twenty-eight people are killed by drunken drivers every day. _____

PRACTICE

5-8 Read the following paragraph about American poet Walt Whitman. As you read, decide whether each sentence is a statement of fact (*F*) or an opinion (*O*). The first sentence has been answered for you.

(1) I believe Walt Whitman was not only one of the most influential American poets but also one of the most considerate. __O__ (2) In 1862, when he learned that his younger brother George had been injured fighting with the Union army in the American Civil War, he trekked south from New York to Virginia just to visit him. _____ (3) George had only suffered a minor cut to the face. _____ (4) Nevertheless, Whitman could see that other soldiers, both Union and Confederate, desperately needed his help. _____ (5) What Whitman did for the wounded, I would argue, was just as important as what he did for American literature. _____ (6) At overcrowded army hospitals in Virginia and Washington, DC, Whitman visited the sick and dying, running errands for them, helping them to write letters home, and even bringing them small gifts, such as ice cream. _____ (7) Throughout his time as a volunteer, Whitman kept a number of journals. _____ (8) In fact, his best poetry comes from this period of his life. _____ (9) In poems like "The Wound-Dresser" and "A March in the Ranks Hard-Prest, and the Road-Unknown," my personal favorites, he shows how modern war is not grand and heroic, but horrific. _____ (10) He also manages to show his remarkable compassion, precisely what made him such a great poet. _____

FOCUS on reading and writing

Look once again at "The Flight from Conversation," by Sherry Turkle (p. 604). Underline three facts, and then underline three opinions. Are the opinions supported or unsupported? Explain.

Making Inferences

> **WORD POWER**
> **infer** conclude from evidence

When you make an **inference**, you arrive at a conclusion by examining specific pieces of evidence. For example, when you see a car on the side of the road with its hood up and a white cloth tied to its antenna, you infer that the driver needs help. You make this assumption by examining bits of information and drawing a conclusion from that information. When people make inferences, they use what they already know to reach conclusions about what they don't know. For example, because you have seen drivers who needed help before, you know that a stalled car, a raised hood, and a white cloth indicate trouble. As a result, you are able to infer that the driver of the car you are now seeing is in need of help. Because inferences are basic to the way we think, they are part of everyday life. Consider the following examples:

- A doctor will infer the cause of a patient's illness by looking at his or her symptoms.
- A jury will infer a person's guilt or innocence by considering statements by the defendant, witness testimony, and photographs of the crime scene.
- An automobile mechanic will infer the cause of an engine problem by consulting a computer analysis of engine functions.

Writers do not always tell readers everything they need to know to understand a text. They expect readers to consider what the text suggests, not just what it literally states. In other words, writers expect you to "read between the lines" to determine what they are implying, not just what they are stating outright.

Keep in mind that an inference is not just a guess. It is an **educated guess**, a conclusion based on evidence in the text. In fact, the more evidence you can find, the stronger your inference will be. Still, as you read, you need to make sure that the inferences that you are making can be supported by the text. If not, reexamine the text and form more solid conclusions.

Making Inferences

The following questions will help you go beyond the literal level of a text and make inferences:
- What do you already know about the subject being discussed?
- What facts can you identify in the text?
- What inferences can you make from the information in the text?
- Is there enough evidence to support your inference? If not, do you need to change your thinking?

PRACTICE 5-9

Look at the public service advertisement on page 150 from the Humane Society of the United States. After examining the image and the words, fill in the inference diagram that follows it. Be prepared to discuss and explain the items in your list.

150 5e Chapter 5 Thinking, Reading, and Writing Critically

> "I'VE NEVER UNDERSTOOD WHY MY HUMAN WON'T LEAVE THE HOUSE WITHOUT HER LEASH. I THINK SHE'S AFRAID OF GETTING LOST. BUT IT'S OK, I KIND OF LIKE SHOWING HER AROUND."
>
> —HARPER
> adopted 08-18-09

A PERSON IS THE BEST THING TO HAPPEN TO A SHELTER PET

adopt

theshelterpetproject.org

Ad Council

The Humane Society of the United States, Maddie's Fund and the Advertising Council; theshelterproject.org

Inference Diagram

Describe the images
_____
_____
_____

Summarize the text
_____
_____
_____

Summarize what you already know
_____
_____
_____

Inference
_____
_____
_____
_____
_____

PRACTICE 5-10

In the following passage from the essay "Mother Tongue" (page 590), Amy Tan takes a position on the issue of defining the kind of English her mother speaks. Read the passage, and then answer the questions that follow it.

> Lately, I've been giving more thought to the kind of English my mother speaks. Like others, I have described it to people as "broken" or "fractured" English. But I wince when I say that. It has always bothered me that I can think of no other way to describe it other than "broken," as if it were damaged and needed to be fixed, as if it lacked a certain wholeness and soundness. I've heard other terms used, "limited English," for example. But they seem just as bad, as if everything is limited, including people's perceptions of the limited English speaker.

1. What do you already know about the subject Tan is discussing?
2. What point is Tan making about the kind of English her mother speaks?
3. Based on the information in this passage, what inference can you make about Tan's opinion of limited English speakers? What evidence in the passage leads you to your conclusion?
4. What is Tan likely to think of people who judge others solely on their ability to speak English? How do you know?

FOCUS on reading and writing

Look once again at "The Flight from Conversation," by Sherry Turkle (p. 604). Based on your reading of this essay, what can you infer about Turkle's attitude toward texting and social media? About her attitude toward face-to-face communication? Be prepared to explain your conclusions.

Michael Ventura/Alamy Stock Photo

Identifying Bias

Bias is a tendency to base conclusions on preconceived ideas rather than on evidence. For example, some people vote for one candidate over another simply because he or she is a Democrat or a Republican. Other people think that one television news program is fairer than another, and still others are convinced that one brand of gasoline is superior to all others. Without evidence, there is no way to support these assumptions.

Keep in mind, however, that there is a difference between *bias* and *point of view*. A **point of view** is a position on a particular issue; any time you voice an opinion, you are expressing a point of view. For example, if someone states that the death penalty is wrong, his or her point of view is clear. When the person goes on to support this position with **evidence**, this point of view may seem reasonable, even persuasive. If, on the other hand, the person provides no supporting evidence and does not consider opposing arguments, you can assume that bias has gotten in the way of his or her ability to think clearly.

Of course, writers do not usually announce that they are biased; often, you have to infer bias. For example, if in an essay on gun violence a writer states that he or she cannot understand why anyone would want to own a gun, you should be prepared for a one-sided discussion of the issue. A writer also demonstrates bias if he or she includes information that only supports his or her position and leaves out (or ignores) information that does not. And of course, a writer who makes overtly disparaging remarks about a particular group of people is clearly expressing bias.

You would also suspect bias if a writer uses language that expresses a value judgment. Consider the following statements:

> The United States entered into the Iraq War in response to the World Trade Center attack.
>
> The United States foolishly entered into the Iraq War in response to the World Trade Center attack.
>
> The United States courageously entered into the Iraq War in response to the World Trade Center attack.

The first sentence is a statement of fact, while the second and third sentences use words that express the biases of the individuals who wrote them. Even if you agree with these sentiments, noting the writers' biases should alert you to the likelihood that you are getting a one-sided, and possibly distorted, picture.

To one degree or another, everyone is biased. When you read, you have to determine if the extent of the writer's bias makes it impossible for him or her to discuss a subject fairly or logically.

FYI

Confirmation bias is a tendency that people have to accept information that confirms their beliefs and to reject information that does not. In other words, people have a tendency to believe what they want to believe. When you read (or write), be alert for confirmation bias, and do not accept information just because it supports your ideas. As a critical thinker, you have an obligation to consider all sides of an issue, not just the side that reinforces your preconceived views.

Identifying the Writer's Bias

The following questions can help you identify a writer's bias:
- Does the writer promote a particular point of view without supplying evidence for his or her opinions?
- Does the writer consider opposing points of view?
- Does the writer make offensive statements?
- Does the writer use language that expresses a value judgment?

FOCUS on reading and writing

Look back at "The Flight from Conversation," by Sherry Turkle (p. 604). Do you detect any bias? If so, where and what kind of bias? How does this bias affect your response to Turkle's essay?

Michael Ventura/Alamy Stock Photo

5f Reading and Writing Critically

There are times when you read just to find information—for example, when you read a textbook. Other kinds of reading—for instance, editorials and opinion essays, journal articles, and works of fiction—require you to read critically. When you **read critically**, you go beyond reading for facts. As a critical reader, you engage in a systematic process that enables you to determine how a text does what it does, how successful it is in achieving its purpose, and how your interaction with the text changes your view of a subject.

> **Steps in the Critical Reading Process**
>
> When you read a text critically, follow these steps:
>
> 1. **Summarize**   Identify the main idea of the text, and state it in your own words.
> 2. **Analyze**   Break the text into its parts, and consider how the parts relate to one another.
> 3. **Synthesize**   Integrate your own ideas with the ideas of the text.
> 4. **Evaluate**   Determine how successful the writer is in presenting his or her ideas.

Summarizing

When you **summarize** a text, you briefly restate its main idea in your own words. Because a summary forces you to condense a text's ideas, it helps you to understand its meaning. Keep in mind, though, that a summary should focus on the ideas of the text, not on your own interpretations or opinions, and it should use your own original wording, not the language of the text. (See 1c for more information on summarizing.)

PRACTICE

5-11   Write your own one-sentence summary of the following paragraph from "The Flight from Conversation," by Sherry Turkle (p. 604). Make sure your summary includes just the ideas in the text and not your own ideas or opinions, and be careful not to use any distinctive language from the original.

> In today's workplace, young people who have grown up fearing conversation show up on the job wearing earphones. Walking through a college library or the campus of a high-tech start-up, one sees the same thing: we are together, but each of us is in our own bubble, furiously connected to keyboards and tiny touch screens. A senior partner at a Boston law firm describes the scene at his office. Young associates lay out their suite of technologies: laptops, iPods and multiple cell phones. And then they put their earphones on. "Big ones. Like pilots. They turn their desks into cockpits." With the young lawyers in their cockpits, the office is quiet, a quiet that does not ask to be broken.

FOCUS on reading and writing

Reread the essay "The Flight from Conversation," by Sherry Turkle (p. 604). Then, write a one- or two-sentence summary of the essay.

Analyzing

After you summarize a text, you **analyze** it, dividing it into its parts to help you better understand it. When you analyze a text, you focus not only on what the text says but also on *how* it says it, and you focus on the text itself, not on your reaction to the text or what it means to you. In a sense, analyzing a text is like putting it under a microscope: You look at its structure, its main idea, its support for this idea, its conclusion, its use of words, and its purpose. You can also examine the writer's purpose and audience and the context or situation that created the need for the text.

By analyzing a text, you see how the parts of the text work together, and as a result, you gain an understanding of what the writer is trying to say. This is true whether you are reading an essay, a letter, a work of fiction, an article in a magazine, or a discussion in an online journal.

Analyzing a Text

Consider these questions when you analyze a text:

- **Who is the writer's audience?** Is the writer targeting general readers or a particular group?
- **Who is the writer?** Is the writer an expert or a person with limited knowledge of the subject? Does the writer try to identify with readers, or does he or she remain aloof?
- **What are the key characteristics of the text?** How is the text organized? What strategies does the writer use to make his or her point? What kind of language does the writer use? What types of evidence does the writer use? How effective is this evidence? How effective is the overall presentation or argument?
- **What is the context for the text?** What are the historical, political, economic, or social forces that shaped the text?
- **What motivated the writer?** What events led the writer to compose the text? In the case of an argument, what issue (or issues) caused the writer to begin thinking about the topic? Does the writer hold a set of values or beliefs that motivated him or her?

Notice how the following excerpt from a student's analysis of Martin Luther King Jr's "Letter from Birmingham Jail" addresses some of these questions.

> Martin Luther King Jr.'s most compelling argument in favor of nonviolent protest occurs in his 1963 "Letter from Birmingham Jail." At the time he wrote the letter, King, who was the leader of the Southern Christian Leadership Conference, was in prison after being arrested during a march against segregation in Birmingham, Alabama. The letter is addressed to moderate white clergymen, who considered King an outside agitator. It is also aimed at other readers who King assumes are sympathetic to his cause. Overall, the letter is organized as an argument. King begins his argument by stating his thesis—that he is in Birmingham, Alabama, "because injustice is here" (3). King then addresses the charge that his actions are extreme and untimely. If anything, says King, his actions are not timely enough—after all, African Americans have waited hundreds of years for their "constitutional and God-given rights" (14). He addresses the charge that he is breaking the law and draws the distinction between just and unjust laws. Because he considers laws upholding racial segregation to be unjust, he believes that he has a moral obligation to disobey them. King then makes the point that white moderates should follow his example and peacefully protest racial segregation in the South. King ends his letter by reinforcing his solidarity with the church and with the white clergy. Eventually, "Letter from Birmingham Jail" became an important document in the struggle for civil rights.

The student who wrote this paragraph examines some of the strategies King uses to construct his argument. In the rest of the analysis, the student goes on to discuss the specific evidence that King uses to support his points as well as the stylistic techniques he employs to make his argument more persuasive.

Michael Ventura/Alamy Stock Photo

FOCUS on reading and writing

Choose two or three paragraphs from "The Flight from Conversation," by Sherry Turkle (p. 604). Then, write a one- or two-paragraph analysis of these paragraphs. Be sure to consult the box on page 155 as you plan your analysis.

Synthesizing

After you analyze a text, your next step is to **synthesize**, to see how ideas from the text relate to your own ideas. As you synthesize, you think of new ideas and arrive at new insights, piecing the parts of a text together in new ways and seeing ideas (or even the entire text) differently. In a sense, synthesizing ideas is like putting the pieces of a puzzle together so that you can see the complete picture.

Synthesizing is part of a critical reading strategy that enables you to build on prior knowledge to develop new opinions, new insights, and possibly new interpretations. When you read, you gain information, and you keep this information in mind as you read further. Throughout the process, you consider material in the text as well as information you already know; eventually, you draw conclusions.

For example, as you read an essay on green campuses, you gain factual information. This information enables you to understand more of the essay as you read further. Eventually, you consider the information in the essay alongside what you already know about green campuses—for example, that your own school is installing solar cells and sustainable heating and cooling units on campus—and you realize that although the process is desirable, it is also expensive. As you read further, you might conclude that although the initial cost of a green campus is high, it is offset by reduced energy costs and reduced environmental damage. Of course, depending on your previous knowledge of the subject, you could draw the opposite conclusion—that despite its advantages, achieving a green campus may not be worth the money.

Not only can you synthesize information from a single text with what you already know, but you can also synthesize ideas from more than one text. For example, you might read two articles about online instruction. One article might support it, and the other might be critical of it. You would begin by summarizing each article and then analyzing them to identify their major points. Then, you would compare the ideas in the two articles and measure them against what you already know about online instruction—for example, what you have learned from taking two online courses. Finally, you might conclude that although online instruction may not be for every student, it could be beneficial for some. Thus, synthesizing information from different sources can enable you to expand your view of the topic, to generate ideas that you didn't have before, and to form your own ideas about a subject.

| PRIOR INFORMATION | → | NEW INFORMATION | → | SYNTHESIS |

> **Writing a Synthesis**
>
> 1. Decide on the point you want to develop.
> 2. Select at least two or three sources to support your point.
> 3. Read each source carefully, noting how they are alike, how they are different, and how they relate to your point.
> 4. Begin drafting your synthesis by clearly stating the point you are going to develop.
> 5. Use specific examples (paraphrases, summaries, and quotations) from your sources to support your point.
> 6. When you revise, make sure that you have used appropriate transitions to indicate the movement from one source to another. Also be sure that you have clearly identified each source that you discuss.
> 7. Document all words and ideas that you take from your sources.

In the following synthesis, taken from the research essay in 14a, the student writer supports her points with ideas from a variety of sources.

> What most people choose to ignore is that buying counterfeit items is stealing. In 2016, U.S. Customs and Border Protection and U. S. Immigration and Customs Enforcement seized a record number of counterfeit goods. Leading the list of seized items were designer watches and jewelry as well as handbags and wallets ("CBP, ICE Seize Record Number of Shipments"). The FBI estimates that in the United States alone, companies lose about $250 billion as a result of counterfeits (Wallace). In addition, buyers of counterfeit items avoid state and local taxes that legitimate companies pay. Thus, New York City alone loses about a billion dollars a year as a result of counterfeit merchandise ("Counterfeit Goods"). When this happens, everyone loses. After all, a billion dollars would pay for a lot of police officers and teachers, would fill a lot of potholes, and would pave a lot of streets. Even though buyers of designer counterfeit designer goods do not think of themselves as thieves, that is exactly what they are.

This paragraph synthesizes the student's own ideas about counterfeit merchandise with material from three different articles. Notice that the student is careful to identify and to document all the information she borrowed from her sources. (For information about documentation, see Chapter 14.)

> **FOCUS on reading and writing**
>
> Look back at the essay "The Flight from Conversation," by Sherry Turkle (p. 604), and synthesize the information in this essay with your own ideas. Then, write several sentences explaining how reading this essay has changed your thinking about how technology has influenced the way we communicate with one another.

Evaluating

So far, we have focused on understanding the ideas in a text. However, like everything else you encounter in life, texts vary in quality, and for this reason, you need to evaluate them. When you **evaluate** a text, you put it into perspective, assessing its strengths and weaknesses and discussing how successful it is in achieving its purpose. In other words, you form your own judgments about the text and its value as a source of information.

For example, if you were evaluating a newspaper opinion piece about the practicality of driverless cars, you would begin by asking questions. For instance, what is the writer's thesis? What is the writer's tone, and is this tone appropriate? Does the writer appear to be biased? What part of the writer's essay is particularly effective or ineffective? These kinds of questions will lead you toward a fair and critical evaluation of a text.

On the following pages you can see how Henry Yam, a computer science major, evaluated an opinion piece from *The New York Times* about self-driving cars. Below is the article along with Henry's underlining and annotations.

Google Wants Driverless Cars, but Do We?

Jamie Lincoln Kitman

<u>Love was in the air</u> at President-elect Donald J. Trump's summit meeting last week with tech executives. Alphabet, Google's parent company, was really feeling it, coming as it did a day after the company announced that its self-driving technology was ready for commercialization. The meeting was a giant green light for an industry and the multitrillion-dollar investment it will represent, the cost largely to be borne by consumers and government. <u>Automobile</u>, telecom, tech and e-commerce industries, and their marketers, have spent the last decade <u>enabling the public's addiction to wired living,</u> working feverishly to <mark>bring</mark> the phone and the internet into the driving environment. And yet this trend has never been voted on or discussed seriously by our politicians. Even when the Senate Committee on Commerce, Science and Transportation brought industry leaders to Washington

Sarcastic tone

Background information

Compares people's love of technology to drug addiction

Fair?

**interlocutor =
person involved in a
conversation**

cliché = sarcasm

**Thesis
Quotation marks =
sarcasm**

**Evidence = not enough
facts or expert
opinion**

**Concedes opposing
argument**

**Are these fair
assumptions?**

**He asks questions
but provides few
definite answers.**

?

for hearings last spring, congressional <u>interlocutors</u> sought mainly to have their guests tell them how government could help usher in this new age of driverless technology. The assumption was: game on.

In <u>the glorious future,</u> we are assured that driverless cars will save lives, reduce accidents, ease congestion, curb energy consumption and lower harmful emissions. These purported benefits contain elements of truth. But the data is nowhere near complete. Even stipulating that all the claimed benefits will one day materialize, the near- and midterm picture from a public-interest perspective is not the same favorable one that industry sees. [Legitimate areas of question and concern remain.]

Take, for instance, the "<u>safety</u>" benefits of self-driving cars that include avoiding tens of thousands of highway deaths each year. The truth is, no one knows for sure how many lives could be saved by driverless cars, because data on the role of human error in crashes is incomplete and misleading, relying heavily on self-reporting. The types of accidents we'll face in this automated future, in which these cars are meant to run together in proximity at high speed, may be fewer, but they'll be new, different, unpredictable and, on occasion, larger and more grisly than the ones we know today. When 1,700 people leave the New Jersey Turnpike at more or less the same moment, all headed for the same parking spot near the food court at the Vince Lombardi rest area, you don't want to be there.

<u>Yes, jobs will be created</u> by these new cars, but many will be lost. Millions of truck and taxi drivers will be out of work, and owing to the rise of car-sharing and app-based car services, people may buy fewer vehicles, meaning automakers and their suppliers could be forced to shed jobs.

Then there's infrastructure. Huge investments in new infrastructure are a given, but huge investments in old infrastructure will also still be needed. Many of these new-generation cars require smooth roads, with clearly painted lines, to safely position themselves. Potholes, worn paint and other irregularities—standard fare on too many of today's roads—will <u>potentially</u> become even greater safety hazards than they are now. Where will the resources to maintain and repair roads and bridges, an effort already underfunded by more than a trillion dollars, come from?

And have we thought about security? Today's cars can be hacked easily. New protocols must be agreed on, and even then, nefarious actors will learn how to remotely start and stop cars, steer them, steal them, crash them or even take them hostage. Senator Edward J. Markey, Democrat of Massachusetts, attempted to address security issues at the hearings last spring—proposing rules governing consumer privacy and antihacking requirements—but the invited companies balked at regulation. For those of a <u>dystopian</u> bent, imagine the day when the local constable locks your doors and instructs your car to drive you to the station for questioning.

And what about the interim period when conventional vehicles share the road with automated ones? One of the claims made for autonomous cars is that they can be lighter, shedding heavy metal crash cells and expensive safety gear, like airbags, saving fuel. That's great until the old-school pickup with the old-fashioned drunken driver T-bones your Google car.

What's more, are we ready to give up on mass transit? In a world where our elected officials can't see fit to fund and fairly price much-needed public transportation, it's hard to imagine these new automated-car expenses will free up money for trains and trams. And yet many cities are so crowded they don't have room for more cars—even automated, electric cars congest.

We humans can't seem to put our phones down, and industry leaders don't want us to. The risk of distracted driving may be one of the strongest arguments for driverless cars. But distracted driving could be reduced simply by disabling phones in moving cars.

When it comes to the practical direction of technology, <u>the government too often defers to industry.</u> Shouldn't society have a say in what amounts to a public works project larger than the Interstate System of highways—run by and for private industry, but underwritten by taxpayers? Congress needs to articulate their goals and answer this burning question: Are driverless cars really what we need?

Jamie Lincoln Kitman, a lawyer, is the New York bureau chief for Automobile Magazine.

Examples?

★ ★ ★

After reading and annotating Kitman's opinion piece on self-driving cars, Henry wrote the following evaluation.

In "Google Wants Driverless Cars, but Do We?" Jamie Lincoln Kitman provides too little evidence and is too sarcastic to be convincing. He does, however, make an interesting point: Self-driving cars may not live up to their early hype. For instance, supporters claim that self-driving cars will save lives, cut down on accidents, lessen traffic congestion, reduce energy consumption, and improve air quality. According to Kitman, however, these predictions are unrealistic. He thinks that driverless vehicles will create more problems than they actually solve. He wonders, for example, if the safety benefits of self-driving vehicles are actually real, or if the economic benefits of this new technology will outweigh their cost in lost jobs. These are legitimate concerns, but Kitman does not provide enough evidence to make his essay persuasive. For example, how much will it cost to prepare roads to accommodate self-driving cars? How safe will these cars be? How many jobs will be lost as a result of this new technology? Surely, there are answers to these questions, but Kitman does not provide them. Because Kitman is a reporter and an expert in the area of driverless vehicles, his opinions carry weight. Even so, he needs to provide more support. Although his essay does lead me to think more critically about self-driving cars, to convince me that they are not feasible, Kitman needs to do more than raise questions and make sarcastic comments.

Even though you might disagree with a writer, you should acknowledge the strengths as well as the weaknesses of the text. Remember that an effective evaluation relies on information in the text, not just on your own ideas or opinions. In other words, unsupported opinions and preconceived ideas about an issue should not form the basis of your evaluation.

FOCUS on reading and writing

Look back at "The Flight from Conversation," (p. 604), and write a one-paragraph evaluation of the essay.

TEST revise edit

Review your evaluation of Turkle's essay. TEST what you have written, and then revise, edit, and proofread your work.

CHAPTER REVIEW

REVIEW ACTIVITY

Read the passage below, from Deborah Tannen's 1994 *New York Times* article "The Triumph of the Yell," following the critical reading process outlined in this chapter. Then, write an essay in which you evaluate the passage. Briefly summarize and analyze the passage, synthesizing its ideas with what you already know. When you have finished, **TEST** and revise what you have written. Then, edit and proofread your work.

From "The Triumph of the Yell"
Deborah Tannen

In many university classrooms, "critical thinking" means reading someone's life work, then ripping it to shreds. Though critique is surely one form of critical thinking, so are integrating ideas from disparate fields and examining the context out of which they grew. Opposition does not lead to truth when we ask only "What's wrong with this argument?" and never "What can we use from this in building a new theory and a new understanding?"

Several years ago I was on a television talk show with a representative of the men's movement. I didn't foresee any problem, since there is nothing in my work that is anti-male. But in the room where guests gather before the show I found a man wearing a shirt and tie and a floor-length skirt, with waist-length red hair. He politely introduced himself and told me he liked my book. Then he added: "When I get out there, I'm going to attack you. But don't take it personally. That's why they invite me on, so that's what I'm going to do."

When the show began, I spoke only a sentence or two before this man nearly jumped out of his chair, threw his arms before him in gestures of anger and began shrieking—first attacking me, but soon moving on to rail against women. The most disturbing thing about his hysterical ranting was what it sparked in the studio audience: they too became vicious, attacking not me (I hadn't had a chance to say anything) and not him (who wants to tangle with someone who will scream at you?) but the other guests: unsuspecting women who had agreed to come on the show to talk about their problems communicating with their spouses.

This is the most dangerous aspect of modeling intellectual interchange as a fight: it contributes to an atmosphere of animosity that spreads like a fever. In a society where people express their anger by shooting, the result of demonizing those with whom we disagree can be truly demonic.

COLLABORATIVE ACTIVITY

Working in a group of three or four students, select an image of a piece of fine art from the options provided by your instructor, or find one using an online resource, such as Art Resource, Bridgeman Art Library, or Google Art Project. Challenge yourselves by choosing a piece of art that is not open to easy interpretation. Discuss as a group what you see, and then share your observations with the rest of the class. Select one group member to record your group's observations, listing all the observations on one side, and all the inferences on the other side of the board. As a class, discuss the differences between the two lists.

Review checklist

- ✔ Identify a writer's audience, purpose, and tone. (See 5a.)
- ✔ Distinguish between the denotations and connotations of words. (See 5b.)
- ✔ Identify a text's main idea—often expressed in a thesis statement. (See 5c.)
- ✔ Identify major and minor supporting points. (See 5d.)
- ✔ Evaluate the writer's ideas, distinguishing between fact and opinion, making inferences, and identifying bias. (See 5e.)
- ✔ When you *read and write critically*, you go beyond reading for facts. You summarize, analyze, synthesize, and evaluate. (See 5f.)

6 Reading and Writing about Different Kinds of Texts

Ivonne Wierink/Shutterstock; sbarabu/Shutterstock; Lauren Burke/Getty Images; Photodisc/Getty Images

FOCUS on reading and writing

The images above come from a chapter opener of a psychology textbook. Brainstorm to discover what you already know about what makes a good textbook. In this chapter you will learn strategies for reading and writing about textbooks and a variety of other texts.

> **PREVIEW**
>
> In this chapter, you will learn to
> - apply active reading strategies to written texts (6a).
> - apply active reading strategies to visual texts (6b–6c).

6a Reading Written Texts

A **written text** is composed of printed words. (**Visual texts**, such as those discussed in **6b**, are composed largely of images.) Although the active reading process you were introduced to in Chapter 1 can generally be applied to almost all texts, some kinds of texts require slightly different strategies during the previewing stage. One reason for this is that different texts often have different purposes—for example, to present information or to persuade. Another reason is that the various texts you read (including visuals) are aimed at different audiences, who often require different content and emphasis. For these reasons, when you **preview** different kinds of texts, you need to look for their characteristic features. Keep in mind that you will often read texts in order to write about them. Reading a text carefully—and with a critical eye—will help you write about it accurately and convincingly.

Textbooks

Much of the reading you do in college is in textbooks (like this one). The purpose of a textbook is to present information, and when you read a textbook, your goal is to locate, understand, and remember that information. To do this, you need to determine which ideas are most important as well as which points support those key ideas and which examples illustrate them.

Before you look at individual sections or pages of a textbook, you should skim the preface to see what the authors' purpose and emphasis is, and you should also look through the table of contents, which shows how the book is organized. In addition, you should consult any end-of-chapter study questions and perhaps look at the book's glossary, which defines key terms. Familiarizing yourself with these features will help you get oriented to your textbook so you can use it more easily to find the information you need.

Checklist

> **Reading Textbooks**
>
> Look for the following features as you preview:
>
> ✔ Chapter titles
>
> ✔ Section headings and subheadings
>
> ✔ **Boldfaced** and *italicized* words, which can indicate terms to be defined
>
> ✔ Boxed checklists or summaries, which may appear at the ends of sections or chapters
>
> ✔ Bulleted or numbered lists, which may list key reasons or examples or summarize important material
>
> ✔ Diagrams, charts, tables, graphs, photographs, and other visuals that illustrate the writer's points
>
> ✔ Marginal quotations and definitions
>
> ✔ Marginal cross-references
>
> ✔ Web links

Look at the textbook excerpt on the next page, which was taken from Hockenbury and Hockenbury's *Psychology*, Eighth Edition. It has been annotated to show some of the features you should look for when previewing material from a textbook.

PRACTICE 6-1 Using the Reading Textbooks Checklist above as a guide, preview a page from one of your textbooks. Then, following the active reading process outlined in Chapter 1, mark up and annotate the page, writing your comments on small sticky notes. Finally, make an informal outline of the information presented on the page.

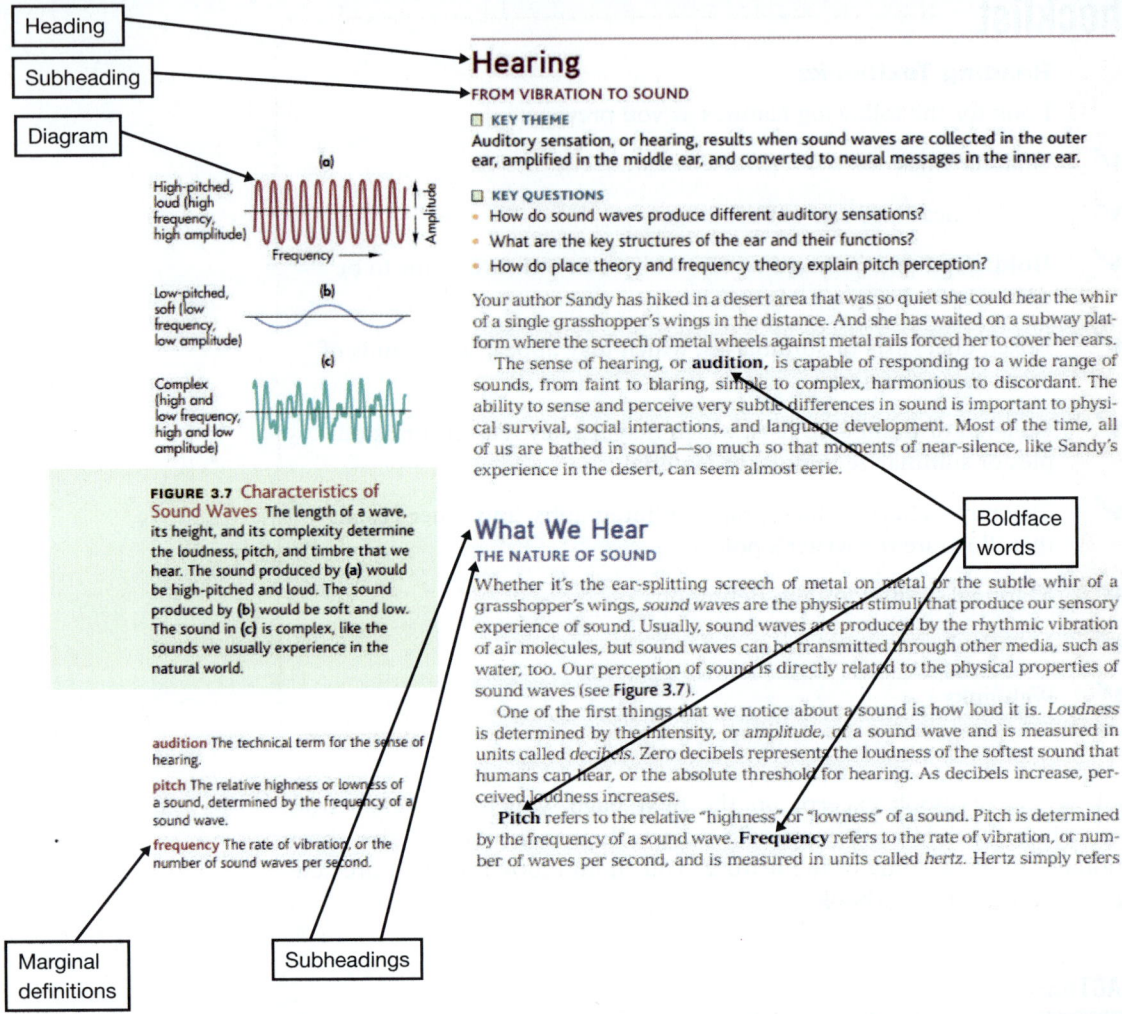

News Articles

As a student, as an employee, and as a citizen, you read school, community, local, and national newspapers in print and online. Like textbooks, news articles communicate information. In addition, newspapers also publish editorials (which aim to persuade) as well as feature articles (which may entertain as well as inform).

Many people read news articles online rather than in print form. If this is what you usually do, keep in mind that newspaper web pages are often very busy and crowded, so you may have difficulty distinguishing important information from not-so-important material. For example, a news article that you read online may be surrounded by advertising and include links to irrelevant (and potentially distracting) material—such as commercial sites or Facebook pages. For this reason, it is very important to read online material carefully and methodically.

Checklist

Reading News Articles
Look for the following features as you preview:

- ✔ Headlines
- ✔ **Boldfaced headings** within articles
- ✔ Labels like *editorial*, *commentary*, or *opinion*, which indicate that an article communicates the writer's own views
- ✔ Brief biographical information at the end of an opinion piece
- ✔ Phrases or sentences in **boldface** (to emphasize key points)
- ✔ The article's first sentence, which often answers the questions *who*, *what*, *why*, *where*, *when*, and *how*
- ✔ The **dateline**, which tells you the date (and sometimes the place) the writer is reporting from
- ✔ Photographs, charts, graphs, and other visuals
- ✔ In *print news articles*, related articles that appear on the same page—for example, boxed information and **sidebars**, short related articles that provide additional background on people and places mentioned in the article
- ✔ In *online news articles*, links to related articles, reader comments, and other useful material

The following online newspaper article from the *StarTribune*, has been annotated to show some of the features you should look for when previewing a newspaper article.

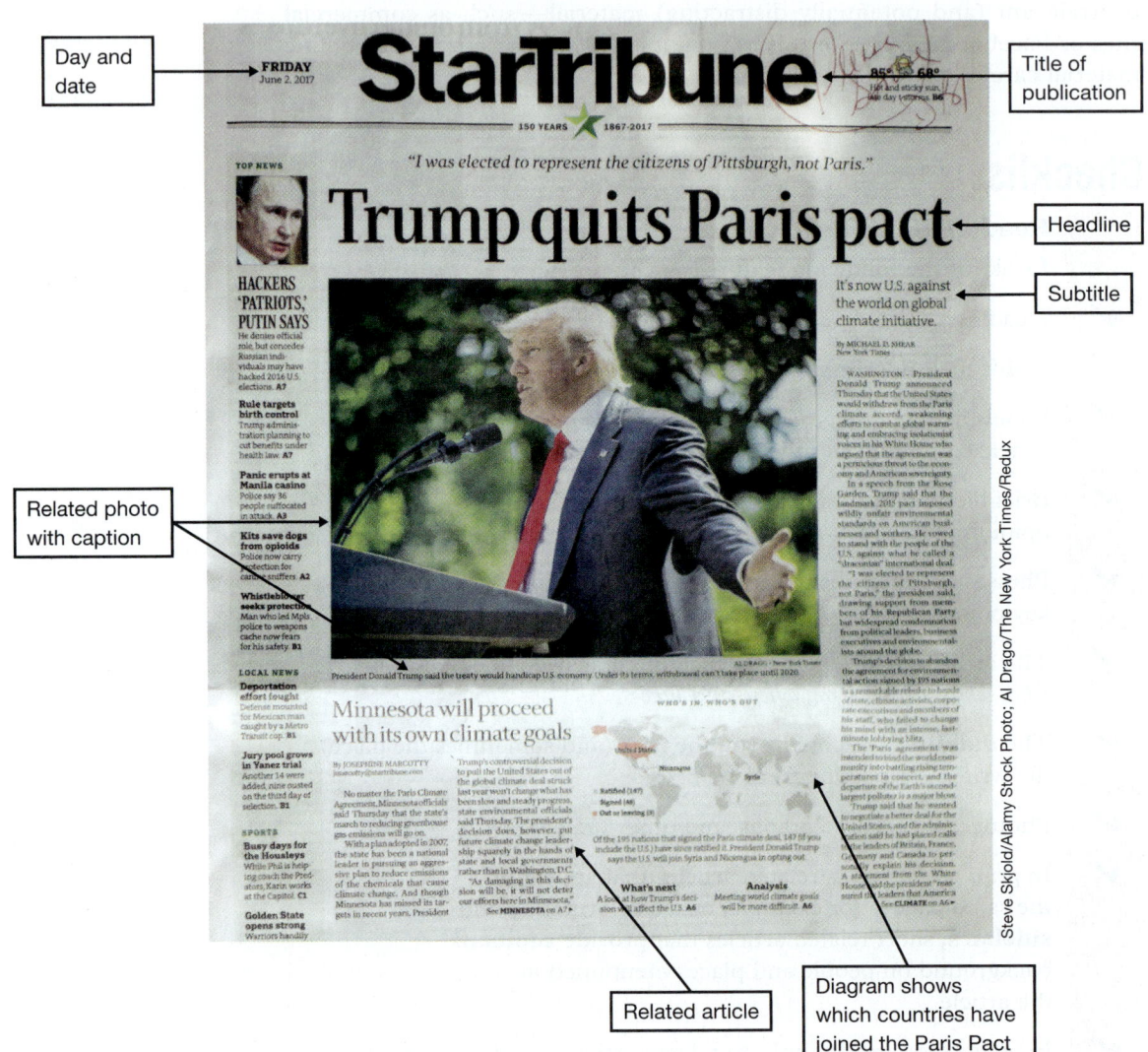

PRACTICE

6-2 Print out a news article from the web. Using the Reading News Articles Checklist on page 169 as a guide, preview the article, and then mark it up and annotate it, following the reading process outlined in Chapter 1. Finally, write a response paragraph commenting on the article's ideas.

Business Documents

In your workplace, you will read memos, letters, emails, reports, and so on. These documents, which may be designed to convey information as well as persuade, are often addressed to a group rather than to a single person. (Note that the most important information often comes *first*—in a subject line or in the first paragraph.)

Checklist

Reading Business Documents

Look for the following features as you preview:

✔ Numbered or bulleted lists of tasks or problems (numbers indicate the order of the items' importance)

✔ In an email, links to the web

✔ In a memo or an email, the person or persons addressed, as well as their titles

✔ In a memo or an email, the subject line

✔ In a memo or a report, headings that might highlight key topics or points

✔ In a memo or report, the **executive summary** and the Conclusions and Recommendations sections

✔ In a letter or an email, the first and last paragraphs and the first sentence of each body paragraph, which often contain key information

✔ **Boldfaced**, underlined, or *italicized* words

The following professional email has been annotated to show some of the features you should look for when previewing a business document.

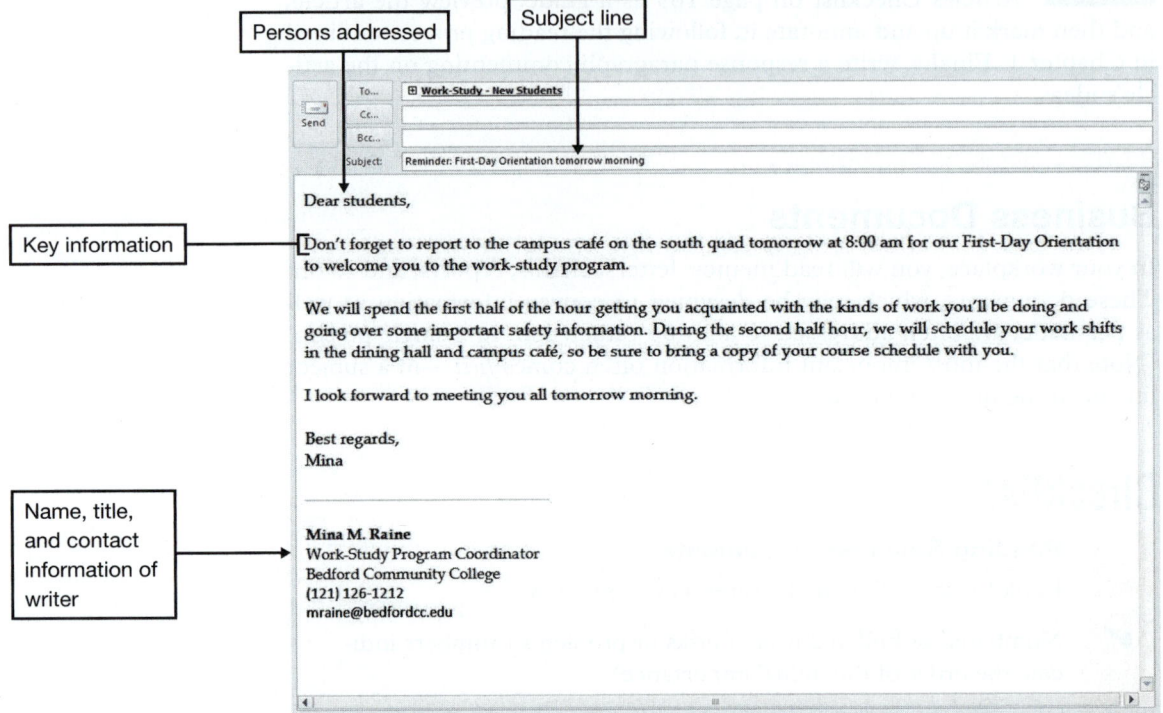

PRACTICE 6-3

Ask your employer or an office worker at your school to share a memo with you. Using the Reading Business Documents Checklist on page 171 as a guide, preview the memo. Following the reading process outlined in Chapter 1, mark up and annotate the memo, and then write a one-sentence summary that conveys its main idea.

Web Pages

Web pages can be written to provide information (as in a page from the website of a charity or a government office), to provoke a response (as in a commercial site advertising a product or a political site advocating a position or course of action), or simply to entertain or amuse.

Web pages are generally not *linear*—that is, they are not laid out neatly on the page in lines or columns (as is the case for textbooks, newspaper articles, and business documents). For this reason, web pages are not likely to be read from left to right, one line at a time. Instead, your eyes wander around the page; sometimes you read a line or two from left to right and then move down vertically or diagonally to read boxed text or look at an advertisement or a visual. Often, you interrupt your reading of a page to follow a link. For this reason, you do not usually read web pages word for word. Instead, you **scan** pages, looking for individual words, sentences, and headings.

It is also important to note that web pages may include irrelevant material—for example, links to articles only tangentially related to the site's topic, advertising, solicitations for donations, and links to free trial offers. One of the most important strategies for reading web pages is learning to recognize—and skip over—irrelevant material.

Checklist

Reading Web Pages

Look for the following features as you preview:

- ✔ Use of color to highlight important information
- ✔ Tabs for drop-down menus
- ✔ "Read more" links that expand summaries or excerpts
- ✔ Search box to help you narrow your focus
- ✔ Boxed information, with box titles in large type
- ✔ **Boldfaced**, underlined, or *italicized* words
- ✔ Bulleted lists (like this one)
- ✔ Images and their captions
- ✔ Links to podcasts, press releases, videos, slideshows, and related articles and reports

Following is the home page of NASA (the National Aeronautics and Space Administration). It has been annotated to show some of the features you should look for when previewing a web page.

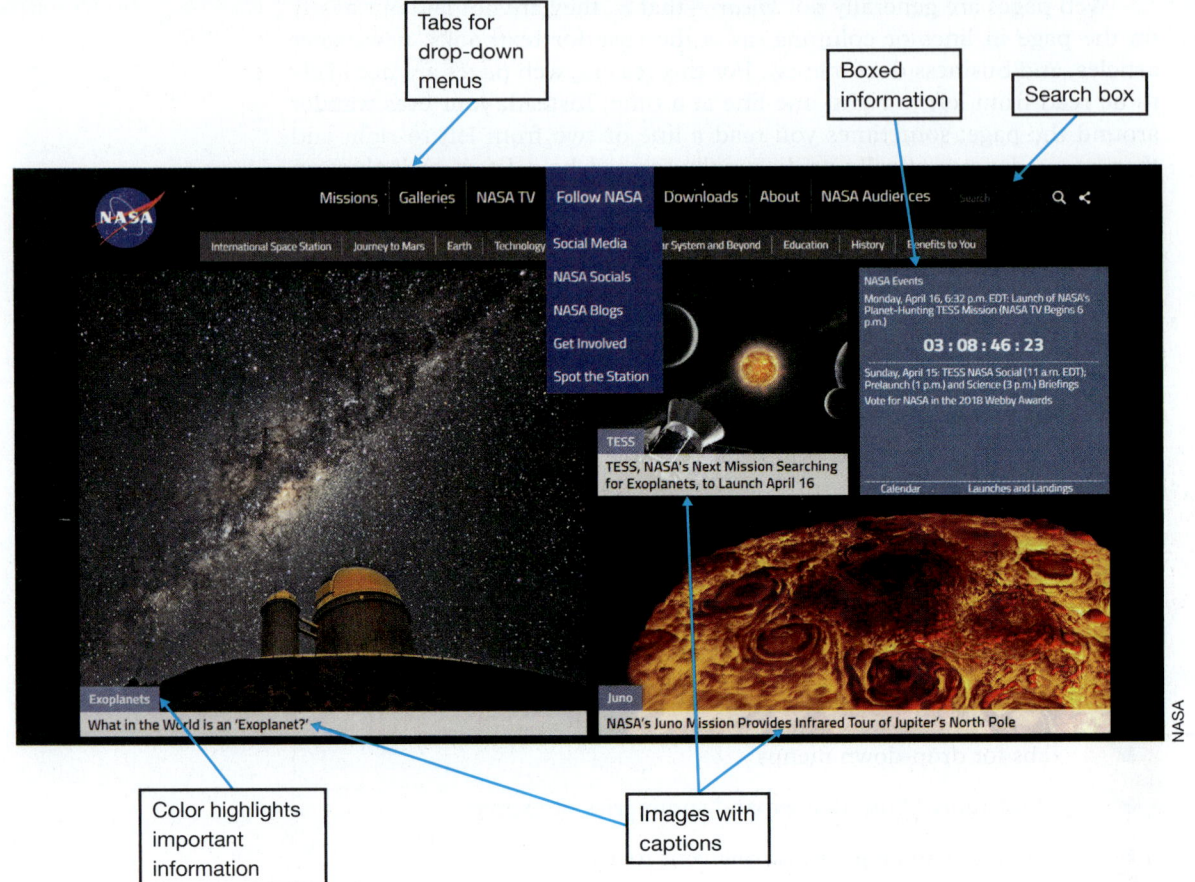

PRACTICE 6-4

Print out a web page. Using the Reading Web Pages Checklist on page 173 as a guide, preview the page, and then mark it up and annotate it, following the reading process outlined in Chapter 1. Finally, write an evaluation of the page assessing the usefulness of its information.

Blogs

Blogs are websites on which bloggers (professional or amateur writers) post information (including visuals) to encourage comments and discussion.

Blog posts, which can range in length from single sentences or paragraphs to pages of text, appear in chronological order, with the most recent post first. An individual or an organization can blog about virtually any topic—sports, politics, education, fashion, or music, for example—and a blog can stand alone or be part of a larger website.

The focus of a blog can be quite narrow—for example, the issues facing kindergarten parents in a particular town or neighborhood. Blogs can also have a wider focus, as is the case with those maintained by elected officials to discuss important issues or by newspapers and magazines to engage their readers. Some of the most popular blogs focus on entertainment gossip, political issues, and business advice. When you read a blog, be careful not to be distracted by advertising or by irrelevant links.

Checklist

Reading Blogs

Look for the following features as you preview:

- ✔ Title of post
- ✔ The first comment (to bring the conversation up-to-date)
- ✔ The farthest-back comment available (to see where the responses to a post began)
- ✔ Links to related blogs or articles
- ✔ "Read more" links that expand summaries or excerpts
- ✔ The Search box, which enables you to search all blog posts
- ✔ Sidebars (Home, About, FAQs, and so on)
- ✔ Monthly archives
- ✔ Photos and other images (some submitted by the author, others by those commenting on the original post)

Look at the following post on a blog about the history of the geology department at Modesto Junior College, written by geology instructor Garry Hayes. It has been annotated to show some of the features you should look for when previewing a blog.

PRACTICE 6-5

Find a blog that interests you on tumblr.com, and print out one post from the blog along with a few of the related comments. Using the Reading Blogs Checklist (p. 175) as a guide, preview the blog post. Then, mark it up and annotate it, following the reading process outlined in Chapter 1. Finally, write your own comment on the writers' ideas.

> ## FOCUS on reading and writing
> What different kinds of reading do you do in a typical week? Do you read for pleasure? To get information? In response to assignments? When—and where—do you generally do your reading? How carefully, and with how much interest, do you read each kind of text? Write a paragraph or two explaining why, when, where, and how you read.

Ivonne Wierink/Shutterstock; sbarabu/Shutterstock; Lauren Burke/Getty Images; Photodisc/Getty Images

 ## 6b Reading Visual Texts

The written texts you read often include **visuals**—graphs, charts, maps, diagrams, photographs, cartoons, or advertisements—to enhance the appeal of the text and convey the writer's ideas. For example, a photograph of an overcrowded prison can make a news article about the inmates' plight more vivid; a diagram of the heart can supplement a biology text's explanation of the circulatory system; and a map can help readers understand an essay's discussion of seventeenth-century explorers' conquests. Sometimes, too, a visual will stand alone, communicating its own message instead of enhancing the message of a written text. For example, an editorial cartoon or advertisement can persuade readers to support a cause, take some type of social action, buy a product, or vote for a particular candidate.

When you "read" a visual—particularly one that will be the subject of class discussion or writing—you should do so with a critical eye. Your primary goal is to understand the point that the creator of the visual is trying to make, but you also need to understand how the information or message is conveyed, as well as how it is intended to affect you. The strategies that will help you achieve these goals are similar to the active reading strategies you were introduced to in Chapter 1.

> **WORD POWER**
> **plight** a difficult or unfortunate situation

Previewing a Visual

When you approach a visual, you should begin by looking for clues to its main idea, or message. Some visuals, particularly advertising images, include written text that conveys the main idea. Apart from words, however, the images themselves can help you to understand the visual's purpose, its intended audience, and the argument (if any) that it is making.

When you preview a visual, considering the following questions will help you understand its content, purpose, and message.

Questions for Previewing

- Who is the visual's target audience?
- What individual images appear in the visual?
- How close together (or far apart) are these images?
- How large is each image? Why are some larger than others?
- How is each image visually connected to the background?
- How is empty space used?
- How are color and shading (for example, contrast between light and dark) used?
- Are any design elements or words repeated?
- Does the visual include any special effects, such as blurring or nonrealistic images?
- Does the visual include people? If so, what do the people's activities, gestures, facial expressions, positions, body language, dress, and the like tell you about the visual's purpose?
- Does the visual include any written text? If so, what purpose does it serve? Is it necessary?
- Are any two images juxtaposed to suggest an association between them — for example, a Prius and a meadow?

WORD POWER
juxtaposed placed side by side for comparison or contrast

When you have considered the items listed in the box above, you should have a sense of why a visual was created and what message it was designed to communicate. Now, look at the following visual:

This editorial cartoon by Nick Anderson was published *in The Houston Chronicle* on May 3, 2013, in response to a shocking industrial accident in Bangladesh: over 1,100 workers were killed and some 2,500 injured, many seriously, in the collapse of a building that housed a clothing factory. This factory was located on the eight-story building's upper floors, which were not strong enough to bear the weight of the factory's heavy machinery. Cracks had been discovered in the building the day before the collapse, but it had been deemed safe, and the factory supervisor had ordered employees to return to work. Because the factory manufactured clothing for a number of American companies, the creator of the cartoon could assume that its subject matter would be of interest to American consumers.

The cartoon has three main visual elements: the message in the upper left-hand corner directed to employers, the central scene of devastation, and the "factory death toll" sign in the lower right-hand corner. These three elements work together to convey the cartoon's message: When clothing is produced under substandard conditions workers pay a terrible price.

The first element sends an ironic (but supposedly positive) message to manufacturers; its bold black-on-white capital letters and even rectangular shape stand in contrast to the random destruction shown in the central scene. The second element, the scene itself, conveys a highly negative message, showing a collapsed building surrounded by rubble and stretcher bearers carrying bodies away. (Additional bodies can be seen lined up in rows in the lower left-hand corner of the image.) Juxtaposed with the seemingly positive message at the upper left is the sign in the lower right-hand corner. Unlike the optimistic invitation to employers, this sign conveys the ugly truth in very straightforward language. Set beside the terrible central image of the collapsed building and the dead bodies, this sign makes the ironic point of the cartoon clear: Manufacturing clothing under unsafe, potentially deadly, conditions can exact a heavy price.

PRACTICE

6-6 Look at the following three visuals and apply the Questions for Previewing to each one. What do you conclude about each visual's purpose and intended message?

Photograph of New York City retired firefighter Jerry Collins and his wife, Suzanne, at the 9/11 Memorial in New York City

Editorial cartoon by award-winning political cartoonist Stuart Carlson

10 ways to protect CORAL REEFS

EDUCATE yourself about coral reefs & the creatures they support.
When you further your own education, you can help others understand the fragility and value of the world's coral reefs.

BE A MARINE DEBRIS CRUSADER.
In addition to picking up your own trash, carry away the trash that others have left behind.

Don't send chemicals into our waterways.
Nutrients from excess fertilizer increases algae growth that blocks sunlight to corals.

Corals are already a gift. Don't give them as presents.
It takes corals decades or longer to create reef structures, so leave them on the reef.

Long-lasting light bulbs ARE A BRIGHT IDEA.
Energy efficient light bulbs reduce greenhouse gas emissions. Climate change is one of the leading threats to coral reef survival.

IF YOU DIVE DON'T TOUCH.
Coral reefs are alive. Stirred-up sediment can smother corals.

Practice safe boating.
Anchor in sandy areas away from coral and sea grasses so that the anchor and chain do not drag on nearby corals.

Choose sustainable seafood.
Learn how to make smart seafood choices at www.FishWatch.gov.

Volunteer!
Volunteer in local beach or reef cleanups. If you don't live near the coast, get involved in protecting your watershed.

CONSERVE WATER
The less water you use, the less runoff and wastewater that eventually find their ways back into the ocean.

oceanservice.noaa.gov

NOAA

Marking Up and Annotating a Visual

Once you have previewed a visual, you should use a highlighter pen to mark it up and then go on to annotate it, focusing your attention on images as well as words.

Begin by identifying key images—by starring, boxing, or circling them—and perhaps drawing lines or arrows to connect related images. Then, go on to make annotations directly on the visual (or on sticky notes), commenting on the effectiveness of its individual images in communicating the message of the whole. As in the case of a written text, your annotations can be in the form of comments or questions.

The following visual, an ad for Discover The Forest, a public service advertising campaign aimed at reconnecting children and their families with nature, has been marked up and annotated by a student.

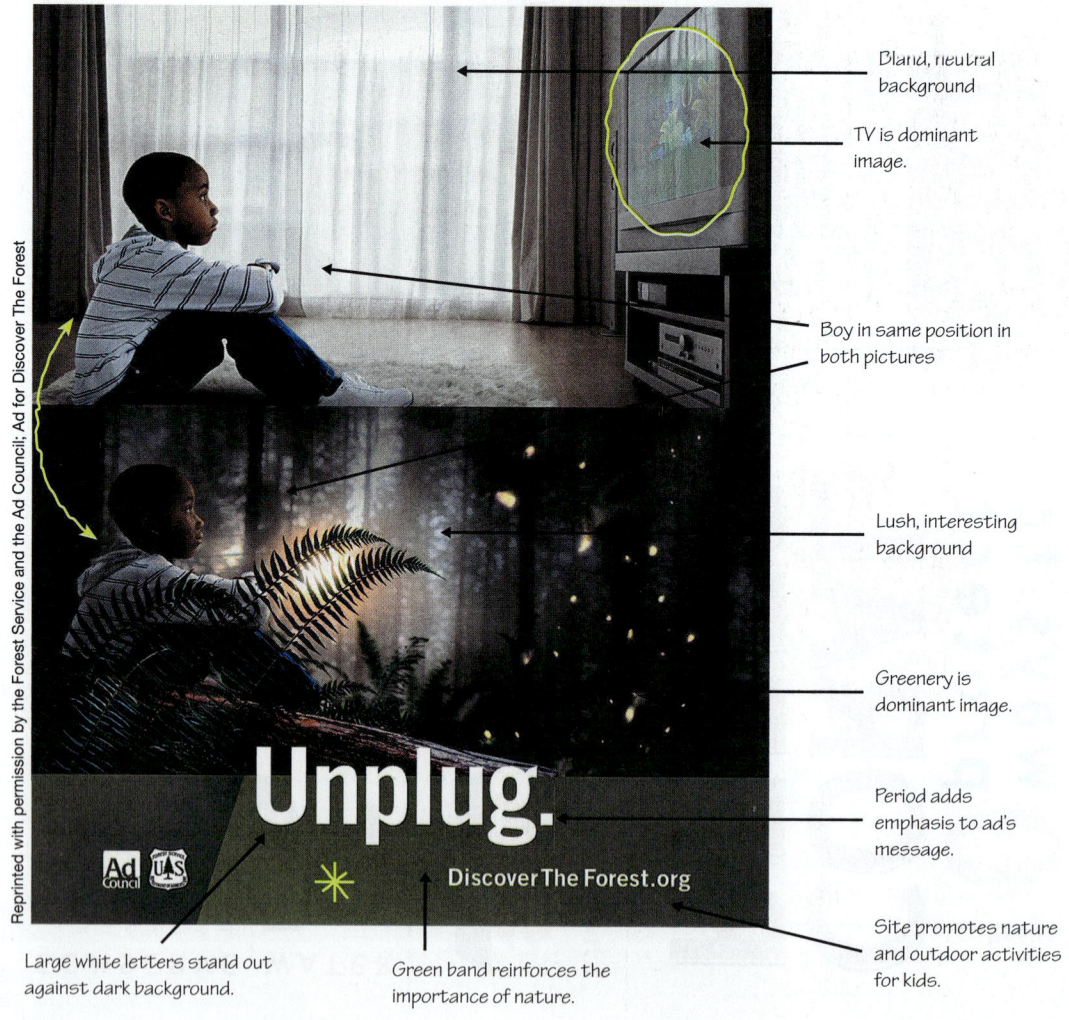

PRACTICE
6-7 Look at the following visual, and then mark up and annotate it to identify its most important images and their relationship to one another. When you have finished, think about how the images work together to communicate information or a central message. What ideas does the visual convey to the audience?

Photograph of some of the devastation caused in central Philippines by Typhoon Haiyan.

6c Types of Visuals

As you learned in 6b, different kinds of visuals call for different approaches. When you examine visual texts, particularly those you plan to write about, consider the special characteristics of each type of visual.

Charts, Graphs, and Tables

Charts, graphs, and tables often appear in textbooks, newspapers, magazines, business reports, and articles on websites. They can be used to present information, to provide support for a position, or to correct misconceptions. Charts, graphs, and tables enable readers to visualize complicated information; it is often easier to understand numerical data when they are presented and organized visually than when the same information is presented in a dense paragraph of description or explanation. (Visuals called **infographics**, or information graphics, such as The Financial

Aid Process on page 181, are especially effective at conveying complex information.)

A **chart**—for example, a pie chart—is a visual representation of statistics or data that illustrates ideas and concepts in a written text. For example, in a discussion of green energy, a chart might show the number of people in a given city who use hybrid, low-gas-mileage, and electric cars. A **graph**—for example, a line graph or a bar graph—also presents data, but it shows the data over time or compares individual bits of data. For example, an economics report could include a graph showing a supply-and-demand curve, a communications text could include a graph showing the increase in Twitter use in the past ten years, and a graph in a government document could show shifts in population in various congressional districts. **Tables** are often used to compare and contrast ideas that are explained in a text, identifying key points so readers can understand concepts more easily. For example, a table in an article in a psychology journal could compare academic performance of well-rested and sleep-deprived students.

Checklist

Reading Charts, Graphs, and Tables

Look for the following features as you preview:

- ✔ Title, caption(s), and legend (which can function as a key)
- ✔ Labels (note the column headings in tables and the labels on the vertical and horizontal axes in graphs)
- ✔ The types of information that are being compared or the type of relationship being shown
- ✔ The units of measurement being used
- ✔ The source of the information being used (look at source lines or footnotes)
- ✔ The way color is used

The graph on the following page shows how much a $15,000 student loan will actually cost a student over a period of ten years, depending on the type of loan and the interest rate. It has been labeled to show you the key features to look for as you preview a graph, a chart, or a table.

PRACTICE

6-8 Find a chart, graph, or table on the web or in one of your textbooks. Preview it to identify its key features; then, mark it up and annotate it. Finally, write a one- or two-sentence summary of the information it presents.

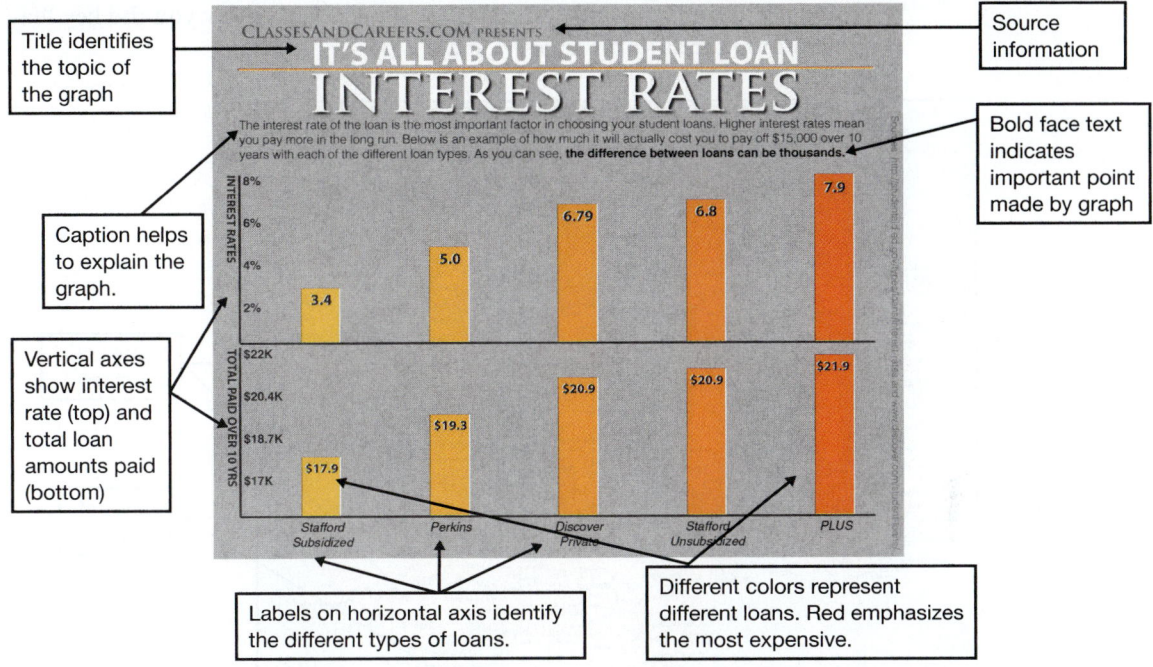

Maps

Maps often appear in textbooks and in newspaper and magazine articles, where they can provide supplementary information or illustrate a discussion. Maps are visual representations of continents, regions, countries, states, cities, or towns (and can also identify smaller features, such as parks or museums). By indicating boundaries, geographical and topographical features, and structures such as roads and bridges, maps provide a geographical context for anything from a discussion of drought conditions in sub-Saharan Africa to the path of explorers on the Silk Road to the relative sizes of the five Great Lakes. Maps can also supplement a discussion of historical, political, or scientific developments by providing comparative information—for example, a pair of maps can show Poland's boundaries before and after World War II, and a series of maps can show changes over time in the size of the polar ice caps.

Checklist

Reading Maps

Look for the following features as you preview:

✔ Names of countries and cities indicated by different type sizes

✔ Shaded or colored areas that distinguish different parts of a region

✔ A legend (often boxed) that explains the map's scale and the meaning of various symbols (such as dots or stars to indicate capital cities)

The following map of Africa has been labeled to show you the key features to look for as you preview a map.

PRACTICE
6-9 Find a map on the web or in one of your textbooks. Preview it to identify its key features; then mark it up and annotate it. Finally, write a sentence that summarizes the information it presents.

Diagrams

Diagrams are often used in textbooks as well as in scientific, engineering, and business reports, where they can supplement a description or explain a process in visual terms. A diagram can represent a structure, mechanism, or piece of equipment, or it can illustrate a process. (A **flowchart** is a diagram used to visually represent a process.) In a biology textbook, a step-by-step process, such as mitosis or photosynthesis, can be represented as a diagram, with arrows indicating the direction of the process. In a business report, a flowchart can show how management and union officials negotiate a contract. Finally, in an engineering report, a diagram of a building could show areas of structural weakness or damage.

Checklist

Reading Diagrams

Look for the following features as you preview:

✔ Title or caption that identifies the subject of the diagram

✔ Labels that identify individual steps in a process or parts of a piece of equipment

✔ Information in the text that discusses what is being illustrated in the diagam

The following diagram shows the process by which living organisms gain energy. It has been labeled to show you the key features to look for as you preview a diagram.

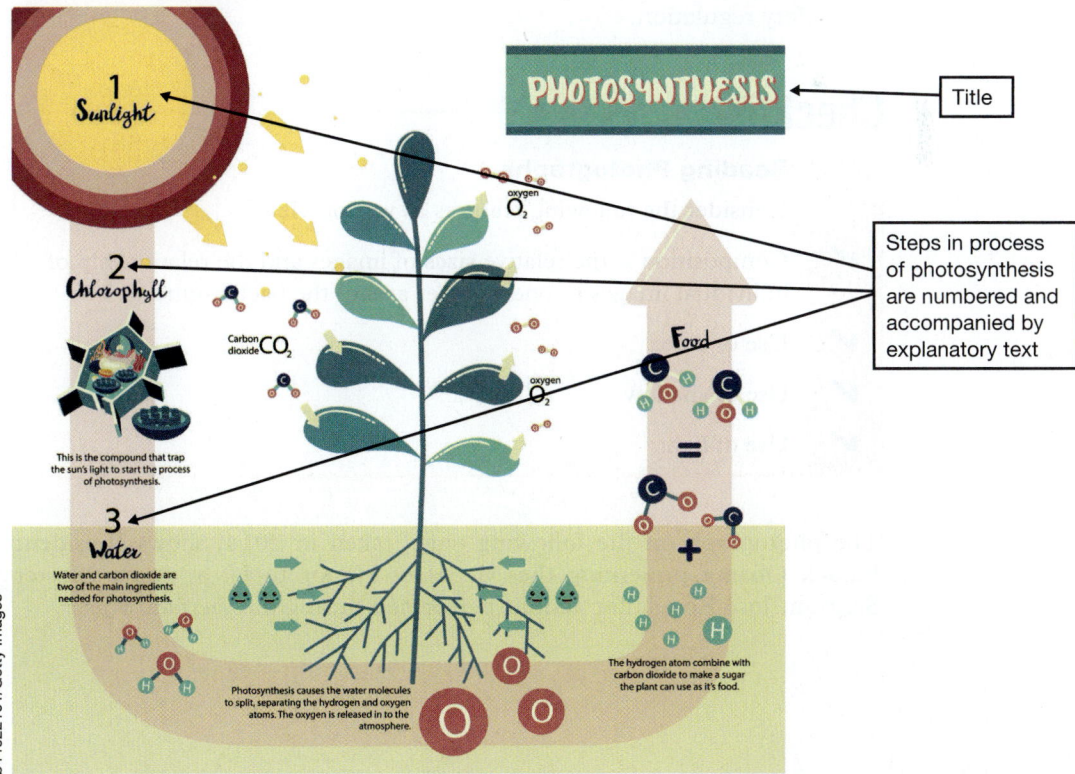

PRACTICE

6-10 Find a diagram on the web or in one of your textbooks. Preview the diagram to identify its key features; then, mark it up and annotate it. Finally, write a paragraph describing the object pictured or explaining the process the diagram illustrates.

Photographs

Photographs are found in textbooks, as well as in magazines and newspapers and on websites, where they can make a discussion more accessible and add visual appeal by breaking up large blocks of text. Photographs are also frequently used to convey information. For example, side-by-side photos of white-only and black-only schools can enrich a textbook description of pre–*Brown v. Board of Education* "separate but equal" schools in the American South. In the same way, a photo of an animal, machine, or landscape can clarify technical discussions in biology, engineering, or earth science, respectively. Photos can also be persuasive, conveying emotion or eliciting sympathy or even shock—as in photos of Appalachia in the 1930s, crowded refugee camps, or victims of violence. Finally, a photo can also be used to advocate a position on a social or political issue. Thus, photos of grieving families of gun-violence victims might be used to make a plea for gun-safety regulation.

Checklist

Reading Photographs

Consider the following features as you preview:

✔ Composition—the relative sizes of images and the relationship of individual images to one another and to the background

✔ Use of color

✔ Use of shadow

✔ Use of light

The photograph on the following page, taken in 2014, shows President Barack Obama presenting the Medal of Honor to U. S. Army Master Sergeant José Rodela for actions performed during the Vietnam War.

PJF Military Collection/Alamy Stock Photo

PRACTICE
6-11 Find a photograph in a newspaper or magazine or on the web. Preview the photograph to identify its key features; then, highlight and annotate it. Finally, write a response paragraph expressing your reaction to the photograph.

Editorial Cartoons

Cartoons can appear in newspapers and magazines, on websites, and even in college textbooks and business reports. Many cartoons are designed solely to entertain or amuse. Thus, a *Dilbert* cartoon might lighten the tone of a business report, and a psychology textbook might use a cartoon to illustrate complicated family dynamics in a lighthearted way.

An **editorial cartoon**, however, is designed to persuade. It takes a position on a controversial issue and conveys that position through an image (often accompanied by a few words of text). Images of people are typically presented as **caricatures**, which exaggerate their most prominent physical features, often for negative effect. Editorial cartoons have a sharp satirical edge, and they are often highly critical of a social or political situation or event, and are designed to provoke discomfort, anger, and even shock. These cartoons, created for newspapers, are often reprinted in other kinds of texts, where they can provide commentary on an issue. For example, a classic editorial cartoon showing a power struggle between Republicans and Democrats that is reprinted in a political science textbook can shed light on today's national political climate.

Checklist

Reading Editorial Cartoons

Consider the following features as you preview:

✔ Presence or absence of written text (in the form of a caption or heading or in dialogue)

✔ How the people depicted are portrayed (sympathetically or negatively)

✔ Facial expressions and body language

✔ Prominent physical features exaggerated for comic or satirical effect

✔ Images that serve as symbols

The following editorial cartoon makes a statement about the issue of steroid use by professional athletes. It has been labeled to show you the key features to look for as you preview an editorial cartoon.

PRACTICE

6-12 Find an editorial cartoon in a print or online newspaper. Preview it to identify its key features; then, mark it up and annotate it. Finally, write a paragraph analyzing its message.

Advertisements

Advertisements appear in newspapers and magazines and on websites and are sometimes reprinted in textbooks to illustrate persuasion techniques. A *public service advertisement*, created by a nonprofit social-action organization such as Mothers Against Drunk Driving, is likely to be informative—for example, citing the decline in highway deaths as a result of the "designated driver" campaign—as well as persuasive, presenting grim pictures of alcohol-related accidents. The purpose of *commercial advertisements* is always persuasive; the creators of these ads want consumers to purchase the products they advertise—anything from designer dresses to dog food—and the ads are designed to make the product appealing (even irresistible) to consumers. Ads created by special-interest groups can get their message across with anything from images that make a simple emotional appeal to shocking images—such as photographs of dead baby seals to protest the annual seal hunt in Alaska.

Checklist

Reading Advertisements

Consider the following features as you preview:

✔ Size and placement of the central image (and its relationship to other images)

✔ The message—such as "Just Do It" or "Friends Don't Let Friends Drive Drunk" (usually appears as a slogan or tagline)

✔ Clues to the ad's intended audience and purpose

✔ Relationship between text and images: How do they work together to convey the ad's central message?

The following public service ad from the U. S. Department of Agriculture has been labeled to show you the key features to look for when you preview an advertisement.

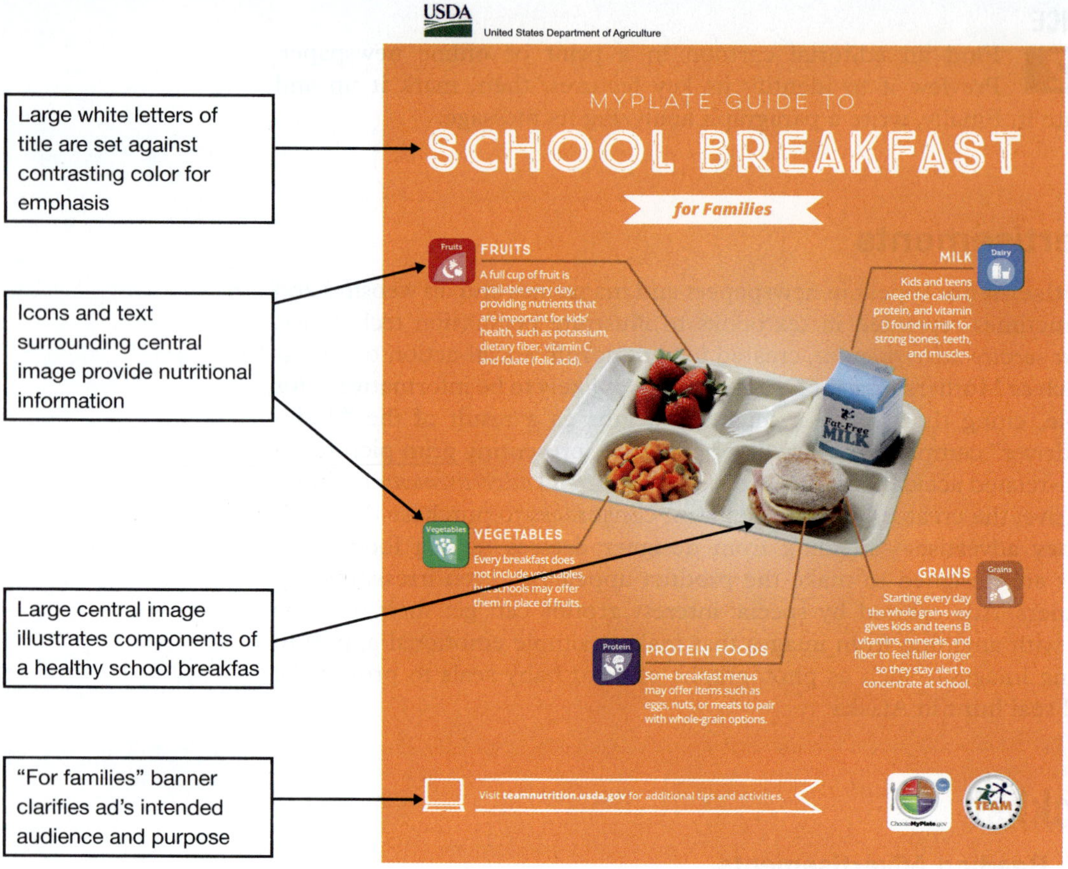

- Large white letters of title are set against contrasting color for emphasis
- Icons and text surrounding central image provide nutritional information
- Large central image illustrates components of a healthy school breakfas
- "For families" banner clarifies ad's intended audience and purpose

USDA, ChooseMyPlate.gov

PRACTICE

6-13 Find an advertisement in a magazine or newspaper or on the web. Preview the ad to identify its key features; then, mark it up and annotate it. Finally, write a paragraph analyzing its purpose, intended audience, and message.

Ivonne Wierink/Shutterstock; sbarabu/Shutterstock; Lauren Burke/Getty Images; Photodisc/Getty Images

FOCUS on reading and writing

Look through your textbooks, and focus your attention on a chapter that is attractively designed and includes visuals as well as written text. Then, write an essay in which you evaluate how the chapter gets its information across. Be sure to consult the Reading Textbooks Checklist on page 167 as well as the relevant checklists for any types of visuals that appear in the textbook chapter you are writing about.

CHAPTER REVIEW

REVIEW ACTIVITY

Graphic Organizer: *Strategies for Previewing Different Kinds of Texts*

Chapter 6 addresses different kinds of texts, both written and visual. In the graphic organizer on pages 194–95, list in the purple box the features you should look for when previewing a written text and in the pink box the features you should look for when previewing a visual text.

Chapter Review

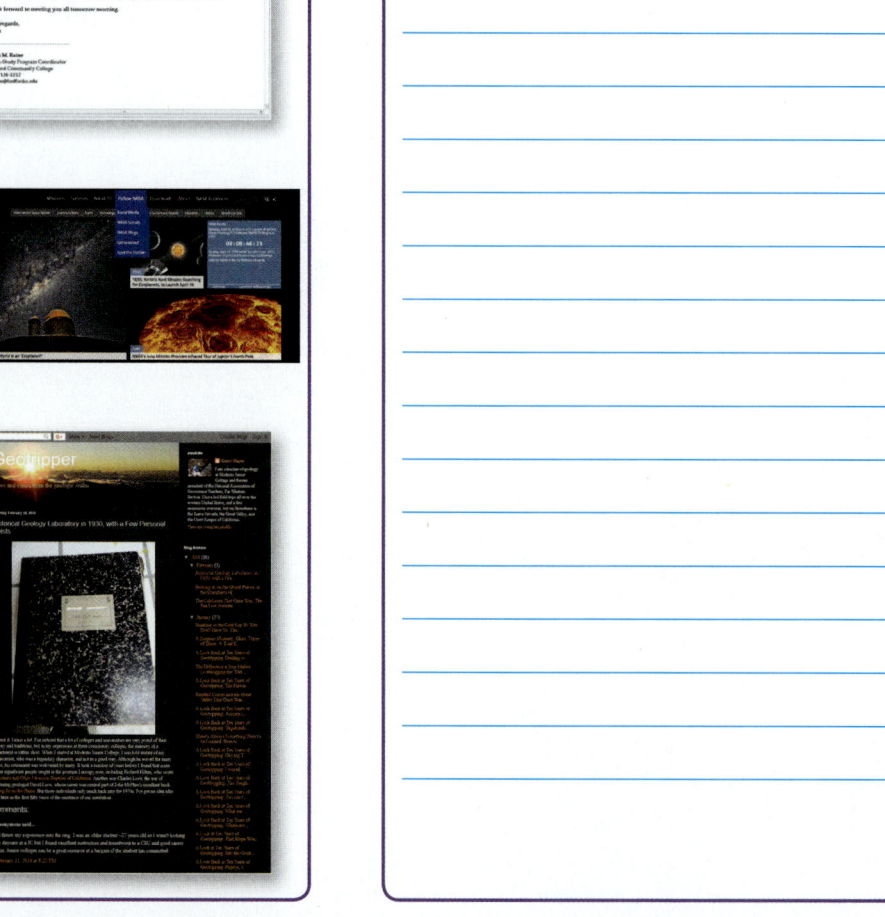

Written Texts

NASA

Geotripper Images

- Chapter titles
- Section headings and subheadings
- Boldfaced and italicized words

Chapter Review

Visuals

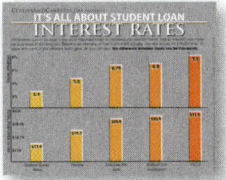

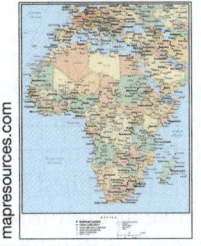

COLLABORATIVE ACTIVITY

Read the following passage from Betty Smith's 1943 novel *A Tree Grows in Brooklyn*. Then, as a group, develop a visual—an ad, cartoon, or diagram, for example—that expresses the passage's main idea.

From *A Tree Grows in Brooklyn*
Betty Smith

The library was a little old shabby place. Francie thought it was beautiful. The feeling she had about it was as good as the feeling she had about church. She pushed open the door and went in. She liked the combined smell of worn leather bindings, library paste and freshly inked stamping pads better than she liked the smell of burning incense at high mass.

Francie thought that all the books in the world were in that library and she had a plan about reading all the books in the world. She was reading a book a day in alphabetical order and not skipping the dry ones. She remembered that the first author had been Abbott. She had been reading a book a day for a long time now and she was still in the B's. Already she had read about bees and buffaloes, Bermuda vacations and Byzantine architecture. For all of her enthusiasm, she had to admit that some of the B's had been hard going. But Francie was a reader. She read everything she could find: trash, classics, time tables and the grocer's price list. Some of the reading had been wonderful; the Louisa Alcott books for example. She planned to read all the books over again when she had finished with the Z's.

Saturdays were different. She treated herself by reading a book not in the alphabetical sequence. On that day she asked the librarian to recommend a book.

Review checklist

Reading and Writing about Different Kinds of Texts

✔ Use active reading strategies to help you understand and write about information in textbooks, news articles, business documents, web pages, and blogs. (See 6a.)

✔ Use active reading strategies to help you interpret and write about information in charts, graphs, and tables; maps; diagrams; photographs; editorial cartoons; and advertisements. (See 6b and 6c.)

unit 2
Reading and Writing Essays

7 Reading and Writing Exemplification Essays 199

8 Reading and Writing Narrative Essays 214

9 Reading and Writing Cause-and-Effect Essays 230

10 Reading and Writing Comparison-and-Contrast Essays 246

11 Reading and Writing Argument Essays 263

12 Additional Options for Organizing Essays 284

7 Reading and Writing Exemplification Essays

travelib/Alamy Stock Photo

FOCUS on reading and writing

Look at this picture of a small-town library, and then brainstorm to discover what you already know about your own community or college library. Is it still relevant in the digital age? What part does it play in your daily life? Later in this chapter, you will read a professional essay on this topic and then have the opportunity to write about it.

PREVIEW

In this chapter, you will learn to
- read an exemplification essay (7a).
- analyze a student exemplification essay (7b).
- write an exemplification essay (7c).

What do we mean when we tell a friend that an instructor is *good* or that a football team is *bad*? What do we mean when we say that a movie is *boring* or that a particular war was *wrong*? To clarify general statements like these, we use **exemplification**—that is, we give **examples** to illustrate a general idea. In daily conversation and in your college courses, you use specific examples to help explain your ideas.

GENERAL STATEMENT	SPECIFIC EXAMPLES
In the future, artificial intelligence is going to help businesses.	In the future, artificial intelligence is going to make businesses leaner, more profitable, and more competitive.
GENERAL STATEMENT	**SPECIFIC EXAMPLES**
Parents should limit their children's access to electronic devices.	Parents should limit screen time on electronic devices such as iPads because they shorten children's attention spans and inhibit social interaction.

Exemplification illustrates a general idea with one or more specific examples. An *exemplification essay* uses specific examples to support a thesis.

7a Read an Exemplification Essay

When you **read** an exemplification essay, follow the active reading process outlined in Chapter 1. You can use **TEST** to help you identify the essay's key elements.

 Thesis In the introduction of an exemplification essay, look for a **thesis** that identifies the writer's main idea—the idea the examples will support. This idea may be explicitly stated in a **thesis statement**, or it may be **implied**, or suggested by the discussion. As you read, ask yourself why the writer chose the option he or she did.

E **Evidence** In the body paragraphs, look for **evidence**—fully developed examples that support the thesis. As you read, note whether the writer uses several short examples or a single long example to support the essay's main idea. Also consider the order in which the writer presents examples. Why was this order chosen? Is it the most effective arrangement? Ask yourself whether there are enough examples. If more are needed, where should they be added? Should the writer have used different examples, or are the ones presented the most effective? In each body paragraph, look for a topic sentence (*often, but not always, at the beginning*) that identifies the example or group of related examples that the paragraph will discuss.

S **Summary** In the concluding paragraphs of an exemplification essay, look for a summary of the writer's key points or a **summary statement** that reinforces the essay's thesis. Does the summary clearly and accurately restate the essay's main idea?

T **Transitions** Try to identify the **transitional words and phrases** that connect examples within paragraphs and between one paragraph and the next. Sometimes a **transitional paragraph** will link sections of the essay. As you read, determine how the transitions connect the different examples. Should the writer have used more transitions? If so, where?

Some Transitional Words and Phrases for Exemplification

Transitional words and phrases introduce examples and indicate how one example is related to another:

also	furthermore	the most important
besides	in addition	example
finally	moreover	the next example
first	one example . . .	
for example	another example	
for instance	specifically	

In an exemplification essay, each body paragraph can develop a single example or discuss several related examples (see the essay maps on the following page). Supporting examples are arranged in **logical order**—for example, from least to most important or from general to specific. The number of examples included depends on the scope of the essay's main idea: A complicated or controversial thesis might require many supporting examples, while a straightforward idea might require just a few.

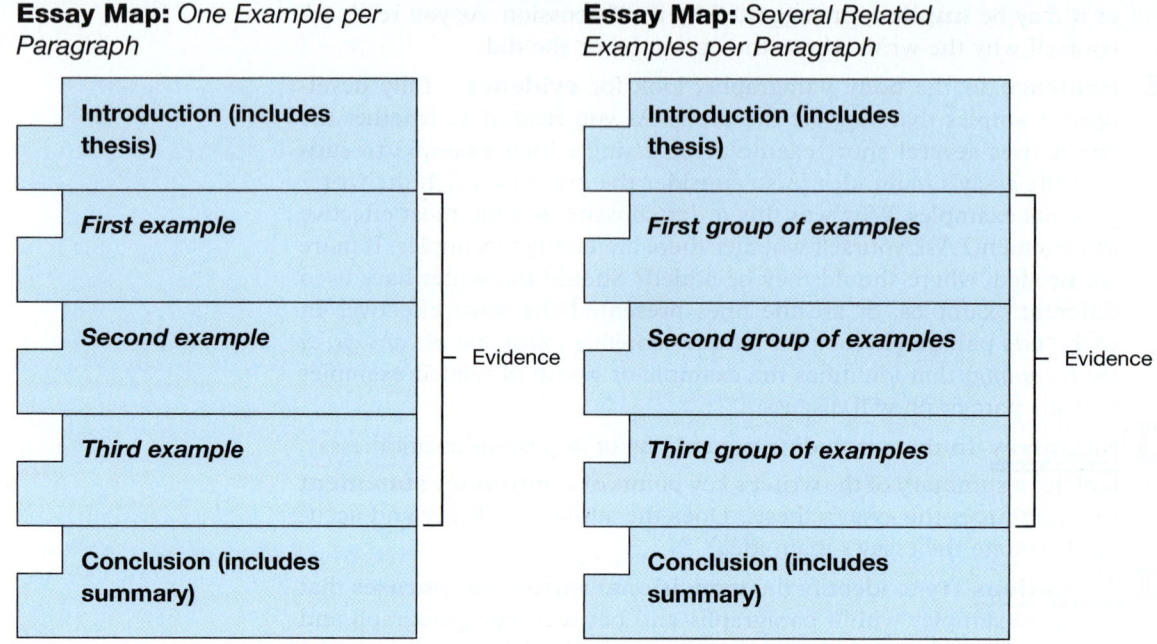

In your college courses, much of your writing will be in response to reading—specifically, to reading texts by professional writers like the one that follows. In this essay, "In Defense of the Small-Town Library," Keshia Mcclantoc supports her thesis with examples. **Read** the essay, following the active reading process outlined in Chapter 1, and then answer the questions that start on page 204. (At the end of this chapter, you will be asked to write an exemplification essay in response to Mcclantoc's ideas.)

In Defense of the Small-Town Library

Keshia Mcclantoc

Keshia Mcclantoc is an M.A. student at the University of Nebraska, Lincoln, focusing on Composition and Rhetoric. She is interested in gender studies, popular culture, and rhetoric. In her essay, "In Defense of the Small-Town Library," published in 2016 in *Odyssey*, Mcclantoc makes the case that neighborhood public libraries serve an important function.

1   In an age where the average five year old can work a smartphone better than me, I feel myself becoming the grumpy old person, rattling off about the "good ol' days" when a book was the best toy ever and the library was

the best playground a kid could ever hope for. When I get this way, I remind myself of those highly exaggerated political comics that portray millennials holding books and asking, "what are these," or "how do I turn this on." The truth is, I gladly embrace technology just as much as I appreciate the feel of a good book in my hands.

2   People who are under the assumption that this is an either/or situation are likely the same people who believe that public libraries are now irrelevant. I do not think libraries are irrelevant, nor do I think they ever will be. Somehow, though, there is an ever-growing assumption that because of the information and access to technology we currently have, we no longer have a need for libraries. Technology does not negate the use of libraries. It adds to them, making the libraries more useful than ever before. Even as technology continues to rise, I believe that the public library has and always will remain the most important part of a town, particularly small towns.

3   The small town that I grew up in is even smaller than the town I currently occupy. When I think of the places I remember the most from childhood, I always have fond thoughts of the library. It essentially functioned as my babysitter when I was a child. When the weekends or summer days were too hot to play outside, my Mom would drop me off at the sweet, air-conditioned oasis where I could be surrounded by a day full of adventure.

4   I always picked out my books first, stacking them near a comfy spot where they would be within easy reach all day. If I grew tired of that, I found myself on the computers, playing around on *MS Paint* or playing *The Oregon Trail*. Without the library in my small town I would not be the person I am today, because I would not have had the early access to books or technology.

5   Like many in that small town we grew up in, we weren't very well off, and the library provided a safe, quiet space where we had access to things that we otherwise wouldn't have had. While I wandered through the books for endless entertainment, the library was providing other people with things that were very necessary. At the library, people could apply for jobs, look up information, or use the computers. While many people like to assume that everyone has access to technology and information, this is not the case. In many small, rural towns—like the one I grew up in, and the one I live in now—the library is the central hub for this.

6   In the town I live in now, Montevallo, the library provides just as much endless entertainment as the library in my hometown did when I was a child. I go to the library about twice a week, the librarians know me by name, and people in the library always greet me with silent nods in hellos of familiarity. In Montevallo, the Parnell Memorial Library provides the same services that my own hometown library provided. People can fill out job applications, find important information, print things, access the internet, find references, or even just browse books for entertainment.

7   This library also functions as a hub for the arts, with an art gallery that constantly displays local artists, and a theater where the Montevallo

Main Street Players put on plays. The library also provides movies nights and other activities for local children, as well as the occasional and very cheap book sale, so that people in the community have the opportunity to own their own books. Parnell Memorial Library rests between Montevallo Elementary School, Orr Park, and The Boys and Girls Club. With placement like that, the library is the center of an area that is brimming with life.

8   I have never entered an empty library. Even on their off days, they have people inside utilizing their services. So why, then, do people believe that libraries are becoming irrelevant? The answer is simple—nostalgia. When people think of libraries, they think of quiet spaces filled only with dusty old bookshelves and cranky librarians. They don't think of libraries as places that provide access to technology and other services, they think only in the limited and thinly veiled terms of nostalgia, when the truth is, libraries are generally at the forefront of technological use.

9   Not only do libraries have access to technology, they often provide services for understanding that technology. At the same time, libraries still have the stacks and stacks of books our nostalgia is familiar with—with many more now available as e-books. Libraries will only become irrelevant if we allow them to, if we allow our nostalgia to overlook the possibility of libraries that are constantly developing and changing to always provide a public good.

10 For me, the biggest defense for the small-town library isn't even all the above information. Instead, my biggest defense for the library is that the library loves anyone and everyone. The small-town public library doesn't demand anything about your background or your beliefs. The library is the ultimate shared space, where anybody, no matter their limitations in life, can find a space that will help them.

Focus on Reading

1. Look back at the work you did when you marked up this essay. Did you number Mcclantoc's key examples? If not, do so now.

2. Now, put a check mark next to the example that most convincingly supports the essay's thesis.

3. **TEST** Mcclantoc's essay. Does she include all four **TEST** elements? If not, why not? What, if anything, does she need to add?

Focus on Meaning

1. According to Mcclantoc, in the age of technology, what assumptions do people make about public libraries? Do you agree with these assumptions?

2. What function do libraries serve in small towns such as the one in which Mcclantoc lives? What, according to Mcclantoc, is "the biggest defense for the small-town library" (para. 10)?

Focus on Strategy

1. Where does Mcclantoc state her thesis? What information does she provide before this? How does this information prepare readers for the thesis?
2. In what order does Mcclantoc present her examples? Does she present the most important example first, or does she begin with the least important example and move to the most important one? What are the advantages (and disadvantages) of her strategy?

Focus on Language and Style

1. In paragraph 8, Mcclantoc says people think that libraries are irrelevant because of nostalgia. What does she mean here by *nostalgia*?
2. What does Mcclantoc mean in paragraph 10 when she says, "The library is the ultimate shared space"?

Focus on the Pattern

1. In paragraph 7, Mcclantoc says that the library in Montevallo is a "hub for the arts." What examples does she give to support this statement?
2. In what paragraphs could Mcclantoc have provided more examples? Are these paragraphs effective as they are, or does the lack of additional examples weaken them?

Focus on Critical Thinking

1. What is the "either/or situation" that Mcclantoc refers to in paragraph 2? Do you agree with her assessment of the situation?
2. Do you think Mcclantoc's points about small-town libraries also apply to libraries in big cities? Why or why not?

7b Analyzing a Student Essay: Exemplification

The following exemplification essay was written by Alison Perry in response to this assignment in a composition class:

> Take a walk around campus, carefully observing people and places. Then, write an exemplification essay that answers the question, "What steps can individual students take to make our campus a better place?"

To help you understand the structure of an exemplification essay, read Alison's essay, following the active reading process outlined in Chapter 1, and then fill in the essay map in Practice 7-1 on pages 207–208. (Note that the **TEST** elements in the essay have been highlighted and color-coded.)

Making a Difference

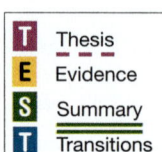

 Thesis

1   Most college students want their campuses to be healthy, productive places to live, work, and learn. Usually, they have opinions about what university leaders should do to make their campuses better. However, many students do not realize how important their own individual contributions can be. In reality, students' attitudes and choices can have a significant impact on the campus culture and environment. This is especially true when it comes to conserving resources and reducing waste. By taking steps to make their schools more energy efficient, students can help to improve the quality of life on campus.

 Transitions

2   First, students can cut down on the amount of electricity they use. This does not require big sacrifices; it just involves a little awareness and a few small changes. Turning off the lights when no one is in the room is a good place to start. However, there are many other ways to avoid waste and save money. For example, students can shut down their computers and electronics rather than putting them in sleep mode. They can also switch off power strips and unplug chargers when they are finished using them. Additionally, students can help their campuses save energy by turning down the thermostat in dorms, offices, and classrooms. Ultimately, by using only the electricity they need, students can make a real contribution to preserving their environment.

Evidence

3   The second way students can help create a more energy-efficient campus is by walking, biking, carpooling, or taking public transportation instead of driving back and forth to school alone. Though these alternatives may require a little more effort (and are not always possible), students can start small. By commuting in one of these ways just once or twice a week, everyone can make a difference and experience the rewards. In addition to reducing their fuel consumption, students who walk or bike to campus get exercise and fresh air, and those who carpool get time to rest or talk with friends. Those who take a bus, subway, or light rail have additional time to study. All of these

alternatives are less expensive, and often less stressful, than driving alone and paying for parking. Moreover, campuses with fewer cars have less traffic and therefore less pollution. They also have less need to put money and resources toward new parking lots and garages. All in all, the payoffs in campus health and happiness make these changes well worth the effort.

4   Finally, students can make a difference by talking to other students about energy-saving choices. For instance, students can let others know why they recycle their used paper rather than throw it in the trash where it cannot be reused. They can explain how filling up water bottles at the tap is less wasteful than buying water in disposable bottles. Furthermore, students can speak up when they see unnecessary energy use, and they can help others come up with creative solutions. For example, if they see an outdoor light left on all night in a campus building, they can talk with someone in charge about using motion-activated lights. If they notice people using Styrofoam takeout containers at the snack bar, they might let diners know that they are allowed to bring their own reusable containers. Often, people are simply not aware that there is another option, and they may be willing to change if they know there is a reasonable, less expensive way. Sharing knowledge and offering new ideas help to create a more thoughtful, more cooperative, and less wasteful community.

5   Though campus-wide projects like constructing new energy-efficient buildings or replacing outdated equipment are important, every student can commit to making small but valuable contributions to energy conservation on his or her own campus. These little changes may seem insignificant. However, when added together, all of the energy-saving choices can strengthen social bonds, encourage cooperation, help students stay fit, and reduce expenses. Students should not underestimate the positive effects of choosing to walk, unplug, turn off, refill, share, and change.

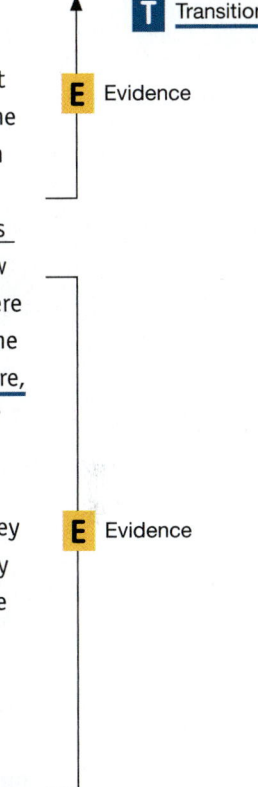

PRACTICE

7-1   Now that you have read Alison's essay, fill in the essay map below to help you understand how she organized her essay. Then, decide whether her organization is effective.

Introduction

First group of examples

Second group of examples

Third group of examples

Conclusion

PRACTICE 7-2

1. Does the thesis statement identify the essay's main idea? Does it indicate that Alison will use exemplification to structure her essay? How?
2. Does she need more examples in any of her body paragraphs? Can you suggest some examples that she could have added?
3. Should any examples be deleted because they are not relevant to the topic or because they are not distinct from other examples?
4. Does the order in which the examples are discussed make sense, or should they be arranged in a different order?
5. What is the essay's greatest strength? What is its greatest weakness?

7c Writing an Exemplification Essay

When you are given a writing assignment, the wording of your assignment may suggest that you write an exemplification essay. For example, you may be asked to *illustrate* or to *give examples*. Once you decide that your assignment calls for exemplification, you need to develop a thesis that reflects this purpose.

ASSIGNMENT	THESIS STATEMENT
Education Should children be taught only in their native languages or in English as well? Support your answer with examples of specific students' experiences.	The success of students in a bilingual third-grade class suggests the value of teaching elementary school students in English as well as in their native languages.
Literature Does William Shakespeare's *Othello* have to end tragically? Illustrate your position with references to specific characters.	Each of the three major characters in *Othello* contributes to the play's tragic ending.
Composition Discuss the worst job you ever had, including plenty of specific examples to support your thesis.	My summer job at a fast-food restaurant was my worst job because of the endless stream of rude customers, the many boring tasks I had to perform, and my manager's insensitivity.

When you **write** an exemplification essay, you follow the process outlined in Chapter 3. The essay you write will include the same elements you have learned to recognize in the exemplification essays you have read. When you finish your draft, you can use **TEST** to make sure it includes all the elements of an exemplification essay.

TESTing Your Exemplification Essay

Thesis Statement Unifies Your Essay

☐ Does your introduction include a thesis statement that identifies your essay's main idea?

☐ Is this main idea expressed in a thesis statement?

Evidence Supports Your Essay's Thesis

☐ Do you have enough evidence—fully developed examples—to support your thesis?

☐ Do all your examples support your thesis?

Summary Statement Reinforces Your Essay's Main Idea

☐ Does your conclusion include a **summary statement** that reinforces your essay's thesis?

Transitions Connect Examples

☐ Do you include transitions that move readers from one example to the next?

Following a Student Writer

Kyle Sims, a student in a first-year writing course, was asked to write an essay about a popular hobby or interest. He decided to use his knowledge by writing about extreme sports.

Once he had settled on a topic, Kyle did some **freewriting** on his laptop. When he read over his freewriting, he saw that he had come up with three kinds of information: ideas about the dangers of extreme sports, about the challenges they present, and about the equipment they require. He then wrote a **thesis statement** that identified the three points he wanted to make. After **brainstorming** about each of these points, he had enough material for a first draft.

As he wrote his **first draft**, Kyle devoted one paragraph to each point, using examples to develop his body paragraphs. When he finished his draft, he **TEST**ed it. He was satisfied with his thesis, which told readers what points he was going to make about extreme sports and also conveyed the idea that they were not like ordinary sports. His summary statement seemed logical and appropriate. However, realizing that his readers might not know much about extreme sports, Kyle added more examples to illustrate a range of different kinds of extreme sports and more **transitions** to lead readers from one example to the next.

When Kyle **revised** his draft, he rewrote his topic sentences so they clearly identified the three points he wanted to make about extreme sports. After he finished his revision, he **edited** and **proofread** carefully and made sure his essay met his instructor's *format* requirements.

The following final draft includes all the elements Kyle looked for when he **TEST**ed his essay. Read Kyle's essay, and then answer the questions in Practice 7-3 on page 211.

Going to Extremes

1   For years, sports like football, baseball, and basketball have been popular in cities, suburbs, and small rural towns. For some young people, however, these sports no longer seem exciting, especially when compared to "extreme sports," such as snowboarding and BMX racing. Extreme sports are different from more familiar sports because they are dangerous, they are physically challenging, and they require specialized equipment.

2   First, extreme sports are dangerous. For example, snowboarders take chances with snowy hills and unpredictable bumps. They zoom down mountains at high speeds, which is typical of extreme sports. In addition, snowboarders and skateboarders risk painful falls as they do their tricks. Also, many extreme sports, like rock climbing, bungee jumping, and skydiving, are performed at very high altitudes. Moreover, the bungee jumper has to jump from a very high place, and there is always a danger of getting tangled with the bungee cord. People who participate in extreme sports accept—and even enjoy—these dangers.

3   In addition, extreme sports are very difficult. For instance, surfers have to learn to balance surfboards while dealing with wind and waves. Bungee jumpers may have to learn how to do difficult stunts while jumping off a high bridge or a dam. Another example of the physical challenge of extreme sports can be found in BMX racing. BMX racers have to learn to steer a lightweight bike on a dirt track that has jumps and banked corners. These extreme sports require skills that most people do not naturally have. These special skills have to be learned, and participants in extreme sports enjoy this challenge.

4   Finally, almost all extreme sports require specialized equipment. For example, surfers need surfboards that are light but strong. They can choose epoxy boards, which are stronger, or fiberglass boards, which are lighter. They can choose shortboards, which are shorter than seven feet and are easier to maneuver, or they can use longboards, which are harder and slower to turn in the water but are easier to learn on. Also, surfers have to get special wax for their boards to keep from slipping as they are paddling out into the water. For surfing in cold water, they need wetsuits that trap their body heat. Other extreme sports require different kinds of specialized equipment, but those who participate in them are willing to buy whatever they need.

5   Clearly, extreme sports are very different from other sports. Maybe it is because they are so different that they have become so popular in recent years. Already, snowboarding, BMX racing, and other extreme sports are featured in the Olympics. The Summer and Winter X Games are televised on ESPN and ABC, and sports like BMX racing, snowboarding, surfing, and snowmobiling get national attention on these programs. With all this publicity, extreme sports are likely to become even more popular—despite their challenges.

PRACTICE 7-3

1. Underline Kyle's thesis statement; then, restate it in your own words.
2. What evidence does Kyle present to support his thesis? For instance, what examples of extreme sports does he give in paragraph 1? What examples of dangers does he give in paragraph 2?
3. Circle some of the transitional words and phrases Kyle uses to move from one example to another.
4. Underline Kyle's summary statement. Then, restate it in your own words.
5. Use **TEST** to evaluate Kyle's essay. What revisions would you suggest he make? Why?

Grammar in context

Exemplification

When you write an exemplification essay, you may introduce your examples with transitional words and phrases like *First* or *In addition*. If you do, be sure to use a comma after the transitional word or phrase.

> <mark>First,</mark> extreme sports are dangerous.
>
> <mark>In addition,</mark> extreme sports are very difficult.
>
> <mark>Finally,</mark> almost all extreme sports require specialized equipment.

For information on using commas with introductory and transitional words and phrases, see 26b.

FOCUS on Reading and Writing: Exemplification

Reread Keshia Mcclantoc's essay, "In Defense of the Small-Town Library," on p. 202. Then, write your own exemplification essay in response to one of the following prompts. (Review the image and text that open this chapter before you choose a topic.) Be sure to follow the writing process outlined in Chapter 3.

1. Write an exemplification essay in which you answer the question, "Do we still need libraries?" Support your thesis with specific examples. You may focus on one example in each body paragraph, or you can combine several related examples in some of your paragraphs.

2. Do you consider your college library a valuable resource? Write an essay in which you answer this question. Be sure to discuss your library's strengths as well as its shortcomings, and illustrate your points with specific examples from your own experience.

If you prefer, you can write on one of the additional topics listed below:

- Reasons to start (or not start) college right after high school
- The three best products ever invented
- Athletes who really are role models
- National or world news events that gave you hope

Reread the draft of your essay, and then **TEST** it. When you have finished, revise, edit, and proofread your essay.

CHAPTER REVIEW

COLLABORATIVE ACTIVITY

Read the essay that another student wrote in response to one of this chapter's writing prompts. Then, work with that student to consider the strengths and weaknesses of both of your exemplification essays. Do you think one of your essays is more effective than the other? If so, why? Based on your reactions to the essays you and your classmate wrote, write a few sentences explaining what an exemplification essay should accomplish.

Review checklist

Reading and Writing Exemplification Essays

✔ When you *read* an exemplification essay, follow the reading process outlined in Chapter 1, and use **TEST** to help you identify the essay's key elements. (See 7a.)

✔ Analyzing a student essay can help you understand the structure of an exemplification essay. (See 7b.)

✔ Keep in mind that in college courses, you often write in response to reading. (See 7c.)

8 Reading and Writing Narrative Essays

© Lynda Barry. Used with permission by Drawn & Quarterly

FOCUS on reading and writing

Look at the image above, which shows four panels from *One! Hundred! Demons!*, a graphic memoir by Lynda Barry about her childhood. Brainstorm to discover what you remember about your own elementary-school experiences. Later in this chapter, you will read an essay on this topic and then have an opportunity to write about it.

> **PREVIEW**
>
> In this chapter, you will learn to
> - read a narrative essay (8a).
> - analyze a student narrative essay (8b).
> - write a narrative essay (8c).

Narration is writing that tells a personal or fictional story or traces a series of events. For example, a narrative could tell how you were changed by an experience you had as a child, how the life of Martin Luther King Jr. helped him to develop as a civil rights leader, or how the Battle of Gettysburg became the turning point in the Civil War.

A narrative usually presents events in chronological (time) order, moving from beginning to end. Sometimes, however, to add interest to a narrative, a writer may decide to start at the end of a story and then move back to the beginning to trace the events that led to the outcome.

> **WORD POWER**
>
> **memoir** a collection of memories about a writer's life

 ## 8a Reading a Narrative Essay

When you **read** a narrative essay, follow the active reading process outlined in Chapter 1. You can use **TEST** to help you identify the essay's key elements.

T **Thesis** In the introduction of a narrative essay, look for a **thesis** that identifies the writer's main idea—the point the narrative is making. This idea may be explicitly stated in a **thesis statement**, or it may be **implied**, suggested by the writer's choice of events and details and the way they are arranged. As you read, ask yourself why the writer chose the option he or she did.

E **Evidence** In the body paragraphs, look for the events that tell the story. Each event will present **evidence**—examples and details—to support the thesis. Events are usually presented in chronological (time) order, but they can be presented in any order—for example, a narrative could begin at the end or in the middle and then move back to the beginning. As you read, consider why the writer chose a particular arrangement of events. Then, determine whether the writer has presented enough events and whether the ones chosen are the most pertinent. If additional events, or more examples and details, are needed, where should they be added? In each body paragraph, look for the topic sentence (often, but not always, at the beginning) that introduces the event or group of related events that the paragraph will discuss.

215

S **Summary** Look for a summary of the key events or a **summary statement** that reinforces the essay's thesis in the concluding paragraph of a narrative essay. Ask yourself whether the summary clearly and accurately restates the essay's main idea.

T **Transitions** Try to identify the **transitional words and phrases** that connect events in time within paragraphs and between one paragraph and the next, showing how one event leads to the next. Sometimes a **transitional paragraph** will link sections of the essay. As you read, determine how the transitions connect the different events. Should the writer have used more transitions? If so, where?

> ### Some Transitional Words and Phrases for Narration
>
> Transitional words and phrases help readers follow a narrative by indicating the order in which events occurred:
>
> | | | |
> |---|---|---|
> | after | eventually | next |
> | as | finally | now |
> | as soon as | first . . . second . . . third | soon |
> | at first | | then |
> | at the same time | immediately | two hours (days, months, years) later |
> | before | later | |
> | by this time | later on | |
> | earlier | meanwhile | when |

In a narrative essay, each body paragraph can discuss one event or several events. The topic sentence of the first body paragraph introduces the first event (or first group of events) that the paragraph will discuss. The events and details presented in the body paragraphs support the essay's thesis, and events are generally arranged in chronological order. (See the essay maps on the following page that illustrate this pattern.)

In your college courses, much of your writing will be in response to reading—specifically, to reading texts by professional writers, such as the one that follows. This essay, "The Sanctuary of School," by Lynda Barry, is a narrative about the writer's childhood. **Read** the essay, following the active reading process outlined in Chapter 1, and then answer the questions that start on page 220. At the end of this chapter, you will be asked to **write** a narrative essay of your own in response to Barry's ideas.

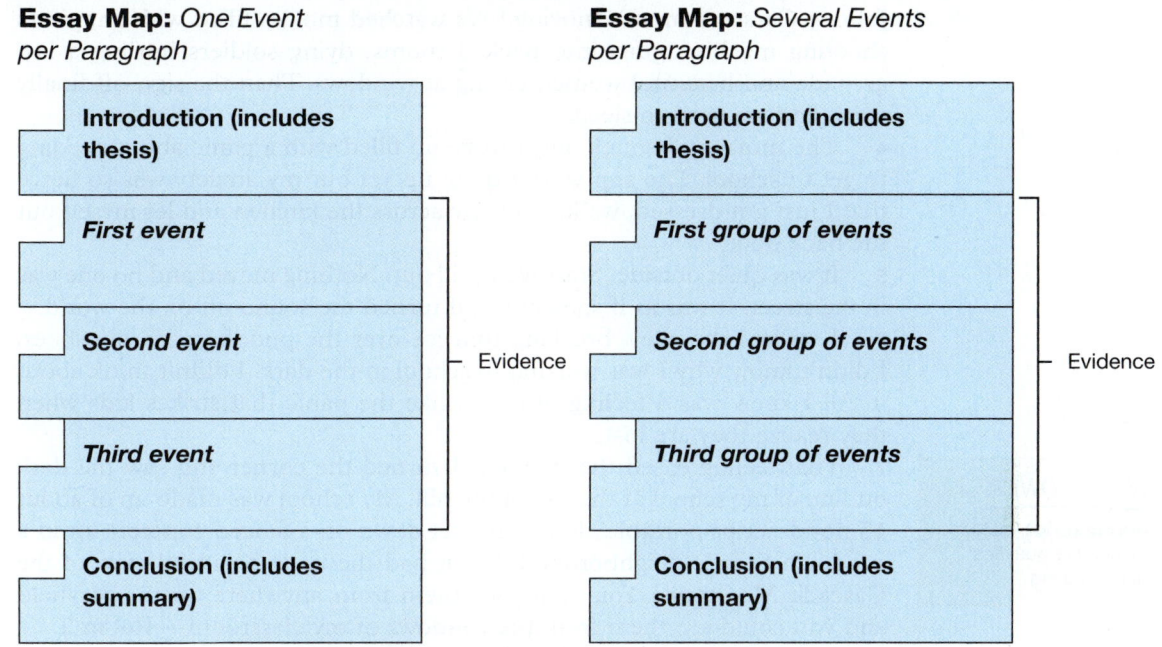

The Sanctuary of School
Lynda Barry

In her many illustrated works — including graphic novels, comic books, and a weekly cartoon strip, *Ernie Pook's Comeek*, which appears in a number of newspapers and magazines — Lynda Barry looks at the world through the eyes of children. Her characters remind adult readers of the complicated world of young people and of the clarity with which they see social situations. In "The Sanctuary of School," first published in *The Baltimore Sun* in 1992, Barry tells a story from her own childhood.

Before you read, think about the strategies you used to cope with difficult periods in your own childhood.

1 I was 7 years old the first time I snuck out of the house in the dark. It was winter and my parents had been fighting all night. They were short on money and long on relatives who kept "temporarily" moving into our house because they had nowhere else to go.

2 My brother and I were used to giving up our bedroom. We slept on the couch, something we actually liked because it put us that much closer to the light of our lives, our television.

3 At night when everyone was asleep, we lay on our pillows watching it with the sound off. We watched Steve Allen's mouth moving. We watched

Johnny Carson's mouth moving.[1] We watched movies filled with gangsters shooting machine guns into packed rooms, dying soldiers hurling a last grenade and beautiful women crying at windows. Then the sign-off finally came and we tried to sleep.

4   The morning I snuck out, I woke up filled with a panic about needing to get to school. The sun wasn't quite up yet but my anxiety was so fierce that I just got dressed, walked quietly across the kitchen and let myself out the back door.

5   It was quiet outside. Stars were still out. Nothing moved and no one was in the street. It was as if someone had turned the sound off on the world.

6   I walked the alley, breaking thin ice over the puddles with my shoes. I didn't know why I was walking to school in the dark. I didn't think about it. All I knew was a feeling of panic, like the panic that strikes kids when they realize they are lost.

7   That feeling eased the moment I turned the corner and saw the dark outline of my school at the top of the hill. My school was made up of about 15 nondescript portable classrooms set down on a fenced concrete lot in a rundown Seattle neighborhood, but it had the most beautiful view of the Cascade Mountains. You could see them from anywhere on the playfield and you could see them from the windows of my classroom—Room 2.

8   I walked over to the monkey bars and hooked my arms around the cold metal. I stood for a long time just looking across Rainier Valley. The sky was beginning to whiten and I could hear a few birds.

9   In a perfect world my absence at home would not have gone unnoticed. I would have had two parents in a panic to locate me, instead of two parents in a panic to locate an answer to the hard question of survival during a deep financial and emotional crisis.

10   But in an overcrowded and unhappy home, it's incredibly easy for any child to slip away. The high levels of frustration, depression and anger in my house made my brother and me invisible. We were children with the sound turned off. And for us, as for the steadily increasing number of neglected children in this country, the only place where we could count on being noticed was at school.

11   "Hey there, young lady. Did you forget to go home last night?" It was Mr. Gunderson, our janitor, whom we all loved. He was nice and he was funny and he was old with white hair, thick glasses and an unbelievable number of keys. I could hear them jingling as he walked across the playfield. I felt incredibly happy to see him.

12   He let me push his wheeled garbage can between the different portables as he unlocked each room. He let me turn on the lights and raise the window shades and I saw my school slowly come to life. I saw Mrs. Holman, our school secretary, walk into the office without her orange lipstick on yet. She waved.

13   I saw the fifth-grade teacher Mr. Cunningham, walking under the breezeway eating a hard roll. He waved.

> **WORD POWER**
> **nondescript** lacking distinctive qualities; uninteresting

[1] Steve Allen and Johnny Carson were late-night television hosts.

14   And I saw my teacher, Mrs. Claire LeSane, walking toward us in a red coat and calling my name in a very happy and surprised way, and suddenly my throat got tight and my eyes stung and I ran toward her crying. It was something that surprised us both.

15   It's only thinking about it now, 28 years later, that I realize I was crying from relief. I was with my teacher, and in a while I was going to sit at my desk, with my crayons and pencils and books and classmates all around me, and for the next six hours I was going to enjoy a thoroughly secure, warm and stable world. It was a world I absolutely relied on. Without it, I don't know where I would have gone that morning.

16   Mrs. LeSane asked me what was wrong and when I said "Nothing," she seemingly left it at that. But she asked me if I would carry her purse for her, an honor above all honors, and she asked if I wanted to come into Room 2 early and paint.

17   She believed in the natural healing power of painting and drawing for troubled children. In the back of her room there was always a drawing table and an easel with plenty of supplies, and sometimes during the day she would come up to you for what seemed like no good reason and quietly ask if you wanted to go to the back table and "make some pictures for Mrs. LeSane." We all had a chance at it—to sit apart from the class for a while to paint, draw and silently work out impossible problems on 11 × 17 sheets of newsprint.

18   Drawing came to mean everything to me. At the back table in Room 2, I learned to build myself a life preserver that I could carry into my home.

19   We all know that a good education system saves lives, but the people of this country are still told that cutting the budget for public schools is necessary, that poor salaries for teachers are all we can manage and that art, music and all creative activities must be the first to go when times are lean.

20   Before- and after-school programs are cut and we are told that public schools are not made for baby-sitting children. If parents are neglectful temporarily or permanently, for whatever reason, it's certainly sad, but their unlucky children must fend for themselves. Or slip through the cracks. Or wander in a dark night alone.

WORD POWER
fend to manage

21   We are told in a thousand ways that not only are public schools not important, but that the children who attend them, the children who need them most, are not important either. We leave them to learn from the blind eye of a television, or to the mercy of "a thousand points of light"[2] that can be as far away as stars.

22   I was lucky. I had Mrs. LeSane. I had Mr. Gunderson. I had an abundance of art supplies. And I had a particular brand of neglect in my home that allowed me to slip away and get to them. But what about the rest of the kids who weren't as lucky? What happened to them?

23   By the time the bell rang that morning I had finished my drawing and Mrs. LeSane pinned it up on the special bulletin board she reserved for drawings from the back table. It was the same picture I always drew—a sun in the corner of a blue sky over a nice house with flowers all around it.

---

[2] Phrase used by former president George Herbert Walker Bush to promote volunteerism.

24   Mrs. LeSane asked us to please stand, face the flag, place our right hands over our hearts and say the Pledge of Allegiance. Children across the country do it faithfully. I wonder now when the country will face its children and say a pledge right back.

Focus on Reading

1. Look back at the work you did when you previewed, marked up, and annotated this essay. What do you think the word *sanctuary* means? Look through the essay for **context clues** that can help you understand this word, and write a brief definition in the margin. (Write a question mark beside your definition to remind yourself to look the word up later on.)
2. Circle the names of the key people featured in this essay. In the margin beside each name, write a few words to identify each person.
3. **TEST** Barry's essay. Does she include all four **TEST** elements? If not, why not? What, if anything, should be added?

Focus on Meaning

1. In paragraph 10, Barry characterizes herself and her brother as "children with the sound turned off." What do you think she means?
2. How are Barry's home and school worlds different? Identify specific negative features of her home life and specific positive features of her school life.
3. A number of adults came to Barry's rescue during her childhood. Who were these adults? What did each one contribute?

Focus on Strategy

1. What point is Barry making in paragraph 10? In paragraphs 20–21? In her conclusion? To whom does she seem to be addressing her comments? Explain.
2. What is the main idea of Barry's essay—the idea she wants to convince readers to accept? Is this idea actually stated in her essay? If so, where? If not, do you think it should be?

Focus on Language and Style

1. Look up the word *sanctuary* in several different dictionaries. Which of the definitions do you think comes closest to Barry's meaning? Why?
2. Now, look up the word *sanctuary* in a thesaurus. What synonyms are listed? Would any other word be a better choice in Barry's title? Explain.

Focus on the Pattern

1. Paragraphs 9–10 and 19–22 interrupt Barry's narrative. What purpose do these paragraphs serve? Do you think the essay would be more effective if paragraphs 9 and 10 came earlier? If paragraphs 19–22 came after paragraph 24? Explain.

2. What transitional words and phrases does Barry use in her narrative to move readers from one event to the next? Do you think her essay needs more transitions? If so, where should they be added?

Focus on Critical Thinking

1. Do you see Barry's narrative primarily as a story of her childhood or as a persuasive essay with a message about needed social change? Why? Specifically, what do you think she expected her essay to accomplish?
2. This essay was first published in *The Baltimore Sun*, a newspaper with a wide general audience. Which sections of the essay do you think would have the strongest impact on this audience? What different reactions would you expect readers to have? Why?

8b Analyzing a Student Essay: Narration

The following narrative essay was written by Erica Sarno in response to this assignment in a first-year writing course.

> Write a literacy narrative, a personal account that traces your development as a reader or writer during a particular period of your life.

To help you understand the structure of a narrative essay, read Erica's essay, following the active reading process outlined in Chapter 1, and then fill in the essay map in Practice 8-1 on page 223. (Note that the **TEST** elements in the essay have been highlighted and color-coded.)

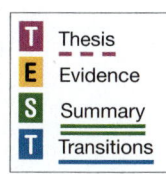

Becoming a Writer

1   I used to think that writing was just about filling pages. Composing an essay for school meant getting the job done and checking it off my to-do list. During my last two years of high school, however, my attitude started to change. Several experiences helped me understand that writing is not a skill that some people are born with and others are not. If I wanted to write, all I needed was a desire to express myself to others and a willing audience. <u>Realizing that there was someone on the other side of the page, eager to listen, helped me develop into a more active reader and more effective writer.</u>

 Thesis

2   <u>My first real lesson in my development as a writer took place in Mrs. Strickland's Junior English class.</u> Mrs. Strickland was hard to approach. She dressed as if she expected to be giving a press conference at the White

 Transitions

House. She wore tan suits and silk scarves and had a helmet of dyed blonde hair. We seemed to disappoint her just because we were high school students. Maybe I saw her lack of interest in us and our work as a challenge because, one day, I took a risk and wrote a very personal essay about losing my aunt to cancer. When I got the paper back, Mrs. Strickland had written only, "Did you read the instructions?" I could not believe it. For the first time, I had actually written about what was important to me rather than just filling the pages with words, and she had not even read past the introduction! Still, I knew then that I had something to say. I just needed someone to listen.

3   The next year, I had Dr. Kelleher for Senior English. My year with Dr. K profoundly changed the way I see myself as a writer (and as a reader). Finally, a teacher was paying attention to what I had written. His only rule for writing was "Don't be boring!" I rewrote sentences, hoping for an exclamation point or one of Dr. K's other special marks in the margin. Dr. K had a whole list of codes and abbreviations, like "BTH" ("Better than Hemingway") or "the knife" (when the writer slayed the opponent in an argument). I also relied on Dr. K to tell me when I was falling into my old habit of just filling the page. He would write a funny comment like, "Come back! Log out of Facebook!" Then, he would give me a chance to try again. Trusting him to be a generous reader and an honest critic helped me develop my voice and my confidence as a writer.

4   Meanwhile, I started to become a better reader, too. I could tell when a writer was writing to me, wanting me to understand. I could also tell when a writer was writing to just get the job done. Instead of just skimming the assigned reading, I got in the habit of writing in the margins and making notes about what I thought. I underlined ideas that spoke to me, and I wrote "Really??" next to ideas that seemed silly. Instead of assuming a reading would be boring, I gave every assignment a chance. Whether I liked the book or not, I felt that I could explain my reasons. I was finally seeing for myself that writing is just another way for people to talk to each other.

Eventually, in the spring of my senior year, I experienced what it feels like to connect with a broader audience. I suggested a column about "senioritis" to the school paper, and even though I had never written for the public before, the editor loved my idea. I knew what I wanted to say, and I knew I could collect plenty of stories to help me illustrate my ideas. What I did not predict was how much I would learn from the experience of writing those six columns. Knowing that hundreds of people would be reading my pieces, I revised them over and over again. When Dr. K read one of my last columns aloud to our class, I got to see how my work affected people. Watching the expressions on my classmates' faces and hearing them laugh at the funny parts helped me understand what good writing is. <u>In that moment</u>, I truly connected with my audience.

Although I still have a lot to learn, I now understand how important the relationship between the writer and the reader is. When I write, I am writing to be heard. When I read, I am reading to understand. The communication may not be perfect, but I know I am not alone in my task. And even though I am not in Dr. K's class anymore, I still sometimes imagine that he will be reading what I have written. Thinking about him reminds me that someone cares about what I have to say.

S Summary

PRACTICE 8-1

Now that you have read Erica's essay, fill in the following essay map to help you understand how she organized her essay. Then, decide whether her organization is effective.

Introduction _____
_____
_____

First event _____
_____
_____

Second event _____
_____
_____

Third event _____
_____
_____

Fourth event _____
_____
_____

Conclusion _____
_____
_____

PRACTICE 8-2

1. Does Erica's thesis statement suggest that she will use narration to structure her essay? If so, how?
2. List the key events in this narrative.
3. Does any body paragraph need additional examples or details? If so, where should additional evidence be added?
4. Does the order in which events are discussed make sense? Could the events have been arranged in any other way?
5. What is the essay's greatest strength? What is its greatest weakness?

8c Writing a Narrative Essay

When you are given a writing assignment, the wording of your assignment may suggest that you write a narrative essay. For example, you may be asked to *tell*, *trace*, *summarize events*, or *recount*. Once you decide that your assignment calls for narration, you need to develop a thesis statement that reflects this purpose.

ASSIGNMENT	THESIS STATEMENT
Composition Tell about a time when you had to show courage even though you were afraid.	In extraordinary circumstances, a person can exhibit great courage and overcome fear.
American history Summarize the events that occurred during President Franklin Delano Roosevelt's first one hundred days in office.	Although many thought they were extreme, the measures enacted by Roosevelt during his first one hundred days in office were necessary to fight the economic depression.
Political science Trace the development of the Mississippi Freedom Democratic Party.	As the Mississippi Freedom Democratic Party developed, it found a voice that spoke for equality and justice.

When you **write** a narrative essay, you follow the process outlined in Chapter 3. The essay you write will include the same elements you have learned to recognize in the narrative essays you read. When you finish your draft, you can use **TEST** to make sure it includes all the elements of a narrative essay.

> ## TESTing your narrative essay
>
> **T**hesis Statement Unifies Your Essay
>
> ☐ Does your introduction include a **thesis statement** that clearly states your essay's main idea?
>
> **E**vidence Supports Your Essay's Thesis Statement
>
> ☐ Does all your **evidence**—events and details—support your thesis, or should some be deleted?
>
> ☐ Have you included enough specific details to make your narrative interesting?
>
> ☐ Are the events you discuss arranged in clear chronological (time) order?
>
> **S**ummary Statement Reinforces Your Essay's Main Idea
>
> ☐ Does your conclusion include a **summary statement** that reinforces your essay's thesis?
>
> **T**ransitions Connect Events
>
> ☐ Do you include enough **transitions** to make the sequence of events clear to your reader?

Following a Student Writer

Elaina Corrato, a returning student who was older than most of her classmates, wasn't sure how to proceed when her writing instructor gave the class an assignment to write about a milestone in their lives. The first topic that came to mind was her recent thirtieth birthday, but she was reluctant to reveal her age to her classmates. However, when she learned that no one except her instructor would read her essay, she decided to write about this topic.

    Elaina began by rereading entries she had made in her **journal** in the days before and after her birthday as well as on the day itself. Even before she began to write, she saw that her essay would be a narrative that traced her reactions to the events she experienced on that day.

    As she **drafted** her essay, Elaina was careful to discuss events in the order in which they occurred and to include transitional words and phrases to move her discussion smoothly from one event to the next. Because she knew what she wanted to say, she found it easy to write a well-developed

> **WORD POWER**
>
> **milestone** an important event; a turning point

first draft that included plenty of information. When she **TEST**ed her essay, however, Elaina saw at once that she had not stated a thesis or included a summary statement to reinforce her main idea.

At this point, Elaina emailed her draft to her instructor and asked him for suggestions. (Her instructor offered this option to students whose off-campus work or family commitments made it difficult for them to schedule face-to-face conferences.) He explained that her thesis should not be just a general overview of the day's events; instead, it should make a point about how those events affected her. With this advice, Elaina found it was not difficult to write a thesis that expressed how she felt about turning thirty. Once she had a **thesis statement**, she was able to add a summary statement that reinforced her main idea, ending her essay on an optimistic note. With all the required elements in place, she continued **revising** and went on to **edit** and **proofread** her essay.

Read Elaina's essay, and then answer the questions in Practice 8-3 on page 227.

Reflections

1   Turning thirty did not bother me at all. My list of "Things to Do before I Die" was far from complete, but I knew I had plenty of time to do them. In fact, turning thirty seemed like no big deal to me. If anything, it was a milestone I was happy to be approaching. Unfortunately, other people had different ideas about this milestone, and eventually their ideas made me rethink my own.

2   As the big day approached, my family kept teasing me about it. My sister kept asking me if I felt any different. She couldn't believe I wasn't upset, but I didn't pay any attention to her. I was looking forward to a new chapter in my life. I liked my job, I was making good progress toward my college degree, and I was healthy and happy. Why should turning thirty be a problem? So, I made no special plans for my birthday, and I decided to treat it as just another day.

3   My birthday fell on a Saturday, and I enjoyed the chance to sleep in. After I got up and had breakfast, I did my laundry and then set out for the supermarket. I rarely put on makeup or fixed my hair on Saturdays. After all, I didn't have to go to work or to school. I was only running errands in the neighborhood. Later on, though, as I waited in line at the deli counter, I caught sight of my reflection in the mirrored meat case. At first, I thought it wasn't really me. The woman staring back at me looked so old! She had bags under her eyes, and she even had a few gray hairs. I was so upset by my reflection that on my way home I stopped and bought a mud mask—guaranteed to make me look younger.

4   As I walked up the street toward my house, I saw something attached to the front railing. When I got closer, I realized that it was a bunch of black balloons. There was also a big sign that said "Over the Hill" in big black letters. I'd been trying to think about my birthday in positive terms, but my family seemed to have other ideas. Obviously, it was time for the mud mask.

5   After quickly unloading my groceries, I ran upstairs to apply the mask. The box promised a "rejuvenating look," and that was exactly what I wanted. I spread the sticky brown mixture on my face, and it hardened instantly. As I sat on my bed, waiting for the mask to work its magic, I heard the doorbell ring. Then, I heard familiar voices and my husband calling me to come down, saying that I had company. I couldn't answer him. I couldn't talk (or even smile) without cracking the mask. At this point, I retreated to the bathroom to make myself presentable for my friends and family. This task was not easy.

6   When I managed to scrub off the mud mask, my face was covered with little red pimples. Apparently, my sensitive skin couldn't take the harsh chemicals. At first, I didn't think the promise of "rejuvenated" skin was what I got. I had to admit, though, that my skin did look a lot younger. In fact, when I finally went downstairs to celebrate my birthday, I looked as young as a teenager—a teenager with acne.

7   Despite other people's grim warnings, I discovered that although turning thirty was a milestone, it wasn't a game-changer. I learned a lot that day, and I learned even more in the days that followed. What I finally realized was that I couldn't ignore turning thirty, but having a thirtieth birthday didn't have to mean that my life was over.

PRACTICE 8-3

1. Underline the thesis statement of "Reflections"; then, rewrite it in your own words.
2. What specific events and details support Elaina's thesis? List as many pieces of evidence as you can.
3. Circle some of the transitional words and phrases Elaina uses to move readers from one event to the next.
4. Underline Elaina's summary statement. Do you think her summary statement effectively reinforces her essay's main idea?
5. Use **TEST** to evaluate Elaina's essay. What revisions would you recommend? Why?

Grammar in context

Narration

When you write a narrative essay, you tell a story. When you get caught up in your story, you might sometimes find yourself stringing details together without proper punctuation, creating a **run-on**.

INCORRECT	As the big day approached, my family kept teasing me about it, my sister kept asking me if I felt any different.
CORRECT	As the big day approached, my family kept teasing me about it. My sister kept asking me if I felt any different.

For information on how to identify and correct run-ons, see Chapter 21.

FOCUS on reading and writing: Narration

Reread Lynda Barry's essay, "The Sanctuary of School," (p. 217). Then, write your own narrative essay in response to one of the following prompts. (Review the images and text that open this chapter before you choose a topic.) Be sure to follow the writing process outlined in Chapter 3.

1. Did you see elementary school as a "sanctuary" or as something quite different? Write a narrative essay that conveys to readers what school meant to you when you were a child.

2. In addition to school, television was a sanctuary for Barry and her brother. Did television watching (or some other activity) serve this function for you when you were younger? Is there some activity that fills this role now? In a narrative essay, write about your own "sanctuary."

If you prefer, you can write on one of the additional topics listed below:

- A perfect day
- A day on which everything went wrong
- A story from your family's history
- A biography of your pet

Reread the draft of your narrative essay, and then **TEST** it. When you have finished, revise, edit, and proofread your essay.

CHAPTER REVIEW

COLLABORATIVE ACTIVITY

Read the essay that another student wrote in response to one of this chapter's writing prompts. Then, work with that student to consider the strengths and weaknesses of both of your narrative essays. Do you think one of your essays is more effective than the other one? If so, why? Based on your assessment of the essays you and your classmate wrote, write a few sentences explaining what a narrative essay should accomplish.

Review checklist

Reading and Writing Narrative Essays

✔ When you *read* a narrative essay, follow the active reading process outlined in Chapter 1, and use **TEST** to help you identify the essay's key elements. (See 8a.)

✔ Analyzing a student essay can help you understand the structure of a narrative essay. (See 8b.)

✔ When you *write* a narrative essay, follow the writing process outlined in Chapter 3, and use **TEST** to make sure you have included all the necessary elements. (See 8c.)

9 Reading and Writing Cause-and-Effect Essays

NICHOLAS KAMM/Getty Images

FOCUS on reading and writing

The photo above shows the interior of a commuter train. Brainstorm about your experiences riding public transportation. What incidents do you recall? What did you observe? Later in this chapter, you will read an essay on this topic and then have an opportunity to write about it.

PREVIEW

In this chapter, you will learn to
- read a cause-and-effect essay (9a).
- analyze a student cause-and-effect essay (9b).
- write a cause-and-effect essay (9b).

Why is the cost of college so high in the United States? How does smoking affect a person's health? What would happen if a city increased its sales tax? How dangerous is the flu? All these questions have one thing in common: They try to determine the causes or effects of an action, event, or situation.

A **cause** is something or someone that makes something happen. An **effect** is a result of a particular cause or event.

CAUSE	EFFECT
Increased airport security	⟶ Long lines at airports
Weight gain	⟶ Health problems
Seat belt laws passed	⟶ Traffic deaths reduced

Of course, a single cause can have multiple effects, and a single effect can be the result of multiple causes. For example, the cause "increased airport security" could also result in fewer terrorist attacks and more job opportunities with the TSA; the effect "traffic deaths reduced" could also be the result of lowering speed limits *and* passing anti-texting laws.

FYI

Tracing a Causal Chain

Sometimes a cause-and-effect essay includes a **causal chain**, a sequence in which one event or situation leads to another, which then leads to another. Thus, each cause is also an effect: A causes B (effect), B causes C (effect), C causes D (effect), and so on. Sometimes an entire essay is structured as a causal chain.

Cause-and-effect essays can identify or analyze causes, and they can also examine or predict effects; sometimes, they do both. Cause-and-effect essays help readers understand why something happened or show how one thing influences another.

9a Reading a Cause-and-Effect Essay

When you **read** a cause-and-effect essay, follow the active reading process outlined in Chapter 1. You can use **TEST** to help you identify its key elements.

T **Thesis** In the introduction of a cause-and-effect essay, look for a **thesis** that communicates the essay's main idea and indicates whether it will focus on causes or on effects. This main idea can be explicitly stated in a **thesis statement**, or it may be **implied**, suggested by the writer's choice of causes and effects and by how they are arranged in the essay.

E **Evidence** In the body paragraphs, look for **evidence**—examples and details—that illustrate and explain the causes or effects the writer examines. As you read, try to identify the most important causes and effects, and consider whether the writer is presenting a **causal chain**. Be sure you understand the relationships between causes and effects. In each paragraph, look for a topic sentence that identifies the causes or effects the paragraph will discuss.

S **Summary** In the conclusion of a cause-and-effect essay, look for a **summary** of the writer's key points or a **summary statement** that reinforces the essay's thesis.

T **Transitions** Try to identify the **transitional words and phrases** that make clear which causes lead to which effects. Sometimes a **transitional paragraph** will link sections of the essay—for example, summarizing key causes before considering other causes or moving along the discussion of effects.

Some Transitional Words and Phrases for Cause and Effect

Transitions are important in cause-and-effect essays because they establish causal connections, telling readers that A caused B and not the other way around:

accordingly	for this reason	the most important cause
another cause	since	
another effect	so	the most important effect
another reason	the first (second, third) cause	
as a result		the most important reason
because	the first (second, third) effect	
consequently		therefore
for		

In a cause-and-effect essay, a full paragraph is usually devoted to each cause or effect. Alternatively, several related causes (or effects) can be grouped together in each body paragraph, as shown in the following essay maps.

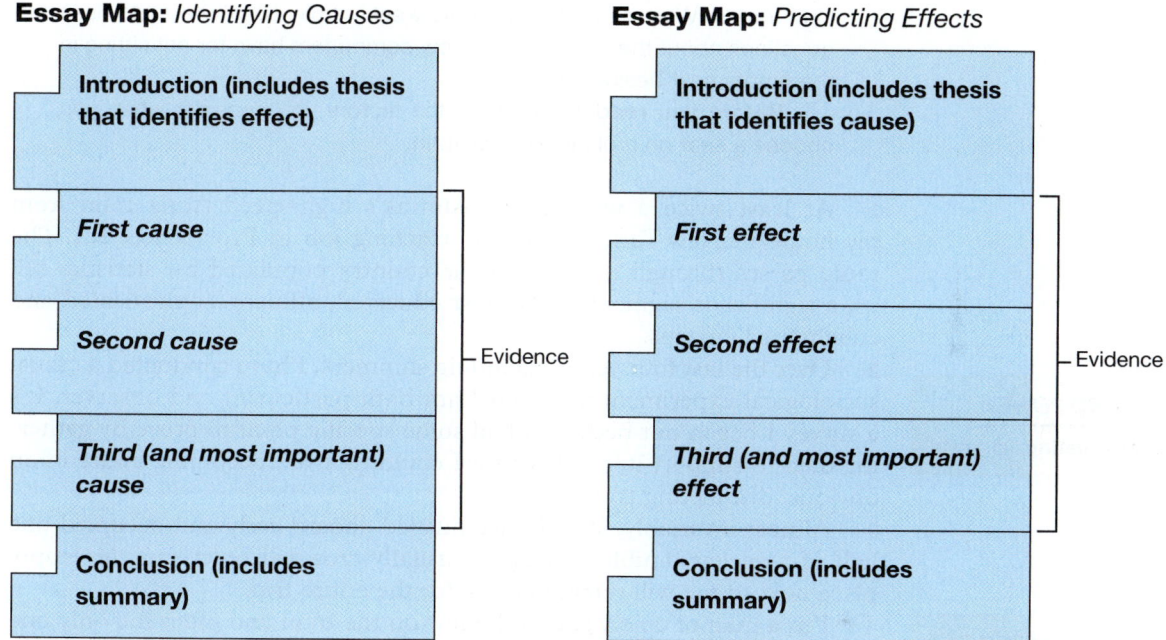

In your college courses, much of the writing you do will be in response to reading—specifically, to reading texts by professional writers, such as the one that follows. In this essay, "The Seat Not Taken," John Edgar Wideman considers why the seat beside him on the train is so often left empty. Read the essay, following the active reading process outlined in Chapter 1, and then answer the questions that start on page 235. At the end of this chapter, you will be asked to write a cause-and-effect essay in response to Wideman's ideas.

The Seat Not Taken

John Edgar Wideman

John Edgar Wideman has published numerous books, both fiction and nonfiction, as well as articles in publications such as *The New York Times*, *The New Yorker*, *Vogue*, *Emerge*, and *Esquire*. Wideman has received the O. Henry Award, the American Book Award for Fiction, the Lannan Literary Fellowship for Fiction, the PEN/Faulkner Award for Fiction (twice — the first person so honored), and a MacArthur Fellowship. He is currently a professor emeritus at Brown University.

In "The Seat Not Taken," an op-ed article first published *in The New York Times*, Wideman reflects on his weekly train commute and raises questions about the motives his fellow commuters have for not sitting in the empty seat beside him.

Before you read, think about the factors you consider when you choose a seat on a plane, bus, or train.

1   At least twice a week I ride Amtrak's high-speed Acela train from my home in New York City to my teaching job in Providence, R.I. The route passes through a region of the country populated by, statistics tell us, a significant segment of its most educated, affluent, sophisticated and enlightened citizens.

2   Over the last four years, excluding summers, I have conducted a casual sociological experiment in which I am both participant and observer. It's a survey I began not because I had some specific point to prove by gathering data to support it, but because I couldn't avoid becoming aware of an obvious, disquieting truth.

3   Almost invariably, after I have hustled aboard early and occupied one half of a vacant double seat in the usually crowded quiet car, the empty place next to me will remain empty for the entire trip.

4   I'm a man of color, one of the few on the train and often the only one in the quiet car, and I've concluded that color explains a lot about my experience. Unless the car is nearly full, color will determine, even if it doesn't exactly clarify, why 9 times out of 10 people will shun a free seat if it means sitting beside me.

5   Giving them and myself the benefit of the doubt, I can rule out excessive body odor or bad breath; a hateful, intimidating scowl; hip-hop clothing; or a hideous deformity as possible objections to my person. Considering also the cost of an Acela ticket, the fact that I display no visible indications of religious preference and, finally, the numerous external signs of middle-class membership I share with the majority of the passengers, color appears to be a sufficient reason for the behavior I have recorded.

6   Of course, I'm not registering a complaint about the privilege, conferred upon me by color, to enjoy the luxury of an extra seat to myself. I relish the opportunity to spread out, savor the privacy and quiet and work or gaze at the scenic New England woods and coast. It's a particularly appealing perk if I compare the train to air travel

WORD POWER
disquieting upsetting

WORD POWER
shun to avoid

or any other mode of transportation, besides walking or bicycling, for negotiating the mercilessly congested Northeast Corridor. Still, in the year 2010, with an African-descended, brown president in the White House and a nation confidently asserting its passage into a postracial era, it strikes me as odd to ride beside a vacant seat, just about every time I embark on a three-hour journey each way, from home to work and back.

7   I admit I look forward to the moment when other passengers, searching for a good seat, or any seat at all on the busiest days, stop anxiously prowling the quiet-car aisle, the moment when they have all settled elsewhere, including the ones who willfully blinded themselves to the open seat beside me or were unconvinced of its availability when they passed by. I savor that precise moment when the train sighs and begins to glide away from Penn or Providence Station, and I'm able to say to myself, with relative assurance, that the vacant place beside me is free, free at last, or at least free until the next station. I can relax, prop open my briefcase or rest papers, snacks or my arm in the unoccupied seat.

8   But the very pleasing moment of anticipation casts a shadow, because I can't accept the bounty of an extra seat without remembering why it's empty, without wondering if its emptiness isn't something quite sad. And quite dangerous, also, if left unexamined. Posters in the train, the station, the subway warn: if you see something, say something.

> **WORD POWER**
> **bounty** generous gift

Focus on Reading

1. Look back at the work you did when you previewed, marked up, and annotated this essay. Circle the words in this essay that refer specifically to race.
2. In the margin beside paragraph 5, list a few reasons you might have for not wanting to sit next to a particular person on a train.
3. **TEST** Wideman's essay. Does he include all four **TEST** elements? If not, why not? What, if anything, should be added?

Focus on Meaning

1. What "casual sociological experiment" (paragraph 2) does Wideman conduct? What are the results of this experiment? How does he interpret these results?
2. Why does Wideman see the empty seat beside him as not simply sad but also dangerous? Do you think he is right to see it this way, or do you think he is overreacting? Why?

Focus on Strategy

1. What do you think Wideman hoped to accomplish in this essay? For example, do you think he was trying to change readers' minds—or their behavior? To issue a warning? To suggest a change in Amtrak policy? Do you think this essay accomplishes his goal?
2. Why does Wideman end his essay with the words "if you see something, say something" (paragraph 8)? In what context does this sentence usually appear? What is the "something" he wants people to say in this case?

Focus on Language and Style

1. Do you think Wideman should have included more references to his own race (and to the races of his fellow passengers)? Why or why not?
2. In paragraph 1, Wideman suggests that his fellow passengers are some of the United States's "most educated, affluent, sophisticated and enlightened citizens." What point is he trying to make by using these adjectives to characterize the other passengers?

Focus on the Pattern

1. What causes does Wideman consider when he examines the possible reasons for "the seat not taken"? What, if anything, determines the order in which he presents these causes in paragraph 5?
2. What do you think might be the *effects* (on Wideman and on society in general) of the behavior he describes?

Focus on Critical Thinking

1. Consider all the reasons you might have (apart from the reasons Wideman lists in paragraph 5) for choosing not to sit next to a particular person on a train, bus, or plane. Might any of these reasons explain why the seat beside Wideman has so often remained empty?
2. In paragraph 5, Wideman mentions the "numerous external signs of middle-class membership" that he, like the other passengers, exhibits. What do you think these "external signs" are? Why do you think he mentions them?
3. In paragraph 6, Wideman, writing during Barack Obama's presidency, refers to our nation's "passage into a postracial era." What does the word *postracial* mean? Is Wideman being serious here, or is his use of this word intended to be ironic? Do you think we are now in a "postracial era"? Why or why not?

9b Analyzing a Student Essay: Cause and Effect

Mehul Shah wrote the following cause-and-effect essay for a history exam. Here is the exam question:

> In the textbook *Ways of the World: A Brief Global History*, author Robert Strayer identifies the years 500–1500 as a time of increasing global connections. Choose one trade network (Silk Roads, Sea Roads, or Sand Roads) that experienced growth during this period, and consider what caused it to expand. What events led to this expansion? In addition, briefly discuss the effects of this growth. What changes did it bring about?

Read Mehul's exam answer, following the active reading process outlined in Chapter 1, and then fill in the essay map in Practice 9-1 on page 239. (Note that the **TEST** elements in the essay exam answer have been highlighted and color-coded.)

Expanding Connections across the Indian Ocean

1 In the years between 500 and 1500, several major trade networks around the world exploded in size. One of those networks connected people as far east as China and as far west as the coast of Africa by way of sea routes across the Indian Ocean. Centered around India, these routes are known as the Sea Roads. Like the land-based Silk Roads of the same era, the Sea Roads brought together people from very different cultures; as a result, those groups of people experienced significant transformations. This increase in sea-based commerce and the resulting changes did not happen without cause, though. Three central factors caused the growth of the Sea Roads between 500–1500.

2 The first reason for the expansion of these sea routes was the development of new knowledge and technology. Understanding the weather patterns in the Indian Ocean was key. Once merchants had this information, they could plan their voyages to take advantage of the best wind currents. Another important factor was the invention of the magnetic compass. Developed by the Chinese in the 11th century, the magnetic compass gave sailors a more accurate and reliable way to tell direction.

T Thesis
E Evidence
S Summary
T Transitions

T Thesis

T Transitions

E Evidence

T Transitions

As a result, they could travel more safely and more quickly across longer distances. At the same time, several societies in the region learned how to build ships that could accommodate bigger, heavier loads. Because they now had these larger ships, merchants could transport more goods to more people. Soon, increased exposure to a diversity of goods led to increased demand for those goods. Together, these developments enabled sea-based commerce in the Indian Ocean to thrive.

3   The second reason the Sea Roads grew and flourished during this time period was the emergence of a stronger Chinese state. After years of instability, China was experiencing economic and political recovery. From the early 7th century to the late 13th century, the country was unified under powerful dynasties. These governments actively supported commerce, particularly sea trade. Under their rule, Chinese merchants delivered iron, silk, porcelain, and other Chinese products to ports all across the Indian Ocean. China also became a valuable market for imports from other regions served by the Sea Roads. Thus, the entire trade network benefited from China's new strength.

Evidence **E**

4   The third and most important reason the Sea Roads grew was the rapid rise of Islam. Founded in the 7th century, the religion spread quickly and led to the emergence of a powerful Arab Empire. By the 16th century, this empire reached beyond the Middle East to Europe, Africa, India, and Southeast Asia. Across the Indian Ocean basin, Arab political rule united diverse groups of people and encouraged greater connections between them. These connections were not just religious, however. Unlike many other religions, Islam was very supportive of commerce, and during this period Muslim traders dominated the Sea Roads. Because Muslims were so prosperous, many more people were attracted to the religion, and this further strengthened the trade networks. The most powerful civilization in the world during this millennium, Islam was a key factor in the expansion of the Sea Roads.

Evidence **E**

5   As a result of this growth in Indian Ocean trade, countless changes took place. People were in contact with each other more than ever before. With more interactions came cultural exchange, political change, and religious conversion. New merchant classes developed. People were introduced to new products, new technology, and new languages. A number of cities gained power as a result of their geographical advantages. For example, the kingdom of Srivijaya in Southeast Asia arose because of its valuable position between China and India and its profitable commercial resources. In addition, cities on the East African coast grew as they became important

Evidence **E**

go-betweens for foreign traders and African producers. The Sea Roads had a lasting impact on religious traditions as well. Although Islam gained the most new followers during this period, Buddhism and Hinduism also widened their influence. Ultimately, the cultural effects of this expanded trade network were immense.

6   The growth in trade across the Indian Ocean, and the changes that followed, resulted from three specific features of the millennium (500–1500). Without the spread of Islam, the powerful Chinese government, and a few well-timed innovations, the Sea Roads would not have developed as they did. Without the Sea Roads, many significant interactions would never have occurred, and the people of this millennium and the following centuries would have led very different lives. Therefore, learning about the causes and effects of this growth is essential to understanding global history.

S Summary

T Transitions

PRACTICE
9-1 Now that you have read Mehul's essay, fill in the essay map below to help you understand how he organized his essay. Then, decide whether his organization is effective.

Introduction _____
_____
_____

First cause _____
_____
_____

Second cause _____
_____
_____

Third cause _____
_____
_____

Conclusion _____
_____
_____

PRACTICE 9-2

1. Reread the exam question on page 237. What words signal that students are to write a cause-and-effect essay?
2. Does the thesis statement make it clear that Mehul will use cause and effect to structure his exam answer?
3. What do you think is the most important cause the essay identifies? What seems to be the most important effect?
4. Do you think the essay's last sentence is necessary? Why or why not?
5. What is the essay's greatest strength? What is its greatest weakness?

9c Writing a Cause-and-Effect Essay

When you are given a writing assignment, the wording of your assignment may suggest that you write a cause-and-effect essay. For example, the assignment may ask you to *explain why, predict the outcome, list contributing factors, discuss the consequences,* or tell what *caused* something else or how something is *affected* by something else. Once you decide that your assignment calls for cause and effect, you need to develop a thesis statement that reflects this purpose.

ASSIGNMENT	THESIS STATEMENT
Women's studies What factors contributed to the rise of the women's movement in the 1970s?	The women's movement of the 1970s had its origins in the peace and civil rights movements of the 1960s.
Public health Discuss the possible long-term effects of smoking.	In addition to its well-known negative effects on smokers themselves, smoking also causes significant problems for those exposed to secondhand smoke.
Media and society How has the Internet affected the lives of those who have grown up with it?	The Internet has created a generation of people who learn differently from those in previous generations.

 A cause-and-effect essay can focus on causes or on effects. When you write about causes, be sure to examine *all* relevant causes. You should emphasize the cause you consider the most important, but do not forget to consider other causes that may be significant. Similarly, when you write about effects, consider *all* significant effects of a particular cause, not just the first few that you think of.

If your focus is on finding causes, as it is in the first assignment in the box on page 240, your introductory paragraph should identify the effect (the women's movement). If your focus is on predicting effects, as it is in the second and third assignments, you should begin by identifying the cause (smoking, the Internet).

When you **write** a cause-and-effect essay, you follow the process outlined in Chapter 3. The essay you write will include the same elements you have learned to recognize in the cause-and-effect essays you have read. When you finish your draft, you can use **TEST** to make sure it includes all the elements of a cause-and-effect essay.

TESTing your cause-and-effect essay

Thesis Statement Unifies Your Essay

☐ Does your introduction include a **thesis statement** that indicates your main idea and makes clear whether your essay will focus on causes or effects?

Evidence Supports Your Essay's Thesis Statement

☐ Does all your **evidence**—examples and details—support your thesis, or should some be deleted?

☐ Do you identify and explain all causes or effects relevant to your topic, or do you need to add any?

☐ Do you arrange causes and effects to indicate which are more important than others?

☐ Does each body paragraph identify and explain one particular cause or effect (or several closely related causes or effects)?

Summary Statement Reinforces Your Essay's Main Idea

☐ Does your conclusion include a **summary statement** that reinforces your essay's thesis?

Transitions Connect Events

☐ Do you include **transitions** that introduce each of your causes or effects and make your essay's cause-and-effect connections clear?

Following a Student Writer

In an orientation course for first-year education majors, Andrea DeMarco was asked to write a personal essay about an event that changed her life. She decided immediately to write about her parents' brief separation, an event that occurred when she was eight years old.

Before she wrote her first draft, Andrea talked to her older sister and brother to see what they remembered about the separation. As they spoke, Andrea **took notes** so she wouldn't forget any details. Armed with her siblings' and her own memories, Andrea **drafted** her essay.

The wording of her assignment—to write about an event that changed her life—told Andrea that her essay would have a cause-and-effect structure. In her draft, she included a **thesis statement**—"My parents' separation made everything different"—that echoed the wording of the assignment. As she wrote, she was careful to include transitional words and phrases like *because* and *as a result* to make the cause-and-effect emphasis clear and to distinguish between the cause (the separation) and its effects. Her summary statement also reinforced the cause-and-effect emphasis of her essay.

When Andrea **TEST**ed her draft, she saw that it included all the required elements—thesis statement, evidence, summary statement, and transitions—so she continued **revising** her draft. When she finished her revisions, she **edited** and **proofread** her essay.

Read Andrea's essay, and then answer the questions in Practice 9-3 on page 243.

How My Parents' Separation Changed My Life

1   Until I was eight, I lived the perfect all-American life with my perfect all-American family. I lived in a suburb of Albany, New York, with my parents, my sister and brother, and our dog, Daisy. We had a Ping-Pong table in the basement, a barbecue in the backyard, and two cars in the garage. My dad and mom were high school teachers, and every summer we took a family vacation. Then, it all changed. My parents' separation made everything different.

2   One day, just before Halloween, when my sister was twelve and my brother was fourteen (Daisy was seven), our parents called us into the kitchen for a family conference. We didn't think anything was wrong at first; they were always calling these annoying meetings. We figured it was time for us to plan a vacation, talk about household chores, or be nagged to clean our rooms. As soon as we sat down, though, we knew this was different. We could tell Mom had been crying, and Dad's voice cracked when he told us the news. They were separating—they called it a "trial separation"—and Dad was moving out of our house.

3   After that day, everything seemed to change. Every Halloween we always had a big jack-o'-lantern on our front porch. Dad used to spend hours at the kitchen table cutting out the eyes, nose, and mouth and hollowing out the insides. That Halloween, because he didn't live with us, things were different. Mom bought a pumpkin, and I guess she was planning to carve it up. But she never did, and we never mentioned it. It sat on the kitchen counter for a couple of weeks, getting soft and wrinkled, and then it just disappeared.

4   Other holidays were also different because Mom and Dad were not living together. Our first Thanksgiving without Dad was pathetic. Christmas was

different, too. We spent Christmas Eve with Dad and our relatives on his side and Christmas Day with Mom and her family. Of course, we got twice as many presents as usual. I realize now that both our parents were trying to make up for the pain of the separation. The worst part came when I opened my big present from Mom: Barbie's Dream House. This was something I had always wanted. Even at eight, I knew how hard it must have been for Mom to afford it. The trouble was, I had gotten the same thing from Dad the night before.

5   The separation affected each of us in different ways. The worst effect of my parents' separation was not the big events but the disruption in our everyday lives. Dinner used to be a family time, a chance to talk about our day and make plans. But after Dad left, Mom seemed to stop eating. Sometimes she would just have coffee while we ate, and sometimes she wouldn't eat at all. She would microwave some frozen thing for us or heat up soup or cook some hot dogs. We didn't care—after all, now she let us watch TV while we ate—but we did notice.

6   Other parts of our routine changed, too. Because Dad didn't live with us anymore, we had to spend every Saturday and every Wednesday night at his apartment, no matter what else we had planned. Usually, he would take us to dinner at McDonald's on Wednesdays, and then we would go back to his place and do our homework or watch TV. That wasn't too bad. Saturdays were a lot worse. We really wanted to be home, hanging out with our friends in our own rooms in our own house. Instead, we had to do some planned activity with Dad, like go to a movie or a hockey game.

7   As a result of what happened in my own family, it is hard for me to believe any relationship is forever. By the end of the school year, my parents had somehow worked things out, and Dad was back home again. That June, at a family conference around the kitchen table, we made our summer vacation plans. We decided on Williamsburg, Virginia, the all-American vacation destination. So, things were back to normal, but I wasn't, and I'm still not. Now, ten years later, my mother and father are all right, but I still worry they'll split up again. And I worry about my own future husband and how I will ever be sure he's the one I'll stay married to.

PRACTICE
9-3

1. Underline Andrea's thesis statement. Does this statement identify a cause or an effect?
2. List the specific effects of her parents' separation that Andrea identifies.
3. Review the transitional words and phrases Andrea uses to make causal connections clear to her readers. Do you think she needs to add more transitions? If so, where?

4. Is Andrea's concluding paragraph effective? Why or why not? Do you think it should be shortened or divided into two paragraphs? If so, would you revise or relocate Andrea's summary statement?

5. Is Andrea's straightforward title effective, or should she have chosen a more creative or eye-catching title? Can you suggest an alternative?

6. Use **TEST** to evaluate Andrea's essay. What revisions would you recommend she make? Why?

Grammar in context

Cause and Effect

When you write a cause-and-effect essay, you may have trouble remembering the difference between *affect* and *effect*.

The worst ~~affect~~ *effect* of my parents' separation was not the big events but the disruption in our everyday lives. (*Effect* is a noun.)

The separation ~~effected~~ *affected* each of us in different ways. (*Affect* is a verb.)

FOCUS on reading and writing

Reread John Edgar Wideman's essay, "The Seat Not Taken," on page 234. Then, write your own cause-and-effect essay in response to one of the following prompts. (Review the image and text that open this chapter before you choose a topic.) Be sure to follow the writing process outlined in Chapter 3.

1. How do you account for the empty seat beside Wideman on so many train trips? Do you agree with his analysis of the situation? What other possible explanations has he not considered? Write a cause-and-effect essay responding to Wideman's essay and its reflections on race.

2. Who would you try to avoid sitting next to on a train? Why? Do you see your objections as reasonable, or do you think some of your objections might be the result of prejudice? Write an essay in which you explain your objections as clearly and thoughtfully as possible.

If you prefer, you can write on one of these topics instead:

- A teacher's positive (or negative) effect on you
- How your life would be different if you dropped out of school (or quit your job)
- How a particular invention has changed (or might change) your life
- How a particular event made you grow up

CHAPTER REVIEW

COLLABORATIVE ACTIVITY

Read the essay that another student wrote in response to one of this chapter's prompts. Work with that student to consider the strengths and weaknesses of both of your cause-and-effect essays. Do you think one of your essays is more effective than the other? If so, why? Based on your reactions to the essays you and your classmates wrote, write a few sentences explaining what a cause-and-effect essay should accomplish.

Review checklist

Reading and Writing Cause-and-Effect Essays

✔ When you *read* a cause-and-effect essay, follow the active reading process outlined in Chapter 1, and use **TEST** to help you identify the essay's key elements. (See 9a.)

✔ Analyzing a student essay can help you understand the structure of a cause-and-effect essay. (See 9b.)

✔ When you *write* a cause-and-effect essay, follow the writing process outlined in Chapter 3, and use **TEST** to make sure you have included all the necessary elements. (See 9c.)

10 Reading and Writing Comparison-and-Contrast Essays

North Wind Picture Archives/Alamy Stock Photo; PRISMA ARCHIVO/Alamy Stock Photo

FOCUS on reading and writing

Look at these portraits of Charles Darwin and Abraham Lincoln. Brainstorm to discover what you already know about some historical figures who have changed the world or some important historical events that have changed your life. Later in this chapter, you will read an essay about Lincoln and Darwin and then have the opportunity to write a comparison-and-contrast essay about some of the people and events you identified in your brainstorming.

> **PREVIEW**
>
> **In this chapter, you will learn to**
> - read a comparison-and-contrast essay (10a).
> - analyze a student comparison-and-contrast essay (10b).
> - write a comparison-and-contrast essay (10c).

When you buy something—for example, a smartphone, a tablet, or a hair dryer—you often comparison shop, looking at various models to determine how they are alike and how they are different. In other words, you *compare and contrast*. When you **compare**, you consider how things are similar. When you **contrast**, you consider how things are different. A **comparison-and-contrast** essay can examine just similarities, just differences, or both.

In order to compare and contrast two things, you need a clear **basis of comparison**. In other words, the two things must have enough in common to justify the comparison. You can, for example, compare and contrast a play and a short story—both are literary works, with characters, dialogue, plots, and settings. You would have a difficult time, however, comparing a television to a car. The two simply do not have enough in common to justify the comparison.

10a Reading a Comparison-and-Contrast Essay

When you **read** a comparison-and-contrast essay, follow the active reading process outlined in Chapter 1. You can use **TEST** to help you identify the essay's key elements.

T **Thesis** In the introduction of a comparison-and-contrast essay, look for a **thesis** that identifies the writer's main idea, indicates that the essay will be a comparison, and tells whether the will writer focus on similarities or differences. This idea may be explicitly stated in a **thesis statement,** or it may be **implied,** suggested by the discussion. As you read, ask yourself why the writer chose the option he or she did.

E **Evidence** In the body paragraphs, look for **evidence,** details and examples that develop the comparison. As you read, note the points the writer chooses to make. Does the writer discuss the same (or similar) points for each subject being compared? Is the essay a **subject-by-subject** or **point-by-point** comparison? Why was this arrangement chosen? Is it the most effective order? In each body paragraph, look for a topic sentence (often, but not always, at the beginning) that identifies the point the writer is comparing or contrasting.

S **Summary** In the concluding paragraphs of a comparison-and-contrast essay, look for a summary of the writer's key points or a **summary statement** that reinforces the essay's thesis. As you read, consider whether the summary clearly and accurately restates the essay's main idea and reinforces the point of the comparison.

T **Transitions** Try to identify the **transitional words and phrases** that connect points within paragraphs and between one paragraph and the next. These transitions enable readers to keep track of the elements of the comparison and to move from one point to another. Sometimes a **transitional paragraph** will link sections of the essay. As you read, determine how the transitions indicate that the writer is moving from one point to the next. Ask yourself whether the writer should have used more transitions. If so, where?

> **Some Transitional Words and Phrases for Comparison and Contrast**
>
> The transitional words and phrases used in a comparison-and-contrast essay tell readers whether an essay is focusing on similarities or on differences and also help move readers through an essay from one subject to the other and from one point of comparison or contrast to the next.
>
> | | |
> |---|---|
> | although | likewise |
> | but | nevertheless |
> | even though | one . . . another |
> | however | on the contrary |
> | in comparison | on the one hand . . . on the other hand |
> | in contrast | similarly |
> | instead | unlike |
> | like | whereas |

A comparison-and-contrast essay can be organized as either a *point-by-point* comparison or a *subject-by-subject* comparison. A **point-by-point** comparison alternates between the two subjects that are being compared or contrasted, first discussing one point about the first subject and then discussing the same (or a similar) point for the second subject. A **subject-by-subject** comparison discusses one subject at a time. The first part of the essay discusses all the points about one subject, and the second part discusses the same (or similar) points for the second subject (see the essay maps on the facing page).

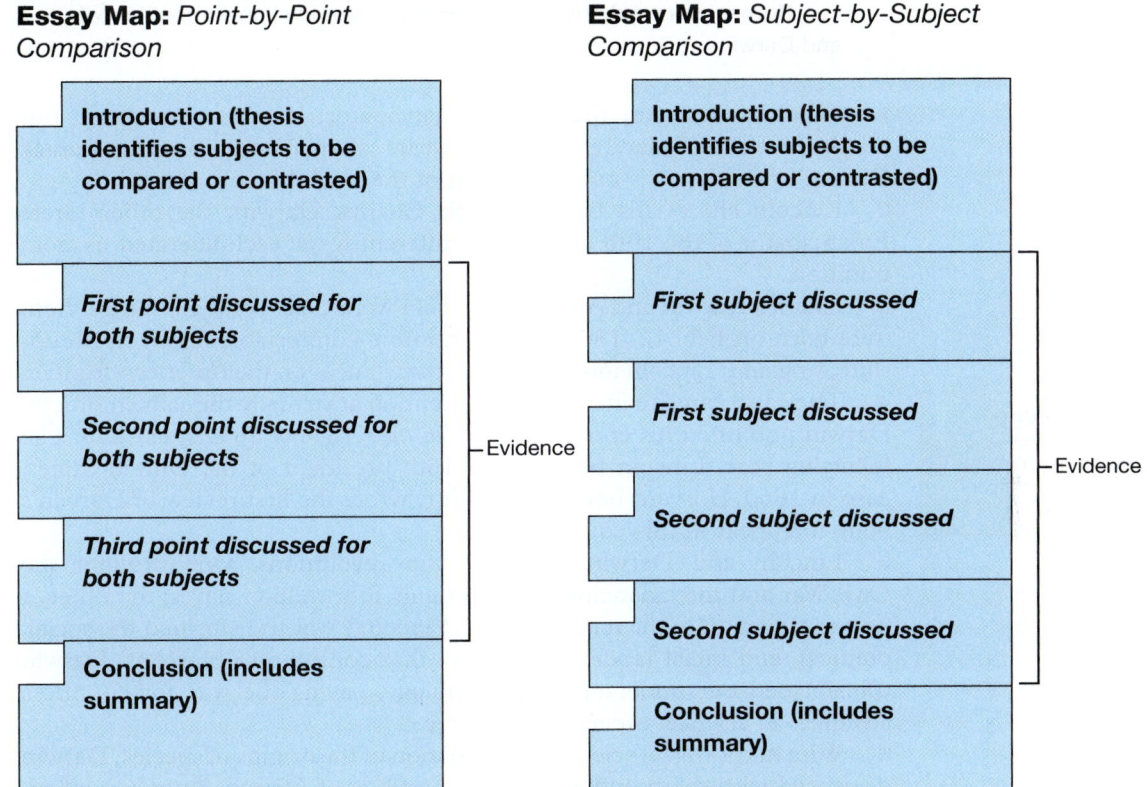

In your college courses, much of your writing will be in response to reading—specifically, to reading texts by professional writers, such as the one that follows. In this essay, "The Twin Revolutions of Lincoln and Darwin," Steven Conn compares two men who had a profound effect on the times in which they lived. Read the essay, following the active reading process outlined in Chapter 1, and then answer the questions starting on page 251. (At the end of this chapter, you will be asked to write an exemplification essay in response to Conn's ideas.)

The Twin Revolutions of Lincoln and Darwin

Steven Conn

Steven Conn is a professor of American cultural and intellectual history and director of the Public History Program at Ohio State University. He is the author of several books, most recently *Americans Against the City: Anti-Urbanism in the Twentieth Century* (2014). In "The Twin Revolutions of Lincoln and Darwin," which first appeared in the *Philadelphia Inquirer* in 2009, Conn compares the lives of two seemingly unrelated historical figures — Abraham Lincoln and Charles Darwin.

Before you read, think about what you already know about Lincoln and Darwin.

1   Abraham Lincoln, the Great Emancipator, has been much on our minds recently. Today, exactly 200 years after Lincoln's birth, Barack Obama's presidency is one fulfillment of the work Lincoln started.

2   Lincoln shares his birthday with Charles Darwin, the other Great Emancipator of the 19th century. In different ways, each liberated us from tradition.

3   Charles Darwin and Abraham Lincoln were exact contemporaries. Both were born on Feb. 12, 1809—Darwin into a comfortable family in Shropshire, England; Lincoln into humble circumstances on the American frontier.

4   They also came to international attention at virtually the same moment. Darwin published his epochal book, *On the Origin of Species*, in 1859. The following year, Lincoln became the 16th president of the United States. Also in 1860, Harvard botanist Asa Gray wrote the first review of Darwin's book to appear in this country.

5   Lincoln and Darwin initiated twin revolutions. One brought the Civil War and the emancipation of roughly four million slaves; the other, a new explanation of the natural world. Lincoln's war transformed the social, political, and racial landscape in ways that continue to play out. Darwin transformed our understanding of biology, paving the way for countless advances in science, especially medicine.

6   With his powerful scientific explanation of the origins of species, Darwin dispensed with the pseudoscientific assertions of African American inferiority. In this way, Darwin provided the scientific legitimacy for Lincoln's political and moral actions.

7   The two revolutions shared a commitment to one proposition: that all human beings are fundamentally equal. In this sense, both Lincoln and Darwin deserve credit for emancipating us from the political and intellectual rationales for slavery.

8   For Lincoln, this was a political principle and a moral imperative. He was deeply ambivalent about the institution of slavery. As the war began, he believed that saving the Union, not abolishing slavery, was the cause worth fighting for. But as the war ground gruesomely on, he began to see that ending slavery was the only way to save the Union without making a mockery of the nation's founding ideals.

9   This is what Lincoln meant when he promised, in the 1863 Gettysburg Address, that the war would bring "a new birth of freedom." He was even more emphatic about it in his second inaugural address, in 1865. Slavery could not be permitted to exist in a nation founded on the belief that we are all created equal.

10   Darwin, for his part, was a deeply committed abolitionist from a family of deeply committed abolitionists. Exposed to slavery during his travels in South America, Darwin wrote, "It makes one's blood boil." He called

---

WORD POWER
epochal extremely important, significant, or influential

WORD POWER
imperative an obligation or duty
ambivalent having mixed feelings

WORD POWER
emphatic forceful and insistent

abolishing slavery his "sacred cause." In some of his first notes about evolution, he railed against the idea that slaves were somehow less than human.

11   For Darwin, our shared humanity was a simple biological fact. Whatever variations exist among the human species—what we call *races*—are simply the natural variations that occur within all species. Like it or not, in a Darwinian world we are all members of one human family. This truth lay at the center of Darwin's science and his abolitionism.

12   That understanding of human equality—arrived at from different directions and for different reasons—helps explain the opposition to the revolutions unleashed by Lincoln and Darwin. It's also why many Americans—virtually alone in the developed world—continue to deny Darwinian science.

13   Many white Southerners never accepted Lincoln's basic proposition about the political equality of black Americans. In the years after the Civil War and Reconstruction, they set up the brutal structures and rituals of segregation. All of the elaborate laws, customs and violence of the segregated South served to deny the basic truth that all Americans are created equal. Most Northerners, meanwhile, didn't care much about the "Southern problem."

14   No wonder, then, that many Americans simply rejected Darwin's insights out of hand. Slavery and segregation rested on the assumption that black Americans were not fully human. Darwinian science put the lie to all that.

15   Lincoln insisted on equality as a political fact. Darwin demonstrated it as a biological fact. In their shared commitment to human equality, each in his own realm, these two Great Emancipators helped us break free from the shackles of the past.

> **WORD POWER**
> **abolitionist** a person who supported ending slavery in the United States

Focus on Reading

1. Look back at the work you did when you previewed, marked up, and annotated this essay. Did you underline the same points about both Lincoln and Darwin?
2. Circle any ideas or references with which you are not familiar. Look them up on the Internet, and add marginal annotations to explain them.
3. **TEST** Conn's essay. Does he include all four **TEST** elements? If not, why not? What, if anything, does he need to add?

Focus on Meaning

1. How are Lincoln and Darwin alike? What are their "twin revolutions"? How are these revolutions similar?
2. How are Lincoln and Darwin different? In Conn's view, is it their similarities or their differences that are most significant?
3. Why, according to Conn, were so many people opposed to both Lincoln's and Darwin's ideas?

Focus on Strategy

1. What is Conn's thesis? Where does he state it? Write a sentence that states the essay's main idea in your own words.
2. Why does Conn compare Lincoln and Darwin? What is the basis for his comparison?

Focus on Language and Style

1. What does the word *emancipator* mean? What associations does this word have for you?
2. What exactly does Conn mean when he calls Lincoln and Darwin "these two Great Emancipators" (paragraph 15)?
3. What does Conn mean by "the shackles of the past" (paragraph 15)? What connotations does the word *shackles* have for you?

Focus on the Pattern

1. Is this a point-by-point or a subject-by-subject comparison? How can you tell?
2. Does Conn make the same points about Lincoln and Darwin, or does he discuss some points for one man and not for the other? If the points he makes do not match exactly, does this weaken the effect of his comparison? Why or why not?

Focus on Critical Thinking

1. Do you think it makes sense to compare Lincoln and Darwin, or do you think they have too little in common to be compared?
2. Who do you see as the more important historical figure, Lincoln or Darwin? Whose legacy is more significant? Why?

10b Analyzing a Student Essay: Comparison and Contrast

The following comparison-and-contrast essay was written by Colin Volpatti, a criminal justice major, in response to this assignment in his composition class:

> Find two websites that interest you. (They could relate to your major, a hobby, your community, or anything else that appeals to you.) Compare and contrast the two sites, taking care to discuss the same or similar points for both. Before you write, decide whether you will organize your essay as a point-by-point or subject-by-subject comparison.

Analyzing a Student Essay: Comparison and Contrast   10b

To help you understand the structure of a comparison-and-contrast essay, read Colin's essay, following the active reading process discussed in Chapter 1, and then fill in the essay map in Practice 10-1 on page 255. (Note that the **TEST** elements in the essay have been highlighted and color-coded.)

Two Very Different Resources

1   The amount of information a person can get from a simple web search can be overwhelming. For example, searching the key words "wrongful conviction" results in thousands of hits. The biggest challenge facing a person carrying out such a search is evaluating the trustworthiness of the information on these sites. A comparison and contrast of two websites that resulted from this search reveals some very interesting differences. The first site, for the People's Law Office, is clearly commercial, while the second site, for the Innocence Project, has a broader purpose. <u>Although both websites claim to help people who have been wrongfully convicted of crimes, they differ significantly in content, purpose, and intended audience.</u>

2   The People's Law Office website presents information about what its lawyers can do for clients. The website is appealing and easy to read; the pages are white and gray with bars of purple and green. The law office's name, logo, and contact information are highlighted at the top of each page. On the site's home page is a bright green bar that contains the main menu. Each of the menu's six tabs takes readers to information about the law office's successes. A tab titled "Victories" leads to a list of cases won. Another page describes the office's "long and illustrious history" of protecting people's civil rights. Under "Areas of Practice" is the office's "remarkable track record" and a discussion of its "decades of experience." Under "News and Commentary," the People's Law Office emphasizes its achievements and includes articles written by its lawyers. Below these tabs is a slide show that displays photos of clients who were freed by the efforts of the firm's lawyers. Throughout these pages, the content emphasizes the dedication and the effectiveness of the firm.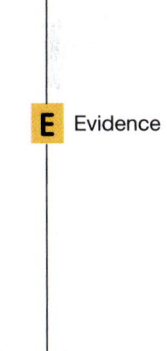

3   The content of the People's Law Office website indicates that its purpose is commercial and that its audience is people who need the services of the firm's lawyers. The website attempts to attract potential clients by appealing to both logic and emotion. By emphasizing its successes, the firm establishes its credibility and tries to convince people that People's Law Office lawyers usually win their cases. The People's Law Office website also appeals to

readers' emotions with a slide show of photos. In one image, a police officer is shown mistreating an unnamed protester. In another, a joyful man, with his smiling lawyers, is pictured leaving a courthouse. The accompanying copy addresses the audience as *you* and declares, "If your constitutional rights have been violated, we can help. . . ." This content makes clear that the purpose of the People's Law Office site is to sell the firm's legal services to people who believe that they have been victimized by the legal system.

4   Although the Innocence Project also presents facts about itself, it offers more extensive and varied content than the People's Law Office. Like the commercial People's Law Office, the nonprofit Innocence Project has mostly white and gray pages accented with bars of color; it also has a slide show on its home page. However, there are many notable differences between the two sites. One difference is that the Innocence Project slide show contains pictures of people who were declared innocent after they had been convicted. Instead of having its address and phone number at the top of each page, the People's Law Office has a search tab and a sign-up button for the organization's email. Another difference is the main menu bar, which has two sides. The slightly larger, rust-colored left side has three tabs: "Know the Cases," "Understand the Causes," and "Fix the System." Each of these tabs directs the reader to an extensive menu of sub-topics. The smaller, mustard-colored right side has four tabs: "Home," "About," "Donate," and "News and Resources." These tabs lead readers to information about the organization as well as to a list of related links. This design is not flashy, but it enables visitors to easily navigate the site.

5   Unlike People's Law Office, the Innocence Project has several purposes and, therefore, multiple audiences. First, the detailed information, including the labeled slide show, indicates that the site's main purpose is to educate. This material is aimed at anyone who is interested in knowing more about wrongful conviction or in reading about individual cases. Second, the organization wants to encourage people to take action. By suggesting numerous ways of getting involved, the site addresses people who already support the organization's cause and want to do more. Finally, the nonprofit Innocence Project wants to offer legal services to people who think they have been wrongly convicted. Unlike People's Law Office, the Innocence Project does not address the reader as *you*. Because this organization is not trying to solicit business, it uses a more straightforward, informative tone.

6   Ultimately, the purpose of the People's Law Office commercial website is to sell services to a specific audience, while the goal of the nonprofit Innocence Project site is to provide free resources to its target audiences. The two organizations share a desire to free innocent people who have been

wrongly convicted. They also have clear agendas. <u>On the one hand</u>, the Innocence Project is interested in addressing and remedying problems with the legal system. <u>On the other hand</u>, People's Law Office is interested in soliciting business for its lawyers. Comparing and contrasting these two sites allows readers to see the objectives of each more clearly and thus to choose a source that meets their needs.

T Transitions

Works Cited

Innocence Project, innocenceproject.org.

People's Law Office, peopleslawoffice.com.

PRACTICE
10-1 Now that you have read Colin's essay, fill in the essay map below to help you understand how he organized his essay. Then, decide whether his organization is effective.

Introduction _____

First subject discussed _____

First subject discussed _____

Second subject discussed _____

Second subject discussed _____

Conclusion _____

PRACTICE 10-2

1. Does the thesis statement identify the essay's main idea? Does it indicate that Colin will use comparison-and-contrast to structure his essay?
2. What specific points about the two websites does Colin compare and contrast?
3. Does Colin organize his essay as a point-by-point or a subject-by-subject comparison? Do you think he made the right choice?
4. Reread the topic sentences of Colin's body paragraphs. How do they indicate the differences between the two sites?
5. What is the essay's greatest strength? What is its greatest weakness?

10c Writing a Comparison-and-Contrast Essay

When you are given a writing assignment, the wording of your assignment may suggest that you write a comparison-and-contrast essay—for example, by asking you to *compare*, *contrast*, *discuss similarities*, or *identify differences*. Once you decide that your assignment calls for comparison and contrast, you need to develop a thesis statement that reflects this purpose.

ASSIGNMENT	THESIS STATEMENT
Philosophy What basic similarities do you find in the beliefs of Henry David Thoreau and Martin Luther King Jr.?	Although King was more politically active, both he and Thoreau strongly supported the idea of civil disobedience.
Nutrition How do the diets of native Japanese and Japanese Americans differ?	As they become more and more assimilated, Japanese Americans consume more fats than native Japanese do.
Literature Contrast the two sisters in Alice Walker's short story "Everyday Use."	Unlike Maggie, Dee—her more successful, better-educated sister—has rejected her family's heritage.

When you **write** a comparison-and-contrast essay, you follow the process outlined in Chapter 3. The essay you write will include the same elements you have learned to recognize in the comparison-and-contrast essays you read. When you finish your draft, you can use **TEST** to make sure it includes all the elements of a comparison-and-contrast essay.

> ### TESTing your comparison-and-contrast essay
>
> **T**hesis Statement Unifies Your Essay
>
> - ☐ Does your introduction include a **thesis statement** that expresses your main idea, identifying the two subjects you will compare and indicating whether your essay will examine similarities or differences?
>
> **E**vidence Supports Your Essay's Thesis Statement
>
> - ☐ Do you discuss all significant points of comparison or contrast that apply to your two subjects, explaining each similarity or difference using specific examples and details?
> - ☐ Does all your **evidence**—examples and details—support your thesis, or should some be deleted?
> - ☐ Have you treated similar points for both of your subjects?
> - ☐ Is your essay's organization consistent with either a point-by-point comparison or a subject-by-subject comparison?
>
> **S**ummary Statement Reinforces Your Essay's Main Idea
>
> - ☐ Does your conclusion include a **summary statement** that reinforces your essay's thesis, reminding readers what your two subjects are, and how they are alike or different?
>
> **T**ransitions Connect Events
>
> - ☐ Do you include **transitional words and phrases** that introduce details and move readers smoothly from one subject to another or from one point to another?

Following a Student Writer

Nisha Jani, a student in a first-year writing course, was given the following assignment.

> Some people claim that males and females are so different that at times they seem to belong to two different species. Do you agree, or do you think males and females are more alike than different? Write an essay that supports your position.

When Nisha read this assignment, the key words *different* and *alike* told her that the assignment called for a comparison-and-contrast essay. After **brainstorming**, she decided to write a humorous essay about the differences between boys and girls—specifically, middle school boys and girls.

Based on her own experiences and those of her younger brother and sister, Nisha thought that the differences between seventh-grade boys and girls would be more interesting (and funnier) than the similarities. So, when she drafted a **thesis statement** for her essay, she made sure that it focused on differences: "The typical boy and girl live very different lives."

Once Nisha had a thesis statement, she **listed** some of the most obvious differences between male and female seventh-graders. When she reviewed the ideas on her list, she decided to follow her two subjects (Johnny and Jane) through a typical school day, and this decision led her to structure her essay as a point-by-point comparison that would humorously contrast boys' and girls' behavior at different points of their day.

When Nisha thought she had enough material to write about, she **wrote a draft** of her essay. Then, she **TEST**ed her draft to see if it included a thesis statement, supporting evidence, a summary statement, and transitional words and phrases. Although her **TEST** showed her that she had included all the required elements, she still needed to **revise** to strengthen her draft. After a **conference** with her instructor, she revised her thesis statement to make it a bit more specific, added more examples and details, sharpened her summary statement so it reinforced her essay's main idea, and added more transitions to make the contrast between her two subjects clearer. After she finished these revisions, she **edited** and **proofread** her essay. Read Nisha's essay, and then answer the questions in Practice 10-3 on page 260.

Another Ordinary Day

1   "Boys are from Jupiter and get stupider/Girls are from Mars and become movie stars/Boys take a bath and smell like trash/Girls take a shower and smell like a flower." As simple playground songs like this one suggest, the two sexes are very different. As adults, men and women have similar goals, values, and occupations, but as children and teenagers, boys and girls often seem to belong to two different species. In fact, from the first moment of the day to the last, the typical boy and girl live very different lives.

2   The sun rises, and the alarm clock signals the beginning of another day for Johnny and Jane, two seventh-grade classmates. Johnny, an average thirteen-year-old boy, wakes up late and has to hurry. He throws on his favorite jeans, a baggy T-shirt, and a baseball cap. Then, he has a hearty high-cholesterol breakfast and runs out of the house to school, usually forgetting some vital book or homework assignment. Jane, unlike Johnny, wakes up early and takes her time. She takes a long shower and then blow-dries her hair. For Jane, getting dressed can be a very difficult process, one that often includes taking everything out of her closet and calling friends for advice. After she

makes her decision, she helps herself to some food (probably low- or no-fat) and goes off to school, making sure she has with her everything she needs.

3   School is a totally different experience for Johnny and Jane. Johnny will probably sit in the back of the classroom with a couple of other guys, throwing paper airplanes and spitballs. These will be directed at the males they do not like and the females they think are kind of cute. (However, if their male friends ever ask the boys about these girls, they will say girls are just losers and deny that they like any of them.) On the opposite side of the classroom, however, Jane is focused on a very different kind of activity. At first, it looks as if she is carefully copying the algebra notes that the teacher is putting on the board, but her notes have absolutely nothing to do with algebra. Instead, she is writing about boys, clothes, and other topics that are much more important to her than the square root of 121. She proceeds to fold the note into a box or other creative shape, which can often put origami to shame. As soon as the teacher turns her back, the note is passed and the process begins all over again.

4   Lunch, a vital part of the school day, is also very different for Johnny and Jane. On the one hand, for Johnny and his friends, it is a time to compare baseball cards, exchange sports facts, and of course tell jokes about every bodily function imaginable. In front of them on the table, their trays are filled with pizza, soda, fries, and chips, and this food is their main focus. For Jane, on the other hand, lunch is not about eating; it is a chance to exchange the latest gossip about who is going out with whom. The girls look around to see what people are wearing, what they should do with their hair, and so on. Jane's meal is quite a bit smaller than Johnny's: it consists of a small low-fat yogurt and half a bagel (if she feels like splurging, she will spread some cream cheese on the bagel).

5   After school, Johnny and Jane head in different directions. Johnny rushes home to get his bike and meets up with his friends to run around and play typical "guy games," like pick-up basketball or touch football. Johnny and his friends play with every boy who shows up, whether they know him or not. They may get into physical fights and arguments, but they always plan to meet up again the next day. In contrast to the boys, Jane and her friends are very selective. Their circle is a small one, and they do everything together. Some days, they go to the mall (they will not necessarily buy anything there, but they will consider the outing productive anyway, because they will have spent

WORD POWER

origami the Japanese art of folding paper into shapes representing flowers or animals

time together). Most days, though, they just talk, with the discussion ranging from school to guys to lipstick colors. When Jane gets home, she will most likely run to the phone and talk for hours to the same three or four girls.

6   At the age of twelve or thirteen, boys and girls do not seem to have very much in common. Given this situation, it is amazing that boys and girls grow up to become men and women who interact as neighbors, friends, and coworkers. What is even more amazing is that so many grow up to share lives and raise families together, treating each other with love and respect.

PRACTICE 10-3

1. Underline Nisha's thesis statement; then, rewrite it in your own words.
2. Does Nisha's introduction identify the two subjects she will discuss? Does it tell whether she will focus on similarities or on differences?
3. Nisha's essay is a point-by-point comparison. What four points does she discuss for each of her two subjects?
4. Circle some of the transitional words and phrases Nisha uses to move from one example to another.
5. Underline Nisha's summary statement. Then, rewrite it in your own words.
6. Use **TEST** to evaluate Nisha's essay. What revisions would you suggest she make? Why?

Grammar in context

Comparison and Contrast

When you write a comparison-and-contrast essay, be sure to present the points you are comparing or contrasting in **parallel** terms to highlight their similarities or differences.

⎯⎯ PARALLEL ⎯⎯

Johnny, an average thirteen-year-old boy, wakes up late and has to hurry.

⎯⎯ PARALLEL ⎯⎯

Jane, unlike Johnny, wakes up early and takes her time.

For information on revising to make ideas parallel, see Chapter 20.

FOCUS on reading and writing

Reread Steven Conn's essay (p. 249). Then, write your own comparison-and-contrast essay in response to one of the following prompts. (Review the image and text that open this chapter before you choose a topic.) Be sure to follow the writing process outlined in Chapter 3.

1. Write a comparison-and-contrast essay in which you compare two historical figures. In your thesis statement, be sure to communicate the significance of your comparison.
2. Write a comparison-and-contrast essay in which you compare your life before and after an important personal or historical event. What changed for you, and what remained the same?

If you prefer, you can write about one of these topics instead:

- Men's and women's body images
- Two fictional characters
- Two ways of studying for an exam
- Country and city living (or, compare suburban living with either)

Reread the draft of your essay, and then **TEST** it. When you have finished, revise, edit, and proofread your essay.

North Wind Picture Archives/Alamy Stock Photo; PRISMA ARCHIVO/Alamy Stock Photo

CHAPTER REVIEW

COLLABORATIVE ACTIVITY

Read the essay that another student wrote in response to one of this chapter's writing prompts. Then, work with that student to consider the strengths and weaknesses of each of your comparison-and-contrast essays. Do you think that one of your comparison-and-contrast essays is more effective than the other? Explain. Based on your reactions to the essays that you and your classmate wrote, what do you think an effective comparison-and-contrast essay should accomplish? Write a few sentences in which you explain what a comparison-and-contrast essay should do.

Review checklist

Reading and Writing Comparison-and-Contrast Essays

- ✔ A comparison-and-contrast essay can examine just similarities, just differences, or both.

- ✔ When you *read* a comparison-and-contrast essay, follow the active reading process outlined in Chapter 1, and use **TEST** to help you identify the essay's key elements. (See 10a.)

- ✔ Analyzing a student essay can help you understand the structure of a compare-and-contrast essay. (See 10b.)

- ✔ When you *write* a comparison-and-contrast essay, follow the writing process outlined in Chapter 3, and use **TEST** to make sure that you have included all the necessary elements. (See 10c.)

- ✔ Keep in mind that in your college courses you often write in response to reading. (See 10c.)

11 Reading and Writing Argument Essays

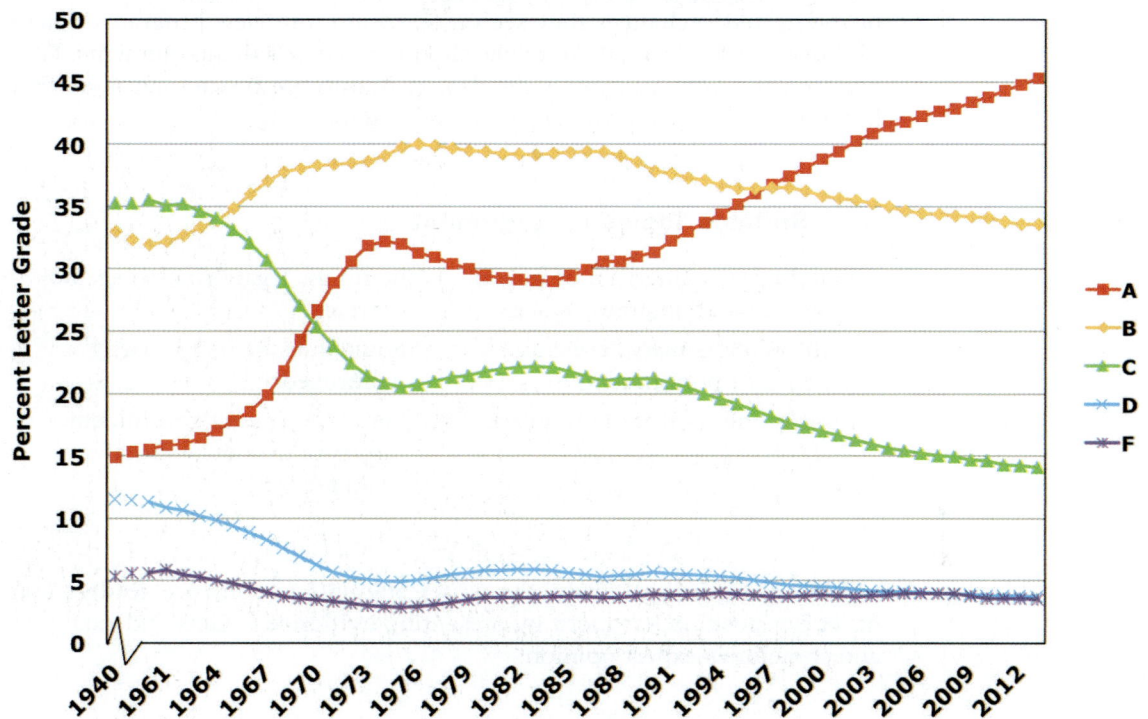

Stuart Rojstaczer

FOCUS on reading and writing

Look at the chart above, which shows the inflation in letter-grade distribution on four-year-college campuses nationwide between 1940 and 2012. Brainstorm to discover what you already know about how instructors grade students and what you think students should do to earn a passing grade. Later in the chapter, you will read an essay on a related topic and then have an opportunity to write about it.

> **PREVIEW**
>
> In this chapter, you will learn to
> - read an argument essay (11a).
> - analyze a student argument essay (11b).
> - write an argument essay (11c).

When most people hear the word *argument*, they think of personal conflicts or the heated exchanges they see on television interview programs. These discussions, however, are more like shouting matches than arguments. True **argument** involves taking a stand on a **debatable issue**—an issue that has at least two sides and can therefore be debated.

> **Suitable Topics for Argument**
>
> Should every American be guaranteed a basic minimum wage?
>
> Is the death penalty "cruel and unusual" punishment?
>
> Should online education replace classroom instruction?
>
> Should the legal drinking age be lowered?
>
> Should guns be more strictly controlled?
>
> Should the federal government do more to control illegal immigration?

In an **argument essay**, the writer attempts to convince readers that his or her position has merit by presenting **evidence**—facts and examples and sometimes expert opinion.

11a Reading an Argument Essay

When you **read** an argument essay, follow the active reading process outlined in Chapter 1. You can use **TEST** to help you identify its key elements. Make sure that you follow the active reading process outlined in Chapter 1.

T **Thesis** Look for a **thesis** that expresses the essay's main idea: the position the writer takes on a debatable issue. This idea may be presented in a **thesis statement**, or it may be **implied**, suggested by the discussion. Although the thesis statement often appears in the introduction, it can, particularly in the case of controversial subjects, appear in the middle or even at the end of the essay. In these situations, the assumption is that readers will not readily accept the thesis, so the writer presents the basic issues before stating his or her position. As you read, identify the writer's strategy and ask yourself why the writer chose the option he or she did.

E **Evidence** In the body paragraphs, look for **evidence**, the information that supports the thesis statement. As you read, keep in mind that evidence can consist of *facts* or *opinions*. **Facts** are statements that can be verified. **Opinions** are judgments or beliefs that are not subject to proof. Opinions do not carry the same weight as facts, but they can be persuasive if they are the opinions of **experts**, people who know a lot about the subject. As you read, consider the arguments the writer is making. Are these arguments supported by evidence, or does the writer just assume that readers will agree? Does the writer consider opposing arguments? How effectively does the writer **refute**—argue against—these opposing arguments? In each body paragraph, look for a topic sentence that identifies the point that the writer is making.

S **Summary** In the concluding paragraphs of an argument essay, look for a **summary** or **summary statement** that reinforces the writer's position. Does the summary clearly and convincingly restate the essay's thesis and reinforce the argument?

T **Transitions** Try to identify the **transitional words and phrases** that connect points within paragraphs and between one paragraph and the next. As you read, determine how transitions enable readers to keep track of the argument and to move from one point to another. For example, do transitions introduce specific points in support of the argument (*first*, *second*, and *finally*), signal refutation (*nevertheless* or *however*), or introduce a conclusion (*therefore* or *consequently*)?

Some Transitional Words and Phrases for Argument

Transitions are extremely important in argument essays because they not only signal the movement from one part of the argument to another but also relate specific points to one another and to the thesis statement.

accordingly	granted	of course
admittedly	however	on the one hand
although	in addition	on the other hand
because	in conclusion	since
but	indeed	therefore

certainly	in fact	so
consequently	in summary	therefore
despite	meanwhile	thus
even so	moreover	to be sure
even though	nevertheless	truly
finally	nonetheless	
first, second . . .	now	

Inductive and Deductive Argument

An argument essay can be organized *inductively* or *deductively*.

An **inductive argument** moves from specific to general. That is, it begins with a series of specific observations (or examples) that lead to a general conclusion based on these observations. For example, an essay that takes the position that your school should do more to address the needs of physically challenged students could be structured as an inductive argument. After discussing the specific hardships that physically challenged students face on campus every day, the essay could lead to the conclusion that in spite of the steps the school has already taken, it should do more to accommodate students with physical disabilities.

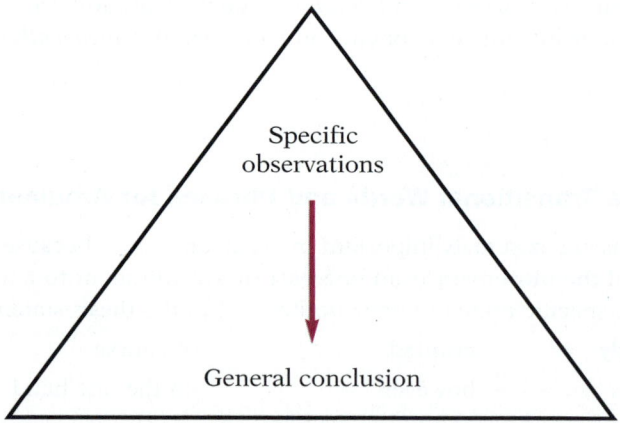

A **deductive argument** moves from general to specific. That is, it begins with a **major premise** (a general statement that the writer believes to be true or believes that readers will accept) and then moves to a **minor premise** (a specific instance of the major premise). It ends with a **conclusion** that logically follows from the two premises. For example, an essay that supports an increase in the federal minimum wage could be structured as a deductive argument. It could begin with the major premise that all workers are entitled to a living wage. It could then go on to state the minor premise that minimum-wage workers are just like other workers. (It could also present facts, examples, and the opinions of experts to make the point that many of these workers live close to the poverty line and, for this reason, are not earning a living wage.) The essay could conclude by saying that minimum-wage workers are, therefore, entitled to an increase in pay.

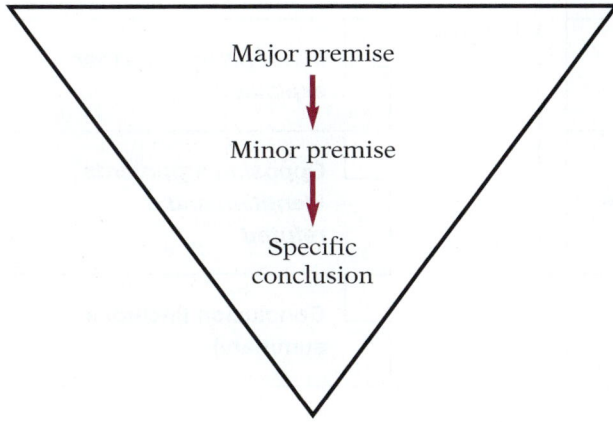

In an argument essay, each body paragraph often begins with a **topic sentence** that clearly states a point in support of the thesis. Throughout the essay, **evidence**—facts, examples, and expert opinions—makes the argument convincing. In addition to taking a position, an argument essay often identifies opposing arguments and then **refutes** them—that is, argues against them by identifying factual errors, errors in logic, and inconsistencies. If an opposing argument is particularly strong, the writer may **concede** (acknowledge) its strengths—and then go on to point out some weaknesses.

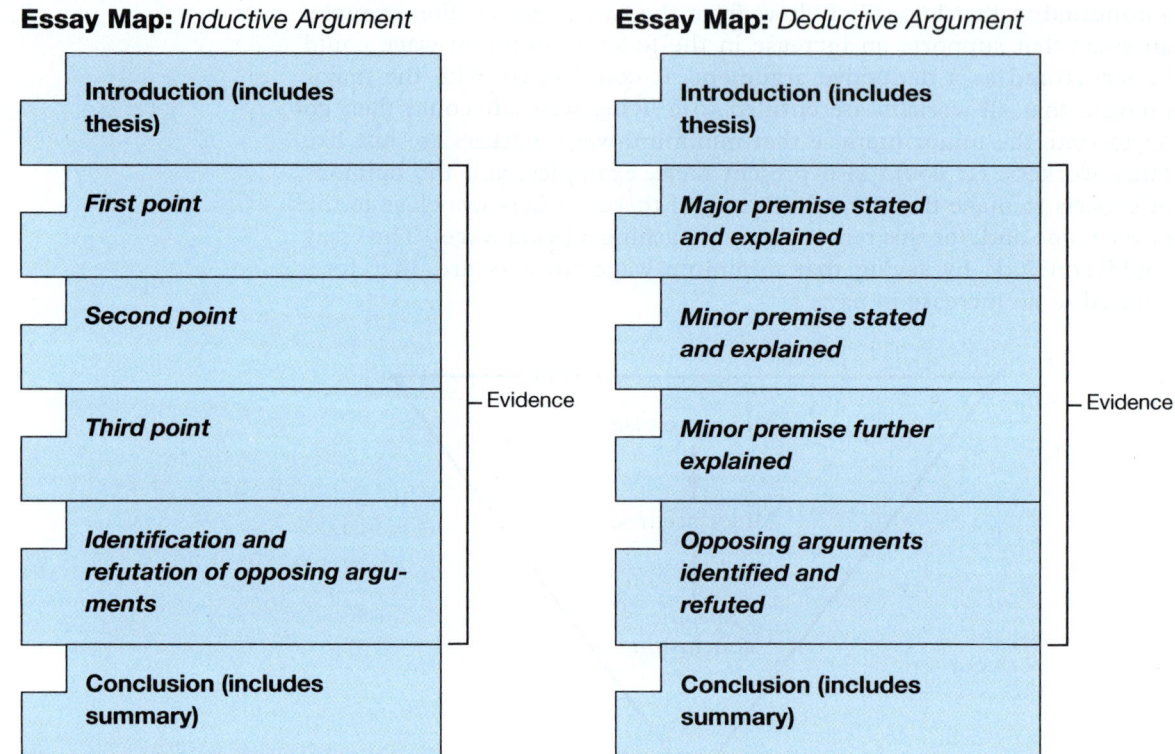

In your college courses, much of your writing will be in response to reading—specifically to reading texts by professional writers like the one that follows. In this essay, "In Praise of the F Word," Mary Sherry takes a stand on a debatable issue, arguing that it is good for students to fail once in a while, and tries to convince readers to accept her position. Read the essay, following the active reading process outlined in Chapter 1, and then answer the questions on pages 271–272. (At the end of this chapter, you will be asked to write an argument essay in response to Sherry's ideas.)

In Praise of the F Word

Mary Sherry

Mary Sherry is a writer and adult literacy educator who is currently working as a tutor in the Learning Center at Mid-State Technical College in Wisconsin Rapids. She has previously taught in both adult basic education and vocational technical programs. In her essay "In Praise of the F Word," which was first published in the "My Turn" column of *Newsweek* in 1991, she argues that it is good for students to fail once in a while because it motivates them to work harder and do better work.

Before you read, consider what you think about failing grades. Do you think they motivate or discourage students?

1   Tens of thousands of 18-year-olds will graduate this year and be handed meaningless diplomas. These diplomas won't look any different from those awarded their luckier classmates. Their validity will be questioned only when their employers discover that these graduates are semiliterate.

2   Eventually a fortunate few will find their way into educational-repair shops—adult-literacy programs, such as the one where I teach basic grammar and writing. There, high-school graduates and high-school dropouts pursuing graduate-equivalency certificates will learn the skills they should have learned in school. They will also discover they have been cheated by our educational system.

3   As I teach, I learn a lot about our schools. Early in each session I ask my students to write about an unpleasant experience they had in school. No writers' block here! "I wish someone would have had made me stop doing drugs and made me study." "I liked to party and no one seemed to care." "I was a good kid and didn't cause any trouble, so they just passed me along even though I didn't read and couldn't write." And so on.

4   I am your basic do-gooder, and prior to teaching this class I blamed the poor academic skills our kids have today on drugs, divorce and other impediments to concentration necessary for doing well in school. But, as I rediscover each time I walk into the classroom, before a teacher can expect students to concentrate, he has to get their attention, no matter what distractions may be at hand. There are many ways to do this, and they have much to do with teaching style. However, if style alone won't do it, there is another way to show who holds the winning hand in the classroom. That is to reveal the trump card of failure.

5   I will never forget a teacher who played that card to get the attention of one of my children. Our youngest, a world-class charmer, did little to develop his intellectual talents but always got by. Until Mrs. Stifter.

6   Our son was a high-school senior when he had her for English. "He sits in the back of the room talking to his friends," she told me. "Why don't you move him to the front row?" I urged, believing the embarrassment would get him to settle down. Mrs. Stifter looked at me steely-eyed over her glasses. "I don't move seniors," she said. "I flunk them." I was flustered

---

WORD POWER
semiliterate barely able to read or write

WORD POWER
trump card a key resource to be used at the right moment

WORD POWER
flustered in a state of worry or confusion
composure calmness

Our son's academic life flashed before my eyes. No teacher had ever threatened him with that before. I regained my composure and managed to say that I thought she was right. By the time I got home I was feeling pretty good about this. It was a radical approach for these times, but, well, why not? "She's going to flunk you," I told my son. I did not discuss it any further. Suddenly English became a priority in his life. He finished out the semester with an A.

7   I know one example doesn't make a case, but at night I see a parade of students who are angry and resentful for having been passed along until they could no longer even pretend to keep up. Of average intelligence or better, they eventually quit school, concluding they were too dumb to finish. "I should have been held back" is a comment I hear frequently. Even sadder are those students who are high-school graduates who say to me after a few weeks of class, "I don't know how I ever got a high-school diploma."

8   Passing students who have not mastered the work cheats them and the employers who expect graduates to have basic skills. We excuse this dishonest behavior by saying kids can't learn if they come from terrible environments. No one seems to stop to think that—no matter what environments they come from—most kids don't put school first on their list unless they perceive something is at stake. They'd rather be sailing.

9   Many students I see at night could give expert testimony on unemployment, chemical dependency, abusive relationships. In spite of these difficulties, they have decided to make education a priority. They are motivated by the desire for a better job or the need to hang on to the one they've got. They have a healthy fear of failure.

10   People of all ages can rise above their problems, but they need to have a reason to do so. Young people generally don't have the maturity to value education in the same way my adult students value it. But fear of failure, whether economic or academic, can motivate both. Flunking as a regular policy has just as much merit today as it did two generations ago. We must review the threat of flunking and see it as it really is—a positive teaching tool. It is an expression of confidence by both teachers and parents that the students have the ability to learn the material presented to them. However, making it work again would take a dedicated, caring conspiracy between teachers and parents. It would mean facing the tough reality that passing kids who haven't learned the material—while it might save them grief for the short term—dooms them to long-term illiteracy. It would mean that teachers would have to follow through on their threats, and parents would have to stand behind them, knowing their children's best interests are indeed at stake. This means no more doing Scott's assignments for him because he might fail. No more passing Jodi because she's such a nice kid.

11   This is a policy that worked in the past and can work today. A wise teacher, with the support of his parents, gave our son the opportunity to succeed—or fail. It's time we return this choice to all students.

> **WORD POWER**
> **merit** value or worth
> **conspiracy** a joining or acting together

Focus on Reading

1. Look back at the work you did when you previewed, highlighted, and annotated this essay. What key points did you identify?
2. Which of Sherry's key points do you agree with? Which do you disagree with? If you have not already done so, indicate your responses with annotations in the margins of the essay.
3. **TEST** Sherry's essay. Does she include all four **TEST** elements? If not, why not? What, if anything, does she need to add?

Focus on Meaning

1. Who or what does Sherry blame for the "meaningless diplomas" (paragraph 1) that are issued each year? What other reasons for this situation can you think of?
2. What does Sherry mean in paragraph 10 when she says, "Flunking as a regular policy has just as much merit today as it did two generations ago"?
3. How does the experience Sherry's son had in high school convince her that the threat of failure is a "positive teaching tool" (paragraph 10)?

Focus on Strategy

1. Where does Sherry state her thesis? Where else could she have stated it? Would it have been more or less effective there? Why?
2. Throughout her essay, Sherry establishes her credentials as a teacher. Why? If she weren't a teacher, would her argument be as convincing?

Focus on Language and Style

1. In her title, Sherry refers to flunking as the "F Word." What point is she making by doing this?
2. In paragraph 4, Sherry calls herself a "do-gooder." What does this term mean? How does Sherry use it in her essay? What other term could she have used instead?

Focus on the Pattern

1. Sherry organizes her argument inductively. List the evidence that she uses to reach her conclusion. Has she provided enough evidence? Explain. (For a discussion of inductive reasoning, see Inductive and Deductive Argument, p. 266.)
2. In paragraph 2, Sherry refers to "educational-repair shops." Why does she think that adult literacy classes are "repair shops"?

Focus on Critical Thinking

In paragraph 9 and 10, Sherry argues that if students do not have a "healthy fear of failure" (9), they will not be motivated to work. What does she mean? Do you have a "healthy fear of failure"? If so, does it motivate you, or does it get in your way? Explain.

11b Analyzing a Student Essay: Argument

The following argument essay was written by Jessica Mar in response to this assignment in her political science class.

> Should the government play a major role in most (or even all) aspects of our lives, or should we be free to make our own rules when it comes to lifestyle choices, such as what we eat or what safety procedures we follow? Choose one issue, and explain why government should (or should not) regulate it.

To help you understand the structure of an argument essay, read Jessica's essay, following the active reading process discussed in Chapter 1, and then fill in the essay map in Practice 11-1 on page 275. (Note that the **TEST** elements in the essay have been highlighted and color-coded.) As you read, notice that Jessica supported some of her points with information from online sources, which she enumerates in a works-cited list. For a discussion of working with sources, see Chapter 13. For a discussion about documenting sources, see Chapter 14.

T Thesis
E Evidence
S Summary
T Transitions

Stop the Regulators, Empower the Consumers

1   One of the primary functions of government is to keep its citizens safe. Elected officials try to fulfill this duty by making and enforcing laws. However, governments can take this obligation too far — particularly when they overregulate personal behavior — and when they do, citizens often object. Although outlawing people's access to dangerous substances, such as drugs and hazardous chemicals, makes sense, restricting people's personal food choices does not. For this reason, the government should treat people like responsible adults and not tell them what they can eat and drink.

Thesis

2   First, no government agency can accurately determine what is healthy for everyone. Different people have different health needs, different calorie requirements, and different abilities to tolerate certain foods. Therefore, any standard that the government adopts is bound to favor some people and penalize others. For example, low-income citizens are at a disadvantage because often they cannot find or afford what the government has decided is "healthy." Organic produce, whole grains, and lean meats are more expensive than processed or fast foods. For this reason, by restricting access to "unhealthy" products, the government makes it difficult for many people to get adequate nourishment. In addition, meeting arbitrary government requirements costs stores and restaurants more money, and this cost is passed on to consumers. As recent article points out, mistakes ion government food policy will cost an average American family "an extra $4,440 each year" (Furth). Government regulation often makes food more expensive, but it does not necessarily result in more nutritious eating.

3   Second, instead of legislating, the government should encourage people to make informed decisions. Good eating habits need to be learned, not imposed. In other words, governments should help educate people but should not make choices for them. At least one state, Mississippi, is trying to uphold its citizens' rights to make their own decisions about what to eat and drink. Recently, Mississippi passed a law that prohibits state regulation of products sold in its restaurants, supermarkets, and convenience stores. The senator who wrote the law explained, "This is about personal responsibility. When I go out to eat with my three daughters they get waters. I don't need the government to tell me to do that" (qtd. in Severson). Certainly, no one is denying that there is a high rate of obesity in this country. However, making it illegal to buy a large soda will not solve this problem. Encouraging individuals to make informed choices will do much more than legislation to improve peoples' long-term health.

4   Finally, consumers must insist that companies provide healthier products and informative labels. It stands to reason that companies want to make products that consumers will buy. So, if consumers insist on more options and more information, then companies will provide those things. For example, there is evidence that companies are listening to consumers' requests for nutritious, low-calorie food and drinks. A recent article in *The Economist* reports that "food companies are keen to show that they take the obesity problem seriously," and "virtually every company has a plan of its own to improve nutrition" ("Food Companies"). Consumers need to support companies in these efforts by buying the best quality food their families can afford. They need to educate themselves about the products

they consume, and demand calorie counts as well as detailed ingredient lists. Most importantly, they need to take responsibility for what they and their children are eating. They do not need the government to do this work for them.

5   Some people point out that consumers do not always have the knowledge to make healthy choices. They maintain that the government is better equipped to make such decisions. After all, the government regulates other aspects of daily life, such as highway safety, so why shouldn't it regulate nutrition too? However, in the case of driving, unsafe driving is a behavior that endangers the safety of others. In contrast, eating too much fatty, sugary, or salty food does not put others at risk. Moreover, the argument that consumers do not know enough to feed themselves properly is offensive. Such a claim assumes that people are as helpless as children. In fact, most people are capable of making mature choices for themselves and should be allowed to do so. Insisting that people need the government to tell them how to eat well is an unwarranted expansion of government into the lives of its citizens. In the end, this kind of overprotection produces dependent, insecure, and even resentful citizens.

6   The government needs to stop telling people what they can and cannot eat and drink. People should have the freedom to decide for themselves what to eat, considering whether a particular food or beverage is affordable, if it is healthy, and if the portion size is appropriate. The only legislation that is needed now is a wide-reaching ban, like Mississippi's, on further regulations of food and beverages. Laws that restrict what individuals can eat or drink prevent people from taking responsibility for their own health, insult the public's intelligence, and can result in higher food prices. If government officials genuinely want to improve people's health, they should stop trying to control their citizens' eating habits and provide them the information they need to make informed choices.

Works Cited

"Food Companies Play an Ambivalent Part in the Fight against Flab." *The Economist*, 15 Dec. 2015, economist.com/news/ special-report/21568064-food-companies-play-ambivalent-part-fight-against-flab-food-thought.

Furth, Salim. "Costly Mistakes: How Bad Policies Raise the Cost of Living." *The Heritage Foundation*, 23 Nov. 2015, heritage. org/government-regulation/report/costly-mistakes-how-bad-policies-raise-the-cost-living.

Severson, Kim. "'Anti-Bloomberg Bill' in Mississippi Bars Local Restrictions on Food and Drink." *The New York Times*, 13 Mar. 2013, nytimes.com/2013/03/14/us/anti-bloomberg-bill-in-mississippi-bars-local-restrictions-on-food-and-drink.html.

PRACTICE 11-1 Now that you have read Jessica's essay, fill in the map that follows to help you to understand how she organized her writing. Then, decide whether her organization is effective.

Introduction _____
_____
_____
_____

First point _____
_____
_____
_____

Second point _____
_____
_____
_____

Third point _____
_____
_____
_____

Opposing arguments and refutation
_____
_____
_____

Conclusion _____
_____
_____
_____

PRACTICE 11-2

1. Does Jessica's thesis statement indicate the position she will take? Draft another thesis statement that she could have used. Which do you think is more effective?
2. What arguments does Jessica make? What other arguments could she have made?
3. What evidence does Jessica include? Does she include enough evidence? What other types of evidence could she have used?
4. What arguments against her thesis does Jessica address? How effectively does she refute them? What other arguments could she have refuted?
5. What points does Jessica reinforce in her conclusion? Should she have emphasized another point? Why or why not?
6. What is the essay's greatest strength? What is its greatest weakness?

11c Writing an Argument Essay

When you are given a writing assignment, the wording of your assignment may suggest that you write an argument essay. For example, you may be asked to *debate*, *argue*, *consider*, *give your opinion*, *take a position*, or *take a stand*. Once you decide that your assignment calls for argument, you need to develop a thesis statement that takes a position on the topic you will write about in your essay.

ASSIGNMENT	THESIS STATEMENT
Composition Explain your position on a current social issue.	People should be able to invest some of their Social Security contributions in the stock market.
American history Do you believe that General Lee was responsible for the South's defeat at the Battle of Gettysburg? Why or why not?	Because Lee refused to listen to the advice given to him by General Longstreet, he is largely responsible for the South's defeat at the Battle of Gettysburg.
Ethics Should physician-assisted suicide be legalized?	Although many people think physician-assisted suicide should remain illegal, it should be legal in certain situations.

When you **write** an argument essay, you follow the process outlined in Chapter 3. The essay you write will include the same elements you have learned to recognize in the argument essays you read. When you finish your draft, you can **TEST** it to make sure it includes all the elements of an argument essay.

TESTing your argument essay

Thesis Statement Unifies Your Essay

☐ Does your introduction include a **thesis statement** that clearly expresses the stand you take on the issue you will discuss? Is this issue debatable—that is, does it really have two or more sides?

Evidence Supports Your Essay's Thesis Statement

☐ Does all your **evidence**—facts, examples, and expert opinion—support your thesis, or should some be deleted?

☐ Do you have enough evidence to support your points?

☐ Have you considered whether readers are likely to be hostile toward, neutral toward, or in agreement with your position—and have you chosen your points accordingly?

☐ Is your evidence presented in a clear inductive or deductive order?

Summary Statement Reinforces Your Essay's Main Idea

☐ Does your conclusion include a **summary statement** that reinforces your essay's thesis?

Transitions Connect Events

☐ Do you include **transitions** that introduce your points?

☐ Do you include enough **transitional words and phrases** to help readers follow the logic of your argument?

Following a Student Writer

Alex Norman, a student in a first-year writing course, was asked to write an argument essay on a controversial issue of his choice. His instructor suggested that students find a topic by reading their campus and local newspapers, going online to read national news stories and political blogs, and watching public affairs programs on television. One issue that caught

Alex's interest was the question of whether the government should do more to subsidize the cost of college for low-income students. Although Alex sympathized with students who needed help paying for school, he also questioned whether taxpayers should have to foot the bill. Because this issue clearly had at least two sides, and because he wasn't sure at the outset which position he could best support, Alex thought it would be a good topic to explore further.

Alex began by **brainstorming**, recording all his ideas on this complex issue. In addition to ideas he thought of as he read, he also included ideas he developed as he spoke to his sister, a recent college graduate, and to his boss at the bank where he worked part-time. When he read over his brainstorming notes, he saw that he had good arguments both for and against increasing government funding for low-income students. At this point, he wasn't sure which position to take in his essay, so he scheduled an appointment for a **conference** with his instructor.

Alex's instructor pointed out that he could make a good case either for or against greater government subsidies; like many controversial issues, this one had no easy answers. She encouraged him to support the position that seemed right to him and to use the information on the opposing side to present (and refute) opposing arguments. She also recommended that Alex email his first draft to her so she could review it.

After he thought about his instructor's comments, Alex decided to argue in favor of increasing government grants to help low-income students pay for college. Before he began to draft his essay, he wrote a **thesis statement** that presented his position on the issue; then, he arranged supporting points from his brainstorming notes into an **outline** that he could follow as he wrote. As he **drafted** his essay, Alex made sure to support his thesis with evidence and to explain his position as clearly and thoroughly as possible. He paid special attention to choosing transitional words and phrases that would indicate how his points were logically connected to one another.

When Alex finished his draft, he TESTed it, taking a quick inventory to make sure he had included all four necessary components of an essay. He then went on to **revise** his draft. Next, he emailed his revised draft to his instructor. Following her suggestions, he continued revising his draft, this time focusing on his topic sentences, his presentation (and refutation) of opposing arguments, and his introductory and concluding paragraphs. When he was satisfied with his revisions, he **edited** and **proofread** his essay. Read Alex's essay, and then answer the questions in Practice 11-3 on page 281.

Increase Grant Money for Low-Income College Students

1   The price of college tuition has more than doubled over the last two decades. Today, low-income students are finding it especially difficult (and sometimes impossible) to pay for school. Should the government help these

students more than it does now? If so, what form should that help take? Rather than reducing aid or asking students to borrow more, the government should give larger grants to subsidize tuition for low-income students.

2   If this is a country that is committed to equal opportunity, then college should be affordable for all. To compete in today's high-tech job market, people need a college degree. However, students' access to college is too often determined by their parents' income. This is unfair. Therefore, the government should make it a priority to support students who are being priced out of a college education. Specifically, the government should give larger grants to low-income students. Although some critics see these grants as unnecessary "handouts," such awards are the best way for the government to invest in the future and to maintain our nation's core values. After all, the country's economy benefits when more of its citizens earn college degrees. Even more important, by giving low-income students the same opportunities to succeed as their more affluent peers, the United States keeps its promise to treat all its citizens fairly.

3   Some people argue that the best way to help students who are struggling to pay for college is to offer them more loans at a lower interest rate. However, this solution is inadequate, unfair, and short-sighted. First of all, lowering the interest rate on student loans only reduces the average monthly payments by a few dollars. Second, student loans already unfairly burden low-income students. Why should they have to take on more debt simply because their parents make less money? The government should be trying to reduce the amount these students have to borrow, not increase it. Finally, forcing graduates to start their careers with such a heavy financial burden will hurt the country's economy. Although loans might cost the government less in the short term, in the long term, student debt makes it more difficult for Americans to be successful and competitive.

4   The federal government does have a program in place to help students who demonstrate need, but Pell Grant funding needs to be expanded. Despite the rising cost of tuition, college students now actually receive proportionally less government grant money than ever before. As a recent report points out, the maximum Pell grant in 2016–17 covers only sixty percent of the tuition and fees at a public four-year college. When you add room and

board into the mix, things get even worse, with Pell grants covering only twenty-nine percent of the total. At private colleges, Pell grants cover only thirteen percent of the average tuition, fees, and room and board ("Maximum Pell Grants"). Meanwhile, the education gap between rich and poor is growing. As education policy expert Andrew J. Rotherham observes, while seventy-five percent of wealthy students earn a four-year degree by age twenty-four, less than ten percent of low-income students do. To help close this gap, the government should offer more funding to those most in need of financial assistance.

5   Some would argue, however, that the government should do just the opposite. One of the most common criticisms of government subsidies is that they are in some way to blame for the rising cost of college. Critics point out that government grants only make it easier for schools to charge more. This may be true, but as Andrew J. Rotherham points out, the government could do more to regulate college tuition. For example, the government could offer incentives to schools that keep their costs down or award more generous grants to students who attend affordable schools. Ultimately, withdrawing aid and abandoning students to the free market is irresponsible as well as counterproductive.

6   With the cost of college continuing to rise, now is the time for the government to help the hardest-hit students by offering them more help to pay for their education. Rather than cutting spending on student aid, the government should fund more grants to low-income students. However, it must do so in ways that discourage future increases in tuition. By acting wisely and prudently, the government can improve access to higher education for all and support the country's economic future.

Works Cited

"Maximum Pell Grant and Published Prices at Four-Year Institutions over Time." *College Board*, Apr. 2017, trends.collegeboard.org/student-aid/figures-tables/maximum-pell-grant-and-published-prices-four-year-institutions-over-time.

Rothman, Andrew J. "How to Fix Pell Grants." *Time*, 24 May 2012, ideas.time.com/2012/05/24/how-to-fix-pell-grants.

PRACTICE 11-3

1. Underline Alex's thesis statement. In your own words, restate the position Alex takes in his essay.
2. List the evidence Alex uses to support his thesis. Where does he include facts? Examples? Expert opinion?
3. Circle some of the transitional words and phrases Alex uses to move from one point to another. How do they advance his argument? Where could he have included additional transitions?
4. Underline Alex's summary statement. Then, restate it in your own words.
5. Use **TEST** to evaluate Alex's essay. What revisions would you suggest he make, and why?

Grammar in context

Argument

When you write an argument essay, you need to show the relationships between your ideas by combining sentences to create **compound sentences** and **complex sentences**.

The federal government does have a program in place to help students who demonstrate need*, but* Pell Grant funding needs to be expanded. (compound sentence)

Although some critics ~~Some critics~~ see these grants as unnecessary "handouts,"*, such* ~~Such~~ awards are the best way for the government to invest in the future and to maintain our nation's core values. (complex sentence)

For information on how to create compound and complex sentences, see Chapter 18.

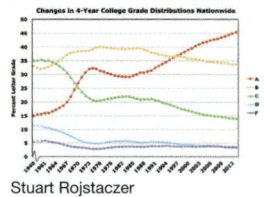
Stuart Rojstaczer

FOCUS on reading and writing

Reread Sherry's essay (p. 268), and then write your own argument essay in response to one of the following prompts. (Review the image and text that open this chapter before you choose a topic.) Be sure to follow the writing process outlined in Chapter 3.

1. Write an argument that supports or opposes the idea of using failure as a teaching tool. Do you, like Sherry, believe that flunking is a policy that "can work today" (paragraph 11)? Or, do you think that there are better ways to motivate students? Try to identify and refute at least two opposing arguments.

2. Write a letter to a teacher who threatened you with failure. Make the case that the teacher's warning either motivated you or did more harm than good. Support your position with specific examples.

3. Do you in any way feel "cheated by our educational system" (paragraph 2)? Write an argument essay in which you answer this question. Use your own experiences as well as ideas from Sherry's essay as evidence.

   If you prefer, you can write about one of these topics instead:

   - The federal government should (or should not) forgive all student loans.
   - Assault-style weapons should (or should not) be banned.
   - Animals should (or should not) be used in medical research.

Reread the draft of your essay, and then **TEST** it. When you have finished, revise, edit, and proofread your essay.

CHAPTER REVIEW

COLLABORATIVE ACTIVITY

Read the essay that another student wrote in response to one of this chapter's writing prompts. Then, work with that student to consider the strengths and weaknesses of each of your argument essays. Do you think that one of your argument essays is more convincing than the other? Explain. Based on your reactions to the essays that you and your classmate wrote, what do you think an effective argument essay should accomplish? Write a few sentences in which you explain what an argument essay should do.

Review checklist

Reading and Writing Argument Essays

- ✔ **Argument** takes a stand on a debatable issue. An **argument essay** attempts to convince readers that the writer's ideas have merit by presenting evidence—facts, examples, and sometimes expert opinion.

- ✔ When you *read* an argument essay, follow the reading process outlined in Chapter 1, and use **TEST** to help you identify the essay's key elements. (See 11a.)

- ✔ Analyzing a student essay can help you understand the structure of an argument essay. (See 11b.)

- ✔ When you *write* an argument essay, follow the writing process outlined in Chapter 3, and use **TEST** to make sure that you have included all the necessary elements. (See 11c.)

12 Additional Options for Organizing Essays

> **PREVIEW**
>
> In this chapter you will learn to
> - read and write a descriptive essay (12a).
> - read and write a process essay (12b).
> - read and write a classification essay (12c).
> - read and write a definition essay (12d).

As you learned in Chapters 7 through 11, writers have a variety of options—often referred to as *patterns*—for developing ideas within an essay. The patterns explained and illustrated in Chapters 7 through 11 are the ones you are most likely to encounter and to use in your academic career. Four additional ways to organize an essay—*description*, *process*, *classification*, and *definition*—are discussed and illustrated in this chapter.

 ## 12a Description

Description tells what something looks, sounds, smells, tastes, or feels like. There are two types of description: *objective* and *subjective*.

An **objective** description is primarily factual, omitting the writer's reactions or responses. It relies on precise observations and uses direct and unemotional language. A **subjective** description reflects the writer's thoughts, emotions, and perspective. It uses language that conveys (or suggests) the writer's personal feelings and reactions to what is being described.

> **OBJECTIVE DESCRIPTION**
> The columns were ten feet tall and made of white marble.
>
> **SUBJECTIVE DESCRIPTION**
> The columns were tall and powerful looking, and their glistening white marble surfaces reflected the harsh glare of the afternoon sun.

Keep in mind that no description is totally objective or subjective. An objective description often includes language that expresses the writer's mood, and a subjective description can include factual details and neutral language.

> ## FYI
>
> **Figures of Speech**
>
> Descriptive writing, particularly subjective description, is frequently enriched by **figures of speech**—language that creates special or unusual effects:
>
> - A **simile** uses *like* or *as* to compare two unlike things.
>
>   Her smile was like sunshine.
>
> - A **metaphor** compares two unlike things without using *like* or *as*.
>
>   Her smile was a light that lit up the room.
>
> - **Personification** suggests a comparison between a nonliving thing and a person by giving the nonliving thing human traits.
>
>   The sun smiled down on the crowd.
>
> See 5b for more on figurative language.

Reading a Descriptive Essay

When you **read** a descriptive essay, follow the active reading process outlined in Chapter 1. You can use **TEST** to help you identify its key elements.

T **Thesis**—In the introduction of a descriptive essay, look for a **thesis** that expresses the essay's main idea—the point the writer is making about the setting, object, or person described. This idea may be explicitly stated in a **thesis statement**, or it may be **implied**, suggested by the choice and arrangement of details. As you read, consider which of these two options the writer used, and why.

E **Evidence**—In the body paragraphs, look for **evidence**, descriptive details that support the thesis. Details are likely to be arranged in **spatial order**—for example, from far to near or from bottom to top. As you read, consider whether the writer has included enough details and whether the details create a clear picture for the reader.

S **Summary**—In the essay's conclusion, look for a **summary** of the writer's impressions or a **summary statement** that reinforces the essay's thesis, reminding readers of the point the writer is making about the subject described.

T **Transitions**—As you read, try to identify the **transitional words and phrases** that connect details within and between body paragraphs and show how they are related. Sometimes you will notice a **transitional paragraph** that moves readers from one section or feature of the subject to another.

> ### Some Transitional Words and Phrases for Description
>
> Transitional words and expressions connect details and show how they work together to create a full picture for readers. Many of these useful transitions indicate location or distance:
>
> | | | |
> |---|---|---|
> | above | in front of | outside |
> | behind | inside | over |
> | below | nearby | the least important |
> | between | next to | the most important |
> | beyond | on | under |
> | in | on one side . . . on | |
> | in back of | the other side | |

In a descriptive essay, details enable readers to see what the writer sees, hear what the writer hears, and feel what the writer has experienced. Often, the writer's goal is to create a single **dominant impression**, a central theme or idea to which all the details relate—for example, the liveliness of a street scene

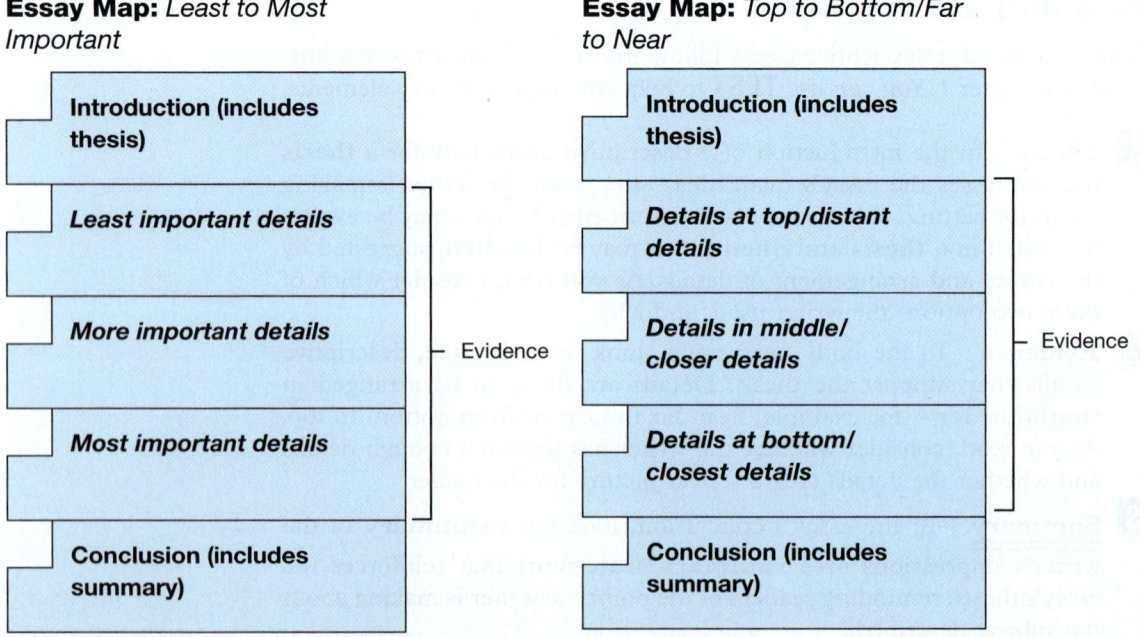

or the tranquility of a summer night. The dominant impression unifies the description and gives readers an overall sense of what the person, place, object, or scene looks like (and perhaps what it sounds, smells, tastes, or feels like).

The details in a descriptive essay can be arranged in many different ways—for example, from least to most important details, from top to bottom (or from bottom to top), or from near to far (or from far to near). Each of the essay's body paragraphs may focus on one key characteristic of the subject being described or on several related descriptive details.

In your college courses, much of your writing will be in response to reading—specifically, to reading texts such as the one that follows. In this essay, "A Fable for Tomorrow," Rachel Carson describes a typical small town "in the heart of America." By doing so, she tries to change the way people look at nature and to stimulate a debate about the environment. Read the essay, following the active reading process outlined in Chapter 1, and then answer the questions that follow on pages 288–289. At the end of section 12a, you will be asked to **write** a descriptive essay in response to Carson's ideas.

A Fable for Tomorrow

Rachel Carson

Rachel Carson (1907–1964) is often credited with starting the modern-day environmental movement. Her book *Silent Spring* (1962) exposed the devastating effects of pesticides on the environment. In the excerpt that follows, part of the introduction to that book, Carson uses specific details to create a powerful picture of the place she describes.

Before you read, consider what reactions today's readers might have to this essay. How would they be different from the reactions of readers in 1962?

1   There was once a town in the heart of America where all life seemed to live in harmony with its surroundings. The town lay in the midst of a checkerboard of prosperous farms, with fields of grain and hillsides of orchards where, in spring, white clouds of bloom drifted above the green fields. In autumn, oak and maple and birch set up a blaze of color that flamed and flickered across a backdrop of pines. Then foxes barked in the hills and deer silently crossed the fields, half hidden in the mists of the fall mornings.

2   Along the roads, laurel, viburnum and alder, great ferns and wildflowers delighted the traveler's eye through much of the year. Even in winter the roadsides were places of beauty, where countless birds came to feed on the berries and on the seed heads of the dried weeds rising above the snow. The countryside was, in fact, famous for the abundance and variety of its bird life, and when the flood of migrants was pouring through in spring and fall people traveled from great distances to observe them. Others came to fish the streams, which flowed clear and cold out of the hills and contained shady pools where trout lay. So it had been from the days many years ago when the first settlers raised their houses, sank their wells, and built their barns.

> **WORD POWER**
>
> **viburnum** a type of shrub with large, white, cream, or pink flower clusters

WORD POWER

moribund dying

3   Then a strange blight crept over the area and everything began to change. Some evil spell had settled on the community: mysterious maladies swept the flocks of chickens; the cattle and sheep sickened and died. Everywhere was a shadow of death. The farmers spoke of much illness among their families. In the town the doctors had become more and more puzzled by new kinds of sickness appearing among their patients. There had been several sudden and unexplained deaths, not only among adults but even among children, who would be stricken suddenly while at play and die within a few hours.

4   There was a strange stillness. The birds, for example—where had they gone? Many people spoke of them, puzzled and disturbed. The feeding stations in the backyards were deserted. The few birds seen anywhere were moribund; they trembled violently and could not fly. It was a spring without voices. On the mornings that had once throbbed with the dawn chorus of robins, catbirds, doves, jays, wrens, and scores of other bird voices there was now no sound; only silence lay over the fields and woods and marsh.

5   On the farms the hens brooded, but no chicks hatched. The farmers complained that they were unable to raise any pigs—the litters were small and the young survived only a few days. The apple trees were coming into bloom but no bees droned among the blossoms, so there was no pollination and there would be no fruit.

6   The roadsides, once so attractive, were now lined with browned and withered vegetation as though swept by fire. These, too, were silent, deserted by all living things. Even the streams were now lifeless. Anglers no longer visited them, for all the fish had died.

7   In the gutters under the eaves and between the shingles of the roofs, a white granular powder still showed a few patches; some weeks before it had fallen like snow upon the roofs and the lawns, the fields and streams.

8   No witchcraft, no enemy action had silenced the rebirth of new life in this stricken world. The people had done it themselves.

9   This town does not actually exist, but it might easily have a thousand counterparts in America or elsewhere in the world. I know of no community that has experienced all the misfortunes I describe. Yet every one of these disasters has actually happened somewhere, and many real communities have already suffered a substantial number of them. A grim specter has crept upon us almost unnoticed, and this imagined tragedy may easily become a stark reality we all shall know. . . .

Focus on Reading

1. Look back at the work you did when you previewed, marked up, and annotated this essay. What did you underline? Why?

2. Place a check mark next to words that are particularly descriptive. In the margin, write a synonym for each of the words you selected. In each case, which do you think is more effective, your synonym or Carson's original word?

3. **TEST** Carson's essay. Does she include all four of the **TEST** elements? If not, why not? What, if anything, should be added?

Focus on Meaning

1. What is a *fable*? In what sense was this essay—written for the introduction to Carson's 1962 book *Silent Spring*, which exposed the dangerous effects of pesticides on the environment—a "fable for tomorrow"?
2. What does Carson mean when she says, "The people had done it themselves" (paragraph 8)?

Focus on Strategy

1. Why do you suppose Carson opened *Silent Spring* with this story? How do you think she expected readers to react? Do you think today's readers would be likely to react differently from those reading in 1962? If so, how? If not, why not?
2. In paragraph 9, Carson admits that the town she has been describing does not exist. Do you think this admission weakens her essay? Why or why not?

Focus on Language and Style

1. This essay is called "A Fable for Tomorrow," but except for the last paragraph, it is written in past tense. Why do you think Carson uses past tense?
2. Throughout this essay, Carson uses strong language, such as "evil spell" (3) and "grim specter" (9), to get her point across. Identify other examples of such language. Do you think these expressions are effective, or do you think Carson goes too far?

Focus on the Pattern

1. How does Carson indicate to readers that she is moving from positive to negative description?
2. Is this a subjective or an objective description? How can you tell?

Focus on Critical Thinking

1. Where might the town "in the heart of America" (para. 1) actually be located? Do you think Carson should have provided more identifying information about this town? Why or why not?
2. Is there a situation affecting our environment today that you see as just as alarming as the one Carson writes about? In what sense do you see this situation as a threat?

Analyzing a Student Essay: Description

The following descriptive essay was written by Rida Sikander in response to this assignment in her composition class.

> Search the Internet to find a work of art that appeals to you. Then, write an essay in which you describe this work of art. Your essay should combine objective and subjective description and should include enough detail so that someone who is not familiar with the work will be able to visualize it.

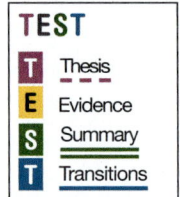

Read Rida's essay, following the active reading process discussed in Chapter 1, and then fill in the essay map in Practice 12-1 on page 292. (Note that the **TEST** elements in the essay have been highlighted and color-coded.)

A Message of Peace and Love

1   Many people think that to be an artist, a person has to go to art school and make money selling his or her work. However, there are plenty of artists who do not fit this description. They are known as "outsider artists," and their work is called "outsider art." Outsider artists are self-taught, they often use found or homemade materials, and they rarely get recognition. In spite of these disadvantages, many outsider artists create impressive works with strong messages. Elijah Pierce is one of these artists. An African American barber, Pierce used his pocketknife to carve pictures in relief on wood; then, he painted the carvings with bright colors. In his woodcarving *"Love" (Martin Luther King, Jr.)*, Pierce shows King protected by an angel. This portrait shows Dr. King embraced by the love and kindness that he embodied when he was alive.

 Thesis

 Transitions

2   At the top of *"Love" (Martin Luther King, Jr.)* is an angel, floating above and behind Dr. King. Although only her upper body is visible, the angel's image fills up most of the top half of the frame. The tips of her paint-spattered wings reach up into the two highest corners of the frame, and her hands spread out to the sides. She looks almost like a protective tree; behind her head, a patch of green is carved to look like leaves. Yet, she seems familiar and human. Her small face is simply drawn, and her expression is calm and kind. Like King, she has brown skin and black hair. Below her face, her open arms stretch her angel's white robe wide. Acting as a background for King's head, the robe resembles a cloud-like pillow. To either side, her open hands reach out to encircle him. In each of these

details, the artist shows the angel's mission to love and protect the fallen leader's spirit.

3   <u>Halfway down</u> on the left-hand side of the picture is the word "LOVE." Written on a raised rectangle and surrounded by a turquoise background, the word looks like a large sign posted in the sky. As with the angel, the message here is unmistakable. Love is what King spread, and love is what embraces him now. <u>In addition</u>, the word tells the viewer to love, and it <u>also</u> tells the viewer to see the love in the artist's work. Elijah Pierce created every element of this image by hand. Each of the black letters is roughly carved and hand-painted. The rectangle is decorated with bright splotches of orange and green. The irregular, uneven lines and edges show his use of simple tools. Through these imperfect images, Pierce expresses his love for King and his accomplishments.

4   The dominant image in the picture is Martin Luther King Jr. sitting on a brown wooden chair. <u>Although</u> the chair is turned sideways, King is facing the viewer. <u>In the center</u> of the frame, his large, gentle face looks a bit too big for his body. Simply carved, his features are out of proportion as well; <u>for instance</u>, his eyes are uneven, and they gaze in slightly different directions. <u>However</u>, these details do not make him look silly or odd. <u>On the contrary</u>, these imperfections, and his very slight smile, make him look human and strangely appealing. <u>Below</u>, he is formally dressed; he wears a dark blue suit, a red tie, and a white shirt. <u>However</u>, he seems at ease. His posture is calm and relaxed, and his hands rest comfortably at his sides. <u>Just below</u> his hands, the picture ends. The artist does not show King's feet or the bottoms of the chair legs, and no ground or horizon is visible. Dr. King seems to float in space, accompanied by the angel and the word "LOVE."

5   <u>In his woodcarving, Pierce surrounds Martin Luther King, Jr. with the love that he exhibited when he was alive.</u> Rather than idealizing its subject, Pierce's simple carving expresses the artist's admiration for the martyred civil rights leader. Although most outsider artists remain unknown, Pierce was recognized when he was alive. Although he was well known in his community, he was not widely appreciated until someone from outside the community noticed his remarkable artwork hanging in his barbershop. As a result, Pierce was "discovered."

T Transitions

E Evidence

E Evidence

S Summary

PRACTICE

12-1 Now that you have read Rida's essay, fill in the essay map on the following page to better understand how she organized her essay. Then, decide whether her organization is effective.

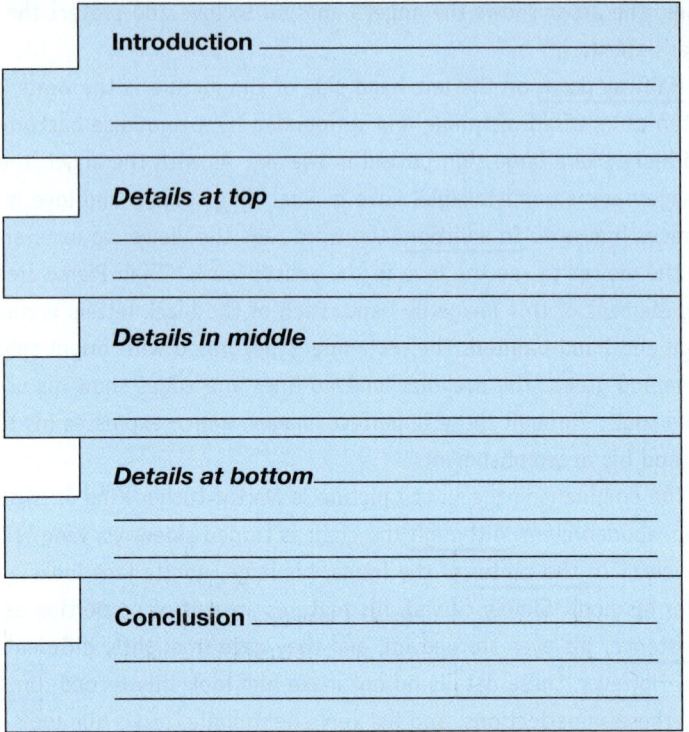

Writing a Descriptive Essay

When you are given a writing assignment, the wording of your assignment may suggest that you write a descriptive essay. For example, it may ask you to *describe* or to *tell what an object looks like*. Once you decide that your assignment calls for description, you need to develop a thesis statement that reflects this purpose.

ASSIGNMENT	THESIS STATEMENT
Scientific writing Describe a piece of scientific equipment.	The mass spectrometer is a complex instrument, but each part is ideally suited to its function.
Art history Choose one modern painting and describe its visual elements.	The disturbing images crowded together in Pablo Picasso's *Guernica* suggest the brutality of war.

When you **write** a descriptive essay, you follow the process outlined in Chapter 3. The essay you write will include the same elements you have learned to recognize in the descriptive essays you read. When you finish your draft, you can **TEST** it to make sure it includes all the elements of a descriptive essay.

TESTing Your Descriptive Essay

Thesis Statement Unifies Your Essay

- [ ] Does your introduction identify the subject of your description?
- [ ] Does your introduction include a **thesis statement** that communicates your essay's main idea?

Evidence Supports Your Essay's Thesis Statement

- [ ] Does all your **evidence**—your descriptive details—support the essay's dominant impression (communicated by your thesis), or are some details irrelevant?
- [ ] Do you describe your subject in enough detail, or do you need to add details to create a more vivid picture?
- [ ] Are your supporting details arranged in a meaningful order within your essay and within your body paragraphs?

Summary Statement Reinforces Your Essay's Main Idea

- [ ] Does your conclusion include a **summary statement** that reinforces your essay's thesis?

Transitions Connect Events

- [ ] Do you include **transitions** that introduce your details and move readers smoothly from one aspect of your subject to another?

The following essay was written by James Greggs in his first-year composition course. Read James's essay, and then answer the questions in Practice 12-2 on page 295.

Building and Learning

1   Throughout the United States, houses reflect not only the lives of the people who live in them but also the diversity of the American population. Some are large and elaborate, others are modest but well maintained, and still others are in need of repair. Unfortunately, most college students know little about homes other than those in their own neighborhood. I too was fairly sheltered until I participated in a service-learning project for my sociology class. For this project, I, along with some classmates, added a deck to a trailer that was the home of three elderly sisters living on Social

Security and disability. It was hard work, but my experience convinced me that all college students should be required to do some kind of service-learning project.

2   The trailer we worked on was located at the end of a small dirt road about thirty minutes from campus. Patches of green and brown grass dotted the land around the trailer, and in the far right-hand corner of the property stood three tall poplar trees. Although the bushes in front of the trailer were trimmed, the woods behind the trailer were beginning to overrun the property. (We were told that members of a local church came once a month to trim the hedges and cut back the trees.) Dominating the right front corner of the lawn, a circular concrete basin looked like a large birdbath. The basin housed a white well pipe with a rusted blue cap. About thirty feet to the left of the concrete basin stood a telephone pole and a bright red metal mailbox.

3   Like the property on which it stood, the trailer was well maintained. It was approximately thirty-five feet long and seven feet high; it rested on cinderblocks, which raised it about three feet off the ground. Under the trailer was an overturned white plastic chair. The trailer itself was covered with sheets of white vinyl siding that ran horizontally, except for the bottom panels on the right side, which ran vertically. The vinyl panels closest to the roof were slightly discolored by dirt and green moss.

4   At the left end of the trailer was a small window—about two feet wide and one foot high. Next to the window was a dark red aluminum door that was outlined in green trim. It had one window at eye level divided by metal strips into four small sections. The number "24" in white plastic letters was glued to the door below this window. To the right of the door was a light-bulb in a black ceramic socket. Next to the light was a large window that was actually two vertical rows of three windows—each the same size as the small window on the left. Further to the right were two smaller windows. Each of these small windows tilted upward and was framed with silver metal strips. On either side of each of these windows was a pair of green metal shutters.

5   The deck we built replaced three wooden steps that had led up to the trailer. A white metal handrail stood on the right side of these steps. It had been newly painted and was connected to the body of the trailer by a heart-shaped piece of metal. In front of the steps, two worn gray wooden boards led to the road.

6   Building the deck was hard work, but the finished deck provided a much better entranceway than the steps did and also gave the trailer a new look. The deck was not very large — ten feet by eight feet — but it extended from the doorway to the area underneath the windows immediately to the right of the door. We built the deck out of pressure-treated lumber so that it wouldn't rot or need painting. We also built three steps that led from the deck to the lawn, and we surrounded the deck with a wooden railing that ran down the right side of the steps. After we finished, we bought two white plastic chairs at a local thrift store and put them on the deck.

7   Now that I look back at the project, I believe that activities like this should be part of every student's college education. Both the residents of the trailer and our class benefited from the service-learning project. The residents of the trailer were happy with the deck because it gave them a place to sit when the weather was nice. They also liked their trailer's new look. Those of us who worked on the project learned that a few days' work could make a real difference in other people's lives.

PRACTICE 12-2

1. Underline James's thesis statement; then, rewrite it in your own words.
2. What details does James provide to describe the property, the trailer, and the deck? What determines the order in which James arranges the details in his description?
3. Circle some of the transitional words and phrases James uses to move from one detail to another. Do you think he includes enough transitions? Could he have added more? Explain.
4. This essay is primarily an objective description. Where does it include some subjective description? What do these subjective details add to the essay?
5. Use **TEST** to evaluate James's essay. What revisions would you suggest he make? Why?

Grammar in context

Description

When you write a descriptive essay, you may use **modifiers**—words and phrases that describe other words in the sentence—to create a picture of your subject. If you place a modifying word or phrase too far from the word it is supposed to describe, you create a potentially confusing **misplaced modifier**.

CONFUSING Next to the window outlined in green trim was a dark red aluminum door. (Was the window outlined in green trim?)

CLEAR Next to the window was a dark red aluminum door outlined in green trim.

For information on how to identify and correct misplaced modifiers, see Chapter 25.

FOCUS on reading and writing: Description

Reread Rachel Carson's essay, "A Fable for Tomorrow" (p. 287). Then, write your own descriptive essay in response to one of the following prompts. Be sure to follow the writing process outlined in Chapter 3.

1. Write your own "fable for tomorrow" describing the likely effects on our environment of the unchecked piling up of nonbiodegradable garbage and trash in our landfills. In your thesis statement, encourage your readers to recycle to avoid the problems you describe.

2. Some people see climate change as a destructive problem of epic proportions—as an even greater problem than the pesticides that Carson warns against. Write a "fable for tomorrow" in which you describe an extreme scenario that could result from an increase in global warming.

    If you prefer, you can write on one of these topics instead:
    - An object you cherish
    - A historical site or monument
    - The home page of a website you visit often

 ## 12b Process

A **process** is a series of chronologically arranged steps that produces a particular result. **Process essays** explain the steps in a procedure, telling how something works or how something is (or was) done—for example, how an optical scanner works, how to hem a pair of jeans, or how to log into an online course. Depending on the writer's purpose, a process essay can be organized as either a *process explanation* (telling how something is or was done) or a set of *instructions* (telling readers how to perform the process themselves).

Reading a Process Essay

When you **read** a process essay, use **TEST** to help you identify its key elements. Be sure to follow the active reading process outlined in Chapter 1.

T **Thesis**—In the introduction of a process essay, look for a **thesis** that identifies the process to be explained and expresses the essay's main idea—for example, the significance of the process or the reason the process is being performed. Sometimes the main idea is stated explicitly in a **thesis statement**; at other times, it is **implied**, suggested by the discussion. As you read, note which of these two options is used, and evaluate the writer's choice.

E **Evidence**—In the body paragraphs, look for **evidence**, examples and details that explain the steps in the process and support the essay's thesis. In each body paragraph, look for a topic sentence that identifies the step (or group of related steps) that the paragraph will explain. Steps are presented in strict chronological (time) order.

S **Summary**—In the conclusion of a process essay, look for a **summary** of the steps in the process or a **summary statement** that reinforces the essay's thesis.

T **Transitions**—As you read, try to identify the **transitional words and phrases** that link the steps in the process and show how they are related. Sometimes you will notice a **transitional paragraph** that sums up a group of steps before moving on to the next stage of the process.

> **Some Transitional Words and Phrases for Process**
>
> Transitions in process essays enable readers to follow the sequence of steps in the process and, in the case of instructions, to perform the process themselves.
>
> | | | |
> |---|---|---|
> | after that | immediately | the final step |
> | as | later | the first (second, |
> | as soon as | meanwhile | third) step |
> | at the end | next | then |
> | at the same time | now | the next step |
> | before | once | ultimately |
> | finally | soon | when |
> | first | subsequently | while |

Whether an essay is a process explanation or a set of instructions, it can either devote a full paragraph to each step of the process or group a series of minor steps together in a single paragraph. (Instructions usually include a list of materials someone needs to perform the process.)

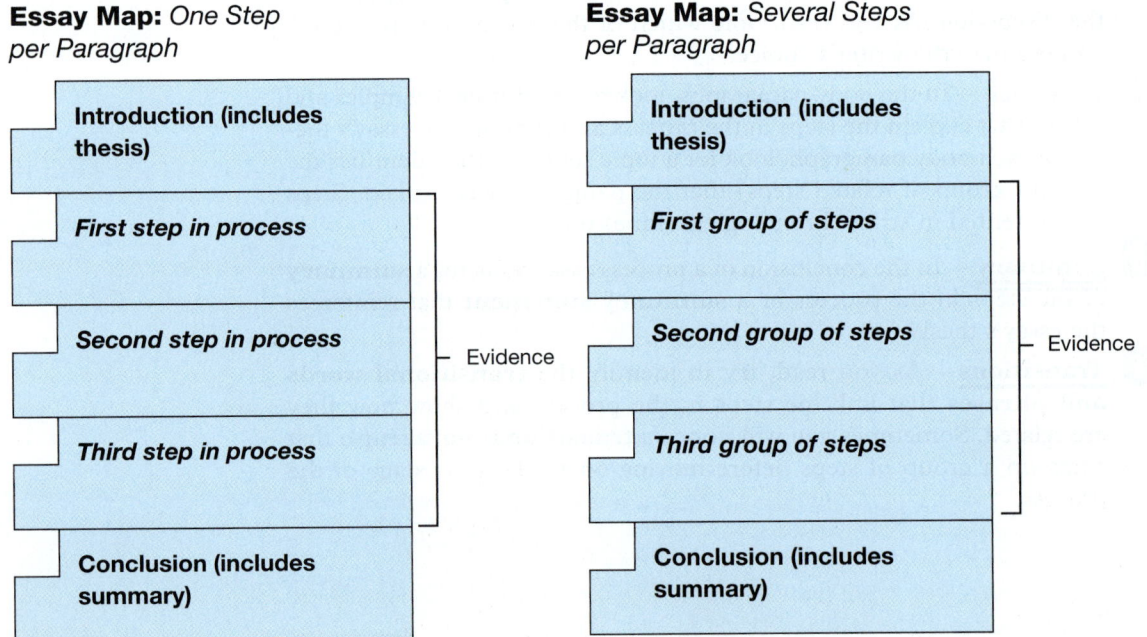

In your college courses, most of your writing will be in response to reading—specifically, to reading texts such as the one that follows. In this essay, "My Grandmother's Dumpling," Amy Ma explains a process. Read the essay, following the active reading process outlined in Chapter 1, and then answer the questions on pages 304–305. At the end of section 12b, you will be asked to write a process essay in response to Ma's ideas.

My Grandmother's Dumpling

Amy Ma

Amy Ma is a writer who trained as a pastry chef in New York City and now lives in Hong Kong. This article, which first appeared in *The Wall Street Journal* in 2009, provides both information about how to make dumplings and the story of several generations of Ma's family.

Before you read, take some time to think about how cooking and family intersect in your own life.

1   There was no denying a dumpling error. If the meat tumbled out of a poorly made one as it cooked, Grandmother could always tell who made it because she had personally assigned each of us a specific folding style at the onset of our dumpling-making education. In our house, a woman's folding style identified her as surely as her fingerprints.

2   "From now on, you and only you will fold it in this way," she instructed me in our Taipei kitchen in 1994, the year I turned 13. That is when I had reached a skill level worthy of joining the rest of the women — 10 in all, from my 80-year-old grandmother, Lu Xiao-fang, to my two middle-aged aunts, my mother and the six children of my generation — in the folding of *jiao zi*, or dumplings, for Chinese New Year. Before then I had been relegated to prep work: mixing the meat filling or cutting the dough and flattening it.

3   Cousin Mao Mao, the eldest daughter of my grandmother's first son, had been away for four years at college in the U.S. But with casual ease, she fashioned her dumplings in the style of the rat, tucking in the creases and leaving a small tail that pinched together at one end. Two distinct pleats in a fan-shaped dumpling marked the work of Aunt Yee, Mao Mao's mother, who had just become a grandmother herself with the birth of a grandson. A smaller purse-like dumpling with eight folds toward the center was my mother's. Grandmother's dumplings were the simplest of the bunch — flat, crescent-shaped with no creases and a smooth edge. And as I was the youngest in my generation, she'd thought it appropriate to make my signature design a quirky variation of her own, with an added crimping to create a rippling *hua bian*, or flower edge.

4   "A pretty little edge, for a pretty little girl," she said.

5   While dumplings graced our tables year-round, they were a requisite dish during the Lunar New Year holidays. The Spring Festival, as it is known in China — *chun jie* — is arguably the most important celebration of the year: It is a time to be with family, to visit friends and start life anew — and eat dumplings.

6   The length of observance varies. Today in Taiwan, the national holiday stretches to nine days — including two weekends — with all businesses and

WORD POWER
relegated assigned [to a lower position]

WORD POWER
requisite necessary

government offices closed. In mainland China, officials rearrange the working calendar to give the public seven consecutive days off, while in Hong Kong there are three public holidays and in Singapore, two. Unofficially, many Chinese people consider the traditional period of the first 15 days appropriate to welcome the new year.

7   My family celebrated the first three days of the Spring Festival in a traditional way: Everyone came "home," which meant to my grandfather's house. We were already home—my father, mother, brother and I lived in Taipei with my father's parents, who had moved from China in the late 1940s. Most of my father's family lived nearby. On *chu yi*, the first day of the new year, friends came to our house to extend greetings. For *chu er*, the second day, married women returned to their parents' house. The third day, *chu san*, was always celebrated united, as a family. And on each of those days, dumplings were the main food served during lunch and dinner. There might be other side dishes—leftovers from New Year's Eve—but no other food was prepared from scratch during the holiday. It was considered bad luck to do any work during this time; to ensure a peaceful year ahead, you had to rest and that meant no cooking.

8   Though it isn't known exactly when dumplings came into being, author and Chinese food expert Fuchsia Dunlop says *jiao zi* date as far back as 1,100 years ago. "In the city of Turpan, a tomb was uncovered that had boiled dumplings from the Tang dynasty (618–907) preserved in much the same shape with similar fillings as they are today," says Ms. Dunlop.

9   Many people believe the practice of eating these dumplings on Chinese New Year became popular in the Yuan and Ming dynasties, which stretched from 1271 to 1644, when *yuan bao*—gold and silver ingots—began to take hold as currency in China; the dumplings take the shape of those coins. During new year celebrations, filling your stomach with edible replicas of ingots was thought to ensure a year of prosperity ahead. The packaged bites also celebrated a letting go of the past, since the word *"jiao"* also means "the end of something."

10   Traditions have relaxed: Not every family eats only dumplings for three days. They also vary regionally: In the south of China, *nian gao*, or rice cakes, are often served instead of these dough-swaddled morsels at Chinese New Year. Still, hefty portions of dumplings undoubtedly remain a big attraction this time of year in many Chinese households.

11   Even now, that initial bite of any dumpling transports me back to our Taipei kitchen: The women packed like sardines working on their craft with a Zen-like rhythm, the flour-dusted countertops, the air redolent with the scent of dough, and the faded brown ceramic tiles on the floor polished smooth by countless footsteps over the years.

12   The great dumpling cook-off commenced each year following Lunar New Year's Eve dinner, a family meal of Grandmother's best dishes—sweet soy-braised pork, *ru yi cai* (10 vegetables tossed together with a soy-sauce vinaigrette), and always steamed fish since its term in Mandarin, "*yu*," is a

WORD POWER

ingots solid metal bars

WORD POWER

redolent fragrant

homonym for "plenty." By 9 p.m., the plates were cleared and washed, and the women were clustered in the kitchen.

13 The men, forbidden to enter the cooking area, dispersed to their separate corners to talk politics and play dice or mahjong while awaiting the countdown to midnight. Every room of the house swelled with festivity as the whole family of more than 30 members—four generations—gathered for this night in my grandparents' house.

14 Amid the bustle, the kitchen alone had an air of serenity and purpose as the women worked through the night. Before dawn of the next morning, there would be enough dumplings to cover two large dining room tables and every kitchen countertop.

15 To start, Grandmother unloaded from the refrigerator the large ball of dough made from flour, cold water and a dash of egg white (her secret ingredient) that she had prepared the day before. Setting it onto the butcher block with her plump and sturdy hands, she ripped off two large balls and rolled each into a log, starting her gentle kneading from the center and stretching out to both sides. The remaining dough she kept covered under a damp towel.

16 Meanwhile, the rest of the women—my mother and two aunts and my cousins and me—picked over bunches of coriander and peeled off the wilted layers of scallions and cabbages. A liberal dose of salt sprinkled over the cabbage drew out the excess water, and the chopped confetti-like bits were hand-squeezed to prevent a watery dumpling filling. The butcher knife rocked repeatedly back and forth on the ginger and garlic until it was almost a paste. Likewise, the vegetables had to be diced as finely as possible so they would be evenly spread through every bite of the final product.

17 Ignoring the slew of innovative options for fillings popular in contemporary restaurants—shrimp and chives, shark's fin and vermicelli—we filled our no-frills dumplings with minced pork. Into the pink ground meat went the chopped speckles of vegetables and herbs along with sesame oil, Shaoxin wine, salt, soy sauce, a pinch of sugar, white pepper, five-spice powder and an egg. Nothing was measured, yet it always tasted the same.

18 "That's enough mixing," Grandmother cautioned. My mother was using a pair of wooden chopsticks to combine the ingredients in large circular motions. Grandmother insisted on only combing through the filling in one direction—clockwise—so as to not over-mix, which would make it tough.

19 Then like a carefully orchestrated master plan, a natural assembly line formed. First, Grandmother cut off equal-size segments of her log of dough and then passed them to my mother, who used a wooden roller to flatten them into circles, a process called *gan mien*. Two aunts continued to fashion new dough into logs on one end of the kitchen counter, and three cousins lined up on the other end to begin filling and folding dumplings. The positions would alternate periodically, and makers would move up the line over the years as their skills improved. At 5 years old, my job had been the menial task of pressing the just-cut dough segments into flat disks so

they would be easier to roll out, but I had since graduated to a dumpling folder. All together, we women stood, each ready to play her part in this culinary theater.

20 "Every step requires its own *kung fu*," Grandmother instructed in Mandarin. She was short, but her chubby silhouette held the solid stance of a symphony conductor. The process was tedious, but a mere mention of serving a frozen dumpling from a supermarket would be confronted with a gaze that screamed: uncultured, unbelievable, un-*Chinese*. The matriarch in her kitchen was doing more than just cooking; she was training the next generation of wives, daughters and mothers as her mother-in-law had taught her.

21 "Use your palm to control the roller, not your fingertips," she barked. "Keep a steady rhythm, consistent like your pulse." The dumpling skins weren't flattened in one fell swoop like a pie crust. Each one had to be rolled just around the rim and rotated so that the resulting circle was thinner on the edges than in the center. When folded in half the two sides met; the dumpling skin was uniform in thickness. It was a painstaking task when repeated over the span of many hours, and my mother once showed me her swollen palms after a night of *gan mien*.

22 The amount of meat filling had to be just right. Not too much—"too greedy!"—and not too little: "too stingy!"

23 And dumplings had to be folded with both hands. "It's a superstition," Grandmother told us. "Women who fold dumplings with one hand won't have children. Your right and left hand have to work together to be a good mother." Grandmother demonstrated how she used the fleshy part of the index finger and thumb to press together the dough. Fresh dough, unlike frozen dough, didn't need water to seal the seams. Only a firm pinch.

24 "Beautifully folded," Grandmother commented on the dumpling of the newest granddaughter-in-law, Mei Fang. "But it took you too long to make. What good is a wife who makes lovely dumplings if there's not enough to feed everyone?" Grandmother asked.

25 The women smirked at the acrid words—she had been equally harsh to all of them when they first joined the family. Grandmother had taken her lumps, too: After she married grandfather, her mother-in-law had harassed her on the ways of making a proper dumpling. Now, Grandmother reigned over her kitchen; it was a classroom and crucible we all endured.

26 "It's better that I am more strict on you girls now," she sighed. "Lest you get criticized by someone else even worse than me." My mother looked over her shoulder to check on me, her only daughter, and smiled when I gave her an assuring nod.

27 When no one was looking, Grandmother washed a small coin and hid it in one of the dumplings to be discovered by a lucky winner, who was said to be blessed with extra good fortune for the new year. Despite my best efforts, I never chanced upon it.

> **WORD POWER**
> **acrid** sharp

> **WORD POWER**
> **crucible** severe test

28   Working until the early hours of the next morning in the kitchen brought out the juicier stories, ones laced with family secrets, scandals, gossips and tall tales, all soaked up by my youthful ears.

29   "Did you hear? Second uncle's daughter got a tattoo."

30   "So-and-so's sister is really her daughter."

31   By the time the echoes of popping firecrackers filled the streets signaling the stroke of midnight, hundreds of dumplings, ready for boiling, were lined up on the kitchen sheet pans like tiny soldiers pending a final command.

32   With only the boiling of the dumplings left to do, the women then took turns cleaning up and bathing, all the while trailing after their children and lulling them to bed. But the majority of the family didn't sleep. The custom of *shou sui*, or staying up all night to symbolize having unlimited energy for the upcoming year, was usually followed.

33   Around 5 a.m., the tables were set in preparation for the midmorning dumpling brunch. But there was no counting of bowls or chopsticks. "You're not allowed to count anything during the first day of the year," reminded Grandmother. "If you don't count anything today, then the amount of possessions you have will be countless for next year." So we grabbed chopsticks by the handfuls—some wooden, some metal, all mixed in a pile—and laid them on the table alongside stacks of blue and white porcelain bowls and plates.

34   Before long, the first doorbell rang, and along with it came the boisterous greetings from guests, friends and neighbors. The words *gong xi fa cai* ("congratulations and be prosperous") were audible even from inside the kitchen, and they drew out the younger girls, who were eager for their *hong bao*, or red packets. These waxy packets stuffed with money were given by elders to children as a gift, and the youngest in the house could often rack up what seemed to them a small fortune. Their flour-covered fingerprints dotted the envelopes as they calculated the year's gains.

35   At 9 a.m. or when the guest count reached 10—enough to fill a table—we slid the dumplings into the stainless steel pot, careful not to let the boiling water splatter onto our bare toes, peeking out from house slippers. Grandmother insisted on never stirring the pot, and to ensure the dumplings wouldn't stick together, she slid a spatula through the bubbling broth just once in a pushing motion. Thrice the water came to a boil and each time we added more water. By the fourth time, the dumplings bobbed merrily on the surface. They were done.

36   Grandmother fished out the broken dumplings before turning to Cousin Jia Yin, often the culprit, in half jest. "Ah . . . thanks to you, the dumpling soup will be especially tasty this year since you've flavored it with all the filling that busted out." The casualties were fished out and quickly disposed of; broken dumplings are considered bad luck if served. To save Jia Yin's face, her father, grandmother's second son, often said at the table, "Dumplings are great, but my favorite is still the dumpling soup," ladling up another bowl.

37 Guests and grandparents ate first and the two large tables in the dining room were seated by gender. My grandfather took the head seat at one table with his friends, and my grandmother with hers at the other. After they ate, the tables were reset and the second generation took its turn, with my father and uncles at one table, my mother and aunts at the other. The third and fourth generations had less strict table assignments and took whatever empty chairs opened up—it could be two or three hours before it was our turn to eat.

38 Steaming plates were heaped high with dumplings still glistening from their hot-water bath. Diners readied themselves with their own taste-tinkering rituals in concocting the perfect dipping sauce—a combination of soy sauce, vinegar, minced garlic and sometimes sesame oil or chili paste. Grandmother's special *la ba* vinegar, marinated with whole garlic cloves, was the most coveted condiment.

39 Before the first bite, everyone gathered around Grandfather, who made a toast—usually with tea though sometimes he would sneak in some Chinese wine—to ring in the new year. Then, he took the first pick of the dumplings—something of an honor among the women, who held their breath in hopes that his choice of the perfect dumpling would be their own. It would have to have the ideal skin-to-filling ratio, every bite an equal portion of meat and dough, and expert craftsmanship—a balanced and symmetrical shape with firmly sealed seams.

40 "This one looks good to me," my grandfather decided, gently lifting the plump parcel with the tips of his chopsticks. It was Grandmother's dumpling, and she stood poker-faced next to him, not revealing her triumph.

41 She remembered a time when her dumplings were the only ones on the platter. As her family grew, so too did the styles of dumplings until the plate resembled an eclectic family tree, and each doughy pouch carried within it the cross-generational memoirs of its maker. The dumpling ritual slowly faded after Grandmother's passing in 1999; Grandfather died soon after and the family scattered. But every Chinese New Year, I still make dumplings in Grandmother's way, repeating her lessons in my head.

42 "Eat more! Eat more! There's magic in these dumplings," Grandmother would say. And she meant it truly.

Focus on Reading

1. Look back at the work you did when you previewed, marked up, and annotated this essay. Now, number the major steps in the process Ma explains. (Begin with paragraph 15.)

2. In the margin beside paragraph 12, write a few words that make a connection between what Ma describes and something in your own life.

3. **TEST** Ma's essay. Does she include all four **TEST** elements? If not, why not? What, if anything, should be added?

Focus on Meaning

1. What different kinds of dumpling "folding style" do the various women have? Why are these differences important?
2. What significance do dumplings have in Chinese culture? What significance do dumplings (and the dumpling-making process) have to Ma?

Focus on Strategy

1. What type of information does Ma provide in paragraphs 1–11 (before she focuses on the process)? Why do you think she provides all this information?
2. What do paragraphs 5–10 tell you about Ma's purpose in writing this essay? About her intended audience?

Focus on Language and Style

1. At various points, Ma quotes her grandmother. What do these quotations tell you about Ma's grandmother? About Ma herself?
2. In paragraph 19, Ma describes the process of making dumplings as "a carefully orchestrated master plan"; in paragraph 20, she calls the process "tedious." Identify other descriptions of the process in this essay, and then write a single sentence that sums up Ma's impression of the process.

Focus on the Pattern

1. How can you tell this is an explanation of a process rather than a set of instructions?
2. Why do you think Ma did not write this essay as a set of instructions? If it were written as instructions, what cautions or reminders might she have had to add?

Focus on Critical Thinking

1. This essay's title is "My Grandmother's Dumpling," but it also discusses other people (and other people's dumplings). Who or what do you think is the essay's central focus? What makes you think so? Do you think the essay should have a different title? Explain.
2. In paragraph 41, Ma refers to the dumplings on the plate as "an eclectic family tree" and says that "each doughy pouch carried within it the cross-generational memoirs of its maker." What does she mean? Do you think she is making too much of the significance of the ritual she describes? Why or why not?

Analyzing a Student Essay: Process

The following process essay was written by Owen McCann in response to the following assignment in a study skills class.

> Write a set of instructions telling how to perform a process that will help students succeed in college.

Read Owen's essay, following the active reading process outlined in Chapter 1, and then fill in the essay map in Practice 12-3 on page 308. (Note that the **TEST** elements in the essay have been highlighted and color-coded.)

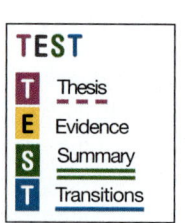

How to Take Effective Notes

1 Most students want to do well in college and graduate on time. However, some students do not have the skills they need to succeed, including the ability to take good notes. To excel in most courses, effective note taking is crucial. Fortunately, with practice and a little knowledge, you can learn how to listen productively in lectures and write down the information you need. <u>Following a few important steps will improve your note-taking skills and help you succeed in your college classes.</u>

2 <u>First</u>, set yourself up for success. Go to class, and arrive on time. Instructors often make important announcements at the beginning of class, so you do not want to miss those first critical minutes. If you prefer to take notes by hand, bring two or three different colored pens. If you are using a laptop or tablet, be sure to close all unrelated applications before coming to class. <u>At the same time</u>, minimize your distractions by silencing your phone and removing it from your desk. <u>Finally</u>, make sure to sit where you can see and hear the instructor. You are more likely to stay focused if you are not sitting at the back of a large, echoey lecture hall. Using these suggestions will prepare you to get the most out of the day's class.

3 <u>Next</u>, get ready to pay attention. <u>Before class</u>, take a couple of minutes to reread your notes from the previous class. Orient yourself to the subject matter, and remind yourself of any questions you may have had after the last lecture. <u>Then</u>, turn to a new page, or open a new file, and set up a simple layout. To make your notes easier to reference later, put the date at the top of the page, and include a title for that day's subject, if there is one. To keep your notes organized, try creating two columns; you can keep your notes on one side and your questions and responses on the other side. <u>Once</u> you have taken these steps, you are ready for the lecture to begin.

4 Now, listen carefully and write down the important ideas. Do not try to get everything down. If you try to record the instructor's every word, you will undoubtedly miss some critical points. Make your note taking efficient by using abbreviations and symbols, and pay close attention to what the instructor emphasizes. Often, he or she will repeat a significant concept or indicate which material will be on the next test. In your notes, underline or boldface these tips, perhaps putting important announcements or reminders in all caps. In addition, include examples in your notes whenever possible; examples will help you better remember abstract concepts. For instance, if you are listening to a lecture on nonviolent resistance, write down a few words to remind you of real-world occurrences, such as "Gandhi-Quit India Movement." Meanwhile, throughout class, use the right-hand column of your page to jot down questions you want to ask the instructor. At the end of class, you will have a clear record of issues that need further attention as well as a complete and concise account of the main ideas covered in that class period.

5 Finally, review what you have recorded. If possible, reread your notes right after class or soon afterwards. At this point, give yourself a chance to fill in gaps, insert examples, and write down additional questions. You are much more likely to understand and absorb the information if you spend a few minutes reviewing what you have written. Be sure to look over your questions while the material is still fresh in your mind. Once you have done all you can on your own, find a classmate or TA to explain any confusing or difficult concepts. You can also see your instructor during office hours or send questions to him or her in an email. All in all, taking the time to clarify and complete your notes will make studying less frustrating and more efficient.

6 Following these steps to establish good note-taking habits will improve your understanding of the course material and help you succeed in college. Take the time to try them out for yourself. Make adjustments to fit your needs and to accommodate the structure of different classes. Share your strategies with others, and learn new methods from them. Ultimately, taking and having reliable notes makes learning easier and more enjoyable, and mastering the note-taking process will make your college experience more productive and satisfying.

PRACTICE
12-3 Now that you have read Owen's essay, fill in the essay map on the following page to help you understand how he organized his essay and to decide whether his organization is effective.

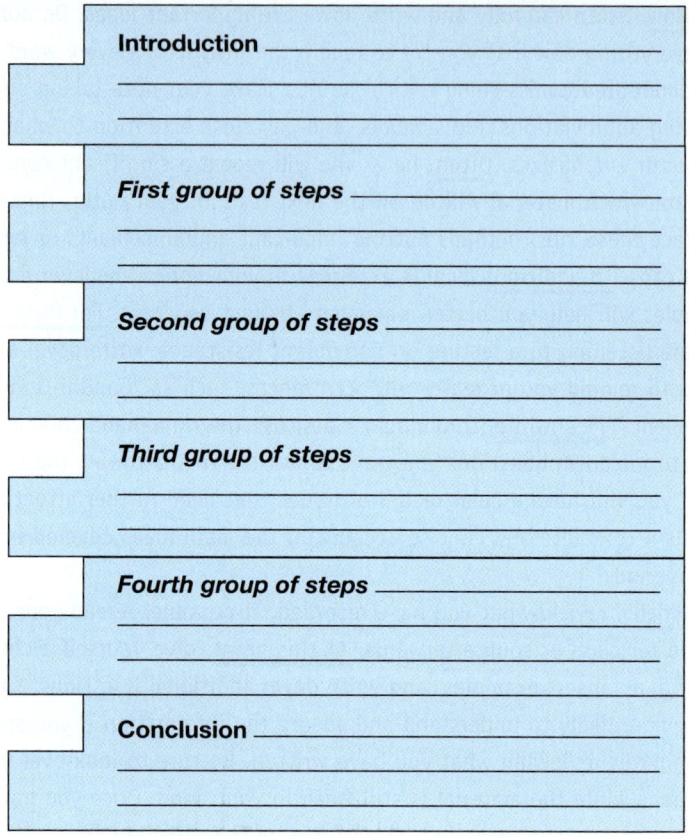

Writing a Process Essay

When you are given a writing assignment, the wording of your assignment may suggest that you write a process essay. For example, you may be asked to *explain a process, give instructions, give directions,* or *give a step-by-step account.* Once you decide that your assignment calls for process, you need to develop a thesis statement that reflects this purpose.

ASSIGNMENT	THESIS STATEMENT
Pharmacy practice Summarize the procedure for conducting a clinical trial of a new drug.	To ensure that drugs are safe and effective, scientists follow strict procedural guidelines for testing and evaluating the drugs.
Technical writing Write a set of instructions for applying for a student internship in a government agency.	Students who want to apply for a government internship need to follow several important steps.

If your purpose is simply to help readers understand a process, not actually perform it, you will write a process explanation. **Process explanations**, like the first example in the box above, often use present tense verbs ("A scientist first *submits* a funding application") to explain how a procedure is generally carried out. However, when a process explanation describes a procedure that was completed in the past, it uses past tense verbs ("The next thing I *did*").

If your purpose is to enable readers to actually perform the steps in a process, you will write instructions. **Instructions**, like the technical writing example in the box above, always use present tense verbs—in the form of commands—to tell readers what to do ("First, *meet* with your adviser").

In your process essay, discuss each step in the order in which it is performed, making sure your topic sentences clearly identify each step or group of steps. If you are writing instructions, you may also include reminders or warnings that readers might need to keep in mind when performing the process.

When you **write** a process essay, you follow the process outlined in Chapter 3. The essay you write will include the same elements you have learned to recognize in the process essays you read. When you finish your draft, you can **TEST** it to make sure it includes all the elements of a process essay.

TESTing Your Process Essay

Thesis Statement Unifies Your Essay

☐ Does your introduction identify the process you will explain and indicate why you are writing about it?

☐ Does your introduction include a **thesis statement** that expresses your essay's main idea?

Evidence Supports Your Essay's Thesis Statement

☐ Does all your **evidence** support your thesis, or are some details or examples irrelevant?

☐ Do you identify and explain every step readers need to understand (or perform) the process?

☐ Are the steps in the process presented in strict chronological order?

☐ If you are writing instructions, have you included all necessary warnings or reminders?

Summary Statement Reinforces Your Essay's Main Idea

☐ Does your conclusion include a **summary statement** that sums up the key steps in the process and reinforces your essay's thesis?

Transitions Connect Events

☐ Do you include **transitional words and phrases** that introduce the steps in the process and clearly show how they are related?

The following essay was written by Jen Rossi in her first-year writing course. Read Jen's essay, and then answer the questions in Practice 12-4 on page 311.

For Fun and Profit

1 Selling items at a flea market can be both fun and profitable. In fact, it can lead to a hobby that will be a continuing source of extra income. Your first flea market can take a lot of work, but establishing a routine will make each experience easier and more rewarding than the last one.

2 The first step in the process is to call to reserve a spot at the flea market. If possible, try to get a spot near the entrance, where there is a lot of foot traffic. Once you have your spot, recruit a helper—for example, one of your roommates—and get to work.

3 The next step is sorting through all the items you've managed to accumulate. Your helper will come in handy here, encouraging you to sell ugly or useless things that you may want to hold on to. Make three piles—keep, sell, and trash—and, one by one, place each item in a pile. (Before you decide to sell or discard an item, check with roommates and family members to make sure you aren't accidentally throwing out one of their prized possessions.)

4 Next, price the items for sale. This can actually be the hardest step in the process. It's always difficult to accept the fact that you might have to set a low price for something that has sentimental value for you (a giant-sized stuffed animal, for example). It can be just as hard to set a high price on the ugly lamp or old record album that might turn out to be someone's treasure. In all likelihood, you will return from your first flea market with a lot of unsold items. You will also probably realize, too late, that you sold some items too cheaply. (Don't worry; you won't make these mistakes again.)

5 The next step is packing up items to be sold. You may want to borrow a friend's truck or van for the heavy, bulky items (boxes of books or dishes, for example). The small items (knickknacks, silk flowers, stray teaspoons) can be transported by car.

6 The final steps in your preparation take place on the day before the event. Borrow a couple of card tables. Then, go to the bank and get lots of dollar bills and quarters, and collect piles of newspaper and grocery bags. Now, your planning is complete, and you are ready for the big day.

7   On the day of the flea market, get up early, and (with your trusty helper's assistance) load your vehicle. When you arrive at the site where the event is to be held, have your helper unload the car. Meanwhile, set things up, placing small items (such as plates or DVDs) on the card tables and large items (such as your parents' old lawnmower) on the ground near the tables.

8   Now, the actual selling begins. Before you can even set up your tables, people will start picking through your items, offering you cash for picture frames, pots and pans, and old video games. Don't panic! Try to develop a system: One of you can persuade buyers that that old meat grinder or vase is just what they've been looking for; the other person can negotiate the price with prospective buyers. Then, while one of you wraps small items in the newspapers or bags you brought, the other person can take the money and make change.

9   Finally, at the end of the day, the process will come to an end. Now, count your money. (Don't forget to give a share to your helper.) Then, load all the unsold items into your vehicle, and bring them back home. The process ends when you store the unsold items in the back of your closet, ready to pack them all up again and follow the same routine for the next flea market.

PRACTICE 12-4

1. Underline Jen's thesis statement; then, rewrite it in your own words.
2. What identifies Jen's essay as a set of instructions rather than a process explanation?
3. Circle some of the transitional words and phrases Jen uses to move from one step in the process to another. Are any other transitions needed? If so, where?
4. Underline Jen's summary statement. Then, rewrite it in your own words.
5. Use **TEST** to evaluate Jen's essay. What, if anything, does she need to revise? Why?

Grammar in context

Process

When you write a process essay, you may have problems keeping tense, person, and voice consistent throughout. If you shift from one tense, person, or voice to another without good reason, you will confuse your readers:

CONFUSING <mark>Make</mark> three piles—keep, sell, and trash—and, one by one, every item <mark>should be placed</mark> in a pile. (shift from active to passive voice and from present to past tense)

CLEAR <mark>Make</mark> three piles—keep, sell, and trash—and, one by one, <mark>place</mark> each item in a pile. (consistent voice and tense)

For information on how to avoid illogical shifts in tense, person, and voice, see Chapter 24.

FOCUS on reading and writing

Reread Amy Ma's essay, "My Grandmother's Dumpling" (p. 299). Then, write your own process essay in response to one of the following prompts. Be sure to follow the writing process outlined in Chapter 3.

1. Explain the process of preparing a meal or dish that is traditional in your culture or in your family. Begin with several paragraphs of background to help readers understand what the preparation process means to you.

2. Rewrite Ma's process explanation as a set of instructions to be followed by her daughters. Remember to include any necessary cautions and reminders.

   If you prefer, you can write on one of these topics instead:
   - Applying for a job
   - A religious ritual or cultural ceremony
   - Your own writing process

12c Classification

When we **classify**, we sort things (individual people, items, or ideas) into categories or groups. In our daily lives, we classify when we organize bills into those we must pay immediately and those we can pay later, or when we sort clothing in a drawer into socks, T-shirts, and underwear.

Classification essays divide a whole (the subject) into parts and sort various items into categories. Each category must be **distinct**. In other words, none of the items in one category should also fit into another category. For example, it is not logical to classify novels into the categories *fantasy novels*, *romance novels*, and *e-books*, because fantasy and romance novels can also be e-books.

Every classification essay has a **principle of classification**—something the items being classified have in common. For example, parents can be classified on the basis of their parenting styles (authoritarian, permissive, and so on.) The writer's purpose determines the principle of classification that is chosen.

Reading a Classification Essay

When you **read** a classification essay, follow the active reading process outlined in Chapter 1. You can use **TEST** to help you identify its key elements.

T **Thesis**—In the introduction of a classification essay, look for a **thesis** that communicates the essay's main idea and indicates what the essay will classify (and perhaps also examines the purpose or significance of the classification). The thesis may be explicitly stated in a **thesis statement**, or it may be **implied**, suggested by the way the categories are selected and how they are arranged. As you read, note which of these two options was chosen, and evaluate the writer's choice.

E **Evidence**—In the body paragraphs, look for **evidence**, examples and details that support the thesis. In each paragraph, look for a topic sentence that identifies the category the paragraph will discuss and perhaps indicates how it is different from other categories.

S **Summary**—In the conclusion, look for a **summary** that reviews the categories discussed or a **summary statement** that reinforces the thesis.

T **Transitions**—As you read, note the **transitional words and phrases** that show how categories are related to one another and to the essay's thesis.

> **Some Transitional Words and Phrases for Classification**
>
> Transitional words and phrases signal movement from one category to the next and may also tell readers which categories are more (or less) important:
>
> | | | |
> |---|---|---|
> | one kind . . . | the first (second, | the most important |
> | another kind | third) category | component |
> | the final type | the last group | the next part |

As a rule, each paragraph of a classification essay examines a separate category—a different part of the whole. For example, a paragraph could focus on one kind of course in the college curriculum, one component of the blood, or one type of voter. Within each paragraph, the writer discusses the individual items that have to be put into a particular category—for example, accounting courses, red blood cells, or Independent voters. If a writer considers some categories less important than others, he or she may decide to discuss those minor categories together in a single paragraph, devoting full paragraphs only to the most significant categories.

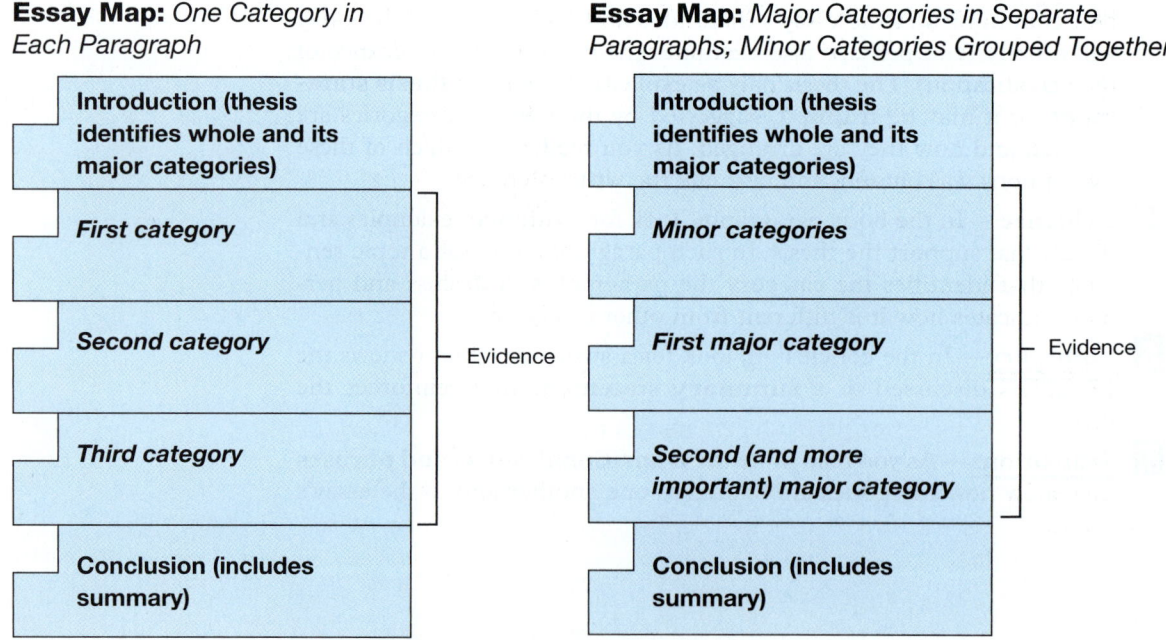

Essay Map: One Category in Each Paragraph

Essay Map: Major Categories in Separate Paragraphs; Minor Categories Grouped Together

In your college courses, much of the writing you do will be in response to reading—specifically, to reading texts such as the one that follows. This essay, "The Men We Carry in Our Minds," by Scott Russell Sanders, classifies the workers he has known. Read the essay, following the active reading process outlined in Chapter 1, and then answer the questions on pages 318–319. At the end of section 12c, you will be asked to write a classification essay in response to Sanders's ideas.

The Men We Carry in Our Minds
Scott Russell Sanders

Scott Russell Sanders is a Distinguished Professor Emeritus at Indiana University, a children's book author, and an essayist. His essays are often personal reflections that include social and philosophical commentary. In the classic essay "The Men We Carry in Our Minds," first published in the *Milkweed Chronicle* in 1984, Sanders reflects on the working lives of the men he knew as a boy and classifies them according to the kind of work they do. His essay discusses not only his boyhood impressions of the men's jobs but also the direction his own professional life has taken.

Before you read, think about the jobs held by men and women you know.

1   The first men, besides my father, I remember seeing were black convicts and white guards, in the cottonfield across the road from our farm on the outskirts of Memphis. I must have been three or four. The prisoners wore dingy gray-and-black zebra suits, heavy as canvas, sodden with sweat. Hatless, stooped, they chopped weeds in the fierce heat, row after row, breathing the acrid dust of boll-weevil poison. The overseers wore dazzling white shirts and broad shadowy hats. The oiled barrels of their shotguns flashed in the sunlight. Their faces in memory are utterly blank. Of course those men, white and black, have become for me an emblem of racial hatred. But they have also come to stand for the twin poles of my early vision of manhood—the brute toiling animal and the boss.

2   When I was a boy, the men I knew labored with their bodies. They were marginal farmers, just scraping by, or welders, steelworkers, carpenters; they swept floors, dug ditches, mined coal, or drove trucks, their forearms ropy with muscle; they trained horses, stoked furnaces, built tires, stood on assembly lines wrestling parts onto cars and refrigerators. They got up before light, worked all day long whatever the weather, and when they came home at night they looked as though somebody had been whipping them.

> **WORD POWER**
> **sodden** soaked with liquid or moisture
> **acrid** bitter and unpleasant in taste or smell
> **overseers** people who watch over the work of others

> **WORD POWER**
>
> **tilling** preparing land for growing crops

In the evenings and on weekends they worked on their own places, tilling gardens that were lumpy with clay, fixing broken-down cars, hammering on houses that were always too drafty, too leaky, too small.

3   The bodies of the men I knew were twisted and maimed in ways visible and invisible. The nails of their hands were black and split, the hands tattooed with scars. Some had lost fingers. Heavy lifting had given many of them finicky backs and guts weak from hernias. Racing against conveyor belts had given them ulcers. Their ankles and knees ached from years of standing on concrete. Anyone who had worked for long around machines was hard of hearing. They squinted, and the skin of their faces was creased like the leather of old work gloves. There were times, studying them, when I dreaded growing up. Most of them coughed, from dust or cigarettes, and most of them drank cheap wine or whiskey, so their eyes looked bloodshot and bruised. The fathers of my friends always seemed older than the mothers. Men wore out sooner. Only women lived into old age.

4   As a boy I also knew another sort of men, who did not sweat and break down like mules. They were soldiers, and so far as I could tell they scarcely worked at all. During my early school years we lived on a military base, an arsenal in Ohio, and every day I saw GIs in the guardshacks, on the stoops of barracks, at the wheels of olive drab Chevrolets. The chief fact of their lives was boredom. Long after I left the Arsenal I came to recognize the sour smell the soldiers gave off as that of souls in limbo. They were all waiting—for wars, for transfers, for leaves, for promotions, for the end of their hitch—like so many braves waiting for the hunt to begin. Unlike the warriors of older tribes, however, they would have no say about when the battle would start or how it would be waged. Their waiting was broken only when they practiced for war. They fired guns at targets, drove tanks across the churned-up fields of the military reservation, set off bombs in the wrecks of old fighter planes. I knew this was all play. But I also felt certain that when the hour for killing arrived, they would kill. When the real shooting started, many of them would die. This was what soldiers were *for*, just as a hammer was for driving nails.

5   Warriors and toilers: those seemed, in my boyhood vision, to be the chief destinies for men. They weren't the only destinies, as I learned from having a few male teachers, from reading books, and from watching television. But the men on television—the politicians, the astronauts, the generals, the savvy lawyers, the philosophical doctors, the bosses who gave orders to both soldiers and laborers—seemed as removed and unreal to me as the figures in tapestries. I could no more imagine growing up to become one of these cool, potent creatures than I could imagine becoming a prince.

6   A nearer and more hopeful example was that of my father, who had escaped from a red-dirt farm to a tire factory, and from the assembly line to the front office. Eventually he dressed in a white shirt and tie. He carried himself as if he had been born to work with his mind. But his body, remembering the earlier years of slogging work, began to give out on him in his fifties, and it quit on him entirely before he turned sixty-five. Even

such a partial escape from man's fate as he had accomplished did not seem possible for most of the boys I knew. They joined the Army, stood in line for jobs in the smoky plants, helped build highways. They were bound to work as their fathers had worked, killing themselves or preparing to kill others.

7   A scholarship enabled me not only to attend college, a rare enough feat in my circle, but even to study in a university meant for the children of the rich. Here I met for the first time young men who had assumed from birth that they would lead lives of comfort and power. And for the first time I met women who told me that men were guilty of having kept all the joys and privileges of the earth for themselves. I was baffled. What privileges? What joys? I thought about the maimed, dismal lives of most of the men back home. What had they stolen from their wives and daughters? The right to go five days a week, twelve months a year, for thirty or forty years to a steel mill or a coal mine? The right to drop bombs and die in war? The right to feel every leak in the roof, every gap in the fence, every cough in the engine, as a wound they must mend? The right to feel, when the layoff comes or the plant shuts down, not only afraid but ashamed?

8   I was slow to understand the deep grievances of women. This was because, as a boy, I had envied them. Before college, the only people I had ever known who were interested in art or music or literature, the only ones who read books, the only ones who ever seemed to enjoy a sense of ease and grace were the mothers and daughters. Like the menfolk, they fretted about money, they scrimped and made-do. But, when the pay stopped coming in, they were not the ones who had failed. Nor did they have to go to war, and that seemed to me a blessed fact. By comparison with the narrow, ironclad days of fathers, there was an expansiveness, I thought, in the days of mothers. They went to see neighbors, to shop in town, to run errands at school, at the library, at church. No doubt, had I looked harder at their lives, I would have envied them less. It was not my fate to become a woman, so it was easier for me to see the graces. Few of them held jobs outside the home, and those who did filled thankless roles as clerks and waitresses. I didn't see, then, what a prison a house could be, since houses seemed to me brighter, handsomer places than any factory. I did not realize—because such things were never spoken of—how often women suffered from men's bullying. I did learn about the wretchedness of abandoned wives, single mothers, widows; but I also learned about the wretchedness of lone men. Even then I could see how exhausting it was for a mother to cater all day to the needs of young children. But if I had been asked, as a boy, to choose between tending a baby and tending a machine, I think I would have chosen the baby. (Having now tended both, I know I would choose the baby.)

9   So I was baffled when the women at college accused me and my sex of having cornered the world's pleasures. I think something like my bafflement has been felt by other boys (and by girls as well) who grew up in dirt-poor farm country, in mining country, in black ghettos, in Hispanic barrios, in the shadows of factories, in Third World nations—any place where the fate of men is as grim and bleak as the fate of women. Toilers and warriors.

> **WORD POWER**
> **undertow** an underlying force or pull

I realize now how ancient these identities are, how deep the tug they exert on men, the undertow of a thousand generations. The miseries I saw, as a boy, in the lives of nearly all men I continue to see in the lives of many—the body-breaking toil, the tedium, the call to be tough, the humiliating powerlessness, the battle for a living and for territory.

10   When the women I met at college thought about the joys and privileges of men, they did not carry in their minds the sort of men I had known in my childhood. They thought of their fathers, who were bankers, physicians, architects, stockbrokers, the big wheels of the big cities. These fathers rode the train to work or drove cars that cost more than any of my childhood houses. They were attended from morning to night by female helpers, wives and nurses and secretaries. They were never laid off, never short of cash at month's end, never lined up for welfare. These fathers made decisions that mattered. They ran the world.

11   The daughters of such men wanted to share in this power, this glory. So did I. They yearned for a say over their future, for jobs worthy of their abilities, for the right to live at peace, unmolested, whole. Yes, I thought, yes yes. The difference between me and these daughters was that they saw me, because of my sex, as destined from birth to become like their fathers, and therefore as an enemy to their desires. But I knew better. I wasn't an enemy, in fact or in feeling. I was an ally. If I had known, then, how to tell them so, would they have believed me? Would they now?

Focus on Reading

1. Look back at the work you did when you previewed, marked up, and annotated this essay. **Scan** paragraphs 1 through 6, looking for the specific jobs held by the men Sanders knew when he was young. Circle those job titles.
2. Review your highlighting of paragraph 8, revising it if necessary. Now, write a one-sentence summary of the paragraph in the margin. Be sure to use your own words.
3. **TEST** Sanders's essay. Does he include all four **TEST** elements? If not, why not? What, if anything, should be added?

Focus on Meaning

1. What two types of men did Sanders know when he was young? How were they different? What did they have in common?
2. What were the grievances of the women Sanders met at college? Why did he have trouble understanding these grievances?

Focus on Strategy

1. Sanders opens his essay with a description of "black convicts and white guards." Why?
2. This essay closes with two questions. Is this an effective concluding strategy? Explain.

Focus on Language and Style

1. What connotations do the words *warriors* and *toilers* have?
2. Suggest two or three alternative pairs of names for the categories *warriors* and *toilers*. Do you think your suggestions are better than Sanders's choices? If so, why?

Focus on the Pattern

1. What kinds of men mentioned in this essay do not fit into either of the two categories Sanders identifies in paragraphs 2–4? Why don't they fit?
2. Sanders does not categorize the women he discusses. Can you think of a few categories into which these women could fit?

Focus on Critical Thinking

Who do you believe has an easier life, men or women? Why?

Analyzing a Student Essay: Classification

The following classification essay was written by Jessica Thomas in response to this assignment in her communication course.

> What kinds of videos go viral on YouTube? Classify some of the most popular videos according to criteria such as their purpose, their intended audience, and their content.

Read Jessica's essay, following the active reading process outlined in Chapter 1, and then fill in the essay map in Practice 12-5 on page 321. (Note that the **TEST** elements in the essay have been highlighted and color-coded.)

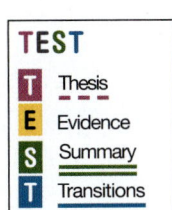

TEST
T Thesis
E Evidence
S Summary
T Transitions

What Kinds of Videos Go Viral?

1   Viral videos usually appear suddenly and spread quickly. Passed from friend to friend or coworker to coworker, these videos can attract millions of hits in just a few months or (even weeks). Although many people want their videos to go viral, predicting which ones will grab people's attention is difficult. Generally speaking, the most popular videos show viewers something they have not seen before. They also trigger a strong reaction. <u>Essentially, videos that go viral fall into three basic categories: outrageous, funny, or inspiring.</u>

 Thesis

T Transitions

Evidence E

2   The first kind of viral video shocks or amazes viewers. Sometimes the content of these videos is extreme; sometimes, it is just plain bizarre. In any case, people have a hard time looking away. "Felix Baumgartner's Supersonic Freefall" is a good example. Millions of people around the world have viewed this skydiver's record-breaking fall and been amazed by his success. The widely shared "Facebook Parenting: For the Troubled Teen" astonishes for different reasons. This homemade film shows a father getting revenge against his disrespectful teenager by shooting her laptop with a pistol. While some viewers are impressed by this man's action and others are horrified, everyone who sees it reacts strongly. Another example is "What's Inside a Rattlesnake's Rattle?" In this video, the host cuts open a rattlesnake's rattle only to discover there is nothing inside. As the host explains, it is the interlocking rings in the rattle hitting against each other that produce the characteristic sound the snake makes when it is startled. This unlikely video has attracted over twenty-one million viewers.

Evidence E

3   The second kind of viral video makes people laugh. Some of these humorous videos are simply clips from comedy shows, such as *Saturday Night Live* or *The Daily Show*. Others are amateur productions that show animals or people doing silly things. For example, one very popular video presents cats being scared with cucumbers. Although some cats don't respond to the hidden vegetable, others leap into the air or engage in hilarious acrobatics. Another viral video in this category shows an octopus moving along the ocean floor carrying two halves of a coconut. It suddenly stops, pulls the two halves together, and climbs inside. Finally, "Chewbacca Mom" shows Candace Payne, a thirty-seven-year-old mother, laughing while wearing a *Star Wars* Chewbacca mask. For some reason, this video became so popular that stores sold out of the mask just days after the video was posted. As of 2016, the video had over 140 million views on *Facebook*.

Evidence E

4   The third kind of viral video spreads not because it is shocking or amusing but because it is inspiring. One example of an emotionally powerful video that went viral is "Bailey Matthews Finishes a Triathlon." Encouraged by his father, eight-year-old Bailey Matthews, who has cerebral palsy, is shown using a specially constructed frame to help him complete a triathlon. The most famous example of this kind of video is "The Last Lecture," delivered in 2007 by Randy Pausch, a professor of computer science at Carnegie Mellon University, a month after he was diagnosed with terminal cancer. In his lecture, he discusses his childhood dreams and the things he wants his children to know about him. His primary message is that people should live life to the fullest because they never know when their lives might end.

Other videos in this category inspire by presenting speeches, often by famous people such as Oprah or Steve Jobs, in which the speakers share the secrets of their success. Like "The Last Lecture," these videos become popular because they make a strong emotional connection with viewers, sometimes inspiring them to change their lives.

5   Although no one can predict exactly which videos will go viral, the ones that spread the most quickly attract people in three notable ways. They appeal to our curiosity, our need to laugh, or our desire to be inspired. Of course, each individual video is unique, and the next videos to sweep the Internet will surely surprise people in one respect or another. However, viral videos will continue to affect viewers in the same basic ways. And, eager to share their experiences, viewers will continue to share the links with others.

S Summary

PRACTICE

12-5 Now that you have read Jessica's essay, fill in the essay map below to better understand how she organized her essay. Then, decide whether her organization is effective.

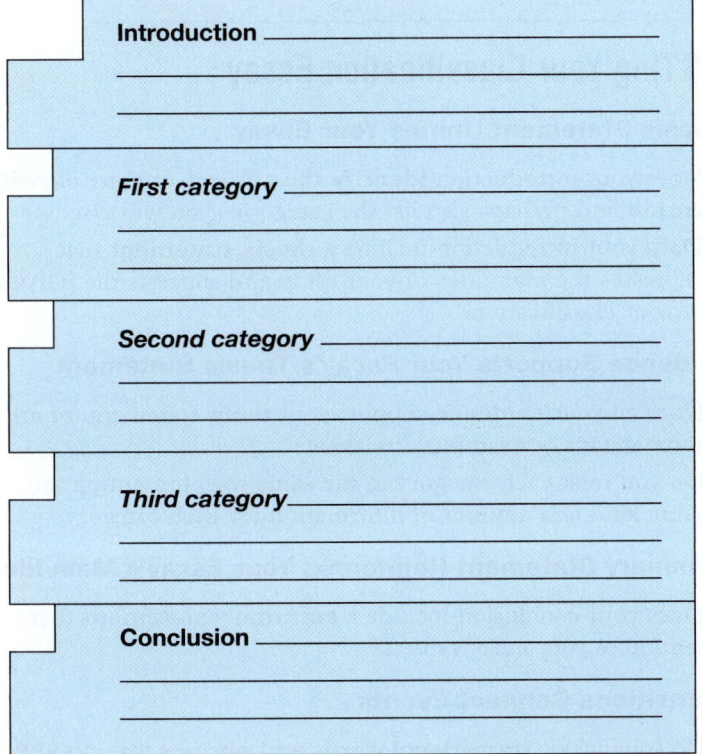

Writing a Classification Essay

When you are given a writing assignment, the wording of your assignment may suggest that you write a classification essay. For example, you may be asked to consider *kinds*, *types*, *categories*, *components*, *segments*, or *parts of a whole*. Once you decide that your assignment calls for classification, you need to develop a thesis statement that reflects this purpose.

ASSIGNMENT	THESIS STATEMENT
Business What kinds of courses are most useful for students planning to run their own businesses?	Courses dealing with accounting, management, and computer science offer the most useful skills for future business owners.
Biology List the components of blood and explain the function of each.	Red blood cells, white blood cells, platelets, and plasma have distinct functions.

When you **write** a classification essay, you follow the process outlined in Chapter 3. The essay you write will include the same elements you have learned to recognize in the classification essays you read. When you finish your draft, you can **TEST** it to make sure it includes all the elements of a classification essay.

TESTing Your Classification Essay

Thesis Statement Unifies Your Essay

- ☐ Does your introduction **identify the subject of your classification** and perhaps also list the categories you will discuss?
- ☐ Does your introduction include a **thesis statement** that expresses the main idea of your essay and suggests the purpose of your classification?

Evidence Supports Your Essay's Thesis Statement

- ☐ Does all your **evidence** support your thesis statement, or are some details or examples irrelevant?
- ☐ Do you treat each category in the same way, presenting the same kind and amount of information for each category?

Summary Statement Reinforces Your Essay's Main Idea

- ☐ Does your conclusion include a **summary statement** that reinforces your essay's thesis?

Transitions Connect Events

- ☐ Do you include **transitional words and phrases** that introduce each category and lead readers from one category to the next?

The following essay was written by Rob O'Neal for his first-year writing course. Read Rob's essay, and then answer the questions in Practice 12-6 on page 324.

Selling a Dream

1   The earliest automobiles were often named after the men who manufactured them—Ford, Studebaker, Nash, Olds, Chrysler, Dodge, Chevrolet, and so on. Over the years, however, American car makers began competing to see what kinds of names would sell the most cars. Many car names seem to have been chosen simply for how they sound: Alero, Corvette, Neon, Probe, Caprice. Many others, however, are designed to sell specific dreams to consumers. Americans always seem to want to be, do, and become something different. They want to be tough and brave, to explore new places, to take risks. The names auto manufacturers choose for their cars appeal to Americans' deepest desires.

2   Some American cars are named for places people dream of traveling to. Park Avenue, Malibu, Riviera, Seville, Tahoe, Yukon, Aspen, and Durango are some names that suggest escape—to New York City, California, Europe, the West. Other place names—Sebring, Daytona, and Bonneville, for example—are associated with the excitement of car racing. And then there is the El Dorado, a car named for a fictional paradise: a city of gold.

3   Other car names convey rough and tough, even dangerous, images. Animal names fall into this category, with models like Ram, Bronco, and Mustang suggesting powerful, untamed beasts. The "rough and tough" category also includes car names that suggest the wildness of the Old West: Wrangler and Rodeo, for example. Because the American auto industry was originally centered near Detroit, Michigan, where many cities have Indian names, cars named for the cities where they are manufactured inherited these names. Thus, cars called Cadillac, Pontiac, and Cherokee recall the history of Indian nations, and these, too, might suggest the excitement of the untamed West.

4   The most interesting car names in terms of the dream they sell, however, were selected to suggest exploration and discovery. Years ago, some car names honored real explorers, like DeSoto and LaSalle. Now, model names only sell an abstract idea. Still, American car names like Blazer, Explorer, Navigator, Journey, Mountaineer, Expedition, Caravan, and Voyager (as well as the names of foreign cars driven by many Americans, such as

Nissan's Pathfinder and Quest and Honda's Passport, Pilot, and Odyssey) have the power to make drivers feel they are blazing new trails and discovering new worlds — when in fact they may simply be carpooling their children to a soccer game or commuting to work.

5   Most people take cars for granted, but manufacturers still try to make consumers believe they are buying more than just transportation. Today, however, the car is just an ordinary piece of machinery, a necessity for many people. Sadly, the automobile is no longer seen as the amazing invention it once was.

PRACTICE 12-6

1. Underline Rob's thesis statement and summary statement; then, rewrite each in your own words.
2. Is Rob's treatment of the three categories of car names similar? Does he present the same kind of information for each kind of car name? Is each category distinct from the others?
3. How do Rob's topic sentences move readers from one category to the next? How do they link the three categories?
4. Circle some of the transitional words and phrases Rob uses to move from one category to another. Are any other transitions needed? If so, where?
5. Use **TEST** to evaluate Rob's essay. What, if anything, does he need to revise? Why?

Grammar in context

Classification

When you write a **classification essay**, you may want to list the categories you are going to discuss or the examples in each category. If you do, use a **colon** to introduce your list, and make sure that a complete sentence comes before the colon.

Many car names seem to have been chosen simply for how they sound: Alero, Corvette, Neon, Probe, Caprice.

For information on how to use a colon to introduce a list, see 29g.

FOCUS on reading and writing

Reread Scott Russell Sanders's essay, "The Men We Carry in Our Minds," (p. 315). Then, write a classification essay of your own in response to one of the following prompts. Be sure to follow the writing process outlined in Chapter 3.

1. Write a classification essay in which you identify and discuss three or four categories of workers (females as well as males) you observed in your community when you were growing up. In your thesis statement, draw a conclusion about the relative status and rewards of these workers' jobs.
2. Write an essay in which you categorize the workers in your current place of employment or on your college campus.

    If you prefer, you can write on one of these topics instead:

    - Traits of oldest children, middle children, and youngest children
    - Types of teachers (or bosses)
    - Types of reality shows

12d Definition

During a conversation, you might say that a friend is stubborn, that a stream is polluted, or that a neighborhood is dangerous. In order to make yourself clear, you have to define what you mean by *stubborn*, *polluted*, or *dangerous*. Like conversations, academic assignments also may involve definition. In a history paper, for example, you might have to define *imperialism*; on a biology exam, you might be asked to define *mitosis*.

Definition explains the meaning of a term or concept. When most people think of definitions, they think of the kinds of definitions they see in a dictionary. These **formal definitions** have the following three-part structure:

- The term to be defined
- The general class to which the term belongs
- The qualities that make the term different from all other items in the general class to which the term belongs

TERM	CLASS	DIFFERENTIATION
Ice hockey	is a game	played on ice by two teams on skates who use curved sticks to try to hit a puck into the opponent's goal.
Spaghetti	is a pasta	made in the shape of long, thin strands.

A single-sentence definition like those above is often not enough to define a specialized term (*point of view* or *premeditation*), an abstract concept (*happiness* or *success*), or a complex subject (*stem-cell research*). In these cases, you may need to move beyond a formal definition to a **definition essay**, which uses various patterns of development to expand a basic dictionary definition.

Reading a Definition Essay

When you **read** a definition essay, follow the active reading process outlined in Chapter 1. You can use **TEST** to help you identify its key elements.

- **T** **Thesis**—In the introduction of a definition essay, look for a **thesis** that identifies the term to be defined and communicates the essay's main idea—for example, the point the writer is making about the term, or the reason the term is being defined. Sometimes the thesis is stated explicitly in a **thesis statement**; at other times, it is **implied**, suggested by the discussion. As you read, note whether the thesis is stated or implied, and consider why.

- **E** **Evidence**—In the body paragraphs, look for **evidence**, examples and details that develop the definition and support the thesis. The structure of a definition essay can follow any of the patterns discussed in this book. In fact, each body paragraph may use a different pattern of development. As you read, identify these patterns and consider why each was used.

- **S** **Summary**—In the conclusion of a definition essay, look for a **summary** of the term's meaning or a **summary statement** that reinforces the essay's thesis.

- **T** **Transitions**—As you read, identify the **transitional words and phrases** that connect ideas and move readers from one section of the definition to the next.

> **Some Transitional Words and Phrases for Definition**
>
> The kinds of transitions used in a definition essay depend on the specific pattern or patterns of development in the essay:
>
> | | |
> |---|---|
> | also | like |
> | for example | one characteristic . . . another characteristic |
> | in addition | one way . . . another way |
> | in particular | specifically |

To explain the meaning of a term, concept, or item, you can develop a definition essay in a number of different ways:

- By giving examples (exemplification)
- By telling how something occurred (narration or cause and effect)
- By describing its appearance (description)
- By telling how it is different from something else (comparison and contrast)
- By discussing its parts (classification)

Some definition essays use a single pattern of development; others combine several patterns of development, perhaps using a different pattern in each paragraph.

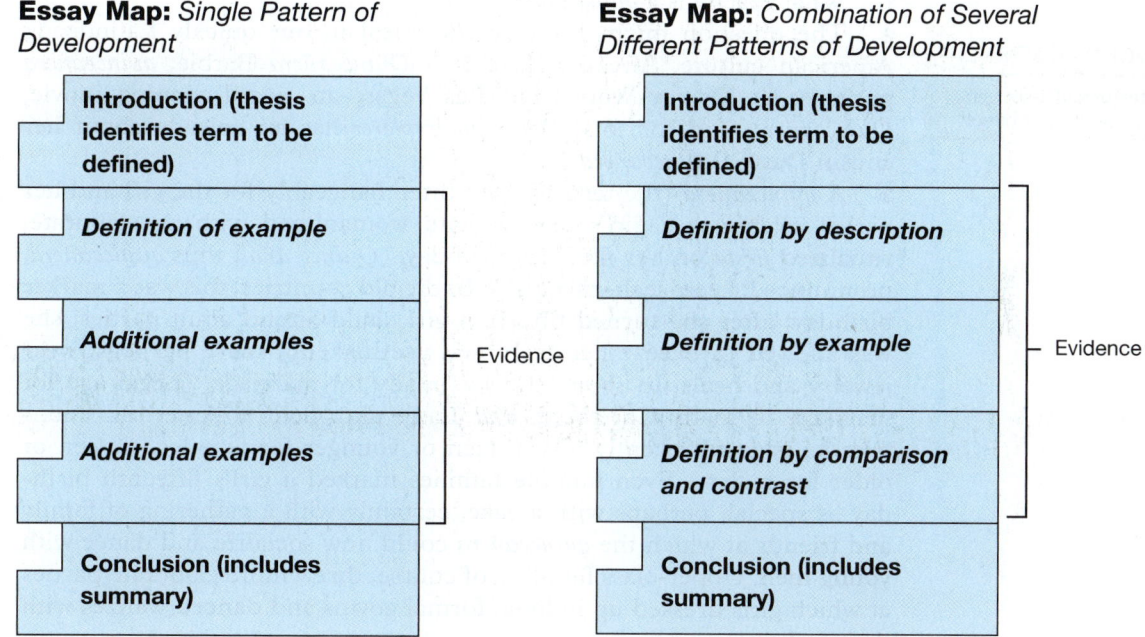

In your college courses, much of the writing you do will be in response to reading—specifically, to reading texts such as the one that follows. In this essay, "What Is a Quinceañera?," Julia Alvarez defines a coming-of-age ritual. Read the essay, following the active reading process outlined in Chapter 1, and then answer the questions on pages 330–331. At the end of section 12d, you will be asked to write a definition essay in response to Alvarez's ideas.

What is a *Quinceañera*?

Julia Alvarez

Born in New York City to Dominican parents, Julia Alvarez has published numerous works of fiction and nonfiction, including poetry, children's stories, novels, and essays. One of her most famous books, *In the Time of the Butterflies* (1994), offers a fictionalized account of the tragic story of three sisters who became revolutionary leaders in the Dominican Republic under the dictatorship of Rafael Trujillo. (Alvarez's own family fled this regime in 1960.) This excerpt is from the nonfiction work *Once Upon a Quinceañera: Coming of Age in the USA* (2007).

Before you read, think about a ritual or celebration in your own life and how you might define it.

> **WORD POWER**
> **rhetorical** used simply for style or effect

1 What exactly is a *quinceañera*?

2 The question might soon be rhetorical in our quickly Latinoizing American culture. Already, there is a *Quinceañera* Barbie; *quinceañera* packages at Disney World and Las Vegas; an award-winning movie, *Quinceañera*; and for tots, *Dora the Explorer* has an episode about her cousin Daisy's *quinceañera*.

3 A *quinceañera* (the term is used interchangeably for the girl and her party) celebrates a girl's passage into womanhood with an elaborate, ritualized *fiesta* on her fifteenth birthday. (*Quince años*, thus *quinceañera*, pronounced: keen-seah-gnéer-ah.) In the old countries, this was a marker birthday: after she turned fifteen, a girl could attend adult parties; she was allowed to tweeze her eyebrows, use makeup, shave her legs, wear jewelry and heels. In short, she was ready for marriage. (Legal age for marriage in many Caribbean and Latin and Central American countries is, or until recently was, fifteen or younger for females, sixteen or older for males.) Even humble families marked a girl's fifteenth birthday as special, perhaps with a cake, certainly with a gathering of family and friends at which the *quinceañera* could now socialize and dance with young men. Upper-class families, of course, threw more elaborate parties at which girls dressed up in long, formal gowns and danced waltzes with their fathers.

4 Somewhere along the way these fancier parties became highly ritualized. In one or another of our Latin American countries, the *quinceañera* was crowned with a tiara; her flat shoes were changed by her father to heels; she was accompanied by a court of fourteen *damas* escorted by fourteen *chambelanes*, who represented her first fourteen years; she received a last doll, marking both the end of childhood and her symbolic readiness to bear her own child. And because our countries were at least

nominally Catholic, the actual party was often preceded by a Mass or a blessing in church or, at the very least, a priest was invited to give spiritual heft to the *fiesta*. These celebrations were covered in newspapers, lavish spreads of photos I remember poring over as a little girl in the Dominican Republic, reassured by this proof that the desire to be a princess did not have to be shed at the beginning of adulthood, but could in fact be played out happily to the tune of hundreds upon thousands of Papi's *pesos*.

5   In the late sixties, when many of our poor headed to *el Norte*'s land of opportunity, they brought this tradition along, and with growing economic power, the no-longer-so-poor could emulate the rich back home. The spin-offs grew (*quinceañera* cruises, *quinceañera* resort packages, *quinceañera* videos and photo shoots); stories of where this *quinceañera* custom had come from proliferated (an ancient Aztec tradition, an import from European courts); further elaborations were added (Disney themes, special entrances, staged dance routines à la Broadway musicals); and in our Pan-Hispanic mixing stateside, the U.S. *quinceañera* adopted all the little touches of specific countries to become a much more elaborate (and expensive) ceremony, exported back to our home countries. But rock-bottom, the U.S. *quinceañera* is powered by that age-old immigrant dream of giving the children what their parents had never been able to afford back where they came from.

6   In fact, the *quince* expression notwithstanding, many of us older first-generation Latinas never had a *quinceañera*. There was no money back when we were fifteen, or we had recently arrived in the United States and didn't want anything that would make us stand out as other than all-American. Or we looked down our noses at such girly-girl fuss and said we didn't want a *quince* because we didn't understand that this was not just about us.

7   These cultural celebrations are also about building community in a new land. Lifted out of the context of our home cultures, traditions like the *quinceañera* become malleable; they mix with the traditions of other cultures that we encounter here; they become exquisite performances of our ethnicities within the larger host culture while at the same time reaffirming that we are not "them" by connecting us if only in spirit to our root cultures. In other words, this tradition tells a larger story of our transformation into Latinos, a Pan-Hispanic group made in the USA, now being touted as the "new Americans."

Focus on Reading

1. Look back at the work you did when you previewed, marked up, and annotated this essay. If you have not already done so, underline the formal (dictionary) definition of *quinceañera* that Alvarez includes. In the margin, rewrite this definition in your own words.

WORD POWER
nominally in name only
heft significance or importance

WORD POWER
emulate try to be like or better than
proliferate to quickly increase in number or amount

WORD POWER
touted promoted

2. Circle all the Spanish words Alvarez uses. If any of them are not familiar to you, look them up, and then write a brief definition of each word in the margin.
3. **TEST** Alvarez's essay. Does she include all four **TEST** elements? If not, why not? What, if anything, should be added?

Focus on Meaning

1. In paragraph 5, Alvarez explains how the *quinceañera* grew and changed as Latino families settled in the United States. What is her attitude toward these changes? For example, does she seem to suggest that they have somehow lessened the meaning of the ritual?
2. According to Alvarez, what is the value of the *quinceañera* for Latinas? For the culture of which they are a part?

Focus on Strategy

1. Alvarez opens her essay with a one-sentence paragraph that asks the question, "What exactly is a *quinceañera*?" What are the advantages and disadvantages of this opening strategy?
2. Do you think Alvarez expects her readers to be familiar with the term she is defining? How can you tell? What does your answer tell you about her intended audience and purpose?

Focus on Language and Style

1. Alvarez uses a number of Spanish words other than *quinceañera* in this essay, but she does not define them. Do you think she should have? Why or why not?
2. In paragraph 4, Alvarez observes that the *quinceañera* has become "highly ritualized." What does the word *ritualized* mean in this context? Is it a positive, negative, or neutral term?

Focus on the Pattern

1. Where does Alvarez give information about the origin of the term *quinceañera*?
2. Where does Alvarez develop her definition with examples? Where does she use description? Does she use any other patterns of development?

Focus on Critical Thinking

At different points in her essay, Alvarez sees the *quinceañera* as a "passage into womanhood" (paragraph 3), a traditional religious celebration (para. 4), a way of "building community in a new land" (para. 7), and the realization of an "age-old immigrant dream" (para. 5). Which of these different impressions does her definition communicate most strongly? Explain.

Analyzing a Student Essay: Definition

The following definition essay was written by Jacob Miller in response to a question on a take-home Introduction to Literature exam. Here is the exam question.

> Define a literary movement, term, or concept that you learned about in this course. You may select a topic from the list below or a topic of your choice. Assume that your readers are not familiar with the term you are defining.
>
> **POSSIBLE TOPICS**
>
> Naturalism   The graphic novel
> Imagism   The short-short story
> Stream of consciousness The ten-minute play
> Point of view   Found poetry
> Staging   Parody

Read Jacob's essay, following the active reading process outlined in Chapter 1, and then fill in the essay map in Practice 12-7 on page 333. (Note that the **TEST** elements in the essay have been highlighted and color-coded.)

TEST
T Thesis
E Evidence
S Summary
T Transitions

The Graphic Novel

1   Many people think that any story that includes pictures must be written for children. However, the graphic novel has a long and respected tradition. Although the concept itself is not new, the term — which is often applied broadly and includes both fiction and nonfiction (usually in the form of graphic memoirs) — only started to take hold in the mid-twentieth century. Now, articles in respected literary journals discuss graphic novels, which are also taught in many college literature courses. Today, with bookstores and websites devoting entire sections to graphic novels, more people are discovering these innovative works and enjoying the invitation to participate as active readers. What they are finding is that the graphic novel is a legitimate form of imaginative literature with its own distinctive conventions, using both words and pictures to tell a complex story.

 Thesis

T Transitions

Evidence **E**

2   The most obvious characteristic of a graphic novel is the use of words and images together on the page. Each page contains panels, generally rectangles made up of individual drawings and handwritten words. However, panels can vary widely in shape, size, and number, making each page look different. Even within one book, an artist frequently varies the layout. By doing so, he or she is able to convey changes in mood, time, or setting. This shifting appearance of graphics is part of what draws readers in and invites them to participate. Readers not only have to imagine the untold story between each page or panel, but they also have to fill in gaps between the words and the images. Looking at either words or images alone would give the reader only fragments of the story, and he or she and would fail to appreciate the hybrid nature of this literary genre.

Evidence **E**

3   Another way to define graphic novels is by recognizing how they are different from and similar to other kinds of illustrated literary works. Graphic novels are not like cartoons or comic books. First of all, graphic novels are not usually written for children; they often have sophisticated subject matter and are created for an adult audience. Second, although cartoons and comics tend to use pictures simply to illustrate their stories, the images in graphic novels are an integral part of the stories. In fact, drawings in graphic novels convey crucial information that is never explained through words; the illustrations are part of the story's narrative framework. The graphic novel is, however, similar to other forms of literature. Like writers of traditional novels, short stories, and memoirs, graphic novelists use literary devices, such as symbols and metaphors, and explore important themes. Rather than telling the reader what a story means, these writers frequently offer visual and written clues; then, they ask the readers to use their imaginations to figure out the meaning for themselves. These features qualify the graphic novel as serious literature.

Evidence **E**

4   Two recent, well-reviewed graphic novels in particular demonstrate how complex, creative, and interactive this form of literature can be. The first example, Alison Bechdel's graphic memoir *Fun Home: A Family Tragicomic*, includes clever humor and references to classic literature. Much like writers of traditional memoirs, Bechdel also gives the audience access to her inner thoughts and questions. She treats the reader like an intimate friend and invites the audience into the unique world of her mind and memory. In this world, her drawings and her written thoughts are inseparable. Another remarkable example of the graphic novel is Chris Ware's *Building Stories*. Unique in its design, this graphic novel comes in a large flat box containing fourteen distinct pieces. Through art and writing, each piece tells part of

the story. The pieces, however, can be read in any order, so in addition to filling in the gaps, the audience has to physically construct the narrative. Like Bechdel's memoir, Ware's "book" shows how graphic literature, like all great literature, invites readers to become co-inventors.

5   The graphic novel deserves recognition and should be treated not as a novelty but as serious literature. Through rich stories and creative approaches, graphic novels engage audiences. Graphic novelists do not treat their subjects in shallow or trivial ways, and readers of graphic novels are not passively entertained. On the contrary, the artists who create graphic literature frequently examine some of humanity's most difficult themes. In addition, readers of these works are active participants, using their own creativity to make sense of the story. In the years to come, the graphic novel is certain to attract more and more readers with its challenging, entertaining, and multilayered tales.

S Summary

PRACTICE

12-7   Now that you have read Jacob's essay, fill in the essay map below to help you understand how he organized his essay. Then, decide whether his organization is effective.

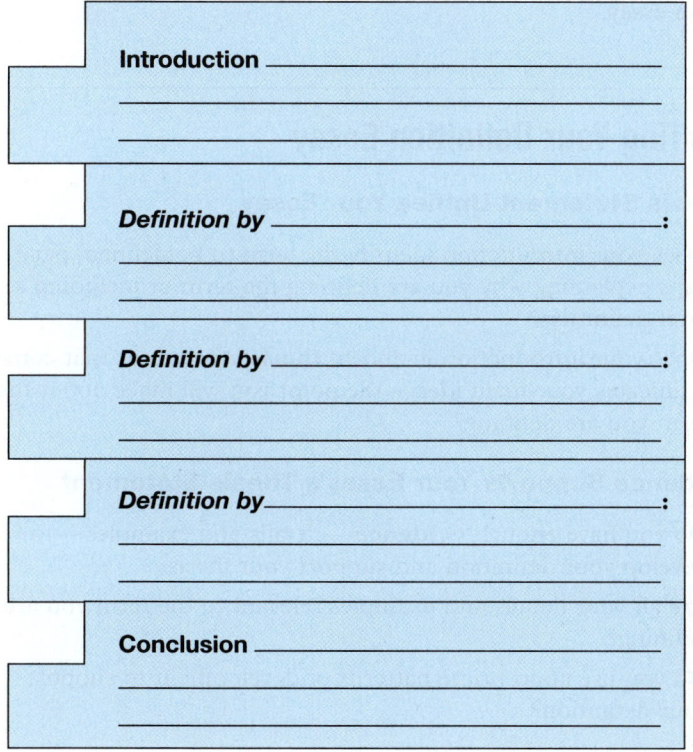

Introduction _____

Definition by _____:

Definition by _____:

Definition by _____:

Conclusion _____

Writing a Definition Essay

When you are given a writing assignment, the wording of your assignment may suggest that you write a definition essay. For example, you may be asked to *define* or *explain* or to answer the question *What is x?* or *What does x mean?* Once you decide that your assignment calls for definition, you need to develop a thesis statement that reflects this purpose.

ASSIGNMENT	THESIS STATEMENT
Art Explain the meaning of the term *performance art*.	Unlike more conventional forms of art, *performance art* extends beyond the canvas.
Biology What did Darwin mean by the term *natural selection*?	*Natural selection*, popularly known as "survival of the fittest," is a good deal more complicated than most people think.

When you **write** a definition essay, you follow the process outlined in Chapter 3. The essay you write will include the same elements you have learned to recognize in the definition essays you read. When you finish your draft, you can **TEST** it to make sure it includes all the elements of a definition essay.

TESTing Your Definition Essay

Thesis Statement Unifies Your Essay

☐ Does your introduction identify the term to be defined, perhaps explaining why you are defining the term or including a brief definition?

☐ Does your introduction include a **thesis statement** that communicates your main idea—the point you will make about the term you are defining?

Evidence Supports Your Essay's Thesis Statement

☐ Do you have enough **evidence**—details and examples—to develop your definition and support your thesis?

☐ Are all your details and examples relevant to the term you are defining?

☐ Do you use appropriate patterns of development to support your definition?

> **S**ummary Statement Reinforces Your Essay's Main Idea
>
> ☐ Does your conclusion include a **summary** of your definition or a **summary statement** that reinforces your essay's thesis, perhaps emphasizing the importance of your definition or explaining why you defined the term?
>
> **T**ransitions Connect Events
>
> ☐ Do you use **transitional words and phrases** to introduce your points and link your ideas?
>
> ☐ Do you have enough transitions to move readers smoothly through your definition?

The following essay was written by Kristin Whitehead in her first-year writing course. Read Kristin's essay, and then answer the questions in Practice 12-8 on page 336.

Street Smart

1   I grew up in a big city, so I was practically born street smart. I learned the hard way how to act and what to do, and so did my friends. To us, being *street smart* meant having common sense. We wanted to be cool, but we needed to be safe, too. Now I go to college in a big city, and I realize that not everyone here grew up the way I did. Many students are from suburbs or rural areas, and they are either terrified of the city or totally ignorant of city life. The few suburban or rural students who are willing to venture downtown are not street smart — but they should be. Being street smart is a vital survival skill, one that everyone should learn.

2   For me, being street smart means knowing how to protect my possessions. Friends of mine who are not used to city life insist on wearing all their jewelry when they go downtown. I think this is asking for trouble, and I know better. I always tuck my chain under my shirt and leave my gold earrings home. Another thing that surprises me is how some of my friends wave their money around. They always seem to be standing on the street, trying to count their change or stuff dollars into their wallets. Street-smart people make sure to put their money safely away in their pockets or purses before they leave a store. A street-smart person will also carry a backpack, a purse strapped across the chest, or no purse at all. A person who is not street smart carries a purse loosely over one shoulder or dangles it by its handle. Again, these people are asking for trouble.

3   Being street smart also means protecting myself. It means being aware of my surroundings at all times and looking alert. A lot of times, I have been downtown with people who kept stopping on the street to talk about where they should go next or walking up and down the same street over and over again. A street-smart person would never do this. It is important that I look as if I know where I am going at all times, even if I don't. Whenever possible, I decide on a destination in advance, and I make sure I know how to get there. Even if I am not completely sure where I am headed, I make sure my body language conveys my confidence in my ability to reach my destination.

4   Finally, being street smart means protecting my life. A street-smart person does not walk alone, especially after dark, in an unfamiliar neighborhood. A street-smart person does not ask random strangers for directions; when lost, he or she asks a shopkeeper for help. A street-smart person takes main streets instead of side streets. When faced with danger or the threat of danger, a street-smart person knows when to run, when to scream, and when to give up money or possessions to avoid violence.

5   Being street smart is vitally important—sometimes even a matter of life and death. Some people think it is a gift, but I think it is something almost anyone can learn. Probably the best way to learn how to be street smart is to hang out with people who know where they are going.

PRACTICE 12-8

1. Underline Kristin's thesis statement; then, rewrite it in your own words.
2. In your own words, define the term *street smart*. Why does this term require more than a one-sentence definition?
3. Where does Kristin use examples to develop her definition? Where does she use comparison and contrast?
4. Kristin's conclusion is somewhat shorter than her other paragraphs. Do you think she should expand this paragraph? If so, what should she add?
5. Use **TEST** to evaluate Kristin's essay. What, if anything, does she need to revise? Why?

Grammar in context

Definition

When you write a definition essay, you may begin with a one-sentence definition that you expand in the rest of your essay. When you write your definition sentence, do not use the phrase *is when* or *is where*.

For me, being street smart ~~is when I know~~ *means knowing* how to protect my possessions.

Being street smart ~~is~~ also ~~where I protect~~ *means protecting* myself.

FOCUS on reading and writing

Reread Julia Alvarez's essay (p. 328). Then, write your own definition essay in response to one of the following prompts. Be sure to follow the writing process outlined in Chapter 3.

1. Write an essay defining a coming-of-age ritual that is significant in your own community, culture, or religion. Assume that your readers are not familiar with the ritual you are defining, and develop your definition with **exemplification** and **description**. (You can also use **comparison and contrast** if you think explaining your ritual by showing how it is like a more familiar practice will be helpful to your readers.)

2. Write an essay defining a coming-of-age ritual with which you are familiar. Develop your definition primarily through **narration**—by telling the story of your own introduction to this ritual.

    If you prefer, you can write on one of these topics instead:
    - The American Dream
    - Procrastination
    - Success

Review checklist

Additional Options for Organizing Essays

✔ When you *read* or *write* a **descriptive** essay, use **TEST** to help you identify the essay's key elements and to make sure you have included all these elements in your own writing. In descriptive writing, details enable readers to see what the writer sees, hear what the writer hears, and feel what the writer has experienced. Often, the writer's goal is to create a single dominant impression to which all the details relate. (See 12a.)

✔ When you *read* or *write* a **process** essay, use **TEST** to help you identify the essay's key elements and to make sure you have included all these elements in your own writing. Process writing explains the steps in a procedure, telling how something works or how something is (or was) done. Depending on the writer's purpose, a process essay can be organized as either a *process explanation* (telling how something is or was done) or a set of *instructions* (telling readers how to perform the process themselves). (See 12b.)

✔ When you *read* or *write* a **classification** essay, use **TEST** to help you identify the essay's key elements and to make sure you have included all these elements in your own writing. Classification writing divides a whole (the subject) into parts and sorts various items into distinct categories using a principle of classification—something the items being categorized have in common. (See 12c.)

✔ When you *read* or *write* a **definition** essay, use **TEST** to help you identify the essay's key elements and to make sure you have included all these elements in your own writing. Definition writing explains the meaning of a term or concept and follows a three-part structure: the term being defined, the class to which the term belongs, and the qualities that differentiate the term from other members of the general class. (See 12d.)

unit 3
Research

13 Finding and Evaluating Sources 341

14 Documenting Sources in MLA or APA Style 358

unit 3

13 Finding and Evaluating Sources

PREVIEW

In this chapter you will learn to
- find and evaluate information in the library and on the Internet (13a).
- use sources in your writing (13b).
- use sources ethically (13c).

When you write, you can sometimes use your own ideas and observations to support your points. At many other times, however, you have to move beyond your own experience and support your points with information you find either in the library or on the Internet. In other words, you have to do **research**. Although the idea of research can be intimidating, it shouldn't be. When you carry out research, you are looking at what other people who have thought long and hard about your subject have to say about it. By doing research, you build on what you already know about a subject as you react to what you read.

As you do research, keep in mind that the essay you write should not be just a collection of other people's ideas. It should present an original thesis that you support with your own insights and opinions. The material you get from your sources should help you develop your ideas about your topic. Of course, you can include the insights of experts, but it is up to you to build on them. In other words, your voice, not the voices of your sources, should control the discussion.

 ## 13a Finding Information

When most students do research, they go straight to the Internet and do a Google search. In some cases—for example, for a short, informal essay—this may be fine. If you do this regularly, however—especially for longer assignments—you'll ignore a valuable resource: your college library. Your library gives you access to many important resources—for instance, books, journals, and electronic databases—that are available nowhere else, including on the Internet. For this reason, when you do research, you should use your college library as well as the Internet.

Finding Information in the Library

For the best results, you should do your library research systematically. Once you get a sense of your topic, you should consult the library's **online catalog**—a comprehensive information system that gives you access to the resources housed in the library. The online catalog is not as "open" as the Internet, where anything and everything is posted. Library resources have been screened by librarians as well as instructors, and in many cases, are written by experts in a particular field and conform to academic standards of reliability.

You search the online catalog just as you would search the Internet—by carrying out a *keyword search* or a *subject search*. You do a **keyword search** the same way you would search using Google or About.com—by entering your keywords in a Search box to retrieve a list of books, periodicals, and other materials that are relevant to your topic. The more specific your keywords, the more focused your search will be. Thus, the keywords *Facebook privacy* will yield more specific (and useful) results than *social networking*.

You do a **subject search** by entering a subject heading related to your topic. Unlike keywords, subject headings are predetermined and come from a list of subject headings published by the Library of Congress. Many online catalogs provide lists of subject headings that you can use. A subject search is best when you want information about a general topic—for example, *rap music*, *discography*, or *Mark Twain*.

After consulting the online catalog, you should look at the **electronic databases**—such as *InfoTrac* and *ProQuest*—that your college library subscribes to. These databases enable you to obtain information from newspapers, magazines, and journals that you often cannot access by doing a web search. Most of the library's electronic databases enable you to retrieve the full text of articles. (You can usually search them remotely, from home or from anywhere on campus.)

Most online catalogs list the databases to which the library subscribes, along with descriptions of the type of material the databases contain.

FYI

Using *WorldCat Discovery*

Find out if your college library subscribes to *WorldCat Discovery*, a mega-search tool that enables you to search all the print and electronic holdings of your college library as well as books and articles outside the library. Unlike the library catalog, which searches for titles, authors, and subjects, *WorldCat Discovery* searches for specific articles, e-book chapters, magazine articles, and journal articles. Because it searches all the library's electronic databases at once, *WorldCat Discovery* eliminates the need to choose a database that is appropriate for your topic. It uses a single search box that gives users a search experience like using Google.

For example, a database may contain articles on a wide variety of subjects, or it may focus on a specific subject area.

Evaluating Library Sources

In general, the sources in library databases are more reliable than the sources you access on the Internet. Even so, you should still **evaluate** them—that is, determine their usefulness and reliability—before you use them in your paper. For example, an article in a respected periodical, such as *The New York Times* or *The Wall Street Journal*, is more trustworthy and credible than one in a tabloid, such as *The National Enquirer* or *The Sun*. Your instructor or college librarian can help you select sources that are both appropriate and reliable.

> **WORD POWER**
> **tabloid** a newspaper that emphasizes stories with sensational content

Questions to Ask When Evaluating Library Sources

When you evaluate library sources, you should consider each source's purpose and audience, author, publisher, citations, and date of publication. You can ask the following questions to help you evaluate your sources:

PURPOSE AND AUDIENCE
- Does the source aim to inform, entertain, persuade, or sell a product or service?
- Who is the intended audience?
- Is the information intended for scholars or for a general audience?

AUTHOR
- Who is the author?
- Is the author well known in the field?
- Is the author an authority on the subject?

PUBLISHER
- Who published the source? For example, is it a university press? A commercial press?
- Is the publisher reputable?
- Is the publisher known to have an editorial bias? (See 5e for more information on bias.)
- How might the publisher's bias impact the information in the source?

CITATIONS
- What sources does the author cite?
- Does the author document these sources? Does the author include a bibliography?
- Does the author use a fair range of sources (that is, not just those that support his or her position)?

DATE

- When was the source published?
- How current is the information in the source?
- For your topic, how important is it that source information be current?
- (See 5e for more information about evaluating a writer's ideas.)

Finding Information on the Internet

The Internet can give you access to a great deal of information that can help you support your ideas and develop your essay. However, you have to be extremely careful when using the Internet because it is an open source; anyone can create a website and upload material. Unlike the resources available in your college library, the resources available on the Internet have not been screened; no one is responsible for checking the accuracy of information or the credentials of people who post on the Internet. For this reason, it is your responsibility (and obligation) to determine the trustworthiness of an Internet source, and to decide whether it is credible (believable).

Once you are online, you need to connect to a **search engine**, which helps you find information by sorting through the millions of documents that are available on the Internet. Among the most popular search engines are Google, Yahoo!, and Bing.

There are two ways to use a search engine to access information:

1. *You can do a keyword search.* All search engines let you do a keyword search. You type a term or terms into a box, and the search engine looks for documents that contain the term, listing all the hits that it finds.

2. *You can paste a URL.* Every web page has a unique electronic address called a **URL** (uniform resource locater). You can copy a URL and paste it into your browser's search box. Click Search, and you will be connected to the website or web page you want.

Evaluating Internet Sources

In general, you evaluate Internet sources the same way you evaluate print sources. With the Internet, however, you have problems that you don't have with the sources available in your college library. Because anyone can publish on the Internet, it is often difficult—if not impossible—to determine, let alone judge, the credentials of an author or the accuracy of his or her claims. To make matters worse, websites sometimes have no listed author. Dates can also be missing, so it may be difficult to tell when information was originally posted and when it was updated. Finally, it is often hard to determine if a website has a purpose other than providing information. For example, is the site trying to sell something or advance a political or social agenda? If it is, it may contain information that is biased or even incorrect.

FYI

Acceptable vs. Unacceptable Internet Sources

Before you use an Internet source, you should consider if it is acceptable for college-level work:

Acceptable Sources

- Websites sponsored by reliable organizations, such as academic institutions, the government, and professional organizations
- Websites sponsored by academic journals and reputable magazines or newspapers
- Blogs by recognized experts in their fields
- Research forums

Unacceptable Sources

- Information on anonymous websites
- Information found in chatrooms or on discussion boards
- Information on personal web pages
- Poorly written web pages
- Most commercial websites that exist solely to sell something

You can evaluate websites by asking some basic questions:

- *Who is the author of the site?* Avoid information from unnamed authors or from authors with questionable credentials.
- *Who is the sponsoring organization?* Be especially careful of using information from websites sponsored by companies selling something, or organizations that have a particular agenda.
- *Can you verify information posted on the site?* Make sure you are able to check the source of the information. For example, you should make sure an article on a site includes documentation. Also, cross-check information you find on the site. Does the same information appear in other reliable sources?
- *Does the site contain errors?* In addition to factual errors, look out for mistakes in grammar or spelling. Errors such as these should raise a red flag about the accuracy of the information on the site you are visiting.
- *Do the links on the site work?* Make sure that the links on the site are "live"—ones that work. The presence of "dead" links is a good indication that a site is not being properly maintained.
- *Is the information up-to-date?* Make sure the site's information is current. Avoid sites that contain information that is outdated. A reliable site will usually include the date that information was posted and the date it was revised.

FYI

Using Google Scholar

Google Scholar is a valuable research resource. If you use it, however, you should be aware of its drawbacks:

- *It includes some non-scholarly publications.* Because it does not accurately define *scholar*, some material may not conform to academic standards of reliability.
- *It does not index all scholarly journals.* Many academic journals are available only through a library's databases and are not accessible on the Internet.
- Google Scholar *is uneven across scholarly disciplines—that is, it includes more information from some disciplines than others.* In addition, Google Scholar does not perform well for publications before 1990.
- Google Scholar *does not screen for quality.* Because Google Scholar uses an algorithm, not a human being, to select sources, it does not always filter out junk journals.
- *Some of the articles in* Google Scholar *are pay-per-view.* Before you pay to download an article, check to see if your college library gives you free access.

When in doubt, check with a reference librarian or with your instructor. Unless you can be certain that a site is reliable, do not use it as a source.

FYI

Using Wikipedia as a Source

Most college students regularly consult Wikipedia, the open-source online encyclopedia. The rationale behind Wikipedia is that if a large number of people review information, errors will eventually be discovered and corrected. Because there are no full-time professional editors, however, Wikipedia articles can (and do) contain inaccurate as well as biased information. In addition, anyone—not just experts—can write and edit entries. Understandably, some instructors distrust—or at least question—the accuracy of Wikipedia entries. For this reason, they do not consider it suitable for academic research. Even though Wikipedia is not a credible research source, however, you can use it to familiarize yourself with a topic or to find acceptable sources by checking the bibliographic entries at the end of an article. (Keep in mind that many instructors do not consider articles from any encyclopedia—print or electronic—acceptable for college research.)

13b Using Sources in Your Writing

Once you have gathered the source material you will need, read it carefully, recording any information you think you can use. (You can record your notes either in computer files or on index cards.)

Remember that taking notes involves more than just copying down or downloading information. As you record information, you should put it into a form that you can use when you write your paper. For this reason, you should always *paraphrase*, *summarize*, or *quote* relevant information from your sources.

FYI

Avoiding Plagiarism

When you transfer information from websites into your notes, you may carelessly copy-and-paste text without recording where the material came from. If you then paste this material into your paper without citing the source, you are committing **plagiarism**—stealing someone else's ideas. Also keep in mind that you must document *all* material that you get from the Internet, just as you document material that you get from print sources. For more information on plagiarism, see 13c. For information on documenting, see Chapter 14.

Paraphrasing

When you **paraphrase**, you use your own words to convey a source's key ideas. You paraphrase when you want to include detailed information from the source but not the author's exact words. Paraphrasing is useful when you want to make a difficult discussion easier to understand while still presenting a comprehensive overview of the original. (See 1c for more information on paraphrasing sources.)

Here is a passage from the article "Hot Fakes," by Joanie Cox, followed by a student's paraphrase.

> **ORIGINAL**
>
> Always pay close attention to the stitching. On a Kate Spade bag, the logo is stitched perfectly straight; it's not a sticker. Most designers stitch a simple label to the inside of their purses. On Chanel bags, however, the interior label is usually stamped and tends to match the color of the exterior. Study the material the bag is made from. A real Chanel Ligne Cambon multipocket bag, for example, is constructed from buttery lambskin leather, not vinyl.

> **PARAPHRASE**
>
> It is often possible to tell a fake designer handbag from a genuine one by looking at the details. For example, items such as logos should not be crooked. You should also look for the distinctive features of a particular brand of handbag. Counterfeiters will not take the time to match colors, and they may use vinyl instead of expensive leather (Cox).

Note that this paraphrase doesn't simply change a word here and there. Instead, the student has taken the time to make sure she fully understands the main idea and supporting points of the passage and has restated the writer's ideas in her own words.

Summarizing

Unlike a paraphrase, which presents the key points of a source in detail, a **summary** is a general restatement in your own words of the main idea of a passage. For this reason, a summary is always much shorter than the original. (See 1c for more information on summarizing sources.)

Here is a student's summary of the original passage on page 347.

> **SUMMARY**
>
> Buyers who want to identify fake handbags should check details, such as the way the label is sewn and the material the item is made from (Cox).

Quoting

When you **quote**, you use the author's exact words as they appear in the source, including all punctuation and capitalization. Enclose all words from your source in quotation marks—*followed by appropriate documentation*. Because quotations can distract readers, use them only when you think that the author's exact words will add something to your discussion.

> **When to Quote**
>
> 1. Quote when the words of a source are so memorable that to put them into your own words would lessen their impact.
> 2. Quote when the words of a source are so precise that a paraphrase or summary would change the meaning of the original.
> 3. Quote when the words of a source add authority to your discussion. The exact words of a recognized expert can help you make your point convincingly.

Here is how a student writer incorporated a quotation from the original passage on page 347 into her notes.

> **QUOTATION**
>
> Someone who wants to buy an authentic designer handbag should look carefully at the material the purse is made from. For example, there is a big difference between vinyl and Chanel's "buttery lambskin leather" (Cox).

Working Sources into Your Writing

When you use material from a source, you don't simply drop it into your paper. To show readers why you are using a source and to help you integrate source material smoothly into your essay, introduce paraphrases, summaries, and quotations with **identifying tags**, phrases that name the source or its author. You can position an identifying tag at various places in a sentence.

- <u>As one celebrity fashion columnist points out,</u> "A real Chanel Ligne Cambon multipocket bag, for example, is constructed from buttery lambskin leather, not vinyl" (Cox).
- "A real Chanel Ligne Cambon multipocket bag, for example," <u>says one celebrity fashion columnist,</u> "is constructed from buttery lambskin leather, not vinyl" (Cox).
- "A real Chanel Ligne Cambon multipocket bag, for example, is constructed from buttery lambskin leather, not vinyl," <u>observes one celebrity fashion columnist</u> (Cox).

FYI

Identifying Sources

Instead of repeating the word *says*, you can use one of the words or phrases below to identify the source of a quotation, paraphrase, or summary.

admits	concludes	points out
believes	explains	remarks
claims	notes	states
comments	observes	suggests

Synthesizing

When you **synthesize**, you combine ideas from two or more sources with your own ideas. The goal of a synthesis is to use sources to develop your own point about a topic. In a synthesis, your own ideas, not those of your sources, should dominate the discussion. In a sense, every time you weave together a paraphrase, summary, or quotation to support a point, you are writing a synthesis. (See 5f for more information on synthesizing sources.)

Here is a paragraph from a student's research paper in which she incorporates material from three different sources. (You can read the full paper in Chapter 14 starting on page 364.) Notice how she uses source material (underlined) to develop her point that buying counterfeit items is really stealing.

> What most people choose to ignore is that buying counterfeit items is stealing. In 2016, U.S. Customs and Border Protection and U.S. Immigration and Customs Enforcement seized a record number of counterfeit goods. Leading the list of seized items were designer watches and jewelry as well as handbags and wallets ("CBP"). The FBI estimates that in the United States alone, companies lose about $250 billion as a result of counterfeits (Wallace). In addition, buyers of counterfeit items avoid the state and local sales taxes that legitimate companies pay. Thus, New York City alone loses about a billion dollars every year as a result of the sale of counterfeit merchandise ("Counterfeit Goods"). When this happens, everyone loses. After all, a billion dollars would pay for a lot of police officers and teachers, would fill a lot of potholes, and would pave a lot of streets. Even though buyers of counterfeit designer goods do not think of themselves as thieves, that is exactly what they are.

13c Using Sources Ethically

When you write a research essay, you must use your sources responsibly. In other words, you must **document** (give source information for) all words, ideas, or statistics from an outside source. You must also document all visuals — tables, graphs, photographs, and so on — that you do not create yourself. (It is not necessary, however, to document **common knowledge**, factual information widely available in reference works.)

When you present information from another source as if it is your own (whether you do it intentionally or unintentionally), you commit **plagiarism** — and plagiarism is theft. Although most plagiarism is accidental, the penalties can be severe. You can avoid plagiarism by understanding what you must document and what you do not have to document. (See Chapter 14 for information about documentation.)

> ## FYI
>
> ### What to Document
>
> You should document
>
> - all quotations from a source.
> - all summaries and paraphrases of source material.
> - all ideas—opinions, judgments, and insights—of others.
> - all tables, graphs, charts, and statistics from a source.
>
> You do not need to document:
>
> - your own ideas.
> - common knowledge.
> - familiar quotations.

Read the following paragraph from "Agencies Can Improve Efforts to Address Risks Posed by Changing Counterfeit Markets," a report by the United States Senate Committee on Finance, and the four guidelines that follow it. This material will help you understand the most common causes of plagiarism and show you how to avoid it.

ORIGINAL

Counterfeit goods may pose risks to the health and safety of consumers. CBP [U.S. Customs and Border Protection] and ICE [U.S. Immigration and Customs Enforcement] have seized and investigated counterfeit goods, such as health and personal care products and consumer electronics, that carried a number of health and safety risks. For example, CBP has seized counterfeit versions of personal care products such as contact lenses, perfume, hair removal devices, hair curlers and straighteners, skin cleansing devices, and condoms, which pose risks to the consumer that include damage to skin or eyes caused by dangerous chemicals and bacteria, burning, or electrocution due to nonstandardized wiring, or ineffectual family planning protection. ICE has also investigated IP crimes involving counterfeit airbags, phone accessories, pharmaceuticals, and other items that present risks to the health and safety of consumers. Counterfeit electronics and batteries can also pose significant risks, including the risk of injury or death, according to CBP. For instance, in December 2015, CBP seized 1,378 hoverboards with counterfeit batteries that carried a risk of causing fires.

Guideline 1: Document Ideas from Your Sources

PLAGIARISM

Counterfeit goods — especially personal care products and pharmaceuticals — may pose a great risk to consumers.

Even though the student writer does not quote her source directly, she must identify the article as the source of this material because it expresses the article's ideas, not her own.

CORRECT

Counterfeit goods — especially personal care products and pharmaceuticals — can be dangerous (Senate Committee on Finance 8).

Guideline 2: Place Borrowed Words in Quotation Marks

PLAGIARISM

Counterfeit goods, such as personal care products and pharmaceuticals, may pose risks to the health and safety of consumers (Senate Committee on Finance 8).

Although the student writer cites the source, the passage incorrectly uses the source's exact words without quoting them. In order to avoid plagiarizing her source, she must quote the borrowed words.

CORRECT (BORROWED WORDS IN QUOTATION MARKS)

Counterfeit goods, such as personal care products and pharmaceuticals, "may pose risks to the health and safety of consumers" (Senate Committee on Finance 8).

Guideline 3: Use Your Own Phrasing

PLAGIARISM

Is buying counterfeit goods without risk? Not at all. The counterfeit goods, such as personal care products and pharmaceuticals, can create problems for consumers. In addition, The CBP and ICE have seized counterfeit contact lenses as well as hair straighteners and skin cleansing devices. Other consumer products, such as batteries and airbags, can actually be dangerous (Senate Committee on Finance 8).

Even though the student writer acknowledges her source, and even though she does not use the source's exact words, her passage closely follows the order, emphasis, sentence structure, and phrasing of the original.

In the following passage, the student writer uses her own wording, quoting one distinctive phrase from the source.

> **CORRECT**
>
> According to a report from the Senate Committee on Finance, counterfeit goods are not an insignificant problem. In fact, they "may pose risks to the health and safety of consumers." The poor quality of most counterfeit goods ensures that they will cause harm. For example, counterfeit contact lenses can damage a person's eyes and counterfeit airbags can cause injury or even death when they don't deploy properly (Senate Committee on Finance 8).

Note: The quotation does not require separate documentation because the identifying tag, "According to a report from the Senate Committee on Finance," makes it clear that all the borrowed material in the passage is from the same source.

Guideline 4: Distinguish Your Ideas from the Source's Ideas

> **PLAGIARISM**
>
> The CPB and ICE have investigated many cases of counterfeit merchandise being smuggled into the United States. These goods include personal care products, electronic items, and pharmaceuticals. The poor quality of these goods makes it likely that they will "pose significant risks to the health and safety of consumers" (Senate Committee on Finance 8).

In the passage above, it appears that only the quotation in the last sentence is borrowed from the Senate Committee repost. In fact, however, the ideas in the first two sentences also come from the source.

In the following passage, the student writer uses an identifying tag to acknowledge the borrowed material in the second sentence.

> **CORRECT**
>
> According to a report from the Senate Committee on Finance, the CPB and ICE have investigated many cases of counterfeit merchandise being smuggled into the United States. These goods include personal care products, electronic items, and pharmaceuticals. The poor quality of these items makes it likely that they will "pose significant risks to the health and safety of consumers" (Senate Committee on Finance 8).

CHAPTER REVIEW

READING AND WRITING ACTIVITY

Read the paragraph below from *The New York Times* article "The New Math on Campus," by Alex Williams. Then, read the three student paragraphs that use this article as a source. In each of these paragraphs, student writers have accidentally committed plagiarism. On the line below each student paragraph, explain the problem. Then, edit the paragraph so that it correctly documents the source and avoids plagiarism.

> North Carolina, with a student body that is nearly 60 percent female, is just one of many large universities that at times feel eerily like women's colleges. Women have represented about 57 percent of enrollments at American colleges since at least 2000, according to a recent report by the American Council on Education. Researchers there cite several reasons: Women tend to have higher grades; men tend to drop out in disproportionate numbers; and female enrollment skews higher among older students, low-income students, and black and Hispanic students.

1. About 60% female, the University of North Carolina is an example of large universities with many more women than men. According to a report from the American Council on Education, one reason is that "female enrollment skews higher among older students, low-income students, and black and Hispanic students" (Williams). If this is true, what will this mean for the black and Hispanic communities?

   _____
   _____
   _____

2. In recent years, colleges and universities have taken on a very different atmosphere. The reason is clear to anyone who takes a casual look around at just about any college campus. Women now outnumber men, so much so that some colleges at times feel eerily like women's colleges (Williams). This situation seems likely to continue in the years to come.

   _____
   _____

3. Why do women outnumber men in today's colleges? Researchers at the American Council on Education mention a few reasons: Women often have higher grades, men tend to drop out in larger numbers, and female enrollment is especially high for some groups such as older students, low-income students, and black and Hispanic students (Williams). These reasons may all be true at our school, which certainly has more women than men.

COLLABORATIVE ACTIVITY

Working in groups of three or four students, complete the following quiz. When you are finished, share your results with the class.

_____ 1. Why should you use your college library?
   a. The reference librarian screens library resources.
   b. Library resources are generally more reliable than sources found on the Internet.
   c. Library resources often meet academic standards of reliability.
   d. All of the above.

_____ 2. Which of these sources is **not** an acceptable research source?
   a. an article in an academic journal
   b. an article in Wikipedia
   c. a chemistry blog written by a noted chemist
   d. an article in *The New York Times*

_____ 3. How can you use a search engine to find information?
   a. You can do a keyword search.
   b. You can paste in a URL.
   c. Both of the above.

4. What is the difference between a paraphrase and a summary?
   _____
   _____
   _____

5. When should you quote a source?
   _____
   _____
   _____
   _____

_____ 6. What information needs to be documented? (There could be more than one answer to this question.)

   a. your own ideas
   b. common knowledge
   c. the ideas of others
   d. direct quotations

_____ 7. Which two of these sources is acceptable for a college research project? (You might have to do some research to find this answer.)

   a. An article about climate change in *Nature*
   b. An article about climate change in *Parade Magazine*
   c. An article about climate change in the environmental blog *Grist*

_____ 8. Which of the following constitutes plagiarism?

   a. Failing to document a direct quotation
   b. Using the exact words of a source without quotation marks
   c. Using the exact words of a source without quotation marks but including documentation
   d. All of the above

Review checklist

- ✔ When you do research, find and evaluate sources from the library as well as from the Internet. (See 13a.)

- ✔ Once you locate source information, put it into a form that you can use in your paper—for example, paraphrases, summaries, or quotations from your sources. (See 13b.)

- ✔ Document all material that you use from outside sources. If you use information from a source and do not document it, you commit **plagiarism**. (See 13c.)

14 Documenting Sources in MLA or APA Style

> **PREVIEW**
>
> In this chapter you will learn to
> - use MLA documentation style (14a).
> - use APA documentation style (14b).

Whenever you use information from a source, you have to **document** it—that is, you need to indicate to readers where you found it. By doing this, you identify your source and you enable readers to locate the information you use. Because conventions differ from discipline to discipline, there is no single documentation style that you can use in all of your courses. For this reason, you should ask your instructors which format they require. Two of the most widely used documentation styles are those recommended by the Modern Language Association (MLA), preferred in the humanities, and the American Psychological Association (APA), preferred in the social sciences.

14a MLA Documentation Style

MLA documentation requires you to place brief references to sources (**in-text citations**) in the body of your essay immediately following material you are using from other authors. Readers can use these citations to find detailed information on specific sources in your works-cited list at the end of the paper.

MLA In-Text Citation

An in-text citation (details about a source set within parentheses) should include enough information to lead readers to a specific entry in your works-cited list. A typical in-text citation consists of the author's last name and the page number (Brown 2). Notice that there is no comma and no *p* or *p*. before the page number.

Whenever possible, introduce information from a source with a phrase that includes the author's name. (If you do this, include only the page number in parentheses.) Place documentation so that it does not interrupt the flow of your ideas, preferably at the end of a sentence.

> As Jonathan Brown observes in "Demand for Fake Designer Goods Is Soaring," as many as 70 percent of buyers of luxury goods are willing to wear designer brands alongside fakes (2).

FYI

Formatting Quotations

1. **Short quotations** Quotations of less than four typed lines are inserted into the text of your paper. End punctuation comes after the parenthetical reference, which follows the quotation marks.

   According to Dana Thomas, customers often "pick up knockoffs for one-tenth the legitimate bag's retail cost, then pass them off as real" (A23).

2. **Long quotations** Quotations of more than four lines are set off from the text of your paper. Begin a long quotation on a new line, indented half an inch from the left-hand margin, and do not enclose it in quotation marks. Do not indent the first line of a single paragraph. If a quoted passage has more than one paragraph, indent the first line of each paragraph, including the first, an extra one-quarter inch. Introduce a long quotation with a complete sentence followed by a colon, and place the parenthetical reference one space *after* the end punctuation. Double-space the text throughout.

   The editorial "Terror's Purse Strings" describes a surprise visit to a factory that makes counterfeit purses:

   > On a warm winter afternoon in Guangzhao, I accompanied Chinese police officers on a raid in a decrepit tenement. We found two dozen children, ages 8 to 13, gluing and sewing together fake luxury-brand handbags. The police confiscated everything, arrested the owner and sent the children out. Some punched their timecards, hoping to still get paid. (Thomas A23)

Sample In-Text Citations

Here are specific guidelines for four special situations:

1. CITING A WORK BY TWO AUTHORS

> Instead of buying nonbranded items of similar quality, many customers are willing to pay extra for the counterfeit designer label (Grossman and Shapiro 79).

2. CITING A WORK WITHOUT PAGE NUMBERS

A seller of counterfeited goods in California "now faces 10 years in prison and $20,000 in fines" (Cox).

3. CITING A WORK WITHOUT A LISTED AUTHOR OR PAGE NUMBERS

More counterfeit goods come from China than from any other country ("Counterfeit Goods").

4. CITING A STATEMENT BY ONE AUTHOR THAT IS QUOTED IN A WORK BY ANOTHER AUTHOR

Speaking of consumers' buying habits, designer Miuccia Prada says, "There is a kind of an obsession with bags" (qtd. in Thomas A23).

The Works-Cited List

The works-cited list includes all the works you cite (refer to) in your essay. Use the guidelines in the Preparing a Works-Cited List box on page 363 to help you prepare your list.

The following sample works-cited entries cover the situations you will encounter most often.

Sample Works-Cited Entries

PERIODICALS

Journals When citing an article from a journal, include the journal's volume number and issue number, using the abbreviations *vol.* and *no.* After the publisher, include the date of publication and the page numbers (if there are any). For online sources, cite a URL or DOI (digital object identifier, a unique label that provides a permanent link to specific content).

Article in a Print Journal

Gioia, Dana. "Robert Frost and the Modern Narrative." *Virginia Quarterly Review*, vol. 89, no. 2, 2013, pp. 185-93.

Article in an Online Journal

Wineapple, Brenda. "Ladies Last." *American Scholar*, vol. 82, no. 3, 2013, theamericanscholar.org/ladies-last/#.WniBVZM-dsY.

Magazines Include the complete date of publication and page numbers. Frequently, an article in a magazine is not printed on consecutive pages. For example, it may begin on page 40, skip to page 47, and continue on page 49. If this is the case, your citation should include only the first page, followed by a plus sign.

Article in a Print Magazine

> Poniewozik, James. "Why I Watch Reality TV with My Kids." *Time*, 17 June 2013, pp. 54–55.

Article in an Online Magazine

> Dobb, Edwin. "The New Oil Landscape." *National Geographic*, Mar. 2013, ngm.nationalgeographic.com/2013/03/bakken-shale-oil/dobb-text.

Newspapers List page numbers, section numbers, and any special edition information (such as late ed.), as provided by the source. If the article falls into a special category, such as an editorial, letter to the editor, or review, add this label to your entry.

Article in a Print Newspaper

> Shah, Neil. "More Young Adults Live with Parents." *The Wall Street Journal*, 28 Aug. 2013, A2.

Article from an Online Newspaper

> Marklein, Mary Beth. "Colleges Are Toughening up on Student Borrowing." *USA Today*, 26 Aug. 2013, www.usatoday.com/story/news/nation/2013/08/25/colleges-student-loan-defaults/2666173/.

BOOKS

Books by One Author

List the author, last name first. Italicize the book's title. In the publisher's name, omit business words like *Company*, and use the abbreviation *UP* for *University Press*, as in *Princeton UP* or *U of Chicago P*. Include the date of publication.

> Mantel, Hilary. *Bring up the Bodies*. Holt, 2012.

Books by Two or More Authors

For books with two authors, list the second author with first name first. List the authors in the order in which they are listed on the book's title page.

> Mooney, Chris, and Sheril Kirshenbaum. *Unscientific America: How Scientific Illiteracy Threatens Our Future*. Basic Books, 2009.

For books with three or more authors, list only the first author, followed by the abbreviation *et al.* ("and others").

Two or More Books by the Same Author

List two or more books by the same author in alphabetical order according to title. In each entry after the first, use three unspaced hyphens (followed by a period) instead of the author's name.

> Eggers, Dave. *The Circle*. Random House, 2013.
> ---. *A Hologram for the King*. McSweeney's, 2012.

Edited Book

> Austen, Jane. *Persuasion: An Annotated Edition*. Edited by Robert Morrison, Belknap-Harvard UP, 2011.

Anthology

> Adler, Frances P., et al., editors. *Fire and Ink: An Anthology of Social Action Writing*. U of Arizona P, 2009.

Essay in an Anthology or Chapter of a Book

> Weise, Matthew J. "How the Zombie Changed Videogames." *Zombies Are Us: Essays on the Humanity of the Walking Dead*, edited by Christopher M. Moreman and Cory James Rushton, McFarland, 2011, pp. 151–68.

INTERNET SOURCES

Full source information is not always available for Internet sources. For this reason, when citing Internet sources, include whatever information you can find—ideally, the name of the author (or authors), the title of the article or other document (in quotation marks), the title of the site (italicized), the sponsor or publisher, and the date of publication or last update. If the site does not have a date of publication, include the date on which you accessed the source.

Include a web address (URL) when citing an electronic source, omitting *http://* or *https://*. When possible, cite a digital object identifier (DOI), preceded by *doi:*, rather than a URL.

Article in an Online Periodical

Wilbon, Michael. "The 'One and Done' Song and Dance." *Washington Post*, 25 June 2009, www.washingtonpost.com/wp-dyn/content/article/2009/06/24/AR2009062403396.html.

Document within a Website

Robbins, Michael. "Reimagining Education through Summer Learning Partnerships." *Homeroom*, U.S. Department of Education, 26 Aug. 2013, blog.ed.gov/2013/08/reimagining-education-through-summer-learning-partnerships/.

Personal Site

Heffernan, Margaret. Home page. www.mheffernan.com. Accessed 10 June 2018.

Preparing a Works-Cited List

- Begin the works-cited list on a new page after the last page of your paper.
- Number the works-cited page as the next page of your paper.
- Center the heading Works Cited one inch from the top of the page; do not italicize the heading or place it in quotation marks.
- Double-space the list.
- List entries alphabetically, according to the author's last name.
- Alphabetize unsigned articles according to the first major word of the title.
- Type each entry at the left-hand margin.
- Indent second and subsequent lines of each entry one-half inch.
- Separate major divisions of each entry—author, title, and publication information—by a period and one space.

Sample MLA-Style Paper

On the pages that follow is a student's essay on the topic of counterfeit designer goods. The paper uses MLA documentation style and includes a works-cited page. It has been annotated to show you the proper formatting and elements of a research paper.

May Compton

Professor DiSalvo

English 100

29 Apr. 2018

Compton 1

The True Price of Counterfeit Goods

At purse parties in city apartments and suburban homes, customers can buy "designer" handbags at impossibly low prices. On street corners, sidewalk vendors sell name-brand perfumes and sunglasses for much less than their list prices. On the internet, buyers can buy luxury watches for a fraction of the prices charged by manufacturers. Is this too good to be true? Of course it is. All of these "bargains" are knockoffs — counterfeit copies of the real thing. What the people who buy these items do not know (or prefer not to think about) is that the money they are spending supports organized crime — and sometimes, terrorism. For this reason, people should not buy counterfeit designer merchandise, no matter how tempted they are to do so.

People who buy counterfeit designer merchandise defend their actions by saying that designer products are expensive. This is certainly true. According to Dana Thomas, the manufacturers of genuine designer merchandise charge more than ten times what it costs to make it (A23). A visitor from Britain, who bought an imitation Gucci purse in New York City for fifty dollars, said, "The real thing is so overpriced. To buy a genuine Gucci purse, I would have to pay over a thousand dollars" (qtd. in "Counterfeit Goods"). Even people who can easily afford to pay the full amount buy fakes. For example, movie stars like Jennifer Lopez openly wear counterfeit goods, and many customers think that if it is all right for celebrities like Lopez to buy fakes, it is all right for them too (Malone). However, as the well-known designer Giorgio Armani points out, counterfeiters create a number of problems for legitimate companies because they use the brand name but do not maintain quality control.

Compton 2

What most people chose to ignore is that buying counterfeit items is stealing. In 2016, U.S. Customs and Border Protection and U. S. Immigration and Customs Enforcement seized a record number of counterfeit goods. Leading the list of seized items were designer watches and jewelry as well as handbags and wallets ("CBP"). The FBI estimates that in the United States alone, companies lose about $250 billion as a result of counterfeits (Wallace). In addition, buyers of counterfeit items avoid state and local taxes that legitimate companies pay. Thus, New York City alone loses about a billion dollars a year as a result of counterfeit merchandise ("Counterfeit Goods"). When this happens, everyone loses. After all, a billion dollars would pay for a lot of police officers and teachers, would fill a lot of potholes, and would pave a lot of streets. Even though buyers of counterfeit designer goods do not think of themselves as thieves, that is exactly what they are.

> Paragraph synthesizes May's own ideas with material from three articles.

Buyers of counterfeit merchandise also do not realize that the sale of knockoffs is a criminal activity. Most of the profits go to the criminal organization that either makes or imports the counterfeit goods — not to the person who sells them. In fact, the biggest manufacturer and distributor of counterfeit items is organized crime (Nellis). Michael Kessler, who heads a company that investigates corporate crime, makes this connection clear when he describes the complicated manufacturing system that is needed to make counterfeit perfume:

> They need a place that makes bottles, a factory with pumps to fill the bottles, a printer to make the labels, and a box manufacturer to fake the packaging. Then, they need a sophisticated distribution network, as well as all the cash to set everything up. (qtd. in Malone)

Kessler concludes that only an organized crime syndicate — not an individual — has the money to support this illegal activity. For this reason,

> Long quotation is set off one-half inch from the left-hand margin. No quotation marks are used.

Compton 3

anyone who buys counterfeits may also be supporting activities such as prostitution, drug distribution, smuggling of illegal immigrants, gang warfare, extortion, and murder (Nellis). In addition, the people who make counterfeits often work in sweatshops where labor and environmental laws are ignored. As Dana Thomas points out, a worker in China who makes counterfeits earns only a fraction of the salary of a worker who makes the real thing (A23).

> Paragraph contains May's own ideas as well as a paraphrase and a quotation.

Finally, and perhaps most shocking, is the fact that some of the money earned from the sale of counterfeit designer goods also supports international terrorism. For example, Kim Wallace reports in her *Times Daily* article that during Al-Qaeda training, terrorists are advised to sell fake goods to get money for their operations. According to Interpol, an international police organization, the bombing of the World Trade Center in 1993 was paid for in part by the sale of counterfeit T-shirts. Also, evidence suggests that associates of the 2001 World Trade Center terrorists may have been involved with the production of imitation designer goods (Malone). Finally, the 2004 bombing of commuter trains in Madrid was financed in part by the sale of counterfeits. In fact, an intelligence source states, "It would be more shocking if Al-Qaeda *wasn't* involved in counterfeiting. The sums involved are staggering—it would be inconceivable if money were not being raised for their terrorist activities" (qtd. in Malone).

> Conclusion contains May's original ideas, so no documentation is necessary.

Consumers should realize that when they buy counterfeits, they are breaking the law. By doing so, they are making it possible for organized crime syndicates and terrorists to earn money for their illegal activities. Although buyers of counterfeit merchandise justify their actions by saying that the low prices are impossible to resist, they might reconsider if they knew the uses to which their money was going. The truth of the matter is that counterfeit designer products, such as handbags, sunglasses, jewelry, and T-shirts, are luxuries, not necessities. By resisting the temptation to buy knockoffs, consumers could help to eliminate the companies that hurt legitimate manufacturers, exploit workers, and even finance international terrorism.

Works Cited

Armani, Giorgio. "10 Questions for Giorgio Armani." *Time*, 12 Feb. 2009, content.time.com/time/magazine/article/0,9171,1879189,00.html.

"CBP, ICE Seize Record Number of Shipments with Intellectual Property Rights Violations in FY2016." *U.S. Customs and Border Protection, Department of Homeland Security*, 24 Nov. 2017, https://www.cbp.gov/newsroom/national-media-release/cbp-ice-seize-record-number-shipments-intellectual-property-rights.

"Counterfeit Goods Are Linked to Terror Groups." *International Herald Tribune*, 12 Feb. 2007, www.nytimes.com/2007/02/12/business/worldbusiness/12iht-fake.4569452.html.

Malone, Andrew. "Revealed: The True Cost of Buying Cheap Fake Goods." *Daily Mail*, 29 July 2007, www.dailymail.co.uk/news/article-471679/Revealed-The-true-cost-buying-cheap-fake-goods.html.

Nellis, Cynthia. "Faking It: Counterfeit Fashion." *About.com*, 2009, fashion.about.com/cs/tipsadvice/a/fakingit.htm. Accessed 24 Mar. 2014.

Thomas, Dana. "Terror's Purse Strings." Editorial. *The New York Times*, 30 Aug. 2007, late ed., A23, www.nytimes.com/2007/08/30/opinion/30thomas.html.

Wallace, Kim. "A Counter-Productive Trade." *Times Daily*, 28 July 2007, www.timesdaily.com/archives/a-counter-productive-trade/article_26e06caa-c44b-5c45-83b7-7ba617729631.html.

> Works-cited list starts on a new page. Title is centered, entries are listed alphabetically by authors' last names or first words of titles, and double-spaced throughout.

> First lines of entries are set flush left; subsequent lines are indented one-half inch.

14b APA Documentation Style

APA documentation requires you to place brief references to sources (**in-text citations**) in the body of your essay immediately following material you are using from other authors. Readers can use these citations to find detailed information on specific sources in your references list at the end of the paper.

APA In-Text Citation

In-text citations (details about a source set within parentheses) refer readers to sources in the list of references at the end of the paper. In general, parenthetical references include the author's last name and the year of publication (Diamond, 2012). If you are quoting directly from a source, the reference should also include page numbers: (Diamond, 2012, p. 137). If, however, you refer to the author's name in your text, include only the year of publication in parentheses: Diamond asserted . . . (2012). When quoting directly, include the page number as well: Diamond asserted . . . (2012, p. 137).

Once you have cited a source, you can refer to the author again within that same paragraph, without the publication date, so long as it is clear you are referring to the same source: Diamond also found. . . .

Here are some specific guidelines for five special situations.

Sample In-Text Citations

1. CITING A WORK BY MULTIPLE AUTHORS

When a work has two authors, cite both names and the year (Reid & Boyer, 2013). Use the word *and* between the authors' names when you mention the authors in your text, but use an ampersand (&) in the parenthetical reference. For three to five authors, cite all authors in the first reference, along with the year (Jung, Pick, Schluter-Muller, Schmeck, & Goth, 2013). For subsequent references, cite only the first author followed by et al. and the year (Jung et al., 2013).

When a work has six or more authors, use only the first author's name, followed by *et al.* and the year (Malm et al., 2012).

2. CITING A WORK THAT HAS NO PAGE NUMBERS

Omit page numbers if you are quoting from a source that does not include them, as is the case with many online sources. (Try to find a PDF version of an online source if it is an option; it will usually include page numbers.) If a source shows paragraph numbers, you can use these instead of page numbers, preceded by the abbreviation *para*. If a source has neither page nor paragraph numbers but has headings, you can cite a shortened version of the heading in quotation marks followed by the number of the paragraph.

3. CITING A WORK THAT HAS NO NAMED AUTHOR

If no author is identified, use a shortened version of the title of the work ("Mind," 2013).

4. **CITING A SOURCE THAT IS QUOTED IN ANOTHER SOURCE**

   If you quote a source found in another source, indicate the original author and the source in which you found it.

   As Hatzes asserted, "If one analysis produces a planet and another doesn't, that's not robust" (as cited in Cowen, 2013, p. 25).

5. **CITING PERSONAL COMMUNICATIONS**

   Include in-text references to personal communications and interviews that you conducted by providing the person's name, the phrase *personal communication*, and the date (J. Smith, personal communication, February 12, 2014). Do **not** include these sources in your reference list.

FYI

Formatting Quotations:

1. **Short quotations** If a direct quotation is fewer than forty words long, set it within quotation marks without separating it from the rest of the text. The parenthetical reference follows, and if the quotation is at the end of the sentence, the period follows the final parenthesis.

   Scientists use mice in these experiments on smell because "the rodent olfactory system provides a good functional model for at least some aspects of the human system" (Yantis, 2014, p. 438).

2. **Long quotations** When quoting a passage that is forty or more words long, set it off from the rest of your paper. Indent the entire block of quoted text one-half inch from the left margin, begin it on a new line, and do not enclose it in quotation marks. If a quoted passage has more than one paragraph, indent the first line of subsequent paragraphs an extra half-inch. The quoted passage should be double-spaced, like the rest of the paper. Place your parenthetical reference after the final punctuation of the quotation.

   Perceptual organization is critical to vision, as Yantis has noted:
   > Perceptual organization is the visual system's way of dealing with scenes containing multiple overlapping objects—it makes object recognition within complex scenes possible. Without perceptual organization, the visual system would be overwhelmed by the jumbled pattern of brightness and color in the retinal image of most real scenes. (2014, p. 123)

The Reference List

The reference list includes all the works you cite in your essay. Use the guidelines in the Preparing a Reference List box on page 372 to help you prepare your list.

The following sample reference list entries cover the situations you will encounter most often.

Note: For all sources with authors, give the authors' last name first, followed by a comma and initials. The authors' names are followed by the publication year in parentheses.

Sample Reference List Entries

PERIODICALS

Capitalize only the first word of the title and subtitle and any names; do not use quotation marks or italics. Give the title of the publication (journal, magazine, or newspaper) in italics, with all major words capitalized. For journals and magazines, add the volume number, italicized and preceded by a comma, and, if the issue paginates the publication, follow the volume number with the issue number in parentheses. After a comma, give the page numbers of the article. Use the abbreviation *p.* or *pp.* only for newspaper articles.

Because websites change and disappear without warning, many publishers, particularly journal publishers, have started adding a digital object identifier (DOI) to their articles. A DOI is a unique number that can be retrieved no matter where the article ends up on the web. If an article, electronic or print, has a DOI, include it at the end of your reference list entry, with no final period.

Article in a Print Journal

> Heyns, C., & Srinivasan, S. (2013). Protecting the right to life of journalists: The need for a higher level of engagement. *Human Rights Quarterly, 35,* 304–332. doi: 10.1353/hrq.2013.0030

Article in a Journal Accessed through an Online Database

The name and URL of the database are not required for citations. If the article has a DOI, use the DOI. If no DOI is available, provide the home page URL of the journal or other periodical.

> Almeroth, K., & Zhang, H. (2013). Alternatives for monitoring and limiting network access to students in network-connected classrooms. *Journal of Interactive Learning Research, 24,* 237–265. Retrieved from http://www.aace.org/pubs/jilr/

Article in a Print Magazine

Kenny, P. J. (2013, September). The food addiction. *Scientific American*, *309*(3), 44–49.

Article in a Print Newspaper

Smith, P. A. (2013, August 27). A quest for even safer drinking water. *The New York Times*, p. D3.

BOOKS

Give book titles in italics, and capitalize only the first word of the title and subtitle and any names. For place of publication, give the city followed by a comma and the two-letter abbreviation for the state. Following a colon, give a shortened form of the publisher's name.

Books by One Author

McCrum, R. (2010). *Globish: How the English language became the world's language*. New York, NY: Norton.

Books by Two to Seven Authors

For works with up to seven authors, give all authors' names, with an ampersand before the last author.

Acemoglu, D., & Robinson, J. (2012). *Why nations fail: The origins of power, prosperity, and poverty*. New York, NY: Crown.

Books by Eight or More Authors

Include the names of the first six authors and then add three ellipsis points and the name of the last author.

Wolfe, J. M., Kluender, K. R., Levi, D. M., Bartoshuk, L. M., Herz, R. S., Klatzky, R. L., . . . Merfeld, D. M. (2012). *Sensation & perception* (3rd ed.). Sunderland, MA: Sinauer.

Edited Book

Sarat, A., Douglas, L., & Umphrey, M. M. (Eds.). (2011). *Law as punishment/ Law as regulation*. Stanford, CA: Stanford University Press.

Essay or Chapter in an Edited Book

Gleiser, M. (2012). We are unique. In J. Brockman (Ed.), *This will make you smarter* (pp. 3–5). New York, NY: Harper.

INTERNET SOURCES

Include the information that your readers will need in order to be able to retrieve your sources. As discussed above, when a DOI is not available, provide a URL.

Document within a Website

In your retrieval statement, give the website and its URL.

Roushdy, R., Sieverding, M., & Radwan, H. (2012). *The impact of water supply and sanitation on child health: Evidence from Egypt* (Poverty, Gender, and Youth Working Paper No. 24). Retrieved from Population Council website: http://www.popcouncil.org/

Blog Post or Video Blog Post

In brackets after the title, describe the source type—for example, as *Web log post* or *Video file*.

Siegel, E. (2013, August 30). How would you figure out whether global warming is real? Part 3 [Web log post]. Retrieved from http://scienceblogs.com/startswithabang/2013/08/30/how-would-you-figure-out-whether-global-warming-is-real-part-3/

Preparing a Reference List

- Start your list of references on a separate page at the end of your paper.
- Center the title References at the top of the page.
- Begin each reference flush with the left margin, and indent subsequent lines one-half inch.
- Double-space the list.
- List your references alphabetically by the author's last name (or by the first major word of the title if no author is identified).

- If the list includes references for two sources by the same author, list them in order by the year of publication, starting with the earliest.
- Italicize the titles of books and periodicals. Do not italicize article titles or enclose them in quotation marks.
- For the titles of books and articles, capitalize only the first word of the title and subtitle as well as any proper nouns. Capitalize words in a periodical title as in the original.

Sample APA-Style Paper

On the pages that follow are annotated excerpts from the student essay on the topic of counterfeit designer goods used to illustrate MLA documentation style (see p. 364), showing the differences in formatting between APA and MLA.

Title page

Running head: THE TRUE PRICE OF COUNTERFEIT GOODS   1

[Title of paper appears top left on each page in capital letters. On the title page, it follows the words "Running head:" If the title is more than 50 characters, use a shortened version. Page number is placed top right.]

The True Price of Counterfeit Goods

May Compton

Drexel University

[Full title of paper, author's name, and school are centered halfway down the page. Do not bold, underline, or italicize.]

Author Note

[Author note with course title and instructor's name can be placed at the bottom of the page. Check with your instructor for his or her preferences.]

This paper was prepared for English 100, taught by Professor Mandell

Abstract page

THE TRUE PRICE OF COUNTERFEIT GOODS   2

Abstract

[The abstract, a brief summary of the paper, appears on the second page.]

Many people buy "designer" goods, such as watches, jewelry, handbags, and wallets, at bargain prices online or from street vendors. Few are aware that they are committing theft and aiding criminals. Mass production of fake goods requires significant capital and is often financed by organized crime. Goods are produced by low-paid workers in sweatshops, no state or local taxes are paid, and the profits are often used to subsidize illegal activities, such as prostitution, drug distribution, gang warfare, the smuggling of illegal immigrants, and even terrorism. This paper explores the consequences of buying counterfeit goods and the arguments for avoiding participation in illegal activities by refusing to buy discounted "designer" items.

First page of paper

THE TRUE PRICE OF COUNTERFEIT GOODS   3

                      The True Price of Counterfeit Goods

> The running head and the title, centered, appear on page 3, followed by the text of the paper.

Paragraph showing APA in-text citations

People who buy counterfeit designer merchandise defend their actions by saying that designer products are expensive. This is certainly true. According to Thomas (2007), the manufacturers of genuine designer merchandise charge more than ten times what it costs to make it (p. A23). A visitor from Britain, who bought an imitation Gucci purse in New York City for fifty dollars, said, "The real thing is so overpriced. To buy a genuine Gucci purse, I would have to pay over a thousand dollars" (as cited in "Counterfeit goods," 2007). Even people who can easily afford to pay the full amount buy fakes. For example, movie stars like Jennifer Lopez openly wear counterfeit goods, and many customers think that if it is all right for celebrities like Lopez to buy fakes, it is all right for them too (Malone, 2007). However, as the well-known designer Giorgio Armani (2009) points out, counterfeiters create a number of problems for legitimate companies because they use the brand name but do not maintain quality control.

> Note that in APA style, the authors' names and/or dates of publication appear in in-text citations, separated by commas. Titles are used if there is no author.

References page

                              References

Armani, G. (2009, February 12). 10 questions for Giorgio Armani. *Time*. Retrieved from time.com/

> Start the reference list on a new page, center the title, and double-space throughout. List sources alphabetically by last names of authors or editors or first word of title, if no one is named.

CBP, ICE seize record number of shipments with intellectual property rights violations in FY2016. (2017, November 24). Retrieved from U.S. Customs and Border Protection, Department of Homeland Security: https://www.cbp.gov/

Counterfeit goods are linked to terror groups. (2007, February 12). *International Herald Tribune.* Retrieved from https://www.nytimes.com/

Malone, A. (2007, July 29). Revealed: The true cost of buying cheap fake goods. *Daily Mail.* Retrieved from www.dailymail.co.uk/

Nellis, C. (2009). Faking it: Counterfeit fashion. *About.com.* Retrieved from fashion.about.com/

Thomas, D. (2007, August 30). Terror's purse strings [Editorial]. *The New York Times,* p. A23. Retrieved from https://www.nytimes.com/

Wallace, K. (2007, July 28). A counter-productive trade. *Times Daily.* Retrieved from www.timesdaily.com/

> First lines of entries are set flush left; subsequent lines are indented one-half inch. Note that titles are set lowercase, except for the first word of the title or subtitle, dates are included after author names, and "Retrieved from" is placed before URLs. Review the Sample Reference List Entries section for more details.

CHAPTER REVIEW

READING AND WRITING ACTIVITY

Using the following three sources, first create an MLA works-cited list and then create an APA references list. Make sure that you arrange the entries in alphabetical order and that you use the correct format for each type of source based on the relevant documentation style.

Article in a Journal Accessed through a Library Database

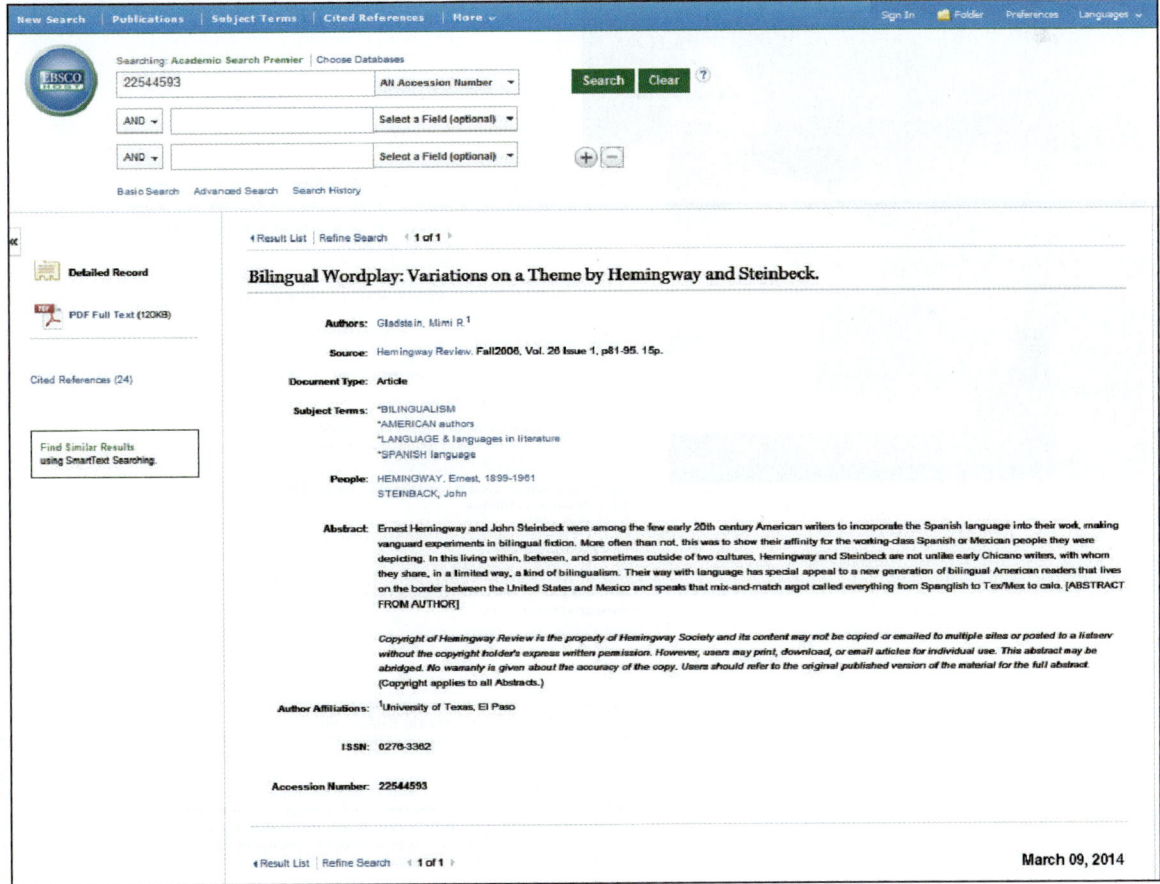

377

Book (Print)

Document within a Website

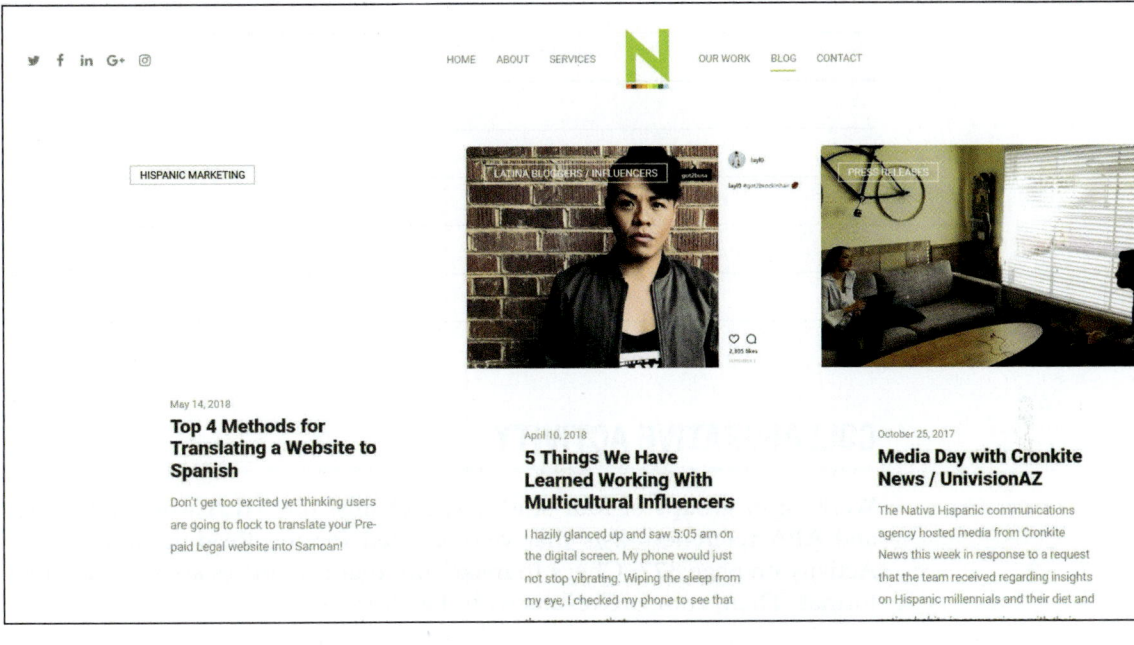

This is a screenshot from the homepage for *Nativa* (thenativa.com/blog/), a multicultural marketing agency.

Works Cited

References

_____
_____
_____
_____
_____
_____

COLLABORATIVE ACTIVITY

Working in groups of four students, exchange the MLA works-cited lists and APA references lists that were created for the Reading and Writing Activity on page 377. Check to make sure that the entries are in the correct format. Then, compare results with the class.

Review checklist

- ✔ Whenever you use information from a source in your writing, you have to document it, indicating for readers where you found it so they can also locate it. Documentation styles vary by discipline, but two of the most common are MLA (see 14a) and APA (see 14b). Before writing, check what style your instructor requires.

- ✔ Both MLA and APA use in-text citations, brief parenthetical references within the body of the text that lead readers to alphabetized listings of complete source information at the end of the paper (see MLA In-Text Citation, p. 358, and APA In-Text Citation, p. 368, for details).

- ✔ In MLA, the list of works you cited in your paper is titled Works Cited (see The Works-Cited List on p. 360 for details).

- ✔ In APA, the list of works you cited in your paper is titled References (see The Reference List on p. 370 for details).

unit 4
Basic Grammar Guide

15 **Understanding Verbs** 383
16 **Understanding Nouns and Pronouns** 398
17 **Understanding Adjectives and Adverbs** 421
18 **Writing Simple, Compound, and Complex Sentences** 430
19 **Writing Varied Sentences** 453
20 **Using Parallelism** 467
21 **Using Words Effectively** 474
22 **Run-Ons** 491
23 **Fragments** 504
24 **Subject-Verb Agreement** 521
25 **Illogical Shifts** 534
26 **Misplaced and Dangling Modifiers** 542
27 **Using Commas** 549
28 **Using Apostrophes** 564
29 **Understanding Mechanics** 571

Parts of Speech

Bailey (1993–2010)

The English language has eight basic parts of speech: nouns, pronouns, verbs, adjectives, adverbs, prepositions, conjunctions, and interjections.

Nouns

A **noun** names a person, an animal, a place, an object, or an idea.

Christine brought her dog Bailey to obedience school in Lawndale.
 noun   noun noun   noun   noun

Pronouns

A **pronoun** refers to and takes the place of a noun or another pronoun.

Bailey did very well in her lessons and seemed to enjoy them.
 noun   pronoun noun   pronoun

Verbs

A **verb** tells what someone or something does, did, or will do.

Sometimes Bailey rolls over, but earlier today she refused.
                        verb   verb

Maybe she will change someday.
              verb

Adjectives

An **adjective** identifies or describes a noun or a pronoun.

This dog is a small beagle with a brown and white coat and long ears.
 adj noun   adj   noun   adj   adj   noun   adj noun

Adverbs

An **adverb** identifies or describes a verb, an adjective, or another adverb.

Bailey is old, so she moves very slowly and seldom barks.
                         verb adverb adverb   adverb verb

Prepositions

A **preposition** is a word—such as *to*, *on*, or *with*—that introduces a noun or pronoun and connects it to other words in a sentence.

Bailey likes sitting quietly in her box at the foot of the stairs.

Conjunctions

A **conjunction** is a word that connects parts of a sentence.

People say you can't teach an old dog new tricks, but Bailey might be an exception.

Interjections

An **interjection** is a word—such as *Oh!* or *Hey!*—that is used to express emotion.

Wow! Bailey finally rolled over!

The eight basic parts of speech can be combined to form **sentences**, which always include at least one **subject** and one **verb**. The subject tells who or what is being talked about, and the verb tells what the subject does, did, or will do.

Bailey graduated from obedience school at the head of her class.
  S   V

15 Understanding Verbs

Tense is the form a verb takes to show when an action or situation takes place. The **past tense** indicates that an action occurred in the past.

15a Regular Verbs

Regular verbs form the past tense by adding either *-ed* or *-d* to the **base form** of the verb (the present tense form of the verb that is used with *I*).

We register<u>ed</u> for classes yesterday.

Walt Disney produce<u>d</u> short cartoons in 1928.

Regular verbs that end in *-y* form the past tense by changing the *y* to *i* and adding *-ed*.

| try | tr<u>ied</u> |
| apply | appl<u>ied</u> |

PRACTICE 15-1   Change the regular verbs below to the past tense.

Example: Every year, my mother ~~visits~~ *visited* her family in Bombay.

(1) My mother always <u>returns</u> from India with henna designs on her hands and feet. (2) In India, henna artists <u>create</u> these patterns. (3) Henna <u>originates</u> in a plant found in the Middle East, India, Indonesia, and northern Africa. (4) Many women in these areas <u>use</u> henna to color their hands, nails, and parts of their feet. (5) Men <u>dye</u> their beards as well as the manes and hooves of their horses. (6) They also <u>color</u> animal skins with henna. (7) In India, my mother always <u>celebrates</u> the end of the Ramadan religious fast by going to a "henna party." (8) A professional henna artist <u>attends</u> the party to apply new henna decorations to the women. (9) After a few weeks, the henna designs <u>wash</u> off. (10) In the United States, my mother's henna designs <u>attract</u> the attention of many people.

15b Irregular Verbs

Unlike regular verbs, whose past tense forms end in *-ed* or *-d*, **irregular verbs** have irregular forms in the past tense. In fact, their past tense forms may look very different from their present tense forms.

Irregular Verbs in the Past Tense

BASE FORM	PAST	BASE FORM	PAST
awake	awoke	hear	heard
be	was, were	hide	hid
beat	beat	hold	held
become	became	hurt	hurt
begin	began	keep	kept
bet	bet	know	knew
bite	bit	lay (to place)	laid
blow	blew	lead	led
break	broke	leave	left
bring	brought	let	let
build	built	lie (to recline)	lay
buy	bought	light	lit
catch	caught	lose	lost
choose	chose	make	made
come	came	meet	met
cost	cost	pay	paid
cut	cut	quit	quit
dive	dove (dived)	read	read
do	did	ride	rode
draw	drew	ring	rang
drink	drank	rise	rose
drive	drove	run	ran
eat	ate	say	said
fall	fell	see	saw
feed	fed	sell	sold
feel	felt	send	sent
fight	fought	set	set
find	found	shake	shook
fly	flew	shine	shone (shined)
forgive	forgave	sing	sang
freeze	froze	sit	sat
get	got	sleep	slept
give	gave	speak	spoke
go (goes)	went	spend	spent
grow	grew	spring	sprang
have	had	stand	stood

BASE FORM	PAST	BASE FORM	PAST
steal	stole	tell	told
stick	stuck	think	thought
sting	stung	throw	threw
swear	swore	understand	understood
swim	swam	wake	woke
take	took	wear	wore
teach	taught	win	won
tear	tore	write	wrote

PRACTICE 15-2

Fill in the correct past tense form of each irregular verb in parentheses, using the chart above to help you. If you cannot find a particular verb on the chart, look it up in a dictionary.

Example: Security on Campus __was__ (be) founded in 1987.

(1) After their daughter, Jeanne, _____ (be) murdered at Lehigh University, Connie and Howard Clery _____ (begin) a movement to improve safety on college campuses. (2) Jeanne _____ (think) she was safe. (3) However, her attacker _____ (get) into her dorm room through three different doors that had all been left unlocked. (4) Shockingly, Jeanne's attacker actually _____ (go) to Lehigh. (5) Shattered by the loss of their daughter, her parents _____ (do) not withdraw into their pain. (6) Instead, they _____ (feel) that the best memorial to their daughter would be the prevention of similar crimes, so they founded Security on Campus, Inc. (7) SOC _____ (make) legal information available to victims of crimes on college campuses. (8) Because of the efforts of SOC, Congress _____ (write) a law that forced colleges to disclose their crime statistics.

> **Reading Tip**
>
> This passage provides evidence (details and examples) that explains the founding of Security on Campus, Inc. What main idea does this evidence support?

15c Problem Verbs: *Be*

The irregular verb *be* causes problems because it has two different past tense forms—*was* for singular subjects and *were* for second-person singular subjects as well as for plural subjects. (All other English verbs have just one past tense form.)

Carlo was interested in becoming a city planner. (singular)
They were happy to help out at the school. (plural)

Past Tense Forms of the Verb *Be*

	SINGULAR	PLURAL
First person	I was tired.	We were tired.
Second person	You were tired.	You were tired.
Third person	He was tired.	They were tired.
	She was tired.	
	It was tired.	
	The man was tired.	Frank and Billy were tired.

PRACTICE 15-3

Edit the following passage for errors in the use of the verb *be*. Cross out any underlined verbs that are incorrect, and write the correct forms above them. If a verb form is correct, label it *C*.

Example: Before 1990, there ~~was~~ *were* no female Hispanic astronauts in the NASA program.

(1) Although there had never been a Hispanic woman astronaut, it was impossible for NASA to ignore Ellen Ochoa's long career in physics and engineering. (2) When Ochoa was young, her main interests was music, math, and physics. (3) After getting a degree in physics at San Diego State University, she were considering a career in music or business. (4) However, she was convinced by her mother to continue her education. (5) In

1983, Ochoa was studying for a doctorate in electrical engineering at Stanford University when the first female astronaut, Sally Ride, flew on the space shuttle. (6) Ochoa were inspired by Sally Ride to become an astronaut. (7) In 1993, Ochoa was the first Hispanic woman to fly into space. (8) After retiring as an astronaut, she were appointed Deputy Director of the Johnson Space Center, and in 2013 became its director.

15d Problem Verbs: *Can/Could* and *Will/Would*

The helping verbs *can/could* and *will/would* present problems because their past tense forms are sometimes confused with their present tense forms.

Can/Could

Can, a present tense verb, means "is able to" or "are able to."

> First-year students can apply for financial aid.

Could, the past tense of *can*, means "was able to" or "were able to."

> Escape artist Harry Houdini claimed that he could escape from any prison.

Will/Would

Will, a present tense verb, talks about the future from a point in the present.

> A solar eclipse will occur in ten months.

Would, the past tense of *will*, talks about the future from a point in the past.

> I told him yesterday that I would think about it.

Would is also used to express a possibility or wish.

> If we stuck to our budget, we would be better off.
> Laurie would like a new stuffed animal.

> **FYI**
>
> **Will and Would**
>
> Note that *will* is used with *can* and that *would* is used with *could*.
>
> I will feed the cats if I can find their food.
>
> I would feed the cats if I could find their food.

PRACTICE 15-4 Circle the appropriate helping verb from the choices in parentheses.

Example: Anyone who doesn't want to throw things away (**can**, could) rent a self-storage unit.

(1) Today's self-storage units (can, could) make life easier for people with limited space and many belongings. (2) In the past, warehouse storage (will, would) provide a place to store excess items. (3) However, people (will, would) have to hire moving vans and (can, could) hardly ever have access to their stored items. (4) They (will, would) have to sign an expensive long-term contract. (5) Now, however, they (can, could) take advantage of another option. (6) They (can, could) store possessions in a space as small as a closet or as large as a house. (7) With self-storage, people (can, could) easily move their belongings in and out of the storage unit. (8) When they need more space, they (will, would) be able to get it. (9) In fact, the managers of self-storage facilities (can, could) suggest how much space owners (will, would) need. (10) The only person who (can, could) get into the self-storage unit is the person who has rented it. (11) If people need a hand truck to move their belongings, they (can, could) usually borrow one. (12) All in all, using self-storage (can, could) solve a lot of problems for people.

15e Regular Past Participles

Every verb has a past participle form. The **past participle** form of a regular verb is identical to its past tense form. Both are formed by adding either *-ed* or *-d* to the **base form** of the verb (the present tense form of the verb that is used with the pronoun *I*).

PAST TENSE	PAST PARTICIPLE
He earne<u>d</u> a fortune.	He has earne<u>d</u> a fortune.

PAST TENSE	PAST PARTICIPLE
He create<u>d</u> a work of art.	He has create<u>d</u> a work of art.

PRACTICE 15-5

Fill in the correct past participle form of each regular verb in parentheses.

Example: For years, volunteer vacationers have <u>visited</u> (visit) remote areas to build footpaths, cabins, and shelters.

(1) Recently, vacationers have _____ (discover) some new opportunities to get away from it all and to do good at the same time. (2) Groups such as Habitat for Humanity, for example, have _____ (offer) volunteers a chance to build homes in low-income areas. (3) Habitat's Global Village trips have _____ (raise) awareness about the lack of affordable housing in many countries. (4) Participants in Sierra Club programs have _____ (donate) thousands of work hours all over the United States. (5) Sometimes these volunteers have _____ (join) forest service workers to help restore wilderness areas. (6) They have _____ (clean) up trash at campsites. (7) They have also _____ (remove) nonnative plants. (8) Some volunteer vacationers have _____ (travel) to countries such as Costa Rica, Russia, and Thailand to help with local projects. (9) Other

vacationers have _____ (serve) as English teachers. (10) Volunteering vacations have _____ (help) to strengthen cross-cultural understanding.

15f Irregular Past Participles

Irregular verbs nearly always have irregular past participles. Irregular verbs do not form the past participle by adding -ed or -d to the base form of the verb.

The following chart lists the base form, the past tense form, and the past participle of the most commonly used irregular verbs.

Irregular Past Participles

BASE FORM	PAST TENSE	PAST PARTICIPLE
awake	awoke	awoken
be (am, are)	was (were)	been
beat	beat	beaten
become	became	become
begin	began	begun
bet	bet	bet
bite	bit	bitten
blow	blew	blown
break	broke	broken
bring	brought	brought
build	built	built
buy	bought	bought
catch	caught	caught
choose	chose	chosen
come	came	come
cost	cost	cost
cut	cut	cut
dive	dove, dived	dived
do	did	done
draw	drew	drawn
drink	drank	drunk
drive	drove	driven
eat	ate	eaten
fall	fell	fallen
feed	fed	fed

Irregular Past Participles

BASE FORM	PAST TENSE	PAST PARTICIPLE
feel	felt	felt
fight	fought	fought
find	found	found
fly	flew	flown
forgive	forgave	forgiven
freeze	froze	frozen
get	got	got, gotten
give	gave	given
go	went	gone
grow	grew	grown
have	had	had
hear	heard	heard
hide	hid	hidden
hold	held	held
hurt	hurt	hurt
keep	kept	kept
know	knew	known
lay (to place)	laid	laid
lead	led	led
leave	left	left
let	let	let
lie (to recline)	lay	lain
light	lit	lit
lose	lost	lost
make	made	made
meet	met	met
pay	paid	paid
quit	quit	quit
read	read	read
ride	rode	ridden
ring	rang	rung
rise	rose	risen
run	ran	run
say	said	said
see	saw	seen
sell	sold	sold
send	sent	sent
set	set	set
shake	shook	shaken

(continued)

(continued from previous page)

BASE FORM	PAST TENSE	PAST PARTICIPLE
shine	shone, shined	shone, shined
sing	sang	sung
sit	sat	sat
sleep	slept	slept
speak	spoke	spoken
spend	spent	spent
spring	sprang	sprung
stand	stood	stood
steal	stole	stolen
stick	stuck	stuck
sting	stung	stung
swear	swore	sworn
swim	swam	swum
take	took	taken
teach	taught	taught
tear	tore	torn
tell	told	told
think	thought	thought
throw	threw	thrown
understand	understood	understood
wake	woke, waked	woken, waked
wear	wore	worn
win	won	won
write	wrote	written

PRACTICE

15-6 Edit the following paragraph for errors in irregular past participles. Cross out any underlined past participles that are incorrect, and write in the correct form above them. If the verb form is correct, label it *C*.

    Example: In recent years, some people have ~~standed~~ *stood* up against overseas sweatshops.

(1) Buying products from overseas sweatshops has <u>became</u> controversial over the last few decades. (2) American manufacturers have <u>sended</u> their materials to developing countries where employees work under terrible conditions for very low wages. (3) Violations of basic U.S. labor laws—such as getting extra pay for overtime and being paid on time—have

lead to protests. (4) Low-wage workers in developing countries have finded themselves facing dangerous working conditions as well as verbal and sexual abuse. (5) Even well-known retailers—such as Walmart, Nike, Reebok, Tommy Hilfiger, and Target—have gotten in trouble for selling items made in sweatshops. (6) Recently, colleges have be criticized for using overseas sweatshops to make clothing featuring school names. (7) Students have spoke out against such practices, and schools have had to respond. (8) While some manufacturers may have losed money by increasing wages for overseas workers, they have understood that this is the right thing to do. (9) They have made a promise to their customers that they will not employ sweatshop labor. (10) Critics have argue, however, that in developing countries sweatshop jobs are often an improvement over other types of employment.

 ## 15g The Present Perfect Tense

The past participle can be combined with the present tense forms of *have* to form the **present perfect tense**.

The Present Perfect Tense

(*have* or *has* + past participle)

SINGULAR
I have gained.
You have gained.
He has gained.
She has gained.
It has gained.

PLURAL
We have gained.
You have gained.
They have gained.

- Use the present perfect tense to indicate an action that began in the past and continues into the present.

   PRESENT PERFECT The <u>nurse</u> <u>has worked</u> at the Welsh Mountain clinic for two years. (The working began in the past and continues into the present.)

- Use the present perfect tense to indicate that an action has just occurred.

   PRESENT PERFECT <u>I</u> <u>have</u> just <u>eaten</u>. (The eating has just occurred.)

PRACTICE 15-7

Circle the appropriate verb tense (past tense or present perfect) from the choices in parentheses.

Example: When I was in Montreal, I (**heard**, have heard) both English and French.

(1) When I (visited, have visited) Montreal, I was surprised to find a truly bilingual city. (2) Montreal (kept, has kept) two languages as a result of its history. (3) Until 1763, Montreal (belonged, has belonged) to France. (4) Then, when France (lost, has lost) the Seven Years' War, the city (became, has become) part of England. (5) When I was there last year, most people (spoke, have spoken) both French and English. (6) Although I (knew, have known) no French, I (found, have found) that I was able to get along quite well. (7) For example, all the museums (made, have made) their guided tours available in English. (8) Most restaurants (offered, have offered) bilingual menus. (9) There (were, have been) even English radio and television stations and English newspapers. (10) In Montreal, I (felt, have felt) both at home and in a foreign country.

15h The Past Perfect Tense

The past participle can also be used to form the **past perfect tense**, which consists of the past tense of *have* plus the past participle.

> **The Past Perfect Tense**
>
> (*had* + past participle)
>
> **SINGULAR**
> I had returned.
> You had returned.
> He had returned.
> She had returned.
> It had returned.
>
> **PLURAL**
> We had returned.
> You had returned.
> They had returned.

Use the past perfect tense to show that an action occurred before another past action.

          PAST PERFECT TENSE   PAST TENSE
Chief Sitting Bull had fought many battles before he defeated General Custer. (The fighting was done before Sitting Bull defeated Custer.)

PRACTICE 15-8

Underline the appropriate verb tense (present perfect or past perfect) from the choices in parentheses.

Example: Although he (has missed/<u>had missed</u>) his second free throw, the crowd cheered for him anyway.

1. Meera returned to Bangladesh with the money she (has raised/had raised).
2. Her contributors believe that she (has shown/had shown) the ability to spend money wisely.
3. The planner told the commission that she (has found/had found) a solution to the city's traffic problem.
4. It seems clear that traffic cameras (have proven/had proven) successful in towns with similar congestion problems.
5. Emily says she (has saved/had saved) a lot of money by driving a motor scooter instead of a car.

CHAPTER REVIEW

EDITING PRACTICE

Read the following student essay, which includes errors in past tense verb forms and in the use of past participles and perfect tenses. Decide whether each of the underlined verbs or participles is correct. If it is correct, write *C* above it. If it is not, write in the correct verb form. The first error has been corrected for you.

> **READING TIP**
>
> As you read, keep a list of details that support the main idea of this student essay. For example, one supporting detail is the purpose of the first flash mob: to express social commentary.

The Flash Mob Phenomenon

The first flash mob ~~had take~~ *took* place in 2003 when two hundred people assembled in a New York City Macy's store. Since then, these strange spontaneous gatherings <u>had popped</u> up in cities around the world and <u>have involve</u> all kinds of unusual behaviors. Occasionally, a group <u>has organized</u> a flash mob for criminal purposes, but in most cases, flash mobs <u>had been</u> harmless acts of group expression.

Organizer Bill Wasik <u>had</u> actually <u>intend</u> the first flash mob to be a social commentary. Wasik <u>has wanted</u> to make fun of "hipster" New Yorkers who showed up at events simply because other people did. However, almost no one <u>had saw</u> the first flash mob that way. In fact, people mostly <u>have thought</u> it was cool. As a result, admirers started organizing their own flash mobs.

So far, few of the subsequent flash mobs <u>had have</u> a political or social purpose. Typically, people <u>had participate</u> simply because these gatherings are fun. For example, over the years, people <u>have gathered</u> in cities around the world to dance to Michael Jackson's "Thriller." People <u>had</u> also <u>enjoyed</u> getting together in public spaces for massive pillow fights. In addition, several groups <u>have coordinated</u> group "freeze frames," in which participants all "freeze" at the same moment. Organized quietly by text messages or social media, most flash mobs <u>have</u> not <u>publicize</u> their plans in traditional media. Consequently, passers-by <u>have enjoyed</u> the feeling that the group <u>had gathered</u> spontaneously.

Although the majority of flash mob organizers have create these brief performances to entertain, people have occasionally use flash mobs to commit crimes. Over the last few years, several groups have robbed stores by entering in large numbers, stealing merchandise, and then separating quickly. Worse, several groups have came together to commit violent acts or destroy property. Most of today's flash mobs, however, are peaceful.

Over the last decade, flash mobs have became more popular than anyone could have imagined. Although they have not had the impact that creator Bill Wasik had hoped for, they have given a lot of people a lot of enjoyment. Flash mobs allow people to be creative, to work together, and to have fun. Although a few flash mobs have done harm, most have offer people a way to be a part of something memorable.

Review Checklist

Verbs

✔ The past tense is the form a verb takes to show that an action occurred in the past.

✔ Regular verbs form the past tense by adding either *-ed* or *-d* to the base form of the verb. (See 15a.)

✔ Irregular verbs have irregular forms in the past tense. (See 15b.)

✔ *Be* has two different past tense forms—*was* for singular subjects and *were* for second-person singular subjects as well as for plural subjects. (See 15c.)

✔ *Could* is the past tense of *can*. *Would* is the past tense of *will*. (See 15d.)

✔ The past participle of regular verbs is formed by adding *-ed* or *-d* to the base form. (See 15e.)

✔ Irregular verbs usually have irregular past participles. (See 15f.)

✔ The past participle is combined with the present tense forms of *have* to form the present perfect tense. (See 15g.)

✔ The past participle is used to form the past perfect tense, which consists of the past tense of *have* plus the past participle. (See 15h.)

16 Understanding Nouns and Pronouns

 ## 16a Identifying Nouns

A **noun** is a word that names a person (*singer*, *Beyoncé*), an animal (*dolphin*, *Flipper*), a place (*downtown*, *Houston*), an object (*game*, *Scrabble*), or an idea (*happiness*, *Darwinism*).

A **singular noun** names one thing. A **plural noun** names more than one thing.

FYI

When to Capitalize Nouns

Most nouns, called **common nouns**, begin with lowercase letters.

    character   holiday

Proper nouns name particular people, animals, places, objects, or events. A proper noun always begins with a capital letter.

    Homer Simpson   Labor Day

 ## 16b Forming Plural Nouns

Most nouns that end in consonants add -*s* to form plurals. Other nouns add -*es* to form plurals. For example, most nouns that end in -*o* add -*es* to form plurals. Other nouns, whose singular forms end in -*s*, -*ss*, -*sh*, -*ch*, -*x*, or -*z*, also add -*es* to form plurals. (Some nouns that end in -*s* or -*z* double the *s* or *z* before adding -*es*.)

SINGULAR	PLURAL	SINGULAR	PLURAL
street	streets	bush	bushes
tomato	tomatoes	church	churches
gas	gases	fox	foxes
class	classes	quiz	quizzes

Irregular Noun Plurals

Some nouns form plurals in unusual ways.

- Nouns whose plural forms are the same as their singular forms

SINGULAR	PLURAL
a deer	a few deer
this species	these species
a television series	two television series

- Nouns ending in *-f* or *-fe*

SINGULAR	PLURAL
each half	both halv<u>es</u>
my life	our liv<u>es</u>
a lone thief	a gang of thiev<u>es</u>
one loaf	two loav<u>es</u>
the third shelf	several shelv<u>es</u>

    Exceptions: *roof* (plural *roofs*), *proof* (plural *proofs*), *belief* (plural *beliefs*)

- Nouns ending in *-y*

SINGULAR	PLURAL
another baby	more bab<u>ies</u>
every worry	many worr<u>ies</u>

    Note that when a vowel (*a, e, i, o, u*) comes before the *-y*, the noun has a regular plural form: *monkey* (plural *monkeys*), *day* (plural *days*).

- Hyphenated compound nouns

SINGULAR	PLURAL
Lucia's sister-in-law	Lucia's two favorite sister<u>s</u>-in-law
a mother-to-be	twin mother<u>s</u>-to-be
the first runner-up	all the runner<u>s</u>-up

    Note that the plural ending is attached to the compound's first word: *sister, mother, runner.*

- Miscellaneous irregular plurals

SINGULAR	PLURAL
that child	all children
a good man	a few good men
the woman	lots of women
my left foot	both feet
a wisdom tooth	my two front teeth
this bacterium	some bacteria

PRACTICE 16-1

Proofread the underlined nouns in the following paragraph, checking to make sure singular and plural forms are correct. If a correction needs to be made, cross out the noun, and write the correct form above it. If the noun is correct, write *C* above it.

                                circuses
Example: Like other ~~circusses~~ around the world, America's first circus featured a variety of animals.

> **READING TIP**
>
> When you read, think about the writer's purpose, which is typically to inform, to explain, or to persuade. In this paragraph, what is the author's purpose, and how is the purpose made clear to the reader?

(1) A tradition for many <u>familys</u> ended on May 21, 2017, when Ringling Brothers and Barnum & Bailey Circus gave its final performance. (2) The <u>origines</u> of "The Greatest Show on Earth" go back to 1806, when Hachaliah Bailey first established his traveling show. (3) Selling <u>tickets</u> for Bailey was a young P. T. Barnum, who became one of the <u>founderrs</u> of Barnum & Bailey's Circus. (4) The Ringling <u>brothers</u> started their own circus and then bought Barnum & Bailey and combined the two <u>companys</u>. (5) Under the big top, the ringmaster announced the show by calling out, "<u>Ladys</u> and <u>Gentleman</u>! <u>Children</u> of all ages!" (6) The millions of fans answering the call over the <u>years</u> were amazed by the <u>skillz</u> of both <u>humans</u> and <u>animals.</u> (7) <u>Audience</u> cheered as <u>performeres</u> were shot out of <u>cannons</u>, walked across <u>tightropes</u>, and flew from one trapeze to another. (8) The circus was as famous for <u>clownes</u>, <u>acrobats</u>, and <u>jugglers</u> as it was for <u>tigers</u>, <u>horsess</u>, <u>lions</u>, and of course, <u>elephantes</u>. (9) In 2016, the <u>elephants</u> performed for the last time and then were moved to a preserve where they would spend the rest of their <u>lifes</u>. (10) Ringling Bros. and Barnum & Bailey closed within a year, citing high operating <u>costes</u> and declining ticket <u>sale</u>, after the <u>elephants</u> left the show.

16c Identifying Pronouns

A **pronoun** is a word that refers to and takes the place of a noun or another pronoun. In the following sentence, the pronouns *she* and *her* take the place of the noun *Michelle*.

Michelle was really excited because <u>she</u> had finally found a job that made <u>her</u> happy. (*She* refers to *Michelle; her* refers to *she*.)

Pronouns, like nouns, can be singular or plural.

- Singular pronouns (*I*, *he*, *she*, *it*, *him*, *her*, and so on) always take the place of singular nouns or pronouns.

    Geoff left his jacket at work, so <u>he</u> went back to get <u>it</u> before <u>it</u> could be stolen. (*He* refers to *Geoff*; *it* refers to *jacket*.)

- Plural pronouns (*we*, *they*, *our*, *their*, and so on) always take the place of plural nouns or pronouns.

    Jessie and Dan got up early, but <u>they</u> still missed <u>their</u> train. (*They* refers to *Jessie and Dan*; *their* refers to *they*.)

- The pronoun *you* can be either singular or plural.

    When the volunteers met the mayor, they said, "We really admire <u>you</u>." The mayor replied, "I admire <u>you</u>, too." (In the first sentence, *you* refers to *the mayor*; in the second sentence, *you* refers to *the volunteers*.)

FYI

Demonstrative Pronouns

Demonstrative pronouns—*this*, *that*, *these*, and *those*—point to one or more items.

- *This* and *that* point to one item: <u>This</u> is a work of fiction, and <u>that</u> is a nonfiction book.
- *These* and *those* point to more than one item: <u>These</u> are fruits, but <u>those</u> are vegetables.

PRACTICE 16-2

In the following sentences, fill in each blank with an appropriate pronoun.

Example: Installing operating system updates can help <u>you</u> protect <u>your</u> personal information.

(1) ____ can help keep ____ personal information safe online by following some "always" and "never" rules. (2) When ____ are shopping or banking online, always check to make sure that the site is encrypted.

(3) If _____ is secure, the web address will begin with "https." (4) Always be sure to shop only at well-known retailers; _____ are more likely to offer protection in case of fraud. (5) Never send _____ bank account number or other sensitive information over a public Wi-Fi network. (6) Always protect _____ passwords by keeping _____ private and secure. (7) Even if _____ have created the perfect password, never use _____ for more than one account. (8) Always copy important data onto a backup drive and then store _____ in a safe place so you can get to _____ even if your device is compromised. (9) Always ensure that apps are safe before you install _____, and never click on suspicious email links or websites. (10) Finally, always disconnect from the Internet and turn off _____ computer when you are finished using _____.

16d Pronoun-Antecedent Agreement

The word that a pronoun refers to is called the pronoun's **antecedent**. In the following sentence, the noun *leaf* is the antecedent of the pronoun *it*.

The leaf turned yellow, but it did not fall.

A pronoun must always agree with its antecedent. If an antecedent is singular, as it is in the sentence above, the pronoun must be singular. If the antecedent is plural, as it is in the sentence below, the pronoun must also be plural.

The leaves turned yellow, but they did not fall.

If an antecedent is feminine, the pronoun that refers to it must also be feminine.

Melissa passed her driver's exam with flying colors.

If an antecedent is masculine, the pronoun that refers to it must also be masculine.

Matt wondered what courses he should take.

If an antecedent is **neuter** (neither masculine nor feminine), the pronoun that refers to it must also be neuter.

The car broke down, but they refused to fix it again.

Identifying Problem Areas with Agreement 16e 403

PRACTICE 16-3

Fill in each blank in the following passage with an appropriate pronoun.

Example: Americans celebrate July 4 because __it__ is Independence Day.

(1) For some Germans, November 9 is a day to celebrate positive change; for others, _____ recalls the human potential for violence and destruction. (2) November 9, designated "World Freedom Day," is important because _____ is the day the Berlin Wall fell. (3) On that day in 1989, residents of East and West Germany were allowed to cross the barrier that had separated _____ since the end of World War II. (4) However, Germans have mixed feelings about this date because November 9 also reminds _____ of a dark moment in their history. (5) On the night of November 9, 1938, Nazis took sledgehammers and axes to as many Jewish businesses, synagogues, and homes as _____ could find. (6) In German, this violent event is called *Kristallnacht*; in English, _____ is known as "the Night of Broken Glass." (7) Because November 9 has been so important in German history, journalists sometimes refer to _____ as Germany's "day of fate." (8) Coincidentally, Albert Einstein, a German Jew, received the Nobel Prize on November 9, 1921; the theories _____ described have changed the way scientists think. (9) Thus, November 9 in Germany is a day of opposites; like so many dates in human history, _____ marks both triumph and tragedy.

16e Identifying Problem Areas with Agreement

Certain kinds of antecedents can cause problems for writers because they cannot easily be identified as singular or plural.

Compound Antecedents

A **compound antecedent** consists of two or more words connected by *and* or *or*.

- Compound antecedents connected by *and* are plural, and they are used with plural pronouns.

    During World War II, <u>Belgium and France</u> tried to protect <u>their</u> borders.

- Compound antecedents connected by *or* may take a singular or a plural pronoun. The pronoun always agrees with the word that is closer to it.

    It is possible that European nations or <u>Russia</u> may send <u>its</u> [not *their*] troops?

    It is possible that Russia or European <u>nations</u> may send <u>their</u> [not *its*] troops?

PRACTICE 16-4

In each of the following sentences, underline the compound antecedent, and circle the connecting word (*and* or *or*). Then, underline the appropriate pronoun in parentheses.

Example: <u>Romeo</u> (and) <u>Juliet</u> fell in love against the wishes of (his or her/<u>their</u>) families.

1. Both Savannah, Georgia, and Charleston, South Carolina, are popular tourist destinations because of (its/their) Southern charm.

2. In *Game of Thrones*, Jon Snow and Daenerys Targaryen are portrayed as strong leaders who want the best for (his or her/their) people.

3. When you travel to a new place, either TripAdvisor or Yelp can be helpful for (its/their) online reviews of restaurants and hotels.

4. In 1903, Marie and Pierre Curie were awarded the Nobel Prize for Physics for (his or her/their) work on radioactivity.

5. One challenge for either vegetarians or vegans can be including enough protein in (his or her/their) diets.

6. For more than a hundred years, Sherlock Holmes and John Watson have entertained (his/their) fans as they investigate mysterious cases.

7. On Cyber Monday, shoppers may go to Amazon or another online retailer offering (its/their) products at bargain prices.

8. This summer, Katie and her sister Liz are planning to drive to Denver to visit (her/their) cousin.

9. Weather forecasters predicted that either the Virgin Islands or Puerto Rico could be devastated if Hurricane Maria continued (its/their) course.

Indefinite Pronoun Antecedents

Most pronouns refer to a specific person or thing. However, **indefinite pronouns** do not refer to any particular person or thing.

Most indefinite pronouns are singular.

Singular Indefinite Pronouns

another	everybody	no one
anybody	everyone	nothing
anyone	everything	one
anything	much	somebody
each	neither	someone
either	nobody	something

When an indefinite pronoun antecedent is singular, use a singular pronoun to refer to it.

Everything was in its place. (*Everything* is singular, so it is used with the singular pronoun *its*.)

FYI

Indefinite Pronouns with *Of*

The singular indefinite pronouns *each, either, neither,* and *one* are often used in phrases with *of*—*each of, either of, neither of,* or *one of*—followed by a plural noun. Even in such phrases, these indefinite pronoun antecedents are always singular and take singular pronouns.

Each of the routes has its [not *their*] own special challenges.

A few indefinite pronouns are plural.

> **Plural Indefinite Pronouns**
> both
> few
> many
> others
> several

When an indefinite pronoun antecedent is plural, use a plural pronoun to refer to it.

They all wanted to graduate early, but **few** received <u>their</u> diplomas in January. (*Few* is plural, so it is used with the plural pronoun *their*.)

FYI

Using *His* or *Her* with Indefinite Pronouns

Even though the indefinite pronouns *anybody, anyone, everybody, everyone, somebody, someone,* and so on are singular, many people use plural pronouns to refer to them.

<u>Everyone</u> must hand in <u>their</u> completed work before 2 p.m.

This usage is widely accepted in spoken English. Nevertheless, indefinite pronouns like *everyone* are singular, and written English requires a singular pronoun.

However, using the singular pronoun *his* to refer to *everyone* suggests that *everyone* refers to a male. Using *his or her* is more accurate because the indefinite pronoun can refer to either a male or a female.

<u>Everyone</u> must hand in <u>his or her</u> completed work before 2 p.m.

When used over and over again, *he or she, him or her,* and *his or her* can create wordy or awkward sentences. Whenever possible, use plural forms.

<u>All students</u> must hand in <u>their</u> completed work before 2 p.m.

PRACTICE 16-5

Edit the following sentences for errors in pronoun-antecedent agreement. When you edit, you have two options: either substitute *its* or *his or her* for *their* to refer to the singular antecedent, or replace the singular antecedent with a plural word.

Examples: Everyone can help prevent the spread of germs by washing his or her ~~their~~ hands.

All
~~Each~~ of the passengers presented their tickets at the gate.

1. Each of the programs has their advantages and disadvantages.

2. Anyone who tries out for the play is responsible for learning their lines.

3. Everyone had to show their registration card to attend the free seminar.

4. Several people agreed to meet at the rally but few kept his or her promise because of the rain.

5. Everybody waits until fall to get their flu shots.

6. Every school in the district changed their starting times to 8:30.

7. Neither of the buildings had their own parking lot.

8. Anyone who needs to take a make-up test must write their name on the list.

9. One of the companies moved their headquarters across town.

10. Each employee had a chance to ask questions about their benefits.

Collective Noun Antecedents

Collective nouns are words (such as *band* and *team*) that name a group of people or things but are singular. Because they are singular, collective noun antecedents are used with singular pronouns.

The band played on, but it never played our song.

Frequently Used Collective Nouns

army	class	family	jury
association	club	gang	mob
audience	committee	government	team
band	company	group	union

PRACTICE 16-6

Circle the collective noun antecedent in each of the following sentences. Then, circle the correct pronoun in parentheses.

Example: The (jury) returned with (its)/their) verdict.

1. The company offers good benefits to (its/their) employees.
2. All five study groups must hand in (its/their) projects by Tuesday.
3. Any government should be concerned about the welfare of (its/their) citizens.
4. The Asian Students Union is sponsoring a party to celebrate (its/their) twentieth anniversary.
5. Every family has (its/their) share of problems.
6. To join the electricians' union, applicants had to pass (its/their) test.
7. Even the best teams have (its/their) bad days.
8. The orchestra just signed a contract for (its/their) first recording.
9. The math class did very well with (its/their) new teacher.
10. The club voted to expand (its/their) membership.

16f Vague and Unnecessary Pronouns

Vague and unnecessary pronouns clutter up your writing and make it hard to understand. Eliminating them will make your writing clearer and easier for readers to follow.

Vague Pronouns

A pronoun should always refer to a specific antecedent. When a pronoun—such as *they* or *it*—has no antecedent, readers may be confused.

VAGUE PRONOUN On the news, they said baseball players would strike. (Who said baseball players would strike?)

VAGUE PRONOUN It says in today's paper that our schools are overcrowded. (Who says schools are overcrowded?)

If a pronoun does not refer to a specific word in the sentence, replace the pronoun with a noun:

REVISED On the news, the <u>sportscaster</u> said baseball players would strike.

REVISED An <u>editorial</u> in today's paper says that our schools are overcrowded.

Unnecessary Pronouns

When a pronoun comes directly after its antecedent, it is unnecessary.

UNNECESSARY PRONOUN The librarian, <u>he</u> told me I should check the database.

In the sentence above, the pronoun *he* serves no purpose. Readers do not need to be directed back to the pronoun's antecedent (the noun *librarian*) because it appears right before the pronoun. The pronoun should therefore be deleted:

REVISED The librarian told me I should check the database.

PRACTICE 16-7

The following sentences contain vague or unnecessary pronouns. Revise each sentence on the line below it.

Example: On their website, they advertised a special offer.

On its website, the Gap advertised a special offer.

1. In Jamaica, they love their spectacular green mountains.

2. My hamster, he loves his exercise wheel.

3. On *Jeopardy!* they have to give the answers in the form of questions.

4. On screens all over the world, they watched the moon landing.

5. In Sociology 320, they do not use a textbook.

16g Understanding Pronoun Case

A **personal pronoun** refers to a particular person or thing. Personal pronouns change form according to their function in a sentence. Personal pronouns can be *subjective*, *objective*, or *possessive*.

Personal Pronouns

SUBJECTIVE	OBJECTIVE	POSSESSIVE
I	me	my, mine
he	him	his
she	her	her, hers
it	it	its
we	us	our, ours
you	you	your, yours
they	them	their, theirs
who	whom	whose
whoever	whomever	

Subjective Case

When a pronoun is a subject, it is in the **subjective case**.

> Finally, <u>she</u> realized that dreams could come true.

Objective Case

When a pronoun is an object, it is in the **objective case**.

> If Joanna hurries, she can stop <u>him</u>. (The pronoun *him* is the object of the verb *can stop*.)

> Professor Miller sent <u>us</u> information about his research. (The pronoun *us* is the object of the verb *sent*.)

> Marc threw the ball to <u>them</u>. (The pronoun *them* is the object of the preposition *to*.)

Possessive Case

When a pronoun shows ownership, it is in the **possessive case**.

> Hieu took <u>his</u> lunch to the meeting. (The pronoun *his* indicates that the lunch belongs to Hieu.)

> Debbie and Kim decided to take <u>their</u> lunches, too. (The pronoun *their* indicates that the lunches belong to Debbie and Kim.)

PRACTICE 16-8

In the following passage, fill in the blank after each pronoun to indicate whether the pronoun is subjective (*S*), objective (*O*), or possessive (*P*).

> **Example:** Between 1932 and 1934, famous criminals Bonnie and Clyde committed their <u>P</u> robberies and murders in broad daylight.

(1) Bonnie Parker and Clyde Barrow are remembered today because they ___ were the first celebrity criminals. (2) With their ___ gang, Bonnie and Clyde robbed a dozen banks as well as many stores and gas stations. (3) In small towns, they ___ terrorized the police. (4) Capturing them ___ seemed impossible. (5) To many Americans, however, their ___ crimes seemed exciting. (6) Because Bonnie was a woman, she ___ was especially fascinating to them ___. (7) During their ___ crimes, Bonnie and Clyde would often carry a camera, take photographs of themselves, and then send them ___ to the newspapers, which were happy to publish them ___. (8) By the time they ___ were killed in an ambush by Texas and Louisiana law officers, Bonnie and Clyde were famous all over the United States.

16h Identifying Problem Areas with Pronoun Case

When you are trying to determine which pronoun case to use in a sentence, three kinds of pronouns can cause problems: pronouns in compounds, pronouns in comparisons, and the pronouns *who* and *whom* (or *whoever* and *whomever*).

Pronouns in Compounds

Sometimes a pronoun is linked to a noun or to another pronoun with *and* or *or* to form a **compound**.

> The teacher and I met for an hour.
>
> He or she can pick up Jenny at school.

To determine whether to use the subjective or objective case for a pronoun in the second part of a compound, follow the same rules that apply for a pronoun that is not part of a compound.

- If the compound is a subject, use the subjective case.

  > Toby and I [not *me*] like jazz.
  >
  > He and I [not *me*] went to the movies.

- If the compound is an object, use the objective case.

  > The school sent my father and me [not *I*] the financial-aid forms.
  >
  > This argument is between Kate and me [not *I*].

> **FYI**
>
> **Choosing Pronouns in Compounds**
>
> To determine which pronoun case to use in a compound that joins a noun and a pronoun, rewrite the sentence with just the pronoun:
>
> Toby and [*I* or *me*?] like jazz.
>
> I like jazz. (not *Me like jazz*)
>
> Toby and I like jazz.

PRACTICE 16-9

In the following sentences, the underlined pronouns are parts of compounds. Check them for correct subjective or objective case. If the pronoun is incorrect, cross it out, and write the correct form above it. If the pronoun is correct, write *C* above it.

Example: My classmates and <u>I</u> were surprised by the results of a study on listening. *[C above I]*

(1) According to a recent study, the average listener remembers only 50 percent of what <u>him</u> or <u>her</u> hears. (2) Two days later, <u>he</u> or <u>she</u> can correctly recall only 25 percent of the total message. (3) My friend Alyssa and <u>me</u> decided to ask our school to sponsor a presentation about listening in the classroom. (4) One point the speaker made was especially helpful to Alyssa and <u>I</u>. (5) We now know that <u>us</u> and the other students in our class each have four times more mental "room" than we need for listening. (6) The presenter taught the other workshop participants and <u>we</u> how to use this extra space. (7) Now, whenever one of our instructors pauses to write on the board or take a sip of water, Alyssa and <u>I</u> remember to silently summarize the last point <u>he</u> or <u>she</u> made. (8) Throughout the class, we pay special attention to the big ideas and overall structure that the instructor wants the other students and <u>us</u> to understand. (9) Above all, we do not waste our mental energy on distractions that other students and <u>us</u> ourselves create, such as dropped books or whispers.

Pronouns in Comparisons

Sometimes a pronoun appears after the word *than* or *as* in the second part of a **comparison**.

John is luckier <u>than I</u>.

The inheritance changed Raymond as much <u>as her</u>.

- If the pronoun is a subject, use the subjective case.

    John is luckier than I [am].

- If the pronoun is an object, use the objective case.

    The inheritance changed Raymond as much as [it changed] her.

> **FYI**
>
> **Choosing Pronouns in Comparisons**
>
> Sometimes the pronoun you use can change your sentence's meaning. For example, if you say, "I like Cheerios more than *he*," you mean that you like Cheerios more than the other person likes them.
>
>   I like Cheerios more than he [does].
>
> If, however, you say, "I like Cheerios more than *him*," you mean that you like Cheerios more than you like the other person.
>
>   I like Cheerios more than [I like] him.

PRACTICE

16-10 Each of the following sentences includes a comparison with a pronoun following the word *than* or *as*. Write in each blank the correct form (subjective or objective) of the pronoun in parentheses. In brackets, add the word or words needed to complete the comparison.

Example: Many people are better poker players than ___I [am]___ (I/me).

1. No one enjoys shopping more than _____ (she/her).

2. My brother and Aunt Cecile were very close, so her death affected him more than _____ (I/me).

3. No two people could have a closer relationship than _____ (they/them).

4. My neighbor drives better than _____ (I/me).

5. He may be as old as _____ (I/me), but he does not have as much work experience.

6. That jacket fits you better than _____ (I/me).

7. The other company had a lower bid than _____ (we/us), but we were awarded the contract.

Who and Whom, Whoever and Whomever

To determine whether to use *who* or *whom* (or *whoever* or *whomever*), you need to know how the pronoun functions within the clause in which it appears.

- When the pronoun is the subject of the clause, use *who* or *whoever*.

    I wonder <u>who</u> wrote that song. (*Who is the subject of the clause who wrote that song.*)

    I will vote for <u>whoever</u> supports the youth center. (*Whoever is the subject of the clause whoever supports the youth center.*)

- When the pronoun is the object, use *whom* or *whomever*.

    <u>Whom</u> do the police suspect? (*Whom is the direct object of the verb suspect.*)

    I wonder <u>whom</u> the song is about. (*Whom is the object of the preposition about in the clause whom the song is about.*)

    Vote for <u>whomever</u> you prefer. (*Whomever is the object of the verb prefer in the clause whomever you prefer.*)

> ### FYI
>
> **Who and Whom**
>
> To determine whether to use *who* or *whom*, try substituting another pronoun for *who* or *whom* in the clause. If you can substitute *he* or *she*, use *who*; if you can substitute *him* or *her*, use *whom*.
>
> [**Who**/Whom] wrote a love song? <u>He</u> wrote a love song.
>
> [Who/**Whom**] was the song about? The song was about <u>her</u>.
>
> The same test will work for *whoever* and *whomever*.

PRACTICE 16-11

Circle the correct form—*who* or *whom* (or *whoever* or *whomever*)—in parentheses in each sentence.

Example: With (who/**whom**) did Rob collaborate?

1. The defense team learned (who/whom) was going to testify for the prosecution.

2. (Who/Whom) does she think she can find to be a witness?

3. The contestant (who/whom) eats the most hot dogs will be the winner.

4. They will argue their case to (whoever/whomever) will listen.

5. It will take time to decide (who/whom) is the record holder.

6. Take these forms to the clerk (who/whom) is sitting at the front desk.

7. We will have to penalize (whoever/whomever) misses the first practice.

8. (Who/Whom) did Kobe take to the prom?

9. We saw the man (who/whom) fired the shots.

10. To (who/whom) am I speaking?

16i Reflexive and Intensive Pronouns

Two special kinds of pronouns, *reflexive pronouns* and *intensive pronouns*, end in *-self* (singular) or *-selves* (plural). Although the functions of the two kinds of pronouns are different, their forms are identical.

Reflexive and Intensive Pronouns

Singular Forms

ANTECEDENT	REFLEXIVE OR INTENSIVE PRONOUN
I	myself
you	yourself
he	himself
she	herself
it	itself

Plural Forms

ANTECEDENT	REFLEXIVE OR INTENSIVE PRONOUN
we	ourselves
you	yourselves
they	themselves

Reflexive Pronouns

Reflexive pronouns indicate that people or things did something to themselves or for themselves.

Rosanna lost herself in the novel.

You need to watch yourself when you mix those solutions.

Mehul and Paul made themselves cold drinks.

Intensive Pronouns

Intensive pronouns always appear directly after their antecedents, and they are used for emphasis.

I myself have had some experience in sales and marketing.

The victim himself collected the reward.

They themselves were uncertain of the significance of their findings.

PRACTICE 16-12 Fill in the correct reflexive or intensive pronoun in each of the following sentences.

Example: The opening act was exciting, but the main attraction ___itself___ was boring.

1. Morticia welcomed her visitors and told them to make _____ at home.

2. Migrating birds can direct _____ through clouds, storms, and moonless nights.

3. The Queen _____ gave a speech at the ceremony.

4. We all finished the project without injuring _____.

5. Even though the government promised to help flood victims, the residents _____ did most of the rebuilding.

6. Sometimes he finds _____ daydreaming in class.

7. The guide warned us to watch _____ on the slippery path.

8. The senators were not happy about committing _____ to a shorter recess.

9. She gave _____ a manicure.

10. Although everyone else in my family can sing or play a musical instrument, I _____ am tone-deaf.

CHAPTER REVIEW

EDITING PRACTICE

Read the following student essay, which includes noun and pronoun errors. Check for errors in plural noun forms, pronoun case, and pronoun antecedent agreement. Then, make any editing changes you think are necessary. The first paragraph has been edited for you.

Swimming to Safety

Swimming is a favorite summertime activity for many children and adults, but it is not enjoyable for everyone. For those who cannot swim, being in or near the water can be a terrifying experience. The Swimming Saves Lives Foundation is one organization that is trying to make a difference for a person who never learned how to swim.

It is important for children to start swimming lessons at a young age. Children should learn how to keep himself or herself safe near the water. The Swimming Saves Lives Foundation believes that water-safety lessons are important for all children, but particularly for minorities. Reports suggest that approximately 70 percent of African American children and 60 percent of Latino children are not strong swimmeres. For all children, drowning is a common cause of death. Whom wants to take that risk? Even if a child does not want to swim recreationally, him or her should understand basic water safety.

Some adult seem to think that it is too late to learn how to swim. The Swimming Saves Lives Foundation offers their services to anyone who wants to learn to swim. Local program are available in many states. Anyone who wants to participate can sign themselves up online.

For many adults, learning to swim leads him to a new favorite sport. For these people, the Swimming Saves Lives Foundation offers a Masters Swimming program. In the Masters Swimming program, adults can continue to refine his or her swimming skills.

> **READING TIP**
> Consider the student writer's tone (expression of emotion or feeling) as you read this essay. What words or phrases provide clues to the writer's attitude toward the Saves Lives Foundation?

Approximately 37 percent of adults cannot swim the length of the pool, and it is time for that number to drop. Thanks to the Swimming Saves Lives Foundation, whomever wants to swim has a greater opportunity to learn. Even if adults do not choose to swim recreationally, he or she can still learn practical water safety and teach it to their children.

Review Checklist

Nouns and Pronouns

- ✔ A noun is a word that names something. A singular noun names one thing; a plural noun names more than one thing. (See 16a.)
- ✔ Most nouns add *-s* or *-es* to form plurals. Some nouns have irregular plural forms. (See 16b.)
- ✔ A pronoun is a word that refers to and takes the place of a noun or another pronoun. (See 16c.)
- ✔ The word a pronoun refers to is called the pronoun's antecedent. A pronoun and its antecedent must always agree. (See 16d.)
- ✔ Compound antecedents connected by *and* are plural and are used with plural pronouns. Compound antecedents connected by *or* may take singular or plural pronouns. (See 16e.)
- ✔ Most indefinite pronoun antecedents are singular and are used with singular pronouns; some are plural and are used with plural pronouns. (See 16e.)
- ✔ Collective noun antecedents are singular and are used with singular pronouns. (See 16e.)
- ✔ A pronoun should always refer to a specific antecedent. (See 16f.)
- ✔ Personal pronouns can be in the subjective, objective, or possessive case. (See 16g.)
- ✔ Pronouns present special problems when they are used in compounds and comparisons. The pronouns *who* and *whom* and *whoever* and *whomever* can also cause problems. (See 16h.)
- ✔ Reflexive and intensive pronouns must agree with their antecedents. (See 16i.)

17 Understanding Adjectives and Adverbs

17a Identifying Adjectives and Adverbs

Adjectives and adverbs are words that modify (identify or describe) other words. They help make sentences more specific and more interesting.

An **adjective** answers the question *What kind? Which one?* or *How many?* Adjectives modify nouns or pronouns:

The Turkish city of Istanbul spans two continents. (*Turkish* modifies the noun *city*, and *two* modifies the noun *continents*.)

It is fascinating because of its location and history. (*Fascinating* modifies the pronoun *it*.)

FYI

Demonstrative Adjectives

Demonstrative adjectives—*this, that, these,* and *those*—do not describe other words. They simply identify particular nouns.

This and *that* identify singular nouns and pronouns.

This website is much more current than that one.

These and *those* identify plural nouns.

These words and phrases are French, but those expressions are Creole.

An **adverb** answers the question *How? Why? When? Where?* or *To what extent?* Adverbs modify verbs, adjectives, or other adverbs.

Traffic moved steadily. (*Steadily* modifies the verb *moved*.)

Still, we were quite impatient. (*Quite* modifies the adjective *impatient*.)

Very slowly, we moved into the center lane. (*Very* modifies the adverb *slowly*.)

> **FYI**
>
> **Distinguishing Adjectives from Adverbs**
>
> Many adverbs are formed when *-ly* is added to an adjective form.
>
> | ADJECTIVE | ADVERB |
> |---|---|
> | slow | slowly |
> | nice | nicely |
> | quick | quickly |
> | real | really |
>
> **ADJECTIVE** Let me give you one quick reminder. (*Quick* modifies the noun *reminder*.)
>
> **ADVERB** He quickly changed the subject. (*Quickly* modifies the verb *changed*.)

PRACTICE 17-1

In the following sentences, circle the correct form (adjective or adverb) from the choices in parentheses.

Example: Beatles enthusiasts all over the world have formed tribute bands devoted to the (**famous**/famously) group's music.

(1) Tribute bands go to (great/greatly) lengths to show appreciation for their favorite musicians. (2) Fans who have a (real/really) strong affection for a particular band may decide to play its music and copy its style. (3) Sometimes they form their own groups and have successful careers (simple/simply) performing that band's music. (4) These groups are (usual/usually) called *tribute bands*. (5) Most tribute bands are (passionate/passionately) dedicated to reproducing the original group's work. (6) They not only play the group's songs but (careful/carefully) imitate the group's look. (7) They study the band members' facial expressions and body movements and create (exact/exactly) copies of the band's costumes

and instruments. (8) Some more (inventive/inventively) tribute bands take the original band's songs and interpret them (different/differently). (9) For example, by performing Beatles songs in the style of Metallica, the tribute band Beatallica has created a (unique/uniquely) sound. (10) Some people believe such tributes are the (ultimate/ultimately) compliment to the original band; others feel (sure/surely) that tribute groups are just copycats who (serious/seriously) lack imagination.

> ## FYI
>
> ### Good and Well
>
> Be careful not to confuse *good* and *well*. Unlike regular adjectives, whose adverb forms add *-ly*, the adjective *good* is irregular. Its adverb form is *well*.
>
> **ADJECTIVE**   Fred Astaire was a good dancer. (*Good* modifies the noun *dancer*.)
>
> **ADVERB**   He danced especially well with Ginger Rogers. (*Well* modifies the verb *danced*.)
>
> Always use *well* when you are describing a person's health:.
>
> He really didn't feel well [not *good*] after eating the entire pizza.

PRACTICE 17-2

Circle the correct form (*good* or *well*) in the sentences below.

Example: It can be hard for some people to find a (**good**/well) job that they really like.

(1) Some people may not do (good/well) sitting in an office. (2) Instead, they may prefer to find jobs that take advantage of their (good/well) physical condition. (3) Such people might consider becoming smoke jumpers—firefighters who are (good/well) at parachuting from small planes into remote areas to battle forest fires. (4) Smoke jumpers must be able to work (good/well) even without much sleep. (5) They must also handle danger (good/well). (6) They look forward to the (good/well) feeling of saving

a forest or someone's home. (7) As they battle fires, surrounded by smoke and fumes, smoke jumpers may not feel very (good/well). (8) Sometimes things go wrong; for example, when their parachutes fail to work (good/well), jumpers may be injured or even killed. (9) Smoke jumpers do not get paid particularly (good/well). (10) However, they are proud of their strength and endurance and feel (good/well) about their work.

17b   Comparatives and Superlatives

The **comparative** form of an adjective or adverb compares two people or things. Adjectives and adverbs form the comparative with *-er* or *more*. The **superlative** form of an adjective or adverb compares more than two things. Adjectives and adverbs form the superlative with *-est* or *most*.

ADJECTIVES	This film is <u>dull</u> and <u>predictable</u>.
COMPARATIVE	The film I saw last week was even <u>duller</u> and <u>more predictable</u> than this one.
SUPERLATIVE	The film I saw last night was the <u>dullest</u> and <u>most predictable</u> one I've ever seen.
ADVERBS	For a beginner, Jane did needlepoint <u>skillfully</u>.
COMPARATIVE	After she had watched the demonstration, Jane did needlepoint <u>more skillfully</u> than Rosie.
SUPERLATIVE	Of the twelve beginners, Jane did needlepoint the <u>most skillfully</u>.

Forming Comparatives and Superlatives

Adjectives

- One-syllable adjectives generally form the comparative with *-er* and the superlative with *–est*.

    great   greater   greatest

- Adjectives with two or more syllables form the comparative with *more* and the superlative with *most*.

    wonderful   more wonderful   most wonderful

    Exception: Two-syllable adjectives ending in *-y* add *-er* or *-est* after changing the *-y* to an *–i*.

    funny   funnier   funniest

Adverbs

- All adverbs ending in *-ly* form the comparative with *more* and the superlative with *most*.

    efficiently   more efficiently   most efficiently

- Some other adverbs form the comparative with *-er* and the superlative with *–est*.

    soon   sooner   soonest

Solving Special Problems with Comparatives and Superlatives

The following rules will help you avoid errors with comparatives and superlatives.

- Never use both *-er* and *more* to form the comparative or both *-est* and *most* to form the superlative.

    Nothing could have been more awful. (not *more awfuller*)

    Space Mountain is the most frightening (not *most frighteningest*) ride at Disney World.

- Never use the superlative when you are comparing only two things.

    This is the more serious (not *most serious*) of the two problems.

- Never use the comparative when you are comparing more than two things.

    This is the worst (not *worse*) day of my life.

PRACTICE 17-3 Fill in the correct comparative form of the word supplied in parentheses.

Example: Children tend to be noisier (noisy) than adults.

1. Traffic always moves _____ (slow) during rush hour than late at night.

2. The weather report says temperatures will be _____ (cold) tomorrow.

3. Some elderly people are _____ (healthy) than younger people.

4. It has been proven that pigs are _____ (intelligent) than dogs.

5. When someone asks you to repeat yourself, you usually answer _____ (loud).

6. The _____ (tall) of the two buildings was damaged by the earthquake.

7. They want to teach their son to be _____ (respectful) of women than many young men are.

8. Las Vegas is _____ (famous) for its casinos than for its natural resources.

9. The WaterDrop is _____ (wild) than any other ride in the amusement park.

10. You must walk _____ (quick) if you expect to catch the bus.

> **READING TIP**
>
> When you come across an unfamiliar word, such as *empowered*, take a few minutes to study the words, phrases, and sentences surrounding the unfamiliar word. These **context clues** can help you to figure out the meaning of the unfamiliar word.

PRACTICE 17-4

Fill in the correct superlative form of the word supplied in parentheses.

Example: The first remote controls came with only the *most expensive* (expensive) televisions.

(1) The invention of the remote control in the 1950s was one of the _____ (important) developments in television history. (2) The remote was especially welcomed by lazy viewers, who were the _____ (empowered) by the new device. (3) Even the _____ (lazy) people could now change channels without getting off the couch. (4) However, as remote controls developed, even the _____ (simple) devices could sometimes confuse the _____ (skilled) users. (5) The large number of buttons became one of the _____ (irritating) features. (6) Even today, remotes remain one of the _____ (unnecessarily) complicated of our modern electronic devices. (7) According to one critic, the TV remote is one of the _____ (poorly) designed inventions of all time. (8) Improving the remote is one of the _____ (challenging) projects inventors face. (9) Already, the _____ (innovative) companies are adding voice and motion control to the _____ (late) remotes. (10) One of

the _____ (astonishing) possible new developments may be a remote control operated entirely by the viewer's mind.

FYI

Good/Well and Bad/Badly

Most adjectives and adverbs form the comparative with *-er* or *more* and the superlative with *-est* or *most*. The adjectives *good* and *bad* and their adverb forms *well* and *badly* are exceptions.

ADJECTIVE	COMPARATIVE FORM	SUPERLATIVE FORM
good	better	best
bad	worse	worst

ADVERB	COMPARATIVE FORM	SUPERLATIVE FORM
well	better	best
badly	worse	worst

PRACTICE 17-5

Fill in the correct comparative or superlative form of *good*, *well*, *bad*, or *badly*.

Example: My sister is a *better* (good) runner than I am.

1. Neela was certain she was the _____ (good) chef in the competition.
2. Because he studied more, Helio earned _____ (good) grades than his sister.
3. An optimist, Mara always thinks she will do _____ (well) next time.
4. Many people drive the _____ (badly) when they are in a hurry.
5. Of all the mortgage companies Ramon researched, Plains Bank had the _____ (good) interest rate.
6. I feel bad when I get rejected, but I feel _____ (bad) when I do not try.
7. For nontraditional students, access to education is _____ (good) than it used to be.
8. Jamie sings badly, but Simon sings _____ (badly).
9. I learn the _____ (well) when I am not distracted.
10. After looking at every painting in the gallery, they decided that the landscapes were definitely the _____ (bad) paintings there.

CHAPTER REVIEW

EDITING PRACTICE

> **READING TIP**
>
> In this student essay, the main idea is not immediately apparent. To identify the main idea of an essay like this one, ask yourself what point the writer is trying to make.

Read the following student essay, which includes errors in the use of adjectives and adverbs. Make any changes necessary to correct adjectives incorrectly used for adverbs and adverbs incorrectly used for adjectives. Also, correct any errors in the use of comparatives and superlatives and in the use of demonstrative adjectives. Finally, try to add some adjectives and adverbs that you feel would make the writer's ideas clearer or more specific. The first sentence has been edited for you.

Starting Over

A wedding can be the ~~joyfullest~~ *most joyful* occasion in two people's lives, the beginning of a couple's ~~most~~ happiest years. For some unlucky women, however, a wedding can be the worse thing that ever happens; it is the beginning not of their happiness but of their battered lives. As I went through the joyful day of my wedding, I wanted bad to find happiness for the rest of my life, but what I hoped and wished for did not come true.

I was married in the savannah belt of the Sudan in the eastern part of Africa, where I grew up. I was barely twenty-two years old. The first two years of my marriage progressed peaceful, but problems started as soon as our first child was born.

Many American women say, "If my husband hit me just once, that would be it. I'd leave." But those modern attitude does not work in cultures where tradition has overshadowed women's rights and divorce is not accepted. All women can do is accept their sadly fate.

Battered women give many reasons for staying in their abusive marriages, but fear is the commonest. Fear immobilizes these women, ruling their decisions, their actions, and their very lives. This is how it was for me.

Of course, I was real afraid whenever my husband hit me. I would run to my mother's house and cry, but she would always talk me into going back and being more patiently with my husband. Our tradition discourages divorce, and wife-beating is taken for granted. The situation is really quite ironic: The religion I practice sets harsh punishments for abusive husbands, but tradition has so overpowered religion that the laws do not really work very good.

One night, I asked myself whether life had treated me fair. True, I had a high school diploma and two of the beautifullest children in the world, but all this was not enough. I realized that to stand up to the husband who treated me so bad, I would have to achieve a more better education than he had. That night, I decided to get a college education in the United States. My husband strongly opposed my decision, but with the support of my father and mother, I was able to begin to change my life. My years as a student and single parent in the United States have been real difficult for me, but I know I made the right choice.

Review Checklist

Adjectives and Adverbs

✔ Adjectives modify nouns or pronouns. (See 17a.)

✔ Demonstrative adjectives—*this*, *that*, *these*, and *those*—identify particular nouns. (See 17a.)

✔ Adverbs modify verbs, adjectives, or other adverbs. (See 17a.)

✔ To compare two people or things, use the comparative form of an adjective or adverb. To compare more than two people or things, use the superlative form of an adjective or adverb. (See 17b.)

✔ The adjectives *good* and *bad* and their adverb forms *well* and *badly* have irregular comparative and superlative forms. (See 17b.)

18 Writing Simple, Compound, and Complex Sentences

Simple Sentences

A **sentence** is a group of words that expresses a complete thought. Every sentence includes both a subject and a verb. A **simple sentence** consists of a single **independent clause**: one <u>subject</u> and one <u>verb</u>.

<u>Chase Utley</u> <u>plays</u> baseball.

 ### 18a Identifying Subjects in Simple Sentences

Every sentence includes a subject. The **subject** of a sentence tells who or what is being talked about in the sentence. Without a subject, a sentence is not complete. In the following three sentences, the subject is underlined:

<u>Derek Walcott</u> won the Nobel Prize in Literature.

<u>He</u> was born in St. Lucia.

<u>St. Lucia</u> is an island in the Caribbean.

The subject of a sentence can be a noun or a pronoun. A **noun** names a person, place, or thing—*Derek Walcott, St. Lucia*. A **pronoun** takes the place of a noun—*I, you, he, she, it, we, they*, and so on.

The subject of a sentence can be *singular or plural*. A **singular subject** is one person, place, or thing (*Derek Walcott, St. Lucia, he*).

A **plural subject** is more than one person, place, or thing (*poets, people, they*).

<u>Readers</u> admire Walcott's poems.

430

A plural subject that joins two subjects with *and* is called a **compound subject**.

<u>St. Lucia and Trinidad</u> are Caribbean islands.

PRACTICE 18-1

Underline the subject in each sentence. Then, write *S* above singular subjects and *P* above plural subjects. Remember, compound subjects are plural.

Example: <u>Renewable energy sources</u> [P] are being developed to replace fossil fuels.

1. For years, <u>fossil fuels</u> have been the main source of energy around the world.

2. <u>Fossil fuels</u>, such as coal, oil, and natural gas, are nonrenewable.

3. In other words, <u>they</u> are not replenished after each use.

4. In contrast, <u>the sun and wind</u> are renewable energy sources.

5. <u>The sun's energy</u> can be collected through solar panels and converted into electricity.

6. <u>Solar power</u> can produce electricity without being connected to a grid.

7. <u>Structures</u> called turbines capture the wind's energy and convert it into electricity.

8. <u>Wind turbines</u> must be located in areas with strong and consistent winds.

9. <u>Other renewable energy sources</u> include hydropower, biomass, and geothermal energy.

10. Despite some obstacles, <u>renewable energy</u> will play an important role in the future.

18b Identifying Prepositional Phrases in Simple Sentences

A **prepositional phrase** consists of a **preposition** (a word such as *on, to, in,* or *with*) and its **object** (the noun or pronoun it introduces).

PREPOSITION	+	OBJECT	=	PREPOSITIONAL PHRASE
on		the stage		on the stage
to		Nia's house		to Nia's house
in		my new car		in my new car
with		them		with them

Because the object of a preposition is a noun or a pronoun, it may seem to be the subject of a sentence. However, the object of a preposition is never the subject of a sentence. To identify a sentence's true subject, cross out each prepositional phrase. (Remember, every prepositional phrase is introduced by a preposition.)

<u>SUBJECT</u>   PREP PHRASE
The <u>cost</u> ~~of the repairs~~ was astronomical.

PREP PHRASE   PREP PHRASE   SUBJECT
~~At the end of the novel~~, ~~after an exciting chase~~, the <u>lovers</u> flee
PREP PHRASE
~~to Mexico~~.

Frequently Used Prepositions

about	before	except	on	underneath
above	behind	for	onto	until
across	below	from	out	up
after	beneath	in	outside	upon
against	beside	inside	over	with
along	between	into	through	within
among	beyond	like	throughout	without
around	by	near	to	
as	despite	of	toward	
at	during	off	under	

PRACTICE 18-2

Each of the following sentences includes at least one prepositional phrase. To identify each sentence's subject, cross out each prepositional phrase. Then, underline the subject of the sentence.

Example: <u>Bicycling</u> ~~on busy city streets~~ can be dangerous.

(1) In many American cities, cyclists are concerned about sharing the road with cars. (2) For this reason, people are becoming more interested in "green" lanes. (3) These bike lanes are different from traditional bike lanes

in one important way. (4) Green lanes are separated from the road by curbs, planters, or parked cars. (5) For years, people in Europe have been creating and using these protected bike lanes. (6) Until recently, however, few green lanes were created in the United States. (7) Now, with the help of the Bikes Belong Foundation and the Federal Highway Administration, several U.S. cities are installing green lanes. (8) For their supporters, these bike lanes are a positive step toward healthier, safer cities. (9) However, some critics worry about reduced space for traffic lanes and parking. (10) Still, despite the criticism, green lanes are increasing the number of bike riders and reducing the number of bike accidents.

18c Identifying Verbs in Simple Sentences

In addition to its subject, every sentence also includes a verb. This **verb** (also called a **predicate**) tells what the subject does or connects the subject to words that describe or rename it. Without a verb, a sentence is not complete.

Action Verbs

An **action verb** tells what the subject does, did, or will do.

> Venus Williams <u>plays</u> tennis.
>
> Amelia Earhart <u>flew</u> across the Atlantic.
>
> Todd <u>will drive</u> to Tampa on Friday.

Action verbs can also show mental and emotional actions.

> Travis always <u>worries</u> about his job.

Sometimes the subject of a sentence performs more than one action. In this case, the sentence includes two or more action verbs that form a **compound predicate**.

> He <u>hit</u> the ball, <u>threw</u> down his bat, and <u>ran</u> toward first base.

PRACTICE 18-3

In the following sentences, underline each action verb twice. Some sentences contain more than one action verb.

Example: Invasive species <u>cause</u> billions of dollars in damage every year.

1. Invasive plant species <u>include</u> weeds as well as flowering plants, shrubs, trees, and vines.
2. Invasive plants <u>thrive</u> outside their native range.
3. These plants <u>tolerate</u> many soil types and weather conditions.
4. They <u>grow</u> rapidly and <u>spread</u> easily, usually by wind, water, or animals.
5. They <u>outcompete</u> native species for food, sunlight, soil, and space.
6. Typically, human actions <u>introduce</u> an invasive plant species to a habitat.
7. People often <u>choose</u> these plants because of their unique qualities.
8. For instance, Americans first <u>imported</u> Japanese honeysuckle and kudzu for erosion control.
9. Unfortunately, these invasive vines <u>smother</u>, <u>strangle</u>, and <u>kill</u> other vegetation.
10. Invasive plants <u>harm</u> the environment, the economy, and even human health.

Linking Verbs

A **linking verb** does not show action. Instead, it connects the subject to a word or words that describe or rename it. The linking verb tells what the subject is (or what it was, will be, or seems to be).

A *googolplex* <u>is</u> an extremely large number.

Many linking verbs, like *is*, are forms of the verb *be*. Other linking verbs refer to the senses (*look, feel,* and so on).

The photocopy <u>looks</u> blurry.

Some students <u>feel</u> anxious about the future.

Frequently Used Linking Verbs

act	feel	seem
appear	get	smell
be (am, is, are, was, were)	grow	sound
	look	taste
become	remain	turn

PRACTICE 18-4

In each of the following sentences, underline every verb twice. Remember that a verb can be an action verb or a linking verb.

Example: Airplane pilots and investment bankers <u>use</u> checklists.

(1) In *The Checklist Manifesto*, surgeon Atul Gawande argues for using checklists in operating rooms. (2) Gawande reminds readers of the complexity of modern medicine. (3) Currently, there are 6,000 drugs and 4,000 medical and surgical procedures. (4) Each year, the number of drugs and procedures increases. (5) As a result, even knowledgeable and highly trained surgeons make mistakes. (6) For some types of patients, the error rate is very high. (7) For example, doctors deliver inappropriate care to 40 percent of patients with coronary artery disease. (8) Luckily, checklists make a big difference for these and other patients. (9) In fact, checklists reduce complications by more than one-third. (10) It is hard to imagine an argument against such a simple and effective tool.

> **READING TIP**
> This paragraph includes a number of transitional words and phrases, which help provide clarity and show the relationships between ideas. Identify at least six transitional words and phrases in this paragraph.

Helping Verbs

Many verbs consist of more than one word. For example, the verb in the following sentence consists of two words:

Minh <u>must make</u> a decision about his future.

In this sentence, *make* is the **main verb**, and *must* is a **helping verb**.

Frequently Used Helping Verbs

does	was	must	should
did	were	can	would
do		could	will
is	have	may	
are	has	might	
am	had		

A sentence's **complete verb** is made up of a main verb plus any helping verbs that accompany it. In the following sentences, the complete verb is underlined twice, and the helping verbs are checkmarked.

Minh should have gone earlier.

Did Minh ask the right questions?

Minh will work hard.

Minh can really succeed.

FYI

Helping Verbs with Participles

Participles, such as *going* and *gone*, cannot stand alone as main verbs in a sentence. They need a helping verb to make them complete.

INCORRECT	Minh going to the library.
CORRECT	Minh is going to the library.
INCORRECT	Minh gone to the library.
CORRECT	Minh has gone to the library.

PRACTICE 18-5

The verbs in the sentences that follow consist of a main verb and one or more helping verbs. In each sentence, underline the complete verb twice, and put a check mark above each helping verb.

Example: In 1954, the Salk polio vaccine was given to more than a million schoolchildren.

(1) By the 1950s, polio had become a serious problem throughout the United States. (2) For years, it had puzzled doctors and researchers. (3) Thousands had become ill each year in the United States alone. (4) Children should have been playing happily. (5) Instead, they would get very sick. (6) Polio was sometimes called infantile paralysis. (7) In fact, it did cause paralysis in children and in adults as well. (8) Some patients could breathe only with the help of machines called iron lungs. (9) Others would remain in wheelchairs for life. (10) By 1960, Jonas Salk's vaccine had reduced the incidence of polio in the United States by more than 90 percent.

Compound Sentences

As you have seen, the most basic kind of sentence, a **simple sentence**, consists of a single **independent clause**: one subject and one verb.

Many European immigrants arrived at Ellis Island.

A **compound sentence** is made up of two or more simple sentences (independent clauses).

18d Forming Compound Sentences with Coordinating Conjunctions

One way to create a compound sentence is by joining two independent clauses with a **coordinating conjunction** preceded by a comma.

Many European immigrants arrived at Ellis Island, but many Asian immigrants arrived at Angel Island.

Coordinating Conjunctions			
and	for	or	yet
but	nor	so	

WORD POWER

coordinate (verb) to link two or more things that are equal in importance, rank, or degree

> **FYI**
>
> Use the letters that spell *FANBOYS* to help you remember the coordinating conjunctions:
>
> | | |
> |---|---|
> | F | for |
> | A | and |
> | N | nor |
> | B | but |
> | O | or |
> | Y | yet |
> | S | so |

Coordinating conjunctions join two ideas of equal importance. They describe the relationship between two ideas, showing how and why the ideas are related. Different coordinating conjunctions have different meanings.

- To indicate addition, use *and*.

    He acts like a child, <u>and</u> people think he is cute.

- To indicate contrast or contradiction, use *but* or *yet*.

    He acts like a child, <u>but</u> he is an adult.

    He acts like a child, <u>yet</u> he wants to be taken seriously.

- To indicate a cause-and-effect relationship, use *so* or *for*.

    He acts like a child, <u>so</u> we treat him like one.

    He acts like a child, <u>for</u> he needs attention.

- To present alternatives, use *or*.

    He acts like a child, <u>or</u> he is ignored.

- To eliminate alternatives, use *nor*.

    He does not act like a child, <u>nor</u> does he look like one.

> **FYI**
>
> **Commas with Coordinating Conjunctions**
>
> When you use a coordinating conjunction to join two independent clauses into a single compound sentence, always put a comma before the coordinating conjunction.
>
> We can stand in line all night, or we can go home now.

PRACTICE 18-6

Join each of the following pairs of independent clauses with a coordinating conjunction. Be sure to place a comma before the coordinating conjunction.

Example: A computer makes drafting essays easier/ It also makes revision easier. *(, and it)*

1. Training a dog to heel is difficult. Dogs naturally resist strict control from their owners.

2. A bodhran is an Irish drum. It is played with a wooden stick.

3. Students should spend two hours studying for each hour in class. They may not do well in the course.

4. Years ago, students wrote their lessons on slates. The teacher was able to correct each student's work individually.

5. Each state in the United States has two senators. The number of representatives in Congress depends on a state's population.

6. In 1973, only 2.5 percent of those in the U.S. military were women. Today, that percentage has increased to almost 20 percent.

7. A small craft advisory warns boaters of bad weather conditions. These conditions can be dangerous to small boats.

8. A DVD looks just like a CD. It can hold fifteen times as much information.

9. Hip-hop fashions include sneakers and baggy pants. These styles are still very popular among some young men.

10. Multiple births have become more and more common. Even some septuplets and octuplets now survive.

PRACTICE 18-7

Add coordinating conjunctions to combine some of the simple sentences in the following paragraph. Remember to put a comma before each coordinating conjunction you add.

Example: Years ago, few Americans lived to be one hundred/ ~~Today~~, there are over 70,000 centenarians. *(, but today,)*

(1) Diet, exercise, and family history may explain centenarians' long lives. (2) This is not the whole story. (3) A recent study showed surprising

similarities among centenarians. (4) They did not all avoid tobacco and alcohol. (5) They did not have low-fat diets. (6) In fact, they ate relatively large amounts of fat, cholesterol, and sugar. (7) Diet could not explain their long lives. (8) They did, however, share four key traits. (9) First, all the centenarians were optimistic about life. (10) All were positive thinkers. (11) They also had deep religious faith. (12) In addition, they had all continued to lead physically active lives. (13) They remained mobile even as elderly people. (14) Finally, all were able to adapt to loss. (15) They had all lost friends, spouses, or children. (16) They were able to get on with their lives.

18e Forming Compound Sentences with Semicolons

Another way to create a compound sentence is by joining two simple sentences (independent clauses) with a **semicolon**. A semicolon connects clauses whose ideas are closely related.

> The AIDS Memorial Quilt contains thousands of panels; each panel represents a life lost to AIDS.

Also use a semicolon to show a strong contrast between two ideas.

> With new drugs, people can live with AIDS for years; many people, however, cannot get these drugs.

FYI

Avoiding Fragments

A semicolon can only join two complete sentences (independent clauses). A semicolon cannot join a sentence and a fragment:

INCORRECT — FRAGMENT — Because millions worldwide are still dying of AIDS; more research is needed.

CORRECT — SENTENCE — Millions worldwide are still dying of AIDS; more research is needed.

Forming Compound Sentences with Semicolons **18e** 441

PRACTICE 18-8

Each of the following items consists of one simple sentence. Create a compound sentence for each item by changing the period to a semicolon and then adding another simple sentence.

Example: My brother is addicted to fast food**/ ; he eats it every day.**

1. Fast-food restaurants are an American institution. _____
_____

2. Families often eat at these restaurants. _____
_____

3. Many teenagers work there. _____
_____

4. McDonald's, Burger King, and Wendy's are known for their hamburgers.
_____

5. KFC is famous for its fried chicken. _____
_____

6. Taco Bell serves Mexican-style food. _____
_____

7. Pizza Hut specializes in pizza. _____
_____

8. Subway restaurants promote their healthy options. _____
_____

9. Some offer recyclable packaging. _____
_____

10. Some even have playgrounds. _____
_____

18f Forming Compound Sentences with Transitional Words and Phrases

Another way to create a compound sentence is by combining two simple sentences (independent clauses) with a **transitional word or phrase**. When you use a transitional word or phrase to join two sentences, always place a semicolon *before* the transitional word or phrase and a comma *after* it.

Some college students receive grants; in addition, they often have to take out loans.

He had a miserable time at the party; besides, he lost his wallet.

Frequently Used Transitional Words

also	instead	still
besides	later	subsequently
consequently	meanwhile	then
eventually	moreover	therefore
finally	nevertheless	thus
furthermore	now	
however	otherwise	

Frequently Used Transitional Phrases

after all	in comparison
as a result	in contrast
at the same time	in fact
for example	in other words
for instance	of course
in addition	on the contrary

Adding a transitional word or phrase makes the connection between ideas in a sentence clearer and more precise than it would be if the ideas were linked with just a semicolon. Different transitional words and phrases convey different meanings.

Forming Compound Sentences with Transitional Words and Phrases   18f

- Some signal addition (*also, besides, furthermore, in addition, moreover,* and so on).

    I have a lot on my mind; <u>in addition</u>, I have a lot of things to do.

- Some make causal connections (*as a result, consequently, therefore, thus,* and so on).

    I have a lot on my mind; <u>therefore</u>, it is hard to concentrate.

- Some indicate contradiction or contrast (*however, in contrast, nevertheless, still,* and so on).

    I have a lot on my mind; <u>still</u>, I must try to relax.

- Some present alternatives (*instead, on the contrary, otherwise,* and so on).

    I have a lot on my mind; <u>otherwise</u>, I could relax.

    I will try not to think; <u>instead</u>, I will relax.

- Some indicate time sequence (*at the same time, eventually, finally, later, meanwhile, now, subsequently, then,* and so on).

    I have a lot on my mind; <u>meanwhile</u>, I still have work to do.

PRACTICE 18-9

Consulting the lists of transitional words and phrases on page 442, choose a word or phrase that logically connects each pair of simple sentences in the following paragraph into one compound sentence. Be sure to punctuate appropriately.

Example: Red-light cameras are used worldwide*;* however, ~~Some~~ some people believe these cameras should be illegal.

(1) Red-light cameras are a form of traffic enforcement. The cameras have proven to be controversial. (2) Cars trigger the camera. The camera photographs the car. (3) A law-enforcement official reviews the photos. The officer issues tickets to drivers who ran the red light. (4) The cameras enforce traffic rules. They should reduce the number of crashes. (5) Some say the cameras are not a safety feature. They primarily increase revenue. (6) Opponents are concerned about danger. Drivers may stop to avoid

> **READING TIP**
>
> This passage provides a number of supporting details about red-light cameras. Considering the types of supporting details provided, what do you think is the author's purpose (to inform, to explain, or to persuade) in this passage?

running a red light. (7) Some people are concerned about the pictures. They think the cameras violate their privacy. (8) The risks and rewards of red-light cameras are not necessarily clear. Several states have banned their use. (9) The red-light camera controversy will likely continue for years to come. It is every driver's responsibility to drive safely. (10) Drivers should obey traffic rules. Everyone should want safe roads.

PRACTICE 18-10

Using the specified transitional words and phrases, create two compound sentences for each of the topics listed below. Be sure to punctuate appropriately.

Example
Topic: gluten-free menu items
Transitional phrases: for example; moreover

Many restaurants now offer gluten-free menu items; for example, they provide main courses and desserts that use rice, corn, and tapioca instead of wheat or barley. Consumer demand from people with gluten allergies seems to have prompted this change; moreover, there is a growing belief that less gluten is better for everyone.

1. *Topic:* male nurses
   Transitional phrases: in addition; after all

   _____

   _____

2. *Topic:* gay couples as adoptive parents
   Transitional words: however; now

   _____

   _____

3. *Topic:* dangerous high-school sports
   Transitional words: also; consequently

   _____

   _____

Complex Sentences

As you learned earlier in this chapter, an **independent clause** can stand alone as a sentence.

INDEPENDENT CLAUSE   The museum exhibit was controversial.

However, a **dependent clause** cannot stand alone as a sentence.

DEPENDENT CLAUSE   Because the exhibit was controversial

What happened because the exhibit was controversial? To answer this question, you need to add an independent clause that completes the idea begun in the dependent clause. The result is a **complex sentence**—a sentence that consists of one independent clause and one or more dependent clauses.

COMPLEX SENTENCE
DEPENDENT CLAUSE: Because the exhibit was controversial, many
INDEPENDENT CLAUSE: people came to see it.

18g Forming Complex Sentences with Subordinating Conjunctions

One way to form a complex sentence is to use a **subordinating conjunction**—a word such as *although* or *because*—to join two simple sentences (independent clauses). When the subordinating conjunction is added to the beginning of the simple sentence, the sentence becomes dependent for its meaning on the other simple sentence.

> **WORD POWER**
>
> **subordinate** (adj) lower in rank or position; secondary in importance

TWO SIMPLE SENTENCES   Muhammad Ali was stripped of his heavyweight title for refusing to go into the army. Many people admired his antiwar position.

COMPLEX SENTENCE   DEPENDENT CLAUSE: Although Muhammad Ali was stripped of his heavyweight title for refusing to go into the army, many people admired his antiwar position.

Frequently Used Subordinating Conjunctions

after	even though	since	whenever
although	if	so that	where
as	if only	than	whereas
as if	in order that	that	wherever
as though	now that	though	whether
because	once	unless	while
before	provided that	until	
even if	rather than	when	

As the chart below shows, different subordinating conjunctions express different relationships between dependent and independent clauses.

RELATIONSHIP BETWEEN CLAUSES	SUBORDINATING CONJUNCTION	EXAMPLE
Time	after, before, since, until, when, whenever, while	<u>When the whale surfaced</u>, Ahab threw his harpoon.
Reason or cause	as, because	Scientists scaled back the project <u>because the government cut funds</u>.
Result or effect	in order that, so that	<u>So that students' math scores will improve</u>, many schools have begun special programs.
Condition	even if, if, unless	The rain forest may disappear <u>unless steps are taken immediately</u>.
Contrast	although, even though, though	<u>Although Thomas Edison had almost no formal education</u>, he was a successful inventor.
Location	where, wherever	Pittsburgh was built <u>where the Allegheny and Monongahela Rivers meet</u>.

> **FYI**
>
> **Punctuating with Subordinating Conjunctions**
>
> In a complex sentence, use a comma after the dependent clause.
>
>   DEPENDENT CLAUSE   INDEPENDENT CLAUSE
>
> Although she wore the scarlet letter, Hester carried herself proudly.
>
> Do not use a comma after the independent clause.
>
>   INDEPENDENT CLAUSE   DEPENDENT CLAUSE
>
> Hester carried herself proudly although she wore the scarlet letter.

PRACTICE 18-11

Combine each of the following pairs of sentences to create one complex sentence. Use a subordinating conjunction from the list on page 446 to indicate the relationship between the dependent and independent clauses in each sentence. Make sure you include a comma where one is required.

> **Example:** Orville and Wilbur Wright built the first powered plane/
>   *although they*
> ~~They~~ had no formal training as engineers.

1. Professional midwives are used widely in Europe. In the United States, they usually practice only in areas with few doctors.

2. John Deere constructed his first steel plow in 1837. A new era began in farming.

3. Stephen Crane describes battles in *The Red Badge of Courage*. He never experienced war.

4. Elvis Presley died in 1977. Thousands of his fans gathered in front of his mansion.

5. The salaries of baseball players rose in the 1980s. Some sportswriters predicted a drop in attendance at games.

18h Forming Complex Sentences with Relative Pronouns

Another way to form a complex sentence is to use **relative pronouns** (*who, that, which,* and so on) to join two simple sentences (independent clauses).

TWO SIMPLE SENTENCES	Harry Potter is an adolescent wizard. He attends Hogwarts School of Witchcraft and Wizardry.
COMPLEX SENTENCE	Harry Potter, who attends Hogwarts School of Witchcraft and Wizardry, is an adolescent wizard.

Note: The relative pronoun always refers to a word or words in the independent clause. (In the complex sentence above, *who* refers to *Harry Potter*.)

Relative Pronouns

that	which	whoever	whomever
what	who	whom	whose

Relative pronouns indicate the relationships between the ideas in the independent and dependent clauses they link.

TWO SIMPLE SENTENCES	Nadine Gordimer lived in South Africa. She won the Nobel Prize in Literature in 1991.
COMPLEX SENTENCE	Nadine Gordimer, who won the Nobel Prize in Literature in 1991, lived in South Africa.
TWO SIMPLE SENTENCES	Last week I had a job interview. It went very well.
COMPLEX SENTENCE	Last week I had a job interview that went very well.
TWO SIMPLE SENTENCES	Transistors have replaced vacuum tubes in radios and televisions. They were invented in 1948.
COMPLEX SENTENCE	Transistors, which were invented in 1948, have replaced vacuum tubes in radios and televisions.

PRACTICE 18-12

In each of the following complex sentences, underline the dependent clause once, and underline the relative pronoun twice. Then, draw an arrow from the relative pronoun to the word or words to which it refers.

Example: Research shows that vampire legends, <u><u>which</u> you may have thought were fiction</u>, have some truth to them.

1. Vampires, which were thought to be terrifying but imaginary, have been proven to be "real."

2. Recently released research debunks the myth that vampires are only found in fiction.

3. These vampires did not suck anyone's blood, which is important to note, or return from the dead.

4. Vampire rumors, which began when a person died, started because close family members often died at the same time.

5. Fear quickly turned into panic that inspired the vampire folklore.

6. People assumed that the deceased, who were returning as vampires, wanted to consume the blood of their family members.

7. The real issue, which many people did not understand at the time, was germs.

8. Poor hygiene, which came from a lack of basic health knowledge, led to diseases that spread quickly.

9. Doctors, who were limited by the knowledge of the era, thought that exhuming the bodies and removing the heart of the deceased was the only way to prevent the rise of vampires.

10. Researchers, who are still discovering "real" vampire stories, now know that the vampire myth began with misinformation.

FYI

Forming Compound-Complex Sentences

A **compound-complex sentence** combines two or more independent clauses with one or more dependent clauses.

When students enter college, they often find it hard to adjust, but they become more confident by the end of their first year.

CHAPTER REVIEW

EDITING PRACTICE

Read the following student essay. Then, revise it by combining pairs of simple sentences to create compound or complex sentences. Create compound sentences by using a coordinating conjunction, a semicolon, or a transitional word or phrase. Create complex sentences by using subordinating conjunctions or relative pronouns that indicate the relationship between the two simple sentences. Be sure to punctuate correctly. The first two sentences have been combined for you.

> **READING TIP**
> In this student essay, the writer's tone (emotion and feeling) is emphasized through specific word choices. How would you describe the writer's tone? Identify several words that help you determine the tone.

Community Art

When a ~~A~~ city has a crime problem, ~~The~~ the police and the courts try to solve it. Some cities have come up with creative ways to help young people stay out of trouble. One example is the Philadelphia Mural Arts Program. It offers free art education for high school students.

In the 1960s, Philadelphia had a serious problem. The problem was graffiti. Graffiti artists had painted on buildings all over the city. A solution to the problem was the Philadelphia Anti-Graffiti Network, which offered graffiti artists an alternative. The artists would give up painting graffiti. They would not be prosecuted for defacing buildings. The artists enjoyed painting. They could paint murals on public buildings instead. They could create beautiful landscapes, portraits of local heroes, and abstract designs. The graffiti artists had once been lawbreakers. They could now help beautify the city.

The Mural Arts Program began in 1984 as a part of the Philadelphia Anti-Graffiti Network. By 1996, the Philadelphia Anti-Graffiti Network was focusing on eliminating graffiti. Its Mural Arts Program was working to improve the community. It no longer worked with graffiti offenders. It ran after-school and summer programs for students. The Mural Arts Program gained national recognition in 1997. That is when President Bill Clinton helped paint a mural. Now, because of the Mural Arts Program's success, Philadelphia is known as the "City of Murals."

Over 20,000 students have taken part in the Mural Arts Program. The students come from all parts of the city. Sometimes students work alongside professional artists. They get to paint parts of the artists' murals themselves. The artwork is on public buildings. It can be seen by everyone.

The Mural Arts Program continues to build a brighter future for students and their communities. It is now over a quarter of a century old. Students help bring people together to create a mural. They feel a stronger connection to their community and more confidence in themselves. They leave the program. They are equipped to make a positive difference in their communities and in their own lives.

Review checklist

Writing Simple, Compound, and Complex Sentences

✔ Every sentence expresses a complete thought and includes a subject and a verb. A **simple sentence** consists of a single independent clause: one subject and one verb. (See Simple Sentences on page 430).

✔ The subject of a sentence tells who or what is being talked about. (See 18a.)

✔ A prepositional phrase consists of a preposition and its object (the noun or pronoun it introduces). The object of a preposition cannot be the subject of the sentence. (See 18b.)

✔ An action verb tells what the subject does, did, or will do. (See 18c.)

✔ A linking verb connects the subject to a word or words that describe or rename it. (See 18c.)

✔ Many verbs are made up of more than one word. The complete verb in a sentence includes the main verb plus any helping verbs. (See 18c.)

(Continued)

Chapter Review

(*Continued from previous page*)

✔ A **compound sentence** is made up of two simple sentences (independent clauses.) (See Compound Sentences on page 437.)

✔ A coordinating conjunction—*and, but, for, nor, or, so,* or *yet*—can join two independent clauses into one compound sentence. A comma always comes before the coordinating conjunction. (See 18d.)

✔ A semicolon can join two independent clauses into one compound sentence. (See 18e.)

✔ A transitional word or phrase can also join two independent clauses into one compound sentence. When it joins two independent clauses, a transitional word or phrase is always preceded by a semicolon and followed by a comma. (See 18f.)

✔ A **complex sentence** consists of one independent clause (simple sentence) combined with one or more dependent clauses. (See Complex Sentences on page 445.)

✔ Subordinating conjunctions—dependent words such as *although, after, when, while,* and *because*—can join two independent clauses into one complex sentence. (See 18g.)

✔ Relative pronouns—dependent words such as *who, which,* and *that*—can also join two independent clauses into one complex sentence. The relative pronoun shows the relationship between the ideas in the two independent clauses that it links. (See 18h.)

✔ A **compound-complex sentence** consists of two or more independent clauses and one or more dependent clauses. (See FYI: Forming Compound-Complex Sentences on page 449.)

19 Writing Varied Sentences

Sentence variety is important because a paragraph of varied sentences flows more smoothly, is easier to read and understand, and is more interesting than one in which all the sentences are structured in the same way.

19a Varying Sentence Types

Most English sentences are **statements**. Others are **questions** or **exclamations**. One way to vary your sentences is to use an occasional question or exclamation where it is appropriate.

In the following paragraph, a question and an exclamation add variety:

> Jacqueline Cochran, the first woman pilot to break the sound barrier, was one of the most important figures in aviation history. In 1996, the United States Postal Service issued a stamp honoring Cochran; the words "Pioneer Pilot" appear under her name. <u>What did she do to earn this title and this tribute?</u> Cochran broke more flight records than anyone else in her lifetime and won many awards, including the United States Distinguished Service Medal in 1945 and the United States Air Force Distinguished Flying Cross in 1969. During World War II, she helped form the WASPs, the Women's Air Force Service Pilots program, so that women could fly military planes to their bases (even though they were not allowed to go into combat). Remarkably, she accomplished all this with only three weeks of flying instruction. She only got her pilot's license in the first place because she wanted to start her own cosmetics business and flying would enable her to travel quickly around the country. Although she never planned to be a pilot, once she discovered flying she quickly became the best. <u>Not surprisingly, when the Postal Service honored Jacqueline Cochran, it was with an airmail stamp!</u>

Question (marginal note for underlined question)

Exclamation (marginal note for underlined exclamation)

PRACTICE 19-1

Revise the following paragraph by changing one of the statements into a question and one of the statements into an exclamation.

Example:

The cell phone may be making the wristwatch obsolete. (statement)

<u>Is the cell phone making the wristwatch obsolete? (question)</u>

(1) As cell phones and other small electronic devices become more common, fewer people are wearing watches. (2) Most cell phones, iPads, and MP3 players display the time. (3) Moreover, cell-phone clocks give very accurate time. (4) This is because they set themselves with satellite signals. (5) They also adjust automatically to time-zone changes. (6) Wristwatches cannot compete with these convenient features. (7) After all, unlike the newer devices, watches are not computers. (8) However, watches do remain appealing for other reasons. (9) For many people, they are fashion accessories or status symbols. (10) For some, watches are still essential for telling time.

19b Varying Sentence Openings

> **WORD POWER**
> **amphibians** cold-blooded vertebrates, such as frogs, that live both in the water and on land

When all the sentences in a paragraph begin the same way, your writing is likely to seem dull and repetitive. In the following paragraph, for example, every sentence begins with the subject:

> Scientists have been observing a disturbing phenomenon. The population of frogs, toads, and salamanders has been declining. This decline was first noticed in the mid-1980s. Some reports blamed chemical pollution. Some biologists began to suspect that a fungal disease was killing these amphibians. The most reasonable explanation seems to be that the amphibians' eggs are threatened by solar radiation. This radiation penetrates the thinned ozone layer, which used to shield them from the sun's rays.

Beginning with Adverbs

Instead of opening every sentence in a paragraph with the subject, you can try beginning some sentences with one or more **adverbs**.

Scientists have been observing a disturbing phenomenon. <u>Gradually but steadily</u>, the population of frogs, toads, and salamanders has been declining. This decline was first noticed in the mid-1980s. Some reports blamed chemical pollution. Some biologists began to suspect that a fungal disease was killing these amphibians. <u>However</u>, the most reasonable explanation seems to be that the amphibians' eggs are threatened by solar radiation. This radiation penetrates the thinned ozone layer, which used to shield them from the sun's rays.

PRACTICE

19-2 Underline the adverb in each of the following sentences, and then rewrite the sentence so that the adverb appears at the beginning. Be sure to punctuate correctly.

Example:

An internship is <u>usually</u> a work or service experience related to a student's career plans.

Usually, an internship is a work or service experience related to a student's career plans..

1. Internships are sometimes paid or counted for academic credit.

2. A prospective student intern should first talk to an academic adviser.

3. The student should next write a résumé listing job experience, education, and interests.

4. The student can then send the résumé to organizations that are looking for interns.

5. Going to job fairs and networking are often good ways to find internships.

Beginning with Prepositional Phrases

Another way to create sentence variety is to begin some sentences with prepositional phrases. A **prepositional phrase** (such as *along the river* or *near the diner*) is made up of a preposition and its object.

<u>In recent years</u>, scientists have observed a disturbing phenomenon. Gradually but steadily, the population of frogs, toads, and salamanders has been declining. This was first noticed in the mid-1980s. <u>At first</u>, some reports blamed chemical pollution. <u>After a while</u>, some biologists began to suspect that a fungal disease was killing them. However, the most reasonable explanation seems to be that the amphibians' eggs are threatened by solar radiation. This radiation penetrates the thinned ozone layer, which used to shield them from the sun's rays.

> **READING TIP**
>
> This paragraph includes a number of supporting details about José Julián Martí. What do these supporting details tell you about the writer's attitude toward Martí?

PRACTICE 19-3

Every sentence in the following paragraph begins with the subject, but several contain prepositional phrases or adverbs that could be moved to the beginning. To vary the sentence openings, move prepositional phrases to the beginnings of four sentences, and move adverbs to the beginnings of two other sentences. Be sure to place a comma after these introductory phrases.

Example: *By the end of the 1800s,* Spain ~~by the end of the 1800s~~ had lost most of its colonies.

(1) People in the Cuban American community often mention José Julián Martí as one of their heroes. (2) José Martí was born in Havana in 1853, at a time when Cuba was a colony of Spain. (3) He had started a newspaper demanding Cuban freedom by the time he was sixteen years old. (4) The Spanish authorities forced him to leave Cuba and go to Spain in 1870. (5) He published his first pamphlet calling for Cuban independence while in Spain, openly continuing his fight. (6) He then lived for fourteen years in New York City. (7) He started the journal of the Cuban Revolutionary Party during his time in New York. (8) Martí's essays and poems argued for Cuba's freedom and for the individual freedom of Cubans. (9) He died in battle against Spanish soldiers in Cuba, passionately following up his words with actions.

19c Combining Sentences

You can also create sentence variety by experimenting with different ways of combining sentences.

Using *-ing* Modifiers

A **modifier** identifies or describes other words in a sentence. You can use an *-ing* modifier to combine two sentences.

TWO SENTENCES	Duke Ellington composed more than a thousand songs. He worked hard to establish his reputation.
COMBINED WITH *-ING* MODIFIER	Composing more than a thousand songs, Duke Ellington worked hard to establish his reputation.

When the two sentences above are combined, the *-ing* modifier (*composing more than a thousand songs*) describes the new sentence's subject (*Duke Ellington*).

PRACTICE 19-4

Use an *-ing* modifier to combine each of the following pairs of sentences into a single sentence. Eliminate any unnecessary words, and place a comma after each *-ing* modifier.

Example: Many American colleges are setting an example for the rest of the country. They are going green.

Setting an example for the rest of the country, many American colleges are going green.

1. Special lamps in the dorms of one Ohio college change from green to red. They warn of rising energy use.

_____

_____

2. A Vermont college captures methane from dairy cows. It now needs less energy from other sources.

_____

_____

3. Student gardeners at a North Carolina college tend a campus vegetable plot. They supply the cafeteria with organic produce.

_____

_____

4. A building on a California campus proves that recycled materials can be beautiful. It is built from redwood wine casks.

_____

_____

5. Some colleges offer courses in sustainability. They are preparing students to take the green revolution beyond campus.

_____

_____

Using *-ed* Modifiers

You can also use an *-ed* modifier to combine two sentences.

TWO SENTENCES	Nogales is located on the border between Arizona and Mexico. It is a bilingual city.
COMBINED WITH *-ED* MODIFIER	Located on the border between Arizona and Mexico, Nogales is a bilingual city.

When the two sentences above are combined, the *-ed* modifier (*located on the border between Arizona and Mexico*) describes the new sentence's subject (*Nogales*).

PRACTICE 19-5

Use an *-ed* modifier to combine each of the following pairs of sentences into a single sentence. Eliminate any unnecessary words, and use a comma to set off each *-ed* modifier. When you are finished, underline the *-ed* modifier in each sentence.

Example: Potato chips were invented purely by accident. They are one of America's most popular foods.

<u>Invented purely</u> by accident, potato chips are one of America's

most popular foods.

1. George Crum was employed as a chef in a fancy restaurant. He was famous for his french fries.

   _____

   _____

2. A customer was dissatisfied with the fries. He complained and asked for thinner fries.

   _____

   _____

3. The customer was served thinner fries. He was still not satisfied and complained again.

   _____

   _____

4. Crum was now very annoyed. He decided to make the fries too thin and crisp to eat with a fork.

   _____

   _____

5. The customer was thrilled with the extra-thin and crisp potatoes. He ate them all.

_____

6. Potato chips were invented to get even with a customer. They are the most popular snack food in America today.

_____

_____

Using a Series of Words

Another way to vary your sentences is to combine a group of sentences into one sentence that includes a **series** of words (nouns, verbs, or adjectives). Combining sentences in this way eliminates a boring string of similar sentences and repetitive phrases and also makes your writing more concise.

GROUP OF SENTENCES	College presidents want to improve athletes' academic performance. Coaches too want to improve athletes' academic performance. The players themselves also want to improve their academic performance.
COMBINED (SERIES OF NOUNS)	College <u>presidents</u>, <u>coaches</u>, and the <u>players</u> themselves want to improve athletes' academic performance.
GROUP OF SENTENCES	Arundhati Roy published her first novel, *The God of Small Things*, in 1997. She won the Man Booker Prize for Fiction that year. She published her second novel, *The Ministry of Utmost Happiness*, in 2017.
COMBINED (SERIES OF VERBS)	Arundhati Roy <u>published</u> her first novel, *The God of Small Things*, in 1997; <u>won</u> the Man Booker Prize for Fiction that year; and <u>published</u> her second novel in 2017.
GROUP OF SENTENCES	As the tornado approached, the sky grew dark. The sky grew quiet. The sky grew threatening.
COMBINED (SERIES OF ADJECTIVES)	As the tornado approached, the sky grew <u>dark</u>, <u>quiet</u>, and <u>threatening</u>.

PRACTICE 19-6

Combine each of the following groups of sentences into one sentence that includes a series of nouns, verbs, or adjectives.

Example: Many years ago, Pacific Islanders from Samoa settled in Hawaii. Pacific Islanders from Fiji also settled in Hawaii. Pacific Islanders from Tahiti settled in Hawaii, too.

Many years ago, Pacific Islanders from Samoa, Fiji, and Tahiti settled in Hawaii.

1. In the eighteenth century, the British explorer Captain Cook came to Hawaii. Other explorers also came to Hawaii. European travelers came to Hawaii, too.

2. Explorers and traders brought commerce to Hawaii. They brought new ideas. They brought new cultures.

3. Missionaries introduced the Christian religion. They introduced a Hawaiian-language bible. Also, they introduced a Hawaiian alphabet.

4. In the mid-nineteenth century, pineapple plantations were established in Hawaii. Sugar plantations were established there as well. Other industries were also established.

5. By 1900, Japanese people were working on the plantations. Chinese people were also working on the plantations. In addition, native Hawaiians were working there.

   _____

   _____

6. People of many different races and religions now live in Hawaii. People of many different races and religions now go to school in Hawaii. People of many different races and religions now work in Hawaii.

   _____

   _____

7. Schoolchildren still study the Hawaiian language. They learn about the Hawaiian kings and queens. They read about ancient traditions.

   _____

   _____

8. Today, Hawaii is well known for its tourism. It is well known too for its weather. It is especially well known for its natural beauty.

   _____

Using Appositives

> **WORD POWER**
>
> **adjacent** next to

An **appositive** is a word or word group that identifies, renames, or describes an adjacent noun or pronoun. Creating an appositive is often a good way to combine two sentences about the same subject.

TWO SENTENCES	C. J. Walker was the first American woman to become a self-made millionaire. She marketed a line of hair-care products for black women.
COMBINED WITH APPOSITIVE	C. J. Walker, the first American woman to become a self-made millionaire, marketed a line of hair-care products for black women.

In the preceding example, the appositive appears in the middle of a sentence. However, an appositive can also come at the beginning or at the end of a sentence.

The first American woman to become a self-made millionaire, C. J. Walker marketed a line of hair-care products for black women. (appositive at the beginning)

Several books have been written about C. J. Walker, the first American woman to become a self-made millionaire. (appositive at the end)

PRACTICE 19-7

Combine each of the following pairs of sentences into one sentence by creating an appositive. Note that the appositive may appear at the beginning, in the middle, or at the end of the sentence. Be sure to use commas appropriately.

Example: *Wikipedia* ~~is~~ a popular online information source*,* ~~It~~ is available in nearly three hundred languages.

(1) *Wikipedia* is one of the largest reference sites on the web. It is different from other encyclopedias in many ways. (2) This site is a constant work-in-progress. It allows anyone to add, change, or correct information in its articles. (3) For this reason, researchers have to be careful when using information from *Wikipedia*. *Wikipedia* is a source that may contain factual errors. (4) The older articles are the ones that have been edited and corrected the most. These often contain the most trustworthy information. (5) Despite some drawbacks, *Wikipedia* has many notable advantages. These advantages include free and easy access, up-to-date information, and protection from author bias.

19d Mixing Long and Short Sentences

A paragraph of short, choppy sentences—or a paragraph of long, rambling sentences—can be monotonous. By mixing long and short sentences, perhaps combining some simple sentences to create **compound** and **complex sentences**, you can create a more interesting paragraph.

In the following paragraph, the sentences are all short, and the result is boring and hard to follow.

The world's first drive-in movie theater opened on June 6, 1933. This drive-in was in Camden, New Jersey. Automobiles became more popular. Drive-ins did, too. By the 1950s, there were more than four thousand drive-ins in the United States. Over the years, the high cost of land led to a decline in the number of drive-ins. So did the rising popularity of television. Soon, the drive-in movie theater had almost disappeared. It was replaced by the multiplex. In 1967, there were forty-six drive-ins in New Jersey. Today, only one is still open. That one is the Delsea Drive-in in Vineland, New Jersey.

The revised paragraph that follows is more interesting and easier to read. (Note that the final short sentence is retained for emphasis.)

> The world's first drive-in movie theater opened on June 6, 1933, in Camden, New Jersey. As automobiles became more popular, drive-ins did, too, and by the 1950s, there were more than four thousand drive-ins in the United States. Over the years, the high cost of land and the rising popularity of television led to a decline in the number of drive-ins. Soon, the drive-in movie theater had almost disappeared, replaced by the multiplex. In 1967, there were forty-six drive-ins in New Jersey, but today, only one is still open. That one is the Delsea Drive-in in Vineland, New Jersey.

PRACTICE 19-8

The following paragraph contains a series of short, choppy sentences that can be combined. Revise the paragraph so that it mixes long and short sentences. Be sure to use commas and other punctuation appropriately.

> **Example:** Kente cloth has special significance for many African Americans/~~Some~~ ^, but some^ other people do not understand this significance.

(1) Kente cloth is made in western Africa. (2) It is produced primarily by the Ashanti people. (3) It has been worn for hundreds of years by African royalty. (4) They consider it a sign of power and status. (5) Many African Americans wear kente cloth. (6) They see it as a link to their heritage. (7) Each pattern on the cloth has a name. (8) Each color has a special significance. (9) For example, red and yellow suggest a long and healthy life. (10) Green and white suggest a good harvest. (11) African women may wear kente cloth as a dress or head wrap. (12) African-American women, like men, usually wear strips of cloth around their shoulders. (13) Men and women of African descent wear kente cloth as a sign of racial pride. (14) It often decorates college students' gowns at graduation.

CHAPTER REVIEW

EDITING PRACTICE

The following student essay lacks sentence variety. All of its sentences begin with the subject, and the essay includes a number of short, choppy sentences. Using the strategies discussed in this chapter as well as strategies for creating compound and complex sentences, revise the essay to achieve greater sentence variety. The first sentence has been edited for you.

Toys by Accident

Many popular toys and games are the result of accidents. ~~People~~ *when people* try to invent one thing, but discover something else instead. Sometimes they are not trying to invent anything at all. They are completely surprised to find a new product.

Play-Doh is one example of an accidental discovery. Play-Doh is a popular preschool toy. Play-Doh first appeared in Cincinnati. A company made a compound to clean wallpaper. They sold it as a cleaning product. The company then realized that this compound could be a toy. Children could mold it like clay. They could use it again and again. The new toy was an immediate hit. Play-Doh was first sold in 1956. Since then, more than two billion cans of Play-Doh have been sold.

The Slinky was discovered by Richard James. He was an engineer. At the time, he was trying to invent a spring to keep ships' instruments steady at sea. He tested hundreds of springs of varying sizes, metals, and tensions. None of them worked. One spring fell off the desk, and "walked" down a pile of books. It went end over end onto the floor. He thought his children might enjoy playing with it. James took the spring home. They loved it. Every child in the neighborhood wanted one. The first Slinky was demonstrated at Gimbel's Department Store in Philadelphia in 1945. All four hundred Slinkys were sold within ninety

> **READING TIP**
>
> Before you read "Toys by Accident," preview the essay by reading only the first sentence of each paragraph. Then, read the essay closely for full comprehension. Previewing an essay before you read it helps you to understand it better and retain more information about it.

minutes. The Slinky is simple and inexpensive. The Slinky is still popular with children today.

The Frisbee was also discovered by accident. According to one story, a group of Yale University students were eating pies from a local bakery. The bakery was called Frisbies. They finished eating the pies. They started throwing the empty pie tins around. A carpenter in California made a plastic version. He called it the Pluto Platter. The Wham-O company bought the patent on the product. Wham-O renamed it the Frisbee after the bakery. This is how the Frisbee came to be.

Some new toys are not developed by toy companies. Play-Doh, the Frisbee, and the Slinky are examples of very popular toys that were discovered by accident. Play-Doh started as a cleaning product. The Slinky was discovered by an engineer who was trying to invent something else. The Frisbee was invented by students having fun. The toys were discovered unexpectedly. All three toys have become classics.

Review checklist

Writing Varied Sentences

✔ Vary sentence types. (See 19a.)

✔ Vary sentence openings. (See 19b.)

✔ Combine sentences. (See 19c.)

✔ Mix long and short sentences. (See 19d.)

20 Using Parallelism

 20a Recognizing Parallel Structure

Parallelism is the use of matching words, phrases, clauses, and sentence structure to highlight similar ideas in a sentence. When you use parallelism, you are telling readers that certain ideas are related and have the same level of importance. By repeating similar grammatical patterns to express similar ideas, you create sentences that are clearer, more concise, and easier to read.

In the following examples, the parallel sentences highlight similar ideas; the other sentences do not.

PARALLEL	NOT PARALLEL
Please leave <u>your name</u>, <u>your number</u>, and <u>your message</u>.	Please leave <u>your name</u>, <u>your number</u>, and <u>you should also leave a message</u>.
I plan to <u>graduate</u> from high school and <u>become</u> a nurse.	I plan to <u>graduate</u> from high school, and then <u>becoming</u> a nurse would be a good idea.
The grass was <u>soft</u>, <u>green</u>, and <u>sweet smelling</u>.	The grass was <u>soft</u>, <u>green</u>, and <u>the smell was sweet</u>.
<u>Making</u> the team was one thing; <u>staying on it</u> was another.	<u>Making the team</u> was one thing, but it was very difficult <u>to stay on it</u>.
<u>We can register</u> for classes in person, or <u>we can register</u> by email.	<u>We can register</u> for classes in person, or <u>registering</u> by email is another option.

PRACTICE 20-1

In the following sentences, decide whether the underlined words and phrases are parallel. If so, write *P* in the blank. If not, rewrite the sentences so that the underlined ideas are presented in parallel terms.

Examples: The missing dog had <u>brown fur</u>, <u>a red collar</u>, and <u>a long tail</u>. ___*P*___

Signs of drug abuse in teenagers include <u>falling grades</u>, <u>mood swings</u>, and <u>~~they lose~~ weight</u> _____
                                                                  loss.

467

1. The food in the cafeteria is <u>varied</u>, <u>tasty</u>, and <u>it is healthy</u>.
   _____

2. Do you want the job done <u>quickly</u>, or do you want it done <u>well</u>?
   _____

3. Last summer <u>I worked at the library</u>, <u>babysat for my neighbor's daughter</u>, and <u>there was a soup kitchen where I volunteered</u>.
   _____

4. <u>Pandas eat bamboo leaves</u>, and <u>eucalyptus leaves. are eaten by koalas</u>.
   _____

5. Skydiving is <u>frightening</u> but <u>fun</u>. _____

6. A number of interesting people work at the co-op with me, including <u>an elderly German man</u>, <u>there is a middle-aged Chinese woman</u>, and <u>a teenaged Mexican boy</u>. _____

7. <u>The bell rang</u>, and <u>the students stood up</u>. _____

8. To conserve energy while I was away, I <u>unplugged the television</u>, <u>closed the curtains</u>, and <u>the thermostat was set at 65 degrees</u>. _____

9. I <u>put away the dishes</u>; will you <u>put away the laundry</u>? _____

10. For several weeks after the storm, the supermarkets had <u>no eggs</u>, <u>they were out of milk</u>, and <u>they did not have any bread</u>. _____

20b Using Parallel Structure

Parallel structure is especially important in *paired items*, *items in a series*, and *items in a list or in an outline*.

Paired Items

Use parallel structure when you connect ideas with a **coordinating conjunction**—*and*, *but*, *for*, *nor*, *or*, *so*, and *yet*.

George believes in <u>doing a good job</u> and <u>minding his own business</u>.

You can <u>pay me now</u> or <u>pay me later</u>.

You should also use parallel structure for paired items joined by *both . . . and*, *not only . . . but also*, *either . . . or*, *neither . . . nor*, and *rather . . . than*.

Jan is both skilled in writing and fluent in French.

The group's new recording not only has a dance beat but also has thought-provoking lyrics.

Louis XVI was a weak monarch who would rather repair locks than govern.

Items in a Series

Use parallel structure for items in a series—words, phrases, or clauses. (Be sure to use commas to separate three or more items in a series. Never put a comma after the final item.)

The immediate causes of World War I were imperialism, militarism, and nationalism. (three words)

Increased demand, high factory output, and a strong dollar will help the economy. (three phrases)

She is a champion because she stays in excellent physical condition, puts in long hours of practice, and has an intense desire to win. (three clauses)

Items in a List or in an Outline

Use parallel structure for items in a numbered or bulleted list.

There are three reasons to open an Individual Retirement Account (IRA):

1. To save money
2. To reduce taxes
3. To be able to retire

Use parallel structure for the elements in an outline.

A. Types of rocks
   1. Igneous
   2. Sedimentary
   3. Metamorphic

PRACTICE 20-2

Fill in the blanks in the following sentences with parallel words, phrases, or clauses of your own that make sense in context.

Example: At the lake, we can <u>go for a swim</u>, <u>paddle a canoe</u>, and <u>play volleyball</u>.

1. When I get too little sleep, I am _____, _____, and _____.

2. I am good at _____ but not at _____.

3. My ideal mate is _____ and _____.

4. I personally define success not only as _____ but also as _____.

5. I use my computer for both _____ and _____.

6. I like _____ and _____.

7. You need three qualities to succeed in college: _____, _____, and _____.

8. I enjoy not only _____ but also _____.

9. I would rather _____ than _____.

10. Football _____, but baseball _____.

CHAPTER REVIEW

EDITING PRACTICE

Read the following student essay, which contains examples of faulty parallelism. Identify the sentences you think need to be corrected, and make the changes required to achieve parallelism. Be sure to supply all words necessary for clarity, grammar, and sense. Add punctuation as needed. The first error has been edited for you.

Self-Made Men and Women Helping Others

Many self-made people go from poverty to achieving success. Quite a few of them not only achieve such success but also they help others. Three of these people are Oprah Winfrey, Alfredo Quiñones-Hinojosa, and Geoffrey Canada. Their lives are very different, but all possess great strength, being determined, and concern for others.

Oprah is one of the most influential people in the world, and she has more money than almost anyone in the world. She came from a very poor family. First, she lived with her grandmother on a Mississippi farm, and then her mother in Milwaukee. During this time, she was abused by several relatives. When she was thirteen, she was sent to Nashville to live with her father. He used strict discipline, and she was taught by him to value education. Through her own determination and because she was ambitious, Winfrey got a job at a local broadcasting company. This started her career. However, Oprah was not satisfied with being successful. Through Oprah's Angel Network and the Oprah Winfrey Leadership Academy, she helps others and making the world a better place.

Today, Alfredo Quiñones-Hinojosa is a top brain surgeon and conducting research on new ways to treat brain cancer. At age nineteen, he was an illegal immigrant from Mexico, worked in the fields, and without any English. When he told his cousin he wanted to learn English and get a better job, his cousin

> **READING TIP**
> This student essay includes several supporting details about self-made men and women. Compare and contrast the supporting details provided for each person. What do Winfrey, Quiñones-Hinojosa, and Canada have in common? How are they different?

told him he was crazy. Then, while a welder on a railroad crew, he fell into an empty petroleum tank and was almost dying from the fumes. However, Alfredo overcame these hardships. He enrolled in a community college, and with determination and by working hard, he began to change his life. He won a scholarship to Berkeley, went on to medical school at Harvard, and eventually winding up as director of the brain tumor program at Johns Hopkins University. In 1997, he became a citizen of the United States. At each step of the way, he has made a special effort to reach out to students from low-income backgrounds and to inspire others.

Geoffrey Canada grew up in a New York City neighborhood that was poor, dangerous, and where violence was not uncommon. His mother was a single parent who struggled to support Geoffrey and his three brothers. Geoffrey learned to survive on the streets, but he also studied a lot in school. Thanks to this hard work, he won a scholarship to college in Maine and went on to a career in education. Deciding to leave his neighborhood in New York wasn't hard, but to decide to come back wasn't hard either. He wanted to help children in poor families to succeed in school and so they could have better lives. With this in mind, he started the Harlem Children's Zone (HCZ). HCZ includes (1) workshops for parents, (2) a preschool and three charter schools, and (3) running health programs for children and families. President Obama has said he would like to see more programs like HCZ.

Oprah Winfrey, Alfredo Quiñones-Hinojosa, and Geoffrey Canada have very different careers—in entertainment, in medicine, and educating children. However, all three overcame great adversity, all three have achieved enormous success, and they have helped others. They have helped their communities, their country, and have contributed to the world.

Review checklist

Using Parallelism

- ✔ Use matching words, phrases, clauses, and sentence structure to highlight similar items or ideas. (See 20a.)
- ✔ Use parallel structure with paired items. (See 20b.)
- ✔ Use parallel structure for items in a series. (See 20b.)
- ✔ Use parallel structure for items in a list or in an outline. (See 20b.)

21 Using Words Effectively

21a Using Specific Words

Specific words refer to particular people, places, things, ideas, or qualities. **General words** refer to entire classes or groups. Sentences that contain specific words are more precise and vivid than those that contain only general words.

SENTENCES WITH GENERAL WORDS	SENTENCES WITH SPECIFIC WORDS
While walking in the woods, I saw an <u>animal</u>.	While walking in the woods, I saw a <u>baby skunk</u>.
<u>Someone</u> decided to run for Congress.	<u>Vivienne</u> decided to run for Congress.
<u>Weapons</u> are responsible for many murders.	<u>Unregistered handguns</u> are responsible for many murders.
Plessy v. Ferguson was a <u>bad</u> Supreme Court decision.	*Plessy v. Ferguson* <u>institutionalized the "separate but equal" doctrine</u>.
Acid rain is a <u>problem</u>.	Acid rain <u>erodes buildings</u>, <u>damages crops</u>, and <u>creates pollution</u>.
Almost from the beginning, Europeans <u>deceived</u> Native Americans.	Almost from the beginning, Europeans <u>lied</u>, <u>broke treaties</u>, and <u>stole land</u> from Native Americans.

> **FYI**
>
> **Using Specific Words**
>
> One way to strengthen your writing is to avoid general words like *good*, *nice*, or *great*. Take the time to think of more specific words. For example, when you say the ocean looked *pretty*, do you really mean that it *sparkled*, *glistened*, *rippled*, *foamed*, *surged*, or *billowed*?

PRACTICE 21-1

In the blank beside each of the five general words below, write a more specific word. Then, use the more specific word in an original sentence.

Example: child *six-year-old*
All through dinner, my six-year-old chattered excitedly about his first day of school.

1. emotion _____
_____

2. building _____
_____

3. said _____
_____

4. animal _____
_____

5. went _____
_____

PRACTICE 21-2

The following one-paragraph job-application letter uses many general words. Rewrite the paragraph, substituting specific words and adding details where necessary. Start by making the first sentence, which identifies the job, more specific; For example: "I would like to apply for the <u>dental technician</u> position you advertised on <u>March 15 on monster.com</u>." Then add information about your background and qualifications. Expand the original paragraph into a three-paragraph letter.

    I would like to apply for the position you advertised in today's paper. I graduated from high school and am currently attending college. I have taken several courses that have prepared me for the duties the position requires. I also have several personal qualities that I think you would find useful in a person holding this position. In addition, I have had certain experiences that qualify me for such a job. I would appreciate the opportunity to meet with you to discuss your needs as an employer. Thank you.

21b Using Concise Language

Concise language says what it has to say in as few words as possible. Too often, writers use words and phrases that add nothing to a sentence's meaning. A good way to test a sentence for these words is to see if crossing them out changes the sentence's meaning. If the sentence's meaning does not change, you can assume that the words you crossed out are unnecessary.

It is clear that the United States was not ready to fight World War II.

In order to follow the plot, you must make an outline.

Sometimes you can replace several unnecessary words with a single word.

Due to the fact that I was tired, I missed my first class.

Einstein believed but could not confirm the existence of black holes.

FYI

Using Concise Language
The following wordy phrases add nothing to a sentence. You can usually delete or condense them with no loss of meaning.

WORDY	CONCISE
It is clear that	(delete)
It is a fact that	(delete)
The reason is because	Because
The reason is that	Because
It is my opinion that	I think/I believe
Due to the fact that	Because
Despite the fact that	Although
At the present time	Today/Now
At that time	Then
In most cases	Usually
In order to	To
In the final analysis	Finally
Subsequent to	After

Unnecessary repetition—saying the same thing twice for no reason—can also make your writing wordy. When you revise, delete repeated words and phrases that add nothing to your sentences.

> My instructor told me the book was ~~old-fashioned and~~ outdated. (An old-fashioned book *is* outdated.)

> The ~~terrible~~ tragedy of the fire could have been avoided. (A tragedy is *always* terrible.)

PRACTICE 21-3

To make the following sentences more concise, eliminate any unnecessary repetition, and delete or condense wordy expressions.

> **Example:** When the movie *Hidden Figures* came out ~~a few years ago~~ in 2016, people ~~in audiences everywhere~~ were introduced to three heroes ~~heroic individuals~~ in NASA's space program.

(1) Based on a book written by Margot Lee Shetterly, the movie version is about the story of NASA mathematicians Katherine Johnson, Dorothy Vaughan, and Mary Jackson. (2) At the time that these women worked for NASA, segregation laws were still very much in effect. (3) Because of the fact that they were African-Americans, they came face to face with discrimination in their jobs as "human computers." (4) On top of that, as women, they faced sexist attitudes typical of that time in history. (5) Despite having to confront many difficulties and challenges, the women were able to overcome the obstacles and achieve several milestones during their careers at NASA. (6) Dorothy Vaughan became the first African-American supervisor at the space center. (7) Mary Jackson rose from her position as a computer and took advanced engineering classes on her way to becoming NASA's first ever African-American female engineer. (8) Katherine Johnson played a key role in many NASA missions. As just an example, she calculated the trajectory for, the first flight to the moon. For

her many, many contributions to the space program, Katherine Johnson, received the Presidential Medal of Freedom in 2015.

21c Using Similes and Metaphors

A **simile** is a comparison of two unlike things that uses *like* or *as*.

His arm hung at his side <u>like</u> a broken branch.
He was <u>as</u> content <u>as</u> a cat napping on a windowsill.

A **metaphor** is a comparison of two unlike things that does not use *like* or *as*.

Invaders from another world, the dandelions conquered my garden.
He was a beast of burden, hauling cement from the mixer to the building site.

The impact of similes and metaphors comes from the surprise of seeing two seemingly unlike things being compared. Used in moderation, similes and metaphors can make your writing more lively and interesting.

PRACTICE 21-4 Think of a person you know well. Using that person as your subject, fill in each of the following blanks to create metaphors. Try to complete each metaphor with more than a single word, as in the example.

Example:

If <u>my baby sister</u> were an animal, <u>she</u> would be <u>a curious little kitten.</u>

1. If _____ were a musical instrument, _____ would be _____

2. If _____ were a food, _____ would be _____ _____

3. If _____ were a means of transportation, _____ would be _____ _____

4. If _____ were a natural phenomenon, _____ would be
   _____

5. If _____ were a toy, _____ would be _____
   _____

 ## 21d Avoiding Slang

Slang is nonstandard language that calls attention to itself. It is usually associated with a particular social group—Twitter users or skateboarders, for example. Some slang eventually spreads beyond its original context and becomes widely used. Often, it is used for emphasis or to produce a surprising or original effect. In any case, because it is very informal, slang is not acceptable in your college writing.

>   *easy.*
> My psychology exam was really ~~sweet.~~
>
>   *relax*^
> On the weekends, I like to ~~chill~~ and watch movies on my laptop.

If you have any question about whether a term is slang or not, look it up in a dictionary. If the term is identified as *slang* or *informal*, find a more suitable term.

FYI

Avoiding Abbreviations and Shorthand

While abbreviations and shorthand, such as *LOL*, *BTW*, *IMO*, and *2day*, are acceptable in informal electronic communication, they are **not** acceptable in your college writing, in emails to your instructors, or in online class discussions.

> IMO your essay needs a strong thesis statement.
>
> I would like to meet with u for a conference 2day.

PRACTICE

21-5 Edit the following sentences, replacing the slang expressions with clearer, more precise words and phrases.

>   *yelled at me*
> **Example:** My father ~~lost it~~ when I told him I crashed the car.

1. Whenever I get bummed, I go outside and jog.
2. Tonight I'll have to leave by 11 because I'm wiped out.
3. I'm not into movies or television.
4. Whenever we argue, my boyfriend knows how to push my buttons.
5. I really lucked out when I got this job.

21e Avoiding Clichés

Clichés are expressions—such as "it is what it is" and "last but not least"—that have been used so often that they have lost their meaning. These worn-out expressions get in the way of clear communication.

When you identify a cliché in your writing, replace it with a direct statement—or, if possible, with a fresher expression.

CLICHÉ When school was over, she felt ~~free as a bird~~ liberated.

CLICHÉ These days, you have to be ~~sick as a dog~~ seriously ill before you are admitted to a hospital.

FYI

Avoiding Clichés

Here are examples of some clichés you should avoid in your writing:

a perfect storm	play God
back in the day	pushing the envelope
better late than never	reality check
bottom line	skill set
connect the dots	think outside the box
cutting edge	throw under the bus
drink the Kool-Aid	to die for
give 110 percent	touch base
groupthink	tried and true
it is what it is	water under the bridge
keep your eye on the ball	what goes around comes around

PRACTICE 21-6

Cross out any clichés in the following sentences. Then, either substitute a fresher expression or restate the idea more directly.

Example: Lottery winners often think they will be ~~on easy street~~ *free of financial worries* for the rest of their lives.

(1) Many people think that a million-dollar lottery jackpot allows the winner to stop working like a dog and start living high on the hog. (2) All things considered, however, the reality for lottery winners is quite different. (3) For one thing, lottery winners who hit the jackpot do not always receive their winnings all at once; instead, yearly payments—for example, $50,000—can be paid out over twenty years. (4) Of that $50,000 a year, close to $20,000 goes to taxes and anything else the lucky stiff already owes the government, such as student loans. (5) Next come relatives and friends with their hands out, leaving winners between a rock and a hard place. (6) They can either cough up gifts and loans or wave bye-bye to many of their loved ones. (7) Adding insult to injury, many lottery winners lose their jobs because employers think that, now that they are "millionaires," they no longer need to draw a salary. (8) Many lottery winners wind up way over their heads in debt within a few years. (9) In their hour of need, many might like to sell their future payments to companies that offer lump-sum payments of forty to forty-five cents on the dollar. (10) This is easier said than done, however, because most state lotteries do not allow winners to sell their winnings.

> **READING TIP**
> The uncorrected version of this passage includes many clichéd expressions. How do these clichés affect your reaction to the writer's ideas?

21f Avoiding Sexist Language

Sexist language refers to men and women in insulting terms. Sexist language is not just words such as *stud* or *babe*, which many people find objectionable. It can also be words or phrases that unnecessarily call attention to gender, or that suggest only a man (or only a woman) hold a job or profession, when it actually is not the case.

You can avoid sexist language by using a little common sense. There is always an acceptable nonsexist alternative for a sexist term.

SEXIST	NONSEXIST
man, mankind	humanity, humankind, the human race
businessman	executive, businessperson
fireman, policeman, mailman	firefighter, police officer, letter carrier
male nurse, woman engineer	nurse, engineer
congressman	member of Congress, representative
stewardess, steward	flight attendant
man and wife	man and woman, husband and wife
manmade	synthetic
chairman	chair, chairperson
anchorwoman, anchorman	anchor
actor, actress	actor

FYI

Avoiding Sexist Language

Do not use *he* when your subject could be either male or female.

SEXIST Everyone should complete his assignment by next week.

You can correct this problem in three ways.

- *Use* he or she *or* his or her.

    Everyone should complete his or her assignment by next week.

- *Use plural forms.*

    Students should complete their assignments by next week.

- *Eliminate the pronoun.*

    Everyone should complete the assignment by next week.

PRACTICE 21-7

Edit the following sentences to eliminate sexist language.

Example: A doctor should be honest with his ∧ patients. *or her (or omit "his")*

1. Many people today would like to see more policemen patrolling the streets.
2. The attorneys representing the plaintiff are Geraldo Diaz and Mrs. Barbara Wilkerson.
3. Every soldier picked up his weapons.
4. Ivy R. Taylor is the female mayor of San Antonio, Texas.
5. Travel to other planets will be a significant step for man.

21g Identifying Commonly Confused Words

Accept/Except *Accept* means "to receive something." *Except* means "with the exception of" or "to leave out or exclude."

"I <u>accept</u> your challenge," said Alexander Hamilton to Aaron Burr.
Everyone <u>except</u> Darryl visited the museum.

Affect/Effect *Affect* is a verb meaning "to influence." *Effect* is a noun meaning "result."

Carmen's job could <u>affect</u> her grades.
Overexposure to sun can have a long-term <u>effect</u> on skin.

All ready/Already *All ready* means "completely prepared." *Already* means "previously, before."

Serge was <u>all ready</u> to take the history test.
Gina had <u>already</u> been to Italy.

Brake/Break *Brake* is a noun that means "a device to slow or stop a vehicle." *Break* is a verb meaning "to smash" or "to detach" and sometimes a noun meaning either "a gap" or "an interruption" or "a stroke of luck."

> Peter got into an accident because his foot slipped off the <u>brake</u>.
>
> Babe Ruth thought no one would ever <u>break</u> his home run record.
>
> The baseball game was postponed until there was a <u>break</u> in the bad weather.

Buy/By *Buy* means "to purchase." *By* is a preposition meaning "close to," "next to," or "by means of."

> The Stamp Act forced colonists to <u>buy</u> stamps for many public documents.
>
> He drove <u>by</u> but did not stop.
>
> He stayed <u>by</u> her side all the way to the hospital.
>
> Malcolm X wanted "freedom <u>by</u> any means necessary."

Conscience/Conscious *Conscience* is a noun that refers to the part of the mind that urges a person to choose right over wrong. *Conscious* is an adjective that means "aware" or "deliberate."

> After he cheated at cards, his <u>conscience</u> started to bother him.
>
> As she walked through the woods, she became <u>conscious</u> of the hum of insects.
>
> Elliott made a <u>conscious</u> decision to stop smoking.

Everyday/Every day *Everyday* is a single word that means "ordinary" or "common." *Every day* is two words that mean "occurring daily."

> *Friends* was a successful comedy show because it appealed to <u>everyday</u> people.
>
> <u>Every day</u>, the six friends met at the Central Perk café.

Fine/Find *Fine* means "superior quality" or "a sum of money paid as a penalty." *Find* means "to locate."

> He sang a <u>fine</u> solo at church last Sunday.
>
> Demi had to pay a <u>fine</u> for speeding.
>
> Some people still use a willow rod to <u>find</u> water.

Hear/Here *Hear* means "to perceive sound by ear." *Here* means "at or in this place."

> I moved to the front so I could <u>hear</u> the speaker.
>
> My great-grandfather came <u>here</u> in 1883.

Its/It's *Its* is the possessive form of *it*. *It's* is the contraction of *it is* or *it has*.

> The airline canceled its flights because of the snow.
> It's twelve o'clock, and we are late.
> Ever since it's been in the accident, the car has rattled.

Know/No/Knew/New *Know* means "to have an understanding of" or "to have fixed in the mind." *No* means "not any," "not at all," or "not one." *Knew* is the past tense form of the verb *know*. *New* means "recent or never used."

> I know there will be a lunar eclipse tonight.
> You have no right to say that.
> He knew how to install a new light switch.

Lie/Lay *Lie* means "to rest or recline." The past tense of *lie* is *lay*. *Lay* means "to put or place something down." The past tense of *lay* is *laid*.

> Every Sunday, I lie in bed until noon.
> They lay on the grass until it began to rain, and then they went home.
> Tammy told Carl to lay his cards on the table.
> Brooke and Cassia finally laid down their hockey sticks.

Loose/Lose *Loose* means "not fixed or rigid" or "not attached securely." *Lose* means "to mislay" or "to misplace."

> In the 1940s, many women wore loose-fitting pants.
> I never gamble because I hate to lose.

Passed/Past *Passed* is the past tense of the verb *pass*. It means "moved by" or "succeeded in." *Past* is a noun or an adjective meaning "earlier than the present time."

> The car that passed me was doing more than eighty miles an hour.
> David finally passed his driving test.
> The novel was set in the past.
> The statement said that the bill was past due.

Peace/Piece *Peace* means "the absence of war" or "calm." *Piece* means "a part of something."

> The British prime minister tried to achieve peace with honor.
> My peace of mind was destroyed when the flying saucer landed.
> "Have a piece of cake," said Marie.

Principal/Principle *Principal* means "first" or "highest" or "the head of a school." *Principle* means "a law or basic assumption."

> She had the principal role in the movie.
>
> I'll never forget the day the principal called me into his office.
>
> It was against his principles to lie.

Quiet/Quit/Quite *Quiet* means "free of noise" or "still." *Quit* means "to leave a job" or "to give up." *Quite* means "actually" or "very."

> Jane looked forward to the quiet evenings at the lake.
>
> Sammy quit his job and followed the girls into the parking lot.
>
> "You haven't quite got the hang of it yet," she said.
>
> After practicing all summer, Tamika got quite good at tennis.

Raise/Rise *Raise* means "to elevate" or "to increase in size, quantity, or worth." The past tense of *raise* is *raised*. *Rise* means "to stand up" or "to move from a lower position to a higher position." The past tense of *rise* is *rose*.

> Carlos raises his hand whenever the teacher asks for volunteers.
>
> They finally raised the money for the down payment.
>
> The crowd rises every time their team scores a touchdown.
>
> Kim rose before dawn so she could see the eclipse.

Sit/Set *Sit* means "to assume a sitting position." The past tense of *sit* is *sat*. *Set* means "to put down or place" or "to adjust something to a desired position." The past tense of *set* is *set*.

> I usually sit in the front row at the movies.
>
> They sat at the clinic waiting for their names to be called.
>
> Elizabeth set the mail on the kitchen table and left for work.
>
> Every semester I set goals for myself.

Suppose/Supposed *Suppose* means "to consider" or "to assume." *Supposed* is both the past tense and the past participle of *suppose*. *Supposed* also means "expected" or "required." (Note that when *supposed* has this meaning, it is always followed by *to*.)

> Suppose researchers were to find a cure for cancer.
>
> We supposed the movie would be over by ten o'clock.
>
> You were supposed to finish a draft of the report by today.

Their/There/They're *Their* is the possessive form of the pronoun *they*. *There* means "at or in that place." *There* is also used in the phrases *there is* and *there are*. *They're* is the contraction of *they are*.

> They wanted poor people to improve <u>their</u> living conditions.
> I put the book over <u>there</u>.
> <u>There</u> are three reasons I will not eat meat.
> <u>They're</u> the best volunteer firefighters I've ever seen.

Then/Than *Then* means "at that time" or "next in time." *Than* is used in comparisons.

> He was young and naive <u>then</u>.
> I went to the job interview and <u>then</u> stopped off for coffee.
> My dog is smarter <u>than</u> your dog.

Threw/Through *Threw* is the past tense of *throw*. *Through* means "in one side and out the opposite side" or "finished."

> Satchel Paige <u>threw</u> a baseball more than ninety-five miles an hour.
> It takes almost thirty minutes to go <u>through</u> the tunnel.
> "I'm <u>through</u>," said Clark Kent, storming out of Perry White's office.

To/Too/Two *To* means "in the direction of." *Too* means "also" or "more than enough." *Two* denotes the numeral 2.

> During spring break, I am going <u>to</u> Disney World.
> My roommates are coming <u>too</u>.
> The microwave popcorn is <u>too</u> hot to eat.
> "If we get rid of the Tin Man and the Cowardly Lion, the <u>two</u> of us can go to Oz," said the Scarecrow to Dorothy.

Use/Used *Use* means "to put into service" or "to consume." *Used* is both the past tense and the past participle of *use*. *Used* also means "accustomed." (Note that when *used* has this meaning, it is followed by *to*.)

> I <u>use</u> a soft cloth to clean my glasses.
> "Hey! Who <u>used</u> all the hot water?" he yelled from the shower.
> Marisol had <u>used</u> all the firewood during the storm.
> After two years in Alaska, they got <u>used</u> to the short winter days.

Weather/Whether *Weather* refers to temperature, humidity, precipitation, and so on. *Whether* is used to introduce alternative possibilities.

> The *Farmer's Almanac* says that the weather this winter will be severe.
> Whether or not this prediction will be correct is anyone's guess.

Where/Were/We're *Where* means "at or in what place." *Were* is the past tense of *are*. *We're* is the contraction of *we are*.

> Where are you going, and where have you been?
> Charlie Chaplin and Mary Pickford were popular stars of silent movies.
> We're doing our back-to-school shopping early this year.

Whose/Who's *Whose* is the possessive form of *who*. *Who's* is the contraction of either *who is* or *who has*.

> My roommate asked, "Whose book is this?"
> "Who's there?" squealed the second little pig as he leaned against the door.
> Who's been blocking the driveway?

Your/You're *Your* is the possessive form of *you*. *You're* is the contraction of *you are*.

> "You should have worn your running shoes," said the hare as he passed the tortoise.
> "You're too kind," said the tortoise sarcastically.

CHAPTER REVIEW

EDITING PRACTICE

Read the following student essay carefully, and then revise it. Make sure that your revision is concise, uses specific words, and includes no slang, sexist language, clichés, or confused words. Add an occasional simile or metaphor if you'd like. The first sentence has been edited for you.

Unexpected Discoveries

When we ~~here~~ *hear* the word "accident," we think of bad things, *like dented fenders and broken glass.* But accidents can be good, too. Modern science has made advances as a result of accidents. It is a fact that a scientist sometimes works like a dog for years in his laboratory, only to make a weird discovery because of a mistake.

The most famous example of a good, beneficial accident is the discovery of penicillin. A scientist, Alexander Fleming, had seen many soldiers die of infections after they were wounded in World War I. All things considered, many more soldiers died due to the fact that infections occurred than from wounds. Fleming wanted to find a drug that could put an end to these terrible, fatal infections. One day in 1928, Fleming went on vacation, leaving a pile of dishes in the lab sink. As luck would have it, he had been growing bacteria in those dishes. When he came back, he noticed that one of the dishes looked moldy. What was strange was that near the mold, the bacteria were dead as a doornail. It was crystal clear to Fleming that the mold had killed the bacteria. He had discovered penicillin, the first antibiotic.

Everyone has heard the name "Goodyear." It was Charles Goodyear who made a discovery that changed and revolutionized the rubber industry. In the early nineteenth century, rubber products became thin and runny in hot weather and cracked in cold weather. One day in 1839, Goodyear

> **Reading Tip**
> "Unexpected Discoveries" includes examples of cause-and-effect relationships. A *cause* is the reason why something happens. An *effect* is the end result of that occurrence. Identify the causes and effects involved in the discoveries discussed in the essay.

accidentally dropped some rubber mixed with sulfur on a hot stove. It changed color and turned black. After being cooled, it could be stretched, and it would return to its original size and shape. This kind of rubber is now used in tires and in many other products.

Another thing was also discovered because of a lab accident involving rubber. In 1953, Patsy Sherman, a female chemist for the 3M company, was trying to find a new type of rubber. She created a batch of man-made liquid rubber. Some of the liquid accidentally spilled onto a lab assistant's new white canvas sneaker. Her assistant used everything but the kitchen sink to clean the shoe, but nothing worked. Over time, the rest of the shoe became dirty, but the part where the spill had hit was still clean. as a whistle. Sherman new that she had found something that could actually keep fabrics clean by doing a number on dirt. The 3M Corporation named it's brand new product Scotchgard.

A scientist can be clumsy, and careless, but sometimes his mistakes lead to great and important discoveries. Penicillin, better tires, and Scotchgard are examples of products that were the result of scientific accidents.

Review checklist

Using Words Effectively

✔ Use specific words that convey your ideas clearly and precisely. (See 21a.)

✔ Use concise language that says what it has to say in the fewest possible words. (See 21b.)

✔ When appropriate, use similes and metaphors to make your writing more lively and more interesting. (See 21c.)

✔ Avoid slang. (See 21d.)

✔ Avoid clichés. (See 21e.)

✔ Avoid sexist language. (See 21f.)

✔ Learn to distinguish between commonly confused words. (See 21g.)

22 Run-Ons

 ## 22a Recognizing Run-Ons

A **sentence** consists of at least one independent clause—one subject and one verb.

> College costs are rising.

A **run-on** is an error that occurs when two sentences are joined incorrectly. There are two kinds of run-ons: *fused sentences* and *comma splices*.

- A **fused sentence** occurs when two sentences are joined without any punctuation.

    FUSED SENTENCE   [College costs are rising] [many students are worried.]

- A **comma splice** occurs when two sentences are joined with just a comma.

    COMMA SPLICE   [College costs are rising], [many students are worried.]

> **WORD POWER**
>
> **fused** joined together
>
> **splice** (verb) to join together at the ends

PRACTICE

22-1   Some of the sentences in the following paragraph are correct, but others are run-ons. In the answer space after each sentence, write *C* if the sentence is correct, *FS* if it is a fused sentence, and *CS* if it is a comma splice.

Example: Using a screen reader is one way for blind people to access the web, two popular programs are JAWS for Windows and Window-Eyes. ___CS___

(1) The Internet should be accessible to everyone, this is not always the case. _____ (2) Many blind computer users have trouble finding

information on the web. _____ (3) Often, this is the result of poor web design it is the designer's job to make the site accessible. _____ (4) Most blind people use special software called screen readers, this technology translates text into speech or Braille. _____ (5) However, screen readers do not always work well the information is sometimes hard to access. _____ (6) Websites need to be understandable to all Internet users. _____ (7) The rights of blind Internet users may be protected by the Americans with Disabilities Act (ADA). _____ (8) We will have to wait for more cases to come to trial then we will know more. _____ (9) Meanwhile, we have to rely on software companies to make the necessary changes, this will take some time. _____ (10) However, there are incentives for these companies, the 1.5 million blind computer users are all potential customers. _____

22b Correcting Run-Ons

FYI

Correcting Run-Ons

You can correct run-ons in five ways:

1. ***Use a period to create two separate sentences.***
   College costs are rising. Many students are worried.
2. ***Use a coordinating conjunction (and, but, or, nor, for, so, or yet) to connect ideas.***
   College costs are rising, and many students are worried.
3. ***Use a semicolon to connect ideas.***
   College costs are rising; many students are worried.
4. ***Use a semicolon followed by a transitional word or phrase to connect ideas.***
   College costs are rising; as a result, many students are worried.
5. ***Use a dependent word (although, because, when, and so on) to connect ideas.***
   Because college costs are rising, many students are worried.

Use a Period to Create Two Separate Sentences

Be sure each sentence begins with a capital letter and ends with a period.

INCORRECT (FUSED SENTENCE)	Elizabeth Bishop wrote the poem "Florida" Maya Angelou wrote a poem called "My Arkansas."
INCORRECT (COMMA SPLICE)	Elizabeth Bishop wrote the poem "Florida," Maya Angelou wrote a poem called "My Arkansas."
CORRECT	Elizabeth Bishop wrote the poem "Florida." Maya Angelou wrote a poem called "My Arkansas."

PRACTICE 22-2

Correct each of the following run-ons by using a period to create two separate sentences. Be sure both of your new sentences begin with a capital letter and end with a period.

Example: Stephen Colbert used to appear on *The Daily Show with Jon Stewart*~~,~~ ~~now,~~ . Now, he hosts *The Late Show*.

1. In 2016, Theresa May became prime minister of the United Kingdom, she replaced David Cameron.

2. New York–style pizza usually has a thin crust Chicago-style "deep-dish pizza" has a thick crust.

3. Last week, Soraya won a text-messaging contest the prize for texting the fastest was five hundred dollars.

4. In some parts of Canada's Northwest Territory, the only way to transport supplies is over frozen lakes, being an ice road trucker is one of the most dangerous jobs in the world.

5. In 1961, the first Six Flags opened in Arlington, Texas, the six flags represent the six former governments of Texas.

Use a Coordinating Conjunction to Connect Ideas

If you want to indicate a particular relationship between ideas—for example, cause and effect or contrast—you can connect two independent clauses with a coordinating conjunction that makes this relationship clear. Always place a comma before the coordinating conjunction.

> **Coordinating Conjunctions**
>
> and   for   or   yet
> but   nor   so

INCORRECT (FUSED SENTENCE) Some schools require students to wear uniforms other schools do not.

INCORRECT (COMMA SPLICE) Some schools require students to wear uniforms, other schools do not.

CORRECT Some schools require students to wear uniforms, but other schools do not. (clauses connected with the coordinating conjunction but, preceded by a comma)

PRACTICE 22-3

Correct each of the following run-ons by using a coordinating conjunction (*and*, *but*, *or*, *nor*, *for*, *so*, or *yet*) to connect ideas. Be sure to put a comma before each coordinating conjunction.

Example: Many college students use Snapchat and Instagram to keep up with their friends ⟨, and⟩ they also use these sites to find new friends.

1. A car with soft tires gets poor gas mileage, keeping tires inflated is a good way to save money on gas.

2. Once it was difficult for football fans to see the first-down line on television, the computer-generated yellow line makes it much easier.

3. Indonesia has more volcanoes than any other country the United States has the biggest volcano in the world, Hawaii's Mauna Loa.

4. Chefs can become famous for cooking at popular restaurants they can gain fame by hosting television shows.

5. Overcrowded schools often purchase portable classrooms or trailers this is only a temporary solution.

Use a Semicolon to Connect Ideas

If you want to indicate a particularly close connection—or a strong contrast—between two ideas, use a semicolon.

INCORRECT (FUSED SENTENCE)	Most professional basketball players go to college most professional baseball players do not.
INCORRECT (COMMA SPLICE)	Most professional basketball players go to college, most professional baseball players do not.
CORRECT	Most professional basketball players go to college; most professional baseball players do not. (clauses connected with a semicolon)

PRACTICE 22-4

Correct each of the following run-ons by using a semicolon to connect ideas. Do not use a capital letter after the semicolon unless the word that follows it is a proper noun.

Example: From 1930 until 2006, Pluto was known as a planet ; it is now known as a "dwarf planet."

1. Of all the states, Alaska has the highest percentage of Native American residents 16 percent of Alaskans are of Native American descent.

2. Satellites and global positioning systems (GPS) can help farmers to better understand the needs of their crops, these new tools are part of a trend called "precision agriculture."

3. Enforcing traffic laws can be difficult some cities use cameras to identify speeding cars.

4. Old landfills can sometimes be made into parks, Cesar Chavez Park in Berkeley, California, is one example.

5. Freestyle motocross riders compete by doing jumps and stunts famous FMX riders include Carey Hart, Nate Adams, and Travis Pastrana.

Use a Semicolon and a Transitional Word or Phrase to Connect Ideas

To show how two closely linked ideas are related, add a transitional word or phrase after the semicolon. The transition will indicate the specific relationship between the two clauses.

INCORRECT (FUSED SENTENCE)	Finding a part-time job can be challenging sometimes it is even hard to find an unpaid internship.
INCORRECT (COMMA SPLICE)	Finding a part-time job can be challenging, sometimes it is even hard to find an unpaid internship.
CORRECT	Finding a part-time job can be challenging; in fact, sometimes it is even hard to find an unpaid internship. (clauses connected with a semicolon followed by the transitional phrase in fact)

Some Frequently Used Transitional Words and Phrases

after all	for this reason	now
also	however	still
as a result	in addition	then
eventually	in fact	therefore
finally	instead	thus
for example	moreover	unfortunately
for instance	nevertheless	

For more complete lists of transitional words and phrases, see 18f.

Correcting Run-Ons **22b** 497

PRACTICE

22-5 Correct each of the following run-ons by using a semicolon, followed by the transitional word or phrase in parentheses, to connect ideas. Be sure to put a comma after the transitional word or phrase.

Example: When babies are first born, they can only see black and
white most baby clothing and blankets are made in pastel colors. (still)
      ^; still,

1. Different condiments are used in different regions of the country, few tables in the Southwest are without a bottle of hot sauce. (for example)

2. Every April, millions of people participate in TV-Turnoff Week by not watching television they read, spend time with family and friends, and generally enjoy their free time. (instead)

3. Today, few people can count on company pension plans, forty years ago, most people could. (however)

4. Many people see bottled water as a waste of money tap water is free. (after all)

5. Owners of "puppy mills" are only concerned with making money they are not concerned with their dogs' well-being. (unfortunately)

FYI

Connecting Ideas with Semicolons

Run-ons often occur when you use a transitional word or phrase to join two independent clauses *without also using a semicolon.*

INCORRECT (FUSED SENTENCE)	It is easy to download information from the Internet however it is not always easy to evaluate the information.
INCORRECT (COMMA SPLICE)	It is easy to download information from the Internet, however it is not always easy to evaluate the information.

To avoid this kind of run-on, always put a semicolon before the transitional word or phrase and a comma after it.

CORRECT	It is easy to download information from the Internet; however, it is not always easy to evaluate the information.

Use a Dependent Word to Connect Ideas

When one idea is dependent on another, you can connect the two ideas by adding a dependent word, such as *when*, *who*, *although*, or *because*.

INCORRECT (FUSED SENTENCE)	American union membership was high in the mid-twentieth century it has declined in recent years.
INCORRECT (COMMA SPLICE)	American union membership was high in the mid-twentieth century, it has declined in recent years.
CORRECT	Although American union membership was high in the mid-twentieth century, it has declined in recent years. (clauses connected with the dependent word *although*)
CORRECT	American union membership, which was high in the mid-twentieth century, has declined in recent years. (clauses connected with the dependent word *which*)

Some Frequently Used Dependent Words

after	even though	until
although	if	when
as	since	which
because	that	who
before	unless	

For complete lists of dependent words, including subordinating conjunctions and relative pronouns, see 18g and 18h.

PRACTICE 22-6

Correct each run-on in the following paragraph by adding a dependent word. Consult the list above to help you choose a logical dependent word. Be sure to add correct punctuation where necessary.

Example: Harlem was a rural area ^until^ improved transportation linked it to lower Manhattan.

(1) Contemporary historians have written about the Harlem Renaissance, its influence is still not widely known. (2) Harlem was populated mostly by European immigrants at the turn of the last century, it saw an influx of African Americans beginning in 1910. (3) This migration from the South continued Harlem became one of the largest African American communities in the United States. (4) Many black artists and writers settled in Harlem during the 1920s. African American art flourished. (5) This "Harlem Renaissance" was an important era in American literary history it is not even mentioned in some textbooks. (6) Scholars recognize the great works of the Harlem Renaissance, they often point to the writers Langston Hughes and Countee Cullen and the artists Henry Tanner and Sargent Johnson. (7) Zora Neale Hurston moved to Harlem from her native Florida in 1925, she began a book of African American folklore. (8) Harlem was an exciting place in the 1920s, people from all over the city went there to listen to jazz and to dance. (9) The white playwright Eugene O'Neill went to Harlem to audition actors for his play *The Emperor Jones*, he made an international star of the great Paul Robeson. (10) The Great Depression occurred in the 1930s, it led to the end of the Harlem Renaissance.

PRACTICE

22-7 Correct each of the following run-ons in one of these four ways: by creating two separate sentences, by using a coordinating conjunction, by using a semicolon, or by using a semicolon followed by a transitional word or phrase. Remember to put a semicolon before, and a comma after, each transitional word or phrase.

Example: Some fish-and-chip shops in Scotland sell deep-fried MARS bars ~~children~~ . Children are the biggest consumers of these calorie-rich bars.

1. Twenty-five percent of Americans under the age of fifty have one or more tattoos 50 percent of Americans under the age of twenty-five have one or more tattoos.

2. The ancient Greeks built their homes facing south this practice took advantage of light and heat from the winter sun.

3. In 1985, a team of musical artists recorded "We Are the World" in support of African famine relief in 2010, artists recorded the same song in support of Haitian earthquake relief.

4. The comic-strip cat Garfield is not cuddly Garzooka, a superhero cat, is even less cuddly.

5. Horse-racing fans love jockey Calvin Borel for his enthusiasm during postrace interviews fellow jockeys respect him for his work ethic.

6. The average Swiss eats twenty-three pounds of chocolate each year the average American eats less than half that amount.

7. Flamenco—a Spanish style of dancing, singing, and clapping—was traditionally informal and unplanned it has been compared to improvisational American jazz.

8. Seattle is considered to have the most-educated population of any major city the smaller city of Arlington, Virginia, has a higher percentage of college graduates.

9. In Acadia National Park in Maine, large stones line the edges of steep trails the stones are called "Rockefeller's teeth" in honor of the trails' patron.

10. Allen Ginsberg was charged with obscenity for his book *Howl* the charges were dismissed.

CHAPTER REVIEW

EDITING PRACTICE

Read the following student essay, and revise it to eliminate run-ons. Correct each run-on in the way that best indicates the relationship between ideas, and be sure to punctuate correctly. The first error has been corrected for you.

Comic-Book Heroes

Comic-book heroes have a long history~~, they~~ . They originated in comic strips and radio shows. In the "Golden Age" of comic books, individual superheroes were the most popular Characters, then teams and groups of superheroes were introduced. Today, some of these superheroes can be found in movies and graphic novels. Over the years, superheroes have remained very popular.

One of the first comic-book heroes was Popeye. Popeye had no supernatural powers, he battled his enemy, Bluto, with strength supplied by spinach. Another early comic-book hero was The Shadow he fought crime in a cape and mask. The Shadow first appeared in comic books in 1930 later the character had his own radio show.

The late 1930s and 1940s are considered the Golden Age of comic books, many famous comic-book heroes were introduced at that time. The first Superman comic appeared in 1939. Superman came out from behind his secret identity as Clark Kent, he could fly "faster than a speeding bullet." Superman was the first comic-book hero who clearly had a superhuman ability to fight evil. Batman was different from Superman he had no real superpowers. Also, Superman was decent and moral, Batman was willing to break the rules. Wonder Woman appeared in 1941, she truly had superhuman qualities. For example, she could catch a bullet in one hand, she could also regrow a limb.

Superheroes sometimes had help. Batman had Robin, Wonder Woman had her sister, Wonder Girl. Sometimes there were superhero teams, these groups of

> **READING TIP**
> This student essay provides a history of comic-book heroes in chronological (time) order. To aid your comprehension, create a bulleted list of the supporting details for each date.

superheroes helped each other fight evil. The first team was the Justice League of America it originally included Superman, Batman, Aquaman, The Flash, Wonder Woman, Green Lantern, and Martian Manhunter. Eventually, the Justice League fought against threats to the existence of the earth these threats even included alien invasions. Another superhero team was the X-Men they were mutants with supernatural abilities.

Now, comic books are not as popular as they used to be, however, superheroes can still be found in popular movies. Superman has been the main character in many movies, a successful Wonder Woman movie was released in 2017. There have also been several successful Batman, Spider-Man, Iron Man, and Fantastic Four movies. In graphic novels, Superman, Batman, and the Fantastic Four are still heroes, recent graphic novels feature Captain America and the Runaways. Apparently, people still want to see superheroes fight evil and win.

Review checklist

Run-Ons

✔ A run-on is an error that occurs when two sentences are joined incorrectly. There are two kinds of run-ons: fused sentences and comma splices. (See 22a.)

✔ A fused sentence occurs when two sentences are incorrectly joined without any punctuation. (See 22a.)

✔ A comma splice occurs when two sentences are joined with just a comma. (See 22a.)

✔ Correct a run-on in one of the following ways:

1. By creating two separate sentences

   _____. _____.

2. By using a coordinating conjunction

   _____, [coordinating conjunction] _____.

3. By using a semicolon

   _____; _____.

4. By using a semicolon followed by a transitional word or phrase

   _____; [transitional word or phrase], _____.

5. By using a dependent word

   [Dependent word] _____, _____.

   _____ [dependent word] _____. (See 22b.)

23 Fragments

23a Recognizing Fragments

A **fragment** is an incomplete sentence. Every sentence must include at least one subject and one verb, and every sentence must express a complete thought. If a group of words does not do *both* these things, it is a fragment and not a sentence—even if it begins with a capital letter and ends with a period.

The following is a complete sentence:

SENTENCE	The actors in the play were very talented. (The sentence includes both a subject and a verb and expresses a complete thought.)

Above "actors" is S and above "were" is V.

Because a sentence must have both a subject and a verb and express a complete thought, the following groups of words are not complete sentences; they are fragments:

FRAGMENT (NO VERB)	The actors in the play. (What point is being made about the actors?)
FRAGMENT (NO SUBJECT)	Were very talented. (Who were very talented?)
FRAGMENT (NO SUBJECT OR VERB)	Very talented. (Who was very talented?)
FRAGMENT (DOES NOT EXPRESS COMPLETE THOUGHT)	Because the actors in the play were very talented. (What happened because they were very talented?)

FYI

Spotting Fragments

Fragments almost always appear next to complete sentences.

COMPLETE SENTENCE	FRAGMENT
Celia took two electives.	Physics 320 and Spanish 101.

The fragment does not have a subject or a verb. The complete sentence that comes before it, however, has both a subject (*Celia*) and a verb (*took*). Often, you can correct a fragment by attaching it to an adjacent sentence that supplies the missing words. (This sentence will usually appear right before the fragment.)

Celia took two electives, Physics 320 and Spanish 101.

WORD POWER
adjacent next to

Recognizing Fragments 23a 505

PRACTICE 23-1

Some of the following items are fragments, and others are complete sentences. On the line following each item, write *F* if it is a fragment and *S* if it is a complete sentence.

Example: Star formations in the night sky. ____F____

1. To save as much as possible for college. _____

2. The judge gave her a two-year sentence. _____

3. A birthday on Christmas Day. _____

4. Because he lost ten pounds on his new diet. _____

5. Working in the garden and fixing the roof. _____

6. Sonya flew to Mexico City. _____

7. Starts in August in many parts of the country. _____

8. And slept in his own bed last night. _____

9. Famous for her movie roles. _____

10. Phones that also play music and take photos. _____

PRACTICE 23-2

In the following paragraph, some of the numbered groups of words are missing a subject, a verb, or both. First, underline each fragment. Then, decide how each fragment could be attached to a nearby word group to create a complete new sentence. Finally, rewrite the entire paragraph, using complete sentences, on the lines provided.

Example: Gatorade was invented at the University of Florida. <u>To help the Florida Gators fight dehydration.</u>

Rewrite: <u>Gatorade was invented at the University of Florida to help the Florida Gators fight dehydration.</u>

(1) Doctors discovered that football players were losing electrolytes and carbohydrates. (2) Through their sweat. (3) They invented a drink. (4) That replaced these important elements. (5) Gatorade tasted terrible. (6) But did its job. (7) The Florida Gators survived a very hot season. (8) And won most of their games. (9) Now, Gatorade is used by many college and professional football teams. (10) As well as baseball, basketball, tennis, and soccer teams.

Rewrite

_____
_____
_____
_____

 ## 23b Missing-Subject Fragments

Every sentence must include both a subject and a verb. If the subject is left out, the sentence is incomplete. In the following example, the first word group is a sentence. It includes both a subject (*He*) and a verb (*packed*). However, the second word group is a fragment. It includes a verb (*took*), but it does not include a subject.

SENTENCE	FRAGMENT
He <u>packed</u> his books and laptop.	And also took an umbrella.

The best way to correct this kind of fragment is to attach it to the sentence that comes right before it. This sentence will usually contain the missing subject.

CORRECT He packed his books and laptop and also took an umbrella.

Another way to correct this kind of fragment is to add the missing subject.

CORRECT He packed his books and laptop. He also took an umbrella.

PRACTICE
23-3 Each of the following items includes a missing-subject fragment. Using one of the two methods explained above, correct each fragment.

Example: Back-to-school sales are popular with students. And with their parents.

Back-to-school sales are popular with students and with their parents. or

Back-to-school sales are popular with students. The sales are also popular

with their parents.

1. Quitting smoking is difficult. But is really worth the effort.

   _____

2. Some retailers make large donations to charity. And even donate part of their profits.

   _____
   _____

3. Geography bees resemble spelling bees. But instead test the contestants' knowledge of countries around the world.

   _____
   _____

4. School uniforms are often preferred by parents. And also favored by many school principals.

   _____
   _____

5. During the Cold War, the Soviet Union and the United States were rivals. But never actually fought a war with each other.

_____

_____

 ## 23c Phrase Fragments

Every sentence must include a subject and a verb. A **phrase** is a group of words that is missing a subject or a verb or both. When you punctuate a phrase as if it is a sentence, you create a fragment.

If you spot a phrase fragment in your writing, you can often correct it by attaching it to the sentence that comes directly before it.

Appositive Fragments

An **appositive** identifies, renames, or describes an adjacent noun or pronoun. An appositive cannot stand alone as a sentence.

To correct an appositive fragment, attach it to the sentence that comes right before it. (This sentence will contain the noun or pronoun that the appositive describes.)

INCORRECT	He decorated the room in his favorite colors. **FRAGMENT** Brown and black.
CORRECT	He decorated the room in his favorite colors, brown and black.

Sometimes a word or expression like *especially, except, including, such as, for example,* or *for instance* introduces an appositive. Even if an appositive is introduced by one of these expressions, it is still a fragment.

INCORRECT	A balanced diet should include high-fiber foods. **FRAGMENT** Such as leafy vegetables, fruits, beans, and whole-grain bread.
CORRECT	A balanced diet should include high-fiber foods, such as leafy vegetables, fruits, beans, and whole-grain bread.

Prepositional Phrase Fragments

A **prepositional phrase** consists of a preposition and its object. A prepositional phrase cannot stand alone as a sentence. To correct a prepositional phrase fragment, attach it to the sentence that comes immediately before it.

INCORRECT   She promised to stand by him. **In sickness and in health.** [FRAGMENT]

CORRECT   She promised to stand by him in sickness and in health.

Infinitive Fragments

An **infinitive** consists of *to* plus the base form of the verb (*to be, to go, to write*). An infinitive phrase (*to be free, to go home, to write a novel*) cannot stand alone as a sentence. You can usually correct an infinitive fragment by attaching it to the sentence that comes directly before it.

INCORRECT   Eric considered dropping out of school. **To start his own business.** [FRAGMENT]

CORRECT   Eric considered dropping out of school to start his own business.

You can also add the words needed to complete the sentence.

CORRECT   Eric considered dropping out of school. **He wanted** to start his own business.

PRACTICE 23-4

In the following paragraph, some of the numbered groups of words are phrase fragments. First, underline each fragment. Then, decide how each fragment could be attached to an adjacent sentence to create a complete new sentence. Finally, rewrite the entire paragraph, using complete sentences, on the lines provided.

Example: Florence Nightingale worked as a nurse. During the Crimean War.

Rewrite: Florence Nightingale worked as a nurse during the Crimean War.

(1) Nurses' uniforms have changed a lot. (2) Over the years. (3) Originally, nurses' uniforms looked like nuns' habits because nuns used to provide care. (4) To sick people. (5) In the late 1800s, a student of Florence

> **READING TIP**
> When you come across an unfamiliar word (or a familiar word used in an unfamiliar way, such as *habits in* Practice 23-4), scan the words, phrases, and sentences surrounding the unfamiliar word for context clues that can help you figure out the meaning of the word.

Nightingale created a brown uniform. (6) With a white apron and cap. (7) This uniform was worn by student nurses at her school. (8) The Florence Nightingale School of Nursing and Midwifery. (9) Eventually, nurses began to wear white uniforms, white stockings, white shoes, and starched white caps. (10) To stress the importance of cleanliness. (11) Many older people remember these uniforms. (12) With affection. (13) Today, most nurses wear bright, comfortable scrubs. (14) To help patients (especially children) feel more at ease.

Rewrite

_____
_____
_____
_____
_____
_____
_____
_____

PRACTICE 23-5

Each of the following items is a phrase fragment, not a sentence. Correct each fragment by adding any words needed to turn the fragment into a complete sentence. (You may add words before or after the fragment.)

Example: During World War I. _A flu epidemic killed millions of people during World War I._ or _During World War I, a flu epidemic killed millions of people._

1. To be the best player on the team. _____

   _____

2. From a developing nation in Africa. _____

   _____

3. Such as tulips or roses. _____

   _____

4. Behind door number 3. _____

   _____

5. Including my parents and grandparents. _____

   _____

23d *-ing* Fragments

Every sentence must include a subject and a verb. If the verb is incomplete, a word group is a fragment, not a sentence.

An *-ing* verb cannot be a complete verb. It needs a **helping verb** to complete it. An *-ing* verb, such as *looking*, cannot stand alone in a sentence without a helping verb (*is looking*, *was looking*, *were looking*, and so on). When you use an *-ing* verb without a helping verb, you create a fragment.

	FRAGMENT
INCORRECT	The twins are full of mischief. Always looking for trouble.

The best way to correct an *-ing* fragment is to attach it to the sentence that comes right before it.

CORRECT	The twins are full of mischief, always looking for trouble.

Another way to correct an *-ing* fragment is to add a subject and a helping verb.

CORRECT	The twins are full of mischief. They are always looking for trouble.

> **FYI**
>
> **Being**
>
> As you write, be careful not to use the *-ing* verb *being* as if it were a complete verb.
>
> INCORRECT I decided to take a nap. The outcome being that I slept through calculus class.
>
> To correct this kind of fragment, substitute a form of the verb *be* that can serve as the main verb in a sentence—for example, *is*, *was*, *are*, or *were*.
>
> CORRECT I decided to take a nap. The outcome was that I slept through calculus class.

PRACTICE 23-6

Each of the following items includes an *-ing* fragment. In each case, correct the fragment by attaching it to the sentence before it.

Example: You can use a number of strategies to repay your student loans early. Saving you money in the long run.

You can use a number of strategies to repay your student loans early, saving you money in the long run.

1. Most student loans have a grace period. Providing time for you to start earning an income before loan payments begin.

   _____

   _____

2. Use this grace period for creating a budget. Building it around how much you owe.

   _____

   _____

3. During the grace period, you can consolidate several different loans. Arranging for just one payment.

   _____

   _____

4. Try to pay more than the minimum. Setting up automatic payments with the extra amount included.

_____

_____

5. Apply any tax refund you receive to your student loan. Using the extra money to reduce your debt.

_____

_____

 ## 23e Dependent-Clause Fragments

Every sentence must include a subject and a verb. Every sentence must also express a complete thought.

A **dependent clause** is a group of words that is introduced by a dependent word, such as *although*, *because*, *that*, or *after*. A dependent clause includes a subject and a verb, but it does not express a complete thought. Therefore, it cannot stand alone as a sentence. To correct a dependent-clause fragment, you must complete the thought.

The following dependent clause is incorrectly punctuated as if it were a sentence:

>   **FRAGMENT**   After Simon won the lottery.

This fragment includes both a subject (*Simon*) and a complete verb (*won*), but it does not express a complete thought. What happened after Simon won the lottery? To turn this fragment into a sentence, you need to complete the thought.

>   **SENTENCE**   After Simon won the lottery, <u>he quit his night job.</u>

Some dependent clauses are introduced by dependent words called **subordinating conjunctions**.

>   **FRAGMENT**   Although Marisol had always dreamed of visiting America.

This fragment includes a subject (*Marisol*) and a complete verb (*had dreamed*), but it is not a sentence; it is a dependent clause introduced by the subordinating conjunction *although*.

To correct this kind of fragment, attach it to an **independent clause** (a simple sentence) to complete the idea. (You can often find the independent clause you need right before or right after the fragment.)

>   **SENTENCE**   Although Marisol had always dreamed of visiting America, <u>she did not have enough money for the trip until 2010.</u>

> **Subordinating Conjunctions**
>
> | | | | |
> |---|---|---|---|
> | after | even though | since | whenever |
> | although | if | so that | where |
> | as | if only | than | whereas |
> | as if | in order that | that | wherever |
> | as though | now that | though | whether |
> | because | once | unless | while |
> | before | provided that | until | |
> | even if | rather than | when | |
>
> For information on how to use subordinating conjunctions, see 18g.

FYI

Correcting Dependent-Clause Fragments

The simplest way to correct a dependent-clause fragment is to cross out the dependent word that makes the idea incomplete.

~~Although~~ Marisol had always dreamed of visiting America.

However, when you delete the dependent word, readers may have trouble seeing the connection between the new sentence and the one before or after it. A better way to revise is to attach the dependent-clause fragment to an adjacent independent clause, as illustrated in the example at the bottom of page 513.

Some dependent clauses are introduced by dependent words called **relative pronouns**.

FRAGMENT Novelist Richard Wright, who came to Paris in 1947.

FRAGMENT A quinceañera, which celebrates a Latina's fifteenth birthday.

FRAGMENT A key World War II battle that was fought on the Pacific island of Guadalcanal.

Each of the above fragments includes a subject (*Richard Wright, quinceañera, battle*) and a complete verb (*came, celebrates, was fought*). However, they are not sentences because they do not express complete thoughts. In each case, a relative pronoun creates a dependent clause.

To correct each of these fragments, add the words needed to complete the thought.

SENTENCE   Novelist Richard Wright, who came to Paris in 1947, <u>spent the rest of his life there.</u>

SENTENCE   A quinceañera, which celebrates a Latina's fifteenth birthday, <u>signifies her entrance into womanhood.</u>

SENTENCE   A key World War II battle that was fought on the Pacific island of Guadalcanal <u>took place in 1943.</u>

> **Relative Pronouns**
>
> | that | who | whomever |
> |-------|---------|----------|
> | what | whoever | whose |
> | which | whom | |
>
> For information on how to use relative pronouns, see 18h.

PRACTICE 23-7

Correct each of the following dependent-clause fragments by attaching it to the sentence before or after it. If the dependent clause comes at the beginning of a sentence, place a comma after it.

Example: Before it became a state. West Virginia was part of Virginia.

Before it became a state, West Virginia was part of Virginia.

1. Because many homeless people are mentally ill. It is hard to find housing for them.

   _____

2. People do not realize how dangerous raccoons can be. Even though they can be found in many parts of the United States.

   _____
   _____

3. I make plans to be better organized. Whenever a new semester begins.

   _____

4. Until something changes. We will just have to accept the situation.

   _____

5. Because it is a very controversial issue. My parents and I have agreed not to discuss it.

_____

_____

PRACTICE

23-8 Each of the following is a fragment. Some fragments are missing a subject, some are phrases incorrectly punctuated as sentences, others do not have a complete verb, and still others are dependent clauses punctuated as sentences. Turn each fragment into a complete sentence, writing the revised sentence on the line below the fragment. Whenever possible, try creating two different revisions.

Example: As part of a healthy diet.

Revised: As part of a healthy diet, many people avoid sugary drinks.

Revised: Many people enjoy fruit as part of a healthy diet.

1. To participate in campus activities.

   Revised: _____

   _____

   Revised: _____

   _____

2. Programs that help users create a budget.

   Revised: _____

   _____

   Revised: _____

   _____

3. On the way to the gym.

   Revised: _____

   _____

   Revised: _____

   _____

4. Because many employers want to hire bilingual workers.

   Revised: _____

   _____

   Revised: _____

   _____

5. Taking class notes on a laptop.

   Revised: _____

   _____

   Revised: _____

   _____

6. Tried a new recipe.

   Revised: _____

   _____

   Revised: _____

   _____

CHAPTER REVIEW

EDITING PRACTICE

Read the following student essay, which includes incomplete sentences. Underline each fragment. Then, correct the fragment by attaching it to an adjacent sentence that completes the idea. Be sure to punctuate correctly. The first fragment has been underlined and corrected for you.

> **READING TIP**
> What is the writer's position in this essay? What evidence (examples and reasons) supports this position?

A New Face

Have you ever thought about the people whose portraits appear on our paper money? Most of us are so used to seeing George Washington on the one-dollar bill that we hardly Even notice him. The same goes for the rest of our paper money, ~~Which~~ , which is dominated by presidents and founding fathers. Several denominations will be updated in the near future. So it is time to consider a change. New bills would let us recognize people who have made a mark on history in different ways. Going beyond the usual faces. One person who deserves to be considered is Jeannette Rankin. The first woman elected to Congress.

First, here is some background. About money. The secretary of the treasury selects the people whose faces appear on our currency. By law, only someone who is deceased may appear. On U.S. money. The portraits on paper money today were adopted long ago. In 1929. Bills are being redesigned now to improve security features. And to include a touch feature that will assist blind people.

Former presidents dominate the money we use today. With two exceptions. The $10 bill features Alexander Hamilton, the first treasury secretary. And the $100 bill features Benjamin Franklin, a signer of the Declaration of Independence. The only woman who has appeared (so far) on U.S. paper currency is Martha Washington. Our first First Lady. Her portrait was featured on silver certificates. In the 1880s. Two other women who appeared on American money were Susan B. Anthony and Sacagawea. But their portraits were on coins.

Jeannette Rankin could be one of the first women to appear on modern paper currency. Rankin was a pioneer for women's rights. And a lifelong peace activist. She served two terms in Congress. In 1917–1919 and again in 1940–1942. In her first term, she helped pass the 19th Amendment. Giving women the right to vote. She also argued for a Constitutional amendment banning child labor. And she was the only member of Congress to vote against U.S. participation in both World War I and World War II. After she left politics, she kept working for peace. Leading a march to Capitol Hill at the age of 87 to protest the Vietnam War. She was considering another run for office when she died. at age 92.

In 2020. The United States will celebrate the 100th anniversary of the 19th Amendment. As one of the people who fought hardest for a woman's right to vote. Jeannette Ranking has earned her place in history. The treasury secretary may decide to reveal new currency designs as part of the 100th anniversary celebration. Making it even more appropriate for Jeannette Rankin's face to appear on one of those bills.

The idea of putting a female face on our paper money is not new. And there are many worthy candidates. For example, among the most popular suggestions are Eleanor Roosevelt and Rosa Parks. Jeannette Rankin may not be as well known. But as the first woman in Congress, she paved the way for others. The face of this independent, dedicated American is a fitting choice for the first woman on U.S. paper currency.

Review checklist

Fragments

✔ A fragment is an incomplete sentence. Every sentence must include a subject and a verb and express a complete thought. (See 23a.)

✔ Every sentence must include a subject. (See 23b.)

✔ Phrases cannot stand alone as sentences. (See 23c.)

✔ Every sentence must include a complete verb. (See 23d.)

✔ Dependent clauses cannot stand alone as sentences. (See 23e.)

24 Subject-Verb Agreement

 ## 24a Understanding Subject-Verb Agreement

A sentence's subject (a noun or a pronoun) and its verb must **agree**: singular subjects take singular verbs, and plural subjects take plural verbs.

       s   v
The <u>museum</u> <u>opens</u> at ten o'clock. (singular noun subject *museum* takes singular verb *opens*)

        s   v
Both <u>museums</u> <u>open</u> at ten o'clock. (plural noun subject *museums* takes plural verb *open*)

s   v
<u>She</u> always <u>watches</u> the eleven o'clock news. (singular pronoun subject *she* takes singular verb *watches*)

 s   v
<u>They</u> always <u>watch</u> the eleven o'clock news. (plural pronoun subject *they* takes plural verb *watch*)

> **Subject-Verb Agreement with Regular Verbs**
>
> | | SINGULAR | PLURAL |
> |---|---|---|
> | **First person** | I play | Molly and I/we play |
> | **Second person** | you play | you play |
> | **Third person** | he/she/it plays | they play |
> | | the man plays | the men play |
> | | Molly plays | Molly and Sam play |

PRACTICE 24-1

Underline the correct form of the verb in each of the following sentences. Make sure the verb agrees with its subject.

Example: Sometimes local farmers (<u>grow</u>/grows) unusual vegetables.

(1) Locavores (choose/chooses) to eat locally grown food for a number of reasons. (2) Some locavores (eat/eats) local food simply because they (like/likes) the taste. (3) When food (travel/travels) a long distance, it (lose/loses) some of its flavor and freshness. (4) By eating locally grown food, locavores also (hope/hopes) to decrease the use of fossil fuels. (5) After all, food transportation (require/requires) a lot of energy. (6) In addition, locavores (visit/visits) farmers' markets to support local producers. (7) Local farmers (need/needs) their community's support to survive. (8) In some cases, local food supporters (buy/buys) only food produced within 50 or 100 miles. (9) In colder or drier regions, however, the climate (make/makes) such a strict policy difficult. (10) More often, a locavore diet (contain/contains) a mix of food from local and faraway places.

> **WORD POWER**
> **locavore** a person who eats only locally produced foods

24b Compound Subjects

The subject of a sentence is not always a single word. It can also be a **compound subject**, made up of two or more subjects joined by *and* or *or*. To avoid subject-verb agreement problems with compound subjects, follow these rules.

1. When the parts of a compound subject are connected by *and*, the compound subject takes a plural verb.

    <u>France and Germany</u> <u>share</u> the euro as an official currency.
            S   V

2. When the parts of a compound subject are connected by *or*, the verb agrees with the part of the subject that is closer to it.

>   S   V
> The mayor or the council members meet with community groups.
>   S   V
> The council members or the mayor meets with community groups.

PRACTICE 24-2 Underline the correct form of the verb in each of the following sentences. Make sure that the verb agrees with its compound subject.

Example: Every summer, wind and rain (<u>pound</u>/pounds) the small shack on the beach.

1. Trophies and medals (fill/fills) my sister's bedroom.
2. Mashed potatoes and gravy (come/comes) with all our chicken dinners.
3. The instructor or his graduate students (grade/grades) the final exams.
4. A voice coach and a piano instructor (teach/teaches) each of the gifted students.
5. Pollen or cat hair (trigger/triggers) allergies in many people.
6. Psychologists or social workers (provide/provides) crisis counseling.
7. Exercise and healthy eating habits (lead/leads) to longer lives.
8. Both parents or only the father (walk/walks) the bride down the aisle at a wedding.
9. The restaurant owner and his daughters (greet/greets) customers as they enter.
10. Flowers or a get-well balloon (cheer/cheers) people up when they are ill.

24c   Be, Have, and Do

The verbs *be*, *have*, and *do* are irregular in the present tense. For this reason, they can present problems with subject-verb agreement. Memorizing their forms is the only sure way to avoid such problems.

Subject-Verb Agreement with *Be*

	SINGULAR	PLURAL
First person	I am	we are
Second person	you are	you are
Third person	he/she/it is	they are
	Tran is	Tran and Ryan are
	the boy is	the boys are

Subject-Verb Agreement with *Have*

	SINGULAR	PLURAL
First person	I have	we have
Second person	you have	you have
Third person	he/she/it has	they have
	Shana has	Shana and Robert have
	the student has	the students have

Subject-Verb Agreement with *Do*

	SINGULAR	PLURAL
First person	I do	we do
Second person	you do	you do
Third person	he/she/it does	they do
	Ken does	Ken and Mia do
	the book does	the books do

PRACTICE

24-3 Fill in the blank with the correct present tense form of the verb *be*, *have*, or *do*.

Example: Sometimes people __do__ damage without really meaning to. (do)

(1) Biologists _____ serious worries about the damage that invading species of animals can cause. (have) (2) The English sparrow _____ one example. (be) (3) It _____ a role in the decline in the

number of bluebirds. (have) (4) On the Galapagos Islands, cats _____ another example. (be) (5) Introduced by early explorers, they currently _____ much damage to the eggs of the giant tortoises that live on the islands. (do) (6) Scientists today _____ worried now about a new problem. (be) (7) This _____ a situation caused by wildlife agencies that put exotic fish into lakes and streams. (be) (8) They _____ this to please those who enjoy fishing. (do) (9) Although popular with people who fish, this policy _____ major drawbacks. (have) (10) It _____ one drawback in particular: Many native species of fish have been pushed close to extinction. (have)

24d Words between Subject and Verb

A verb must always agree with its subject. Don't be confused when a group of words (for example, a prepositional phrase) comes between the subject and the verb. These words do not affect subject-verb agreement.

                            S   V
CORRECT   High levels of mercury occur in some fish.

                            S   V
CORRECT   Water in the fuel lines causes an engine to stall.

                            S   V
CORRECT   Food between the teeth leads to decay.

An easy way to identify the subject of the sentence is to cross out the words that come between the subject and the verb.

High levels ~~of mercury~~ occur in some fish.
Water ~~in the fuel lines~~ causes an engine to stall.
Food ~~between the teeth~~ leads to decay.

FYI

Words between Subject and Verb

Look out for words such as *in addition to, along with, together with, as well as, except,* and *including*. Phrases introduced by these words do not affect subject-verb agreement.

             s   v

St. Thomas, ~~along with St. Croix and St. John~~, is part of the United States Virgin Islands.

PRACTICE 24-4

In each of the following sentences, cross out the words that separate the subject and the verb. Then, underline the subject of the sentence once and the verb that agrees with the subject twice.

Example: The <u>messages</u> ~~on the phone~~ (<u><u>say</u></u>/says) that Carol is out of town.

1. Each summer, fires from lightning (cause/causes) great damage.

2. Books downloaded onto an eReader usually (cost/costs) less than print books.

3. One out of ten men (gets/get) prostate cancer.

4. The woodstove in the living room (heat/heats) the entire house.

5. Trans fat in a variety of foods (lead/leads) to increased rates of heart disease.

24e Collective Noun Subjects

Collective nouns are words (such as *family* and *audience*) that name a group of people or things but are singular. Because they are singular, they always take singular verbs.

       s   v

The <u>team</u> <u><u>practices</u></u> five days a week in the gym.

Frequently Used Collective Nouns

army	class	corporation	jury
association	club	family	mob
audience	committee	government	team
band	company	group	union

PRACTICE 24-5 Fill in the blank with the correct present tense form of the verb.

Example: Our government __is__ democratically elected by the people. (be)

1. The Caribbean Culture Club _____ on the first Thursday of every month. (meet)

2. The company no longer _____ health insurance for part-time employees. (provide)

3. The basketball team _____ competing in the division finals next week. (be)

4. After two days, the jury _____ been unable to reach a verdict. (have)

5. The union _____ guaranteed raises for its members. (want)

24f Indefinite Pronoun Subjects

Indefinite pronouns—*anybody, everyone*, and so on—do not refer to a particular person, place, or idea.

Most indefinite pronouns are singular and take singular verbs.

    S   V
No one likes getting up early.

S V
Everyone likes to sleep late.

S V
Somebody likes beets.

> **Singular Indefinite Pronouns**
>
> | another | either | neither | somebody |
> |---------|--------|---------|----------|
> | anybody | everybody | nobody | someone |
> | anyone | everyone | no one | something |
> | anything | everything | nothing | |
> | each | much | one | |

A few indefinite pronouns (*both, many, several, few, others*) are plural and take plural verbs.

S V
Many were left homeless by Hurricane Sandy.

FYI

Indefinite Pronouns as Subjects

If a prepositional phrase comes between the indefinite pronoun and the verb, cross out the prepositional phrase to help you identify the sentence's subject.

S V
Each ~~of the boys~~ has a bike.

S V
Many ~~of the boys~~ have bikes.

PRACTICE

24-6 Underline the correct verb in each sentence.

Example: As my friends and I know, anything (helps/help) when it comes to paying for college.

1. One of my friends (has/have) an academic scholarship.

2. Another (relies/rely) entirely on loans.

3. Several of us (works/work) on weekends.

4. Everybody (says/say) that work-study jobs are best.

5. Many of the most interesting work-study jobs (is/are) located on campus.

6. Others (places/place) students off campus with nonprofits or government agencies.

7. Some of the work-study jobs (tends/tend) to be better than a regular job.

8. Not everyone (understands/understand) the demands of school, but work-study employers do.

9. Nobody (says/say) juggling work and school is simple, but work-study makes it easier.

10. Each of my work-study friends (is/are) glad to have this option.

24g Verbs before Subjects

A verb always agrees with its subject—even if the verb comes *before* the subject. In questions, for example, word order is reversed, with the verb coming before the subject or with the subject coming between two parts of the verb.

>   S V
> Where is the bank?

> V   S   V
> Are you going to the party?

If you have trouble identifying the subject of a question, answer the question with a statement. (In the statement, the subject will come before the verb.)

>   V   S   S V
> Where is the bank? The bank is on Walnut Street.

FYI

There Is and There Are

When a sentence begins with *there is* or *there are*, the word *there* is not the subject of the sentence. The subject comes after the form of the verb *be*.

         V   S

There is one chief justice on the Supreme Court.

         V   S

There are nine justices on the Supreme Court.

PRACTICE

24-7 Underline the subject of each sentence, and circle the correct form of the verb.

Example: Who ((is)/are) the baseball player who broke Hank Aaron's home-run record?

1. Where (do /does) snakes go in the winter?

2. There (is/ are) three branches of government in the United States.

3. There (is /are) some money available for financial aid.

4. What (is /are) the country with the highest literacy rate?

5. Where (do/ does) the football team practice in the off-season?

CHAPTER REVIEW

EDITING PRACTICE

Read the following student essay, which includes errors in subject-verb agreement. Decide whether each of the underlined verbs agrees with its subject. If it does not, cross out the verb and write in the correct form. If it does, write *C* above the verb. The first sentence has been done for you.

> **READING TIP**
> A writer's purpose is often to persuade, explain, or inform the reader. What clues in this essay help you to identify the writer's purpose?

Making your Own Dream Team

Every August, Sean and a group of friends <u>gathers</u> at his place for a very important meeting. There <u>is</u> chili on the stove and there <u>is</u> sodas in the cooler. The centerpiece on Sean's kitchen table <u>is</u> not a bowl of fruit or a vase of flowers. It <u>is</u> a large, golden trophy with the words "League Champion." As people arrive, everyone <u>admire</u> the trophy and some even <u>shake</u> Sean's hand. What <u>are</u> the meeting about? Sean's fantasy football league <u>is</u> kicking off a new season.

Like sports fans everywhere, Sean and his friends <u>has</u> discovered the fun of fantasy sports leagues. (You <u>do</u> not have to be a sports fan to enjoy fantasy sports leagues, but it <u>help</u>.) Fantasy sports leagues have an online component, but friends often <u>joins</u> a league together. Game days <u>is</u> even better when friends <u>has</u> their own dream teams.

There <u>is</u> different stories about how fantasy sports leagues began, but most <u>agree</u> golf was the first fantasy sport. Today, there <u>are</u> a fantasy league for every major sport, including football, baseball, basketball, hockey, tennis, and cricket. People can be in more than one fantasy league for more than one sport. For example, Sean <u>is</u> in two different football leagues with his friends as well as a tennis league with his grandparents.

A fantasy league <u>imitate</u> the real thing. In professional sports, owners and managers <u>create</u> a team with the best players they can get. The same is true for fantasy sports leagues. Participants <u>chooses</u> real players from a professional

531

sport. They researches the players and puts together a team with a player for each position, depending on the sport. Each fantasy player is a real person from a real team, but the fantasy team have a mix of players from different teams. For instance, Sean's fantasy football team have a quarterback from the Atlanta Falcons and a kicker from the Philadelphia Eagles.

The goal is to choose the best performing athletes during a certain season. Participants uses their own knowledge of their favorite sports. In addition, they looks at actual statistics for players, such as speed, agility, and points scored. For a fantasy team draft, participants combine their own knowledge with players' statistics. Each participant choose a line-up and draft (or pick) those players. Everyone take turns selecting players, so it is important to be prepared. Participants may not get their first choice, or even their third.

Once the season start, fantasy teams compete based on how players perform in actual games. Each real-life player gain or lose points for a fantasy team. A fantasy team might get twenty points for a good performance by one player but zero points for a bad performance by another player. Each team's total determine who wins the league that week. If you are the manager of the fantasy team, you makes strategic decisions based on a player's performance. You trade players, cut players from the team, and sign new players. Most fantasy leagues requires you to choose new players every season. Other leagues lets you keep some or all of your players for the next season.

For most people in fantasy sports leagues, the biggest thrill come at the end of the season. Anyone can have a good week, but only one person get the trophy. Everyone else wait until next year.

Review checklist

Subject-Verb Agreement

- ✔ Singular subjects (nouns and pronouns) take singular verbs, and plural subjects take plural verbs. (See 24a.)
- ✔ Special rules govern subject-verb agreement with compound subjects. (See 24b.)
- ✔ The irregular verbs *be*, *have*, and *do* often present problems with subject-verb agreement in the present tense. (See 24c.)
- ✔ Words that come between the subject and the verb do not affect subject-verb agreement. (See 24d.)
- ✔ Collective nouns are singular and take singular verbs. (See 24e.)
- ✔ Most indefinite pronouns, such as *no one* and *everyone*, are singular and take a singular verb when they serve as the subject of a sentence. A few are plural and take plural verbs. (See 24f.)
- ✔ A sentence's subject and verb must always agree, even if the verb comes before the subject. (See 24g.)

25 Illogical Shifts

A **shift** occurs whenever a writer changes **tense**, **person**, or **voice**. As you write and revise, be sure that any shifts you make are **logical**—that is, that they occur for a reason.

 ## 25a Shifts in Tense

Tense is the form a verb takes to show when an action takes place or when a situation occurs. Some shifts in tense are necessary—for example, to indicate a change from the past to the present.

> **LOGICAL SHIFT**   When they first came out, cell phones were large and bulky, but now they are small and compact.

An **illogical shift in tense** occurs when a writer shifts from one tense to another for no apparent reason.

> **ILLOGICAL SHIFT IN TENSE**   The dog walked to the fireplace. Then, he circles twice and lies down in front of the fire. (shift from past tense to present tense)
>
> **REVISED**   The dog walked to the fireplace. Then, he circled twice and lay down in front of the fire. (consistent use of past tense)
>
> **REVISED**   The dog walks to the fireplace. Then, he circles twice and lies down in front of the fire. (consistent use of present tense)

PRACTICE 25-1   Edit the sentences in the following paragraph to correct illogical shifts in tense. If a sentence is correct, write *C* in the blank.

534

Example: The 100th Battalion of the 442nd Infantry is the only remaining United States Army Reserve ground combat unit that fought in World War II. ____C____

(1) During World War II, the 100th Battalion of the 442nd Combat Infantry Regiment was made up of young Japanese Americans who are eager to serve in the U.S. Army. _____ (2) At the start of World War II, 120,000 Japanese Americans were sent to relocation camps because the government feared that they might be disloyal to the United States. _____ (3) However, in 1943, the United States needed more soldiers, so it sends recruiters to the camps to ask for volunteers. _____ (4) The Japanese-American volunteers are organized into the 442nd Combat Infantry Regiment. _____ (5) The soldiers of the 442nd Infantry fought in some of the bloodiest battles of the war, including the invasion of Italy at Anzio and a battle in Bruyères, France, where they capture over two hundred enemy soldiers. _____ (6) When other U.S. troops are cut off by the enemy, the 442nd Infantry soldiers were sent to rescue them. _____ (7) The Japanese-American soldiers suffered the highest casualty rate of any U.S. unit and receive over eighteen thousand individual decorations. _____

25b Shifts in Person

Person is the form a pronoun takes to show who is speaking, spoken about, or spoken to.

Person

	SINGULAR	PLURAL
First person	I	we
Second person	you	you
Third person	he, she, it	they

An **illogical shift in person** occurs when a writer shifts from one person to another for no apparent reason.

ILLOGICAL SHIFT IN PERSON The hikers were told that you had to stay on the trail. (shift from third person to second person)

REVISED The hikers were told that they had to stay on the trail. (consistent use of third person)

ILLOGICAL SHIFT IN PERSON Anyone can learn to cook if you practice. (shift from third person to second person)

REVISED You can learn to cook if you practice. (consistent use of second person)

REVISED Anyone can learn to cook if he or she practices. (consistent use of third person)

PRACTICE 25-2

The sentences in the following paragraph contain illogical shifts in person. Edit each sentence so that it uses pronouns consistently. Be sure to change any verbs that do not agree with the new subjects.

Example: Before a person finds a job in the fashion industry, ~~you have~~ *he or she has* to have some experience.

(1) Young people who want careers in the fashion industry do not always realize how hard you will have to work. (2) They think that working in the world of fashion will be glamorous and that you will make a lot of money. (3) In reality, no matter how talented you are, a recent college

graduate entering the industry is paid only about $22,000 a year. (4) The manufacturers who employ new graduates expect you to work at least three years at this salary before you are promoted. (5) A young designer may get a big raise if you are very talented, but this is unusual. (6) New employees have to pay their dues, and you soon realize that most of your duties are boring. (7) An employee may land a job as an assistant designer but then find that you have to color in designs that have already been drawn. (8) Other beginners discover that you spend most of your time typing up orders. (9) If a person is serious about working in the fashion industry, you have to be realistic. (10) For most newcomers to the industry, the ability to do what you are told to do is more important than your talent.

25c Shifts in Voice

Voice is the form a verb takes to indicate whether the subject is acting or is acted upon. When the subject is acting, the sentence is in the **active voice**. When the subject is acted upon, the sentence is in the **passive voice**.

ACTIVE VOICE	Nat Turner organized a slave rebellion in August 1831. (Subject *Nat Turner* is acting.)
PASSIVE VOICE	A slave rebellion was organized by Nat Turner in 1831. (Subject *rebellion* is acted upon.)

An **illogical shift in voice** occurs when a writer shifts from active to passive voice or from passive to active voice for no apparent reason.

ILLOGICAL SHIFT IN VOICE	J. D. Salinger wrote *The Catcher in the Rye*, and *Franny and Zooey* was also written by him. (active to passive)
REVISED	J. D. Salinger wrote *The Catcher in the Rye*, and he also wrote *Franny and Zooey*. (consistent use of active voice)

ILLOGICAL SHIFT IN VOICE Radium <mark>was discovered</mark> by Marie Curie in 1910, and she <mark>won</mark> a Nobel Prize in chemistry in 1911. (passive to active)

REVISED Marie Curie <mark>discovered</mark> radium in 1910, and she <mark>won</mark> a Nobel Prize in chemistry in 1911. (consistent use of active voice)

FYI

Correcting Illogical Shifts in Voice

You should usually use the active voice in your college writing because it is stronger and more direct than the passive voice.

To change a sentence from the passive to the active voice, determine who or what is acting, and make this noun the subject of a new active voice sentence.

PASSIVE VOICE <mark>Gunpowder</mark> <u>was invented</u> by the Chinese in the ninth century.

(*The Chinese* are acting.)

ACTIVE VOICE <mark>The Chinese</mark> <u>invented</u> gunpowder in the ninth century.

PRACTICE 25-3

The following sentences contain illogical shifts in voice. Revise each sentence by changing the underlined passive voice verb to the active voice.

Example: Two teachers believed they could help struggling students in New York City schools, so "Chess in the Schools" <u>was founded</u> by them.

Two teachers believed they could help struggling students in New York City schools, so they founded "Chess in the Schools."

1. Chess develops critical-thinking skills, and self-discipline and self-esteem <u>are developed</u> by players, too.

_____

_____

2. Because players face complicated chess problems, good problem-solving skills <u>are developed</u> by them.

   _____

   _____

3. Student chess players improve their concentration, and reading and math skills <u>can be improved</u> through this better concentration.

   _____

   _____

4. Chess teaches students how to lose as well as win, and that ability <u>will be needed</u> by students throughout their lives.

   _____

   _____

5. "Chess in the Schools" also helps keep students out of trouble because of the conflict-resolution skills <u>developed</u> by them.

   _____

   _____

CHAPTER REVIEW

EDITING PRACTICE

Read the following essay, which includes illogical shifts in tense, person, and voice. Edit the passage to eliminate the illogical shifts, making sure subjects and verbs agree. The first sentence has been edited for you.

A Different Kind of Vacation

During our upcoming winter break, my sister and I were going to Belize to help build a school. Like many people, we want to travel and see new places, but we did not want to be tourists who only see what is in a guidebook. We also want to help people who are less fortunate than we were. Volunteering gives us the opportunity to combine travel with community service and to get to know a different culture at the same time.

These days, many people are using his or her vacation time to do volunteer work. Lots of charitable organizations offer short-term projects during school or holiday breaks. For most projects, no experience was necessary. All people need is his or her interest in other people and a desire to help.

For example, last year my aunt goes to Tanzania to work in a health clinic. She loved her experience volunteering in a poor rural community where you help local doctors. She also loved the host family who shared their modest house with her. Before she left Tanzania, she and some of the other volunteers climb Mount Kilimanjaro. She said it was the best vacation she had ever had.

Although many volunteer vacations focus on improving schools or health care, a wide range of projects was available. Everyone can find work that suits their interests. For instance, people can volunteer to help preserve the environment, or you can work to protect women's rights. Countries all over the world welcome volunteers because help is needed by a lot of people.

> **READING TIP**
> This essay includes both facts and opinions. Identify at least two facts and two opinions.

My sister and I decided to help with the school in Belize because we believe a clean and safe place to learn is deserved by everyone. We are also eager to do some construction, get to know the local people, and enjoy the warm weather. If we have enough time, we hoped to visit some Mayan ruins as well. All in all, we are looking forward to a rewarding and unforgettable experience.

Review checklist

Illogical Shifts

✔ An illogical shift in tense occurs when a writer shifts from one tense to another for no apparent reason. (See 25a).

✔ An illogical shift in person occurs when a writer shifts from one person to another for no apparent reason. (See 25b).

✔ An illogical shift in voice occurs when a writer shifts from active to passive voice or from passive to active voice for no apparent reason. (See 25c).

26 Misplaced and Dangling Modifiers

A **modifier** is a word or word group that identifies or describes another word in a sentence. Many word groups that act as modifiers are introduced by *-ing* (present participle) or *-ed* (past participle) modifiers. To avoid confusion, a modifier should be placed as close as possible to the word it modifies—ideally, directly before or directly after it.

Working in his garage, Steve Jobs invented the personal computer.

Rejected by Hamlet, Ophelia goes mad and drowns herself.

Used correctly, *-ing* and *-ed* modifiers provide useful information. These types of modifiers can be very confusing when used incorrectly.

The two most common problems with modification are *misplaced modifiers* and *dangling modifiers*.

26a Correcting Misplaced Modifiers

A **misplaced modifier** appears to modify the wrong word because it is placed incorrectly in the sentence. To correct this problem, move the modifier so it is as close as possible to the word it is supposed to modify.

INCORRECT Holden Caulfield went to New York wearing his hunting hat backwards. (Was New York wearing the hunting hat?)

CORRECT Wearing his hunting hat backwards, Holden Caulfield went to New York.

INCORRECT Dressed in a raincoat and boots, I thought my son was prepared for the storm. (Who was dressed in a raincoat and boots?)

CORRECT I thought my son, dressed in a raincoat and boots, was prepared for the storm.

PRACTICE 26-1

Underline the modifier in each of the following sentences. Then, draw an arrow to the word it modifies.

Example: <u>Helping people worldwide</u>, Doctors Without Borders is a group of volunteer medical professionals.

1. Suffering from famine and other disasters, some people are unable to help themselves.

2. Feeding and healing them, Doctors Without Borders improves their lives.

3. Responding to a recent earthquake, doctors arrived within three days to help with the relief effort.

4. Setting up refugee camps in Thailand, the group quickly helped its first survivors.

5. Some doctors, chartering a ship called *The Island of Light*, once provided medical aid to people escaping Vietnam by boat.

PRACTICE 26-2

Rewrite the following sentences, which contain misplaced modifiers, so that each modifier clearly refers to the word it logically modifies.

Example: Mark ate a pizza standing in front of the refrigerator.
Standing in front of the refrigerator, Mark ate a pizza.

1. The cat broke the vase frightened by a noise.

2. Running across my bathroom ceiling, I saw two large, hairy bugs.

3. Lori looked at the man sitting in the chair with red hair.

4. *Wonder Woman* is a 2017 film about a female superhero directed by Patty Jenkins.

5. Ordering an invasion of Russia, the lesson of Napoleon's defeat was forgotten by Hitler.

26b   Correcting Dangling Modifiers

A **dangling modifier** dangles because the word it modifies does not appear in the sentence. Often, a dangling modifier comes at the beginning of a sentence and appears to modify the noun or pronoun that follows it.

Using my computer, the report was finished in two days.

In the sentence above, the modifier *Using my computer* seems to be modifying *the report*. But this makes no sense. (How can the report use a computer?) The word the modifier should logically refer to is missing. To correct this sentence, you need to supply this missing word.

Using my computer, I finished the report in two days.

To correct a dangling modifier, supply a word to which the modifier can logically refer.

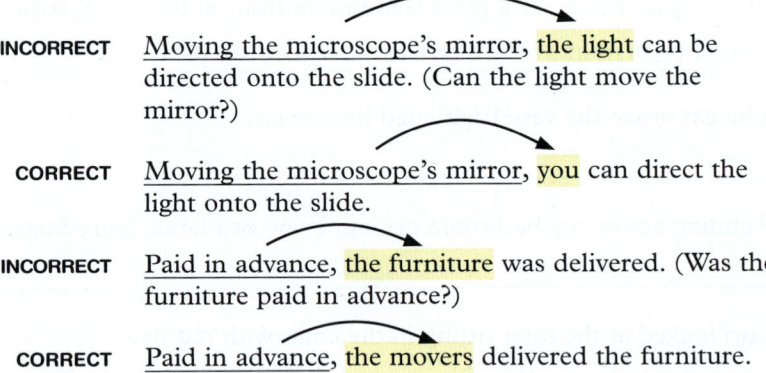

INCORRECT	Moving the microscope's mirror, the light can be directed onto the slide. (Can the light move the mirror?)
CORRECT	Moving the microscope's mirror, you can direct the light onto the slide.
INCORRECT	Paid in advance, the furniture was delivered. (Was the furniture paid in advance?)
CORRECT	Paid in advance, the movers delivered the furniture.

Correcting Dangling Modifiers **26b** 545

PRACTICE
26-3
Each of the following sentences contains a dangling modifier. To correct each sentence, add a word to which the modifier can logically refer.

Example: Waiting inside, my bus passed by.
Waiting inside, I missed my bus.

1. Ordered by the school, the librarians sorted the books.

2. Pushing on the brakes, my car would not stop for the red light.

3. Short of money, the trip was canceled.

4. Working overtime, his salary almost doubled.

5. Angered by the noise, the concert was called off.

PRACTICE
26-4
Complete the following sentences, making sure to include a word to which each modifier can logically refer.

Example: Dancing with the man of her dreams, *she decided it was time to wake up.*

1. Blocked by the clouds, _____
   _____

2. Applying for financial aid, _____
   _____

3. Settled into his recliner chair, _____
   _____

4. Fearing that they might catch a cold, _____
   _____

5. Hearing strange noises through the wall, _____
   _____

CHAPTER REVIEW

EDITING PRACTICE

Read the following student essay, which includes modification errors. Rewrite sentences to correct dangling and misplaced modifiers. In some cases, you will have to supply a word to which the modifier can logically refer. The first sentence has been corrected for you.

Eating as a Sport

After eating a big meal, ~~the food often makes~~ you *often* feel stuffed. Imagine how someone participating in competitive eating feels. To win, you have to eat more food faster than anyone else. Training for days, many different kinds of food are eaten in these contests. For example, contestants eat chicken wings, pizza, ribs, hot dogs, and even matzo balls. Training for events, competitive eating is considered a sport by participants. By winning, a good living can be made by a competitive eater. Considered dangerous by some, competitive eaters and their fans nevertheless continue to grow.

The way it works is that each competitor eats the same weight or portion of food. Giving the signal, the competitors begin eating. Breaking the food in pieces or just eating the food whole, any technique can be used. The competitors, soaked in water, can make the food softer. They can even eat hot dogs separately from their buns. Good competitors are usually not overweight. In fact, some are quite thin. Keeping the stomach from expanding, competitors are hurt by extra fat. By drinking large amounts of water, their stomachs stretch and increase their chances of winning. This is one technique many competitors use when they train.

> **READING TIP**
>
> Previewing an essay by reading only the first sentence of each paragraph and then relating it to your own experiences can help you understand a writer's ideas and remember what you read. Read the first sentence of this essay. Then try to make a connection between this sentence and your own experiences. Continue this process with the first sentence of each subsequent paragraph.

The International Federation of Competitive Eating watches over the contests to make sure they are fair and safe. Providing the dates and locations, contests are listed on its website. Often, contests are held at state fairs. Also listing participants, prizes, and rankings of winners, new participants are invited. Before entering the contests, their eating specialty and personal profile must be indicated by new participants. Competitors must also be at least eighteen years old.

Many competitive eaters participate in lots of contests. For example, weighing only 100 pounds, 8.1 pounds of sausage was eaten in only 10 minutes by Sonya Thomas. At another contest, she ate 46 crab cakes in 10 minutes. Held in the United States, some participants come from other countries. For instance, Takeru Kobayashi, who comes from Japan, once ate 18 pounds of cow brains in 15 minutes. Winners usually get cash prizes. The largest prize, $20,000, was awarded in a hot dog–eating contest at Coney Island, which was televised by ESPN. By eating 72 hot dogs and their buns in 10 minutes, the contest was won by Joey Chestnut, a professional speed eater. Almost 50,000 people attended the contest in person, and millions watched on television.

There is some concern about competitive eating. By stretching the stomach, a person's health may be affected. There is also concern about obesity and overeating. Worried about choking, events should have doctors present some people argue. Still, many people like to watch these contests, and they seem to be getting more popular each year.

Review checklist

Misplaced and Dangling Modifiers

 Correct a misplaced modifier by placing the modifier as close as possible to the word it modifies. (See 26a.)

 Correct a dangling modifier by supplying a word to which the modifier can logically refer. (See 26b.)

27 Using Commas

A **comma** is a punctuation mark that separates words or groups of words within sentences, keeping ideas distinct from one another.

In earlier chapters, you learned to use a comma between two simple sentences (independent clauses) linked by a coordinating conjunction to form a compound sentence.

> Some people are concerned about climate change, but others are not.

You also learned to use a comma after a dependent clause that comes before an independent clause in a complex sentence.

> Although bears in the wild can be dangerous, hikers can take steps to protect themselves.

In addition, commas are used to set off directly quoted speech or writing from the rest of the sentence.

> John F. Kennedy said, "Ask not what your country can do for you; ask what you can do for your country."

As you will learn in this chapter, commas have several other uses as well.

 ## 27a Commas in a Series

Use commas to separate all elements in a **series** of three or more words, phrases, or clauses.

> Leyla, Zack, and Kathleen campaigned for Representative Lewis.
> Leyla, Zack, or Kathleen will be elected president of Students for Lewis.
> Leyla made phone calls, licked envelopes, and ran errands for the campaign.
> Leyla is president, Zack is vice president, and Kathleen is treasurer.

549

> **FYI**
>
> **Using Commas in a Series**
>
> Newspapers and magazines usually omit the comma before the coordinating conjunction in a series. However, in college writing, you should always use a comma before the coordinating conjunction.
>
> Leyla, Zack, and Kathleen worked on the campaign.
>
> Exception: Do not use *any* commas if all the items in a series are separated by coordinating conjunctions.
>
> Leyla or Zack or Kathleen will be elected president of Students for Lewis.

PRACTICE

 Edit the following sentences for the use of commas in a series. If the sentence is correct, write *C* in the blank.

Examples

Costa Rica produces bananas, cocoa, and sugarcane. ____*C*____

The pool rules state that there is no running, or jumping, or diving. _____

1. The musician plays guitar bass and drums. _____

2. The organization's goals are feeding the hungry, housing the homeless and helping the unemployed find work. _____

3. *The Price Is Right*, *Wheel of Fortune*, and *Jeopardy!* are three of the longest-running game shows in television history. _____

4. In native Hawaiian culture, yellow was worn by the royalty red was worn by priests and a mixture of the two colors was worn by others of high rank. _____

5. The diary Anne Frank kept while her family hid from the Nazis is insightful, touching and sometimes humorous. _____

27b Commas with Introductory Phrases and Transitional Words and Phrases

Commas can be used to set off introductory phrases and transitional words or phrases from the other parts of a sentence.

Introductory Phrases

Use a comma to set off an **introductory phrase** from the rest of the sentence.

In the event of a fire, proceed to the nearest exit.
Walking home, Nelida decided to change her major.
To keep fit, people should try to exercise regularly.

PRACTICE 27-2

Edit the following sentences for the use of commas with introductory phrases. If the sentence is correct, write *C* in the blank.

Examples

For some medical conditions, effective treatments are hard to find. _____

After taking placebos, some depressed patients experience relief from their symptoms. __C__

(1) Also known as sugar pills placebos contain no actual medicine. _____ (2) Despite this fact, placebos sometimes have positive effects on patients who take them. _____ (3) For years researchers have used placebos in experiments. _____ (4) To evaluate the effectiveness of a medication scientists test the drug on volunteers. _____ (5) To ensure that the experiment's results are reliable, researchers always have a control group. _____ (6) Instead of taking the drug the control group takes a placebo. _____ (7) Thinking they are taking an actual medicine patients in the control group may experience the "placebo effect." _____ (8) After receiving treatment with a placebo, they feel better. _____

Transitional Words and Phrases

Use commas to set off **transitional words or phrases**, whether they appear at the beginning, in the middle, or at the end of a sentence.

In fact, Thoreau spent only one night in jail.
He was, of course, bailed out by a friend.
He did spend more than two years at Walden Pond, however.

> **FYI**
>
> **Using Commas in Direct Address**
>
> Always use commas to set off the name of someone whom you are addressing (speaking to) directly, whether the name appears at the beginning, in the middle, or at the end of a sentence.
>
> <u>Molly</u>, come here and look at this.
> Come here, <u>Molly</u>, and look at this.
> Come here and look at this, <u>Molly</u>.

PRACTICE

27-3 Edit the following sentences for the use of commas with transitional words and phrases. If the sentence is correct, write *C* in the blank.

Example: Eventually, most people build a personal credit history.

(1) Often establishing credit can be difficult. _____ (2) College students for example often have no credit history of their own, especially if their parents pay their bills. _____ (3) Similarly some older married women have no personal credit history. _____ (4) In fact their credit cards may be in their husbands' names. _____ (5) As a result, they may be unable to get their own loans. _____ (6) Of course one way to establish credit is to apply for a credit card at a local department store. _____ (7) Also, it is relatively easy to get a gas credit card. _____ (8) It is important to pay these credit-card bills promptly however. _____ (9) In addition having checking and savings accounts can help to establish financial reliability. _____ (10) Finally, people who want to establish a credit history can sign an apartment lease and pay the rent regularly to show that they are good credit risks. _____

27c Commas with Appositives

Use commas to set off an **appositive**—a word or word group that identifies, renames, or describes a noun or a pronoun.

> I have visited only one country, Canada, outside the United States. (*Canada* is an appositive that identifies the noun *country*.)
>
> Carlos Santana, leader of the group Santana, played at Woodstock in 1969. (*leader of the group Santana* is an appositive that identifies *Carlos Santana*.)
>
> A really gifted artist, he is also a wonderful father. (*A really gifted artist* is an appositive that describes the pronoun *he*.)

FYI

Using Commas with Appositives

Most appositives are set off by commas, whether they fall at the beginning, in the middle, or at the end of a sentence.

> A dreamer, he spent his life thinking about what he could not have.
>
> He always wanted to build a house, a big white one, overlooking the ocean.
>
> He finally built his dream house, a log cabin.

PRACTICE 27-4

Underline the appositive in each of the following sentences. Then, check each sentence for the correct use of commas to set off appositives, and add any missing commas. If the sentence is correct, write *C* in the blank.

Example: Wendy Kopp, a college student, developed the Teach For America program to help minority students get a better education. _____

1. Guglielmo Marconi a young Italian inventor, sent the first wireless message across the Atlantic Ocean in 1901. _____

2. A member of the boy band 'N Sync Justin Timberlake went on to establish a successful career as a solo musician and an actor. _____

3. HTML hypertext markup language, is the set of codes used to create web documents. _____

4. William Filene, founder of Filene's Department Store, invented the "bargain basement." _____

5. Known as NPR National Public Radio presents a wide variety of programs.

27d Commas with Nonrestrictive Clauses

> **WORD POWER**
> **restrict** to keep within limits
> **restrictive** limiting

Clauses are often used to add information within a sentence. In some cases, commas are needed to set off these clauses; in other cases, commas are not required.

Use commas to set off **nonrestrictive clauses**, those that are not essential to a sentence's meaning. Do not use commas to set off **restrictive clauses**.

- A **nonrestrictive clause** does *not* contain essential information. Nonrestrictive clauses are set off from the rest of the sentence by commas.

    Telephone scams, which cost consumers millions of dollars each year, are becoming increasingly common.

    Here, the clause between the commas (underlined) provides extra information to help readers understand the sentence, but the sentence would still communicate the same idea without this information.

    Telephone scams are becoming increasingly common.

- A **restrictive clause** contains information that is essential to a sentence's meaning. Restrictive clauses are *not* set off from the rest of the sentence by commas.

    Many rock stars who recorded hits in the 1950s made little money from their songs.

    In the sentence above, the clause *who recorded hits in the 1950s* supplies specific information that is essential to the idea the sentence is communicating: It tells readers which group of rock stars made little money. Without the clause, the sentence does not communicate the same idea.

    Many rock stars made little money from their songs.

Compare the meanings of the following pairs of sentences with nonrestrictive and restrictive clauses.

NONRESTRICTIVE Young adults, who text while driving, put themselves and others in danger. (This sentence says that all young adults text while driving and all pose a danger.)

RESTRICTIVE Young adults who text while driving put themselves and others in danger. (This sentence says that only those young adults who text and drive pose a danger.)

NONRESTRICTIVE Student loans, which are based on need, may not be fair to middle-class students. (This sentence says that all student loans are based on need and all may be unfair to middle-class students.)

RESTRICTIVE Student loans that are based on need may not be fair to middle-class students. (This sentence says that only those student loans that are based on need may be unfair to middle-class students.)

FYI

Which, That, and Who

- *Which* always introduces a nonrestrictive clause.

    The job, which had excellent benefits, did not pay well. (clause set off by commas)

- *That* always introduces a restrictive clause.

    He accepted the job that had the best benefits. (no commas)

- *Who* can introduce either a restrictive or a nonrestrictive clause.

    RESTRICTIVE Many parents who work feel a lot of stress. (no commas)

    NONRESTRICTIVE Both of my parents, who have always wanted the best for their children, have worked two jobs for years. (clause set off by commas)

PRACTICE 27-5

Edit the following sentences so that commas set off all nonrestrictive clauses. (Remember, commas are *not* used to set off restrictive clauses.) If a sentence is correct, write *C* in the blank.

Example: A museum exhibition that celebrates the Alaska highway tells the story of its construction. ____C____

_____ (1) During the 1940s, a group of African American soldiers who defied the forces of nature and human prejudice were shipped to Alaska. _____ (2) They built the Alaska highway which stretches twelve hundred miles across Alaska. _____ (3) The troops who worked on the highway have received little attention in most historical accounts. _____ (4) The highway which cut through some of the roughest terrain in the world was begun in 1942. _____ (5) The Japanese had just landed in the Aleutian Islands which lie west of the tip of the Alaska Peninsula. _____ (6) Military officials, who oversaw the project, doubted the ability of the African American troops. _____ (7) As a result, they made them work under conditions, that made construction difficult. _____ (8) The troops who worked on the road proved their commanders wrong by finishing the highway months ahead of schedule. _____ (9) In one case, white engineers, who surveyed a river, said it would take two weeks to bridge. _____ (10) To the engineers' surprise, the soldiers who worked on the project beat the estimate. _____

27e Commas in Dates and Addresses

Commas are used to separate the elements of dates and addresses.

Dates

Use commas in dates to separate the day of the week from the month and the day of the month from the year.

> The first Cinco de Mayo we celebrated in the United States was Tuesday, May 5, 1998.

When a date that includes commas does not fall at the end of a sentence, place a comma after the year.

> Tuesday, May 5, 1998, was the first Cinco de Mayo we celebrated in the United States.

Addresses

Use commas in addresses to separate the street address from the city and the city from the state or country.

> The office of the famous fictional detective Sherlock Holmes was located at 221b Baker Street, London, England.

When an address that includes commas falls in the middle of a sentence, place a comma after the state or country.

> The office at 221b Baker Street, London, England, belonged to the famous fictional detective Sherlock Holmes.

PRACTICE 27-6

Edit the following sentences for the correct use of commas in dates and addresses. Add any missing commas, and cross out any unnecessary commas. If the sentence is correct, write *C* in the blank.

Examples

Usher's album *Hard II Love* was released on September 16, 2016.

_____

The entertainer grew up in Chattanooga, Tennessee. _____

1. On Tuesday June 5, 2012, people around the world witnessed the rare astronomical phenomenon known as the transit of Venus. _____

2. Stefani Joanne Angelina Germanotta, more commonly known as Lady Gaga, was born on March 28 1986 in New York New York. _____

3. Fans from around the world travel to visit Ernest Hemingway's houses in Key West Florida and San Francisco de Paula, Cuba. _____

4. Oprah addressed the graduating class at Smith College on Sunday May 21, 2017 in Northampton Massachusetts. _____

5. To visit the New York Transit Museum, visitors must travel to 130 Livingston Street in Brooklyn New York. _____

27f Unnecessary Commas

In addition to knowing where commas are required, it is also important to know when *not* to use commas.

- Do not use a comma before the first item in a series.

    INCORRECT *Duck Soup* starred, Groucho, Chico, and Harpo Marx.

    CORRECT *Duck Soup* starred Groucho, Chico, and Harpo Marx.

- Do not use a comma after the last item in a series.

    INCORRECT Groucho, Chico, and Harpo Marx, starred in *Duck Soup*.

    CORRECT Groucho, Chico, and Harpo Marx starred in *Duck Soup*.

- Do not use a comma between a subject and a verb.

    INCORRECT Students and their teachers, should try to respect one another.

    CORRECT Students and their teachers should try to respect one another.

- Do not use a comma before the coordinating conjunction that separates the two parts of a compound predicate.

    INCORRECT   The transit workers voted to strike, and walked off the job.

    CORRECT   The transit workers voted to strike and walked off the job.

- Do not use a comma before the coordinating conjunction that separates the two parts of a compound subject.

    INCORRECT   The transit workers, and the sanitation workers voted to strike.

    CORRECT   The transit workers and the sanitation workers voted to strike.

- Do not use a comma to set off a restrictive clause.

    INCORRECT   People, who live in glass houses, should not throw stones.

    CORRECT   People who live in glass houses should not throw stones.

- Finally, do not use a comma before a dependent clause that follows an independent clause.

    INCORRECT   He was exhausted, because he had driven all night.

    CORRECT   He was exhausted because he had driven all night.

PRACTICE 27-7

Some of the following sentences contain unnecessary commas. Edit to eliminate unnecessary commas. If the sentence is correct, write *C* in the blank following it.

Example: Both the Dominican Republic/and the republic of Haiti occupy the West Indian island of Hispaniola. _____

1. The capital of the Dominican Republic, is Santo Domingo. _____

2. The country's tropical climate, generous rainfall, and fertile soil, make the Dominican Republic suitable for many kinds of crops. _____

3. Some of the most important crops are, sugarcane, coffee, cocoa, and rice.

4. Mining is also important to the country's economy, because the land is rich in many ores. _____

5. Spanish is the official language of the Dominican Republic, and Roman Catholicism is the state religion. _____

6. In recent years, resort areas have opened, and brought many tourists to the country. _____

7. Tourists who visit the Dominican Republic, remark on its tropical beauty.

8. Military attacks, and political unrest have marked much of the Dominican Republic's history. _____

9. Because the republic's economy has not always been strong, many Dominicans have emigrated to the United States. _____

10. However, many Dominican immigrants maintain close ties to their home country, and return often to visit. _____

CHAPTER REVIEW

EDITING PRACTICE

Read the following student essay, which includes errors in comma use. Add commas where necessary between items in a series and with introductory phrases, transitional words and phrases, appositives, and nonrestrictive clauses. Cross out any unnecessary commas. The second sentence has been edited for you.

Earn While You Learn

What is an apprentice? If you watch reality TV, you might think of the people on *The Celebrity Apprentice*. On that show celebrities raised money for charity and, competed for the title of "apprentice." If you are a fan of old Disney movies you might picture Mickey Mouse in his role as the "sorcerer's apprentice," the sorcerer's magical assistant in *Fantasia*. In real life though apprentices do not fit either description. Generally an apprentice is someone who works for a skilled person, while learning a trade on the job.

In Europe and around the world apprenticeships have been used for a long time. They have provided a path to jobs in many fields, from skilled trades, to health care, to banking. Apprenticeship programs are a normal part of life in Switzerland for example where seventy percent of teenagers participate in apprenticeships. Australia, has a strong apprenticeship system, as well.

In the United States however apprenticeships were traditionally for jobs in skilled blue-collar trades, such as construction, and plumbing. Today that is changing. A wide variety of industries, offer apprenticeships for both blue-collar and white-collar jobs. In addition to skilled trades apprenticeships are offered by insurance companies hospital systems and cybersecurity firms. All kinds of companies want to take part, in these "earn-and-learn" programs.

No matter what the industry is the focus of an apprenticeship is on hands-on training. Apprentices usually begin with simple tasks which become more complicated as they gain experience skills and knowledge. In a typical apprenticeship program professional skills are taught through a combination of paid on-the-job training, and classroom instruction. The length of an apprenticeship program depends on the employer the job and other factors. Programs can be as short as one year or as long as six years.

In today's market jobs that start with apprenticeships include plumbers electricians and carpenters as well as dental assistants solar panel installers and information-technology specialists. Apprenticeships are offered by corporations and by departments of the federal government including the Centers for Disease Control and Prevention and, the Bureau of Engraving and Printing. Employers who use apprenticeship programs have been pleased with the results reporting higher productivity and lower turnover.

Congress has shown support for apprenticeships setting aside money to go with apprenticeship grants given to colleges states and companies. Apprenticeship programs also got a boost from the original host, of *The Celebrity Apprentice*. In 2017 President Donald Trump signed an executive order expanding access to apprenticeship programs. In addition the order promotes apprenticeships to business leaders, in a wide range of industries, including manufacturing and health care. It, also, encourages colleges and universities to incorporate apprenticeship programs into their courses of study.

Review checklist

Using Commas

✔ Use commas to separate all elements in a series of three or more words or word groups. (See 27a.)

✔ Use commas to set off introductory phrases and transitional words and phrases from the rest of the sentence. (See 27b.)

✔ Use commas to set off appositives from the rest of the sentence. (See 27c.)

✔ Use commas to set off nonrestrictive clauses. (See 27d.)

✔ Use commas to separate parts of dates and addresses. (See 27e.)

✔ Avoid unnecessary commas. (See 27f.)

28 Using Apostrophes

An **apostrophe** is a punctuation mark that is used in two situations: to form a contraction and to form the possessive of a noun or an indefinite pronoun.

28a Apostrophes in Contractions

A **contraction** is a word that uses an apostrophe to combine two words. The apostrophe takes the place of omitted letters.

I <u>didn't</u> (*did not*) realize how late it was.

<u>It's</u> (*it is*) not right for cheaters to go unpunished.

> **Frequently Used Contractions**
>
> I + am = I'm   are + not = aren't
> we + are = we're   can + not = can't
> you + are = you're   do + not = don't
> it + is = it's   will + not = won't
> I + have = I've   should + not = shouldn't
> I + will = I'll   let + us = let's
> there + is = there's   that + is = that's
> is + not = isn't   who + is = who's

PRACTICE 28-1 In the following sentences, add apostrophes to contractions if needed. If the sentence is correct, write *C* in the blank.

Example: ~~Whats~~ What's the deadliest creature on earth? _____

(1) Bacteria and viruses, which we cant see without a microscope, kill many people every year. _____ (2) When we speak about the

deadliest creatures, however, usually were talking about creatures that cause illness or death from their poison, which is called venom. _____ (3) After your bitten, stung, or stuck, how long does it take to die? _____ (4) The fastest killer is a creature called the sea wasp, but it isn't a wasp at all. _____ (5) The sea wasp is actually a fifteen-foot-long jellyfish, and although its not aggressive, it can be deadly. _____ (6) People who've gone swimming off the coast of Australia have encountered this creature. _____ (7) While jellyfish found off the Atlantic coast of the United States can sting, they arent as dangerous as the sea wasp, whose venom is deadly enough to kill sixty adults. _____ (8) A person whos been stung by a sea wasp has anywhere from thirty seconds to four minutes to get help or die. _____ (9) Oddly, it's been found that something as thin as pantyhose worn over the skin will prevent these stings. _____ (10) Also, theres an antidote to the poison that can save victims. _____

 ## 28b Apostrophes in Possessives

Possessive forms of nouns and pronouns show ownership. Nouns and indefinite pronouns do not have special possessive forms. Instead, they use apostrophes to indicate ownership.

Singular Nouns and Indefinite Pronouns

To form the possessive of **singular nouns** (including names) and **indefinite pronouns**, add an apostrophe plus an *-s*.

> Cesar Chavez's goal (*the goal of Cesar Chavez*) was justice for American farmworkers.
> The strike's outcome (*the outcome of the strike*) was uncertain.
> Whether it would succeed was anyone's guess (*the guess of anyone*).

> **FYI**
>
> **Singular Nouns Ending in -s**
>
> Even if a singular noun already ends in -s, add an apostrophe plus an -s to form the possessive.
>
> The class's next assignment was a research paper.
>
> Dr. Ramos's patients are participating in a clinical trial.

Plural Nouns

Most plural nouns end in -s. To form the possessive of **plural nouns ending in –s** (including names), add just an apostrophe (not an apostrophe plus an -s).

The two drugs' side effects (*the side effects of the two drugs*) were quite different.

The Johnsons' front door (*the front door of the Johnsons*) is red.

Some irregular noun plurals do not end in -s. If a plural noun does not end in -s, add an apostrophe plus an -s to form the possessive.

The men's room is right next to the women's room.

PRACTICE 28-2

Rewrite the following phrases, changing the noun or indefinite pronoun that follows *of* to the possessive form. Be sure to distinguish between singular and plural nouns.

Examples

the mayor of the city <u>the city's mayor</u>

the uniforms of the players <u>the players' uniforms</u>

1. the video of the singer _____
2. the scores of the students _____
3. the favorite band of everybody _____
4. the office of the boss _____
5. the union of the players _____
6. the specialty of the restaurant _____
7. the bedroom of the children _____

8. the high cost of the tickets _____
9. the dreams of everyone _____
10. the owner of the dogs _____

28c Incorrect Use of Apostrophes

Be careful not to confuse a plural noun (*boys*) with the singular possessive form of the noun (*boy's*). Never use an apostrophe with a plural noun unless the noun is possessive.

> Termites can be dangerous <u>pests</u> [not *pest's*].
>
> The <u>Velezes</u> [not *Velez's*] live on Maple Drive, right next door to the <u>Browns</u> [not *Brown's*].

Also remember *not* to use apostrophes with possessive pronouns that end in *-s*: *theirs* (not *their's*), *hers* (not *her's*), *its* (not *it's*), *ours* (not *our's*), and *yours* (not *your's*).

Be especially careful not to confuse possessive pronouns with sound-alike contractions. Possessive pronouns never include apostrophes.

POSSESSIVE PRONOUN	CONTRACTION
The dog bit **its** master.	**It's** (*it is*) time for breakfast.
The choice is **theirs**.	**There's** (*there is*) no place like home.
Whose house is this?	**Who's** (*who is*) on first base?
Is this **your** house?	**You're** (*you are*) late again.

PRACTICE
28-3 Check the underlined words in the following sentences for correct use of apostrophes. If a correction needs to be made, cross out the word and write the correct version above it. If the noun or pronoun is correct, write *C* above it.

> **Example:** The <u>governor's</u> views were presented after several other <u>speaker's</u> first presented <u>their's</u>.
> (corrections above: *C* over governor's; *speakers* over speaker's; *theirs* over their's)

1. <u>Parent's</u> should realize that when it comes to disciplining children, the responsibility is <u>there's</u>.

2. <u>It's</u> also important that parents offer praise for a <u>child's</u> good behavior.

3. In <u>it's</u> first few <u>week's</u> of life, a dog is already developing a personality.

4. His and <u>her's</u> towels used to be popular with <u>couple's</u>, but <u>it's</u> not so common to see them today.

5. All the <u>Ryan's</u> spent four <u>year's</u> in college and then got good jobs.

6. She remembered the lyrics "<u>You're</u> the one <u>who's</u> love I've been waiting for."

7. If you expect to miss any <u>class's</u>, you will have to make arrangements with someone <u>who's</u> willing to tell you <u>you're</u> assignment.

8. No other <u>school's</u> cheerleading squad tried as many stunts as <u>our's</u> did.

9. Surprise <u>test's</u> are common in my economics <u>teacher's</u> class.

10. <u>Jazz's</u> influence on mainstream <u>musician's</u> is one of the <u>article's</u> <u>subject's</u>.

CHAPTER REVIEW

EDITING PRACTICE

Read the following student essay, which includes errors in the use of apostrophes. Edit it to eliminate errors by crossing out incorrect words and writing corrections above them. (Note that this essay is an informal response, so contractions are acceptable.) The first sentence has been edited for you.

The Women of Messina

In William ~~Shakespeares'~~ **Shakespeare's** play *Much Ado about Nothing*, the women of Messina, whether they are seen as love objects or as ~~shrew's~~ **shrews**, have very few options. A womans role is to please a man. She can try to resist, but she will probably wind up giving in.

The plays two women, Hero and Beatrice, are very different. Hero is the obedient one. Heroes cousin, Beatrice, tries to challenge the rules of the mans world in which she lives. However, in a place like Messina, even women like Beatrice find it hard to get the respect that should be their's.

Right from the start, we are drawn to Beatrice. Shes funny, she has a clever comment for most situation's, and she always speaks her mind about other peoples behavior. Unlike Hero, she tries to stand up to the men in her life, as we see in her and Benedicks conversations. But even though Beatrice's intelligence is obvious, she often mocks herself. Its clear that she doesn't have much self-esteem. In fact, Beatrice is'nt the strong woman she seems to be.

Ultimately, Beatrice does get her man, and she will be happy—but at what cost? Benedicks' last word's to her are "Peace! I will stop your mouth." Then, he kisses her. The kiss is a symbolic end to their bickering. It is also the mark of Beatrices defeat. She has lost. Benedick has silenced her. Now,

> **WORD POWER**
> **shrew** a scolding woman

> **READING TIP**
> This student essay has a comparison-and-contrast pattern of organization. To help organize the information in the essay, list the traits that Hero and Beatrice have in common (comparison) and the traits that make them different (contrast).

she will be Benedick's wife and do what he wants her to do. Granted, she will have more say in her marriage than Hero will have in her's, but she is still defeated.

Shakespeares audience might have seen the plays ending as a happy one. For contemporary audience's, however, the ending is disappointing. Even Beatrice, the most rebellious of Messinas women, finds it impossible to achieve anything of importance in this male-dominated society.

Review checklist

Using Apostrophes

✔ Use apostrophes to form contractions. (See 28a.)

✔ Use an apostrophe plus an -s to form the possessive of singular nouns and indefinite pronouns, even when a noun ends in -s. (See 28b.)

✔ Use an apostrophe alone to form the possessive of plural nouns ending in -s, including names. If a plural noun does not end in -s, add an apostrophe plus an s. (See 28b.)

✔ Do not use apostrophes with plural nouns unless they are possessive. Do not use apostrophes with possessive pronouns. (See 28c.)

29 Understanding Mechanics

 29a Capitalizing Proper Nouns

A **proper noun** names a particular person, animal, place, object, or idea. Proper nouns are always capitalized. The list that follows explains and illustrates specific rules for capitalizing proper nouns.

- Always capitalize names of **races, ethnic groups, tribes, nationalities, languages,** and **religions**.

    The census data revealed a diverse community of Caucasians, African Americans, and Asian Americans, with a few Latino and Navajo residents. Native languages included English, Korean, and Spanish. Most people identified themselves as Catholic, Protestant, or Muslim.

- Capitalize names of **specific people and the titles that accompany them**. In general, do not capitalize titles used without a name.

    In 1994, President Nelson Mandela was elected to lead South Africa.

    The newly elected fraternity president addressed the crowd.

- Capitalize names of **specific family members and their titles**. Do not capitalize words that identify family relationships, including those introduced by possessive pronouns.

    The twins, Aunt Edna and Aunt Evelyn, are Dad's sisters.

    My aunts, my father's sisters, are twins.

- Capitalize names of **specific countries, cities, towns, bodies of water, streets,** and so on. Do not capitalize words that do not name specific places.

    The Seine runs through Paris, France.

    The river runs through the city.

- Capitalize names of **specific geographical regions**. Do not capitalize such words when they specify direction.

    William Faulkner's novels are set in the South.

    Turn right at the golf course, and go south for about a mile.

- Capitalize names of **specific buildings** and **monuments**. Do not capitalize general references to buildings and monuments.

    He drove past the Liberty Bell and looked for parking near Independence Hall.

    He drove past the monument and looked for a parking space near the building.

- Capitalize names of **specific groups, clubs, teams**, and **associations**. Do not capitalize general references to such groups.

    The Teamsters Union represents workers who were at the stadium for the Republican Party convention, the Rolling Stones concert, and the Phillies-Astros game.

    The union represents workers who were at the stadium for the political party's convention, the rock group's concert, and the baseball teams' game.

- Capitalize names of **specific historical periods, events**, and **documents**. Do not capitalize nonspecific references to periods, events, or documents.

    The Emancipation Proclamation was signed during the Civil War, not during Reconstruction.

    The document was signed during the war, not during the postwar period.

- Capitalize **names of businesses, government agencies, schools,** and **other institutions**. Do not capitalize nonspecific references to such institutions.

    The Department of Education and Apple Computer have launched a partnership project with Central High School.

    A government agency and a computer company have launched a partnership project with a high school.

- Capitalize **brand names**. Do not capitalize general references to kinds of products.

  While Jeff waited for his turn at the Xerox machine, he drank a can of Coke.

  While Jeff waited for his turn at the copier, he drank a can of soda.

- Capitalize **titles of specific academic courses**. Do not capitalize names of general academic subject areas, except for proper nouns—for example, a language or a country.

  Are Introduction to American Government and Biology 200 closed yet?

  Are the introductory American government course and the biology course closed yet?

- Capitalize **days of the week, months of the year,** and **holidays**. Do not capitalize the names of seasons.

  The Jewish holiday of Passover usually falls in April.

  The Jewish holiday of Passover falls in the spring.

PRACTICE

29-1 Edit the following sentences, capitalizing letters or changing capitals to lowercase where necessary.

Example: The third-largest ~~C~~city in the ~~u~~United ~~s~~States is ~~C~~Chicago, ~~I~~illinois.

(1) Located in the midwest on lake Michigan, chicago is an important port city, a rail and highway hub, and the site of o'hare international airport, one of the Nation's busiest. (2) The financial center of the city is Lasalle street, and the lakefront is home to Grant park, where there are many Museums and monuments. (3) To the North of the city, soldier field is home to the chicago bears, the city's football team, and wrigley field is home to the chicago cubs, a national league Baseball Team. (4) In the mid-1600s, the site of what is now Chicago was visited by father jacques marquette, a catholic missionary to the ottawa and huron tribes, who were native to the area. (5) By the 1700s, the city was a trading post run

by john kinzie. (6) The city grew rapidly in the 1800s, and immigrants included germans, irish, italians, poles people, greeks, and chinese, along with african americans who migrated from the south. (7) In 1871, much of the city was destroyed in one of the worst fires in united states history; according to legend, the fire started when mrs. O'Leary's Cow kicked over a burning lantern. (8) Today, Chicago's skyline has many Skyscrapers, built by businesses like the john hancock company, sears, and amoco. (9) I know Chicago well because my Mother grew up there and my aunt jean and uncle amos still live there. (10) I also got information from the Chicago Chamber of Commerce when I wrote a paper for introductory research writing, a course I took at Graystone high school.

29b Punctuating Direct Quotations

A **direct quotation** shows the *exact* words of a speaker or writer. Direct quotations are always placed in quotation marks.

A direct quotation is usually accompanied by an **identifying tag**, a phrase (such as "she said") that names the person being quoted. In the following sentences, the identifying tag is underlined.

<u>Lauren said</u>, "My brother and Tina have gotten engaged."
A <u>famous advertising executive wrote</u>, "Don't sell the steak; sell the sizzle."

When a quotation is a complete sentence, it begins with a capital letter and ends with a period (or a question mark or exclamation point). When a quotation falls at the end of a sentence (as in the two examples above) the period is placed *before* the quotation marks.

If the quotation is a question or an exclamation, the question mark or exclamation point is also placed *before* the closing quotation mark.

The instructor asked, "Has anyone read *Sula*?"
Officer Warren shouted, "Hold it right there!"

If the quotation itself is not a question or an exclamation, the question mark or exclamation point is placed *after* the closing quotation mark.

Did Joe really say, "I quit"?
I can't believe he really said, "I quit"!

The rules for punctuating direct quotations with identifying tags are summarized below.

> **FYI**
>
> **Indirect Quotations**
>
> A direct quotation shows someone's *exact* words, but an **indirect quotation** simply summarizes what was said or written.
> Do not use quotation marks with indirect quotations.
>
> | | |
> |---|---|
> | DIRECT QUOTATION | Martin Luther King Jr. said, "I have a dream." |
> | INDIRECT QUOTATION | Martin Luther King Jr. said that he had a dream. |

Identifying Tag at the Beginning

When the identifying tag comes *before* the quotation, it is followed by a comma.

> Theodore Roosevelt wrote, "Speak softly and carry a big stick."

Identifying Tag at the End

When the identifying tag comes at the *end* of a quoted sentence, it is followed by a period. A comma (or, sometimes, a question mark or an exclamation point) inside the closing quotation mark separates the quotation from the identifying tag.

> "Life is like a box of chocolates," stated Forrest Gump.
> "Is that so?" his friends wondered.
> "That's amazing!" he cried.

Identifying Tag in the Middle

When the identifying tag comes in the *middle* of the quoted sentence, it is followed by a comma. The first part of the quotation is also followed by a comma, placed inside the closing quotation mark. Because the part of the quotation that follows the identifying tag is not a new sentence, it does not begin with a capital letter.

> "This is my life," Bette insisted, "and I'll live it as I please."

Identifying Tag between Two Sentences

When the identifying tag comes *between* two quoted sentences, it is preceded by a comma and followed by a period. (The second quoted sentence begins with a capital letter.)

"Producer Berry Gordy is an important figure in the history of music," Tony explained. "He was the creative force behind Motown records."

PRACTICE 29-2

The following sentences contain direct quotations. First, underline the identifying tag. Then, punctuate the quotation correctly, adding capital letters as necessary.

Example: "Why," Darryl asked, "are teachers so strict about deadlines?"

1. We who are about to die salute you said the gladiators to the emperor.

2. When we turned on the television, the newscaster was saying ladies and gentlemen, we have a new president-elect.

3. The bigger they are said boxer John L. Sullivan the harder they fall.

4. Do you take Michael to be your lawfully wedded husband asked the minister.

5. Lisa Marie replied I do.

6. If you believe the *National Enquirer* my friend always says then you'll believe anything.

7. When asked for the jury's verdict, the foreperson replied we find the defendant not guilty.

8. I had felt for a long time that if I was ever told to get up so a white person could sit Rosa Parks recalled I would refuse to do so.

9. The reports of my death Mark Twain supposedly wrote have been greatly exaggerated.

10. Quality is much better than quantity Steve Jobs said one home run is better than two doubles.

 ## 29c Setting Off Titles

Some titles are typed in *italics*. Others are enclosed in quotation marks. The following box shows how to set off different kinds of titles.

> **Italics or Quotation Marks?**
>
> **ITALICIZED TITLES**
>
> Books: *How the Garcia Girls Lost Their Accents*
> Newspapers: *Miami Herald*
> Magazines: *People*
> Long poems: *John Brown's Body*
> Plays: *Death of a Salesman*
> Films: *The Rocky Horror Picture Show*
> Television or radio series: *Game of Thrones*
> Paintings and sculpture: *American Gothic*; *Pietà*
> Video games: *Call of Duty: WWII*; *Halo 6*
>
> **TITLES IN QUOTATION MARKS**
>
> Book chapters: "Understanding Mechanics"
> Short stories: "The Tell-Tale Heart"
> Essays and articles: "The Suspected Shopper"
> Short poems: "Richard Cory"
> Songs and speeches: "America the Beautiful"; "The Gettysburg Address"
> Individual episodes of television or radio series: "The Montgomery Bus Boycott" (an episode of the PBS series *Eyes on the Prize*)

> **FYI**
>
> **Capital Letters in Titles**
>
> Capitalize the first letters of all important words in a title. Do not capitalize an **article** (*a*, *an*, *the*), a **preposition** (*to*, *of*, *around*, and so on), the *to* in an infinitive, or a **coordinating conjunction** (*and*, *but*, and so on)—unless it is the first or last word of the title or subtitle (*On the Road*; "To an Athlete Dying Young"; *No Way Out*; *And Quiet Flows the Don*).

PRACTICE 29-3

Edit the following sentences, capitalizing letters as necessary in titles.

Example: *The New York Times* best-seller *Three Cups of Tea* is about Greg Mortenson's work building schools in Pakistan and Afghanistan.

1. In 2009, Aziz Ansari began appearing in *parks and recreation,* and he later starred as Dev Shah in the netflix series *master of none.*

2. In 1948, Eleanor Roosevelt delivered her famous speech "the struggle for human rights" and published an article titled "toward human rights throughout the world."

3. Before being elected president, Barack Obama wrote and published two books: *dreams from my father* and *the audacity of hope.*

4. English actor Daniel Craig plays secret agent James Bond in the films *casino royale, quantum of solace,* and *skyfall.*

5. *janis joplin's greatest hits* includes songs written by other people, such as "piece of my heart," as well as songs she wrote herself, such as "mercedes benz."

PRACTICE 29-4

In the following sentences, underline titles to indicate italics or place them in quotation marks. (Remember that titles of books and other long works are italicized, and titles of stories, essays, and other shorter works are enclosed in quotation marks.)

Example: In an article in <u>The New Yorker</u> called "Scoop Dreams," Shonda Rhimes recalls a job she had when she was a teenager.

1. <u>Business Week</u> reports that many young workers do not contribute regularly to a retirement account.

2. At the beginning of most major American sporting events, the crowd stands for The Star-Spangled Banner.

3. People who want to purchase new cars often compare the different models in Consumer Reports magazine.

4. U2's song Pride (in the Name of Love) is about Martin Luther King Jr.

5. Edgar Allan Poe wrote several mysterious short stories, two of which are called The Tell-Tale Heart and The Black Cat.

6. The popular Broadway show Hamilton was based on Ron Chernow's 2004 book Alexander Hamilton.

7. Aasif Mandvi, a comedian who was a correspondent on The Daily Show, also wrote the book No Land's Man.

8. In a college textbook called Sociology: A Brief Introduction, the first chapter is titled The Essence of Sociology.

29d Using Hyphens

A hyphen has two uses: to divide a word at the end of a line and to join words in compounds.

- Use a **hyphen** to divide a word at the end of a line. If you need to divide a word, divide it between syllables. (Check your dictionary to see how a word is divided into syllables.) Never break a one-syllable word, no matter how long it is.

    When the speaker began his talk, the people seated in the <u>auditorium</u> grew very quiet.

- Use a hyphen in a **compound**—a word that is made up of two or more words.

    This theater shows <u>first-run</u> movies.

PRACTICE 29-5

Add hyphens to join words in compounds in the following sentences.

Example: The course focused on nineteenth-century American literature.

1. The ice skating rink finally froze over.

2. We should be kind to our four legged friends.

3. The first year students raised money for charity.

4. The well liked professor gave a speech to new students during orientation.

5. The hand carved sculpture looked like a pair of doves.

29e Using Abbreviations

An **abbreviation** is a shortened form of a word. Although abbreviations are generally not used in college writing, it is acceptable to abbreviate the following:

- Titles — such as Mr., Ms., Dr., and Jr. — that are used along with names
- a.m. and p.m.
- CE (Common Era) and BCE (Before the Common Era) in dates such as 43 CE
- Names of organizations (NRA, CIA) and technical terms (DNA). Note that some abbreviations, called **acronyms**, are pronounced as words: AIDS, FEMA.

Keep in mind that it is *not* acceptable to abbreviate days of the week, months, names of streets and places, names of academic subjects, or titles that are not used along with names.

PRACTICE

 Edit the incorrect use of abbreviations in the following sentences.

Example: In leap years, ~~Feb.~~ February has twenty-nine days.

1. The dr. diagnosed a case of hypertension.

2. Nov. 11 is a federal holiday.

3. Derek registered for Eng. literature and a psych elective.

4. The museum was located at the corner of Laurel Ave. and Neptune St.

5. The clinic is only open Tues. through Thurs. and every other Sat.

29f Using Numbers

In college writing, most numbers below one hundred are spelled out (*forty-five*) rather than written as numerals (*45*). However, numbers more than two words long are always written as **numerals** (*4,530*, not *four thousand five hundred thirty*).

In addition, you should use numerals in the following situations.

DATES	January 20, 1976
ADDRESSES	5023 Schuyler Street
EXACT TIMES	10:00 a.m. (If you use *o'clock*, spell out the number: *ten o'clock*)
PERCENTAGES AND DECIMALS	80% 8.2
DIVISIONS OF BOOKS	Chapter 3 Act 4 page 102

Note: Never begin a sentence with a numeral. Use a spelled-out number, or reword the sentence so the numeral does not come at the beginning.

PRACTICE 29-7

Edit the incorrect use of numbers in the following sentences.

Example: The population of the United States is over ~~three hundred~~ 300 million.

1. Only 2 students in the 8 o'clock lecture were late.

2. More than seventy-five percent of the class passed the exit exam.

3. Chapter six begins on page 873.

4. The wedding took place on October twelfth at 7:30.

5. Meet me at Sixty-five Cadman Place.

29g Using Semicolons, Colons, Dashes, and Parentheses

Correct usage of semicolons, colons, dashes, and parenthese will help you to communicate your ideas effectively.

Semicolons

Use a **semicolon** to join independent clauses in a compound sentence.

> Twenty years ago, smartphones did not exist; today, many people cannot imagine life without them.

Also use a semicolon (not a comma) to separate items in a series when one or more of those items already contain a comma.

> The tour group visited Toulouse, France; Cordoba, Spain; and San Remo, Italy.

Colons

- Use a **colon** to introduce a quotation.

    > Our family motto is a simple one: "Accept no substitutes."

- Use a colon to introduce an explanation, a clarification, or an example.

    > Only one thing kept him from climbing Mt. Everest: fear of heights.

- Use a colon to introduce a list.

    > I left my job for four reasons: boring work, poor working conditions, low pay, and a terrible supervisor.

Dashes

Use **dashes** to set off important information.

> She parked her car—a red Firebird—in a towaway zone.

Parentheses

Use **parentheses** to enclose material that is relatively unimportant.

> The weather in Portland (a city in Oregon) was overcast.

PRACTICE 29-8

Add semicolons, colons, dashes, and parentheses to the following sentences where necessary.

Example: Megachurches (those with more than two thousand worshippers at a typical service) have grown in popularity since the 1950s.

1. Megachurches though they are Protestant are not always affiliated with the main Protestant denominations.

2. Services in megachurches are creative preaching is sometimes accompanied by contemporary music and video presentations.

3. Although many of these churches are evangelical actively recruiting new members, people often join because of friends and neighbors.

4. Megachurches tend to keep their members because they encourage a variety of activities for example, hospitality committees and study groups.

5. Worshippers say that their services are upbeat they are full of joy and spirituality.

6. Megachurches in nearly all cases use technology to organize and communicate with their members.

7. The largest of these churches with ten thousand members would be unable to function without telecommunications.

8. Some even offer services in a format familiar to their younger members the podcast.

9. Critics of megachurches and there are some believe they take up too much tax-exempt land.

10. Other critics fear that smaller churches already struggling to keep members will lose worshippers to these huge congregations and eventually have to close.

CHAPTER REVIEW

EDITING PRACTICE

Read the following student essay, which includes errors in capitalization and punctuation and in the use of direct quotations and titles. Correct any errors you find. The first sentence has been edited for you.

A Threat to Health

Pandemics are like Epidemics, only more widespread, perhaps even spreading throughout the World. In a pandemic, a serious Disease spreads very easily. In the past, there have been many pandemics. In the future, in spite of advances in Medicine, there will still be pandemics. In fact, scientists agree that not every pandemic can be prevented, so pandemics will continue to be a threat.

Probably the best-known pandemic is the bubonic plague. It killed about one-third of the Population of europe during the middle ages. Some areas suffered more than others. According to Philip ziegler's book *the black Death*, at least half the people in florence, Italy, died in one year. Many years later, in 1918, a flu pandemic killed more than fifty million people worldwide, including hundreds of thousands in the United states.

Unfortunately, pandemics have not disappeared. AIDS, for example, is a current pandemic. *Philadelphia* the 1993 movie starring denzel washington and tom hanks is still one of the most moving depictions of the heartbreak of AIDS. The rate of AIDS infection is over 30% in parts of africa, the disease continues to spread on other Continents as well. So far, efforts to find an AIDS vaccine have failed. Dr. anthony s. Fauci discussed recent AIDS research on NPR's series *All things considered* in a program called Search for an HIV vaccine expands.

READING TIP

This essay provides numerous supporting details about specific pandemics. To aid your comprehension, identify at least two supporting details about each pandemic discussed in the essay.

Although some pandemic diseases, such as Smallpox, have been wiped out by Vaccination, new pandemics remain a threat. Many viruses and Bacteria change in response to treatment, so they may become resistant to Vaccination and Antibiotics. Also, with modern transportation, a disease can move quickly from Country to Country. For example, the disease known as severe acute respiratory syndrome (SARS) began in china but was spread to other countries by travelers. Hundreds died as a result of the SARS pandemic between November 2002 and july 2003. Birds also remain a threat because they can transmit disease. It is obviously impossible to prevent birds from flying from one country to another. Markos kyprianou, health commissioner of the European union, has said that I am concerned that birds in Turkey have been found with the bird flu Virus. He said, There is a direct relationship with viruses found in Russia, Mongolia and china. If this Virus changes so that it can move easily from birds to Humans, bird flu could become the next pandemic.

Public Health Officials are always on the lookout for diseases with three characteristics: they are new, they are dangerous, and they are very contagious. Doctors try to prevent them from becoming Pandemics. However, they continue to warn that some Pandemics cannot be prevented.

Review checklist

Understanding Mechanics

- ✔ Capitalize proper nouns. (See 29a.)
- ✔ Always place direct quotations within quotation marks. (See 29b.)
- ✔ In titles, capitalize all important words. In text, use italics or quotation marks to set off titles. (See 29c.)
- ✔ Use a hyphen to divide a word at the end of a line or to join words in compounds. (See 29d.)
- ✔ Abbreviate titles used with names, a.m. and p.m., CE and BCE names of organizations, and technical terms. (See 29e.)
- ✔ Use numerals for numbers more than two words long and in certain other situations. (See 29f.)
- ✔ Use semicolons to join independent clauses in a compound sentence or in a series whose elements include commas. (See 29g.)
- ✔ Use colons, dashes, and parentheses to set off material from the rest of the sentence. (See 29g.)

unit 5
Reading Essays

30 Readings for Writers 588

Reading and Writing 590

Amy Tan, *Mother Tongue* 590

Richard Lederer, *The Case for Short Words* 596

Noah Lewis, *For Trans People Like Me, Pronouns Are about More Than Grammatical Correctness* 600

Technology and Science 604

Sherry Turkle, *The Flight from Conversation* 604

Alex Hern, *Don't Know the Difference between Emoji and Emoticons? Let Me Explain* 610

Michael Pollan, *Why 'Natural' Doesn't Mean Anything Anymore* 613

Working and Learning 618

Toni Morrison, *The Work You Do, the Person You Are* 618

Jennine Capó Crucet, *Taking My Parents to College* 622

Naomi Rosenberg, *How to Tell a Mother Her Child Is Dead* 626

Identity and Self-Image 629

Nikita, *Growing Up a Desi Girl: What It Means to Be between Two Worlds* 629

Jacqueline Woodson, *When a Southern Town Broke a Heart* 633

Umapagan Ampikaipakan, *That Oxymoron, the Asian Comic Superhero* 637

30 Readings for Writers

The following twelve essays by professional writers offer interesting perspectives on four general themes:

- Reading and Writing
- Technology and Science
- Working and Learning
- Identity and Self-Image

The essays are collected here for you to read, react to, think critically about, discuss, and write about. In addition, these essays illustrate some of the ways you can develop ideas in your own writing.

Each essay is preceded by a short **headnote**, an introduction that tells you something about the writer, and a **"Before you read"** sentence that suggests what to focus on as you approach the essay. Following each reading are six sets of questions and a set of writing prompts.

- **Focus on Reading** questions encourage you to review your marked-up text and annotations.
- **Focus on Meaning** questions help you to assess your understanding of the essay's basic ideas.
- **Focus on Strategy** questions ask you to consider the writer's purpose and intended audience as well as the essay's opening and closing strategies and the thesis statement.
- **Focus on Language and Style** questions ask you to think about the writer's stylistic decisions and word choices as well as the words' **denotations** (dictionary definitions) and **connotations** (meanings associated with the words).
- **Focus on the Patterns** questions help you to see how the writer arranged ideas within the essay.
- **Focus on Critical Thinking** questions encourage you to move beyond what is on the page to consider the essay's wider implications or the connections between the writer's ideas and your own.
- **Focus on Writing** prompts offer suggestions for writing in response to each essay.

As you read each of the essays in this chapter, follow the active reading process outlined in Chapter 1, previewing, marking up, and annotating each essay to help you understand what you are reading and prepare for writing an essay of your own. You can use **TEST** to help you identify the essay's key elements.

T **Thesis**—Look for the thesis or **main idea**, which is sometimes stated directly, often (but not always) in the opening paragraphs. Try to decide why the writer placed the main idea where it is. If the main idea is **implied** (suggested), try to decide why it is not explicitly stated. Try to write a sentence that states the main idea in your own words.

E **Evidence**—Look for the evidence that supports the writer's main idea. This evidence can be in the form of examples, statistics, anecdotes based on the writer's observations or experiences, or the opinions of experts. Think about why the writer chose these types of evidence rather than others. Consider whether different evidence or additional support is needed and whether any evidence is irrelevant or unnecessary. Think about what you can **infer** from the evidence presented (see 5e).

S **Summary**—Look for a statement that lists or summarizes the writer's key points or the essay's main idea. Often, this summary appears in the closing paragraphs. If no summary is included, write a sentence that could serve as a summary statement.

T **Transitions**—Look for transitional words and expressions that connect ideas within and between paragraphs. How do these transitions help you to understand the writer's ideas and follow his or her train of thought? Look for **transitional paragraphs**, paragraphs whose purpose is not to supply evidence, but rather to move readers from one section of the essay to the next.

READING AND WRITING

"Mother Tongue," Amy Tan   590
"The Case for Short Words," Richard Lederer   596
"For Trans People Like Me, Pronouns Are about More Than Grammatical Correctness," Noah Lewis   600

TECHNOLOGY AND SCIENCE

"The Flight from Conversation," Sherry Turkle   604
"Don't Know the Difference between Emoji and Emoticons? Let Me Explain," Alex Hern   610
"Why 'Natural' Doesn't Mean Anything Anymore," Michael Pollan   613

WORKING AND LEARNING

"The Work You Do, the Person You Are," Toni Morrison   618
"Taking My Parents to College," Jennine Capó Crucet   622
"How to Tell a Mother Her Child Is Dead," Naomi Rosenberg   626

IDENTITY AND SELF-IMAGE

"Growing Up a Desi Girl: What It Means to Be between Two Worlds," Nikita   629
"When a Southern Town Broke a Heart," Jacqueline Woodson   633
"That Oxymoron, the Asian Comic Superhero," Umapagan Ampikaipakan   637

 # Reading and Writing

Mother Tongue

Amy Tan

Amy Tan was born in 1952 in Oakland, California, the daughter of Chinese immigrants. In 1987, she published *The Joy Luck Club*, a best-selling novel about four immigrant Chinese women and their American-born daughters. Her later works include the novels *The Bonesetter's Daughter* (2001), *Saving Fish from Drowning* (2005), and *The Valley of Amazement* (2013) as well as the memoirs *The Opposite of Fate: A Book of Musings* (2003) and, most recently, *Where the Past Begins* (2017). In the following essay, Tan considers her mother's heavily Chinese-influenced English as well as the different "Englishes" she herself uses, especially in communicating with her mother. She then discusses the potential limitations of growing up with immigrant parents who do not speak fluent English.

Before you read, think about the different kinds of language you use when talking with friends, family members, employers, and teachers.

1   I am not a scholar of English or literature. I cannot give you much more than personal opinions on the English language and its variations in this country or others.

2   I am a writer. And by that definition, I am someone who has always loved language. I am fascinated by language in daily life. I spend a great deal of my time thinking about the power of language—the way it can evoke an emotion, a visual image, a complex idea, or a simple truth. Language is the tool of my trade. And I use them all—all the Englishes I grew up with.

3   Recently, I was made keenly aware of the different Englishes I do use. I was giving a talk to a large group of people, the same talk I had already given to half a dozen other groups. The nature of the talk was about

my writing, my life, and my book, *The Joy Luck Club*. The talk was going along well enough, until I remembered one major difference that made the whole talk sound wrong. My mother was in the room. And it was perhaps the first time she had heard me give a lengthy speech, using the kind of English I have never used with her. I was saying things like, "The intersection of memory upon imagination" and "There is an aspect of my fiction that relates to thus-and-thus"—a speech filled with carefully wrought grammatical phrases, burdened, it suddenly seemed to me, with nominalized forms, past perfect tenses, conditional phrases, all the forms of standard English that I had learned in school and through books, the forms of English I did not use at home with my mother.

4   Just last week, I was walking down the street with my mother, and I again found myself conscious of the English I was using, and the English I do use with her. We were talking about the price of new and used furniture and I heard myself saying this: "Not waste money that way." My husband was with us as well, and he didn't notice any switch in my English. And then I realized why. It's because over the twenty years we've been together I've often used that same kind of English with him, and sometimes he even uses it with me. It has become our language of intimacy, a different sort of English that relates to family talk, the language I grew up with.

5   So you'll have some idea of what this family talk I heard sounds like, I'll quote what my mother said during a recent conversation which I videotaped and then transcribed. During this conversation my mother was talking about a political gangster in Shanghai who had the same last name as her family's, Du, and how the gangster in his early years wanted to be adopted by her family, which was rich by comparison. Later, the gangster became more powerful, far richer than my mother's family, and one day showed up at my mother's wedding to pay his respects. Here's what she said in part: "Du Yusong having business like fruit stand. Like off the street kind. He is Du like Du Zong—but not Tsung-ming Island people. The local people call putong, the river east side, he belong to that side local people. The man want to ask Du Zong father take him in like become own family. Du Zong father wasn't looking down on him, but didn't take seriously, until that man big like become a mafia. Now important person very hard to inviting him. Chinese way, come only to show respect, don't stay for dinner. Respect for making big celebration, he shows up. Mean gives lots of respect. Chinese custom. Chinese social life that way. If too important won't have to stay too long. He come to my wedding. I didn't see. I heard it. I gone to boy's side, they have YMCA dinner. Chinese age I was nineteen."

6   You should know that my mother's expressive command of English belies how much she actually understands. She reads the *Forbes* report, listens to *Wall Street Week*, converses daily with her stockbroker, reads all of Shirley MacLaine's books with ease—all kinds of things I can't begin to understand. Yet some of my friends tell me they understand 50 percent of what my mother says. Some say they understand 80 to 90 percent. Some

say they understand none of it, as if she were speaking pure Chinese. But to me, my mother's English is perfectly clear, perfectly natural. It's my mother's tongue. Her language, as I hear it, is vivid, direct, full of observation and imagery. This was the language that helped shape the way I saw things, expressed things, made sense of the world.

7   Lately, I've been giving more thought to the kind of English my mother speaks. Like others, I have described it to people as "broken" or "fractured" English. But I wince when I say that. It has always bothered me that I can think of no way to describe it other than "broken," as if it were damaged and needed to be fixed, as if it lacked a certain wholeness and soundness. I've heard other terms used, "limited English," for example. But they seem just as bad, as if everything is limited, including people's perceptions of the limited English speaker.

8   I know this for a fact, because when I was growing up, my mother's "limited" English limited *my* perception of her. I was ashamed of her English. I believed that her English reflected the quality of what she had to say. That is, because she expressed them imperfectly her thoughts were imperfect. And I had plenty of empirical evidence to support me: the fact that people in department stores, at banks, and at restaurants did not take her seriously, did not give her good service, pretended not to understand her, or even acted as if they did not hear her.

9   My mother has long realized the limitations of her English as well. When I was fifteen, she used to have me call people on the phone to pretend I was she. In this guise, I was forced to ask for information or even complain and yell at people who had been rude to her. One time it was a call to her stockbroker in New York. She had cashed out her small portfolio and it just so happened we were going to go to New York the next week, our very first trip outside California. I had to get on the phone and say in an adolescent voice that was not very convincing, "This is Mrs. Tan."

10   And my mother was standing in the back whispering loudly, "Why he don't send me check, already two weeks late. So mad he lie to me, losing me money."

11   And then I said in perfect English, "Yes, I'm getting rather concerned. You had agreed to send the check two weeks ago, but it hasn't arrived."

12   Then she began to talk more loudly. "What he want, I come to New York tell him front of his boss, you cheating me?" And I was trying to calm her down, make her be quiet, while telling the stockbroker, "I can't tolerate any more excuses. If I don't receive the check immediately I am going to have to speak to your manager when I'm in New York next week." And sure enough, the following week there we were in front of this astonished stockbroker, and I was sitting there red-faced and quiet, and my mother, the real Mrs. Tan, was shouting at his boss in her impeccable broken English.

13   We used a similar routine just five days ago, for a situation that was far less humorous. My mother had gone to the hospital for an appointment, to find out about a benign brain tumor a CAT scan had revealed a month ago. She said she had spoken very good English, her best English,

no mistakes. Still, she said, the hospital did not apologize when they said they had lost the CAT scan and she had come for nothing. She said they did not seem to have any sympathy when she told them she was anxious to know the exact diagnosis, since her husband and son had both died of brain tumors. She said they would not give her any more information until the next time and she would have to make another appointment for that. So she said she would not leave until the doctor called her daughter. She wouldn't budge. And when the doctor finally called her daughter, me, who spoke in perfect English—lo and behold—we had assurances the CAT scan would be found, promises that a conference call on Monday would be held, and apologies for any suffering my mother had gone through for a most regrettable mistake.

14   I think my mother's English almost had an effect on limiting my possibilities in life as well. Sociologists and linguists probably will tell you that a person's developing language skills are more influenced by peers. But I do think that the language spoken in the family, especially in immigrant families which are more insular, plays a large role in shaping the language of the child. And I believe that it affected my results on achievement tests, IQ tests, and the SAT. While my English skills were never judged as poor, compared to math, English could not be considered my strong suit. In grade school I did moderately well, getting perhaps B's, sometimes B-pluses, in English and scoring perhaps in the sixtieth or seventieth percentile on achievement tests. But those scores were not good enough to override the opinion that my true abilities lay in math and science, because in those areas I achieved A's and scored in the ninetieth percentile or higher.

15   This was understandable. Math is precise; there is only one correct answer. Whereas, for me at least, the answers on English tests were always a judgment call, a matter of opinion and personal experience. Those tests were constructed around items like fill-in-the-blank sentence completion, such as "Even though Tom was _____, Mary thought he was _____." And the correct answer always seemed to be the most bland combinations of thoughts, for example, "Even though Tom was shy, Mary thought he was charming," with the grammatical structure "even though" limiting the correct answer to some sort of semantic opposites, so you wouldn't get answers like, "Even though Tom was foolish, Mary thought he was ridiculous." Well, according to my mother, there were very few limitations as to what Tom could have been and what Mary might have thought of him. So I never did well on tests like that.

16   The same was true with word analogies, pairs of words in which you were supposed to find some sort of logical, semantic relationship—for example, "*Sunset* is to *nightfall* as _____ is to _____." And here you would be presented with a list of four possible pairs, one of which showed the same kind of relationship: *red* is to *stoplight, bus* is to *arrival, chills* is to *fever, yawn* is to *boring*. Well, I could never think that way. I knew what the tests were asking, but I could not block out of my mind the images already created by the first pair, "*sunset* is to

nightfall"—and I would see a burst of colors against a darkening sky, the moon rising, the lowering of a curtain of stars. And all the other pairs of words—red, bus, stoplight, boring—just threw up a mass of confusing images, making it impossible for me to sort out something as logical as saying: "A sunset precedes nightfall" is the same as "a chill precedes a fever." The only way I would have gotten that answer right would have been to imagine an associative situation, for example, my being disobedient and staying out past sunset, catching a chill at night, which turns into feverish pneumonia as punishment, which indeed did happen to me.

17   I have been thinking about all this lately, about my mother's English, about achievement tests. Because lately I've been asked, as a writer, why there are not more Asian Americans represented in American literature. Why are there few Asian Americans enrolled in creative writing programs? Why do so many Chinese students go into engineering? Well, these are broad sociological questions I can't begin to answer. But I have noticed in surveys—in fact, just last week—that Asian students, as a whole, always do significantly better on math achievement tests than in English. And this makes me think that there are other Asian-American students whose English spoken in the home might also be described as "broken" or "limited." And perhaps they also have teachers who are steering them away from writing and into math and science, which is what happened to me.

18   Fortunately, I happen to be rebellious in nature and enjoy the challenge of disproving assumptions made about me. I became an English major my first year in college, after being enrolled as pre-med. I started writing nonfiction as a freelancer the week after I was told by my former boss that writing was my worst skill and I should hone my talents toward account management.

19   But it wasn't until 1985 that I finally began to write fiction. And at first I wrote using what I thought to be wittily crafted sentences, sentences that would finally prove I had mastery over the English language. Here's an example from the first draft of a story that later made its way into *The Joy Luck Club*, but without this line: "That was my mental quandary in its nascent state." A terrible line, which I can barely pronounce.

20   Fortunately, for reasons I won't get into today, I later decided I should envision a reader for the stories I would write. And the reader I decided upon was my mother, because these were stories about mothers. So with this reader in mind—and in fact she did read my early drafts—I began to write stories using all the Englishes I grew up with: the English I spoke to my mother, which for lack of a better term might be described as "simple"; the English she used with me, which for lack of a better term might be described as "broken"; my translation of her Chinese, which could certainly be described as "watered down"; and what I imagined to be her translation of her Chinese if she could speak in perfect English, her internal language, and for that I sought to preserve the essence, but neither an English nor a

Chinese structure. I wanted to capture what language ability tests can never reveal: her intent, her passion, her imagery, the rhythms of her speech and the nature of her thoughts.

21 Apart from what any critic had to say about my writing, I knew I had succeeded where it counted when my mother finished reading my book and gave me her verdict: "So easy to read."

Focus on Reading

1. Look back at the work you did when you previewed, marked up, and annotated this essay. What do you think the term *mother tongue* means? Write a definition beside the essay's title. If you aren't sure what the term means, add a question mark to remind yourself to look it up later.
2. In the margin beside your most heavily marked-up paragraph, write a one-sentence summary of the paragraph.
3. TEST Tan's essay. Does she include all four TEST elements? If not, why not? What, if anything, should be added?

Focus on Meaning

1. What day-to-day problems did Tan experience because of her mother's "limited English"?
2. What "different Englishes" does Tan use? How are these "Englishes" different from one another?
3. According to Tan, how were her "possibilities in life" (paragraph 14) limited by her mother's English?

Focus on Strategy

1. What do Tan's first two paragraphs suggest about her purpose for writing this essay?
2. What is Tan's thesis? Is it explicitly stated? If so, where? If not, how would you express the thesis, and where would you place the thesis statement?
3. Does Tan seem to be writing for a primarily Asian-American audience or for a wider audience? How can you tell?

Focus on Language and Style

1. In addition to the standard definition of *mother tongue*, what other meaning does Tan's title suggest? Which meaning (or meanings) do you think Tan intended this term to have? Why?
2. Review the examples of Mrs. Tan's English that appear in this essay. Do you think Amy Tan could have made her point without these examples? Explain.

Focus on the Patterns

1. Among other things, this essay classifies different kinds of "Englishes." Where does this classification appear?
2. Where does Tan use comparison and contrast? What is she comparing? Why?
3. In addition to classification and comparison and contrast, what other patterns of development can you identify in this essay?

Focus on Critical Thinking

1. Do you think the specific kinds of academic problems Tan describes are limited to the children of parents whose first language is not English? Explain.
2. In addition to the situations outlined in the essay, what other challenges do you think are faced by those with "limited English" who live in the United States?
3. Reread paragraph 17. What factors do you think account for how few Asian Americans work in jobs associated with language and literature—and for their strong presence in science and engineering?

Focus on Writing

1. Write a **literacy narrative** tracing your development as a reader or a writer. (For a model of this type of essay, see the student essay "Becoming a Writer" in Chapter 8.)
2. Did your parents' spoken or written language help you become a better reader or writer? Or did their language stand in the way of your development as a reader or writer? Explain.

The Case for Short Words

Richard Lederer

Known for his love of words and wordplay, Richard Lederer began his career teaching English and media at St. Paul's School in New Hampshire. After twenty-seven years, he left teaching and went on to write over thirty popular books on language and trivia, beginning with the humorous *Anguished English* (1989). In "The Case for Short Words," Lederer uses examples ranging from famous literary works to high school students' essays to illustrate the power of short words.

Before you read, think about some of the one-syllable words you use most often in your writing.

1   When you speak and write, there is no law that says you have to use big words. Short words are as good as long ones, and short, old words—like *sun* and *grass* and *home*—are best of all. A lot of small words, more than you might think, can meet your needs with a strength, grace, and charm that large words do not have.

2   Big words can make the way dark for those who read what you write and hear what you say. Small words cast their clear light on big things—night and day, love and hate, war and peace, and life and death. Big words at times seem strange to the eye and the ear and the mind and the heart. Small words are the ones we seem to have known from the time we were born, like the hearth fire that warms the home.

3   Short words are bright like sparks that glow in the night, prompt like the dawn that greets the day, sharp like the blade of a knife, hot like salt tears that scald the cheek, quick like moths that flit from flame to flame, and terse like the dart and sting of a bee.

4   Here is a sound rule: Use small, old words where you can. If a long word says just what you want to say, do not fear to use it. But know that our tongue is rich in crisp, brisk, swift, short words. Make them the spine and the heart of what you speak and write. Short words are like fast friends. They will not let you down.

5   The title of this chapter and the four paragraphs that you have just read are wrought entirely of words of one syllable. In setting myself this task, I did not feel especially cabined, cribbed, or confined. In fact, the structure helped me to focus on the power of the message I was trying to put across.

WORD POWER

wrought crafted

6   One study shows that twenty words account for twenty-five percent of all spoken English words, and all twenty are monosyllabic. In order of frequency they are: *I, you, the, a, to, is, it, that, of, and, in, what, he, this, have, do, she, not, on,* and *they*. Other studies indicate that the fifty most common words in written English are each made of a single syllable.

7   For centuries our finest poets and orators have recognized and employed the power of small words to make a straight point between two minds. A great many of our proverbs punch home their points with pithy monosyllables: "Where there's a will, there's a way," "A stitch in time saves nine," "Spare the rod and spoil the child," "A bird in the hand is worth two in the bush."

WORD POWER

pithy brief but meaningful

8   Nobody used the short word more skillfully than William Shakespeare, whose dying King Lear laments:

> And my poor fool is hang'd! No, no, no life!
> Why should a dog, a horse, a rat have life,
> And thou no breath at all? . . .
> Do you see this? Look on her; look, her lips.
> Look there, look there!

9   Shakespeare's contemporaries made the King James Bible a centerpiece of short words—"And God said, Let there be light: and there was light.

And God saw the light, that it was good." The descendants of such mighty lines live on in the twentieth century. When asked to explain his policy to Parliament, Winston Churchill responded with these ringing monosyllables: "I will say: It is to wage war, by sea, land, and air, with all our might and with all the strength that God can give us." In his "Death of the Hired Man" Robert Frost observes that "Home is the place where, when you have to go there, / They have to take you in." And William H. Johnson uses ten two-letter words to explain his secret of success: "If it is to be, / It is up to me."

10   You don't have to be a great author, statesman, or philosopher to tap the energy and eloquence of small words. Each winter I ask my ninth graders at St. Paul's School to write a composition composed entirely of one-syllable words. My students greet my request with obligatory moans and groans, but, when they return to class with their essays, most feel that, with the pressure to produce high-sounding polysyllables relieved, they have created some of their most powerful and luminous prose. Here are submissions from two of my ninth graders:

> What can you say to a boy who has left home? You can say that he has done wrong, but he does not care. He has left home so that he will not have to deal with what you say. He wants to go as far as he can. He will do what he wants to do.
>
> This boy does not want to be forced to go to church, to comb his hair, or to be on time. A good time for this boy does not lie in your reach, for what you have he does not want. He dreams of ripped jeans, shorts with no starch, and old socks.
>
> So now this boy is on a bus to a place he dreams of, a place with no rules. This boy now walks a strange street, his long hair blown back by the wind. He wears no coat or tie, just jeans and an old shirt. He hates your world, and he has left it.
>
> —Charles Shaffer

> For a long time we cruised by the coast and at last came to a wide bay past the curve of a hill, at the end of which lay a small town. Our long boat ride at an end, we all stretched and stood up to watch as the boat nosed its way in.
>
> The town climbed up the hill that rose from the shore, a space in front of it left bare for the port. Each house was a clean white with sky blue or grey trim; in front of each one was a small yard, edged by a white stone wall strewn with green vines.
>
> As the town basked in the heat of noon, not a thing stirred in the streets or by the shore. The sun beat down on the sea, the land, and the back of our necks, so that, in spite of the breeze that made the vines sway, we all wished we could hide from the glare in a cool, white house. But, as there was no one to help dock the boat, we had to stand and wait.
>
> At last the head of the crew leaped from the side and strode to a large house on the right. He shoved the door wide, poked his head

WORD POWER
obligatory required

through the gloom, and roared with a fierce voice. Five or six men came out, and soon the port was loud with the clank of chains and creak of planks as the men caught ropes thrown by the crew, pulled them taut, and tied them to posts. Then they set up a rough plank so we could cross from the deck to the shore. We all made for the large house while the crew watched, glad to be rid of us.

—Celia Wren

11 You, too, can tap into the vitality and vigor of compact expression. Take a suggestion from the highway department. At the boundaries of your speech and prose place a sign that reads "Caution: Small Words at Work."

Focus on Reading

1. Look back at the work you did when you previewed, marked up, and annotated this essay. If you have not already done so, underline the essay's thesis statement. Then, restate it in your own words.
2. Go through the essay, and circle ten words that have more than one syllable. Try substituting a one-syllable word for each of these words. Do your words strengthen the essay?
3. TEST Lederer's essay. Does he include all four TEST elements? If not, why not? What, if anything, should be added?

Focus on Meaning

1. What "case for short words" is Lederer making in this essay?
2. In paragraph 6, Lederer discusses two studies. What information is provided in these studies? Do you think Lederer needs this information to make his point?

Focus on Strategy

1. Do you think Lederer is writing for a general audience? For students? For teachers? How can you tell?
2. Evaluate Lederer's concluding paragraph. Is his use of "You, too" effective here? Is the closing quotation appropriate for his audience and purpose? Explain.

Focus on Language and Style

1. As Lederer points out in paragraph 5, his essay's title and first four paragraphs are composed entirely of one-syllable words. Is this an effective stylistic choice?
2. In paragraph 7, Lederer says, "For centuries our finest poets and orators have recognized and employed the power of small words to make a straight point between two minds." What does he mean by "a straight point between two minds"? How else could he have expressed this idea?

Focus on the Patterns

1. In addition to his many short examples, Lederer uses longer examples from the Bible, literature, politics, as well as passages from two student writers. How do these examples support his thesis?
2. In paragraphs 2–4, Lederer uses comparison and contrast to point out the differences between long and short words. What key difference does he identify?

Focus on Critical Thinking

1. Which of Lederer's many examples do you find most convincing? Why?
2. Choose a sentence from the essay that is *not* composed entirely of one-syllable words, and rewrite it using words of only one syllable. Is your sentence as clear and effective as Lederer's original? If not, does your rewrite undercut his essay's thesis?
3. Evaluate the "sound rule" Lederer presents in paragraph 4. Is it useful? Practical? Logical?

Focus on Writing

1. In paragraph 10, Lederer reproduces two short student essays that use only one-syllable words. Write a short essay of your own composed entirely of one-syllable words.
2. Write an essay focusing on three or four stylistic choices you habitually make when you write. For example, do you prefer to begin or end your essays with a particular strategy? Do you like to use quotations or anecdotes for support? In your thesis statement, summarize the advantages (or disadvantages) of your writing choices.

For Trans People Like Me, Pronouns Are about More Than Grammatical Correctness

Noah Lewis

Noah Lewis is the founder and executive director of Transcend Legal, an organization that advocates for transgender people. A 2005 graduate of Harvard Law School, he spent five years as the staff attorney at the Transgender Legal Defense & Education Fund. In the following article, which appeared in *The Washington Post* in 2016, Lewis argues in favor of using people's preferred pronouns.

Before you read this essay, read Josh Blackman's essay "The Government Can't Make You Use 'Zhir' or 'Ze' in Place of 'She' or 'He'." (Go to the home page for *The Washington Post* and search for the article or type the title and author's name into your search engine.)

1   When my dad came out to his co-workers about having a transgender son, he showed them a picture of me on my first day at law school. "You may remember that I had a daughter who went to Harvard Law School," he began. Switching to a picture of me and my parents taken in the same spot three year later, he added, "And I have a son who graduated."

2   Despite being the first transgender person to transition at Harvard Law School, I was met—more than a decade ago—with the utmost respect from my classmates and professors. It was disheartening, then, to read recent columns by law professors Josh Blackman and Eugene Volokh arguing in support of referring to transgender people by incorrect pronouns.

3   If I were a fellow professor at one of their law schools, they would defend the ability of themselves or students to refer to me as "Ms. Lewis" and "she" to express the belief—however inaccurate—that I am not male. While those who would intentionally misgender me would look silly, it would convey a more insidious message: transgender people are not welcome at their schools.

4   The normal practice in polite society is to honor the title and pronouns of an individual. Mr. Blackman, for example, prefers male titles and pronouns. If his colleagues and students took to referring to him as "her" or "Ms. Blackman," he might consider it nonsensical at first, and if it persisted, disrespectful or even harassing.

5   We know that potentially benign words such as "sweetheart," "cripple" or "boy"—I wince just writing them—are not permitted in the workplace when their purpose is to harass and demean. We have collectively decided that in order to have a society enriched by the contributions of a diverse group of people, everyone deserves to be respected in the workplace. While people may still harbor prejudices, they cannot express those views in a way that infringes on another's right to work in a safe and equitable environment.

6   What such an environment looks like for transgender people has catapulted into the nation's consciousness in recent months. North Carolina continues to defend its anti-transgender law, while the federal government has moved to protect transgender people nationwide from discrimination.

7   New York City, meanwhile, is building upon its rich history of respect for the diversity of its residents. In December, the NYC Commission on Human Rights issued legal guidance regarding existing gender identity protections under the New York City Human Rights Law. This directive clarifies protections and provides examples of potential violations, such as denying appropriate bathroom use or the "intentional or repeated refusal to use an individual's preferred name, pronoun or title" in the workplace. The commission had issued similar guidelines on this subject in 2006 under the Bloomberg administration.

8   The commission made clear that accidentally using the wrong pronoun is not harassment, while deliberate misuse is. My mom still calls me "she" on occasion. She also accidentally calls me by my brother's name, so I don't

let a neural lapse bother me. My parents were not able to switch pronouns overnight, but because they love and respect me and eventually came to see me for who I am, they did. Calling me "he" has in no way interfered with some of their favorite forms of free expression—namely, watching Fox News and voting Republican.

9   Contrary to those who would paint the guidance as suppressing free speech, no one is being forced to use certain pronouns for transgender people. Those who are strongly opposed to using correct pronouns can make their beliefs known by avoiding pronouns altogether.

10   Language is constantly evolving. The policemen, firemen and stewardesses I grew up with have given way to police officers, firefighters and flight attendants. Newspapers are also adopting gender-neutral language. In an article, the *New York Times* recently used Mx. instead of Mr. or Ms.—a title with its own hard-fought history. *The Post* changed its editorial guidelines to accept "they" as a singular gender neutral pronoun. Its copy editor Bill Walsh called it "the only sensible solution to English's lack of a gender-neutral third-person singular personal pronoun."

11   For transgender people, it's about more than grammatical correctness. It's about being able to work and attend school safely, free from discrimination. Until recently, most transgender people were simply shut out of the workplace or were afraid to let their co-workers and classmates know that they are trans. That's all changing now. Knowing openly transgender friends, family members and colleagues is rapidly becoming the norm.

12   Does it take a little bit of effort to break out of old habits and refer to someone by a new pronoun? Sure. But given the stark realities facing transgender people who are excluded from jobs and education, it's the very least we can do. The simple act of calling me "Mr. Lewis" and "he" adds up to nothing less than creating a society in which transgender people don't merely survive, but thrive.

Focus on Reading

1. Look back at the work you did when you previewed, marked up, and annotated this essay. Did you underline Lewis's thesis statement? If not, do so now.

2. Skim paragraph 10. In the margin, write down a question that you would like to ask about the paragraph's content.

3. **TEST** Lewis's essay. Does he include all four **TEST** elements? If not, why not? What, if anything, should be added?

Focus on Meaning

1. Why does Lewis object to the columns written by Josh Blackman (2) and Eugene Volokh?

2. When it comes to pronoun use, what, according to Lewis, is "the normal practice in polite society" (4)?

3. According to Lewis, how have *The New York Times* and *The Post* addressed the issue of gender-neutral pronouns?
4. In paragraph 11, Lewis says that for transgender individuals, pronoun use is "about more than grammatical correctness." What does he mean?

Focus on Strategy

1. Lewis begins his essay with an anecdote about his father. What does he hope to accomplish here? Does he succeed?
2. Lewis does not state his thesis until the end of his essay. Why does he wait so long?
3. What assumptions about transgender people does Lewis assume his audience has? Do you think he is correct?
4. In his conclusion, Lewis mentions that transgender people face obstacles in employment and education. Why does he end with this information? Should he have discussed these obstacles earlier in his essay?

Focus on Language and Style

1. In paragraph 4, Lewis says using the pronoun *her* to refer to Josh Blackman would be disrespectful and possibly constitute harassment. Do you agree?
2. In paragraph 5, Lewis mentions the "potentially benign words" *sweetheart, cripple*, and *boy*. Why are these words *potentially* benign? In what circumstances could these words be hurtful? Why does Lewis say, "I wince at writing them"?
3. How would you describe Lewis's tone? Is it engaging? Aloof? Sarcastic? Something else? (See 5a for discussion of a writer's tone.)

Focus on the Patterns

1. Lewis relies on his own experience to support his thesis. Should he have included other kinds of support—statistics or expert opinion, for example? Explain.
2. What opposing arguments does Lewis address? How effectively does he deal with these arguments? What other arguments could he have addressed? Should he have included them in his essay?
3. Paragraphs 6 and 7 present a comparison. What two things are being compared? What point does this comparison make?

Focus on Critical Thinking

1. According to Lewis, the New York Commission on Human Rights says using the wrong pronoun accidentally is not harassment. Using the wrong pronoun intentionally, however, is harassment. Can you think of examples where it would be difficult to make this distinction? Explain.

2. In paragraph 8, Lewis says that his parents watch Fox News and vote Republican. Why does he include this information?

3. In paragraph 9, Lewis says that those who object to using "correct pronouns" can register their displeasure by "avoiding pronouns altogether." Is this suggestion reasonable? Is it feasible?

4. In paragraph 7, Lewis discusses the mandates that Blackman criticizes in his essay. How is Lewis's view of these mandates different from Blackman's?

Focus on Writing

1. In paragraph 2, Lewis refers to essays by Josh Blackman and Eugene Volokh. Read both essays (Blackman's essay, "The Government Can't Make You Use 'Zhir' or 'Ze' in Place of 'She' or 'He'," and Volokh's essay, "You Can Be Fined for Not Calling People 'Ze' or 'Hir,' If That's the Pronoun They Demand that You Use" are both available online). Then, write an essay in which you argue for or against using gender-neutral pronouns. Make sure you refer to all three essays and that you document all words and ideas that are not your own (see Chapter 14 for information on MLA documentation style).

2. One objection to requiring people to use gender-neutral pronouns is that it amounts to the government forcing people to conform to its ideas about gender. How would Lewis respond to this objection? Write an essay in which you answer this question. Make sure you document all words and ideas that are not your own (see Chapter 14).

 Technology and Science

The Flight from Conversation

Sherry Turkle

Sherry Turkle received a Ph.D. in sociology and personality psychology from Harvard University. She is a licensed clinical psychologist, a professor at MIT, and the founding director of the MIT Initiative on Technology and Self. Turkle writes about people's relationship with technology. Her books include *Life on the Screen: Identity in the Age of the Internet* (1995), *Alone Together: Why We Expect More from Technology and Less from Each Other* (2011), and *Reclaiming Conversation: The Power of Talk in a Digital Age* (2015). In "The Flight from Conversation," Turkle contrasts face-to-face conversation and technological connection and identifies some of the effects of people's shift in communication styles.

Before you read, think about how much time you spend on social media each day.

1   We live in a technological universe in which we are always communicating. And yet we have sacrificed conversation for mere connection.

2   At home, families sit together, texting and reading email. At work, executives text during board meetings. We text (and shop and go on Facebook) during classes and when we're on dates. My students tell me about an important new skill: it involves maintaining eye contact with someone while you text someone else; it's hard, but it can be done.

3   Over the past 15 years, I've studied technologies of mobile connection and talked to hundreds of people of all ages and circumstances about their plugged-in lives. I've learned that the little devices most of us carry around are so powerful that they change not only what we do, but also who we are.

4   We've become accustomed to a new way of being "alone together." Technology-enabled, we are able to be with one another, and also elsewhere, connected to wherever we want to be. We want to customize our lives. We want to move in and out of where we are because the thing we value most is control over where we focus our attention. We have gotten used to the idea of being in a tribe of one, loyal to our own party.

5   Our colleagues want to go to that board meeting but pay attention only to what interests them. To some this seems like a good idea, but we can end up hiding from one another, even as we are constantly connected to one another.

6   A businessman laments that he no longer has colleagues at work. He doesn't stop by to talk; he doesn't call. He says that he doesn't want to interrupt them. He says they're "too busy on their e-mail." But then he pauses and corrects himself. "I'm not telling the truth. I'm the one who doesn't want to be interrupted. I think I should. But I'd rather just do things on my BlackBerry."

7   A 16-year-old boy who relies on texting for almost everything says almost wistfully, "Someday, someday, but certainly not now, I'd like to learn how to have a conversation."

8   In today's workplace, young people who have grown up fearing conversation show up on the job wearing earphones. Walking through a college library or the campus of a high-tech start-up, one sees the same thing: we are together, but each of us is in our own bubble, furiously connected to keyboards and tiny touch screens. A senior partner at a Boston law firm describes a scene in his office. Young associates lay out their suite of technologies: laptops, iPods and multiple phones. And then they put their earphones on. "Big ones. Like pilots. They turn their desks into cockpits." With the young lawyers in their cockpits, the office is quiet, a quiet that does not ask to be broken.

9   In the silence of connection, people are comforted by being in touch with a lot of people — carefully kept at bay. We can't get enough of one another if we can use technology to keep one another at distances we can control: not too close, not too far, just right. I think of it as a Goldilocks effect.

10   Texting and e-mail and posting let us present the self we want to be. This means we can edit. And if we wish to, we can delete. Or retouch: the voice, the flesh, the face, the body. Not too much, not too little—just right.

11   Human relationships are rich; they're messy and demanding. We have learned the habit of cleaning them up with technology. And the move from conversation to connection is part of this. But it's a process in which we shortchange ourselves. Worse, it seems that over time we stop caring, we forget that there is a difference.

12   We are tempted to think that our little "sips" of online connection add up to a big gulp of real conversation. But they don't. E-mail, Twitter, Facebook, all of these have their places—in politics, commerce, romance and friendship. But no matter how valuable, they do not substitute for conversation.

13   Connecting in sips may work for gathering discrete bits of information or for saying, "I am thinking about you." Or even for saying, "I love you." But connecting in sips doesn't work as well when it comes to understanding and knowing one another. In conversation we tend to one another. (The word itself is kinetic; it's derived from words that mean to move, together.) We can attend to tone and nuance. In conversation, we are called upon to see things from another's point of view.

14   FACE-TO-FACE conversation unfolds slowly. It teaches patience. When we communicate on our digital devices, we learn different habits. As we ramp up the volume and velocity of online connections, we start to expect faster answers. To get these, we ask one another simpler questions; we dumb down our communications, even on the most important matters. It is as though we have all put ourselves on cable news. Shakespeare might have said, "We are consum'd with that which we were nourish'd by."

15   And we use conversation with others to learn to converse with ourselves. So our flight from conversation can mean diminished chances to learn skills of self-reflection. These days, social media continually asks us what's "on our mind," but we have little motivation to say something truly self-reflective. Self-reflection in conversation requires trust. It's hard to do anything with 3,000 Facebook friends except connect.

16   As we get used to being shortchanged on conversation and to getting by with less, we seem almost willing to dispense with people altogether. Serious people muse about the future of computer programs as psychiatrists. A high school sophomore confides to me that he wishes he could talk to an artificial intelligence program instead of his dad about dating; he says the A.I. would have so much more in its database. Indeed, many people tell me they hope that as Siri, the digital assistant on Apple's iPhone, becomes more advanced, "she" will be more and more like a best friend—one who will listen when others won't.

17   During the years I have spent researching people and their relationships with technology, I have often heard the sentiment "No one is listening to me." I believe this feeling helps explain why it is so appealing to have a Facebook page or a Twitter feed—each provides so many automatic

> **WORD POWER**
> **discrete** separate; individual

listeners. And it helps explain why—against all reason—so many of us are willing to talk to machines that seem to care about us. Researchers around the world are busy inventing sociable robots, designed to be companions to the elderly, to children, to all of us.

18   One of the most haunting experiences during my research came when I brought one of these robots, designed in the shape of a baby seal, to an elder-care facility, and an older woman began to talk to it about the loss of her child. The robot seemed to be looking into her eyes. It seemed to be following the conversation. The woman was comforted.

19   And so many people found this amazing. Like the sophomore who wants advice about dating from artificial intelligence and those who look forward to computer psychiatry, this enthusiasm speaks to how much we have confused conversation with connection and collectively seem to have embraced a new kind of delusion that accepts the simulation of compassion as sufficient unto the day. And why would we want to talk about love and loss with a machine that has no experience of the arc of human life? Have we so lost confidence that we will be there for one another?

20   We expect more from technology and less from one another and seem increasingly drawn to technologies that provide the illusion of companionship without the demands of relationship. Always-on/always-on-you devices provide three powerful fantasies: that we will always be heard; that we can put our attention wherever we want it to be; and that we never have to be alone. Indeed our new devices have turned being alone into a problem that can be solved.

21   When people are alone, even for a few moments, they fidget and reach for a device. Here connection works like a symptom, not a cure, and our constant, reflexive impulse to connect shapes a new way of being.

22   Think of it as "I share, therefore I am." We use technology to define ourselves by sharing our thoughts and feelings as we're having them. We used to think, "I have a feeling; I want to make a call." Now our impulse is, "I want to have a feeling; I need to send a text."

23   So, in order to feel more, and to feel more like ourselves, we connect. But in our rush to connect, we flee from solitude, our ability to be separate and gather ourselves. Lacking the capacity for solitude, we turn to other people but don't experience them as they are. It is as though we use them, need them as spare parts to support our increasingly fragile selves.

24   We think constant connection will make us feel less lonely. The opposite is true. If we are unable to be alone, we are far more likely to be lonely. If we don't teach our children to be alone, they will know only how to be lonely.

25   I am a partisan for conversation. To make room for it, I see some first, deliberate steps. At home, we can create sacred spaces: the kitchen, the dining room. We can make our cars "device-free zones." We can demonstrate the value of conversation to our children. And we can do the same thing at work. There we are so busy communicating that we often don't have time to talk to one another about what really matters. Employees asked for casual Fridays; perhaps managers should introduce conversational Thursdays.

WORD POWER

partisan strong supporter

Most of all, we need to remember—in between texts and e-mails and Facebook posts—to listen to one another, even to the boring bits, because it is often in unedited moments, moments in which we hesitate and stutter and go silent, that we reveal ourselves to one another.

26   I spend the summers at a cottage on Cape Cod, and for decades I walked the same dunes that Thoreau once walked. Not too long ago, people walked with their heads up, looking at the water, the sky, the sand and at one another, talking. Now they often walk with their heads down, typing. Even when they are with friends, partners, children, everyone is on their own devices.

27   So I say, look up, look at one another, and let's start the conversation.

Focus on Reading

1. Look back at the work you did when you previewed, marked up, and annotated this essay. If you have not already done so, circle all the words that suggest communication.
2. In the margin beside paragraph 10, write a one-sentence summary of the paragraph.
3. **TEST** Turkle's essay. Does she include all four **TEST** elements? If not, why not? What, if anything, should be added?

Focus on Meaning

1. What does Turkle mean by "'alone together'" (4)? How does she illustrate this **paradox?**
2. What is the "Goldilocks effect" (9)? How does this term help Turkle make her point?
3. What does Turkle mean by "connecting in sips" (12–13)? What, according to her, is wrong with this kind of connection? How is it different from face-to-face conversation?

Focus on Strategy

1. In her essay's first paragraph, Turkle says that we "have sacrificed conversation for mere connection." What distinction is she making? Is this her essay's thesis? Explain.
2. In paragraph 3, Turkle notes that she has studied "technologies of mobile connection" for fifteen years and has interviewed hundreds of people. Later, in paragraph 17, she mentions that she has spent "years . . . researching people and their relationships with technology." Why does she provide this information?
3. In paragraph 25, Turkle makes some recommendations for solving the problem she has described. Do any of these recommendations make sense (or seem feasible) to you? Explain.

Focus on Language and Style

1. In paragraph 15, Turkle mentions the "flight from conversation" that is also the essay's title. Consider the connotations of the word *flight*. Is this the best choice of words? Can you think of another word that might express the concept more clearly and effectively?
2. In paragraph 24, Turkle makes a distinction between being *alone* and being *lonely*. What is the difference?

Focus on the Patterns

1. What has caused the situation Turkle describes? What results of the "flight from conversation" does she identify? Are all these results negative?
2. Central to this essay is a comparison between two kinds of communication. What are they? How are they alike? How are they different?
3. Where does Turkle use narrative? How do her narratives help to get her points across?

Focus on Critical Thinking

1. Do you agree with Turkle that mobile devices "change not only what we do, but also who we are" (3), or do you think she overstates her case?
2. In paragraph 16, Turkle suggests that people today "seem almost willing to dispense with people altogether." Do you think she is being serious here, or do you think she is exaggerating? Explain.
3. This essay was written in 2012. Do you think it is dated, or do you think Turkle's conclusions make sense today? Do they perhaps make *more* sense today? Explain.

Focus on Writing

1. Do you recognize yourself in the scenarios Turkle presents here? For example, have you come to "expect more from technology and less from [others]" (paragraph 20)? Do you find yourself spending more time on social media than in face-to-face conversation? Write an essay in which you consider how social media has affected your life in the years since your early adolescence. Do you see this increased influence as entirely negative, as Turkle seems to, or can you identify some positive effects?
2. Write an essay in which you trace the way a friend of yours has moved from being a face-to-face friend to being just a social-media friend—or vice versa. What led to the change in status?

Don't Know the Difference between Emoji and Emoticons? Let Me Explain

Alex Hern

Alex Hern has been a staff writer for the *New Statesman* and is now a technology reporter for *The Guardian*. His writing covers topics including policy, internet culture, cryptocurrency, and the dark net. In the following 2015 article from *The Guardian*, Hern defines two types of graphic symbols and explains their differences.

Before you read, think about the occasions on which you use emoji or emoticons, and consider when they are appropriate and when they are not.

1   Emoji and emoticons are not the same thing and the continued confusion of the two will not stand.

2   In *The New York Times*, under the headline "At Silk Road Trial, Lawyers Fight to Include Evidence They Call Vital: Emoji," the two were treated as interchangeable.

3   "At issue" in the court's debates "was a piece of information that [the Silk Road founder Ross Ulbricht's] lawyer suggested was critically important, yet was omitted by federal prosecutors: an emoji.

4   "And not just any emoji, or emoticon, as the symbol is sometimes called—it was the gold standard. A version of a smiley face."

5   And on the BBC, under the headline "Emoticons in texts can rack up huge bills" is a news story which exclusively discusses emoji.

6   An **emoticon** is a typographic display of a facial representation, used to convey emotion in a text only medium. Like so: ;-)

7   Invented multiple times over human history, its internet-era genesis is widely considered to have occurred in September 1982, when computer scientist Scott Fahlman suggested to the Carnegie Mellon University message board that :-) and :-(could be used to distinguish jokes from serious statements online. Shortly thereafter came the name, a portmanteau of the phrase "emotion icon".

8   In contrast to the grassroots creation of the emoticon, **emoji** were created in the late 1990s by NTT DoCoMo, the Japanese communications firm. The name is a contraction of the words *e* and *moji*, which roughly translates to pictograph.

9   Unlike emoticons, emoji are actual pictures, of everything from a set of painted nails (💅) to a slightly whimsical ghost (👻). And where emoticons were invented to portray emotion in environments where nothing but basic text is available, emoji are actually extensions to the character set used by most operating systems today, Unicode.

10   In essence, emoji are treated by the computer as letters from a non-western language, in much the same way as Japanese and Chinese

> **WORD POWER**
>
> **portmanteau** a word whose form and meaning are created by a combination of two other words.

> **WORD POWER**
>
> **pictograph** an image that symbolizes a word or phrase

characters are. But that also means that the software has to explicitly support them—otherwise it is forced to display a placeholder icon, or even just a blank space (which you might see between the brackets in the paragraph above if your browser doesn't support emoji).

11 It also means that each company has to provide its own interpretations of what the emoji descriptions should actually look like – and they don't always agree. Take the implementations of the "dancer" emoji: for Twitter and Apple, it's a female flamenco dancer. But for Google, it was, until recently, a John Travolta lookalike dancing disco style. And now it's a weird blobby thing. So if you're about to tell someone "you look gorgeous, like a 💃", make sure they aren't reading it on a new Android phone.

12 To complicate matters, some emoji are also emoticons. The standard for the characters breaks them apart into sets by theme. Most are filed under "Miscellaneous Symbols and Pictographs", but the emoji which depict emotive faces are separated out as "emoticons".

13 There's more.

14 Although the name's not much used in the west, it's probably best to distinguish **kaomoji** from emoticons in general. Independently invented around the same time as emoticons, they make the most of the fuller character set necessary to write in Japanese, and can be read head-on. They may be as simple as (*_*), or as complex as (/●ヮ●)/*:·° ✧. or ಠ_ಠ.

15 Oh, and then there's **stickers**, the custom pictures used in a number of instant messaging clients such as Facebook Messenger or Line. Some apps refer to them as emoji, but they're fully specific to the app, and can't be cut and pasted anywhere else except when they're treated as an image.

16 With that much variation, is it surprising that people get a little (╯°□°)╯︵ ┻━┻ if you confuse :-) with ☺?

Focus on Reading

1. Look back at the work you did when you previewed, marked up, and annotated this essay. If you have not already done so, underline the definitions of the two terms being compared here.
2. Construct a brief outline to identify the main points of contrast between *emoticon* an *emoji*.
3. **TEST** Hern's essay. Does he include all four **TEST** elements? If not, why not? What, if anything, should be added?

Focus on Meaning

1. In one sentence, define *emoticon*; then, define *emoji* in a single sentence.
2. How did emoticons originate? How were emoji created?
3. What are *kaomoji*? How are they different from "emoticons in general" (14)? What are *stickers*? How are they different from emoji?

Focus on Strategy

1. What is Hern's thesis? Where does he state it? Would it be more convincing if it were stated at the end of a full introductory paragraph? Why or why not?
2. Do you think Hern's purpose in this essay is to convince readers of the importance of a linguistic distinction, or do you think he is just trying to amuse or entertain? Explain your conclusion.
3. Does Hern expect his readers to be familiar with both emoticons and emoji? How can you tell?
4. In paragraphs 2 through 6, Hern gives examples of situations in which emoji and emoticons were confused or conflated. Why does he introduce these examples?

Focus on Language and Style

1. Using the example given in paragraph 7 (emotion + icon = emoticon) as a model, try to think of five additional portmanteau words.
2. Some of the paragraphs in this essay are quite short; several, in fact, are each just one sentence long. Is this a strength or a weakness of the essay? Should any of the single-sentence paragraphs be combined with paragraphs that precede or follow them? If so, which ones?

Focus on the Patterns

1. Circle the transitional word and phrases in this essay that signal contrast. Do you think Hern should have used more of these words, or are the specific points of contrast clear?
2. Should Hern have used more examples of emoticons or emoji to define these two terms? Should he have used more visuals—for example, a chart—to distinguish one from the other? If so, where should he have inserted these additions? Are there any images that should be deleted? If so, explain why.
3. Does Hern treat his two subjects equally? Or does he devote more time to one than to the other? If so, do you see this as a problem?

Focus on Critical Thinking

1. Paragraph 12 begins with the phrase "To complicate matters . . ." Does this paragraph just "complicate matters," or does it provide information that is central to Hern's comparison? Does Hern seem to "complicate matters" anywhere else in this essay?
2. Do you think the distinction between emoticons and emoji is important? Why or why not?

Focus on Writing

1. Write an essay in which you compare the kinds of situations in which emoji and emoticons are and are not appropriate or helpful.
2. Construct a sequence of emoticons to convey a specific scenario; then, assemble a sequence of emoji to convey the same scene or action. (You may use other symbols, such as a *plus* or *equals* sign, along with either sequence.) Now, write an essay comparing these two systems of communication. Which do you see as superior in terms of visual appeal, clarity, and ease of use?
3. Assemble emoji so they briefly summarize a familiar fairy tale. Then, use words to retell the same story. Now, write an essay comparing the visual language of emoji with the language of words. What advantages and disadvantages of each can you identify?

Why 'Natural' Doesn't Mean Anything Anymore
Michael Pollan

Michael Pollan was born in 1955 on Long Island, New York, and received an M.A. in English from Columbia University. In his numerous books and articles, Pollan explores the intersection of nature and culture, primarily through humans' relationship with food. His book *The Omnivore's Dilemma* (2006) won the James Beard Foundation's award for best food writing. His most recent book, *Cooked: A Natural History of Transformation* (2013), was adapted into a documentary series on Netflix. Pollan is a contributing writer for the *New York Times Magazine*, where, in this 2015 article, "Why 'Natural' Doesn't Mean Anything Anymore," he discusses multiple meanings people have assigned to the word *natural*.

Before you read, think of some commonly used expressions that include the word *natural*.

1 It isn't every day that the definition of a common English word that is ubiquitous in common parlance is challenged in federal court, but that is precisely what has happened with the word "natural." During the past few years, some 200 class-action suits have been filed against food manufacturers, charging them with misuse of the adjective in marketing such edible oxymorons as "natural" Cheetos Puffs, "all-natural" Sun Chips, "all-natural" Naked Juice, "100 percent all-natural" Tyson chicken nuggets and so forth. The plaintiffs argue that many of these products contain ingredients—high-fructose corn syrup, artificial flavors and colorings, chemical preservatives and genetically modified organisms—that the typical consumer wouldn't think of as "natural."

> **WORD POWER**
> **ubiquitous** found everywhere
> **parlance** talk, speech
> **oxymoron** a combination of two contradictory words

2   Judges hearing these cases—many of them in the Northern District of California—have sought a standard definition of the adjective that they could cite to adjudicate these claims, only to discover that no such thing exists.

3   Something in the human mind, or heart, seems to need a word of praise for all that humanity hasn't contaminated, and for us that word now is "natural." Such an ideal can be put to all sorts of rhetorical uses. Among the antivaccination crowd, for example, it's not uncommon to read about the superiority of something called "natural immunity," brought about by exposure to the pathogen in question rather than to the deactivated (and therefore harmless) version of it made by humans in laboratories. "When you inject a vaccine into the body," reads a post on an antivaxxer website, Campaign for Truth in Medicine, "you're actually performing an unnatural act." This, of course, is the very same term once used to decry homosexuality and, more recently, same-sex marriage, which the Family Research Council has taken to comparing unfavorably to what it calls "natural marriage."

4   So what are we really talking about when we talk about natural? It depends; the adjective is impressively slippery, its use steeped in dubious assumptions that are easy to overlook. Perhaps the most incoherent of these is the notion that nature consists of everything in the world except us and all that we have done or made. In our heart of hearts, it seems, we are all creationists.

5   In the case of "natural immunity," the modifier implies the absence of human intervention, allowing for a process to unfold as it would if we did nothing, as in "letting nature take its course." In fact, most of medicine sets itself *against* nature's course, which is precisely what we like about it—at least when it's saving us from dying, an eventuality that is perhaps more natural than it is desirable.

6   Yet sometimes medicine's interventions are unwelcome or go overboard, and nature's way of doing things can serve as a useful corrective. This seems to be especially true at the beginning and end of life, where we've seen a backlash against humanity's technological ingenuity that has given us both "natural childbirth" and, more recently, "natural death."

7   This last phrase, which I expect will soon be on many doctors' lips, indicates the enduring power of the adjective to improve just about anything you attach it to, from cereal bars all the way on up to dying. It seems that getting end-of-life patients and their families to endorse "do not resuscitate" orders has been challenging. To many ears, "D.N.R." sounds a little too much like throwing Grandpa under the bus. But according to a paper in *The Journal of Medical Ethics*, when the orders are reworded to say "allow natural death," patients and family members and even medical professionals are much more likely to give their consent to what amounts to exactly the same protocols.

8   The word means something a little different when applied to human behavior rather than biology (let alone snack foods). When marriage or certain sexual practices are described as "natural," the word is being strategically deployed as a synonym for "normal" or "traditional," neither of which carries nearly as much rhetorical weight. "Normal" is by now too obviously soaked in moral bigotry; by comparison, "natural" seems to float high above human squabbling, offering a kind of secular version of what used to be called divine law. Of course, that's exactly the role that "natural law" played for America's founding fathers, who invoked nature rather than God as the granter of rights and the arbiter of right and wrong.

9   "Traditional" marriage might be a more defensible term, but traditional is a much weaker modifier than natural. Tradition changes over time and from culture to culture, and so commands a fraction of the authority of nature, which we think of as timeless and universal, beyond the reach of messy, contested history.

10 Implicit here is the idea that nature is a repository of abiding moral and ethical values—and that we can say with confidence exactly what those values are. Philosophers often call this the "naturalistic fallacy": the idea that whatever *is* (in nature) is what *ought to be* (in human behavior). But if nature offers a moral standard by which we can measure ourselves, and a set of values to which we should aspire, exactly what sort of values are they? Are they the brutally competitive values of "nature, red in tooth and claw," in which every individual is out for him- or herself? Or are they the values of cooperation on display in a beehive or ant colony, where the interests of the community trump those of the individual? Opponents of same-sex marriage can find examples of monogamy in the animal kingdom, and yet to do so they need to look past equally compelling examples of animal polygamy as well as increasing evidence of apparent animal homosexuality. And let's not overlook the dismaying rates of what looks very much like rape in the animal kingdom, or infanticide, or the apparent sadism of your average house cat.

> **WORD POWER**
> **implicit** implied, suggested

11 The American Puritans called nature "God's Second Book," and they read it for moral guidance, just as we do today. Yet in the same way we can rummage around in the Bible and find textual support for pretty much whatever we want to do or argue, we can ransack nature to justify just about anything. Like the maddening whiteness of Ahab's whale, nature is an obligingly blank screen on which we can project what we want to see.

12 So does this mean that, when it comes to saying what's natural, anything goes? I don't think so. In fact, I think there's some philosophical wisdom we can harvest from, of all places, the Food and Drug Administration. When the federal judges couldn't find a definition of "natural" to apply to the class-action suits before them, three of them wrote to the F.D.A., ordering the agency to define the word. But the F.D.A. had considered the question several times before, and refused to

attempt a definition. The only advice the F.D.A. was willing to offer the jurists is that a food labeled "natural" should have "nothing artificial or synthetic" in it "that would not normally be expected in the food." The F.D.A. states on its website that "it is difficult to define a food product as 'natural' because the food has probably been processed and is no longer the product of the earth," suggesting that the industry might not want to press the point too hard, lest it discover that *nothing* it sells is natural.

13   The F.D.A.'s philosopher-bureaucrats are probably right: At least at the margins, it's impossible to fix a definition of "natural." Yet somewhere between those margins there lies a broad expanse of common sense. "Natural" has a fairly sturdy antonym—artificial, or synthetic—and, at least on a scale of relative values, it's not hard to say which of two things is "more natural" than the other: cane sugar or high-fructose corn syrup? Chicken or chicken nuggets? G.M.O.s or heirloom seeds? The most natural foods in the supermarket seldom bother with the word; any food product that feels compelled to tell you it's natural in all likelihood is not.

14   But it is probably unwise to venture beyond the shores of common sense, for it isn't long before you encounter either Scylla or Charybdis. At one extreme end of the spectrum of possible meanings, there's nothing *but* nature. Our species is a result of the same process—natural selection—that created every other species, meaning that we and whatever we do are natural, too. So go ahead and call your nuggets natural: It's like saying they're made with matter, or molecules, which is to say, it's like saying nothing at all.

15   And yet at the opposite end of the spectrum of meaning, where humanity in some sense stands outside nature—as most of us still unthinkingly believe— what is left of the natural that we haven't altered in some way? We're mixed up with all of it now, from the chemical composition of the atmosphere to the genome of every plant or animal in the supermarket to the human body itself, which has long since evolved in response to cultural practices we invented, like agriculture and cooking. Nature, if you believe in human exceptionalism, is over. We probably ought to search elsewhere for our values.

> **WORD POWER**
>
> **antonym** a word opposite in meaning to another

Focus on Reading

1. Look back at the work you did when you previewed, marked up, and annotated this essay. If you have not already done so, put a question mark in the margin beside any term or reference whose meaning you do not know.
2. Circle all the phrases Pollan cites that use *natural* as an adjective (for example, *natural immunity*).
3. **TEST** Pollan's essay. Does it include all four **TEST** elements? If not, why not? What, if anything, should be added?

Focus on Meaning

1. Why have so many recent court battles revolved around the definition of the word *natural*?
2. Why, according to Pollan, is the word *natural* used so often, and in so many different situations?
3. Pollan acknowledges that the word *natural* is "impressively slippery" (4). Does he even manage to define it? Explain.
4. How does the FDA define *natural*? What is Pollan's assessment of this definition?

Focus on Strategy

1. If, as the essay's title states, "'natural' doesn't mean anything anymore," what does Pollan hope to accomplish by writing an essay in which he attempts to define it?
2. What point is Pollan trying to make in this essay? Does he state this main idea directly—for example, in his title or in his closing sentence—or does he imply it?
3. Look up *Scylla and Charybdis* online. To what does it refer? For what purpose does Pollan use this allusion in paragraph 14? What, if anything, does its use here—as well as the reference to "Ahab's whale" in paragraph 11—tell you about how Pollan views his audience?

Focus on Language and Style

1. Look up the word *natural*. What is its **denotative** (dictionary) meaning? What **connotations** does the word have (that is, what associations does it suggest)? Are these connotations generally positive or negative?
2. List some of the phrases Pollan uses to illustrate the use of *natural* as a modifier—for example, *natural childbirth*. What does the word *natural* mean in each of these phrases?
3. Some paragraphs in this essay—for example, paragraphs 1, 10, and 12—are quite long. Should any be divided to improve clarity, or are the paragraphs effective as they are?

Focus on the Patterns

1. For the most part, Pollan develops his definition with examples. List some of his key examples.
2. Besides exemplification, what other patterns does Pollan use to develop his definition?

Focus on Critical Thinking

1. Reread paragraph 4. How do you interpret the last sentence? Do you think Pollan expects readers to take this sentence literally? Why or why not?

2. Do you see Pollan as an objective observer of our society, or do you think he takes a particular political or moral stance? Consider, for example, his use of terms such as "the antivaccination crowd" (3), "throwing Grandpa under the bus" (7), and "The F.D.A's philosopher-bureaucrats" (13).

Focus on Writing

1. Write an essay in which you define the term *artificial*, focusing on its use as a modifier. Does this adjective generally have positive or negative connotations? Use exemplification and comparison and contrast to develop your definition.

2. In paragraph 9, Pollan explains why *traditional* is "a much weaker modifier than natural." Taking this distinction into account, write an essay in which you define *traditional*. Develop your definition with examples of this adjective's use as a modifier in various commonly used expressions.

Working and Learning

The Work You Do, the Person You Are

Toni Morrison

Toni Morrison was born in 1931 to a working-class family in Ohio. After earning her master's degree from Cornell University, Morrison spent her early career teaching English and working as an editor. She published her first novel, *The Bluest Eye*, in 1970. Other acclaimed novels centered on African-American experiences followed, including *Song of Solomon* (1977), which won the National Book Critics Circle Award, and *Beloved* (1987), which won the Pulitzer Prize. Morrison was a professor at Princeton University from 1989 to 2006. Her many awards include the Nobel Prize in Literature in 1993, the National Humanities Medal in 2000, and the Presidential Medal of Freedom in 2012. Her most recent works are the novel *God Help the Child* (2015) and a book of essays *The Origin of Others* (2017). In "The Work You Do, the Person You Are," published in *The New Yorker* in 2017, Morrison recalls a childhood job.

Before you read, think about the first job — or the most challenging job — you ever had.

1   All I had to do for the two dollars was clean Her house for a few hours after school. It was a beautiful house, too, with a plastic-covered sofa and chairs, wall-to-wall blue-and-white carpeting, a white enamel stove, a

washing machine and a dryer—things that were common in Her neighborhood, absent in mine. In the middle of the war, She had butter, sugar, steaks, and seam-up-the-back stockings.

2   I knew how to scrub floors on my knees and how to wash clothes in our zinc tub, but I had never seen a Hoover vacuum cleaner or an iron that wasn't heated by fire.

3   Part of my pride in working for Her was earning money I could squander: on movies, candy, paddleballs, jacks, ice-cream cones. But a larger part of my pride was based on the fact that I gave half my wages to my mother, which meant that some of my earnings were used for real things—an insurance-policy payment or what was owed to the milkman or the iceman. The pleasure of being necessary to my parents was profound. I was not like the children in folktales: burdensome mouths to feed, nuisances to be corrected, problems so severe that they were abandoned to the forest. I had a status that doing routine chores in my house did not provide—and it earned me a slow smile, an approving nod from an adult. Confirmations that I was adultlike, not childlike.

4   In those days, the forties, children were not just loved or liked; they were needed. They could earn money; they could care for children younger than themselves; they could work the farm, take care of the herd, run errands, and much more. I suspect that children aren't needed in that way now. They are loved, doted on, protected, and helped. Fine, and yet . . .

> **WORD POWER**
> **doted on** adored

5   Little by little, I got better at cleaning Her house—good enough to be given more to do, much more. I was ordered to carry bookcases upstairs and, once, to move a piano from one side of a room to the other. I fell carrying the bookcases. And after pushing the piano my arms and legs hurt so badly. I wanted to refuse, or at least to complain, but I was afraid She would fire me, and I would lose the freedom the dollar gave me, as well as the standing I had at home—although both were slowly being eroded. She began to offer me her clothes, for a price. Impressed by these worn things, which looked simply gorgeous to a little girl who had only two dresses to wear to school, I bought a few. Until my mother asked me if I really wanted to work for castoffs. So I learned to say "No, thank you" to a faded sweater offered for a quarter of a week's pay.

> **WORD POWER**
> **eroded** gradually worn away

6   Still, I had trouble summoning the courage to discuss or object to the increasing demands She made. And I knew that if I told my mother how unhappy I was she would tell me to quit. Then one day, alone in the kitchen with my father, I let drop a few whines about the job. I gave him details, examples of what troubled me, yet although he listened intently, I saw no sympathy in his eyes. No "Oh, you poor little thing." Perhaps he understood that what I wanted was a solution to the job, not an escape from it. In any case, he put down his cup of coffee and said, "Listen. You don't live there. You live here. With your people. Go to work. Get your money. And come on home."

7   That was what he said. This was what I heard:

1. Whatever the work is, do it well—not for the boss but for yourself.
2. You make the job; it doesn't make you.
3. Your real life is with us, your family.
4. You are not the work you do; you are the person you are.

8   I have worked for all sorts of people since then, geniuses and morons, quick-witted and dull, bighearted and narrow. I've had many kinds of jobs, but since that conversation with my father I have never considered the level of labor to be the measure of myself, and I have never placed the security of a job above the value of home.

Focus on Reading

1. Look back at the work you did when you previewed, marked up, and annotated this essay. If you have not already done so, put an asterisk beside the advice Morrison's father gave her. If you can think of similar advice your own parents gave you, jot down these words of advice in the margin.
2. In the margin beside paragraph 4, summarize the paragraph in one sentence.
3. **TEST** Morrison's essay. Does she include all four **TEST** elements? If not, why not? What, if anything, should be added?

Focus on Meaning

1. Why was work so important to Morrison? What, besides money, did she get from her work?
2. According to Morrison, why were children in the 1940s "not just loved or liked; they were needed" (4)?
3. What specific tasks did Morrison's job entail? How did her employer's demands change as time went on?
4. What specific details tell you that Morrison's family was poor?

Focus on Strategy

1. Morrison opens her essay by describing her employer's home and possessions. Why?
2. Write a sentence that could serve as the thesis of this essay. Does the essay include such a sentence? If not, why not?
3. Do you think Morrison's attitude toward her day-to-day experiences at her job changed after her conversation with her father? Do you think Morrison should have given this information to readers? Why or why not?

Focus on Language and Style

1. Why does Morrison capitalize *She* and *Her* when referring to her employer? What does this usage suggest about her attitude toward the woman she works for? About their relative social status?
2. Morrison quotes her father, but she does not include her employer's words. Why not? Do you think she should have quoted her employer, perhaps reproducing dialogue between herself and her employer? Why or why not?
3. In paragraph 6, Morrison says that her father told her, "You live here. With your people." What did he mean by "your people"? Consider all possible meanings.

Focus on the Patterns

1. Paragraph 5 opens with "Little by little," which serves as a transition that moves readers along in time. What other words and phrases help to move readers through the narrative? Do readers need more transitions? Why or why not?
2. Although Morrison's essay has a narrative structure, it also relies on exemplification and description. Identify uses of each of these patterns. What other patterns does Morrison use in the essay?

Focus on Critical Thinking

1. In paragraph 4, Morrison says that she doesn't think children today are "needed" now as they were in the past. Do you think she is correct?
2. How old do you think Morrison was when she had the experiences she describes here? What details in the essay give you that information?
3. How would you define the relationship between "the work you do" and "the person you are"?

Focus on Writing

1. Write a narrative essay in which you trace your adjustment to a difficult job. How did you respond to challenges? Who gave you advice that helped you come to terms with the tasks and personalities you encountered? What did you learn about work, and about yourself?
2. Write an essay in which you apply each item on the list in paragraph 7 to a challenge you faced in a job you had. Use each statement on the list as a heading to introduce a different section of your essay. (You can write about four different jobs, or you can apply all the items to one job.) Use a narrative to illustrate each piece of advice.

Taking My Parents to College

Jennine Capó Crucet

Jennine Capó Crucet was born in Miami to Cuban immigrants. She graduated with honors from Cornell University in 2003, the first in her family to obtain a college degree. Crucet's writing often focuses on navigating the differences between Spanish, her native language, and English, as well as on the differences between Cuban and American culture. Her first novel, *Make Your Home among Strangers* (2015), is about a young Cuban American struggling to find her identity when she leaves her home in Miami for an elite university, an issue Crucet also writes about in the following 2015 *New York Times* essay.

Before you read, think about the orientation programs and other resources available to first-year students at your school.

1   It was a simple question, but we couldn't find the answer in any of the paperwork the college had sent. How long was my family supposed to stay for orientation? This was 1999, so Google wasn't really a verb yet, and we were a low-income family (according to my new school) without regular Internet access.

2   I was a first-generation college student as well as the first in our family to be born in America—my parents were born in Cuba—and we didn't yet know that families were supposed to leave pretty much right after they unloaded your stuff from the car.

3   We all made the trip from Miami, my hometown, to what would be my new home at Cornell University. Shortly after arriving on campus, the five of us—my parents, my younger sister, my abuela and me—found ourselves listening to a dean end his welcome speech with the words: "Now, parents, please: Go!"

4   Almost everyone in the audience laughed, but not me, and not my parents. They turned to me and said, "What does he mean, *Go*?" I was just as confused as they were: We thought we *all* needed to be there for freshman orientation—the whole family, for the entirety of it. My dad had booked their hotel through the day after my classes officially began. They'd used all their vacation days from work and had been saving for months to get me to school and go through our orientation.

5   Every afternoon during that week, we had to go back to the only department store we could find, the now-defunct Ames, for some stupid thing we hadn't known was a necessity, something not in our budget: shower shoes, extra-long twin sheets, mesh laundry bags. Before the other families left, we carefully watched them—they knew what they were doing—and we made new shopping lists with our limited vocabulary: *Those things that lift up the bed*, we wrote. *That plastic thing to carry stuff to the bathroom.*

WORD POWER

abuela Spanish word for *grandmother*

WORD POWER

Defunct no longer functional

6   My family followed me around as I visited department offices during course registration. *Only four classes?* they asked, assuming I was mistakenly taking my first semester too easy. They walked with me to buildings I was supposed to be finding on my own. They waited outside those buildings so that we could all leave from there and go to lunch together.

7   The five of us wandered each day through the dining hall's doors. "You guys are still here!" the over-friendly person swiping ID cards said after day three. "They sure are!" I chirped back, learning via the cues of my hallmates that I was supposed to want my family gone. But it was an act: We sat together at meals—amid all the other students, already making friends—my mom placing a napkin and fork at each place, setting the table as we did at home.

8   I don't even remember the moment they drove away. I'm told it's one of those instances you never forget, that second when you realize you're finally on your own. But for me, it's not there—perhaps because, when you're the first in your family to go to college, you never truly feel like they've let you go.

9   They did eventually leave—of course they did—and a week into classes, I received the topics for what would be my first college paper, in an English course on the modern novel. I might as well have been my non-English-speaking grandmother trying to read and understand them: The language felt that foreign. I called my mom at work and in tears told her that I had to come home, that I'd made a terrible mistake.

10   She sighed into the phone and said: "Just read me the first question. We'll go through it a little at a time and figure it out."

11   I read her the topic slowly, pausing after each sentence, waiting for her to say something. The first topic was two paragraphs long. I remember it had the word *intersectionalities* in it. And the word *gendered*. And maybe the phrase *theoretical framework*. I waited for her response and for the ways it would encourage me, for her to tell me I could do this, that I would eventually be the first in my family to graduate from college.

12   "You're right," she said after a moment. "You're screwed."

13   Other parents—parents who have gone to college themselves—might have known at that point to encourage their kid to go to office hours, or to the writing center, or to ask for help. But my mom thought I was as alone as I feared.

14   "I have no idea what any of that means," she said. "I don't even know how it's a *question*."

15   While my college had done an excellent job recruiting me, I had no road map for what I was supposed to do once I made it to campus. I'd already embarrassed myself by doing things like asking my R.A. what time the dorm closed for the night. As far as I knew, there'd been no mandatory meeting geared toward first-generation students like me: Aside from a check-in with my financial aid officer when she explained what work-study was (I didn't know and worried it meant I had to join the army or

something) and where she had me sign for my loans, I was mostly keeping to myself to hide the fact that I was a very special kind of lost. I folded the sheet with the paper topics in half and put it in my desk drawer.

16 "I don't know what you're gonna do," my mom almost laughed. "Maybe—have you looked in the dictionary?"

17 I started crying harder, my hand over the receiver.

18 "You still there?" she eventually asked, clearly hiding her own tears. I murmured *Mmmhmm.*

19 "Look, just stick it out up there until Christmas," she said. "We have no more vacation days this year. We can't take off any more time to go get you."

20 "O.K.," I swallowed. I started breathing in through my nose and out through my mouth, calming myself. "I can do that," I said.

21 My mom laughed for real this time and said, "Mamita, you don't really have a choice."

22 She didn't say this in a mean way. She was just telling me the truth. "This whole thing was your idea, remember?" she said. Then she told me she had to go, that she needed to get back to work.

23 So I got back to work, too, and *Get back to work* became a sort of mantra for me. I tackled the paper with the same focus that had landed me, to everyone's surprise—even my own—at Cornell in the first place. I did O.K. on it, earning a "B-/C" (I never found out how a grade could have a slash in it, but now that I'm an English professor I understand what he was trying to say). The professor had covered the typed pages with comments and questions, and it was in his endnote that he listed the various campus resources available to me.

24 My mom didn't ask outright what grade I earned—she eventually stopped asking about assignments altogether—and I learned from my peers that grades were something that I didn't have to share with my parents the way I had in high school.

25 My grades were the first of many elements of my new life for which they had no context and which they wouldn't understand. With each semester, what I was doing became, for them, as indecipherable as that paper topic; they didn't even know what questions to ask. And that, for me, is the quintessential quality of the first-generation college student's experience. It's not even knowing what you don't know.

> **WORD POWER**
>
> **indecipherable** impossible to understand
>
> **quintessential** the most typical example

Focus on Reading

1. Look back at the work you did when you previewed, marked up, and annotated this essay. If you have not already done so, place a question mark in the margin beside any term or expression that is unfamiliar to you.

2. Reread paragraph 15. In the margin, jot down some resources for first-year students at your school, and think about how you learned about them.

3. **TEST** Crucet's essay. Does she include all four **TEST** elements? If not, why not? What, if anything, should be added?

Focus on Meaning

1. How are Crucet and her parents different from her fellow students and their parents? What things do other students know that Crucet and her family do not know?
2. What specific mistakes do Crucet and her family make?

Focus on Strategy

1. Reread the passages of dialogue (paragraphs 16–22 and elsewhere) in this essay. Why do you think Crucet includes this dialogue? What does it contribute to the essay?
2. Why does Crucet include information about herself and her family in paragraph 2? Is this information necessary? Explain.
3. Do you think Crucet should have provided more information about her parents' economic status? About their jobs? About her neighborhood? Why or why not?

Focus on the Pattern

1. What features in this essay tell you it is a narrative?
2. Make a brief outline that lists the main events that make up this narrative. Then, write a short summary of those events. Make sure you include transitional words and phrases to link events in time.
3. Does Crucet need additional transitions to connect events? If so, where?

Focus on Critical Thinking

1. Do you think the specific problems Crucet and her family face are also common in families with parents who grew up in the United States? Why or why not?
2. In paragraph 15, Crucet discusses the apparent absence of resources for new students on her campus. Later, at the end of paragraph 23, she mentions briefly how she learned that such resources did in fact exist. Why do you think she learned about these resources so late? Whom do you think Crucet blames for this apparent communication failure? Who do you think was at fault?
3. Near the end of the essay, Crucet mentions in passing that she is now an English professor. Should she have mentioned this information earlier? Does this detail change the essay's meaning or impact for you? If so, how?

Focus on Language and Style

1. In paragraph 11, Crucet mentions some words and expressions that she does not understand. Define each of these terms. Do you think her not knowing what they mean can be explained by the fact that she is a first-generation college student, or is there some other reason?
2. What is a *mantra* (23)? What does the word mean in the context of the paragraph in which it appears?

Focus on Writing

1. In her conclusion, Crucet identifies the "quintessential quality of the first-generation college student's experience." According to her, "It's not even knowing what you don't know." Write an essay in which you discuss the things you didn't know when you began college, and how you learned to navigate academic life.

2. Write an essay focusing on how you decided which college to attend (or how you decided whether to attend college). Did you consult your parents, teachers, or friends? What factors—for example, geography, finances, academic programs, or social life—influenced your decision?

How to Tell a Mother Her Child Is Dead

Naomi Rosenberg

Naomi Rosenberg is a physician in the emergency department at Temple University Hospital in North Philadelphia and an assistant professor of emergency medicine. After she finished her medical residency at the hospital, she took a writing workshop and began writing about her experiences as a doctor. In "How to Tell a Mother Her Child Is Dead," published in *The New York Times* in 2016, Rosenberg explains how to break the worst possible news to patients' families.

Before you read, think about the doctors you have known and how they have broken bad news to you or your family members.

1   First you get your coat. I don't care if you don't remember where you left it, you find it. If there was a lot of blood you ask someone to go quickly to the basement to get you a new set of scrubs. You put on your coat and you go into the bathroom. You look in the mirror and you say it. You use the mother's name and you use her child's name. You may not adjust this part in any way.

2   I will show you: If it were my mother you would say, "Mrs. Rosenberg. I have terrible, terrible news. Naomi died today." You say it out loud until you can say it clearly and loudly. How loudly? Loudly enough. If it takes you fewer than five tries you are rushing it and you will not do it right. You take your time.

3   After the bathroom you do nothing before you go to her. You don't make a phone call, you do not talk to the medical student, you do not put in an order. You never make her wait. She is his mother.

4   When you get inside the room you will know who the mother is. Yes, I'm very sure. Shake her hand and tell her who you are. If there is time you

shake everyone's hand. Yes, you will know if there is time. You never stand. If there are no seats left, the couches have arms on them.

5 You will have to make a decision about whether you will ask what she already knows. If you were the one to call her and tell her that her son had been shot then you have already done part of it, but you have not done it yet. You are about to do it now. You never make her wait. She is his mother. Now you explode the world. Yes, you have to. You say something like: "Mrs. Booker. I have terrible, terrible news. Ernest died today."

6 Then you wait.

7 You will not stand up. You may leave yourself in the heaviness of your breath or the racing of your pulse or the sight of your shoelaces on your shoe, but you will not stand up. You are here for her. She is his mother.

8 If the mother has another son with her and he has punched the wall or broken the chair, do not be worried. The one that punched the wall or broke the chair will be better than the one who looks down and refuses to cry. The one who punched the wall or broke the chair will be much easier than the sister who looks up and closes her eyes as they fill.

9 Security is already outside the room and when they hear the first loud noise they will know to come in. No, you will not have to tell them. They know about the family room in the emergency department in summer in North Philadelphia. It is all right. They will be kind. If the chair cannot be sat in again that is all right. We have money for new chairs every summer. If he does not break your chair you stay in your chair. If he does you find a new place to sit. You are here for the mother and you have more to do.

10 If she asks you, you will tell her what you know. You do not lie. But do not say he was murdered or he was killed. Yes, I know that he was, but that is not what you say. You say that he died; that is the part that you saw and that you know. When she asks if he felt any pain, you must be very careful. If he did not, you assure her quickly. If he did, you do not lie. But his pain is over now. Do not ever say he was lucky that he did not feel pain. He was not lucky. She is not lucky. Don't make that face. The depth of the stupidity of the things you will say sometimes is unimaginable.

11 Before you leave you break her heart one more time. "No, I'm so sorry, but you cannot see him. There are strict rules when a person dies this way and the police have to take him first. We cannot let you in. I'm so sorry." You do not ever say "the body." It is not a body. It is her son. You want to tell her that you know that he was hers. But she knows that and she does not need for you to tell her. Instead you tell her you will give her time and come back in case she has questions. More questions, or questions for the first time. If she has no questions you do not give her the answers to the questions she has not asked.

12 When you leave the room, do not yell at the medical student who has a question. When you get home, do not yell at your husband. If he left his socks on the floor again today, it is all right.

Focus on Reading

1. Look back at the work you did when you previewed, marked up, and annotated this essay. If you have not already done so, write a brief comment at the end of the essay in which you summarize your reactions to it.
2. In the margins of the essay, number the key steps in the process.
3. **TEST** Rosenberg's essay. Does she include all four **TEST** elements? If not, why not? What, if anything, should be added?

Focus on Meaning

1. What caused the death of the young man Rosenberg is writing about? How do you know? Is he a specific person, or is he a typical example of young men who die as he did?
2. Rosenberg says that security staff "know about the emergency department in summer in North Philadelphia" (9). What do they know? What does this comment tell you about Rosenberg?

Focus on Strategy

1. As the headnote explains, Rosenberg is an emergency room doctor, but she does not explicitly identify her profession in the essay. Why not? Should she have included this information in the essay itself? If so, where?
2. Evaluate the essay's introduction and conclusion. Are they consistent in content and tone with the rest of the essay? Do they have to be?
3. This essay does not have a stated thesis. Why not? In one sentence, summarize Rosenberg's main idea.

Focus on Language and Style

1. This essay's vocabulary and syntax are quite simple. Is this style appropriate for the subject matter, or would more complex language and sentence structure be more effective? Explain.
2. Rosenberg uses the pronoun *you* throughout her essay. Is she addressing someone specific? Readers? Another audience? Explain.
3. How would you characterize the **tone** of this essay? (See 5a for information on tone.)
4. In paragraph 10, Rosenberg says, "You do not lie. But do not say he was murdered or he was killed." Instead, she recommends, "You say that he died . . ." Why does she give this advice? What distinction is she making?

Focus on the Patterns

1. What features tell you that this essay is presented as instructions rather than as an explanation of a process?

2. Since Rosenberg does not expect her readers to perform the steps she enumerates, why did she choose to present her essay as a set of instructions?
3. In the essay's first paragraph, Rosenberg cautions readers, "You may not adjust this part in any way." Where else does she include the kind of cautions and reminders that are usually found in instructions?

Focus on Critical Thinking

1. Rosenberg repeats the sentence "She is his mother" at the end of both paragraph 3 and paragraph 7. Why? Should she have used it a third—or even a fourth—time? If so, where?
2. In addition to explaining what to do, Rosenberg also tells what *not* to do. Give some examples. Are all these cautions necessary, or are some (or even most) common sense? Explain.
3. Who do you think might benefit most from reading this essay? Why?

Focus on Writing

1. Write a process explanation that summarizes the events Rosenberg describes. Using past tense, and using the point of view of a sibling of a particular person who died under the circumstances Rosenberg alludes to, explain what happened in the emergency room.
2. Write a set of instructions directed at friends of a young person who died. In your essay, present guidelines for how to behave when visiting family members and at the funeral or memorial service. Be sure to include advice about what *not* to say or do.

Identity and Self-Image

Growing Up a Desi Girl: What It Means to Be between Two Worlds

Nikita

Nikita is a freelance writer with interests in fashion and digital culture. Raised in California by Indian-American parents, Nikita balanced her dual identities and others' perceptions of her. This experience inspired her essay "Growing Up a Desi Girl," which was written while she was a student at New York University and published by *Teen Vogue* in 2015.

Before you read, think about how you define your cultural and ethnic identity.

1   When I'm presented with a "Where are you from?" I usually run through this multiple-choice quiz in my head:
Should I . . .

a. Say that I'm American and be prodded to admit where I'm *really* from, as though being born on native soil isn't enough of a token of my American-ness.

b. Say that I'm Indian and sit through the whole FAQ. ("Wait, red dot Indian or Native American? Do you eat curry every night? Do your parents speak English? Will your marriage be arranged?")

c. Say "around here" and fake that I have to go to the bathroom.

2   I roll the dice with options A–C, depending on how much energy I have that day. But, the truth is? I'm not sure myself some days.

3   Being a woman of color, people often press you even harder on that "Where are you from?" question. Questions that are often considered harmless can sometimes result in an awkward, stumbling identity crisis. My standard reply of, "California, around the SF… Bay Area," never seems to placate people, because my tan skin, big dark eyes, and thick eyebrows betray me. I don't look like I'm *really* American to a lot of people (read: sun-kissed, California-beach-blonde beauty), and so the label never *quite* fits. Add in the fact that my name is "Nikita" and I've truly thrown the audience a plot twist. Is she from here? Is she mixed-race? Is she an alien? Stay tuned to find out!

4   I've lived in four big cities in under 18 years: Chicago, New Delhi, San Francisco, and New York. New York is now home, and technically because my family is in California, so is San Francisco. It's odd to juggle specific regional identities that pertain to the U.S. only while negotiating the complications of my ethnic and cultural identities as well. Saying I'm from California means something different to people than "American," and saying I'm Indian carries other implications. Plus, the "Indian" identity is an umbrella term for a series of different identities all woven together by a similar overarching cultural thread and a political boundary. India is a vast country with dozens of languages, cuisines, and more—no two Indian experiences can ever neatly intersect.

5   Perhaps if I were entirely born and raised in America, I'd feel as though I wasn't *too* Indian to fit under "American" neatly. And, maybe if I didn't spend the better part of my 21 years in America, I'd feel better just saying I am Indian. I love being Indian, but sometimes I don't feel Indian enough, really. I am Indian. I am American. I am Indian-American. Neither there, nor there—but somewhere in between.

6   I lived in India for the better part of the first 5 years of my life, and once I moved back to the U.S., I immediately felt alien amongst my classmates. With my broken English, my funny accent, and the fact that I had no idea who Pikachu was, I may as well have been from another planet. I was a quick study, though: I laboriously repaired my accent, always making sure

---

WORD POWER

placate soothe; make less angry

WORD POWER

pertain relate to
overarching dominating all else

to pronounce my Vs and Ws correctly, and never allowing my Rs to linger on my tongue for too long; I watched all the "Blue's Clues" I could get my hands on; I asked my parents to take me to movies, the works. However, despite all my efforts otherwise, I felt culturally inept.

> **WORD POWER**
> **inept** incompetent

7 So I stepped up my efforts. I began shirking my Indian-ness and wholly adopting American culture in an attempt to fit in. I spent the better part of my teenage years acting as though my own culture was backwards, primitive, and something worth being ashamed of. I turned up my nose at Indian food, maligned religion, and was just kind of a brat. "I'm like, the whitest Indian girl like, ever," and all that jazz. I tried so desperately to lose all the things that made me different so that I could fall into a dominant narrative that wasn't mine and didn't *need* to be mine—despite how much the world sometimes made (and still makes) me feel otherwise.

> **WORD POWER**
> **shirking** neglecting a duty
> **maligned** made harmful statements about

8 I had made an error in naively assuming that assimilating wholeheartedly would make my life easier, but the truth is: whiteness didn't fit. And somehow, full on Indian-ness didn't either, given that I was (mostly) raised and schooled in America. I didn't feel as though I could relate to either fairly. In retrospect? As much as I desperately wanted one label or the other to fit in an absolutist fashion, they never needed to: it's okay to be who I am, the way I am. I think I fall somewhere in between Indian and American; I am the definition of a hyphenated, hybrid identity.

9 The truth is, it's okay to feel like you're neither here nor there—we are all shaped by the experiences we've lived through. There is no right way to be Indian, and there is no right way to be American. We're formed by our individual experiences and beliefs, and it's daunting to collapse millions of experiences into one label for a curious stranger (or even yourself!). It is normal to feel confused by your own identity from time to time, to feel like an enigma. Trust me though—as much as the world keeps making you feel like an absolute weirdo, you are not. Learning and knowing that I have a place in this world has been healing; finding people who have shared similar struggles, experiences, and stories has been instrumental. Know that you are not entirely alone, and as you go through life you will encounter your people.

> **WORD POWER**
> **daunting** intimidating
> **enigma** something mysterious or puzzling

10 I still don't know how to *really* answer that dreaded question, though. I'll keep rolling the dice and get back to you.

Focus on Reading

1. Look back at the work you did when you previewed, marked up, and annotated this essay. If you have not already done so, place check marks in the margins beside the various terms Nikita uses to identify herself.
2. Write a two-sentence summary of paragraph 9. What distinctive words or terms did you place in quotation marks?
3. **TEST** Nikita's essay. Does she include all four **TEST** elements? If not, why not? What, if anything, should be added?

Focus on Meaning

1. What is a Desi girl? Does Nikita ever define this term? If so, where? If not, should she have?
2. Between what "two worlds" does Nikita say she is caught? Why does she have trouble making various possible labels fit?
3. Why did Nikita try so hard to assimilate into American culture? How successful was she?

Focus on Strategy

1. In what sense is Nikita caught between more than two worlds? Explain.
2. Toward the end of her essay, Nikita says, "The truth is, it's okay to feel like you're neither here nor there . . ." (9). Is this statement her essay's thesis? Explain.
3. This essay was originally published in *Teen Vogue*. What features might make it appeal to *Teen Vogue* readers—even if they do not feel caught "between two worlds"?

Focus on Language and Style

1. Nikita uses the word *alien* in paragraph 3 and again in paragraph 6. What different meanings does the word *alien* have in these two contexts? Generally speaking, what connotations does this word have?
2. Nikita uses very informal language, including slang and contractions. Give some examples. Does this informal style weaken her essay? Why or why not?

Focus on the Patterns

1. Nikita refers to herself as "the definition of a hyphenated, hybrid identity" (8). What does she mean? In one sentence, define this identity.
2. Review the bulleted list in at the beginning of 8d. Which of the listed strategies does Nikita use to develop her definition?

Focus on Critical Thinking

1. Nikita says that when she is asked, "Where are you from?," she is "not sure [herself] some days" (2). Do you think she is being honest about her inability to define her ethnic and cultural identity? Why or why not?
2. How do you respond when people ask, "Where are you from?" Do you find it difficult to pin down your own ethnic origin or explain it to others?

Focus on Writing

1. Write an essay in which you define your own ethnic, religious, racial, and cultural identity, explaining your connections to all the "worlds" you identify with.
2. What does it mean to be a "hyphenated American"? Write an essay defining this term and explaining why you believe it is (or is not) a useful and appropriate designation.

When a Southern Town Broke a Heart

Jacqueline Woodson

Jacqueline Woodson grew up in South Carolina and Brooklyn, New York, in the 1960s and '70s. She is known for her children's literature for a range of ages. Woodson's writing includes picture books such as *Each Kindness* (2012), middle grade titles such as Newbery Honor-winning *After Tupac and D Foster* (2008), and young adult books such as *Brown Girl Dreaming* (2014), winner of the Coretta Scott King Award and the National Book Award. Her most recent book is the novel *Another Brooklyn* (2016). Woodson is the 2018–2019 National Ambassador for Young People's literature. In her 2016 *New York Times* article "When a Southern Town Broke a Heart," Woodson describes a childhood memory and a shifting perception of home.

Before you read, think about a place where you felt safe when you were a child.

1   Greenville, S.C., in the 1970s is a rolling green dream in my memory now. Always in that memory are the smell of pine and the red dirt wafting up around our summer shoes — new blue Keds with thick white soles, red by the end of our first day "home." Because for me, South Carolina had always been home. Even years after my family joined the Great Migration and my mother moved us from Greenville to Brooklyn, each summer we returned to the Southern town of my mother's childhood.

2   There, the friendly neighbors who knew us before we "were even a thought" and remembered our mama "when she was a little girl in pigtails" opened their arms to us every summer, welcoming us home. Vegetable gardens filled with collards, berries, pole beans and cucumbers grew beside the small houses. Raised flower beds brightened front yards. And, always, the smell of honeysuckle beckoned my siblings and me to its vine where we sipped sweet nectar from the flowers until, as always, my grandmother called from the kitchen window, "Let that honeysuckle grow like y'all trying to grow," and we ran off to whatever next thing the summer brought us. We were safe. We were home.

> **WORD POWER**
>
> **morphed** turned into

3   But the summer I was 9 years old, the town I had always loved morphed into a beautifully heartbreaking and complicated place. That summer, like other summers and many Brooklyn children, we left the city only days after school ended.

4   My mother was a single mom whose days were spent as a customer service rep at Con Edison in downtown Brooklyn. When school ended with a half-day party of sugary Kool-Aid, cookies and report cards, my sister, brothers and I took the No. 52 Gates Avenue bus to downtown Brooklyn, waiting outside of J. W. Mays until my mother, nearly six feet tall, appeared in the crowd of people moving along Fulton Street.

5   Mays was a discount chain that eventually, like other discount chains—Orbach's, Korvettes, Alexander's—went out of business. But back then, it was an affordable one-stop shopping spot where my mother, in anticipation of our trip home and wanting to make sure her four children represented what it meant to leave the oppressive Jim Crow South for the economic and educational opportunity of New York, filled a cart with blue Keds, cotton dresses, T-shirts and underwear. We would return home well-dressed and well-spoken, products of the North's unbroken promise.

6   In other years, we had traveled back to Greenville by bus, but that year, for the first time, we took a train home, our uncle accompanying my sister, brothers and me. For the four of us, an overnight train brought a freedom we'd never dreamed—our overly permissive uncle letting us run from train car to train car, eat the small bags of candy he'd bought us before we even pulled the waxed paper-wrapped sandwiches and fruit my mother had packed from our new school bags.

7   The train left New York in the late afternoon, arriving in Greenville before daybreak. As we disembarked, my sleepy-eyed siblings and I exaggerated deep inhalations of "country air."

> **WORD POWER**
>
> **tendrils** long, thin, curling strands (usually of hair)

8   The fleeting moments of childhood are etched deep in my memory—the salty indentations of baby teeth newly gone, the tug of hairbrushes through knotted hair, the heat and smell of the straightening comb, my mother's broad shoulders and easy smile—and a summer in South Carolina, when the deep green beauty revealed my place and time in history and laid claim to that moment all children know, when the tendrils of adulthood move toward us, showing themselves long before we are ready to see.

9   For so many summers, we'd been warned to stay away from the small patch of poison ivy that grew around the base of the one tree in my grandparents' backyard. But until that year, the consequence had been as theoretical as the segregation surrounding us. We saw the white people when we went downtown or as we drove through their neighborhoods on our way to visit relatives.

10   We knew the ones our family members worked for as maids and handymen and how they sometimes sent home bags of not so gently-used clothing that were thankfully accepted then redonated. A "No thank you" would have been as unacceptable as leaving off a "Ma'am" or "Sir" or heading downtown to march against Jim Crow. The poison ivy crept up the base of the tree on the roadside but grew low to the ground on the house side.

"Don't go on the other side of that tree," our grandmother warned us. "And don't touch those leaves."

11   I would love to write that I remember the tree—that it was an old, solid oak or a stunning pine tree. Or one of the beautiful willows that seemed to weep all over South Carolina. I would love to bring the metaphor sorrowfully back somehow to Billie Holiday's "Strange Fruit" or Buffy Sainte-Marie's "Tall Trees in Georgia."

12   But what I remember of that summer is not the actual tree but the sap running from it, the thick shine of it moving along a gnarled and blackened trunk. And at the foot of that trunk, the poison ivy's oily leaves circling the base then climbing up into the tree on the road side. At 5, 6 and 7, I spent long periods of the day bent over the ivy, fascinated by the promise of its danger—a danger I believed I was protected from—and would continue to be.

13   But that summer, the poison ivy found its way to my older brother's legs, then along his hands and arms. As he suffered what we discovered was an allergic reaction to the ivy, the clammy heat rose in South Carolina and a fiery rash settled itself over my brother's neck and throat until, finally, my grandmother took him to the one white doctor who would treat black patients in our segregated town.

14   Dr. M. had a jar in the reception room filled with rock candy that he gave out to both his patients and their sugar-loving siblings. He's a kind man, my grandmother said. Other doctors wouldn't even look at colored people, let alone treat them. It was the early '70s. In our Brooklyn school we were being taught that segregation was a thing of the past, that what King and Parks, Tubman and Turner, Phillis Wheatley and Crispus Attucks had struggled for was all behind us. But in Greenville, we lived in Nicholtown, a segregated neighborhood inside of a segregated town. I realized that either Greenville was cheating or Brooklyn was lying.

15   Coming home from Dr. M.'s my grandmother trailed the four of us to the back of the bus where other blacks had settled themselves. I sat, as I always did, in a window seat leaning into my grandmother—for safety? For assuredness? For comfort? For love. I watched downtown Greenville become Nicholtown again. We had left "home" the first time with my mother for the dream of New York. At 9, I felt as though home was turning its back on me now without so much as a wave goodbye.

Focus on Reading

1. Look back at the work you did when you previewed, marked up, and annotated this essay. If you have not already done so, circle *Great Migration* in paragraph 1. In the margin, briefly identify this term.
2. In the margin beside paragraph 11, write a question about the paragraph's content that you would like Woodson to answer.
3. **TEST** Woodson's essay. Does it include all four **TEST** elements? If not, why not? What, if anything, should be added?

Focus on Meaning

1. What is the meaning of the essay's title? How did Greenville break Woodson's heart?
2. What does Woodson mean by "the North's unbroken promise" (5)? In what respects, according to Woodson, were she and her family products of this promise?
3. What is the Great Migration (1)? What is Jim Crow (10)? Why are these references important for this essay?
4. In paragraph 14, Woodson says, "I realized that either Greenville was cheating or Brooklyn was lying." What does she mean? Which of these two alternatives does her essay support?

Focus on Strategy

1. What is this essay's main idea—the central point or dominant impression that Woodson wants to make about her subject?
2. In paragraph 1, Woodson says that for her, "South Carolina had always been home"; in her concluding paragraph, she says that she "felt as though home was turning its back on me now. . ." (15). What, specifically, changed her mind?

Focus on Language and Style

1. In addition to describing what things look like, Woodson gives a great deal of information on the way things smelled. Give some examples. How do these memories of odors help to paint a picture of Greenville?
2. In paragraphs 10 through 14, Woodson discusses the poison ivy the children were warned against. In what sense is this poison ivy a symbol as well as an actual plant? Beyond its literal significance, what might the poison ivy stand for?
3. Descriptive essays frequently use figures of speech, such as **metaphors** and **similes** to enhance their descriptions (see 21c). Identify some of the figures of speech Woodson uses in this essay. How do they strengthen the essay?

Focus on the Patterns

1. Is this essay primarily a subjective or an objective description? How do you know?
2. Woodson develops a comparison between Brooklyn and Greenville. How are the two places different?
3. Where does Woodson use narration? How do the narrative passages support the impression of Greenville she wants to convey?

Focus on Critical Thinking

1. In paragraph 12, Woodson says that when she looked at the poison ivy, she was "fascinated by the promise of its danger." What exactly do you think "fascinated" her? What kind of danger do you think she was anticipating?
2. In what sense do you see this essay as a description of a time (the early 1970s) as well as a place?

Focus on Writing

1. Find the lyrics to the two songs Woodson mentions in paragraph 11. Then, write a descriptive essay in which you analyze the lyrics of one of these songs.
2. In paragraph 2, Woodson says that when she was a child in Greenville, she and her three siblings "were safe. We were home." In what childhood location did you feel "safe" and "at home"? Why? Write an essay describing that place and the sense of security it gave you.

That Oxymoron, the Asian Comic Superhero
Umapagan Ampikaipakan

Umapagan Ampikaipakan is a Malaysian journalist, cultural critic, and radio producer. He hosted the TV documentary *Every Street Tells a Story*, which explored his native city of Kuala Lumpur, and is the long-time host of the literary radio show *Bookmark*. In his 2015 *New York Times* essay "That Oxymoron, the Asian Comic Superhero," Ampikaipakan argues that the attempt to diversify comics is misguided.

Before you read, think about the comic superhero with whom you most identify and why.

1   THE final page of the first issue of the new Ms. Marvel comic is pitch perfect. A strange mutagenic mist pervades the streets of Jersey City, activating a secret alien gene that triggers a transformation within our teenage protagonist. She punches her way out of a chrysalis to find that she has mutated into another body: The Pakistani-American Muslim Kamala Khan, with her newly minted superpowers, has been transmogrified into a tall, leggy blonde.

2   It is a fantastic visual gag. And it is the perfect metaphor for the teenage immigrant who is struggling both in her skin and to find her place in America.

3   But it doesn't take long—three issues or so—for Kamala to realize that her brown Muslim self is as potent as can be. All she needed to become super, besides a costume and a mask, was a strong sense of individualism,

righteousness, a can-do spirit and a purpose. The superhero comic is an inherently egalitarian genre, even though its lead characters are exceptional: After a bout with a radioactive spider or some Terrigen Mist, it could be you or it could be me.

4   Which is why the recent push by Marvel and DC for greater diversity in comics doesn't make much sense. Or maybe it does in the United States, where real-life anxieties about race, gender and identity politics are often played out in popular culture. Captain America is black. Thor is a woman. Iceman is gay.

5   But for some of us non-Americans, the genre doesn't need to apologize for itself, no matter how quintessentially American it is. The superhero comic is the American dream illustrated, and by definition the American dream must be accessible to all. However monochromatic its characters, the superhero comic's message has always seemed universal.

6   You could say I was primed to buy into all this. I'm Hindu and grew up on the adventures of gods with formidable features: the elephant-like Ganesh; the monkey-faced Hanuman; the blue-skinned, butter-eating Krishna. But they always remained out of reach: I could never be Ganesh or Krishna; they were deities. Yet I could be Spider-Man, because I already was Peter Parker.

7   In fact, I became a superhero in Damansara Heights, a middle-class neighborhood of Kuala Lumpur, in the waning months of 1989, when, at age 8, I crawled out a bloodied mess from underneath the mangled remains of my jet-black BMX Dyno D-Tour. I had crashed on my way to the corner store to pick up my monthly stash of comic books. The brakes on my brand-new bicycle had failed somehow—sabotage, I was sure. In my comic-addled mind, it was the perfect origin story.

8   Back then, there was just one news agent in my neighborhood that stocked Spider-Man comics. The selection was limited, wedged between an abundance of Archies and displayed in no particular order. Most issues came a month or two late. Would our hero escape the clutches of Doctor Octopus? I might never know. But I might wind up with the stunning finale to some saga I'd never read.

9   I didn't care. Plot and continuity were of little concern. My problem was that there were three other comic-book freaks in the neighborhood and just that one news agent. Each of us would try to make under-the-counter deals with him. We would secrete away issues behind copies of National Geographic and Esquire, hiding them until we had collected enough pocket money to buy them. And we would mess with one another's brakes.

10   The Bloody Bicycle Incident of 1989 led to a truce, the Great Summit on the Hill, then to the realization that we'd be better off pooling resources, and finally to the formation of the Bicycle Brotherhood—Kuala Lumpur's first and only superhero team. We didn't have special names that I can recall, but we had electric blue bedsheets we'd knot around our necks, and costumed in those second skins, we'd ride around dreaming up worlds, righting wrongs, saving lives.

> **WORD POWER**
> **monochromatic** containing only one color

11 We were Hindu, Muslim, Buddhist and Christian. We were brown and yellow. But we didn't mind that our role models were all white. We were Spider-Man. We were Batman. We were Superman. We were Captain America. We were always, happily, obliviously, super. I suppose the current push to draw diversity into comics and add variety to the canon is meant to reinforce the notion that anyone can be a superhero. But that only risks undercutting the genre's universal appeal.

12 It can't be an accident that so many efforts to create an Asian superhero have failed. The first attempt, back in 1944, was called the Green Turtle. He fought for China, America's ally, against the invading Japanese Army, and reportedly was drawn to look Chinese. There was no way to know, though, because he always had his back to the reader, plus he wore a mask. The Green Turtle disappeared after five issues.

13 Then came the Great Ten, Lady Shiva, Tsunami and Collective Man, among others. Mostly sidekicks or secondary characters, they failed to generate much of a following, partly because though Asian in name and looks—yellow skin, slanted eyes—they were not in spirit or essence.

14 As recently as 2004, "Spider-Man: India" transposed Peter Parker's story to Pavitr Prabhakar, a poor Indian boy in Mumbai. Aunt May became Aunt Maya. Mary Jane, Meera Jain. It was a near-literal translation of American tropes into an Indian setting, and made no use of India's rich mythological traditions or particular class and caste struggles.

15 The same goes for the heroes of major Japanese mangas, like Astro Boy and Devilman. Though their origin stories tend to be mystical or supernatural—as opposed to familial (Batman, the orphan myth), societal (Superman, the immigration myth) or political (The Incredible Hulk, the nuclear disaster myth)—in most other respects these characters are just rip-offs of the American comic book canon.

16 The current Ms. Marvel is the most successful rendition of an Asian superhero. But Kamala is Asian-American, and her struggles to balance her duties as both a superhero and a good Muslim girl are merely another retelling of the classic American immigrant experience.

17 Try to adapt the superhero comic's conventions to an Asian context and the genre collapses under the weight of traditional Asian values: humility, self-effacement, respect for elders and communal harmony. American comic book heroes also act in the service of the collective good, but they do so, unabashedly, out of a heightened sense of self. How can an Asian superhero take down the bad guy without embarrassing both the bad guy's family and his own? How do you save the world and save face at the same time? The Asian comic superhero is a contradiction in terms.

18 We geeks out here in the Asian hinterlands have always readily bought into American ideals because the American comic book makes us believe we can be special, too. The Asian superhero, steeped in our cultural baggage, would only undermine the fantasy.

Focus on Reading

1. Look back at the work you did when you previewed, marked up, and annotated this essay. Did you highlight and number Ampikaipakan's key points? If not, do so now.
2. Write *refutation* in the margin next to the paragraph (or paragraphs) in which Ampikaipakan refutes opposing arguments.
3. TEST Ampikaipakan's essay. Does he include all four TEST elements? If not, why not? What, if anything should be added?

Focus on Meaning

1. Why, according to Ampikaipakan, does the push for greater diversity in comics make sense in the United States?
2. In paragraph 6, Ampikaipakan says, "I already was Peter Parker." What does he mean? What does this comment tell you about him?
3. Why is the Asian comic superhero "a contradiction in terms" (20)? According to Ampikaipakan, why is it difficult to adapt the superhero's comic conventions to the norms of Asian society?

Focus on Strategy

1. Where does Ampikaipakan state his thesis? What information does he provide before stating it? How does this information set the stage for his thesis?
2. In his essay, Ampikaipakan, a resident of Malaysia, discusses Asian superheroes. What relevance does his essay have for Americans? For Asians? For Asian Americans?
3. What point does Ampikaipakan emphasize in his conclusion? Why? How else could he have ended his essay?

Focus on Language and Style

1. Evaluate the essay's title. What does *oxymoron* mean? What other title could Ampikaipakan have used?
2. What does the term *superhero* mean to you? How is your definition similar to or different from Ampikaipakan's?
3. In paragraph 5, Ampikaipakan says the characters in superhero comics are "monochromatic." What does he mean? Is Ampikaipakan correct in his assessment of these characters? Explain.

Focus on the Patterns

1. In paragraphs 7–12, Ampikaipakan recounts an incident that occurred when he was eight years old. What does this long narrative add to his argument?

2. Ampikaipakan relies on evidence from his own experience to support his argument. Should he have included statistics or expert opinion? Why or why not?
3. Does Ampikaipakan structure his argument inductively or deductively? What are the advantages and disadvantages of his organization?
4. What arguments against his position does Ampikaipakan discuss? How effectively does he refute these arguments?

Focus on Critical Thinking

1. In paragraph 5, Ampikaipakan says, "The superhero comic is the American dream illustrated." What does he mean? Do you agree?
2. A **paradox** is a statement that seems senseless or self-contradictory. In paragraph 13, Ampikaipakan says that the effort to make comics racially and ethnically diverse could undercut "the genre's universal appeal." Is this statement a paradox? Explain.
3. Do you think Ampikaipakan understates the importance of having greater ethnic diversity in comics? Why or why not?

Focus on Writing

1. In an article in *Wired*, Greg Pak, a writer for *Action Comics* and creator of a title about an Asian American gunfighter, says, "Diversity isn't just a catchphrase—it's actually just the way we all live our lives. Letting the stories and creative teams reflect that just makes sense as a way to nurture good, honest storytelling for everybody." Do you agree with him, or do you agree with Ampikaipakan? Write an essay supporting your position. Make sure you refute the opposing argument.
2. Suppose you were asked to create a superhero comic strip that would appear each week in your school newspaper. The editor of the newspaper has made it clear that the comic strip should reflect the school's diverse student body. Write an email to the editor of the paper in which you discuss the nature of your comic strip and the characters who will appear in it. Be sure to address the issue of diversity and how you intend to deal with this issue. If possible, include a reference to Ampikaipakan's essay. Make sure you document all words and ideas that are not your own (see Chapter 14).

Acknowledgments

Julia Alvarez, "What Is a Quinceañera?" From *Once Upon a Quinceañera: Coming of Age in the USA*. Copyright © 2007 by Julia Alvarez. Published by Plume, an imprint of Penguin Random House, and in hardcover by Viking. By permission of Susan Bergholz Literary Services, New York, NY, and Lamy, NM. All rights reserved.

Umapagan Ampikaipakan, "That Oxymoron, the Asian Comic Superhero," *The New York Times*, December 25, 2015. Copyright © 2015 by The New York Times. All rights reserved. Used by permission and protected by the Copyright Laws of the United States. The printing, copying, redistribution, or retransmission of this Content without express written permission is prohibited.

Lynda Barry, "The Sanctuary of School" by Lynda Barry, from *The New York Times*, January 5, 1992. Copyright © 1992 by Lynda Barry. All Rights Reserved. Used with permission.

Rachel Carson, "A Fable for Tomorrow" from *Silent spring*. Copyright © 1962 by Rachel L. Carson, renewed 1990 by Roger Christie. Reprinted by permission of Houghton Mifflin Harcourt Publishing Company and Frances Collin, Trustee. All rights reserved. Unauthorized redistribution of this text is expressly forbidden.

Steven Conn, "The Twin Revolutions of Lincoln and Darwin" from the *Philadelphia Inquirer*, February 12, 2009. Reprinted by permission of the author.

Jennine Capo Crucet, "Taking My Parents to College," *The New York Times*, August 22, 2015. Copyright © 2015 by The New York Times. All rights reserved. Used by permission and protected by the Copyright Laws of the United States. The printing, copying, redistribution, or retransmission of this Content without express written permission is prohibited.

Aimee Groth, "Why Working at Starbucks for Three Weeks Was the Toughest Job I've Ever Had" from *Business Insider*, December 15, 2011. Copyright © 2014 Business Insider, Inc. Reprinted by permission of Wright's Media.

Alex Hern, "Don't Know the Difference Between Emoji and Emoticons? Let Me Explain," *The Guardian*, February 6, 2015. Copyright © 2015 by The Guardian. Used with permission.

Jamie Lincoln Kitman, "Google Wants Driverless Cars, but Do We?" *The New York Times*, December 18, 2016. Copyright © 2016 by The New York Times. All rights reserved. Used by permission and protected by the Copyright Laws of the United States. The printing, copying, redistribution, or retransmission of this Content without express written permission is prohibited.

Richard Lederer, "The Case for Short Words." From *The miracle of language* by Richard Lederer. Copyright © 1991 by Richard Lederer. Reprinted with the permission of Atria Books, a division of Simon & Schuster, Inc. All rights reserved.

Noah Lewis, "For Trans People Like Me, Pronouns Are about More Than Grammatical Correctness," originally appeared in *The Washington Post*, June 24, 2016. Copyright © 2016 by Noah Lewis Used with permission.

Amy Ma, "My Grandmother's Dumpling," *Wall Street Journal*, January 30, 2009. Copyright © 2009 by Dow Jones & Company. Permission conveyed through Copyright Clearance Center, Inc.

Keshia Mcclantoc, "In Defense of the Small-Town Library," originally appearing on *Odyssey.com*, June 1, 2016. Copyright © 2016 by Keshia Mcclantoc. Used with permission.

"portage." By permission. From Merriam-Webster.com © 2018 by Merriam-Webster, Inc. https://www.merriam-webster.com/dictionary/portage.

Toni Morrison, "The Work You Do, The Person You Are," by Toni Morrison. Copyright © 2017 by Toni Morrison. Reprinted by permission of ICM Partners.

Nikita, "Growing Up a Desi Girl: What It Means to Be between Two Worlds," *Teen Vogue*, July 24, 2015. Copyright © 2015 by Nikita. Used with permission.

Michael Pollan, "Why 'Natural' Doesn't Mean Anything Anymore," *The New York Times*, April 28, 2015. Copyright © 2015 by The New York Times. All rights reserved. Used by permission and protected by the Copyright Laws of the United States. The printing, copying, redistribution, or retransmission of this Content without express written permission is prohibited.

Colin Powell, "What American Citizenship Makes Possible," *The Wall Street Journal*, July 26, 2016. Copyright © 2016 by Dow Jones & Company. Republished with permission of Dow Jones & Company; permission conveyed through Copyright Clearance Center, Inc.

Naomi Rosenberg, "How to Tell a Mother Her Child Is Dead," *The New York Times*, September 3, 2016. Copyright © 2016 by The New York Times. All rights reserved. Used by permission and protected by the Copyright Laws of the United States. The printing, copying, redistribution, or retransmission of this Content without express written permission is prohibited.

Scott Russell Sanders, "The Men We Carry in Our Minds." Copyright © by Scott Russell Sanders. Used with permission.

Mary Sherry, "In Praise of the F Word." Used with permission from the author.

Amy Tan, "Mother Tongue" first appeared in *The Threepenny Review*. Copyright © 1989 by Amy Tan. Reprinted by permission of the author and the Sandra Dijkstra Literary Agency.

Deborah Tannen, "The Triumph of the Yell," excerpt, from *The New York Times*, January 14, 1994. Copyright Deborah Tannen. Reprinted with permission of the author.

Sherry Turkle, "The Flight from Conversation," *The New York Times*, April 21, 2012. Copyright © 2012 by The New York Times. All rights reserved. Used by permission and protected by the Copyright Laws of the United States. The printing, copying, redistribution, or retransmission of this Content without express written permission is prohibited.

John Edgar Wideman, "The Seat Not Taken." Copyright © 2010 by John Edgar Wideman, originally appeared in *The New York Times*, reprinted with permission of The Wylie Agency, LLC.

Jacqueline Woodson, "When a Southern Town Broke a Heart," *The New York Times*, July 26, 2016. Copyright © 2016 by The New York Times. All rights reserved. Used by permission and protected by the Copyright Laws of the United States. The printing, copying, redistribution, or retransmission of this Content without express written permission is prohibited.

Index

Note: Page numbers in **bold** type indicate pages on which terms are defined.

A

abbreviations, **580**
  when to avoid, 479
  when to use, 580
accept, except, 483
accurate support, 147
acronyms, **580**
action verbs, **433**
active reading, **4**
  assessing prior knowledge, 6
  purpose, understanding 7
  scanning, guidelines for, 8–9
  skimming, guidelines for, 7–8
  Stage 1: before you read
    creating a schedule, 4–7
    previewing, 7–9
    understanding your purpose, 7
  Stage 2: as you read
    annotating a text, 18–20
    marking up a text, 15–17
    TESTing a text, 11–15
  Stage 3: after you read
    outlining, 21–22
    reviewing and self-quizzing, 25–26
  summarizing and paraphrasing, 23–25
  writing a response paragraph, 26–27
  verbal signals, **8**, 15–16
  visual signals, **8**, 15
  textbooks, 166–67
active voice, 537–39
addition, transitional words indicating, 120
addresses, commas with, 556–58
adjectives, **421**
  vs. adverbs, 422
  comparatives and superlatives, 424–27
  demonstrative, 421
  editing practice, 428–29
adverbs, **421**
  vs. adjectives, 422
  comparatives and superlatives, 424–27
  editing practice, 428–29
  varying opening sentences with, 454–55
advertisements, reading, 191–92
affect, effect, 244, 483
agreement. *See* pronoun-antecedent agreement; subject-verb agreement

all ready, already, 483
Alvarez, Julia, "What Is a *Quinceañera?*," 328–29
Ampikaipakan, Umapagan, "That Oxymoron, the Asian Comic Superhero," 637–39
am, are (in subject-verb agreement), 524
analyzing texts, 155–56
annotating a text, **18**
  in active reading, 18–20
  visual texts, 182
antecedents. *See* pronoun-antecedent agreement
antonyms, **39**
  concept cards, 45–46
  as contrast clues, 44–45
  in thesauri, 42
  vocabulary building, 39–40
anybody, anyone, everybody, somebody, someone, 406
apostrophes, **564**
  in contractions, 564–65
  editing practice, 569–70
  incorrect use of, 567–68
  in possessives, 565–66
appositives, **553**
  combining sentences with, 462–63
  commas with, 553–54
  fragments, 508
are, is (subject-verb agreement), 530
argument essays
  analyzing, 272–75
  collaborative activity, 283
  reading, 264–72
  sample essays
    "In Praise of the F Word" (Sherry), 269–70
    "Increase Grant Money for Low-Income College Students" (Norman), 278–80
    "Stop the Regulators, Empower the Consumers" (Mar), 272–75
  writing, 276–80
articles. *See* periodicals
assessing prior knowledge, **6**
assignments, 64–66
audience, **64**, 133–34, 138

B

bad/badly, 427
Barry, Lynda, "The Sanctuary of School, The," 217–20

645

base forms of verbs
  irregular verbs, 384–85
  past participles
    irregular, 390–93
    regular, 389
  regular verbs, 383
basis of comparison, **247**
Battle Hymn of the Tiger Mother, from (Chua), 120
be
  forms of, 386–87
  subject-verb agreement), 524
"Becoming a Writer" (Sarno), 221–23
"Becoming Chinese American" (Chu), 61–62
being, 512
bias, **152**, 153
blogs, reading, 174–76
body of essay, defined, **60**
body paragraph, **60**
  assessing while reading, 108
  writing, guidelines for, 114–24
books
  citing
    APA style, 371–72
    MLA style, 361–62
  library sources, evaluating, 343–44
brainstorming, **67**
  guidelines for, 67–68
brake, break, 483, 483–84
business documents, reading, 171–72
buy, by, 484

C

can, could, 387
capitalization, 398, 571–73
caricatures, **189**
Carson, Rachel, "A Fable for Tomorrow," 287–88
cartoons, 189–90
"Case for Short Words, The" (Lederer), 596–99
catalogs, online library, 343–44
cause-and-effect essays
  analyzing, 237–39
  collaborative activity, 245
  defined, 231
  reading, 232–36
  sample essays
    "Expanding Connections across the Indian Ocean" (Shah)
    "The Seat Not Taken" (Wideman), 233–35
    "How My Parents' Separation Changed My Life" (DeMarco), 242–43
  writing, 240–44
causes, transitional words indicating, 232
charts, reading, 184

checklists
  documenting sources, 380
  essays, organizing, 338
  grammar
    fragments, 520
    illogical shifts in tense, 541
    misplaced and dangling modifiers, 548
    nouns and pronouns, 420
    parallelism, 473
    run-ons, 502
    simple, compound, and complex sentences, 451
    subject-verb agreement, 533
    verbs, 397
  punctuation
    apostrophes, using, 570
    commas using, 563
    mechanics, understanding, 586
  reading different kinds of texts
    blogs, 175
    business documents, 171
    news articles, 169
    textbooks, 167
    visual texts
      advertisements, 191
      charts, graphs, and tables, 184
      diagrams, 187
      editorial cartoons, 190
      maps, 185
      web pages, 172–74
  reading process
    active reading, 32
    critical reading, 164
  research, 357
  specific essay types
    argument, 283
    cause-and-effect, 245
    comparison-and-contrast, 262
    exemplification, 213
    narrative, 229
  using, for revision, 90
  vocabulary building, 57
  writing process
    editing an essay, 96
    effective word use, 490
    introductions and conclusions, 131
    revising an essay, 92
    varied sentences, 466
    writing an essay, 105
Chu, Jennifer, "Becoming Chinese American," 61–62
Chua, Amy, from *Battle Hymn of the Tiger Mother,* 120

classification essays, **313**
　analyzing, 319–21
　reading, 313–18
　sample essays
　　"The Men We Carry in Our Minds" (Sanders), 315–18
　　"Selling a Dream" (O'Neal), 323–24
　　"What Kinds of Videos Go Viral?" (Thomas), 319–21
　writing, 322–24
clichés, 479–81
clustering, **70**
coherent body paragraphs, 119–21
collaborative brainstorming, **68**
collective nouns
　frequently used, 407, 527
　subject-verb agreement, 526–27
colons
　for lists, 324
　mechanics of using, 582–83
combining sentences
　using appositives, 462–63
　using -*ed* modifiers, 458–60
　using -*ing* modifiers, 457–58
　using a series of words, 460–62
commas, **549**
　for appositives, 553–54
　with dates and addresses, 556–58
　with direct address, 552
　editing practice, 561–62
　with introductory words and phrases, 212, 550–51
　with nonrestrictive clauses, 554–56
　with quoted speech or writing, 549
　run-ons, correcting with, 494–95
　in a series, 549–50
　with transitional words and phrases, 551–52
　unnecessary, 558–60
comma splice, **491**. *See also* run-ons
common knowledge, **350**
commonly confused words, 483–88
comparative adjectives and adverbs, 424–27
comparison-and-contrast essays
　analyzing, 252–55
　reading, 247–52
　sample essays
　　"Another Ordinary Day" (Jani), 258
　　"Twin Revolutions of Lincoln and Darwin, The" (Conn), 247–52
　　"Two Very Different Resources" (Volpatti), 253–55
　writing, 256–60
comparisons
　pronouns in, 413–14
　transitional words indicating, 120

complete verbs, 436–37
complex sentences
　in argument essays, 281
　editing practice, 450–51
　mixing long and short sentences, 463–64
　overview, 445
　relative pronouns and, 448–49
　subordinating conjunctions and, 445–47
compound antecedents, 404
compound-complex sentences, **449**
compound nouns and pronouns, 412
compound predicates, **433**
compound sentences
　in argument essays, 281
　coordinating conjunctions with, 437–40
　editing practice, 450–51
　mixing long and short sentences, 463–64
　semicolons with, 440–41
　with transitional words and phrases, 442–44
compound subjects, **431**
　commas with, 559
　subject-verb agreement and, 522–23
compound words, hyphens for, 579–80
Compton, May, "The True Price of Counterfeit Goods," 374–76
concept cards, 45–46
concise language, **476**
concise words, 476–78
conclusions, **60**
　assessing while reading, 108
　guidelines for, 124–27
　transitional words indicating, 121
conference with instructor/tutor, 91–92
confirmation bias, **153**
conjunctions
　coordinating
　　commas with, 494, 549–50, 559
　　in compound sentences, 437–40
　　paired items, 468–69
　　correcting run-ons, 492, 494–95
　　editing practice, 450
　subordinating
　　commas with, 447
　　forming complex sentences with, 445–47
　　sentence fragments and, 513–14
Conn, Steven, "Twin Revolutions of Lincoln and Darwin, The," 247–52
connotations, **38**, **139**
　identifying, 139
　vocabulary building, 38–39
conscious, conscience, 484
context clues, **41**, 42–45
contractions, 564–65
contrast context clues, 44, 121

coordinating conjunctions, 494
    commas with, 550
    in compound sentences, 437–40
    correcting run-ons with, 494–95
Corrato, Elains, "Reflections," 226–27
could, can, 387
critical reading
    audience, purpose, and tone, 133–38
    connotations and figurative language, 139–40
    essays
        "Google Wants Driverless Cars, but Do We?" (Kitman), 159–61
        "Mother Tongue," from (Tan), 151
        "Triumph of the Yell, The," from (Tannen), 163
    evaluating ideas
        fact versus opinion, 145–47
        identifying bias, 152–53
        main idea, 141–42
        making inferences, 148–50
    processes
        analyzing, 155–56
        evaluating, 159–62
        summarizing, 154
        synthesizing, 157–58
        supporting points, 143–45
Crucet, Jennine Capó, "Taking My Parents to College," 622–24

D

dangling modifiers, **544**
    correcting, 544–46
    editing practice, 547–48
dashes, 582–83
databases, electronic. *See* electronic databases
dates, using commas in, 556–58
debatable issue, **264**
definition, **325**
definition essays
    analyzing, 331–33
    reading, 326–29
    sample essays
        "Street Smart" (Whitehead), 335–36
        "The Graphic Novel" (Miller), 331–33
        "What Is a *Quinceañera*?" (Alvarez), 328–29
    TESTing, 334–35
    thesis statements, 334
    writing, 334–37
definitions
    in introduction, 111
    vocabulary building, 38, 43
definition/synonym context clues, 43
demonstrative adjectives, 421
demonstrative pronouns, 401

DeMarco, Andrea, "How My Parents' Separation Changed My Life," 242–43
demonstrative adjectives, 421
demonstrative pronouns, 401
denotations, 37–38
dependent-clause fragments, 513–17
dependent word
    to correct a run-on, 492, 498–500
    frequently used words, 498
description, **284**
description essays, 284–95
    analyzing, 290–92
    reading, 285–89
    sample essays
        "Fable for Tomorrow, A" (Carson), 287–88
        "Message of Peace and Love" (Sikander), 290–91
        "Building and Learning" (Greggs), 293–95
    TESTing, 292–93
    thesis statement, 292
    writing, 292–95
diagrams, reading, 186–87
dictionaries, **41**
direct address, comma with, 552
direct quotations, **574**
do, does (subject-verb agreement), 524
documenting sources
    APA style
        in-text citations, 368–69
        reference list, 369–73
        sample paper, 373–76
    collaborative activity, 380
    ethical issues, guidelines for, 350–53
    guidelines for, 350–53
    MLA style
        in-text citation, 358–59, 358–60
        sample paper, 360–67
        works-cited list, 360–63
    reading and writing activity, 377–80
does, do (subject-verb agreement), 524
"Don't Know the Difference between Emoji and Emoticons? Let Me Explain" (Hern), 610–11
drafting an essay, 82–84. *See also* patterns of development

E

each, either, neither, one, 405
-ed, -d, for past tense, 383
editing, writing process and, 95–96
editorial cartoons, reading, 189–90
-ed modifiers, to combine sentences, 458–60
educated guesses, **149**
effect, **231**
effect, affect, 244, 483

effects, transitional words indicating, 232
either of, 469
electronic databases, **342.** *See also* Internet
emails, avoiding abbreviations, 479. *See also* business documents
-er or *more,* 424–27
essays, **59**
   pattern of development, 82
   structure of, 59–62
   writing process, 59–64
-est and *most,* 424–27
evaluate, **159**
evaluating ideas
   distinguishing facts from opinions, 145–47
   identifying bias, 152–53
   making inferences, 148–49
evaluating sources
   Internet, 344–47
   library, 343–44
evaluating support, 147
evaluating texts, **26**
every day, everyday, 484
evidence, **11, 60, 78**
   critical analysis and
      bias vs. points of view, 152–53
      evaluating quality of, 159
      for facts vs. opinions, 145–47
      inductive vs. deductive arguments, 266–68
      inferences, 148–49
      questions to consider, 149
   essay structure and
      body paragraphs, 108, 114–15, 122–23
      minor supporting points, 143–45
      support for opinions, 146–47
      support for topic sentences, 27
   reading
      looking for, when annotating, 19
      in response paragraphs, 27
   in specific essay types
      argument, 273–74
      classification, 320
      cause and effect, 232, 233
      comparison and contrast, 247, 249
      definition, 332–33
      descriptive, 291
      exemplification, 206–7
      narrative, 222–23
      process, 306–7
   supporting points and, 78–79, 143–45
   TESTing for, 11, 60, 85–86
example clues, 43
examples
   active reading
      annotating a text, 20
      marked-up text, 16–17
      outline, 22
      paraphrasing, 25
      response paragraph, 26
      summary, 24
   body paragraphs
      coherence, 119–20
      transitional words and phrases, 119–21
      unified, 117–18
      well-developed, 122–23
   conclusions, 125–126
   critical reading
      analysis of an essay, 156
      bias of writer, 152
      synthesis of an essay, 158
      evaluation of a text, 161
      making inferences, 149
   definition, to begin an introduction, 111
   figurative language, 140
   introductions, 110–12
   thesis statement, 141
      body paragraphs to support, 115
      transitional words for, 121
   vocabulary building, 43–44
   working with sources
      incorporating identifying tags, 349
      plagiarism, avoiding, 351–53
      summarizing, 348
   writing an introduction, 110–12
   writing process
      avoiding plagiarism, 351–53
      brainstorming, 68
      clustering, 70
      freewriting, 67
except, accept, 483
exclamations, as type of sentence, **453**
exemplification essays
   analyzing, 205–208
   collaborative activity, 213
   reading, 200–205
   sample essays
      "Going to Extremes" (Sims), 210–11
      "In Defense of the Small-Town Library" (Mcclantoc), 202–4
      "Making a Difference" (Perry), 206–7
   writing, 208–211
expert opinion, **146,** 265
"Expanding Connections across the Indian Ocean" (Shah)
explaining, as purpose of writing, 134–35
expressive vocabulary, 35

F

"Fable for Tomorrow, A" (Carson), 287–88
facts vs. opinions, 145–47

figurative language (figures of speech), **140**
  connotations and 139–40
  effective word use, 478–79
  similes, 140, 285, 478
find, fine, 484
finding sources
  Internet, 344
  library, 342–43
fine, find, 484
finding ideas, 66
  brainstorming, 67–68
  clustering, 70–71
  freewriting, 66–67
  journaling, 69
finding sources
  Internet, 344–46
  library, 343–44
"Flight from Conversation" (Turkle), 604–608
flowcharts, **187**
focused freewriting, 66–67
formal definitions, **37, 325**
formal outlines, **21, 81**
format, **96**
"For Trans People Like Me, Pronouns Are about More Than Grammatical Correctness" (Lewis), 600–602
fragments
  avoiding, 440
  vs. complete sentences, 504
  dependent-clause fragments, 513–17, 515
  editing practice, 518–19
  -ing fragments, 511–13
  missing-subject fragments, 506–8
  phrase fragments
    appositive fragments, 508–9
    infinitive fragments, 509–11
    prepositional phrase fragments, 509
  recognizing, 504–6
freewriting, 66–67
"Fun and Profit, For" (Rossi), 310–11
fused sentence, **491**. *See also* run-ons

G

general information clues, 43–44
general vs. specific words, 474
"Going Back to School" (White), 83–84
"Going to Extremes" (Sims), 210–11
good, well, 423, 427
Google Scholar, using as a source, 346
"Google Wants Driverless Cars, but Do We?" (Kitman), 159–61
"Graphic Novel, The" (Miller), 331–33
graphs, reading, 184
Greggs, James, "Building and Learning," 293–95

Groth, Aimee, "Why Working at Starbucks for Three Weeks Was the Toughest Job I've Ever Had," 62–64
"Growing Up a Desi Girl: What It Means to Be between Two Worlds" (Nikita), 629–31

H

have, has (subject-verb agreement), 524
hear, here, 484
helping verbs, 435–37
Hern, Alex, "Don't Know the Difference between Emoji and Emoticons? Let Me Explain," 610–11
highlighting, 29
his or her versus *their,* 406
"How My Parents' Separation Changed My Life" (DeMarco), 242–43
"How to Take Effective Notes" (McCann), 306–307
"How to Tell a Mother Her Child Is Dead" (Rosenberg), 626–27
hyphens, 579–80

I

ideas. *See also* main ideas
  connecting with semicolons, 497
  connecting, with coordinating conjunctions, 494–95
  finding, for writing, 66–71
ideas in source materials
  distinguishing from own writing, 353
  documenting, 352
identifying tags, **349**
  incorporating sources into writing, 349
  punctuating, in direct quotations, 574–77
illogical shifts
  editing practice, 540–41
  in tense, person, or voice, 312, 534–39
implied main idea, 142
"Increase Grant Money for Low-Income College Students" (Norman), 278–80
indefinite pronouns
  apostrophe placement for possessive forms, 565–66
  indefinite pronoun antecedents, 405–6
  singular, 528
  subject-verb agreement, 527–29
  as subjects, identifying, 528
"In Defense of the Small-Town Library" (Mcclantoc), 202–4
independent clause, **430, 445**. *See also* compound sentences
inductive argument, **266**
inferences, **148**

inferential questions, **26**
infinitive fragments, 509–11
infographics, 183–84
informal outline, **21, 80**
informing, as purpose of writing, 134–35
-ing and *-ed* modifiers
    to begin sentences, 457–60
    correcting misplaced and dangling modifiers, 542–46
    fragments, 511–13
"In Praise of the F Word" (Sherry), 269–70
instructions, present tense verbs for, 309
instructor/tutor, conference with, 91–92
intended audience, **133**
intensive pronouns, 416–17
Internet sources
    citing
        APA style, 372
        MLA style, 362–63
    evaluating, 345–46
    finding, 344
    vocabulary building, 42
in-text citations
    APA style, 368–69
    MLA style, 358–60
introductions, **60, 107**
    collaborative activity, 129–30
    commas with, 550–51
    guidelines for, 109–14
    narrative, beginning with, 110
    quotation, beginning with, 111
    reading, 107
    surprising statement, beginning with, 111–12
irregular noun plurals, 399
irregular past participles, 390–92
is when, is where, 337
it's, its, 485
items in a series, and parallelism, 469–70

J

James, "Building and Learning" (Greggs), 293–95
Jani, Nisha, "Another Ordinary Day," 258
journal articles
    citing
        APA style, 370–71
        MLA style, 360–61
journaling, **69**

K

keyword search, **342**
know, no, knew, new, 484

L

lay, lie, 485
Lederer, Richard, "Case for Short Words, The," 596–99
Lewis, Noah, "For Trans People Like Me, Pronouns Are about More Than Grammatical Correctness," 600–602
libraries
    evaluating, for research, 341–44
    finding sources, 342–43
    WorldCat Discovery, 342
lie, lay, 485
linking verbs, **434**, 435
listening vocabulary, **34**
literal questions, **26**
logical order, transitional words indicating, 119
long quotations, formatting
    APA style, 369
    MLA style, 359, 369
long sentences, 463–64
loose, lose, 485

M

Ma, Amy, "My Grandmother's Dumpling," 299–304
magazine articles
    citing
        APA style, 371
        MLA style, 361
main idea, **11**
    supporting points, 143–44
    TESTing a thesis, 11
main verbs, **435**
"Making a Difference" (Perry), 206–7
major premise, **267**
major supporting points, **143**
making inferences, 148–49
maps, reading, 185–86
Mar, Jessica, "Stop the Regulators, Empower the Consumers," 272–75
marking up text, 15
McCann, Owen, "How to Take Effective Notes," 306–7
McClantoc, Keshia, "In Defense of the Small-Town Library," 202–4
mechanics
    abbreviations, 580
    capitalizing proper nouns, 571–73
    editing practice, 584–85
    hyphens, 579–80
    punctuating direct quotations, 574–77
    semicolons, colons, dashes, and parentheses, 582–83
    titles, setting off, 577–79
    using numbers, 581

memos. *See* business documents
"Men We Carry in Our Minds, The" (Sanders), 315–18
"Message of Peace and Love" (Sikander), 290–91
metaphor, **285, 478**
Miller, Jacob, "The Graphic Novel," 331–33
minor premise, **267**
minor supporting points, **143**
misplaced modifiers, **296**
   correcting, 542–46
   in descriptive writing, 296
   editing practice, 547–48
missing-subject fragments, 506–8
MLA documentation style
   collaborative activity, 380
   parenthetical text references, 358–60
   sample paper, 363–67
   works-cited list, 360–63
mnemonics, **25,** 46–47
modifiers, **296**
   combining sentences with
      -ed modifiers, 458–60
      -ing modifiers, 457–58
   in descriptive writing, 296
   misplaced and dangling, 542–48
more or *-er,* 424–27
Morrison, Toni, "The Work You Do, the Person You Are," 618–20
"Mother Tongue" (Tan), 36–37, 151, 590–95
"My Grandmother's Dumpling" (Ma), metaphor, **140**

N

narrative
   to begin an introduction, 110
   in a conclusion, 125
narrative essays
   analyzing a student essay, 221–23
   collaborative activity, 229
   reading, 215–216
   sample essays
      "Becoming a Writer" (Sarno), 221–23
      "Reflections" (Corrato), 226–27
      "Sanctuary of School, The" (Barry), 217–20
   TESTing, 215–16
   writing, 224–28
news articles, reading, 168–70
newspapers
   citing
      APA style, 371
      MLA style, 361
Nikita, "Growing Up a Desi Girl: What It Means to Be between Two Worlds," 629–31
no, know, new, knew, 485
nonrestrictive clauses, commas with, 554–56

Norman, Alex, "Increase Grant Money for Low-Income College Students," 278–80
nouns, **398**
   capitalizing, 398, 571–73
   collective, and subject-verb agreement, 526–27
   editing practice, 419–20
   as object of prepositional phrase, 432
   plural forms, 398
      of irregular nouns, 399
   possessive forms
      of plural nouns, 566–67
      of singular nouns and indefinite pronouns, 565
      of singular nouns ending in *-s,* 566
   and pronouns
      in compounds, 412
      in comparisons, 413–14
numbers, spelling out, 581
numerals, 581

O

object, **431**
objective case of pronouns, 410
objective description, **284**
objective tone, 136
O'Neal, Rob, "Selling a Dream," 323–24
online tools for time management, 9–10
opening remarks, **60,** 109
opinions, **265**
online library catalogs, 342
organizers for time management, 9–10
outline, **21**
   formal, 81
   informal (scratch), 80
   writing, 21–22

P

paired items, 468–69
parallel structures, **467**
   comparison-and-contrast essays, 260
   editing practice, 471–72
   using for
      items in a list or outline, 469–70
      items in a series, 469
      paired items, 468–69
paraphrasing, **24**
   guidelines for, 24–25
   of sources, 347–48
parentheses, 582–83
participles
   helping verbs with, 436
   irregular past participles, 390–92
   regular past participles, 389–90
passed, past, 485

passive versus active voice, 537–39
past participles
   irregular, 390–92
   regular, 389–90
past perfect tense, 395
past tense
   of *be,* 386
   of *can, could,* 387
   of irregular verbs, 384–85, 390–92
   of regular verbs, 389
   of *will* and *can,* 387–88
   of *will* and *would,* 387
patterns of development, **82.** *See also* cause-and-effect essays; classification essays; comparison-and-contrast essays; definition essays; description essays; exemplification essays; narration essays; process essays; reading and writing argument essays; organizing essays
peace, piece, 485
peer review, 90
periodicals
   citing
      APA style, 370–71
      MLA style, 360–61
periods, 493
Perry, Alison, "Making a Difference," 206–7
person (first, second, third)
   illogical shifts in voice, 535–37
   subject-verb agreement and, 521, 524
personal pronouns, **410**
personification, **140,** 285
persuading, as purpose of writing, 134–35
photographs, reading, 188–89
piece, peace, 485
plagiarism, 347, 350–53
plural indefinite pronouns, 406
plural nouns, 398–99
   apostrophe placement for possessive form, 566–67
   avoiding sexist language with, find page number
   forming, find page number
plural pronouns, 401
plural subjects, **430**
point of view, **152**
point-by-point comparisons, **247,** 249
Pollan, Michael, "Why 'Natural' Doesn't Mean Anything Anymore," 613–16
possessive case of pronouns, 411
possessive forms, 565–66
Powell, Colin, "What American Citizenship Makes Possible," 12–14
predictions, in conclusions, 126
prefixes, **49,** 49–50
prepositions
   beginning sentences with, 456
   frequently used, 432
   prepositional phrase fragments, 509

present perfect tense, 393–94
present tense verbs, for instructions, 309
previewing a text
   active reading and, 7–9
   different kinds of texts, 166
   visual texts, 177–79
   writer's purpose, 134
principle, principal, 486
prior knowledge, assessing, **6**
problem verbs
   be, was, were, 386
   can, could, 387
   will, would, 387–88
process essays
   analyzing, 306–308
   sample essays
      "Fun and Profit, For" (Rossi), 310–11
      "How to Take Effective Notes" (McCann), 306–307
      "My Grandmother's Dumpling" (Ma), 299–304
   TESTing, 309
   writing, 308–311
process explanations, **308–9**
pronoun case, 410–411
pronoun-antecedent agreement, 402
   collective noun antecedents, 407
   compound antecedents, 404
   editing practice, 419–20
   his or *her* vs. *their,* 406
   indefinite pronoun antecedents, 405–6
pronouns, **400**
   case, understanding, 410–11
   in comparisons, 413–14
   in compounds, 412
   demonstrative, 401
   editing practice, 419–20
   identifying, 400–401
   indefinite
      as antecedents, 405
      possessive forms of, 565–66
      subject-verb agreement, 527–29
      with *of,* 405
   and nouns, in compounds, 412
   as object of prepositional phrase, 432
   personal, 410
   possessive case, 411
   pronoun case
      comparisons and, 413–14
      overview: subjective, objective case, possessive, 410–11
      who and *whom, whoever* and *whomever,* 415–16
   reflexive and intensive, 416–17
   singular and plural, 401
   vague and unnecessary, 408–9
proofreading, 96–98
proper nouns, **398,** 571–73

public service announcements, 191
purpose
  of writer, identifying, 134–36, 138
  in writing, 64

Q

questions
  in introductions, 110
  as type of sentence, 453
quiet, quit, quite, 486
quotation marks, 574–75, 577
quotations
  in a conclusion, 126
  indirect, 575
  in an introduction, 111
quoted speech
  commas with, 549
  punctuating, 574–77
quoting sources, 348–49

R

raise, rise, 486
reading, active. *See* active reading
reading, critical. *See* critical reading
readings
  identity and self-image
    "Growing Up a Desi Girl: What It Means to Be between Two Worlds" (Nikita), 629–31
    "That Oxymoron, the Asian Comic Superhero" (Ampikaipakan), 637–39
    "When a Southern Town Broke a Heart" (Woodson), 633–35
  reading and writing
    "Case for Short Words, The" (Lederer), 596–99
    "For Trans People Like Me, Pronouns Are about More Than Grammatical Correctness" (Lewis), 600–602
    "Mother Tongue" (Tan), 590–95
  technology and science
    "Don't Know the Difference between Emoji and Emoticons? Let Me Explain" (Hern), 610–11
    "Flight from Conversation" (Turkle), 604–608
    "Why 'Natural' Doesn't Mean Anything Anymore" (Pollan), 613–16
  working and learning
    "How to Tell a Mother Her Child Is Dead" (Rosenberg), 626–27
    "Taking My Parents to College" (Crucet), 622–24
    "Reflections" (Corrato), 226–27
reading vocabulary, 34–35

reading to write
  collaborative activity, 30–31
  review activity, 28–29
reference list, APA style. *See also* works-cited list, MLA style
reflexive pronouns, 416–17
regular past participles, 389–90
regular verbs
  forming past tense of, 383
  subject-verb agreement, 521
relative pronouns, **448,** 515
relevant support, 147
reliable support, 147
representative support, 147
research. *See* sources, working with
response paragraph, **26–27**
restrictive clauses, 554–55
reviewing, 25–26
revising, 90–91
roots of words, **48**
Rosenberg, Naomi, "How to Tell a Mother Her Child Is Dead," 626–27
Rossi, Jen, "For Fun and Profit," 310–11
run-ons, **491**
  correcting
    with a coordinating conjunction, 492, 494–95
    using a dependent word, 492, 498–500
    with a period, 492, 493
    using a semicolon, 492, 495–96
    using a semicolon and a transitional word or phrase, 492, 496–97
  in narrative essays, 228
  editing practice, 501–2
  recognizing, 491–92

S

"Sanctuary of School, The" (Barry), 217–20
Sanders, Scott Russell, "The Men We Carry in Our Minds," 315–18
Sarno, Erica, "Becoming a Writer," 221–23
scanning, **8**
schedule for active reading, 4–7
schemata, **35**
  in active reading, 35–36
scratch outline, **80**
search engines, **344**
"Seat Not Taken, The" (Wideman), 233–35
secondary purpose, for a writer, 134
self-assessment checklist, for essay writing, 96
self-quizzing and reviewing, 25–26
"Selling a Dream" (O'Neal), 323–24
semicolons, **440**
  in compound sentences, 440–41
  to connect ideas, 497

correcting run-ons with, 495–97
mechanics of using, 582–83
sentences. *See* complex sentences; compound sentences; fragments; simple sentences; varying sentences
sequence, transitional words for, 120
series of words
combining sentences with, 460–62
commas with, 549–50
parallelism and, 469
-*s*, -*es*, to form plural nouns, 398–99
sexist language, **481**
avoiding, 481–83
sexist vs. nonsexist words, 482
Shah, Mehul, "Expanding Connections across the Indian Ocean"
Sherry, Mary, "In Praise of the F Word," 269–70
shifts, illogical. *See* illogical shifts
short quotations, formatting
APA style, 369
MLA style, 359
short sentences, 463–64
shorthand, avoiding, 479
Sikander, Rida, "Message of Peace and Love," 290–91
simile, **140**, 285, 478. *See also* figurative language
simple sentences
prepositional phrases in, 431–33
subjects, identifying, 430–31
verbs in, 433–37
Sims, Kyle, "Going to Extremes," 210–11
singular and plural. *See* subject-verb agreement
singular indefinite pronouns, 405
singular nouns, **398**
apostrophe placement for possessive forms, 565–66
ending in -*s* and possessive form, 566
singular pronouns, 401
singular subjects, 430–31
sit, set, 486
skimming, 7
slang, 479–80
smartphone apps, 42
Smith, Betty, *A Tree Grows in Brooklyn,* 196
sources, working with. *See also* documenting sources
collaborative activity, 355–56
ethical issues, 350–53
distinguishing between source and writer, 353
documenting ideas, 352
use of quotation marks, 352
use your own phrasing, 352–53
evaluating
Internet, 344–46
library, 343–44
finding
Internet, 344
library, 342–43

plagiarism, avoiding, 350–53
reading and writing activity, 354–55
using in writing
integrating into writing, 349
paraphrasing, 347–48
quoting, 348–49
summarizing, 348
synthesizing, 350
spatial order, transitional words indicating, 119
speaking vocabulary, **35**
specific vs. general words, 474
specific words, using, 474–75
"Starting Over" (White), 98–100. *See also* White, Jared
statements, sentences as, **453**
"Stop the Regulators, Empower the Consumers" (Mar), 272–75
"Street Smart" (Whitehead), 335–36
subject-by-subject comparisons, **247**, 249
subject of sentence, identifying, 430–31
subjective case, **410**
subjective description, **284**
subjective pronouns, 410
subjective tone, 136
subject of sentence, 430–31. *See also* fragments; subject-verb agreement
subject searches
on Internet, 344–46
in library catalogs and databases, 342–43
subject-verb agreement
be, have, and *do,* 523–25
collective-noun subjects, 526–27
with compound subjects, 522–23
editing practice, 531–32
indefinite pronoun subjects, 527–29
with regular verbs, 521–22
there is and *there are,* 530
verbs before subjects, 529–30
words between subject and verb, 525–26
subordinating conjunctions
commas with, 447
forming complex sentences with, 445–46
frequently used, 446
sentence fragments and, 514
sufficient support, 147
suffixes, 50–51
summarizing, **23**
active reading and, 23–24
critical reading and, 154
sources, 348–49
summary statements, 11–15, 87, 108
in body paragraphs, 114
in conclusions, 124–25
transitional words for, 121
superlative adjectives and adverbs, 424–27

suppose, supposed, 486
supported opinion, 146
supporting points
    identifying, in critical reading, 143–45
    organizing an essay and, 78–80
surprising statements, 111–12
synonyms, **39**, 42
synthesizing sources, 350

T

tables, reading, 184
"Taking My Parents to College" (Crucet), 622–24
Tan, Amy, "Mother Tongue," 36–37, 151, 590–95
Tannen, Deborah, from "The Triumph of the Yell," 163
tense, illogical shifts in, 534–35
tenses, verb
    editing practice, 396–97
    illogical shifts in, 534–35
    past
        of *be,* 386
        of *can* and *will,* 387
        of irregular verbs, 384–85
        of regular verbs, 383
    past perfect, 395
    present perfect, 393–94
TESTing, **11**
    defined, 11
    essays, 11–14,
    for evidence, 85–86
    specific essay types
        argument, 264–65
        cause-and-effect, 232
        classification, 322
        comparison-and-contrast, 257
        descriptive, 293
        definition, 334
        exemplification, 201–2
        narrative, 215–216
        process, 309
    for a summary, 87
    for a thesis, 85
    for transitions, 87–89
textbooks, 166–67
texts, types of
    visual
        advertisements, 191–92
        charts, graphs, and tables, 183–84
        diagrams, 186–87
        editorial cartoons, 189–90
        maps, 185–86
        photographs, 188–89

    written
        blogs, 174–77
        business articles, 171–72
        collaborative activity, 196
        news articles, 168–71
        textbooks, 166–68
        web pages, 172–74
"That Oxymoron, the Asian Comic Superhero" (Ampikaipakan), 637–39
that, which, and *who,* 555
their, there, they're, 487
then, than, 487
thesaurus, **42**
thesis-and-support essay structure, **82**
thesis statement, **60, 72, 109**
    evaluating, 74
    examples, by essay type
        argument, 276
        cause-and-effect, 240
        classification, 322
        comparison-and-contrast, 256
        definition essays, 334
        description essays, 292
        exemplification essay, 209
        narrative, 224
        process essays, 308
    in introduction, 60, 107, 109–10
    overview, 72–74
    TESTing for, 11, 85
they're, their, there, 487
thinking critically, **133**
this, that, these, and *those,* 401, 421
Thomas, Jessica, "What Kinds of Videos Go Viral?," 319–21
threw, through, 487
time-management strategies, 9–10
time, transitional words indicating, 119, 120
titles
    of artistic works, 577
    with proper names
        capitalization for, 571
        abbreviations for, 580
    formatting, 97
    working, 82
tone, 136–37
too, to, two, 487
topics
    based on assignment, 64–65
    assessing while reading, 108
    effective, 116
topic sentences, **108**
    guidelines for, 116
    marking up text, 15
    in a unified paragraph, 117–18
transitional paragraphs, **11**

transitional words and phrases, **60**
  assessing while reading, 108
  in body paragraphs, 119–21
  commas in, 551–52
  compound sentences formed with, 442–44
  frequently used, 442
  introductory, and commas, 212
  list of, 120–21
  in specific essay types
    cause-and-effect essay, 232
    classification essays, 314
    comparison-and-contrast essays, 247–48
    comparison-and-contrast essays, 248
    process essays, 298
    definition, 326
    description essay, 286
    exemplification essays, 201
    narrative essays, 216
  TESTing and, 11, 87–89
"Triumph of the Yell, The" from (Tannen), 163
Tree Grows in Brooklyn, A (Smith), 196
"True Price of Counterfeit Goods, The"
    (Compton), 364–67
"Twin Revolutions of Lincoln and Darwin, The"
    (Conn), 247–52
two, too, to, 487
"Two Very Different Resources" (Volpatti), 253–55
Turkle, Shirley, "Flight from Conversation," 604–608
tutor/instructor, conference with, 91–92

U

unified body paragraphs, 117–18
unnecessary commas, 558–60
unnecessary pronouns, 408–9
unnecessary repetition, **477**
use, used, 487
unsupported opinion, **146**

V

vagueness
  of pronouns, 408–9
  in thesis statement, 73
varying sentences
  combining sentences
    using appositives, 462–63
    using a series of words, 460–62
    using *-ed* modifiers, 458–60
    using *-ing* modifiers, 457–58
  editing practice, 465–66
  mixing long and short sentences, 463–64
  by openings
    with adverbs, 454–55
    with prepositional phrases, 456
  types of, 453–54

verbs
  complete verbs, 436–37
  editing practice, 396–97
  irregular verbs, 384–85
  main and helping, 435–37
  past participles
    irregular, 390–93
    regular, 389–90
  past perfect tense, 395
  present perfect tense, 393–94
  problem verbs
    be, was, were, 386–87
    can/could, will/would, 387–88
  regular verbs, 383
  in simple sentences, 433–37
  See also fragments; subject-verb agreement
visual learners, and marking up text, 15
visual signals, **8**, 15
visual texts, **166**
  guidelines for reading
    marking up and annotating, 182
    previewing, 177–79
  types of
    advertisements, 191–92
    charts, graphs, and tables, 183–84
    diagrams, 186–87
    editorial cartoons, 189–90
    maps, 185–86
    photographs, 188–89
vocabulary building
  acquiring new words
    context clues, 42–45
    learning from coursework, 45–47
    learning from reading, 51–52
    learning from roots, prefixes, and suffixes,
      47–50
    reference tools, 41–42
  collaborative activity, 55–56
  denotations, connotations, synonyms, and
    antonyms, 37–40
  essay: "Mother Tongue" (Tan), 36–37
  "knowing" words, 35–40
  listening, reading, speaking, writing, 34–35
  review activity, 55
  schemata, activating your, 35–37
  using new words in writing, 52–53
voice, illogical shifts in, 537–39
Volpatti, Colin, "Two Very Different Resources,"
    253–55

W

was, were, as irregular forms of *be,* 384
weather, whether, 488
web pages, 172–74
well, good, 423

"What American Citizenship Makes Possible" (Powell), 12–14
"What Is a *Quinceañera*?" (Alvarez), 328–29
"What Kinds of Videos Go Viral?" (Thomas), 319–21
"When a Southern Town Broke a Heart" (Woodson), 633–35
where, were, we're, 488
which, that, and *who*, 555
White, Jared
  from assignment to topic, 65
  brainstorming, 68
  final essay: "Starting Over," 98–100
  first draft: "Going Back to School," 83–84
  focused freewriting, 67
  journal entry, 69
  format: sample first page, 87
  TESTing essay: "Starting Over," 93–95
Whitehead, Kristin, "Street Smart," 335–36
who, that, and *which*, 448, 555
who, whom, 415–16
whoever, whomever, 415–16
whose, who's, 488
"Why 'Natural' Doesn't Mean Anything Anymore" (Pollan), 613–16
"Why Working at Starbucks for Three Weeks Was the Toughest Job I've Ever Had" (Groth), 62–64
will, would, 387–88
word use, effective
  clichés, 480–81
  commonly confused words, 483–88
  concise language, 476–78
  editing practice, 489–90
  figurative language (similes and metaphors), 478–79
  sexist language, 481–83
  slang, 479–80
  specific vs. general words, 474–76
working title, 82
WorldCat Discovery, 342
works-cited list, MLA style, 360–63. *See also* reference list, APA style
"Work You Do, the Person You Are, The" (Morrison), 618–20

would, will, 387–88
writing centers, 90
writing process, **95**
  assignment to
  case study: Jared White (*see* White, Jared)
  collaborative activity, 103–4
  essays
    "Becoming Chinese American" (Chu), 61–62
    "Going Back to School" (White), 83–84
    "Starting Over" (White), 98–100
    "Why Working at Starbucks for Three Weeks Was the Toughest Job I've Ever Had" (Groth), 62–64
  essay structure, understanding, 59–61
  Step 1: planning
    finding ideas, 66
      brainstorming, 67–68
      clustering, 70–71
      freewriting, 66–67
      journaling, 69
    moving from assignment to topic, 64–66
    thesis statement, 72–78
  Step 2: organizing
    outlining, 80–82
    supporting points, 78–80
  Step 3: drafting
  Step 4: TESTing and revising
    overview of TESTing, 85–88
    revising an essay, 89–95
  Step 5: editing and proofreading
    editing, 95–96
    proofreading, 96–100
  review activity, 101–3
  overview, 59
writing vocabulary, **35**
written texts, 166
  blogs, 174–77
  business documents, 171–72
  news articles, 168–71
  textbooks, 166–68
  web pages, 172–74

Y

your, you're, 487, 488

Revision Symbols

This chart lists symbols that many instructors use to point out writing problems in student papers. Next to each problem is the chapter or section of *Focus on Reading and Writing*, Second Edition, where you can find help with that problem. If your instructor uses different symbols from those shown here, write them in the space provided.

INSTRUCTOR'S SYMBOL	STANDARD SYMBOL	PROBLEM
	adj	problem with use of adjective 17
	adv	problem with use of adverb 17
	agr	agreement problem (subject-verb) 24 agreement problem (pronoun-antecedent) 16d, 16e
	apos	apostrophe missing or used incorrectly 28
	awk	awkward sentence structure 24, 25
	cap or triple underline [example]	capital letter needed 29a
	case	problem with pronoun case 16g, 16h
	cliché	cliché 21e
	coh	lack of paragraph coherence p. 87, 3h
	combine	combine sentences 19c
	cs	comma splice 22
	d or wc	diction (poor word choice) 21
	dev	lack of paragraph development 3e, 3h
	frag	fragment 23
	fs	fused sentence 22
	ital	italics or underlining needed 29c
	lc or diagonal slash [Example]	lowercase; capital letter not needed 29a
	para or ¶	indent new paragraph 4c
	pass	overuse of passive voice 25c
	prep	nonstandard use of preposition 18b
	ref	pronoun reference not specific 16e
	ro	run-on sentence 22
	shift	illogical shift 25
	sp	incorrect spelling 21g
	tense	problem with verb tense 25a
	trans	transition needed p. 3h, p. 87
	unity	paragraph not unified 3h
	w	wordy, not concise 21b
	//	problem with parallelism 20
	⊙	problem with comma use 27
	⊙	problem with semicolon use 18e, 29g
	" "	problem with quotation marks 29b, 29c
	⌒ [ex ample]	close up space
	∧	insert
	[exa⧸mple]	delete
	∽ [words example]	reversed letters or words
	X	obvious error
	✓	good point, well put
	# [example#words]	add a space